NATIONAL GEOGRAPHIC

10 *the* BEST
of EVERYTHING

National
Parks

800 TOP PICKS FROM PARKS COAST TO COAST

introduction by
FRAN P. MAINELLA
16th Director of the National Park Service

NATIONAL GEOGRAPHIC
WASHINGTON, D.C.

table of
contents

Page 2: The Milky Way twinkles over Natural Bridges National Monument, Utah.

Snow and ice turn the Many Glacier region of Montana's Glacier National Park into a winter wonderland.

about this book

Our national parks are busy places, hosting millions of people every year, sustaining countless varieties of creatures, balancing the rumbling weight of ancient rock formations, and giving annual nutrients to vast fields of colorful plants and towering trees. Everyone and everything that partakes in the grandeur of these parks gains a unique sense of wonder. They are living, learning playgrounds for eager active children, dream expanses of roads and summits for hikers and bikers, stunning raw visions for painters, and, very simply, homes for some of our most endangered species.

To sum this vastness and diversity of use into lists of "ten best parks" is near impossible. For the group of renowned nature writers and outdoor enthusiasts working in close contact with the expertise and passion of editors at National Geographic, however, these lists became a labor of love and a record of lifetimes spent enjoying the National Park System. The individual lists are simply one person's opinion, backed by nothing more than personal knowledge, interest, and experience, and perhaps suggestions from friends and editors. You'll also find fact notes from the National Parks website *(www.nps.gov)*.

This book is a starting point, rather than a checklist, for first-time explorers and regular adventurers to best discover the many offerings. From climbs, fishing, kayaking, or drives to the most unusual places to sleep and eat, to say "I do" or "I will," or to stare at a star-splashed nighttime sky, all are present in our national parks.

introduction

Our national parks are the soul of our nation and tell the history of our country. As the 16th Director of the National Park Service and the first woman to serve in that position in its nearly hundred-year history, I was honored to work alongside the 20,000 NPS employees and thousands of volunteers to "preserve unimpaired our natural and cultural resources for the enjoyment, education, and inspiration of this and future generations."

The National Geographic Society has long been a supporter of our country's "best idea." *The 10 Best of Everything National Parks* is the next chapter in this strong relationship.

During my time as director it was clear that our nation was well acquainted with our national parks. From the geysers of Yellowstone to the hallowed ground of Gettysburg, this wonderful guide celebrates the iconic parks, yet gives us ways to appreciate the uniqueness of many of our lesser known jewels. Through this book, readers will discover many diverse recreational opportunities in some of the most dynamic and beautiful places of our country.

Throughout my tenure at the National Park Service, I was frequently asked which parks were my favorites. Of course I said, "I have 390!" Even though I did not choose the categories or parks included in this guide, National Geographic has helped the reader identify 80 areas of interest and the ten best parks within each category. Today as we work to get our children, adults, and families back outdoors, it is important to find diverse ways to

visit our national parks and enjoy them from all perspectives. It is my hope that through experiencing our national parks the public will develop a greater sense of stewardship and obligation toward these beloved lands.

Today I serve as a Visiting Scholar at Clemson University in South Carolina, where I have had the chance to teach many young college students about the value of parks while also conveying this message as a board member of many nonprofits, including Children & Nature Network, the National Park Trust, and the U.S. Play Coalition. From my early days as a playground counselor to my service as National Park Service Director, I have seen and experienced the overwhelmingly positive changes that parks can make in our lives. I truly believe that *The 10 Best of Everything National Parks* will serve as an excellent guide to exploring and enjoying our National Park System throughout life while leaving the parks unimpaired for future generations.

Fran P. Mainella
Visiting Scholar, Clemson University
16th Director of the National Park Service

chapter one

natural wonders

landmarks

Distinctive, prominent, and instantly recognizable natural landmarks

Landmarks have long served as beacons for travelers, providing reassuring markers on great journeys and standing as symbols to signify important places. This remains true. Modern maps tell us how to get somewhere, but landmarks tell us where we are, from Devils Tower to Mount McKinley.

☆ Grand Canyon ☆
NATIONAL PARK
Cape Royal and Angels Window

Angels don't need windows, but if they ever wanted to frame a great view, they might choose the North Rim's Cape Royal and its noble companion parapet in Arizona. Thrust far above the immense luminous space of the canyon, this natural arch overlooks the big bend where the canyon turns west, carving ever deeper into the heart of the Kaibab Plateau. No viewpoint offers a better perspective on the contrast between the dizzying verticality of the gorge and the horizontal rock layers through which it was carved. Red-and-yellow cliffs march across bays and escarpments for mile after astounding mile. Wotans Throne is in the foreground. That distant green ribbon is the Colorado River. The southern horizon is the South Rim, 9 miles away and almost 1,000 feet lower. Adding to its appeal, the North Rim is forested, wildflower strewn, and pleasantly cooler in summer than the South Rim. Cape Royal is a prime spot to watch cloud formations sail across the void, but beware of thunderstorms. Angels may be a matter for faith, but lightning strikes are high-voltage reality at this most exposed geologic extremity.

☆ Yosemite ☆
NATIONAL PARK
Half Dome

Like all good landmarks, Half Dome is an eye magnet. It towers over the other grand monoliths of Yosemite Valley and demands attention. The others in the pantheon, including El Capitan, Sentinel Rock, and Cathedral Spires, are no less illustrious; however, there's something special about Half Dome. It has undeniable stage presence. View it from the valley floor, beside the winding Tuolomne River. Or drive up to Glacier Point to watch it glow in the sunset as night falls. Best of all, see it from its own bald top. The trail, which takes in the glories of Vernal and Nevada Falls along the way, ends on a cable-protected pathway nailed to smooth granite slabs. Eight miles and 4,800 vertical feet each way, it's a long day—but entirely worth the effort.

Chimney Rock marked the entrance to the West for travelers on the Oregon and California Trails.

✶ Denali ✶
NATIONAL PARK & PRESERVE
Mount McKinley

The mountain sprawls across the Alaska tundra like half a planet, gleaming white and broad shouldered. How big is it really? It's hard to tell by looking. And one can read the facts, and accept them, and still not know the measure of the place. Alaska natives expressed their awe with a single word, Denali, which means "the high one." With all due respect to the 25th American President, the mountain remains the ineffable Denali in the eyes of many. The summit towers 20,320 feet above sea level, more than 18,000 feet above the base. This gives the mountain an all-in-one-view vertical rise more than a mile greater than Mount Everest, which begins its grand ascent at an already lofty elevation of about 17,000 feet. But comparisons are good only for discussion. A true understanding of the mountain and its relationship to those gazing at it in wonderment lies somewhere in the experience of being near it. Climbers, hikers, and travelers of all types have tried to understand it. It's safe to say, as with Everest, that no one has fully succeeded.

✶ Grand Teton ✶
NATIONAL PARK
Grand Teton and
the Central Peaks

Grand Teton, the central crag of the Teton Range, scrapes the clouds nearly 7,000 feet above the Wyoming valley floor. Then consider the other mighty crags surrounding the 13,770-foot peak. Together they compose a formidable alpine stronghold of snow, rock, and ice, a seemingly untouchable and remote world. But looks can be deceiving. Knowing the stories—from mysterious Native American vision-quest sites found high on "The Grand" to modern feats of endurance and skill, such as hiking the nine central peaks in a Grand Traverse—coupled with spending some time on even the lower trails, makes it clear. That far summit, so easy to look at but difficult to comprehend, is a human place after all.

✶ Mount Rainier ✶
NATIONAL PARK
Mount Rainier

Now you see it, now you don't. Mount Rainier, true to its name, disappears behind cloud banks, stays hidden for days and weeks at a time, and reappears in most dramatic fashion. Sometimes, it floats above the clouds, visible only to mountaineers on its glacier-decked slopes and to thrilled passengers of flights climbing south from Seattle. When weather permits, 14,410-foot-high Rainier is visible from most of western Washington and far out to sea. It looms above the skyline of downtown Seattle as if its glaciers were invading suburban neighborhoods. Of course the best encounters are from park roads and trails, notably on the south side in the area called Paradise, known for its wildflower meadows, views of the mountain, prodigious snowfall, and the occasional rainstorm.

☆ Cumberland Gap ☆
NATIONAL HISTORICAL PARK
Gateway to the West

This landmark is the opposite of a high prominence, but to American immigrants in the late 1700s, it was an extremely important geographic feature. Settlement of the bluegrass region of Kentucky was held up for decades by Native American tribes, who prized it as a hunting territory, and also by the physical barrier of the Cumberland mountains. Eventually, war and politics ended the claims of native people, and a flood of settlers poured through the Cumberland Gap. The route was originally a Native American footpath called the Warriors' Path. In 1775, Daniel Boone hacked out a wider track that became famous as the Wilderness Road. By 1820, despite sporadic warfare and the inherent challenge of life on the frontier, some 300,000 settlers had passed through the gap on their way west. Today the highway runs underground, leaving the gap almost as peaceful as

ever. Modern travelers get a fine view of it and the surrounding mountains from the Pinnacle Overlook, a 4-mile drive from the park visitor center.

☆ Chimney Rock ☆
NATIONAL HISTORIC SITE
Significant Trails West Landmark

Days could get long for immigrants headed to Utah, Oregon, and California. Starting at Independence, Missouri, where wagon trains formed up so people could travel together, trundling toward the sunset at the pace of a walking ox, settlers entered a world more open than most could imagine: no trees, little water, and grass that grew thinner as the miles went by. What Francis Parkman described in 1846 as "the same wild endless expanse" stretched through tomorrow into forever. On a route with few notable mileposts, Chimney Rock, in today's Nebraska, stood out. Most diarists commented on the sight of it. Quite a few people climbed the slope at its base to scratch their names in the soft sandstone. Needle-shaped, 326 feet high, and a short walk from their camps on the North Platte River, the rock told travelers that they were nearing the end of the prairies and would soon be in the mountains. Hooray, you have made it this far. Carry on bravely!

☆ Devils Tower ☆
NATIONAL MONUMENT
Sacred Native American Site

As a landform, it seems almost impossible. From the relatively flat surrounding land, the tree-stump-like tower's sides form smooth upward arcs, drawing our thoughts to the sky. The summit, hovering 1,267 feet above Wyoming's Belle Fourche River, is flat, not visible from below, and therefore mysterious. Plains tribes—Lakota, Shoshone, Crow, Blackfeet, Kiowa, Arapaho, and others—consider the tower a sacred object and call it by evocative names like Bear's Lodge, Mythic-owl Mountain, Grey Horn Butte, Ghost Mountain, and Tree Rock. Legends tell of heroes, creation, and redemption. The tower's ongoing importance is reflected by ceremonies and rituals conducted every year by regional tribes. The geologic story, not fully understood, credits an intrusion of molten igneous rock that took shape beneath overlying sedimentary layers, where it hardened and was eventually exposed by erosion. In the process of cooling, the rock formed vertical hexagonal columns that, parallel but separate, give the tower its distinctive striated appearance. Rock climbers find the columns irresistible. Most are happy to gaze upward from the base where, in 1906, President Theodore Roosevelt proclaimed the first national monument.

> [A]long the [Oregon] trail, emigrants encountered Chimney Rock. "[T]he only way I can describe it" wrote S.E. Hardy in 1850, "is it looks like a big sweet potatoe hill with a pile of rocks on top something like a chimney."

☀ Canyonlands ☀
NATIONAL PARK
Island in the Sky:
Intricately Carved Yet Massive in Scale

One pleasure of being in the red rocks of Utah is how intimate the landscape can be. Narrow canyons, room-size alcoves, little rounded peaks, streams you can step across, waterfalls and pools sized for a single person. Or two. The opposite pleasure is to get far above it all, up in the wind and weather, where the view is limited only by the arc of the Earth. Such a place is Island in the Sky. It is reached by driving south toward the tip of a huge triangular mesa. Side roads beckon toward Mineral Bottom, on the Green River, and Dead Horse Point State Park, perched above the Colorado River. Save them for later. Carry on to the apex where the triangle, clawed by erosion from both sides, comes to a jaw-dropping halt overlooking the confluence of the two great rivers and a vast spill of brightly colored sediments, intricately carved and at the same time massive in scale. The sediments lie in orderly horizontal layers. The carving slices them into psychedelic patterns. The rivers lend a sense of life and motion, and the sky—well, you just have to go and see for yourself.

☀ Bering Land Bridge ☀
NATIONAL PRESERVE
A Geographic Landmark
in Human History

Whether, in the days of its use, anyone viewed the Bering Land Bridge as a landmark is doubtful. It wasn't a bridge at all but rather a 1,000-mile-wide connector between Asia and North America. Sea level fell when Ice Age glaciers took up vast quantities of water and rose when those glaciers melted. In turn, the bridge appeared and disappeared. People lived on it and moved east across it as conditions permitted. Some continued south as the continental glaciers melted. Genetic evidence indicates that these Asian immigrants were the true first Americans. The bridge is still there, beneath the relatively shallow waters of the Bering Sea. The landmark means more to modern people as we ponder our heritage, study our maps, and consider the mere 50-mile separation between Asia and North America. The preserve, not precisely on the tip of Alaska's Seward Peninsula, is a larger-than-Yellowstone chunk of pure roadless arctic wildness.

Considered a sacred site by many Native American peoples, Devils Tower is also America's first national monument.

amazing trees

To marvel at trees is to marvel at nature itself.

Forests come in all shapes and guises in the parks, from the moist hardwood forests of the Smokies to austere stands of saguaros in Arizona. The parks contain the biggest, tallest, girthiest, and oldest trees in the world. But for all the wonders of the grand trees, one fact is clear—trees don't stand alone. Their health signals the health of the environment.

✳ Redwood ✳
NATIONAL AND STATE PARKS
Coastal Redwoods

When John Steinbeck stood in the presence of the tallest living thing on the planet, he described the sensation as a "cathedral hush." The writer was describing a reverential awe more than any sound-damping effect. Among the trees preserved in California's Redwood National Park, a quilt of national and state park parcels, are the oldest, largest, and tallest of coast redwoods—"ambassadors from another time," Steinbeck called them, because their relatives stood in the Jurassic era. Only 4 percent of their historic 2-million-acre range remains, mostly in the park. All of the trees are magnificent, and it's almost impossible to gauge and compare their height without special instruments. The tallest tree, the 371-foot Hyperion tree, was only "discovered" in 2006. If you hike 8 miles up Redwood Creek Trail to the Tall Trees Grove, you'll be near Hyperion and the 368-foot Libby Tree, as well as numerous other giants, all of which elicit that cathedral hush.

✳ Big Cypress ✳
NATIONAL PRESERVE
Bald Cypresses on the Gator Hook Trail

About a third of Big Cypress is covered with cypress trees, but not too many of them qualify as "big" anymore. Most of southern Florida's giant bald cypress trees, 900-year-old, 150-foot behemoths, fell to loggers' axes in the first half of the 20th century. The trees were coveted for their water resistance and used for pickle barrels, decking, stadium seats, and even early World War II PT boats. Though most of the preserve's cypresses are a dwarf variety, some giants do remain. The best place to see them is on the Gator Hook Trail off the Loop Road south of Monroe Station. It can be a wet, water-to-the-knees walk even in the winter dry season, particularly since the giants grow from water-filled depressions; the term "cypress dome" refers to their appearance from afar. Slosh on in. Some people even float on their backs to savor the silent grandeur of a veritable cathedral of buttressed, moss-draped giants.

☆ Joshua Tree ☆
NATIONAL PARK
Joshua Trees on the
Upper Covington Flats

They are the "most repulsive tree in the vegetable kingdom," said Capt. John C. Frémont in 1844, but when you see Joshua trees silhouetted in the soft light of a desert sunset, or their creamy white-green springtime flowers, or a Scott's oriole nesting in the crook of a tree's branches, you begin to gain affection for these hardy desert survivors. Legend has it that they got their name from Mormon settlers in the mid-19th century who saw in their outstretched limbs the biblical figure Joshua guiding them westward. The trees are a species of yucca *(Yucca brevifola)* and grow only in the high desert, mainly in the Mojave, between 3,000 and 4,000 feet. They grow in sparse stands loosely called forests throughout the north part of this southeastern California park, but not in the lower elevations of the south. The densest copses of Joshua trees can be found in Upper Covington Flats—as can the biggest Joshua trees. One is 40 feet tall, 14 feet around, and believed to be 300 years old. Note that it has long outlived the unappreciative Captain Frémont.

Otherworldly Joshua trees stand silhouetted against a night sky at the national park named after them.

You might not expect weed pulling to be high on the National Park Service's conservation agenda, but when those weeds are non-native, the NPS Invasive Species Branch is all over them. The challenge isn't obvious to park visitors, but biologists are well aware of the toll bad-guy species can take on those that naturally belong. They do their best to get rid of the pests and to restore the rightful residents. Case in point is Point Reyes National Seashore, where plants like pampas grass, Scotch broom, and iceplant can overwhelm some of the park's 46 rare plant species. (Enter the weed pullers.)

The process gets trickier when the non-natives are kind of cute, like Point Reyes's non-native deer that threaten the livelihood of native tule elk. (Enter contraceptives, a humane solution to the problem.) In the Channel Islands, a decline in bald eagles (due to DDT) led to an influx of golden eagles, which in turn feasted on endemic island foxes. Happily, bald eagles are again on the rise in the park, and the park has eliminated non-native feral pigs, another favorite golden eagle meal. Fewer golden eagles means more foxes and more bald eagles.

Parks like Great Smoky Mountains, home to 100 native species of trees (more than in all of northern Europe) and 30 species of salamanders slithering on the forest floor, work hard to protect their natives, because they're what make each park unique.

☆ Olympic ☆
NATIONAL PARK
Giant Denizens of Primeval Forests

Part of Olympic National Park's charter was to protect the "finest sample of primeval forests." The cool, damp Washington State park is a huge nursery for giant trees, and something of a hall of fame for several immense species that thrive in deep, shaded, ferny forests. One Douglas-fir—the former national champion (a bigger one has been found) is 200 feet tall, 600 inches around. It's located off the Queets Trail. The national champion western redcedar, 159 feet tall, 260 inches around, is just off U.S. 101 about 5 miles north of Kalaloch Lodge, where a sign proclaims "Big Cedar Tree." And the co-champ western hemlock, 172 feet tall, 335 inches around, is up the East Fork Quinault, 2 miles east of Enchanted Valley Chalet. But you don't need to be into numbers and records to appreciate the park's majestic forests. In general, the biggest trees (Sitka spruce is another giant species) are in the Lake Quinault area along short, easy north-shore trails.

☆ Saguaro ☆
NATIONAL PARK
Sonoran Desert Cacti
Worthy of Being Called Trees

Saguaros are technically cacti, not trees, but their stoic majesty, virtually the symbol of the Old West, earns them a rightful place in this chapter. And to the envy of many a tree, they stand as tall as 50 feet and live up to 200 years. The biggest can sprout up to 40 arms. Their range, however, is small—only in the Sonoran Desert in Arizona and only below 4,000 feet. And many fell victim to cattle grazing in years past—it takes ten years for one to grow to the size of a fist. Saguaro are basically water storage tanks; they'll soak up 200 gallons after a brief, intense rain. The park's two units near Tucson, Arizona, contain 1.6 million saguaros, so you can't miss them, but the greatest concentration is along the Bajada Loop Drive in Saguaro West, with the densest stand right behind that unit's visitor center. The Valley View Trail gives a great overhead view of the giant stiff-armed cactus.

⭐ Sequoia ⭐
NATIONAL PARK
Giant Forest Grove and
the General Sherman Tree

The world's largest living thing merits the short walk it takes to pay respects. The General Sherman Tree is the largest representative of the largest species of tree in the world as measured by volume, the giant sequoia; its cousin, the coast redwood, grows taller, but its trunk is much more slender. Sherman is 274.9 feet tall, 102 feet in circumference, 36.5 feet in diameter, 52,000 cubic feet in volume, and probably more than 3,000 years old. Why is such a giant protected by a low fence? Because sequoia roots are quite shallow; years of trampling could damage it. But the Sherman doesn't stand alone: Other giant sequoias, which are rarely found in such abundance, grow all around in this southeastern California park's Giant Forest Grove. Giant sequoias grow only on the western slopes of the Sierra Nevada from 4,000 to 8,000 feet, in a narrow belt that extends about 250 miles.

⭐ Great Basin ⭐
NATIONAL PARK
Long-lived Bristlecone Pines

The world's longest living trees look nothing like mighty sequoias or giant oaks. Bristlecone pines are twisted, gnarled, forlorn looking, and stand only 15 to 30 feet high. But these heroic survivors date

The General Sherman Tree in Sequoia National Park takes top honors as the world's largest giant sequoia.

from the time of the pyramids. They grow on just a few high, dry mountain slopes in the West. Some of the oldest are in Nevada's Great Basin National Park. Because they grow on exposed slopes that get hammered by wind and snow, many appear to be dead. Some have only a single thin strip of bark and a single living branch. But they're alive, and actually live longest where conditions are the harshest. That includes high on 13,063-foot Wheeler Peak. One tree removed from the Wheeler Peak grove in 1964 was more than 4,900 years old. The best places to see the trees are along the gentle Sky Islands Forest Trail and the longer 2.8-mile Bristlecone Trail.

Everglades
NATIONAL PARK
Magnificent Mangroves

The emblematic tree of the tropics, certainly of tropical swamps, is the mangrove, and nowhere else in the Western Hemisphere does the tree grow in such abundance as in the Everglades. Mangroves can be an acquired taste. Their bizarre growth habits and sheer density make them appear foreign, almost sinister. The spidery taproots of red mangroves look like tiny legs about to stage a march. Black mangrove roots are even stranger—they sink into the muck, then send pneumatophores back above the surface to obtain oxygen. But the mangroves foster an amazing habitat that is home to the American crocodile; to sport fish like snook, redfish, and tarpon; and to exotic birds like roseate spoonbills and mangrove coocoos. It's hard to miss these trees since they dominate the Everglades coastlines. They're easily seen afoot on the West Lake Trail, on canoe trails such as Hells Bay and Bear Lake, and throughout the Wilderness Waterway labyrinth.

Great Smoky Mountains
NATIONAL PARK
Abundance and Diversity

While some other parks feature a superstar tree species, Great Smoky is all about abundance and diversity. The conditions are perfect: elevation ranging from 875 feet to 6,000 feet and higher; sunny south-facing ridges as well as moist north-facing slopes; terrain that was never scoured by glaciers; and abundant rainfall ranging from 60 to 80 inches. The park is 95 percent forested, of which 20 percent is old growth and contains 15 national champions

Some of the specific accomplishments of the [CCC] during its existence included 3,470 fire towers erected, 97,000 miles of fire roads built, 4,235,000 man-days devoted to fighting fires, and more than three billion trees planted.

and eastern hemlocks taller than 170 feet. The trees, in fact, are responsible for the blue haze for which the park was named; it's the result of the natural transpiration of vapors from trees. Albright Grove is one of the best places to see old-growth stands, including eastern hemlock trees that are threatened by blight elsewhere. The grove also contains champion maples up to 140 feet high. In the Cove Hardwood Forest, trails wind among some of the country's largest tulip trees, yellow buckeye, Frazier magnolia, red maple, and black cherry trees.

Congaree
NATIONAL PARK
One of the Tallest Temperate
Deciduous Forest Canopies in the World

Some of the tallest trees in the eastern United States are in Congaree, home to 11,000 acres of extremely dense old-growth bottomland (meaning subject to river flooding) hardwood forest. In fact, South Carolina's Congaree contains one of the tallest temperate deciduous forest canopies in the world. The park has 90 species of trees that thrive on rich nutrients provided by the flooding of the Congaree River, which happens two or three times a year. Congaree has six national champions, including a 162-foot swamp tupelo, a 160-foot sweet gum, and a 143-foot water hickory. Walk any of the park's 20 miles of trail, including the wonderful 2.6-mile Western Lake Loop boardwalk, and you'll encounter giant trees. Even in summer, their shade and a breeze blowing across the water combine to provide a refreshing sense of natural air-conditioning.

ten best parks
waterfalls

The irresistible allure of water, falling

From thundering cataracts to fine veils of mist, falling water has the power to rest our eyes and hearts. We stop. We gaze. We pose in front of them, arms linked with friends and family, and take pictures for posterity. The great ones strike us with awe. The small, misty ones speak to us of peace and contentment.

✳ Yosemite ✳
NATIONAL PARK
Yosemite, Bridalveil, Vernal,
Nevada, Ribbon, and Horsetail Falls

It's no coincidence that great scenery and great waterfalls go together. The water needs something to fall from, which usually means cliffs and mountains and canyon walls. California's Yosemite Valley claims them all and produces spectacular waterfalls at every turn. They fall from dizzying heights. Yosemite Fall drops a total of 2,425 feet over two vertical drops separated by a cascade. Bridalveil, near the entrance to the valley, is 620 feet high. A torrent in spring, it becomes a diaphanous, shifting veil as the summer season wears on. Vernal and Nevada come as a pair. For close views, hike the Mist Trail to the top of Vernal, then onward to the top of Nevada: 5.4 miles round-trip with a 2,000-foot elevation gain. Other falls visible without hiking include well-named Ribbon Fall, 1,612 feet high, and Horsetail Fall, 1,000 feet high and known for its fiery glow during winter sunsets.

✳ Haleakala ✳
NATIONAL PARK
Waimoku Falls

Waimoku Falls could be a natural haiku, minimal and eloquent but at the same time powerful. It slips rather than falls, sliding 400 feet down a near-vertical lava wall painted with bright green vegetation. Getting there is a delight. The falls is located in the Kipahulu area of the park, on the southeast coast of the island of Maui, reached by driving the Hana Road, which itself is a sort of waterfall alley. Practically every watercourse along the coast offers one or more falls and cascades. When you come to Oheo Gulch, also known as Seven Sacred Pools, set off hiking up the Pipiwai Trail, renowned as one of the best short hikes on the island and very popular. Get an early start if you want solitude. The trail climbs 650 feet through green forest, including several groves of bamboo—non-native, but visually striking—along a chain of rock-rimmed pools, waterfalls, and cascades. Hikers often stop for a cooling swim in the pools. There are more than

Framed by autumn's colors, Cuyahoga Valley's Brandywine Falls tumbles 65 feet in a bridal veil pattern.

seven, and they continue right down to the ocean. Along the way, the trail passes 185-foot-tall Makahiku Falls, a fine sight in its own right.

✷ Glacier ✷
NATIONAL PARK
McDonald, Redrock, Bird Woman, and Running Eagle Falls

With its many high mountains, northwest Montana's Glacier is a wonderland of waterfalls. They include McDonald Falls, a roadside cascade thundering through beautifully carved rock walls. Another gem is Redrock Falls in the Many Glacier area, an easy hike in a hiking paradise. Bird Woman Falls can be seen along the Going-to-the-Sun Road. A high ribbon of white that falls nearly 1,000 feet in two main drops, Bird Woman is typical of the park's numerous hanging valley waterfalls. Hanging valleys result when a large glacier cuts deeper than a tributary glacier. The tributary, in effect, is left hanging high above the main valley, a perfect recipe for dramatic waterfalls. Bird Woman could be a top choice, but Running Eagle Falls in the Two Medicine area edges it by dint of a peculiarity: It was once called Trick Falls because it doubles its height depending on water level. Early in the summer, when runoff is abundant, the water comes down in a single frothing curtain. Later, when flows diminish, most or all of the water follows a secondary channel that bypasses the high rim and emerges from a cave in the middle of the rock face. At high water, the upper stream completely obscures the lower; at low water, there is no upper falls at all. A good trick.

✸ Katmai ✸
NATIONAL PARK & PRESERVE
Brooks Falls

Brooks Falls might warrant no special attention were it not for the brown bear show. Together with leaping salmon and the Alaska landscape, the scene ranks among the world's top wildlife-viewing experiences. The falls is a simple ledge a few feet high that spans the Brooks River. In summer, great numbers of sockeye salmon return from the ocean to spawn. Making their way upriver, they encounter the falls—and a gang of hungry bears waiting for them, sometimes a dozen or more. The bears plunge into the pool below the falls where the fish mass, waiting for a chance to jump the falls; or they stand on top and catch the airborne fish as they literally fly into their mouths. A viewing platform allows you to survey the action at close range. There is no road access to the falls. You normally fly from Anchorage to the settlement of King Salmon, then transfer to a seaplane for the last leg.

✸ Cuyahoga Valley ✸
NATIONAL PARK
Brandywine Falls

When water levels are low in this Ohio national park, 65-foot Brandywine Falls makes the best use of it. Hardly more than a trickle is needed in the smooth sandstone bed of Brandywine Creek above the falls to become a lovely sheet of water. Below

the sandstone, a series of step-like shale ledges at the top spread the water, then set it loose to whisper down the sloping ramp to a lucid pool at its base. In times of high flow, the falls becomes a thundering spectacle. Yet there is something eminently satisfying in the elegant beauty of the low-water flow. A wooden walkway (wheelchair accessible) leads an eighth of a mile from the parking area under the forested rim of the gorge to a viewing platform perfectly situated halfway down the falls; it's part of a 1.5-mile loop trail that circles the gorge. The popular Brandywine is one of nearly 70 falls that can be found in Cuyahoga Valley.

☆ Birds of the Mist ☆

If you look closely at a waterfall, not so much at the falling water but rather at the things around it, you may see a small gray bird—a dipper, or water ouzel. Short-legged with a stubby tail, it perches on mist-drenched rocks, making little bouncing motions. It doesn't look like a waterbird but it rivals any duck for riparian affinity. Watch closely; now you see it, now you don't. In a twinkle, the bird vanishes beneath the water, where it walks on the gravel bottom snapping up aquatic bugs. Then *poink!* up it comes, wings whirring, to perform its best avian trick. Flying straight at the falling curtain of water, it disappears, gone behind the weighty sheet of thundering water as if through a puff of smoke, to its nest on an unseen ledge. Its hatchlings grow up in a zone of security where no predator can follow.

Yellowstone
NATIONAL PARK
Lower Falls
of the Yellowstone

Waterfalls often mark the point in a river valley where hard rock gives way to softer rock. The river erodes the soft rock more quickly while the hard rock resists erosion. Nowhere is this more dramatically illustrated than in the Grand Canyon of the Yellowstone, where the Lower Falls drops 308 feet to the bottom of a bright yellow canyon. All of the surrounding stone is volcanic rhyolite, the hard, dark rock that covers most of the park. In this case, an ancient geyser basin altered the rhyolite through heat and chemical action. In effect, the rock was cooked until soft and yellow, and easily eroded. Viewing the falls from Lookout Point, you can see that the rock at the brink of the falls is unaltered dark rhyolite, while everything downstream—so fortunate for artists and photographers—is a palette of yellows and earth tones. You can see this up close, from a dizzying perspective, by hiking the paved Brink of the Falls Trail. Or try Uncle Tom's Trail, a long metal stairway that ends at a misty viewpoint perched in front of the roaring falls.

> *Sensing the possibilities of profit, D. B. May of Billings, Montana, in March, 1889, applied to the Secretary of the Interior for permission to erect an elevator at the lower falls of the Yellowstone River.*

Grand Canyon
NATIONAL PARK
Deer Creek Falls

In the enormous sharp-edged gorge of the Grand Canyon there exist hidden grottoes rounded by water, decorated with tender moisture-loving vegetation, frequented by creatures like tree frogs and warblers. The epic landscape hides sweet delicacies. Places like Elves Chasm, Thunder River, and Havasu Canyon stand out. In fact, Havasu Falls, so beautifully set among red cliffs and travertine terraced pools, would probably take top honors if it were not just outside the park boundary on the Havasupai Reservation. But that doesn't take anything away from the beauty of Deer Creek Falls. Pouring down from the North Rim, it falls over cliffs and waters the roots of cottonwood groves until just before it hits the Colorado River, where it cuts a smooth slot canyon in the limestone. Its last act is a fitting climax. Seeming to burst from the cliff face, it falls in one clean sweep 100 feet to a beautiful pool at river level. Most who visit the falls are on wilderness river trips. It's also possible to hike down from the rim, a minimum three-day trek.

Little River Canyon
NATIONAL PRESERVE
Little River Falls
and Grace's High Falls

They call Little River a mountaintop river because it flows for most of its length on Lookout Mountain in northeast Alabama. But it's also a canyon river, running beneath sandstone walls hundreds of feet high. The Little River Falls stands in the middle. Upstream, the country is more gentle, the river relatively placid. Downstream, it becomes a significant white-water river with boulder-bed rapids. The 45-foot-high falls pours over a 100-foot-wide ledge that spans the river. In autumn, when water levels are low, the falls is a peaceful white curtain surrounded by bright yellow and red foliage. Spring floods transform it into a roaring maelstrom. That would also be the time to visit Grace's High Falls, a 133-foot seasonal free-falling plume of water that can be seen from an overlook.

⭐ Zion ⭐
NATIONAL PARK
Temple of Sinawava Waterfalls

Speaking of ephemeral flows, a wondrous magic happens in the desert Southwest during heavy rainstorms. Dry streambeds suddenly burst into life. Waterfalls appear where hours ago there was nothing. Where cliffs are high, the result is unforgettable, as in the Temple of Sinawava at the upper end of Zion Canyon in Utah. The red-rock temple is a stunning place any time. High walls glow with reflected light, giving a particular luminescence to leaves of trees and flowers, be they green in the summer or gold in the fall. But when it rains— and summer thunderstorms can be torrential—an elegant and very high bridal veil falls tumbles from a cleft far overhead, falling into the upper reaches of the North Fork of the Virgin River. Appreciate it now; in a few hours it will be gone.

⭐ Great Smoky Mountains ⭐
NATIONAL PARK
Grotto, Indian Creek, Toms Branch, Laurel, and Rainbow Falls

Mountains everywhere are rain catchers, and the higher the better. On average, the upper elevations of the Great Smoky Mountains in Tennessee/North Carolina pull down 85 inches of rain each year. The runoff feeds more than 2,000 miles of streams, which makes for a lot of waterfalls. Seeing the best of them requires some hiking. It's a pleasant feeling, on a hot summer day, to arrive in a zone of cool, forest-fragrant mist. The delightful Grotto Falls drops 25 feet from a ledge that overhangs enough for the

Trillium Gap Trail to go behind the water curtain; it's a 3-mile round-trip. A shorter walk on the Deep Creek Trail (1.6 miles round-trip) takes hikers to 25-foot-high Indian Creek Falls. Along the way, the trail passes Toms Branch Falls, a side stream that slides gracefully down a series of ledges. Laurel Falls rewards hikers on one of the park's most popular trails, a paved 2.6-mile round-trip path named after the falls. And popular Rainbow Falls, also on an eponymously named trail, drops 80 feet, turning the waters of Le Conte Creek into a broad veil that hikers can walk behind. In winter, the veil becomes a freestanding ice pillar.

Seasonal rains create curtains of water that fall down the red-rock sandstone walls of Zion.

chasing photographs

To get the most from a national park, think like a photographer.

It's summer at the Grand Canyon. You arrive in the middle of the day, road weary but eager to see the legendary wonder. The air is hot. The roads are crowded, and the kids are cranky after hours in the car. Find a parking space. Hike out to an overlook. And there it lies, the awesome gulf in its full glory. Well, not quite full. Although the Grand Canyon is an impressive sight at any time, you might feel a bit let down, squinting in the glare of midday light.

Where are the bright colors, the deep shadows, the luminous voids, not to mention rainbows and billowing storm clouds? It sure doesn't look like the pictures in travel magazines.

But the canyon often does look that way. The pictures are not exaggerations; they were not manipulated with the latest computer software. Rather, they hold out a promise that applies to all the national parks and all their magnificent sights. If you think like the people who made those pictures—that is, if you approach the national parks like a nature photographer—not only will you get memorable images, but also you'll experience the parks at their inspiring best.

Jeff Foott knows this as well as anyone. Filmmaker, photographer, and naturalist, he has spent his life making sure he is in the right place at the right time. His work for the likes of National Geographic, BBC, Discovery, and the International League of Conservation Photographers represents a parade of natural wonders, animate and inanimate, all of which he has experienced in person.

He has no option. By definition, a photographer has to be in the thick of things. Foott can't conjure events from imagination. The pod of orcas launching themselves from the sea in a graceful ballet, the bald eagle snatching a fish from a grizzly bear, the double rainbow spanning the canyon rim to rim: He has to be there while it's happening before he can capture the first image.

The lesson for the rest of us, whether or not we chase photographs, is that knowing what to look for and being there at the right time can lead to enrichment beyond our expectation.

Foott says it takes effort. "Sometimes you find a place that's inherently beautiful but the light is wrong. You get an idea of what it could look like, so you keep going back. It might not work out but the chances increase the more you know and the more you plan."

IMPROVING THE ODDS

There are ways to improve the odds of getting a fabulous photograph. Consider spring in the Mojave Desert, where very specific weather conditions can lead to extravagant eruptions of wildflowers. Blooms might last only a few days. Catching them at their peak requires more than luck. It requires networking.

"On the Internet you can find what the flowers are doing almost anywhere in the country. Websites predict months in advance, and there are also reports from people who have just been there. You can wait for the reports, then jump in the car. This goes for autumn colors and wildlife sightings too."

Among his important tools are a compass and astronomical charts. Suppose you want to see Delicate Arch, the iconic symbol of Utah's red-rock country, as thousands of photos show it—glowing in warm sunlight against a deep blue sky framing a snowy view of the La Sal Mountains.

"To get it right, you need to know that the arch faces northwest, and where the sun will be at different times of the year." He says the arch catches good light at sunset, not sunrise, in June but not October. Solar calculators available on the Internet provide all the needed details, even to the extent of indicating when the full moon will rise perfectly positioned behind the arch.

Of course, clouds could spoil the view. Or improve it.

"Landscape people look for weather," he says. "For drama, weather is key. Sometimes when it looks like it's going to be worst it's the best time to go out. There might be lightning, cloud formations, other interesting atmospheric things happening."

He mentions Zion Canyon as an example, where rainstorms create ephemeral waterfalls. One minute the walls are dry. The next, they come alive with cascading water. The storms pass, the waterfalls disappear, "and if you weren't out in the rain, you wouldn't know that you missed something special."

KNOW YOUR ECOLOGY

In general, nature photographers avoid midday, preferring what they call "God's light," the rich tones of early morning and late evening. The same applies to seasons and animal movements.

"Go to Yellowstone for the elk rut in September, or Point Reyes for whales in mid-February, which also happens to be a good time for wildflowers." He recommends going to Yosemite in spring for the dogwoods bloom, and Theodore Roosevelt, Yellowstone, and Wind Cave in May to see new bison calves. "During early summer, big horn sheep are common on the Highline Trail in Glacier. There's a famous steelhead run in Olympic National Park where they jump the falls in spring. Trail Ridge Road in Rocky Mountain is the place for seeing pikas at close range.

"It helps to know your ecology," he says, "where the animals are, what they're doing." This leads to a deeper understanding of the natural world and our place in it. That gift, he believes "is the best reward of all for visiting national parks."

volcanic wonders

Vast badlands of lava, cinder cones, lava tubes, and thermal sites

Some of the most fascinating and alien landscapes in the national parks are volcanic. Many of them defy conventional notions of beauty, but they have a particular lure of their own. Happily, the volcanic parks do an outstanding job of interpreting their geology, and a compelling story of ongoing creation begins to emerge.

☀ Chiricahua ☀
NATIONAL MONUMENT
Rhyolitic Rock Pinnacles

Chiricahua is one of Arizona's "sky islands"—discrete, isolated volcanic mountain ranges that rise 9,000 feet or so above the surrounding desert grasslands. "Isolated" is an operative word. This is a quiet park of 12,000 acres. Volcanically speaking, the park's most amazing feature is its wonderland of rock pinnacles—balanced rocks and stacks hundreds of feet tall that look like giant stone totem poles. The Apache called this the "land of standing-up rocks." The formations are composed of rhyolite—superheated and solidified volcanic ash. The park's 8-mile scenic drive features overlooks of the pinnacles at Echo Canyon and Massai Point. For a closer look, hike the 7.3-mile Heart of Rocks Trail. Take the shuttle to Echo Canyon and hike down to the visitor center. Rangers drive the van, so you'll get a crash course in volcanism, then a great look at the rocks—some weigh up to 3,000 pounds yet are perched on bases just inches around.

☀ Yellowstone ☀
NATIONAL PARK
Geyser Basins and Hot Springs:
10,000 Thermal Features

Yellowstone country is a gigantic volcanic playground in northwest Wyoming comprising three calderas produced by three super eruptions between 600,000 and 3,000,000 years ago. The northwest quadrant of the park is the nexus of an immense hot spot, a growing underground bulge that spreads hundreds of miles, and which is effectively one of the largest volcanoes in the world. Because its magma chamber is just a couple of miles below the surface, a constant source of heat is constantly meeting circulating water that migrates down through cracks, and presto—geyser. And the world's most astounding concentration of thermal features, 10,000 of them, including hot springs, mud pots (a blend of sulfuric acid, silica, and clay), and fumaroles. All are on vivid display at the park's two main geyser basins, Upper and Norris, and the Mammoth Hot Springs area. Norris contains the world's tallest active geyser, Steamboat; Upper is the home of the world-famous Old Faithful geyser and many others; Mammoth's flowing waters have formed beautiful travertine limestone terraces.

✳ Haleakala ✳
NATIONAL PARK
A Massive Cinder Cone Volcano

Haleakala is a teenager to Kilauea's infant, so naturally the older volcano on the island of Maui has a more complex story to tell than the work in progress on the Big Island of Hawaii. Haleakala is something of a volcano's greatest hits—a massive (10,023 feet) volcanic mountain with a gaping crater that displays all manner of lava types and formations. A road winds to the top, where the big picture is revealed: This enormous mountain—which actually rises 30,000 feet from the ocean's floor—is in fact a cinder cone vent that once spewed volcanic particles like popcorn from a popper. Traversing across a series of cinder vents, the Keonehe'ehe'e (Sliding Sands) Trail leads past sharp a'a lava, ropy pahoehoe, and globby lava bombs, lava formations as large as a small car, spewed out by eruptions peppered across the landscape. The bombs are old enough to be peeling away, revealing their inner structure.

The desolate landscape of Haleakala is made beautifully colorful by the mineral content of the volcanic cinders.

Lassen Volcanic
NATIONAL PARK
A Showcase of Volcanoes and Volcanism

Located in northeastern California about 50 miles from Shasta, Lassen Volcanic National Park gladdens the hearts of volcano lovers because among its 60 identifiable volcanoes are all four major types: plug dome, shield, cinder cone, and composite—and it contains numerous thermal areas, making it a highly concentrated showcase of volcanism. The crown jewel of the park is Lassen Peak, among the world's largest plug dome volcanoes. Its last major eruption occurred in 1914–17, peaking in 1915; it has been quiet since 1921. A 5-mile round-trip hike climbs nearly 2,000 feet to the 10,457-foot summit. The Bumpass Hell thermal area is the park's most popular attraction, full of colorful boiling pools, the noisy Big Boiler fumarole, and Boiling Springs, the largest thermal lake outside of Yellowstone. Get there early in the morning when specters of steam rise up in small whorls. Devil's Kitchen is equally compelling but draws fewer people, and there one can move around without boardwalks. Count on a strong rotten-egg smell at both places. If all this activity suggests, well, volcanic activity, it's true; scientists believe Lassen Peak or Mount Shasta—farther north—could join Mount St. Helens as the next active volcanoes in the Cascade Range.

> *"[T]he Devil's Vomit" is how one Oregon- bound pioneer described his encounter with Craters of the Moon. Hundreds of pioneers travelled through the area on the Goodale's Cutoff section of the Oregon trail in the 1850's and 1860's.*

Crater Lake
NATIONAL PARK
A Dazzling Lake-filled Caldera

Crater Lake is such a dazzling sight that it's easy to forget its origins. The lake comprises snowmelt and rainwater that filled a 1,932-foot-deep crater left by the eruption of Mount Mazama about 7,700 years ago. Drive Rim Drive (or take the Trolley Tour)—it traces the caldera of the volcano—with that dimension in mind and you get a sense of the mountain's immense scope. The top of the mountain would have been 12,000 feet high; the surface of the lake today is 6,173 feet. Mazama's eruptions had 42 times the force of Mount St. Helens's in 1980. Later eruptions inside the crater created Wizard Island and the submerged Merriam Cone. If you can't quite picture a volcano here, drive to Pumice Desert north of the lake. The swath of pumice and ash, 50 feet deep, covers 5.5 square miles.

Craters of the Moon
NATIONAL MONUMENT & PRESERVE
Spatter and Cinder Cones

"Where's the volcano?" is high atop the list of FAQs at Craters of the Moon in Idaho. Instead of a single peak, look for spatter cones and cinder cones aligned along what is known as the Great Rift—a 50-mile fissure that permitted lava to well up and flow across half a million acres of landscape. Spatter cones are the monument's signature feature, created by globs of lava that shot up through the rift and adhered to one another. Trails lead to several of them, including one called Snow Cone whose magma chamber is filled with ice. A walk on Caves Trail leads to four different lava tubes—underground chambers through which rivers of lava once ran—including massive Indian Tunnel, 800 feet long with a 30-foot ceiling. Adventurous backpackers can follow the Wilderness Trail to Echo Crater, where they can savor the extraordinary experience of sleeping inside a volcanic crater.

☆ Lava Beds ☆
NATIONAL MONUMENT
Lava Tubes

The name may be Lava Beds, but lava tube "caves"— underground conduits through which lava once flowed—are the star of the show here. The monument is home to more than 750 caves, of which more than 20 are easily accessible. That doesn't mean every cave is a cakewalk. The caves are rated, and a down-and-dirty experience is guaranteed in a challenging cave—duckwalking, crawling, ceilings as low as 12 inches. Helmets (the park sells "bump hats"), knee pads, and flashlights are de rigueur. But the features are similar in all the caves, so the less adventurous can opt for Mushpot Cave or Skull Cave, whose second-tier floor is coated permanently with ice. These caves played a part in history, as they served as hiding places for the Modoc people during the Modoc War of 1872–73.

☆ Hawaii Volcanoes ☆
NATIONAL PARK
Kilauea

It's not every day one gets to see land being born, which is why a walk near flowing lava in Hawaii Volcanoes National Park is a thrilling experience. Start by driving to the top of Kilauea's often billowing caldera, which last erupted with lava in 1982, via the Crater Rim Drive. There you can gaze into Halemaumau, the 400-foot crater pit and traditional

☆ Know Your Volcanoes ☆

Among the fascinations of visiting volcanic parks is the opportunity to play amateur geologist, which entails a detective hunt for clues about the origins of the rocks and formations you encounter. For example, Lassen Volcanic National Park in California is famous for having all four major volcano types— formations that also occur throughout the parks. So how do you identify them, and what do they mean?

A *cinder cone* is an accumulation of volcanic fragments spewed out through a vent. They can be small, like the cones lined up along the Great Rift in Craters of the Moon, or large, like Sunset Volcano. A showcase version in Lassen Volcanic is cleverly called Cinder Cone.

A *shield volcano* is a broadly sloping mountain built up by the eruption of fluid lava. Prospect Peak in Lassen is one. Kilauea in Hawaii Volcanoes National Park is an example of one that remains under construction.

A *plug dome* is a dome-shaped volcano formed by viscous magma. Domes often erupt from the flanks of composite volcanoes, which was the case with Lassen Peak, a plug dome that formed on its ancestor, a mountain called Tehama that was 1,000 feet taller than Lassen.

A *composite*, or *stratovolcano*, is created by the eruption of viscous lava flows, tephra (fragments), and pyroclastic flows. It is typically built up over thousands of years and consists of a number of vents that may spew separate cones and domes on the composite's flank. Brokeoff Mountain in Lassen is a composite volcano, as is Mount St. Helens.

home of Pele, goddess of the volcano—an experience all the more stunning after dark. The famous lava flows are 12 miles east, and everything about walking here is subject to the caprices of nature. Lava seekers might walk a mile from a vehicle to the flowing lava, or several dicey miles across craggy hardened lava, or never get close at all. But to get close is to hear the brittle, glassy, scraping sound of new pieces of lava being dragged along a flow, the noise of rocks cracking as a new flow starts from within, to smell the sulfury odors, the vaguely metallic smell of an active flow—a total sensory experience. The park posts daily updates and cautions, but if possible, try to witness the sight of lava flowing into the ocean near the end of Chain of Craters Road, especially at twilight when the lava glows red against the deep blue backdrop of dusk.

✵ Sunset Crater Volcano ✵
NATIONAL MONUMENT
A Colorful Volcanic Cone
and Lava Fields

Sunset Crater, a classically shaped cinder cone, erupted circa 1040–1100, making it the most recent volcanic event in north-central Arizona's San Francisco Volcanic Field. When explorer John Wesley Powell first saw the cone in 1885, he remarked that it "seems to glow with a light of its own"—the result of the cinders being oxidized to reddish, sunset-like colors. Hence the cone's name, which Powell is credited with naming. Only sparse vegetation has grown around the cone's lower slopes, and the top is so pristine and so little eroded that it is off-limits—a trail closed in the 1970s still scars its slopes. But you can hike to nearby Lenox

Crater—a steep half-mile path leads to the top—and across the Bonito Lava Flow at the base of Sunset. The visitor center shows a video reenactment of the crater's eruption as it would have been witnessed by native people nearly a thousand years ago.

✵ El Malpais ✵
NATIONAL MONUMENT
Lava Flows, Cinder Cones,
and Lava Tubes

Its name literally means "the bad land," and El Malpais in New Mexico is really bad, particularly if you try to walk across the park's 110,000 acres of jagged lava. The easiest way to do it is via the 7.5-mile Zuni-Acoma Trail. Rock cairns, some placed by Zuni and Acoma people more than 800 years ago, mark the way. The going is arduous—figure on a mile an hour—and good boots are needed to protect against the sole-shredding lava. But even a short jaunt on the trail gives appreciation for the rugged geology of the badlands, which represent the fruit of a series of eruptions that ended about 2,000 years ago. A short cairn-marked trail in the Lava Falls area takes you over the youngest lava flow in the park. Alternatively, you can don a headlamp and follow a half-mile, cairn-marked trail to Big Skylight and Four Windows Caves, 600 feet and 1,200 feet long respectively, both part of a 17-mile lava-tube system in the Big Tubes area. A cinder cone, Bandera Crater, and an ice cave are in private hands but open to the public. Both are short, easy walks. You can get a great overlook of the lava fields and crater from Sandstone Bluffs Overlook on N. Mex. 117.

fossils & dinosaurs

Ancient times preserved in the natural archives of our planet

Centuries ago, people in China found huge bones exposed on the ground and decided they were the skeletons of dragons. We know them as dinosaurs. Their fossil remains are found on every continent, along with gangly proto-birds, tiny rodents, horses, fish, flowers, ferns, insects, tree trunks—even algae.

☀ Dinosaur ☀
NATIONAL MONUMENT
A Spectacular Quarry of Fossil Bones

We start with the big ones. The supposed dragons. They lived from about 245 million years ago until 65 million years ago, when a natural catastrophe—evidence supports that a huge meteorite hit Earth—caused their extinction. Dinosaurs, of course, existed in a huge variety of sizes and shapes; however, it's the big ones that stir our imaginations. This Colorado monument is best known for its spectacular quarry, a steeply angled rock wall that displays a dense concentration of partially excavated fossil bones. The bones are in the Morrison formation, a mix of sandstone and conglomerate deposited during the Jurassic period 150 million years ago. The concentration here is thought to have been a sandbar in an ancient river where carcasses came to rest during floods. Among the bony roll call: *Stegosaurus,* with its protruding spinal plates and spiked tail; *Apatosaurus,* also called *Brontosaurus,* whose long neck and longer tail gave it a total length

up to 75 feet; and *Allosaurus,* the nightmarish relative of *Tyrannosaurus rex.* Paleontologists recently unearthed the first complete North American sauropod skull from the Cretaceous period. Skulls are fragile and rarely found whole. This one belonged to an herbivore called *Abydosaurus* that lived about 105 million years ago. (Note: A new structure enclosing the quarry is expected to open in late 2011.)

☀ Petrified Forest ☀
NATIONAL PARK
Colorful Fossilized Wood and
Other Fossils of the Late Triassic

Staying on the whopping side of things, trees come after dinosaurs. When trees die, they normally decompose quickly. But if they become buried in the right sort of sediment, one fine-grained and rich in silica, decomposition is arrested. Water soaks into the wood, carrying minerals that gradually replace the organic matter, literally turning it to stone. The woody structure remains, but the original colors have been replaced by a glittering crystal rainbow of

A technician outlines dinosaur bones on the steep quarry wall at Dinosaur National Monument.

reds, blues, and yellows. The trees of Petrified Forest in Arizona grew during the late Triassic period about 200 million years ago, early in the age of dinosaurs. Growing conditions were good. Giant conifers rose 200 feet and higher above thickets of lush vegetation. Their fossil remains are scattered among the colorful clay hills of the Chinle formation. Trunks of the genus *Araucarioxylon* stand out for their size (up to 190 feet long) and their awesome petrified beauty. Other fossils help fill out the ancient scene: early dinosaurs, crocodile-like reptiles 40 feet long, half-ton amphibians, horseshoe crabs, clams, and freshwater sharks. Mammals were far in the future.

✳ Florissant Fossil Beds ✳
NATIONAL MONUMENT
A Rich Deposit of Eocene Epoch Fossils

It is impressive that the 5-foot femur of a 30-ton *Apatosaurus* can survive 80-odd million years. For a tiny mayfly wing to do the same is downright boggling. The fossil femur weighs about 600 pounds. It was the size of a small tree trunk and pound-for-pound stronger. The mayfly practically defines its order name, Ephemeroptera, from the Greek *ephemeros,* or short-lived. Yet here it is, 34 million years later, the lightest of gossamer preserved between thin layers of shale. Colorado's Florissant is extraordinarily rich in fossil species; about 1,700 have been identified. They include the leaves of ferns, cypress, maple, mahogany, laurel, cocoa, and many others. Among the insects are dragonflies, cicadas, lacewings, beetles, caddisflies, and yes, cockroaches. Fish are abundant, birds and mammals less so. Not all the fossils are delicate. Several huge petrified redwood stumps still stand upright behind the visitor center, which is loaded with fossil displays. The park has a roster of hands-on paleontology activities. Call ahead for schedules and availability.

☆ Fossil Butte ☆
NATIONAL MONUMENT
Eocene Epoch Fossils
at Fossil Lake

It was 50 million years ago, the Eocene epoch. Dinosaurs had suffered their catastrophic disappearance. In Wyoming and the surrounding region, the climate was subtropical. For about two million years, a large shallow lake, now called Fossil Lake, collected sediments and the bodies of creatures that lived in and around the water. The sediments today make up the Green River formation. Mingled with them are the river and stream sediments of the Wasatch formation. Both formations contain fossils, but the formation created by the lake sediments yields especially good fossils. In the lake's calm water, organisms tended to lie undisturbed and whole. Fine-grained sediments covered them like pages in a book. The monument protects a small piece of that book and features more than 80 opened pages in the visitor center. Every slab of stone is a work of art, revealing fossils galore. Fish are prominent, including *Knightia,* long-snouted gar, and stingrays. Also found are turtles, crocodiles, snakes, snails, birds, the earliest known bat, and an early horse. Insects include plant-hoppers, crickets, wasps, beetles,

weevils, and dragonflies. Palm fronds, sycamore leaves, ferns, horsetails, flowers, and redwood leaves prove the warmer ancient climate.

☆ Agate Fossil Beds ☆
NATIONAL MONUMENT
Miocene Epoch Remains:
Early Mammal Fossils

Two buff-colored hills rise from a grassy plain beside the Niobrara River in Nebraska. They are important not for agates, which are found in other locations nearby, but for Miocene mammal fossils. About 20 million years ago the area was populated by an odd assemblage of herd animals, predators, and rodents. The landscape was a savanna of grass and scattered water holes. Paleontologists theorize that a severe

☆ Prehistoric Fish Trophies ☆

Fossil collecting is not permitted in National Park Service properties, but you can experience the thrill of discovery and take home your findings from privately owned quarries near some parks. One of the best is **Ulrich's Fossil Gallery** (307-877-6466), adjacent to Fossil Butte National Monument in Wyoming. The sediments and fossils are the same as those protected by the monument; however, here fossil fans get to keep what they find, except for species declared by the state of Wyoming to be rare and unusual. According to the gallery, a wannabe paleontologist can expect to find six to eight fish fossils. Digging sessions last about three hours; a staff member supervises at the quarry. The gallery will also give advice for display preparation. The enclosing stone must be painstakingly removed with tiny hand tools to reveal the complete fossil on its rock slab.

drought concentrated the animals near shrinking water sources, where they died close to each other. Some of the animals were similar to modern species; others were downright strange. There was a rhino the size of a dog with two small side-by-side horns on its nose. An 8-foot-tall chalicothere called *Moropus* had a horse-like skull, three-clawed feet like a sloth, and short hind legs. *Dinohyus,* or "terrible pig," was an omnivore described as a "cross between a bison and a pig with a whole lot of mean thrown in" and which stood 6 feet tall. There were little gazelle-like *Stenomylus,* delicate creatures the size of whippets. Land beavers lived away from water, digging corkscrew tunnels deep into dry ground. Imagine a long cat's tail on a heavy-jawed hyena, and you have something like *Daphoenodon,* or "beardog." They exist today only as well-displayed exhibits in the visitor center.

> *Eight National Park System units were established specifically for the protection of important fossils, but the geologic history of plants and animals is preserved in as many as 146 units.*

☀ Hagerman Fossil Beds ☀
NATIONAL MONUMENT
One of the World's Richest Deposits of Late Pliocene Epoch Fossils

Across the Snake River from Hagerman, Idaho, this monument is significant as one of the world's richest deposits of fossils from the late Pliocene epoch, some three to four million years ago. Chief among them is the Hagerman horse *(Equus simplicidens),* a small and strongly built horse with a thick neck and muscular forequarters like an African zebra. The earliest specimens date from 3.5 million years ago. The horse became extinct some 10,000 years ago at the end of the last ice age, along with many other large species. Thirty complete skeletons and many partial ones have been excavated since a local rancher discovered the bones in 1928. Besides horses, more than 220 other species (105 vertebrates) have been located in these strata, which represent a variety of ancient habitats, including grassy plains and wetlands. There were mastodons, saber-toothed cats, ground sloths, giant marmots, camels, bears, otters, muskrats, and peccaries. Of two dog species, one was the ancestor of modern coyotes. The other, *Borophagus,* has no living descendants. It sported a powerful, shortened jaw like that of a hyena, which explains its unofficial name, bone-crushing dog. A visitor center in Hagerman offers displays; ranger-led tours visit the fossil beds in the bluffs across the river.

☀ Guadalupe Mountains ☀
NATIONAL PARK
A Fossilized Marine Reef

Far back in the shadows of the Permian era, 265 million years ago, western Texas was near the Equator. Much of it was covered by the Permian Basin, an inland sea. Around its margins there formed a reef—roughly circular, 400 miles long, built up by tiny lime-secreting organisms. Today, this part of Texas is a desert and the reef is an imposing limestone mountain range that ranks as one of the world's best examples of a fossilized marine reef. Its fine-grained stone contains fossils of sea urchins, crinoids, trilobites, nautiloids, and much more. They are important, in part, because they lived before the Great Dying, a catastrophic series of events that drove some 96 percent of marine species into extinction. Hikers can get a geologic tour of the results via the Permian Reef Trail (8.4 miles round-trip).

✶ John Day Fossil Beds ✶
NATIONAL MONUMENT
More Than 700 Known Fossil Sites
Spanning 40 Million Years

Scattered among the park's three units are more than 700 known fossil sites spanning 40 million years. Fossils reveal the development of flowering plants and mammals. They include 14 genera of ancient horse; also prehistoric turtles, alligators, tapirs, rhinos, peccaries, cougars, bears, hippos, and more. Among plants are primitive horsetails, ferns, and ginkgoes, but also flowering species like dogwood, magnolia, beech, and laurel. Visit the paleontology museum at the Sheep Rock Unit. Then hike among the colorful hills on interpretive trails that offer displays and numerous in situ fossils.

✶ Glacier ✶
NATIONAL PARK
Stromatolites:
Precambrian Fossils

The most scenic fossil sites in America, and among the oldest, lie along the Continental Divide in Montana's Glacier National Park. The fossils themselves aren't much to look at. They are stromatolites, ancient bacterial mats that appear as cabbage-size swirls in the Precambrian rock. If it's Precambrian, it's very old. Stromatolites found in Australia have been dated from 2.7 billion years ago. Other discoveries push the age back to nearly 3.5 billion years ago (keeping in mind that not all stromatolites are caused by living organisms, and they can be difficult to tell apart). In Glacier, stromatolites occur in several rock strata. The Altyn limestone, exposed in areas on the east side of the park, is nearly 1.5 billion years old. The Siyeh, also limestone, dates from 1.1 billion years ago. That's billion with a *b,* back to the time when life on Earth was dominated by simple forms like blobs of bacteria. In some exposures, the Glacier fossils are packed so densely that the rock seems solid fossil, so much so that one could easily overlook the fossils—and many people do, in part because it's hard to ignore Glacier's extravagant alpine scenery for a bunch of stone cabbages. But just remember this: *Tyrannosaurus rex* skulls might be more compelling, but stromatolites are older by a thousand million years.

✶ Theodore Roosevelt ✶
NATIONAL PARK
Paleocene Epoch Swamp Creatures:
Turtles, Crocodilians, Snails, and Clams

In the Paleocene epoch, about 55 million years ago, this part of the Dakota plains was a swamp with a climate resembling that of modern-day southern Louisiana. Dinosaurs had disappeared. Slow-moving rivers coming from the west created a lush delta shaded by sequoia, palm, and magnolia trees. Bald cypresses stood in warm shallows. Turtles and crocodilians swam around their knobby roots. Snails and freshwater clams were abundant. So are their fossils, thanks to the volcanic ash and other sediments exposed in the park's badland canyons. Loop roads in both units of the North Dakota's Theodore Roosevelt park give access to erosional beauties along the Little Missouri River. For walkers, petrified wood can be seen (but never collected) on the Petrified Forest Loop Trail in the South Unit of the park. The Medora South Unit visitor center sports the skeleton of a crocodile-like *Champsosaurus.*

rocks & arches

The natural whimsy and artistry of wind, water, ice, and time

Arches, hoodoos, natural bridges, domes, and other gravity-defying shapes belie the notion that rock is an inanimate material lying hard beneath our feet. The most remarkable natural sculptures are mere remnants, the last bits of large formations that have been carved away by erosion. They will disappear in a geological flash.

✴ Arches ✴
NATIONAL PARK
Delicate Arch and Other
Arches, Spires, and Balanced Rocks

No place on the planet rivals the red-rock country of the American Southwest for the number and beauty of its unusual rock formations. The explanation lies in the geologic history of the Colorado Plateau, which covers southern Utah and parts of adjacent states. Uplifted and rumpled in places, the plateau is a hotbed of erosion. Its soft and easily carved horizontal layers of rock lie exposed to the weather, with underlying softer layers—mudstones and shale—readily undercutting harder layers that collapse along vertical lines, creating the imposing cliffs and layer-cake structures characteristic of the Southwest deserts. At the center of all this geologic folderol is Arches, the best natural sculpture garden in America. Its signature piece, Delicate Arch, is most famous (pictured on Utah license plates), but others of its more than 2,000 arches are equally marvelous. Half the pleasure is getting to them.

Park roads lead to highlights like Double Arch, Courthouse Towers, and Parade of Elephants. For trails, try Devils Garden where the long, slender strand of Landscape Arch challenges belief; or hike to Delicate Arch for a sunset that will never fade from memory.

✴ Capitol Reef ✴
NATIONAL PARK
The Waterpocket Fold
and Sandstone Domes

All rocks have stories, some more interesting than others. The rock of Capitol Reef in south-central Utah ranks fairly high among geologic narratives, but not because of any complex twists of plot. Rather, it's the elegant finish that makes the tale satisfying. This one begins with a rock warp. Ten thousand feet of sedimentary rock—sandstone and shale—were folded when a deep fault moved beneath them to create a monocline, a warp or dip in a region of horizontal rock layers. Fifty to 70 million years of erosion later, the Waterpocket Fold, as the monocline is called, is a steeply angled line of cliffs 100 miles long. From one end to the other, this is elite rock work, spangled with arches, narrow canyons, soaring rock fins, and—explaining the other half of the park's name—gleaming high, white domes crafted out of beautiful Navajo sandstone. Geologists and poets call the stone aeolian, for its origin as dunes. Finely sifted and shaped by the wind in a Sahara-like desert, this stone has an unusual purity and a tendency to form graceful rounded shapes, of which Capitol Dome is an ideal example. The park's 10-mile Scenic Drive roughly parallels a portion of the fold and provides a good introduction to the wondrous formations.

✶ Glen Canyon ✶
NATIONAL RECREATION AREA
Countless Side Canyons,
Large and Small

Conservationists consider the flooding of Glen Canyon to be one of the great environmental losses of our time. The waters of Lake Powell, held back by 710-foot-high Glen Canyon Dam in Arizona, drowned a unique canyon system that stretched deep into Utah, a place with no equivalent. At its heart was the Colorado River, flowing warm and gentle beneath high overhanging walls of Navajo sandstone. Side canyons, many of them supporting

Freestanding and 45 feet tall, Delicate Arch has become the icon of Utah's Arches National Park.

lush gardens of ferns and willows watered by clear, shallow streams, beckoned like secret chapels. The river carved graceful bends, creating deep, concave amphitheaters hundreds of feet high. Drifting in a boat through such an amphitheater, you might see only a distant arc of blue sky. Today, most of this is gone. Yet some remains. The shoreline of Lake Powell is fantastically convoluted, measuring nearly 2,000 miles. That number reflects the intricate winding of its many branching channels. Side canyons narrow the farther up one goes, until some will scarcely permit passage to a canoe, cool echoing

Two hikers venture into Bryce Canyon's fantastical world of fiery colored hoodoos.

spaces filled with reflected light. In some, you can reach the high water line and walk upstream past waterfalls and clearwater pools in a land where every turn brings a new sculpture garden.

✶ Natural Bridges ✶
NATIONAL MONUMENT
Rock Fins
and Natural Bridges

Three easily visited natural bridges stand in two canyons in southeast Utah. A 9-mile loop road meanders along the rims of White and Armstrong Canyons, and short trails drop in for closer views. The canyons are beautifully convoluted, curving tightly around narrow rock fins that make it easy to visualize the creation of a natural bridge. It starts with a bend in the stream. As the water cuts deeper, the bend becomes a hairpin loop. The rock inside the loop becomes thinner as erosion eats away from both sides until the stream punches through and a bridge is born. By twisting itself in serpentine curves, water finds the straight path, the shortest distance. Hydrologists provide explanations for this; yet the bridges, in their airy improbability, encourage thoughts of natural mysteries. These three—Owachomo, Kachina, and Sipapu—are prime subjects.

✶ Rainbow Bridge ✶
NATIONAL MONUMENT
World's Largest Natural Rock Bridge

Graceful Rainbow Bridge in southern Utah seems as remote as the legendary pot of gold. Before the creation of Lake Powell made it possible to get here by motorboat on a day trip, reaching Rainbow Bridge involved a rugged overland foot trip through the Navajo Reservation, or a float down the Colorado River and then a hike up Bridge Canyon. Either way took at least a week and usually more. But Rainbow Bridge was and still is worthy of such effort. In fact, the Navajo and other tribes consider this a significant sacred site. Made of beautiful Navajo sandstone, it stands in near-perfect symmetry—290 feet high and 275 feet across at the base. It is the world's largest natural rock bridge. Rainbow Bridge could be called an arch, except for the manner in which it was born. The difference between natural bridges and arches is that bridges are formed by flowing water. True to their names, they span existing or former watercourses.

☆ Bryce Canyon ☆
NATIONAL PARK
Red-rock Hoodoos
and Natural Amphitheaters

The rock of Utah's Bryce is limestone of the Claron formation and although it does hold some arches, it is most famous for its tightly clustered spires, or hoodoos. Seeing them from a distance, high against the rim of the forested Paunsaugunt Plateau, it becomes clear that Bryce is not a canyon but rather a series of eroded amphitheaters. The plateau is being demolished, by erosion, in a most spectacular fashion. Peering into the hoodoos from the rim, that impression is intensified, and so is the desire to get down amid the fiery colors to experience them close at hand. Numerous trails provide access. The Queens Garden Trail is among the least demanding and most popular; it leads to a formation that reminds some people of Queen Victoria. Combining it with the Navajo Trail adds a little distance and takes in other landmarks, including Wall Street (a narrow passage through the rock), Thors Hammer,

and Two Bridges. A more strenuous route, the 4-mile round-trip Hat Shop Trail, drops off Bryce Point to a cluster of balanced rocks perched like white hats on red pedestals. The Rim Trail offers any number of wonderful views without the cost of having to climb back up.

☆ Devils Postpile ☆
NATIONAL MONUMENT
Basalt Columns

Whoever gave Devils Postpile in California its name might have been picturing the pillars of Hades—black in color, born in fire, massed heavily underfoot. The posts, however, are quite beautiful and better described by their geological names, hexagonal basalt columns. They formed when a lava flow pooled behind a glacial moraine to a depth of several hundred feet. Slow and uniform cooling created the necessary conditions for columnar jointing. Exposed by glacial erosion, the columns appear to have been bundled neatly together. In fact, it's simply the way the rock cracked while cooling. A short trail from the parking area provides views of the exposed cliff of vertical posts, and you can walk on top of the pile where the posts appear like well-fitted tiles.

☆ Canyonlands ☆
NATIONAL PARK
Canyons, Mesas, and Pinnacles

A parade of dramatic rocks marches through Utah's Canyonlands, where you could view the entire park as one dramatic sculpture. Yet if choices must be made, head for the Needles District. A paved road ends at Squaw Flat amid a cluster of reddish-and-tan sandstone pinnacles, the Needles. From here, trails

Arches seem to defy gravity: How can they, with nothing but hollow space underneath them, keep standing? Answer: They don't. Arches are short-lived shapes that seem durable only because the human scale of time is so much shorter than that of geology. Some last longer than others, yet in rock ages, they come and go in a flash. Wall Arch, one of the better known spans at Arches National Park, collapsed in 2008. Next on the worry list: Landscape Arch, an impossibly slender, nearly horizontal strand also in Arches National Park. It spans 290 feet, with a thickness at one point of only 6 feet. Large chunks of rock have fallen from it in recent decades; one incident was captured on video. More than any other major arch, it is hard to comprehend what keeps this one in place. But some day the twin forces of gravity and erosion will bring it down.

enter a three-dimensional playground of smooth rock, narrow canyons, wildflower gardens, shallow streams, and hidden meadows. Distances are moderate, and every mile is a delight. Highlights include the narrow subterranean cracks of the Joints Trail and the full-day excursion to massive Druid Arch.

☆ Zion ☆
NATIONAL PARK
Rock Shapes at Kolob Canyons

Utah's Zion is blessed with a stunning array of rock shapes. Most visitors head straight for Zion Canyon itself, where they find a scenic feast for their eyes and camera. Some make the roundabout trip to the park's remote northwest corner, the Kolob Canyons Unit. From the road, it's a full day's hike of 14 miles round-trip to Kolob Arch, a flat-topped alcove arch similar to Landscape Arch in Arches but considerably more massive and just a few feet shorter (287 feet) in horizontal span. For a shorter option nearby, the Taylor Creek Trail offers a 5-mile round-trip to Double Arch Alcove, a huge overhanging wall beautifully painted with seeping springs. Zion always has something fine to offer.

☆ Badlands ☆
NATIONAL PARK
Array of Canyons,
Buttes, Spires, and Cliffs

Seen from their base at sunrise, the ragged peaks of the South Dakota badlands rise up, seemingly enormous, and glow with an unearthly light. But they are not tall, they only have the proportions of grander summits. It's a lesson in erosion: Large or small, given the right material you get similar forms. As evidenced in Badlands National Park, wind and water have sculpted the rock into buttes, spires, and pinnacles that are a colorful torte of volcanic ash, river sands, flood plain mud, and ocean-deposited shale, with layers in shades of yellow, black, brown, and gray. Dating from 75 to 28 million years ago, they are also loaded with early mammal fossils from the late Eocene and Oligocene epochs, including *Archaeotherium* and titanotheres. The moderately strenuous 0.75-mile Door Trail offers a good introduction to the park's geological formation, entering through an opening in the rock—the Door—and meandering through rugged, eroded badlands. For a longer exploration, hikers will find solitude and some steep formations on the Castle Trail, accessed from the parking area for the Door.

caves

The extravagant, mysterious underground world

Caves lure us into utter blackness, where natural light has never shone, and then reveal exquisite wonders: great halls, long corridors, rooms stacked upon rooms; rivers thundering over high cascades; lakes, hills, and deep yawning pits; and creatures that prefer darkness over light amid gleaming crystals and flowstone formations.

☆ Mammoth Cave ☆
NATIONAL PARK
World's Longest Known Cave System

Mammoth is just that—the biggest cave system by far. No end has yet been found to this vast multilayered labyrinth in Kentucky. Measured passageways total 367 miles, making it the world's longest known cave system. For size alone, Mammoth would top this list. Yet the cave also superbly exemplifies the formation of limestone solution caverns. First, limestone is deposited in the sea. Then, after earth movements push the stone above sea level, seeping fresh water hollows out spaces and decorates them with baroque extravagance. Mammoth has some huge chambers, their area measured in acres beneath ceilings that disappear into darkness overhead. The space called Mammoth Dome is 192 feet high; you climb down it on stairways. There are tight squeezes, too. The walls at Fat Man's Misery, for example, have been polished by thousands of bodies squeezing through. You can choose from a range of tours that last from one to several hours, including the 2.5-hour, 2.5-mile River Styx Tour, which traces the path of water from the surface through sculpted tunnels to the lowest level of the cave. The Frozen Niagara Tour (1.25 hours, 0.25 mile) offers a good introduction, passing a large waterfall-like formation of flowstone and many other decorations. The New Entrance Tour (two hours, 0.75 mile) takes in deep pits, high domes, and a few tight spaces, and visits one of the cave's most decorated sections.

☆ Carlsbad Caverns ☆
NATIONAL PARK
Speleothems and
Flights of Brazilian Free-tailed Bats

Like other solution caves, New Mexico's Carlsbad was carved from limestone bedrock, but this one got a power boost. Hydrogen sulfide gas, rising from deep petroleum deposits, combined with underground water and subterranean microbes to form a potent dissolving bath of sulfuric acid. When the water table fell, the chambers were left high and relatively dry. About a million years ago, fresh water trickling down from the surface began decorating the maze of passageways. Carlsbad is rich in speleothems (the technical word for cave formations) including staple items like stalactites, columns, draperies, and ribbons; also helictites, soda straws, popcorn, and lily pads. For most, the Big Room, also called Hall of the Giants, is the central attraction. You can take an elevator below, or hike down on your own through the Natural Entrance, a descent of more than 750 feet. If interested in less traveled regions, the park offers a range of ranger-led adventure tours. This cave is famous for its flights of Brazilian free-tailed bats. After sunset during summer months, some 400,000 of the half-ounce creatures leave their roosting sites and pour out of the cave in spiraling clouds, headed for a night of foraging. Visitors gather nightly for the show.

✸ Jewel Cave ✸
NATIONAL MONUMENT
Calcite Spar Crystals and
Rare Mineralogical Speleothems

High in the Black Hills of South Dakota stretches the world's second longest cave. More than 150 miles have been surveyed. Jewel gets its name from the blunt calcite spar crystals that cover most of the

With more than 361 miles of passageways, Mammoth Cave in Kentucky is the world's longest known cave system.

cave walls, giving them a glittery sheen. It contains other calcite speleothems—stalactites, flowstone, and such—but its greater treasures include unusual gypsum flowers, needles, spiders; also rare hydro-magnesite balloons and aragonite frostwork so delicate it seems that a baby's breath could destroy it. The standard cave tour, offered year-round, begins with an elevator descent and follows a half-mile loop on a paved trail. During summer months, rangers in historic uniforms hand out lanterns for a step back into 1930s cave exploration. For adventure, join the Wild Caving Tour, a strenuous, sometimes-crawling-in-tight-spaces experience.

☆ Great Basin ☆
NATIONAL PARK
Speleothems at Lehman Caves

Hidden in Nevada's Great Basin National Park, Lehman Caves is a relative boutique among caves: Its entire known length is about 2 miles. It makes up for its small size with an unusual richness of speleothems, however, and a few special treasures. Chief among its rarities are cave shields, large disk-shaped structures resembling flat clam shells, their two matching halves separated by a hairline crack. Standing out from the walls at various angles, they become draped with flowstone of their own making. Lehman has more than 300 of them scattered among a superabundance of dripstone, flowstone, columns, draperies, popcorn, helictites, ribbons, and more. Despite the crowded appearance, the jumble of speleothems is remarkably harmonious. The park offers two tours. Highlights include the Grand Palace and its famous shield called the Parachute; and the Cypress Swamp, a seasonal pond where stalagmites and columns play the role of trees. The cave itself once played Mars in a comically bad sci-fi movie called *Horrors of the Red Planet*.

☆ Cave Ghosts of Mammoth Cave ☆

Caves are perfect places for ghost stories. In the dark dripping underground, slight sounds echo through labyrinthine passageways. What strange things lie in wait beyond the reach of a light? Plenty, according to the stories told about Mammoth Cave. People report strange sounds, vague lights in the blackness, the occasional nudge from behind when no one is around. Figures in old-style clothing, or tattered rags, trail behind tour groups for a distance, then vanish. Legend has it that in the mid-1800s a spurned girl named Melissa took revenge on the object of her affection by luring him deep into the cave and abandoning him there. He was never seen again, and she evidently had second thoughts. Her ghost prowls the cave, miserably searching for him. There's also the leg of Floyd Collins, the cave explorer who in 1925 famously died underground while rescuers worked feverishly to free him. His body, later put on display, was stolen and recovered missing a leg, which is evidently still hopping around looking for a reunion.

☆ Wind Cave ☆
NATIONAL PARK
Large Barometric Wind Cave
With Delicate Boxwork

Caves breathe. Wind Cave, comprising more than 134 miles of passageways under the rolling hills of South Dakota, was named for its barometric puffing, the result of changing atmospheric pressure on the surface; Wind Cave is one of the largest barometric wind caves in the United States. Its outstanding feature is boxwork, a sort of irregular honeycomb structure with delicate calcite fins separating the cells. Other wonders include Calcite Lake, a shallow pond where thin sheets of calcite float like lily pads. Gleaming white clusters of frostwork seem to grow best where air flows strongly. Gypsum crystals sprout like alien cotton candy. Helictites are found in such density that cavers call them helictite bushes. Among the many ranger-led cave tours is a candlelight tour and an adventurous (four-hour) wild cave tour that gives enthusiasts ample opportunity for crawling.

let in light, protect gardens of ferns and other plants that would not survive on the surface. Pictographs, animal bones, and in one case two human skeletons tell of past human habitation. Most caves in the park are open to the public. More than two dozen have been developed with trails to make visiting easier, but only one cave is lighted; bring a flashlight, and a hard hat is recommended. Free ranger-guided tours are offered in the summer.

☆ Lava Beds ☆
NATIONAL MONUMENT
Lava Tube Caves
Born of Fire

Limestone caves are created by water—first hollowing, then filling—over long silent underground years. Lava tubes are at the opposite extreme. They are the products of short-lived violence. Molten lava, flowing in rivers from a volcano, hardens on top but continues to move beneath the surface crust. When the flows ebb, the lava drains away, leaving tunnels that can be miles long. Located in northern California, Lava Beds National Monument features the biggest concentration of lava tubes in North America; more than 700 have been counted. They were created over the past half million years by periodic eruptions of the Medicine Lake volcano, a huge shield volcano that ranks as the largest volcanic peak in the Cascade Range if measured by volume rather than height. The lava tube caves range from crawling size (claustrophobes beware) up to 60 feet in diameter. Some have beautiful ice formations, notably a large frozen waterfall in Crystal Ice Cave. Others, in sections where collapsed roofs

☆ Sequoia & Kings Canyon ☆
NATIONAL PARKS
Wild and Undeveloped
Cave for the Professional

Some of the best caves remain "wild," undeveloped and unsuited for tourists—for reasons of skill, equipment, and/or cave protection. For those spelunkers lucky enough to venture into them, they offer an unsurpassed experience of underground wilderness. In the Sierra Nevada of central California, Sequoia and Kings Canyon (managed as a single unit) protects more than 200 caves. Of them, only Crystal Cave is developed and deserving of the large numbers of people who tour it each year. Other caves are managed under strict guidelines that limit access according to a rating scale. Among the most protected is Hurricane Crawl Cave, which was only discovered in 1988. No recreational caving is permitted. Only qualified researchers with strong justification are allowed to enter what the park calls "some of the most unusual and spectacular cave mineralogy and biology" in the western United States. The rest of us can see it only in pictures and feel good that its treasures are well protected.

✳ Timpanogos Cave ✳
NATIONAL MONUMENT

Three Caverns in a
High-mountain Cave

Interestingly, before climbing into Timpanogos, you have to climb up. The 1.5-mile access trail to Timpanogos ascends more than 1,000 feet above American Fork Canyon in Utah's Wasatch Mountains, affording a grand vista most of the way. Then, into the intricate dark it goes. Three main chambers are accessible on ranger-led tours that last 45–60 minutes: Hansen Cave, Middle Cave, and Timpanogos. The most prominent feature is a tapered flowstone speleothem hanging from the ceiling called the Great Heart of Timpanogos. The cave is also known for its uncommon abundance of helictites (calcite formations that branch, curve, or spiral, seemingly in defiance of gravity) and its rare natural coloration—greens and yellows caused by nickel in the calcite. Because snow covers the trail for much of the year, the cave is open only in warmer months. The park usually recommends that you set aside three hours for the round-trip hike and cave tour.

SEE AMERICA
UNITED STATES TRAVEL BUREAU

✳ Oregon Caves ✳
NATIONAL MONUMENT

A Metamorphosed Marble Wonder

Hidden beneath the lush old-growth rain forest of southwestern Oregon, the Oregon Caves are unusual for being set in marble. The rock began as limestone but was metamorphosed by heat and pressure to become the smooth-grained, white material of classic sculpture. The general 1.5-hour tour only covers a half mile, but it is rated moderately strenuous because the route includes some 500 stairs, many of them steep and uneven. Highlights include Angel Falls, a drapery that glows blue under UV light; Paradise Lost, the cave's most decorated room; and a spiral staircase created by an ancient waterfall. A strenuous three-hour caving adventure to undeveloped areas serves as an introduction to caving—how to move through a cave without damaging either yourself or the underground environment. It can be messy work. Think wet mud, loose rocky slopes, and water dripping from the ceiling. Lots of fun for the right people.

✳ Cumberland Gap ✳
NATIONAL HISTORICAL PARK

Historic Legacies at Gap Cave

Located near where Kentucky, Tennessee, and Virginia meet, Gap Cave offers a historic element in addition to the geologic. A classic solution cave, its features include the 65-foot Pillar of Hercules and the pearly white Frozen Niagara. The ranger-led tour begins with a 1-mile walk on the old Wilderness Trail, pioneered by Daniel Boone along the older Warrior's Path, a Native American route to the hunting grounds of Kentucky. After the Revolutionary War, water from the cave powered the mills of the new town of Cumberland Gap. Inside the cave, a rock face bears signatures of Civil War soldiers from both sides who sheltered here. It was once called Cudjo's Cave, after a character in an antislavery novel of the same name; Cudjo was a runaway slave who was killed in the cave by Confederates. Today, tours are led by lantern light to enhance the historic atmosphere.

wetlands & swamps

Gators and willets, bayous and bogs

More water than land, swamps are unfamiliar but enticing territory. The South claims the best, where dense canopies of cypress and tupelo shelter watery mysteries. Shy creatures disappear behind curtains of Spanish moss. Chorusing birds, frogs, and insects make a happy racket. And then there are marshes, estuaries, mires, bogs . . .

✶ Everglades ✶
NATIONAL PARK
Diversity at River of Grass

Top wetland honors belong to the Everglades, at the southern tip of Florida. Here America dabbles its toe into the exuberant life of the subtropics. There's no topography to speak of; the park's highest point is 8 feet above sea level. Nonetheless, the Everglades presents a stunning diversity of plants and animals. Foremost among its habitats are the broad marshy rivers called freshwater sloughs, which together make up the famous "river of grass" that channels water from Lake Okeechobee to the sea through fields of sawgrass and other marsh vegetation. Sloughs are punctuated by forested islands called hammocks. Cypress trees spread their graceful buttressed roots in shallow water. Mangrove forests thrive in the tidal zone where fresh water mingles with seawater. A tangle of channels, bays, estuaries, and small islands complicate the seashore. The result is an astounding richness of winged, finned, clawed, scaly, and slippery critters living in every conceivable nook and cranny. For curious humans eager to follow them into their world, the park features some remarkable trails and boardwalks, all of them wheelchair accessible: Anhinga, Gumbo Limbo, Pahayokee, Mahogany Hammock, and others. Better yet, explore by boat. Excellent water trails allow canoers and kayakers to move as smoothly and quietly as alligators, and to stay overnight thanks to the park's system of elevated tent platforms called chickees.

✶ Big Cypress ✶
NATIONAL PRESERVE
Wet Prairie, Swampy Sloughs, Hardwood
Hammocks, and Large Stands of Bald Cypresses

Big Cypress shares many of the natural features of its more famous neighbor and partner in southern Florida, Everglades National Park. Water originating from Lake Okeechobee, augmented by thunderstorms, hurricanes, and storm surges along the coast, flows through both parks. The preserve, measuring 720,000 acres, is a big place but its name

Everglades National Park's so-called river of grass—freshwater sloughs—hosts a stunning range of biodiversity.

honors the fragile and threatened nature of these unique wetlands. Most of the big bald cypresses—meaning the old and tall ones—were felled more than half a century ago, long before the preserve was established in 1974. But there are several large stands of bald cypresses—hence the "big" in the park's name—and the forest covers a lot of ground. Given time, its relatively young trees will achieve distinction. Meanwhile, the symphony of the swamps plays in full richness here. Anhingas spread their wings to dry as alligators, inscrutably patient, wait for opportunity. Swamp rabbits, raccoons, bobcats, deer, river otters, and even critically endangered Florida panthers go about the mysterious business of being furred creatures in a scaly world. Birds are everywhere, some flaunting their presence and others moving secretively through the brush. For visitors, two driving tours on the south side of the preserve provide a good sampling. For a full immersion into the watery wonderland, a number of paddling trails lead quietly to the island-studded coast.

☆ Jean Lafitte ☆
NATIONAL HISTORICAL PARK & PRESERVE
Bayous at the Barataria Preserve

Barataria is a 20,000-acre bayou-riddled tract south of New Orleans on the shores of Lakes Cataouatche and Salvador. Originally a Choctaw word, "bayou" describes a very slow-moving body of water, usually in a former river channel or lake, and commonly surrounded by swamp or marshland. Practically speaking, a bayou is a way to get deeper into a swamp; and, one would hope, out of it as well. A good start at exploring Barataria is to walk the half-mile, accessible Bayou Coquille Trail. It starts on dry ground, leads gently through stands of live oak and palmetto to a bald cypress swamp, and ends at a floating prairie. From there another short trail leads to the Marsh Overlook, where alligators, wading birds, and other pleasures await. The intrepid can paddle a pirogue (which elsewhere might be called a canoe; the Louisiana variety has a flat bottom) on one of several water trails meandering through bayous, canals, and trenasses. Warning from the park: At twilight, it can be hard to converse over the din of celebrating frogs.

☆ Big Thicket ☆
NATIONAL PRESERVE
Unparalleled Biological Diversity
of the International Biosphere Reserve

The word "thicket" barely hints at the biological diversity in the 15 scattered units of this east Texas preserve. Forests of pine, cypress, oak, and other hardwoods mingle with meadows, swamps, bogs, lazy rivers, and even some Southwest desert. It's an East-meets-West sort of place, where prickly pear cacti encounter blackwater swamp and midwestern plains find themselves unexpectedly close to the Deep South. Scientists credit cool conditions during the last ice age with compressing different habitats closer together. This fusion leads to unusual biological wealth recognized by the preserve's status as an international biosphere reserve and a globally important bird area. Birdwatchers have a lot to look at, and dream of one day seeing an ivory-billed woodpecker—once thought extinct but recently spotted in Arkansas. The preserve includes a number of watercourses: Neches

River, Turkey Creek, Big Sandy Creek, and Village Creek among them. These and the watery zones along their banks provide good boating opportunities. In addition, the preserve offers 45 miles of hiking trails. Walkers will like trails in the Turkey Creek Unit, particularly the short Pitcher Plant Trail named for its carnivorous botany, which blooms yellow in springtime. The curious might also want to probe a baygall, a highly acidic type of bog named for the commonly found sweet-bay magnolia and gallberry holly and said to be the most dense, impenetrable habitat in the Big Thicket.

☆ Cumberland Island ☆
NATIONAL SEASHORE
Barrier Island Wetlands,
Coastal Birds, and Historic Sites

This barrier island, the largest of Georgia's Golden Isles (3 miles wide and 18 miles long), is known mainly for its historic sites and nearly 20 miles of open sand beach. Several private estates dating back to Gen. Nathanael Greene, who rose to prominence during the American Revolutionary War, and also including a mansion built by the Carnegie family, are now open to the public. At the north end of the island stands a tiny First African Baptist Church built in 1893 to serve a community of African-American workers. The wetlands tucked behind the dunes and maritime forest offer significant rewards, including a chance to see river otters, raccoons, mink, manatees, and even bottlenose dolphins in addition to the full catalog of coastal wetland birds, notably pelicans, herons, shorebirds, gulls, and terns. One of the best areas for wildlife-viewing opportunities lies between the old cemetery near Dungeness and the beach, where a boardwalk skirts the salt marsh. Most of Cumberland is a quiet place. The heart of the island is a wilderness area crossed

☆ Swamp Gas ☆

Swamps are strange places. Not quite water, not quite land, they lie in a twilight zone of bizarre possibility. Legends tell of unexplained and spooky things prowling the murky damp—things swallowed up only to be revealed again in altered form. Enter the phenomenon called swamp gas—or more lyrically, foxfire, will-o'-the-wisp, corpse candles, jack-o'-lantern, and ignis fatuus. The names refer to dimly visible, ghostly lights described for centuries but never well explained. We know that swamps produce methane gas from decaying organic matter. Poke the muddy bottom and a nose-wrinkling whiff of it, mixed with the odors of decay, will escape. Methane is flammable. It burns easily with a yellow or blue color. This would explain the lights except for the igniting part. Is there a natural force capable of torching methane on calm, steamy nights in the bayous? Or is it something else?

by one main road. Vehicles are limited to park staff and the few private residents. You must be content with hiking on the 50-mile-long trails system, or by bicycling on designated roads through forest draped in Spanish moss. The island has both wilderness and developed campsites for people wishing to overnight.

☆ Congaree ☆
NATIONAL PARK
Old-growth
Floodplain Forest

This park occupies a bottomland near the junction of the Congaree and Wateree Rivers, on the coastal plain of South Carolina. With an elevation less than 100 feet, and as many miles from the ocean, seasonal water tends to pool here, under the big trees that rely on it for good growing conditions. The Congaree River floods the relatively flat landscape ten times a year, on average, bringing a wealth of nutrient-rich silt that remains once the waters recede. Floodplain forests were once common in the Southeast but today they are scarce. Congaree happily demonstrates the value of a flooded forest to those who happily paddle through the old-growth bald cypress and tupelo trees when the waters are high. A 2.4-mile elevated boardwalk, standing 6 feet above the ground, provides access in any weather, and even when the park is not flooded, there are creeks, oxbow lakes, and two rivers to explore. The trees are tall, commonly around 100 feet, with six national champions including the tallest loblolly pine (167 feet), laurel oak, water hickory, and swamp tupelo. Birds are abundant; seasonal migrants flood through like the water. Deer, bobcats, river otters, opossums, and raccoons are of interest to all. Snakes, biting insects, and spiders demand their fair share of attention here, too.

> [I]n 1816, Joseph Bailly and his family became one of the first known settlers of the "Indiana Dunes." Bailly, a Canadian fur trapper, was the first to recognize the area's commercial potential, but by the time of his "squatting" on Indian lands, the fur trade was in decline.

☆ Timucuan ☆
ECOLOGICAL & HISTORIC PRESERVE
Coastal Wetlands, Forest, and Grasslands on Barrier Islands

Three Florida rivers—the St. Johns, Nassau, and South Amelia—converge on a tangle of creeks between Jacksonville and the ocean. The result is 46,000 acres of forest, grassland, and coastal wetlands tucked behind a line of barrier islands. A handful of state parks protect the islands and other adjacent land. In addition to its watery wilds, Timucuan offers a 16th-century French fort, a 19th-century plantation, and a 20th-century farmstead turned natural area. Despite the surrounding urban development, the preserve is a remarkably good place for seeing wildlife, with many unique habitats. Brown pelicans sail overhead in graceful phalanxes. Black-crowned night-herons haunt the marsh plants along with egrets, ibises, and other wonderfully named avians: semipalmated plovers, greater yellowlegs, roseate spoongills, painted buntings, pileated woodpeckers, anhingas, whimbrels, godwits, and willets. The park offers numerous coastal saltwater paddling routes for canoes and kayaks, including portions of the Florida Sea Islands Paddling Trail. Nonboaters can enjoy the natural scene from trails, viewpoints, and bird observation platforms.

☆ Indiana Dunes ☆
NATIONAL LAKESHORE
Wetlands of the Great Marsh

If remoteness from human impact gives a wild area extra value, is the opposite extreme also true? A natural system functioning in the shadow of a great city as if it existed in some distant roadless region is arguably the greater treasure. It stands as an example and inspiration not only to hardy adventurers but to the millions who can experience the place with a Sunday picnic. The marshlands of Indiana Dunes have potential, but it will take some time. Within sight of Chicago, and adjacent to the rusting industrial lakefront of Gary, the wetlands that once earned the name Great Marsh are mostly gone. But they are coming back. Restoration is a primary goal of the park. Meanwhile, trails at Cowles Bog and Inland Marsh help you to appreciate what still exists and to see the rebirth of the marsh's fens, sedge meadows, and wet prairies. An early season highlight is the great blue heron rookery beside the Little Calumet River, reached via the 2-mile-long Heron Rookery Trail. Tall wading birds perching awkwardly beside their tree-top nests make an odd and pleasing sight.

☆ Cape Cod ☆
NATIONAL SEASHORE
Marshlands and Kettle Ponds

The sea constantly works at the land. In 1605, the French explorer Samuel de Champlain could sail his ship in what is now the Nauset Marsh in Massachusetts. Since then, the Atlantic Ocean has built an intervening barrier of sand, the Nauset Spit. Seawater still pours in and out with the tides but the entrance has grown smaller. The Fort Hill area offers good access points for viewing the marsh, as does the Salt Pond Trail, which skirts one of Cape Cod's many kettle ponds—depressions created by huge blocks of ice left by retreating Ice Age glaciers. Once a body of fresh water, Salt Pond is now fed by the same tidal flows that support the teeming life of Nauset Marsh.

☆ Glacier ☆
NATIONAL PARK
Fens

Northwestern Montana's Glacier National Park has the odd fen—odd not only because fens are not common in the northern Rockies, but also because they are unusual among wetlands. Fens are basically soggy sponges of peat that offer very low nutrient levels to the plants that live in them—cottongrass, buckler fern, blueberries, stunted shrubs,

and sphagnum moss. And if you're a small insect, beware the murderous bladderwort. Those little tendrils with their floating balloon structures are the plant's roots; it has no others, and they are voracious. Brushing the trigger hairs will cause them to inflate suddenly, sucking little bugs to their doom. In Glacier, the drama unfolds at McGee Meadow on the Camas Creek Road, sometimes attracting moose.

Bald cypresses thrive in the seasonally flooded bottomlands of Congaree National Park.

glaciers

Endangered rivers of ice, shrinking but still magnificent

Not many things move mountains. Glaciers do. Ponderous and powerful, glaciers can reduce them to rubble. Everything about a glacier is spectacular. The ice groans and cracks, revealing its deep blue interior. Great slabs calve with mighty roars. Clear rivulets cross its surface while dark, silt-laden subglacial rivers pour from its snout.

☆ Glacier Bay ☆
NATIONAL PARK & PRESERVE
Grand Pacific Glacier

We begin with an obvious choice, Glacier Bay in southeast Alaska, where large glaciers grind their way to sea level, giving passengers of cruise ships and tour vessels thrilling close-up views of towering ice walls and gleaming slabs crashing into the bay. In such a dynamic landscape, climate change and its effects on environment are a natural subject of conversation. In 1794, Capt. George Vancouver described no bay at all, just an unremarkable ice-bordered recess 5 miles deep. When John Muir visited in 1879, the ice had retreated northward, leaving 48 miles of open water. Today, ships must cruise about 65 miles to reach Grand Pacific Glacier, one of the most distant of Glacier Bay's many tidewater glaciers. To see the park, the great majority travel by water, in everything from giant cruise ships to sea kayaks. They come for the glaciers, but also the extravagant mountain scenery and wildlife. Orcas, humpback whales, minke whales, harbor seals,

Steller sea lions, and sea otters are all present. Kayakers and hikers interested in camping can arrange with the Bartlett Cove day-tour boat to be dropped off at selected locations.

☆ Glacier ☆
NATIONAL PARK
Many Glacier Region
and Grinnell Glacier

You expect glaciers to be a prominent feature at Many Glacier in Glacier National Park. But there is so much more. Three spectacular valleys branch upward toward the Continental Divide. Each boasts a string of icy lakes fed by cascading streams. The wildflower display in July is unsurpassed. The high peaks—Gould, Siyeh, Apikuni, and others—are the very definition of mountain gravitas. And then there are the glaciers, especially Grinnell, which is reached by one of the finest hiking trails the park system has to offer. The trail begins in a deep coniferous forest, skirts the clear green waters of Grinnell Lake, and climbs high up the Garden Wall to

A 50-foot boat is dwarfed by Reid Glacier, one of the many tidewater glaciers that calve into Glacier Bay.

where the glacier sits beside a small lake in the cirque of its own making. The glacier is far smaller than it was just 20 years ago. By some estimates, it will be gone in another 20. Park natural-ists make the point that Glacier was named more for the effects of ice—the hanging valleys, cirques, moraines, and other features—than for the glaciers themselves. It's a good thing to keep in mind, con-sidering that in 1850 there were 150 glaciers in the park; today there are 26. The ice may disappear for a while, but the park won't have to change its name.

> *There are 616 officially named glaciers in Alaska ... The Alaska Almanac estimates that Alaska has 100,000 glaciers.*

☀ Wrangell–St. Elias ☀
NATIONAL PARK & PRESERVE
Malaspina Glacier

Alaskans like to point out that this glacier would cover the state of Rhode Island. The Malaspina is truly huge, about 28 by 40 miles and in places almost 2,000 feet thick. Its size is symbolic of the vast rock-and-ice wilderness of which it is a part. Wrangell–St. Elias and Glacier Bay National Parks together with Canadian neighbors Kluane National Park and Tatshenshini-Alsek Provincial Park com-pose a 24-million-acre contiguous protected area, a World Heritage site ten times the size of Yellowstone National Park. The Malaspina is a piedmont glacier, the largest of its type in North America. "Piedmont" refers to its forming in an open area unrestrained by mountain walls. It can't be seen in its entirety from closer than orbit. From satellite photos, it is possible to see how it flows through the St. Elias Range and spreads out on the coastal plain in a vast sloping disk. In fact, space photos are the only way most of us will ever see it. Access in this exceptionally remote part of the world is difficult in the extreme.

☀ Great Basin ☀
NATIONAL PARK
Wheeler Peak Glacier

You won't find much ice in this glacier. In fact, it's the lack of ice that makes it noteworthy. Nor is the size outstanding; it measures all of 300 by 400 feet. The glacier occupies a cirque at about 11,500 feet elevation on the shaded northeast side of Wheeler Peak. High quartzite walls rise above a steep talus slope ending a jumble of sharp-edged boulders. There it is: a rock glacier. Below the rocks, in the spaces between them, there is ice. It freezes, thaws, expands, and contracts depending on the weather. It pushes and lubricates the rocks and slowly, like a more conventional glacier, the whole mass moves downslope. Getting there involves taking a first-rate scenic road, the Wheeler Peak Scenic Drive, which climbs nearly 5,000 feet from the valley bottom to a cool alpine basin. From there, a pleasant 2-mile trail leads to the glacier and an added bonus: Just shy of the glacier stands a magnificent grove of bristlecone pines, many of them more than 5,000 years old. They have weathered the millennia, recorded the centuries in their gnarled shapes, and witnessed the transient nature of glaciers.

☀ Grand Teton ☀
NATIONAL PARK
Skillet Glacier

The Skillet is not large. Few visitors to the Tetons ever get to appreciate it from close range. It looks more like a snowfield than a glacier. But there are good reasons to include it among the best, all related to your vantage point. The glacier clings to the steep east face of Mount Moran, a kingly sight from miles around. The glacier's name refers to its long-handled fry pan shape, although to some modern eyes it looks more like an electric guitar. The prime viewing location is the Oxbow Bend Turnout on U.S. 89/191/287, a spot along the Snake River just below the Jackson Lake Dam. Here, a slow meander in the river provides an entrancing foreground—sometimes mirror smooth, often busy with wildlife. On cool autumn mornings, the mountains float on an ethereal blanket of mist. The Willow Flats Overlook, a short distance up the same road to the north, is a worthy second choice. Instead of water, the foreground is an expanse of shrub willows that turn warm gold in the fall. Moose, elk, and bears commonly wander into the scene as swans glide past. Few glaciers can claim such a theatrical setting.

✳ Kenai Fjords ✳
NATIONAL PARK
Exit Glacier

Looking at glaciers from a distance is good, but standing on one is better. Exit Glacier offers an up-close-and-personal encounter, easily accessible by road from the town of Seward. A short paved walk from the parking area leads through a stand of cottonwood trees to a panoramic overlook of a living Alaska glacier that is falling in spectacular slow motion from the Harding Icefield. The ice is cracked by its rapid descent, rather like a river tumbling down a cascade. Crevasses glow deep blue. Melting creates fantastic shapes. Dark, silt-laden water rushes from the glacier terminus. A moderately strenuous 1-mile side trail leads to the edge of the glacier for a side-on look at towering blue ice. If the outflow stream is not too high, it's also possible to cross the gravel outwash plain to the actual toe of the glacier (but stay clear of overhanging ice). Those wishing to visit the glacier's birthplace can take the 7.4-mile round-trip Harding Icefield Trail (gaining approximately 3,000 feet on the ascent) for expansive views of the vast icy plain.

✳ Mount Rainier ✳
NATIONAL PARK
Nisqually Glacier

Put high mountains together with wet climates, and glaciers will happen. Mount Rainier gets a lot of precipitation. The annual average snowfall, measured at Paradise on the mountain's south side, is 680 inches. (The record is 1,122 inches, more than 95 feet, received during the winter of 1971–72.) If you consider that Paradise is 9,000 feet below the summit, and higher elevations usually attract more snow, the numbers get more impressive. Rainier supports 25 major glaciers, the greatest single-peak glacial system in the lower 48 states. Of these, Nisqually is the most easily accessed and, being close to the park's main visitor center in the popular Paradise area, the best known. It has been monitored for more than a century. During that time, the ice has advanced and retreated several times. Currently, like glaciers all over the world, its growth is negative, meaning that more ice melts in the summer than the glacier receives in winter—even a Rainier winter. From the Paradise Henry M. Jackson Memorial Visitor Center, Nisqually Vista is an easy 1.2-mile round-trip hike. Glacier Vista, along the 3-mile round-trip Skyline Trail, offers a closer view among lush wildflowers and a broad mountain panorama.

✷ Rocky Mountain ✷
NATIONAL PARK
Tyndall Glacier

If the value of something rises with scarcity then Tyndall Glacier in Colorado's Rocky Mountain National Park has become exceedingly valuable. Once a large alpine glacier, Tyndall survives now as a small cirque glacier in the shelter of 12,713-foot Hallett Peak's steep north face. Hikers can get close to it by trekking to Emerald Lake from the Bear Lake Trailhead, a 1.8-mile moderate climb one way. Recommendation? Start early. This trail is one of the park's most popular hikes, for good reason. Emerald is the highest in a chain of small alpine lakes, strung together along Tyndall Creek beneath the sheer walls of surrounding mountain ridges.

☆ Weighing Glaciers ☆

How much ice is in a glacier? The answer is important to scientists investigating climate change, but it's not so simple as checking to see if a particular glacier is getting longer or shorter, or even thinner. Glaciers behave in complicated ways that defy simple, short-term measurements. The most useful number for climate study is what researchers call the mass balance, a comparison of annual snow accumulation (which adds mass) with annual melting and evaporation, or ablation (which reduces mass). Scientists derive accurate figures from periodic measurements of snowfall, snow depth, runoff, and rate of ablation throughout the year. But they can get an idea of a glacier's condition just by looking at it in late summer. If 60 to 70 percent of its surface area is not covered by snow—that is, if too much snow has melted from the ice during the summer—then the glacier is in negative balance and is losing mass.

Among the scenic highlight of Rocky Mountain, the Bear Lake area ranks near the top, and people flock to it. Not all of the glacier is visible from the end of the trail. The canyon steepens just beyond the lake, and mountaineering skills are needed to climb into the cirque itself. But the beauty of Emerald Lake is ample consolation, a blue jewel of a tarn ringed by stands of emerald green conifers.

✷ Olympic ✷
NATIONAL PARK
Blue Glacier and Other
Mount Olympus Glaciers

There are 60 named glaciers in this Washington State park, most of them draped over the central peak, 7,980-foot Mount Olympus. Taken together, they form the third largest glacier system in the lower 48 states, a mass of ice explained in part by the Olympic Peninsula being the wettest place in the continental United States. It's not easy to get within arm's reach of a glacier here—hiking and climbing are required, as 95 percent of the park is officially designated wilderness—but the park offers a fine opportunity to see both ends of the glacial process. First, check out the glittering panorama of Mount Olympus from Hurricane Ridge. Then drive to Hoh Rain Forest, where the Hoh River carries icy meltwater from the glaciers through giant trees and a rain-soaked wonderland of lush vegetation. The 17.3-mile Hoh River Trail climbs through temperate rain forest (some of the last remaining in the United States), montane forest, and subalpine meadows to Glacier Meadows on the shoulder of Mount Olympus. Above, Blue Glacier reaches down from the mountain's heights. A short trail that gets longer each year the glacier retreats leads to the glacier's toe, and the starting point for many ascents of Mount Olympus.

☆ North Cascades ☆

NATIONAL PARK

Glaciers on Mounts Challenger and Shuksan

The glacier-topped mountains in Washington State's North Cascades are volcanic, well watered, and steep, with names as dramatic as the setting: Fury, Terror, Despair, and Triumph. There's an old saying among climbers and hikers that in the Cascades, a step forward is a step up or down. Nothing is on the level. To see some of the complex's more than 300 glaciers, this means a lot of walking through big-tree forests on the valley bottoms, followed by hard climbs into alpine meadows above tree line. Views like the one from Whatcom Pass across the valley at Challenger Glacier, which covers virtually the whole north side of Mount Challenger, are a happy reward for the long miles. But the view of Mount Shuksan is at least as good, and it can be had from the Mount Baker Highway. Studded with sharp crags, dripping with glaciers, and reflected in the mirror-smooth waters of Picture Lake, Shuksan has become an iconic image of the Pacific Northwest. Compared to the near-perfect volcanic cones in the area, Shuksan has a wilder look, more craggy, more mysterious. Several glaciers are visible on the western face. The most prominent is Upper Curtis and, below it, White Salmon.

Glacier-draped Mount Shuksan rises above Picture Lake in North Cascades National Park.

geological oddities

Inland dunes and colorful rocks, folded and shifted land

The parks are showcases of extraordinary geological phenomena. Some earn greater renown than others, while some are unsung and just plain strange—some mysterious, some that only geologists can fully fathom, but all of them spurring the imagination and helping us appreciate the forces that have shaped our parks and country.

✷ Badlands ✷
NATIONAL PARK
Badlands Wall

The condensed story: Once there were volcanoes and volcanic ash. There were forests and river flood plains. There was a sea, then uplift, then an inland sea, and each episode left a layer on the site of the Badlands in South Dakota. Half a million years ago, rivers began to carve it all into the strange and stratified badlands seen today. The most representative formation in the park, found in the North Unit, is the Badlands Wall—a 60-mile spine of buttes left behind as wind, rain, freezing, and thawing have had their way with the badlands sediments. A scenic drive hugs the wall, providing access to trails such as Door and Window, which lead to openings in the 150- to 450-foot wall that reveal views of the upper grasslands to the north and lower grasslands to the south. Both the drive and the trails are excellent ways to marvel at the park's strange geology, particularly evident in the colorful horizontal layers clearly revealed in the wall's facades.

✷ Death Valley ✷
NATIONAL PARK
The Racetrack

In this California desert park full of geological oddities, from its salt-pan floor to fluted canyons to cinder cone crater, none is stranger or more baffling than Death Valley's mysterious Racetrack. The Racetrack is a playa, a dry lake bed, in the northern part of the park where rocks tumble from a bordering bluff. Then, as evidenced by tracks in the playa, the rocks inexplicably proceed to move on their own across the playa. They zigzag, loop, even cross each other's tracks. The rocks range from golf-ball size to several hundred pounds. The "races" seem to take place overnight; no one has actually witnessed the rocks' movement. The long-standing theoretical explanation: Rain causes the playa surface to become slick, and strong winds blow and push the rocks across its surface. One problem with that theory is the fact that the rocks sometimes seem to move in concert with one another, but other times split up and go their own

Unknown forces are at work at the Racetrack in Death Valley, where rocks mysteriously move across the dry lake bed.

way. No one really knows for sure how they move. The road to Racetrack Valley starts near Ubehebe Crater. Four-wheel drive is necessary to reach the dry lake.

✳ White Sands ✳
NATIONAL MONUMENT
Mile Upon Mile of
Sugary White Sand

Is it possible that White Sands has its own little sandmaking factory that keeps the dunes supplied with sugary white sand? In a way, yes. The sand is made of gypsum, a substance that is soluble in water and easily carried away by rain, snow, and rivers. Normally, that's exactly what happens to it, and it ultimately finds a home on seafloors—which is what the Tularosa Basin was 250 million years ago. The New Mexico mountain-ringed valley where the dunes are situated was once covered by a giant lake geologists call Lake Otero, and its floor contained thick layers of gypsum washed into it from eroded mountains. Briefly speaking, the lake eventually dried up (about 6,500 years ago), and since Tularosa Basin has no outlet to the sea, the gypsum remained in the form of selenite crystals. The crystals began to break down from temperature fluctuations, freezing, contracting, expanding, until they became the fine soft sand that comprises the dunes. What's equally fascinating is that the process continues today, both from the ancient sediments of Otero and from that little gypsum factory called Lake Lucero, a dry lake on the west side of the 275-square-mile dune field. Lucero's surface is covered with selenite crystals that continue to break down, blow, and join the dunes to the east. Once a month, the park offers three-hour ranger-led tours to Lake Lucero, and it's fascinating to see how its coarse crystals compare to the soft dunes of White Sands.

✳ Kobuk Valley ✳
NATIONAL PARK
Great Kobuk Sand Dunes

Hanging out on the sand with temperatures in the 80s would not be unusual in, say, southern California, but in the Alaska Arctic? Strange but possible. The Great Kobuk Sand Dunes in Kobuk Valley National Park stretch for miles just south of the Kobuk River between the villages of Ambler and Kiana, 35 miles north of the Arctic Circle. The inland dunes are the result of two periods of glaciation, during which retreating glaciers pulverized

Rippled by the winds, the dune field of White Sands is trapped in the Tularosa Basin.

rock into sand, which was borne by strong east winds to form the high dunes of the valley floor. The dunes crest at about 100 feet high near the river and rise to 500 feet closer to the Waring Mountains. The youngest, most active dunes are crescent-shaped mounds called barchans, a sand formation that's the result of strong winds prevailing from a single direction. They're reachable by a hike from the river if you're on a float trip, or by air taxi from Bettles or Kotzebue. The park also has two smaller active dune fields that can be visited, the Little Kobuk Sand Dunes and the Hunt River Dunes.

☆ Great Sand Dunes ☆
NATIONAL PARK & PRESERVE
North America's Tallest Dunes

The magnificent dunes that rise from the San Luis Valley against the soaring backdrop of Colorado's Sangre de Cristo Mountains are composed of sand left behind by ancient lakes and blown up against the massive mountain windbreak by prevailing westerly winds that funnel the sand toward three passes in the range. Because the winds occasionally change direction and blow from the mountains back toward the valley, the Great Sand Dunes get sculpted and grow higher than most. They are, in fact, the tallest dunes in North America, up to 750 feet high. Only about 10 percent of the park's sand is actually in the dunes. The rest is in what's known as the sand sheet, grasslands that surround the dunes on three sides. But it's the soaring dunes of the 30-square-mile dune field that capture attention in the park. There dunes are wind sculpted into star dunes, whose crests intersect in star-shaped patterns. The tallest dune in the park is the 750-foot-high star dune called, imaginatively, the Star Dune. Reversing winds also form "Chinese Walls," long, low

☆ A Lot of Work for Hand Soap ☆

For all of its dazzling geological riches, including gold strikes in the Panamint Mountains, it was a mineral called borax that put Death Valley on the map and in the American consciousness. The 1880s were "borax rush" days in Death Valley and in the Nevada desert. Consumer demand for the stuff was huge. It was used to aid digestion, keep milk sweet, improve skin complexion, and remove dandruff and as a purported cure for epilepsy and bunions. Later it was used in powdered soaps called 20 Mule Team Borax and Boraxo, whose manufacturer, the Pacific Coast Borax Company, sponsored a popular radio and television series called *Death Valley Days*—a show hosted by a future President of the United States, Ronald Reagan.

Back in the original Death Valley days, the ore lay on the surface of the desert floor in a compound form known as "cottonball," and it only needed to be scraped up, refined, and hauled away. But hauling anything out of Death Valley was a daunting task. The nearest railhead was in Mojave, 165 miles away. The ore had to be hauled up and over the Panamint Mountains across sand and rocks on extremely primitive roads. The specially made wagons weighed 7,800 pounds empty, 73,000 pounds loaded. William T. Coleman, owner of the Harmony Borax Works on the site of present-day Furnace Creek Ranch, then came up with the idea of using 20-mule teams to haul the borax and the water needed for the grueling, ten-day journey. Though the operation only ran from 1883 to 1889, the mule teams became a symbol of the pluck and persistence of Old West prospectors. Two of the wagons stand on display in the park. Borax is still mined near the park for industrial use, and, yes, still for powdered soap.

ridges that arc across the ridges of high dunes. Getting around in the dunes isn't easy—rangers recommend walking in a zigzag fashion up the ridges—but gaining a vantage on sand summits like High Dune, which looms 650 feet above the valley, or Star Dune yield extraordinary perspectives on the whimsical forms and shapes of their neighbors. (Sandboarding down those dunes is possible on a well-waxed old snowboard or plastic sled.)

> *The geology of the Waterpocket Fold created conditions which allowed unique plant species to evolve here. Six sensitive, threatened or endangered wildflower species are monitored and protected in Capitol Reef National Park.*

⭐ Capitol Reef ⭐
NATIONAL PARK
Waterpocket Fold:
100-mile-long Monocline

Although Utah's Capitol Reef was named for a dome formation flanked by cliffs and ridges that resemble an ocean reef, it's the remarkable Waterpocket Fold that is its main attraction. "Fold" is apt, because it's like a wrinkle in the Earth's crust, of which the dome is one small part. People often come into the park visitor center asking where to see the fold, only to learn that they're standing on it. The 100-mile-long fold is what geologists call a monocline, a long line of cliffs created by faulting action. Erosion over the last 15 to 20 million years has laced the fold with domes and twisting slot canyons. One way to see it is to "loop the fold" on a 147-mile scenic drive. East of the visitor center, Utah 24 runs west right *through* the fold. Then follow Notom-Bullfrog Road south to Burr Trail Road, which makes some spectacular switchbacks up and east over the fold, with fantastic views of its cliffs. Eventually Burr Trail joins Utah 12, which leads back north toward park headquarters. Hikers can plunge into the fold on Upper Muley Twist and Lower Muley Twist Trails. Upper Muley is a 9-miler that starts down in a canyon near the Strike Valley Overlook and climbs to the ridgeline that is the top of the fold. Lower Muley's trailhead is at mile 44.6 on Burr Trail, and the trail zigzags so tightly it can "twist a mule." It runs for 23.4 miles, but even a short hike gives you sense of venturing deep into one of the planet's most interesting formations.

⭐ Mojave ⭐
NATIONAL PRESERVE
Kelso Dunes:
Third Tallest in North America

Many people feel nature speaks to them. In the Kelso Dunes of California's Mojave National Preserve, nature sings. Or, more accurately, it booms, like the musical sound of a tympani roll or a Tibetan prayer gong. The effect is a low vibrational sound emitted when finely polished grains of rose quartz slide over consolidated sand that contains just the right moisture content. You can help initiate the sound by plunge-stepping down the side of a steep sand dune, of which there are plenty. The dunes cover 45 square miles and rise to 600 feet. How they got where they are is quite amazing—their sand is known to have traveled from the Mojave River sink near Afton Canyon, nearly 50 miles west, blown in when Soda Lake dried up, and subsequently trapped by the presence of the Providence Mountains. Rangers offer a weekly 1-mile round-trip guided walk through the dunes, touching on the geologic forces that created them and the plants and animals that live in the ever shifting landscape.

✳ Sleeping Bear Dunes ✳
NATIONAL LAKESHORE
Perched Dunes Atop Glacial Moraines

The presence of sand along a Lake Michigan shoreline is no great surprise, but how did it reach such heights at Sleeping Bear Dunes in Michigan? The answer—these dunes got a boost. From a glacier, no less. Like a child standing atop a father's shoulders, these "perched dunes" stand atop glacial moraines—hills of rock, sand, silt, and clay left behind by continental ice sheets—that once protruded farther into Lake Michigan. Waves cut into the base of the moraine, exposing a steady supply of sand. The sand blew onto the eroded moraine bluffs and perched on top. The Sleeping Bear Plateau spreads 5 miles long, 3 miles wide, and as high as 400 feet at the dune overlooks—Sleeping Bear, Empire, and Pyramid Point. For the full dune experience, you should attempt the 200-foot Dune Climb, the park's favorite kid attraction, and continue on the Dunes Hiking Trail. It winds 3.5 miles through mountains of dunes before coming to an end at an isolated Lake Michigan beach.

✳ Pictured Rocks ✳
NATIONAL LAKESHORE
Colorful Formations:
Chapel Rock and Miner's Castle Members

The colorful patterns on the sandstone bluffs and formations that rise as high as 300 feet above Michigan's Upper Peninsula Lake Superior shoreline are not the product of Chippewa artists. The artist behind these rocks is nature, although geologists can read their hues like a graphic textbook. The most visible layers are the Chapel Rock and Miners Castle members of the Munising formation. The first is comprised of pinkish gray to light brown quartz sandstone, visible at Chapel Rock. The more crumbly Miners Castle sandstone layer hails from a different era and comprises the lakeshore's most prominent wave-cut formation, Miners Castle. One of the castle's crowning turrets collapsed in 2006 and tumbled into Lake Superior, illustrating how the forces that shaped this marvel can also destroy it. The rocks stretch along 15 miles of Lake Superior shoreline, from Munising to Twelvemile Beach, and can be seen by foot or water.

✳ Point Reyes ✳
NATIONAL SEASHORE
Earthquake Trail:
San Andreas Fault Movement

Everyone has heard about the 1906 San Francisco earthquake, but it's sobering to see direct evidence of the fault movement that caused it. The 0.6-mile paved Earthquake Trail at Point Reyes National Seashore provides that opportunity. The loop trail follows a course between Bear Valley Creek and an old wooden pasture fence that was standing at the time of the earthquake. Interpretive signs along the way explain the geological process by which the tectonic plates that meet along the San Andreas Fault moved on April 18, 1906, causing the 7.8 quake that killed 3,000 people. Then comes a brilliant visual aid: a 16-foot offset in the fence, indicating a dramatic shift in the Earth and the line where the North American and Pacific lithospheric plates meet and slide against each other. West of the fence, on the Pacific side, the Earth, and Point Reyes itself, is slowly moving northward toward Alaska, at a rate of just under an inch a year.

chapter two

by land

short backpacking trips

Short backcountry trips that provide wilderness solitude

Stunning backcountry is so accessible in our national parks that a three- or four-day backpacking trip can deliver all the sensations of a true wilderness experience. The following hike descriptions are more illustration than prescription. There's seldom a single magical "right" route. Use these as touchstones, not step-by-step blueprints.

✳ Yosemite ✳
NATIONAL PARK
Wawona Loop

If eastern California's Yosemite has a gentle side, it's Wawona in the southern part of the park. Compared to the High Sierra, these elevations are lower, crowds fewer, and the hiking season longer; it can stretch well into October. This is still majestic country, featuring granite-ringed lakes and tumbling streams, but the setting is more rolling forests of firs and Jeffrey pines than barren alpine of the higher mountains. To forge a 22-mile counterclockwise loop, start hiking from Wawona to Buena Vista Pass (9,300 feet) by way of Chilnualna Falls—a stunning series of foamy tumbles. Once you drop down from the pass you can savor serenity at a choice of lakeside campsites. Buena Vista Lake is a classic alpine cirque at the foot of Buena Vista Peak (9,709 feet). Royal Arch Lake is beautifully set against slabs of exfoliating granite. On the way back, either Johnson or Crescent Lake makes a perfect camp within a day's hike of the trailhead.

✳ Grand Canyon ✳
NATIONAL PARK
Nankoweap Trail

You're not a Grand Canyon hiker till you've plunged from rim to river and back. Do it minus the mobs and mules via the North Rim's Nankoweap Trail, which drops 6,000 feet in 14 miles. Allow one (long) day for the plummet and two for the return ascent, and be sure to spend a day at the Colorado River. After passing through cool groves of aspen and ponderosa pine, the trail enters the canyon proper, corkscrewing down steep faces of Supai sandstone and redwall limestone. Look for cairns when the trail is less than obvious. Be sure to pause to enjoy the amazing canyon views of buttes, hoodoos, and red-rock temples. At 10.6 miles the trail meets perennial Nankoweap Creek. Follow it to the Colorado, where camping is allowed on a sandy beach near Nankoweap Rapids. On your layover day, explore the thousand-year-old granaries built into the cliffs 750 feet above the river by the ancient Pueblo people—you'll see the ruins from camp,

☆ Packs for the Medium Haul ☆

Long-weekend backpacking trips are popular not only because of the constraints of time but also because they allow trail lovers to hike fast and lean without a monster load. The ideal load hauler for such a hike is an internal-frame pack in the neighborhood of 3,000 to 4,000 cubic inches in capacity, which in itself saves weight versus an expedition-style pack.

Fit is crucial to the happiness and well-being of any backpacker, which is why it's a good idea to buy a pack from a mountaineering store; they'll find the perfect backpack to fit a person's general size and frame, then fine-tune it to suit the individual to a tee. A well-fitting pack rests comfortably on the hips, with the shoulder taking a minority of the weight, while a sternum strap keeps the load snugged to your center of gravity. Even a three-day weekend calls for a fair amount of weight, so be sure the pack has a feature that helps deliver most of it to the hips—either built-in stays or a stiff plastic framesheet. Otherwise it feels like a potato sack is hanging from your shoulders.

Most backpacks are top loading and can be expanded vertically to accommodate bigger loads. A separate sleeping-bag compartment aids organization, as do zippered top and front pockets that can handle quick-access snacks. A built-in pouch for a hydration bladder is a handy bonus. Most packs do not have side pockets because the pack maker assumes the hiker wants his or her arms free to swing—or to wield poles if ski touring. Don't sweat the actual pack material too much. Most packs are made of extremely strong Cordura nylon. It is not waterproof, however, so be sure to buy a waterproof overpack if one is not built in to the backpack itself.

just downstream. On your way out of the canyon, plan to camp at Nankoweap Creek, and be sure to top up your water bottles for the last 10.6 dry miles back to the rim.

☆ Great Smoky Mountains ☆
NATIONAL PARK
Big Creek to Hemphill Bald

Allow four days on the trail for this one-way trip that's as diverse as the Tennessee–North Carolina park itself. Many hikers opt for a late start on Big Creek Trail so they can work up enough sweat to relish a dip in the creek's Midnight Hole, a paradisiacal plunge just 1.4 miles from the trailhead. The next 4 miles to Campsite 37 are easy. On Day 2, hikers pick up the Gunter Fork Trail, ford Big Creek, and ogle Gunter Fork Falls as they hike 6 steep miles to Laurel Gap Shelter. Day 3 involves hiking 8 miles to Campsite 39 by way of the Balsam Mountain and Palmer Creek Trails. Day 4 requires an early start for the 9-mile hike out through Cataloochee Valley, which affords surprising sights like elk grazing beside late 19th- and early 20th-century cabins and buildings, including Beech Grove School and Palmer Chapel. The hike concludes by following Big Fork Ridge Trail to Hemphill Bald Trail, finally ending at the Swag, a luxury lodge whose comforts are balm to weary hikers.

☆ Big Bend ☆
NATIONAL PARK
Outer Mountain Loop

This three-day hike into Texas' Chisos Mountains delivers the essence of Big Bend's vastness—100-mile views of the Chihuahuan Desert unsullied by anything man-made. More immediate pleasures include hidden canyons, springs, mountain woodlands, and a profound sense of solitude. In passing through such a variety of habitats, the trail affords hikers the opportunity to truly experience the wonders of Big Bend. The 30-mile loop starts at Chisos Basin and climbs the south rim of the range for a steady succession of heady views—hills, arroyos, and mesas, enormous variations in color, and a powerful sense of expansiveness. It then drops into Juniper Canyon, where a spring may or may not be flowing. The contrasts that define Big Bend are striking as the trail climbs back into the 7,000-foot mountains and a realm of Arizona cypress, maples, oaks, and ponderosa pines. Another drop down dips into Blue Creek Canyon, a veritable Utah of red-rock desert. The return leg is through the open pine country of Chisos Basin. The park is well known for the diversity of its birds, and bird-watchers will especially appreciate the variety they encounter along this hike.

✳ Isle Royale ✳
NATIONAL PARK
Greenstone Ridge Trail

A sense of quest always adds an extra charge to a backpacking trip. In Michigan's Isle Royale National Park, backpackers aim to hike the length of the isolated island that gives the park its name, by way of a 40-mile trail that traces its spine. For the most rewarding approach, start from the southwest corner and work northeast. This way the hike begins in deep woods—birch, aspen, maples—and climbs gradually into mixed conifer forests. The payoff comes when the trail breaks out of the woods for amazing views of Isle Royale, Lake Superior, and sundry barrier islands, most notably from 1,394-foot Mount Desor. Moose are likely to be seen along the way—more than 500 of them hang out on the island, feeding on aquatic plants beside swamps and inland lakes, or simply ambling along the trail—and

the howl of wolves is often heard at night. Campsites are scattered along the trail beside water sources, allowing the hike to be broken into three or four segments. Swimming is possible in most inland lakes, providing a bit of refreshment; just be sure to check for leeches afterward. If that doesn't sound appealing, many side trails lead down to Lake Superior, which offers the opportunity for a cold but leech-free dip. The trail terminates in a dead end, so hikers not wishing to backtrack 3 miles drop down at the Three Mile trail junction, which leads to Rock Harbor and boat transportation back to the mainland.

The trails of Great Smoky Mountains beckon hikers seeking solitude and communion with nature.

✶ North Cascades ✶
NATIONAL PARK
Sahale Arm Trail

Climbers, glacier aficionados, and weekend back-packers alike love this hike to the alpine back-country of Washington State's North Cascades and ultimately to the face of Sahale Glacier. Leaving from a trailhead on the Cascade River Road, the hike begins on the popular Cascade Pass Trail, a path through forests and wildflower-strewn mead-ows that leads to spectacular views of craggy peaks, Stehekin Valley, and possibly even Mount Rainier. At the pass (3.7 miles), most day hikers turn around, so the next 6 miles hiked on the Sahale Arm Trail to the glacier and the trail camp at its base afford wonderful solitude—and the views just keep get-ting better. Many hikers choose to lay over here and simply savor the glorious high-alpine scenery, but the strong and ambitious use the day to proceed up the glacier (ice ax and crampons) and summit Sahale Peak. It's a Class 4 climb, requiring the use of hands at times, to reach the 8,700-foot summit.

✶ Olympic ✶
NATIONAL PARK
Rialto Coast

Long coastal hikes are rare in the United States, which is why the 23 wild miles between Cape Alava and Rialto Beach are so compelling, even in

a park known for mighty forests and mountains. It's no stroll on the beach, however. Scrambling over headlands is hard, slip-pery work, while walking around them might mean waiting on a tide change and slogging through deep, coarse sand. But the superb scenery of the wild "Shipwreck Coast," with its mighty sea stacks, scads of seabirds, and colonies of sea lions is worth the effort. From the Ozette Ranger Station, start for the coast on a 3-mile boardwalk through a boggy for-est of Sitka spruce and western redcedars. At Cape Alava, scan the Pacific for migrating gray whales in the spring and fall. Farther south, look for Indian middens—piles of shells several feet thick—and the so-called Wedding Rocks, covered in petroglyphs. After Yellow Banks, there's a 4-mile run of slippery boulders and ankle-deep gravel—hiking poles are a big help. The route is scattered with eight des-ignated camping areas, some right on the beach; check with rangers beforehand to see which ones allow driftwood fires. The end of the hike is near the point where Hole in the Wall, a massive arch cut into a headland that can only be passed through at low tide, comes into view. If the tide's high, hikers have no choice but to wait patiently and soak up the wild salt air.

✶ Denali ✶
NATIONAL PARK & PRESERVE
Glacier Creek/Contact Creek Loop

Alaska's vast and wild Denali National Park & Preserve doesn't go in much for niceties like trails or trail camps. A backpacking trip here is a true wilderness experience—hikers plot an itinerary (which you must carefully vet with a backcountry ranger) and then forge their way cross-country, setting up campsites wherever they choose (some restrictions apply). The going is difficult, but the reward is a thrilling sense of self-reliance. Such is the case with this loop in Toklat Basin beneath mighty Mount McKinley. Take the park visitor bus to mile 68, disembark, cross the Thorofare River, follow it to Glacier Creek, and proceed up along the creek, all the while paralleling the edge of massive Muldrow Glacier. The landscape is alpine tundra and scree the entire way, so the views are huge, and there's a good chance of spotting Dall sheep, caribou, or a grazing grizzly bear. After about 4.5 miles is Contact Creek, which roughly defines the traversing descent back down the drainage to Eielson Visitor Center to catch the return bus. It's a slow going hike, but one that is supremely rewarding.

> *Much of [Glacier's] early park history is woven around the use of or search for routes across the mountain range. The old Indian trails were not much as we think of park trails today; but they did follow well-defined routes and were often deeply worn by heavy use.*

✳ Glacier ✳
NATIONAL PARK
Cut Bank to Two Medicine

A four-day, 19.8-mile hike in the southeast part of the park, starting at the Cut Bank trailhead and ending at Two Medicine, delves spectacularly into wild Continental Divide country with the option of summiting a couple alpine peaks. From Cut Bank, hike 4 miles to Atlantic Creek Campground. Be sure to allow time to toss flies at the cutthroat trout in Medicine Grizzly Lake. Ambitious hikers can take the next morning (or, better, a layover day) to day hike the spine of the continent at Triple Divide Pass. It's the only place in the United States where water drains not only east to the Atlantic or west to the Pacific but also north to Hudson Bay. Watch for bighorn sheep along the way. The next leg of the hike roughly parallels the North Fork Cut Bank Creek and heads south to Morning Star Campground, where more cutthroat lurk in nearby Katoya Lake. The third segment of the hike takes trekkers above tree line and over Pitamakan and Dawson Passes, the latter on the Continental Divide; in fact the trail parallels the divide for a stretch between the passes. If time permits, do what many hikers do: Stow the backpack at Dawson to climb Flinsch Peak (9,225 feet) by its south face, and then drop down to camp at No Name Lake. The hike out to Two Medicine trailhead traces the shore of Two Medicine Lake, where many hikers don't feel the least bit guilty about snagging a lift on a tour boat for the final few miles.

✳ Rocky Mountain ✳
NATIONAL PARK
North Inlet/Tonahutu Creek Trail Loop

Gasping for oxygen is a way of life in this Colorado park where the *low* elevation is 8,000 feet. Still, with some acclimation, fit hikers can handle this 25-miler that starts at 10,000 feet and tops out at 13,000—one of the country's greatest high-altitude backpacking trips. The hike circles monolithic 12,274-foot Snowdrift Peak in the park's remote southwest corner. On the first night, follow the North Inlet Trail from Grand Lake to July Campsite. Get an early start, because the trail stays in exposed tundra all day, and thunderstorms are always possible. The next day switchback through subalpine forest and alpine tundra in the shadow of Flattop Mountain (12,324 feet), then drop down to the Renegade Campsite. Complete the loop on the equally dazzling Tonahutu Creek Trail, where views take in Ptarmigan Mountain to the south, Cascade Mountain to the west, and shimmering glacier tarn lakes in between.

horseback riding

On the trail with equine friends

Horses often go to places you wouldn't be able to go without their help. But they are more than transport. Horses can be extra eyes and ears, better than our own, their actions alerting riders to pay attention. Also, horses can mingle with wildlife, getting closer than a human could do on foot. (All horse use in the parks requires permits.)

☆ Yellowstone ☆
NATIONAL PARK
Thorofare Region

Thorofare sounds like a busy place, but it's the farthest you can get from a road in the lower 48 states. The area is named for Thorofare Creek, which offers a relatively easy way through Wyoming's Absaroka Mountains. The creek rises on one side of Thorofare Mountain in Teton Wilderness; the Yellowstone River rises on the other. The two streams take different directions from there, but come together just inside the park on their way to a lush delta on Yellowstone Lake. The valley is broad, flat-floored, rimmed by 10,000-foot mountains and blessed with a hearty complement of those things that make the Wyoming wilderness sing—bears, elk, moose, wolves, eagles, wildflower meadows, pine forests, a big sky, and not a motor or electric light to spoil the tranquility. It's country that makes you want to breathe deep and keep some portion of it in your heart forever. Safe to say, most visitors do. A number of trails lead to Thorofare. The route that starts on the northeast shore of Yellowstone Lake and ends miles to the south on U.S. 26 is a classic that should take at least a week.

☆ Olympic ☆
NATIONAL PARK
Hoh River to Sol Duc

Towering trees, cold rivers, damp trails through ferns. In this green shadowed world of the Pacific Northwest temperate rain forest, Sitka spruce and western hemlocks grow 250 feet high. In their shade, maples wear shaggy beards of lichen and thick carpets of epiphytic moss and ferns. The forest is rich and layered with life, while high overhead mountain peaks gleam with glaciers, essentially sterile and seeming as remote as the moon. The contrast is particularly strong along the Hoh River, a beautiful place to linger among the great trunks. Yet it's a natural desire to get above it, up in the blue sky for a view from the top. That's exactly where the Hoh Lake Trail goes: 4,000 vertical feet to a series of high subalpine meadows. Wildflowers abound.

Snowfall blankets Yellowstone National Park, making it tough going for horseback riders.

Wide views of Mount Olympus dominate the southern quarter. The trail winds among sparkling lakes, sometimes tiptoeing along narrow ridges, before plunging back down into the forest and Sol Duc River to complete a magnificent two- or three-night trip.

Olympic maintains 365 miles of trail for horse use. Note that special common-sense conditions apply to some areas (for example, no horse camping above 3,500 feet elevation, and camping only in designated stock camps on sensitive trails) along with the usual minimum-impact camping regulations.

✷ Capitol Reef ✷
NATIONAL PARK
South Draw Road
and Pleasant Creek

If John Ford hadn't been able to film in Monument Valley, he might have come here, and Western movies from then on would have had a different classic look. This central Utah park has enough varying backdrops to keep riders thinking they've passed through a series of extravagant film sets, most of which seem a bit exaggerated, as if the scenery designers got carried away. Ride the Halls Creek drainage south of the Post Corral for a look at the reef—not a former ocean reef but a geologic warp, more specifically a monocline, called the Waterpocket Fold. This great wall of rock has been turned into a strangely sculpted fantasy by wind and water, poked full of holes and gussied up with windows, arches, and domes. Branching slot canyons go deep into the fold, narrowing so much that riders will need to dismount and continue on by foot to marvel

> "[T]here are few sensations I prefer to that of galloping over these rolling limitless prairies . . . or winding my way among the barren, fantastic and grimly picturesque deserts of the so-called Bad Lands."
>
> —THEODORE ROOSEVELT

at the oversize imagination on display. Head for more open country via the Hartnet Road into Cathedral Valley, a fine place to imagine galloping cavalry regiments. On the park's west side, a recommended loop is to follow the South Draw Road (at the end of Scenic Drive) and return by way of Pleasant Creek. The park has no developed facilities for overnight horse use except at the Post Corral, but the park does allow backcountry camping provided campers observe park regulations and restrictions; many trails and hiking routes are closed to horse use.

✷ Theodore Roosevelt ✷
NATIONAL PARK
Maah Daah Hey Trail

Theodore Roosevelt, America's great conservationist President, said his lifelong passion for wild country and its creatures began in the hills of North Dakota. "I heartily enjoy this life," he wrote, "and there are few sensations I prefer to that of galloping over these rolling limitless prairies." Whether riders stay on marked trails or take off across the country, there is reason to believe that horses were made for this sort of terrain. The 96-mile-long Maah Daah Hey Trail connects the North and South Units of the national park named after Roosevelt, with four designated campsites equipped with hitching posts. For about half the distance, it parallels the Little Missouri River. Then, after visiting the site of Roosevelt's Elkhorn Ranch, it crosses the river and loops through badlands and undulating prairie to the northern terminus. Early summer and autumn are the best seasons.

☆ Grand Canyon ☆
NATIONAL PARK
Bright Angel Trail

Bright Angel is arguably the most famous riding trail in the world. However, it's a trail on which riders sit atop mules, not horses. The trip entails heading down, down, down into the wonderland of Arizona's Grand Canyon to spend a night, perhaps two, in the bottom of the canyon at Phantom Ranch. Reservations are stacked up for months in advance, and for good reason. The trail drops off the South Rim, following the Bright Angel Fault and natural weaknesses in the otherwise impregnable cliffs that rise up as you go deeper. At a point some 2,000 feet down, the trail passes through cottonwood-shaded Indian Garden, a popular lunch stop watered by perennial Garden Creek. Looking back toward the rim, it's hard to believe that a trail comes down that way, much less a trail suitable for even these sure-footed mules. Beyond the Indian Garden stretches the Tonto Platform, a broad shelf that runs nearly the length of the canyon. Staying on the Tonto, the mules can reach Plateau Point on the brink of the Inner Gorge, which offers a magnificent view of the Colorado River in a gorge of ancient black rock. The Bright Angel Trail, however, bypasses Plateau Point and descends by twisting pathway to a suspension bridge over the river. Ahead lies Phantom Ranch in a grove of cottonwoods, holding the promise of a steak dinner, a comfy cabin, and a repeat performance by the mules tomorrow, in the reverse direction. Simply put, this trail ride is unforgettable.

THE LURE OF THE NATIONAL PARKS

☆ Haleakala ☆
NATIONAL PARK
Descent Into Haleakala Crater

The Hawaiian island of Maui claims cattle ranches, cowboys, and open mountainous country to ride in. The most unusual terrain is found on the top of the island, in the weird landscape of Haleakala Volcano, an expansive desert of cinders, brightly colored craters, and endemic plants, some of them rare. The Sliding Sands Trail offers a strenuous 2,500-foot descent from the 10,000-foot rim to the crater floor, which makes a horse a valuable companion indeed. A concessionaire—Pony Express Tours (*www.ponyexpresstours.com*)—offers half-day rides. Pack sunblock and, believe it or not, a warm jacket.

☆ Rocky Mountain ☆
NATIONAL PARK
Flattop Mountain Trail

The Rockies reach their greatest elevation in Colorado. The park's scenic Trail Ridge Road offers an excellent opportunity to experience this realm of thin air, climbing above 12,000 feet on a dizzying traverse of the Continental Divide, but doing it on a horse in the wilderness is truly memorable. Glacier Creek Stables (*www.sombrero.com/custompages/glaciercreek.asp*), a horse concessionaire at Sprague Lake, offers the trip in August, after high snowdrifts have melted. The trail follows Glacier Creek, climbs to the divide at Flattop Mountain, and ends after 26 miles of rough, exhilarating country at Grand Lake. It's a challenging ride, recommended for people at least somewhat saddle-hardened.

Below glacier-carved arêtes, a cowboy guide leads pack horses into Glacier National Park's backcountry.

✷ Glacier ✷
NATIONAL PARK
Highline Trail

The unmatched splendor of Montana's Glacier is only hinted at from the roads, and the urge to venture deeper into its beauty strikes many. Park trails are generally open to stock, with limitations to minimize impact in particularly sensitive areas. This leaves a lot of options, including one of the country's finest alpine trails, the Highline, which hugs the Continental Divide from Logan Pass north to Waterton Lake. Birds don't get better views of the mountains than hikers and riders on this trail. The first few miles from Logan Pass are closed to stock (one glance and the reason is obvious) but horseback riders can join the route via the Swiftcurrent Trail from Many Glacier, a superb trail that climbs high over the divide before dropping a short distance to Granite Park Chalet, a classic mountain lodge set near timberline. Swan Mountain Outfitters *(www .swanmountainoutfitters.com)*, the park horse concessionaire, offers it as a one-night trip. For a custom adventure, or for those with their own stock, the Highline continues northward to Goat Haunt on gorgeous Waterton Lake. From there, one trail heads north to Canada (special border regulations apply to horses); another climbs west over Brown and Boulder passes to a trailhead at Kintla Lake. A third trail turns off short of Goat Haunt, crosses Stoney Indian Pass, and heads down the valley toward Belly River. It's possible to turn this into a loop that returns to Many Glacier.

✵ Great Smoky Mountains ✵
NATIONAL PARK
Appalachian Trail

Straddling the Tennessee–North Carolina border, Great Smoky Mountains is a horse-friendly park. With about 550 miles of trails, and more than 40 backcountry campsites approved for horses, trip options abound, including several sections of the Appalachian Trail. Start at one of the park's five roadhead camps set up specially for horses (reservations required). To get a full transect on a day ride, leave Cades Cove on the Anthony Creek Trail, which climbs through deep forest beside the cascading stream to top out on the Appalachian Trail. Fine views open up from Little Bald and other points. Return to Cades Cove on the Russell Field Trail for a loop of about 12 miles, or continue to Gregory Bald, and come down via the Gregory Trail (22 miles with a shuttle at Forge Creek Road). For the complete transit, consider the Benton MacKaye Trail, which runs nearly 100 miles from Twentymile to Big Creek; not heavily used, it is an adventure.

✵ Natchez Trace ✵
NATIONAL SCENIC TRAIL
Leipers Fork Trail

Running from Natchez, Mississippi, to Nashville, Tennessee, the Natchez Trace was a 500-mile footpath established by Native Americans long before either city existed. It remained an important route through the period of European settlement. Traders and travelers could float down rivers eastern cities past St. Louis and all the way to New Orleans with relative ease. But to get back, it was better to walk or ride; the trace was an important part of the route. The footpath is mostly gone today, but four stretches of trail, totaling 65 miles running near or on the original, have been designated a national scenic trail, cutting through habitats such as hardwood and pine forests, creeks, and swamp wetlands. The most scenic section is the 24-mile Leipers Fork Trail near the Nashville end of the trace.

☆ Horse as Pack Animal ☆

Knees get weak. Bodies age. Even once dedicated backpackers eventually find it harder to carry the loads and desire their creature comforts. So time to call in the cavalry, literally. Load up the horses. Send them down the trail with oversize tents, cushy sleeping pads, fresh food, clanking wine bottles, bird books, art supplies, inflatable fishing boats, or anything else your backcountry passions might demand—perhaps even a companion who would rather ride. Outfitters in the parks are always happy to pack in (and later, to pack out) what they call a drop camp. Clients walk in at their own pace with light loads and lighter hearts for a few days of well-supplied wilderness pleasure. If you prefer to explore by horse, many parks allow backcountry stock camping in areas, and some even have designated stock campsites.

day hikes

Stellar scenery and wonderful experiences

The best day hikes have an element of quest, or mission, which is why so many of them climb to the top of a mountain or landmark. Such is the case with many of these hikes. But there's no serious mountain climbing here—the point of each hike is the experience of getting there, and the inspiring view gained at the quest's end.

☆ Acadia ☆
NATIONAL PARK
Sargent Mountain Loop

Can a single hike distill all the beauties of coastal Maine's Acadia? This 5.4-miler comes close, offering a pleasant walk in the woods, a challenging ascent, and a glorious view from 1,373-foot Sargent Mountain, the second highest summit in the park. As an added bonus, the trail provides timely assists in the form of some beautifully crafted stone steps and thoughtfully placed iron rungs. Start at the Jordan Pond House, follow the Spring Trail across the Jordan Cliffs Trail, and take the Sargent Mountain East Cliffs Trail to the summit. Once there, just turn slowly and start identifying. On a clear day Maine's highest mountains, Baxter Peak and Katahdin, are visible far to the north. To the south are the Cranberry Isles, to the west Somes Sound, and to the east the granite domes of Pemetic and Cadillac Mountains. Worked up a sweat? Take a dip in Sargent Pond before returning via the Penobscot Mountain Trail.

☆ Great Smoky Mountains ☆
NATIONAL PARK
Alum Cave Trail to Mount LeConte

Few peaks anywhere are as beloved as Mount LeConte. People return to it year after year. LeConte lovers are slightly chagrined that it's only the third highest peak (6,593 feet) in the Smokies, so they're endeavoring to raise it—hence the growing pile of rocks at its summit. The 5.5-mile (one way) Alum Cave Trail is the shortest, steepest (2,600 feet of gain), and most interesting path to the top. It features more open ridges than other routes, so the views are greater—though always best in the haze-free shoulder seasons. Its wonders include two varieties of rhododendron (rosebay and Catawba), peregrine falcons doing aerobatics at Inspiration Point, and forest habitats that include old-growth hardwoods. The cable handholds along the ledge just below Cliff Top might seem unnecessary on a dry day, but when the rock is slick or icy, you're grateful to have them. Alum Cave, at mile 2.3, is a great slate overhang and site of a Confederate saltpeter mine. The true summit is High Top, site of the huge cairn. But proceed to Myrtle Point for the Great Smoky view that draws visitors back to LeConte time and time again.

✴ Yellowstone ✴
NATIONAL PARK
Specimen Ridge Trail

In northwest Wyoming, the Specimen Ridge Trail off Yellowstone Park's Northeast Entrance Road rises 1,600 feet in 3.5 miles without relief, so only hiking gluttons begin this challenging hike, let alone reach the ridge top and the spectacular views it affords. When standing high on the ridge, the hordes at Old Faithful become a cloudy memory. After the trail passes through some grassy sagebrush meadows and clears a Douglas-fir forest, it emerges into vast open country that's like a secluded grandstand overlooking Yellowstone's northeast quadrant. To the north is Lamar Valley—wolf country. To the south, Mount Washburn (10,243 feet) rises over central Yellowstone. In between are expanses of meadows, and the foreground is special too. The specimens in question are petrified stumps of oaks, redwood, birch, and maple trees as well as conifers—this is one of the world's largest petrified

The first light of day strikes the coastal lands of Acadia National Park in Maine.

forests. Late summer wild-flowers round out the show. As the trail continues, the views magnify. The ridge summit, 9,614-foot Amethyst Mountain, is at mile 11 of the hike, and if you've arranged a car shuttle, you can proceed 7 more miles down to the Lamar River Trailhead. Or just turn around anywhere, anytime. The view's just as good going down.

> *In 1913 and 1914, the animals began to arrive [at Wind Cave]. Fourteen bison came from the New York Zoological Society, twenty-one elk arrived from Wyoming and thirteen pronghorn came from Alberta, Canada.*

☆ Grand Teton ☆
NATIONAL PARK
Cascade Canyon
to Solitude Lake

Beautiful Cascade Canyon in Wyoming's Grand Teton National Park is extremely popular with hikers, and Solitude Lake is the goal for many. Plenty of people set out to explore its depths—first on the shuttle boat across Jenny Lake, and then on the first few miles of the trail. But solitude and its eponymous lake lies at the end. From the boat landing, most hikers will make the steep climb to Inspiration Point for a signature view of Jenny Lake and the mountains that frame Jackson Hole, and perhaps proceed another 3.5 miles along Cascade Creek—prime bear and moose habitat—while towering pinnacles (the Grand, Mount Owen, Teewinot) loom overhead. But by the time a hiker reaches the point where the trail splits, with the North Fork Trail leading another 3 miles to Solitude Lake, the majority of the crowds will have disappeared. And intrepid hikers who reach Solitude get to behold the Grand Teton as no casual tourist ever does—a sheer 1,000 feet of dark, massive, towering rock. Just as moving are the collages of wildflowers—glacier lilies, mountain bluebells, and sticky geraniums—and the flashes of colorful western tanagers in the sky. The strenuous hike to Solitude Lake is 14.4 miles round trip from the boat landing. Hikers desiring a longer day can skip the boat shuttle and skirt the lake on the Jenny Lake Loop to reach the Cascade Canyon Trailhead, adding 2 miles each way.

☆ Wind Cave ☆
NATIONAL PARK
Highland Creek/
Centennial Trail Loop

The aboveground scenery is just as compelling as the subterranean stuff at South Dakota's Wind Cave National Park, and what a remarkable contrast. After their stygian stint, visitors emerge to encounter big skies, wide-open spaces, abundant wildlife, and a solitary, almost elegiac experience of a primal American landscape—the prairies that once covered a third of the North American continent. This 7.3-mile loop starts on the Highland Creek Trail, which later intersects the Centennial Trail; the trailhead for the Centennial is the destination. The hike begins on mixed-grass prairie with distant views of the Black Hills and close-up views of a huge prairie dog colony. The trail then edges some lovely riparian stretches along Beaver Creek and Highland Creek and traverses ponderosa pine forests. Watch for bison wallows or, better yet, the beasts themselves—the park is home to more than 450 of them. But beware: Their docile appearance is deceptive; they can charge at surprising speed. Elk, coyotes, deer, and pronghorn, are also plentiful.

☀ Shenandoah ☀
NATIONAL PARK
Old Rag

Although 50,000 hikers a year summit Old Rag in Virginia, climbing to the 3,291-foot granite peak is no walk in the park. There's nothing easy about it, but everything alluring. It's what one local guide calls a "4WD hike," meaning hikers should plan on employing every available limb and a good healthy ticker on the way up. The 8-mile loop climbs 2,380 feet to the summit and entails some rough, steep scrambling on Yosemite-style granite slabs along the way. From the top, views can stretch 100 miles in any direction. The best trailhead is at Weakley Hollow. Old Rag can be hiked throughout the year, but locals call spring "Old Rag season" for two very good reasons: (1) sunshine and brilliantly clear blue skies, and (2) no snakes, bugs, or poison ivy.

☀ Grand Canyon ☀
NATIONAL PARK
Rim Trail

People come to Arizona to gape into the abyss of Grand Canyon, to see the play of sunlight on rock, clouds on canyon, maybe to watch a rainstorm rush through, leaving a rainbow in its wake. To see the endless buttes and temples and side canyons and amphitheaters of rock. The best way to see it all, while avoiding the pounding of a canyon descent, is to hike the Rim Trail from Maricopa Point (where it becomes a dirt path) west to Hermits Rest—a distance of 6.7 miles. Take the park shuttle to the trailhead and pick it up at trail's end, or at six other spots along the way. As the path undulates along the precipice, versus plummeting to the bottom, it reveals the park's (maybe the world's) most stunning panoramas—canyons within canyons, cauldrons of rapids far below. Do it late in the day and watch

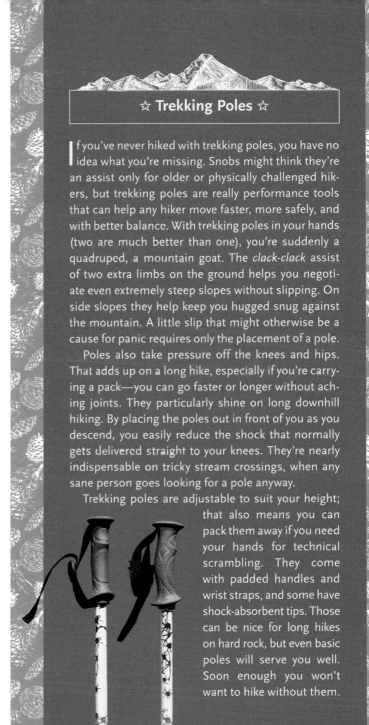

☆ Trekking Poles ☆

If you've never hiked with trekking poles, you have no idea what you're missing. Snobs might think they're an assist only for older or physically challenged hikers, but trekking poles are really performance tools that can help any hiker move faster, more safely, and with better balance. With trekking poles in your hands (two are much better than one), you're suddenly a quadruped, a mountain goat. The *clack-clack* assist of two extra limbs on the ground helps you negotiate even extremely steep slopes without slipping. On side slopes they help keep you hugged snug against the mountain. A little slip that might otherwise be a cause for panic requires only the placement of a pole.

Poles also take pressure off the knees and hips. That adds up on a long hike, especially if you're carrying a pack—you can go faster or longer without aching joints. They particularly shine on long downhill hiking. By placing the poles out in front of you as you descend, you easily reduce the shock that normally gets delivered straight to your knees. They're nearly indispensable on tricky stream crossings, when any sane person goes looking for a pole anyway.

Trekking poles are adjustable to suit your height; that also means you can pack them away if you need your hands for technical scrambling. They come with padded handles and wrist straps, and some have shock-absorbent tips. Those can be nice for long hikes on hard rock, but even basic poles will serve you well. Soon enough you won't want to hike without them.

sunset do a supernova number on the scene, then hop the bus back to Grand Canyon Village. It isn't perhaps the most challenging hike, but it just might be the most memorable.

✶ Yosemite ✶
NATIONAL PARK
Valley Floor Loop

In California's Yosemite National Park, counter to all reasonable expectations, the 13-mile valley trail that circumnavigates Yosemite Valley is lightly used—the park's fabled crowds are in their cars or congregating at a few valley landmarks, leaving this gem wide open. The trail, an old bridle path, is unrelentingly spectacular as it winds in and out of forests, connecting most of the valley's major sights. While the loop is 13 miles in its entirety, it does come with a bailout plan—it intersects park roads numerous times, so it is possible to shorten the loop and catch the park shuttle bus back to the starting trailhead. If starting behind Yosemite Lodge or Camp 4 and proceeding west, the trail hugs the base of mighty El Capitan with it's 3,593-foot vertical wall until reaching Pohono Bridge, where it crosses over the Merced River to the south side of the valley. The trail then turns east and goes past Bridalveil Falls, crosses El Capitan Meadow, and parallels the Merced River until it reaches Swinging Bridge. Here the trail crosses back over the Merced, affording a great look at Upper Yosemite Falls, then winds back to the starting point at Yosemite Lodge.

✶ Big Bend ✶
NATIONAL PARK
Pine Canyon

One of the great pleasures of Big Bend is its ability to deliver the unexpected. The Texas park's 800,000 acres of desert expanse are compelling on their own, but when they yield to woodlands, uplands, or the presence of water, the result is startling and thrilling. All three can be encountered in Pine Canyon, especially in the rainy season, July to October. A high-clearance vehicle is recommended to reach the start of the hike, which begins in open Chihuahuan desert scrubland and climbs steadily into the canyon in the Chisos Mountains. Once inside, the trail winds through a cool, shady realm of ponderosa pine, oak, maple, and madrone. After about 2 miles, it dead-ends at a 200-foot cliff—a "pour-off" in the local parlance—that becomes a waterfall for several days after a rain. It's truly a world within a world.

✶ Point Reyes ✶
NATIONAL SEASHORE
Tomales Point

The hike to Tomales Point is a landlubber's experience of the heart-lifting view that enchanted Spanish explorers—wave-crashed headlands, islands teeming with gulls and cormorants, migrating gray whales *(Jan.–April)*, and the vastness of the Pacific. But the closer pleasures are equally inspiring—the play of sun and fog, brilliant poppies dotting the green meadows, and diffident tule elk across the pasture. The 9.5-mile round-trip starts at Upper Pierce Point Ranch, bisects a narrow peninsula, proceeds past trail's end, and culminates at a dramatic, north-pointing finger of land jutting into Bodega Bay. If it's foggy and/or windy, as it often is, the hike is still an experience of pristine California—cool, damp, and seemingly untouched by man.

great bicycle rides

Fresh air, level trails, and picturesque settings

National parks are blessed with opportunities for unparalleled biking. Trips that can cross the Continental Divide, circle the rim of an ancient volcano, follow the path of an historic canal, or see the waters of the Atlantic beyond the sands of Cape Cod. The diversity and grandeur of the surroundings is awe-inspiring.

✳ Crater Lake ✳
NATIONAL PARK
Rim Drive

Perhaps because the window of opportunity is so very small, the desire to bicycle at Oregon's Crater Lake is so very large. With an average annual snowfall of more than 44 feet, paved Rim Drive is usually closed until late May or early June. When the snow is cleared, the road opens to foot traffic, then bicycles, and then cars until around October when weather begins closing the road again. Riders who slip in through that window will cycle beside America's deepest lake (1,943 feet), which dazzles guests with its rich blue waters shimmering within a 6-mile-wide caldera (volcanic crater) created when Mount Mazama erupted and collapsed about 7,700 years ago. The 33-mile rim road, edged with fir and pines, creates a wonderfully appealing tour for riders who can handle some steep hills and numerous curves. Beginners are pleased to complete a single circuit, experienced cyclists push themselves to pedal three laps to complete a century ride.

✳ Acadia ✳
NATIONAL PARK
Park Loop Road

Thanks to the fortune of John D. Rockefeller, Jr., and the efforts of anonymous road crews, between 1913 and 1940 access around Acadia was made far easier and much lovelier with the addition of 45 miles of stone and gravel carriage roads which, at the time, came with a ban on motorized traffic. The roads designed for horses have since been supplemented by the 27-mile Park Loop Road that tracks the island coast before slicing into the center of the park with a separate road leaping up toward 1,530-foot Cadillac Mountain. In general, the loop road is relatively level while the ascent to reach the peak presents steep grades. As a reward, though, are commanding views of the Maine coast. Depending on the road selected, cyclists may be sprayed by mist from the sea, steering clear of pedestrians, or giving wide berth to equestrian traffic. That's part of the beauty of Acadia. There's something for everyone. And horses.

Heat-defying mountain bikers take to the rugged terrain of Death Valley National Park.

☆ Glacier ☆
NATIONAL PARK
Going-to-the-Sun Road

Considered one of the nation's most stunning *drives,* the fact that cyclists get to experience Going-to-the-Sun Road unencumbered by 4,000 pounds of metal, climate controls, and a blaring sound system also makes this Montana road one of the most impressive *rides*. It's demanding to tackle the one road that bisects the park, and cyclists straining to propel themselves up and over 6,646-foot Logan Pass will wish their bicycle was equipped with cruise control. The payoff is in the sights: the crisp blue sky, the Matterhorn-shaped peak of Mount Reynolds, the alpine flowers and fir trees, and especially a glance back to see the recently conquered thin black ribbon of road snaking around the steep hills. From border to border, the ride's roughly 50 miles so plan on several hours to make the complete stretch (much longer for beginning bicyclists). And planning pays. For about 12 miles between Logan Creek and Logan Pass, east-bound bicycle traffic (the side closest to the cliffs) is prohibited between 11 a.m. and 4 p.m., and bicycling in both directions is stopped during the same time period between the Apgar and Sprague Creek Campgrounds.

☀ Death Valley ☀
NATIONAL PARK
Furnace Creek Area Rides

One iconic image of the America West includes bleached cow skulls resting in the depths of Death Valley—which may nudge some bicyclists away from even considering a ride here. But in addition to rugged paths designed for mountain biking, this California park offers several easygoing rides. Riders may share the main roads with public vehicular traffic, but there are also designated bicycle routes. Among the short (1- to 2-mile) routes of pavement or packed gravel in the Furnace Creek area, bikers can take a Wild West ride by pedaling to the Harmony Borax Works through Mustard Canyon. Farther away is Twenty Mule Team Canyon, which offers a 3-mile loop ride, and you can continue along the road to explore on foot the Salt Creek Interpretive Trail. Countering the obvious drawback of temperatures that have hit 134°F, there is a palpable spiritual essence here. Longer stretches (6 and 7 miles) lead to hidden canyons and overlooks which, for riders with time, stamina, and a generous supply of water, are worth exploring.

☀ Cuyahoga Valley ☀
NATIONAL PARK
Ohio & Erie Canal Towpath Trail

There are four superb trails in Ohio's Cuyahoga Valley, but for bicyclists the standout star is a path that also pleases joggers and pedestrians. Once reserved for barge-towing mules, the Ohio & Erie Canal Towpath Trail rolls for about 20 miles in the park beside the famous waterway, while additional miles of trails extend beyond the park into the Ohio & Erie Canalway. In addition to abundant shade and a wide berth, one thing that makes this family-friendly ride so pleasing is its ease and the chance to enjoy a variety of sights and sounds and feelings. There are marshes and covered bridges, boardwalks and woods, and historic structures like the circa 1836 Boston Store. For riders whose energy flags, it's simply a matter of finding a Cuyahoga Valley Scenic Railroad station and flagging down a passing train (yes, train) that, for $2, takes them and their mount back to their starting point.

☀ Grand Teton ☀
NATIONAL PARK
John D. Rockefeller, Jr.
Memorial Parkway

Travelers entering Grand Teton via the park's main north–south highway U.S. 191 experience an impending sense of, well, grandeur, courtesy of the towering peaks dubbed by French fur traders as Les Trois Tetons—the Three Breasts. The sight

☆ Rules of the Road ☆

With bicycling comes a sense of freedom and independence, a train of thought that's magnified on a ride in a national park. In reality, the rules of the road in most national parks are likely more stringent than when pedaling around a town. Before heading out on a ride, check with rangers. While rules may vary, generally riders are expected to wear a helmet and high visibility clothing, ride single file, have visible headlights and taillights if riding after dark, and stay to the right and ride with traffic. Recognize, too, that along with hazards such as snow, ice, and sand, national parks can present unusual hazards, such as deer, elk, moose, prairie dogs, and an assortment of other wildlife blocking your way. If you see bison or bear on the road, rangers suggest, turn around. Ride safe, ride happy.

of snow laced along broad swatches of granite are all part of the park's larger than life scenery that fuels riders. While the roadway is wide enough to accommodate two lanes of traffic as well as cautious bicyclists, in 2009 new multiuse pathways near the south end of the park improved the ability of riders to hit the road with a heightened sense of ease. The scenic trails include level paths through sagebrush flats that parallel the main road leading to the shores of Jenny Lake and incredible views of the tallest Teton peaks, long-standing landmarks in western Wyoming. While riders needn't be cowed by oncoming traffic, heed the advice of park rangers who suggest steering clear of bison, moose, elk, pronghorn, and bears.

> **MAY 23 1928**
> *President Calvin Coolidge signed legislation authorizing construction of the Mount Vernon Memorial Highway ... This early federal parkway soon became part of the longer George Washington Memorial Parkway.*

the mood of the river on a trail that is more remote and rural and natural. As riders pedal south, the landscape changes and so does the experience. The feel of the ride and dynamic of the river adopt a more urban appearance as it flows through residential and business areas near Minneapolis, introducing city sights like the Stone Arch Bridge and its view of St. Anthony Falls. After following the river's meander through Minneapolis and St. Paul, the trail continues south to Hastings along a stretch of river that blends industry and nature. This ride should please cyclists looking for a country ride in the heart of the city, and a city tour that rolls across the country, and prepare them for the longer bike ride downriver.

☆ Mississippi ☆
NATIONAL RIVER & RECREATION AREA
Mississippi River Trail

Similar to hiking the Appalachian Trail from Maine to Georgia, it's actually possible to bike the length of the Mississippi River from its headwaters at Lake Itasca to the Gulf of Mexico via the Mississippi River Trail. Determined riders could tackle the 3,000-mile series of independent trails across ten states on paved roads, atop levees, through the woods, and beside the water, but that would require a lot of thought and a lot of effort. Instead, in southeast Minnesota, 25 communities have come together with the national recreation area and a series of smaller regional parks to create a 72-mile bike path along the famous waterway. Beginning in Anoka, north of Minneapolis–St. Paul, the ride mirrors

☆ George Washington ☆
MEMORIAL PARKWAY
Mount Vernon Trail

For 18-odd miles the Mount Vernon Trail flows along the Potomac River from Arlington, Virginia, to George Washington's Virginia home at Mount Vernon, and even with an average of 20,000 users a week, it's well worth contending with walkers, runners, and skaters just to experience the history and scenery it delivers. Depart from Theodore Roosevelt Island and a mile later ride toward Arlington National Cemetery by crossing below the Memorial Bridge, the symbolic dividing line of the Union and Confederacy. Shortly after, at Lady Bird Johnson Park is the Lyndon Baines Johnson Memorial and a panoramic view of Washington, D.C. Clock on more miles and pedal past memorials to service personnel, Daingerfield Island, the charm (and conveniences) of Old Town Alexandria's shops and restaurants, the wetlands and hiking of Dyke Marsh, the remains of the Civil War–era Fort Hunt, and, 3 miles later, the historic Mount Vernon. In other words, in just 18 miles riders can travel from America's present into the past.

⋆ Cape Cod ⋆
NATIONAL SEASHORE
Nauset, Head of the Meadow,
and Province Lands Trails

Flexing its long arm 60 miles into the Atlantic and wrapping itself around the eastern coast of mainland Massachusetts, Cape Cod National Seashore continues to guard against development and vigilantly preserve its shoreline and sand dunes. Generally low and long and level, the terrain makes pedaling a pleasure, and its three short, but enjoyable, biking trails give riders *exactly* the kind of carefree riding any visitor expects to find on the cape. The Nauset Trail begins at the Salt Pond Visitor Center, which is the prime spot for park maps and information on programs. The entire ride is only 1.6 miles (double that for a round trip) and leads through the woods and sometimes beneath a canopy of trees on a paved trail that slowly dips and twists like a low-grade roller coaster until, just after a long bridge, comes Coast Guard Beach—and the Atlantic Ocean. The easy 2-mile Head of the Meadow Trail winds from the town of Truro to East Harbor. The 5.4-mile Province Lands Trail features steep hills, sharp curves, and low tunnels in a loop that takes in Beech Forest and Pasture Pond. Caution is definitely called for along certain stretches of the path. The loop has several access points and spur trails, including one to the Old Harbor Lifesaving Station Museum.

⋆ Yellowstone ⋆
NATIONAL PARK
South and East Entrance Roads

Yellowstone National Park is a fascinating place any time of the year, but for bicyclists the high season is springtime. For one brief, shining moment between mid-March and mid-April, as the roads are thawing out from the winter freeze and prior to a mass of travelers filtering into the park, cyclists are granted something spectacular: exclusive access to portions of Yellowstone roads. It's easy to be awed by Yellowstone's geological variety show at peak capacity, but imagine riding in the West Entrance to find the road between here and Mammoth Hot Springs reserved especially for riders, joggers, pedestrians, and other nonmotorized traffic. Sneak in through the south and east entrances for short rides, too, although there may be road crews prepping the asphalt for summer visitors. Since the weather is inclined to be notoriously notorious, for a sure bet give it a few more weeks until all the park services are up and running and the roads are clean and clear. By late spring or early summer all the main roads through the park are open to traffic, although stubborn snowbanks can make riding more dangerous. Even in good weather, drivers on this splendid two-lane figure-eight road may seem less concerned with the safety of bicyclists than their need to stay on schedule. In that case, opt for one of the handful of short designated bicycling/hiking trails that are found in the Mammoth, West Entrance, Old Faithful, Lake, and Tower-Lamar areas; some are paved, while some are gravel.

family-friendly hikes

Easy enough for kids, fun for parents

Finding the right hike for children can be tricky: The trail needs to be safe and not too strenuous, yet interesting enough to keep the young folks' attention. As a bonus, it would be nice if the hike stimulated them to want to learn more about the place. National parks abound in good kids' hikes; these are ten of the best and most diverse.

✴ Great Sand Dunes ✴
NATIONAL PARK & PRESERVE
Dunes Fields

The United States' tallest dunes are found in of all places Colorado, tucked against the east side of the Sangre de Cristo Mountains. Between the westerly winds and some unique geological circumstances the main dune field has spread across about 30 square miles, with dune heights reaching above 700 feet. The dune field is not so much a hiking place as a "Go out and have fun" spot. Kids (adults, too) are welcome to run up the sand dunes and slide or roll down. Certain precautions should be heeded, especially when the sand is scorching hot in summer, but the kids are not likely to hurt themselves if they fall down. To sand sled, or sandboard, all that's really needed is something like a flat-bottomed plastic sled; skis and snowboards work, too; a section of cardboard box does not. If the weather conditions have been too dry, the sand may be too soft for sledding, but the dunes are great to explore any time. People are free to wander, provided they don't impact the vegetation. The summit of High Dune, the second highest dune, is a long mile climb through the shifting sands. Nearby Medano Creek offers a great place to cool off afterward, if it's flowing.

✴ Mount Rainier ✴
NATIONAL PARK
Sourdough Ridge Trail

Fantastic views of western Washington's snow-capped peaks, including Mount Rainier, make the Sourdough Ridge Trail a mini-adventure the whole family will love. Located high in the subalpine zone of the park in the Sunrise area, the trail makes a 1-mile loop with only gentle elevation gain. Passing through flower-filled meadows, it's a great way to introduce kids to the beauty of the high country. They'll feel like mountain climbers when they reach the ridge top for even better panoramic vistas. Snow closes this area most of the year, so plan to visit in the summer or early fall to do this hike; the road to Sunrise may not even open until July.

✳ Mammoth Cave ✳
NATIONAL PARK
Frozen Niagara Tour

Some cave tours are too long for children, or require climbing lots of stairs or squeezing through tight (possibly scary) spaces. The Frozen Niagara Tour at Kentucky's Mammoth Cave is short enough (a quarter-mile round-trip, taking just over an hour) and easy enough for kids, yet offers spectacular cave scenery such as Rainbow Dome, Crystal Lake, the Frozen Niagara flowstone, and the Drapery Room. Young folks can let their imaginations take over here, as formation shapes suggest animals, cartoon characters, and who knows what. With this introduction to underground wonders, a child just might turn into a dedicated caver.

✳ Petrified Forest ✳
NATIONAL PARK
Giant Logs Trail

This northeastern Arizona park has the kind of wide-open space that kids sometimes find unexciting. Get them onto park trails, however, and they're sure to be astonished by close-up looks at enormous "fallen trees"—made of rock. One of the best short hikes for children is the Giant Logs Trail, a 0.4-mile

Mammoth Cave's Booth's Amphitheater is named for actor Edwin Booth, who performed here in the 19th century.

loop that begins at the Rainbow Forest Museum, the park's southern visitor center. This path leads to the largest log in the park: Old Faithful, around 170 feet long and more than 9 feet across at its base. Here, kids can see (and feel) how ancient tree trunks were permeated by water carrying dissolved silica, which crystallized as quartz, exactly replacing the soft plant structure with hard mineral. They'll see bark, knotholes, and growth rings, all in amazingly fine detail. Every color imaginable seems to be represented in the shiny agate logs. Interpretive panels along the way explain the science behind the petrified logs. The Rainbow Forest Museum includes exhibits on dinosaurs, always popular with kids.

⚝ Devils Tower ⚝
NATIONAL MONUMENT
Base Loop Trail

There's a reason that Native Americans have long considered this site in northeastern Wyoming a sacred place, and that it was designated as America's first national monument in 1906: It's awesome, in a way that's truly otherworldly. The solidified magma of an ancient volcano (phonolite porphyry, similar to granite, if you want to be precise), Devils Tower rises 867 feet above the rock rubble at its base in distinctive multisided columns. The molten magma forced its way upward but didn't reach the Earth's surface. Over millennia, it was exposed by erosion, creating this massive, flat-topped geological wonder. Don't just take a couple of photos and drive on. Walk the 1.3-mile loop trail around its base to marvel at this amazing structure from all angles. Kids and parents alike will enjoy seeing how the tower's shape changes from different viewpoints and watching rock climbers scaling its height. One more hint: Take time before your trip to watch the movie *Close Encounters of the Third Kind,* which unforgettably turns Devils Tower into an alien landing site.

⚝ Assateague Island ⚝
NATIONAL SEASHORE
Life of the Marsh
and Woodland Trails

It's probably safe to say that all kids love ponies. At this Atlantic Ocean seashore park—encompassing a 37-mile-long barrier island on the Maryland–Virginia border—parents can promise their children the chance to see "ponies" (small horses, actually) living in picturesque fields and marshes, far from the county fairs and farmyards where they're usually encountered. The famous wild horses of Assateague Island are descended from animals brought to the island in the 1600s by local planters. Their small size is thought to be a result of their restricted diet, and their chubby look comes from the amount of water they must drink to offset the salt they intake. The horses delight visitors young and old with their appealingly shaggy charm—especially those who've

☆ Activities for Kids ☆

Many parks have special activities for young people, including kid-friendly nature walks and essay contests. In the Junior Ranger Program, offered at many National Park Service sites, kids can complete selected parts of a booklet and attend a ranger-led program to earn a badge. Before visiting a park, check out the "For Kids" section of its website (start at *www.nps.gov*) to learn more about fun activities for children.

read the classic book *Misty of Chincoteague* by Marguerite Henry, based on the true story of a pony born here. On the Maryland part of the island the horses wander freely and might be seen anywhere; the half-mile round-trip Life of the Marsh Trail that winds through a salt marsh is a good place to look for them. On the Virginia side the horses are kept in a large enclosure and can be seen from the 1.5-mile-loop Woodland Trail.

☆ Muir Woods ☆
NATIONAL MONUMENT
Trails Along Redwood Creek

Children will feel like they're in the movie *Honey, I Shrunk the Kids* as they walk through the forest of coast redwoods in this park north of San Francisco. Some of the trees here top 250 feet in height and are more than 14 feet across at the base; the average age of the redwoods is 600 to 800 years old. Expect to see lots of people walking around with upturned faces and wide-open eyes. If any landscape in the country can be called magical, this cathedral-like forest qualifies. Easy paved trails run alongside Redwood Creek, crossing it on bridges and making possible loop walks of a half mile to 2 miles in length.

☆ Mount Rushmore ☆
NATIONAL MEMORIAL
Presidential Trail

Kids have seen them in schoolbooks, on television, and in movies. Four gigantic presidential heads—Washington, Jefferson, T. Roosevelt, Lincoln—way up on the mountain, looking just as distinguished as they should. Nobody can fail to be impressed

> *How big are the faces [on Rushmore]?*
> *Heads: approximately 60 feet.*
> *Nose: Washington's is 21 feet the rest are approximately 20 feet.*
> *Eyes: approximately 11 feet wide.*
> *Mouths: approximately 18 feet wide.*

by the first sight of South Dakota's Mount Rushmore through the Avenue of Flags (try to arrive in the morning for best light). To get a closer view, walk the half-mile Presidential Trail, which approaches the base of the mountain and passes the studio where sculptor Gutzon Borglum worked. Consider renting audio wands for a narrated tour of the park as well, to learn lots of fascinating details about the monument's history and creation.

☆ Acadia ☆
NATIONAL PARK
Carriage Roads

Thanks to the actions of oil mogul and philanthropist John D. Rockefeller, Jr., back in the early to mid-20th century, visitors to this park on the Maine coast can enjoy more than 50 miles of carriage roads: broad, smooth gravel paths approximately 16 feet wide open to walkers, horseback riders, and bicyclists but not motorized vehicles. These paths wind throughout much of the park on the east side of Mount Desert Island, passing developed areas as well as more remote spots, and they're perfect for families—even those with strollers to push, as Rockefeller specifically designed the roads to be not too steep or sharply curved for horse-drawn carriages. But rather than a family-friendly hike, consider a family-friendly bike ride. Bikes can be rented in the nearby town of Bar Harbor, making possible a leisurely outing through the wooded landscape of Mount Desert Island. As you ride, stop to admire the striking stone bridges scattered along the routes; there are 17 of them, each designed for its particular setting (and all also courtesy of Rockefeller).

✺ Hawaii Volcanoes ✺
NATIONAL PARK
Thurston Lava Tube

Lots of families visit Hawaii, and those who visit the Big Island can tour the otherworldly landscape of this fascinating park. Because this is one of the most volcanically active places on Earth, a last-minute check about conditions is wise. Parts of the park have been closed since a new vent opened in Kilauea's Halemaumau Crater in March 2008. The great majority of the time, though, the park can be visited with complete safety. Kids will love Thurston Lava Tube, located just off Crater Rim Drive. Very small children might be afraid here, but older kids will find it just creepy enough to be fun. Formed when molten lava flowed out of an underground tunnel, leaving it empty, Thurston is about 450 feet long, and is lit by electric lights to reduce claustrophobia; the path through it is paved. In places the roots of trees hang down inside the cave, adding to the Indiana Jones atmosphere created by the tree ferns outside the entrance. When kids reach the surface again at the end of the tube, they'll definitely have a unique experience to tell their friends.

Some hikers choose to explore the forest-clad Kilauea volcano in Hawaii Volcanoes National Park.

walk-up summits

Peaks where moderate effort brings big rewards

Our national parks are full of peaks that can be reached by nearly anyone in good physical condition, with proper gear and preparation. Some of these are fairly easy hikes, while others are moderately strenuous. As always, know your personal limits and get advice from a park ranger before setting out for a summit.

☆ Kings Canyon ☆
NATIONAL PARK
Lookout Peak

Many of the Sierra Nevada summits in this eastern California park (including 14,505-foot Mount Whitney, the highest point in the lower 48 states) are reached by either very long and strenuous day hikes or overnight backpacking trips. Lookout Peak, however, offers a wonderful vista for far less effort and preparation. You can make a short hike to the 8,531-foot top from the Big Meadows Road in Sequoia National Forest, but a more satisfying (and scenic) approach is via the Don Cecil Trail, which ascends the north-facing slope of Kings Canyon beginning in the Cedar Grove area. The hike climbs about 4,000 feet in 7 miles, passing a lovely cascade on Sheep Creek along the way. The reward for this workout is an eye-popping panorama east toward the head of Kings Canyon, which shows the U-shaped form of a typical glacier-carved chasm. It's truly one of the best views in the combined Sequoia and Kings Canyon National Parks.

☆ Yellowstone ☆
NATIONAL PARK
Avalanche Peak

Located on the eastern boundary of Yellowstone in the Absaroka Range of northwestern Wyoming, 10,568-foot Avalanche Peak can be climbed on a trail that begins near Eleanor Lake, between the east entrance to the park and Yellowstone Lake. (Park at Eleanor Lake; the trail is across the road on the north side.) The hike ascends (somewhat steeply at times) 2,100 feet over 2.5 miles through lush conifer forests of subalpine fir and Englemann spruce—look for deer and elk—and an alpine basin to an above-timberline panorama that includes Yellowstone Lake to the west and the Absarokas to the east, with sharp-topped Hoyt Peak relatively near. The Avalanche Peak Trail may not be snow free until July, but the brief summer season brings a colorful display of subalpine wildflowers, including yellow columbine, purple larkspur, and Indian paintbrush. This is a popular summer hike, so if a degree of solitude is wanted, set out at dawn.

☆ Shenandoah ☆
NATIONAL PARK
Stony Man

The aptly named Stony Man (the top is a mass of boulders and rocky cliffs) isn't the highest point in Virginia's Shenandoah National Park. But at 4,011 feet, it's only 40 feet lower than Hawksbill, which rises in the Blue Ridge Range about 3 miles to the south. Stony Man arguably has better unobstructed views, including the vista west over the seemingly endless Appalachian Mountains, forested ridges stretching to the horizon like green ocean waves. Stony Man can be climbed from a parking area near mile 39 on the park's Skyline Drive, or from the Skyland area a couple of miles south. Either way, it's a hike of less than 2 miles with an elevation gain of less than 1,000 feet. But there's a bonus to starting the hike at the trailhead near mile 39: a short spur trail to the cliffs of Little Stony Man. Get an early start to avoid some of the midday crowds on this popular hike. It is especially pretty in late June, when the mountain laurel is blooming.

☆ Afternoon Storms ☆

While standing atop a mountain peak can be an exhilarating feeling, keep one important point in mind: You're likely to be the tallest thing for many miles around, and that can be very bad if a thunderstorm develops. Summer lightning storms are a common and serious (and potentially deadly) danger in the mountains, especially on high, exposed peaks in the West. To minimize the risk, many hikers begin their climbs at dawn or even earlier, to reach the summit and be back down below tree line before dark clouds form late in the afternoon.

☆ Death Valley ☆
NATIONAL PARK
Wildrose Peak

Some peak-seeking folks are going to head straight for Death Valley's high point: 11,049-foot Telescope Peak, part of eastern California's Panamint Range. It's a hard 14-mile round-trip with a 3,000-foot elevation gain, rewarding hikers with fantastic views of mountains and, of course, Death Valley, including the lowest point in the United States, Badwater Basin at 282 feet below sea level. An alternative, though, is nearby Wildrose Peak, which offers vistas nearly as good for quite a bit less work. The 4.2-mile (one way) trail to the 9,064-foot summit has great views along the way as it climbs 2,200 feet through piñon pine–juniper forest, open ridge tops, and barren scrubland dotted with cacti. The views begin to open up after the first 2 miles. These high-country hikes are among the few outdoor activities possible in summer in Death Valley National Park, where the average July daily high temperature is 115°F. Both trails begin in Wildrose Canyon, east of Wildrose Campground.

☆ Guadalupe Mountains ☆
NATIONAL PARK
Guadalupe Peak

The scenic symbol of this western Texas park is El Capitan, a massive limestone escarpment that rises prominently above the Chihuahuan Desert landscape at the southern terminus of the Guadalupe Mountains. El Capitan isn't the highest point in the park, though: That's 8,749-foot Guadalupe

Peak, which is also the highest point in Texas. To stand atop the Lone Star State requires a hike of 4.2 miles, ascending around 3,000 feet. Don't be discouraged at the start of the climb; the trail actually becomes less steep after the first 1.5 miles. The route doesn't have a lot of shade, but at times it does pass through groves of pine and Douglas-fir. Atop Guadalupe Peak sits an odd aluminum pyramid placed here in 1958, before this site was made a national park; it commemorates overland stage and air travel. On a clear day, the panorama of surrounding desert and mountains seems as big as Texas—and that's plenty big. The round-trip hike takes from six to eight hours, depending on a person's physical condition and desire.

Hallett Peak, the next Continental Divide mountain south of Flattop is also easily seen. To reach that peak means continuing another 0.6 mile and ascending another 400 feet or so. Getting to the top of Hallett does require a bit of boulder scrambling, but it doesn't require anything too difficult. On its summit, a hiker will probably feel more like a "mountain climber" than on the summit of Flattop, which is well described by its name. Both hikes are considered somewhat strenuous, with the round-trip to Flattop taking around eight hours; continuing on to the summit of Hallett would add a couple more hours. Beware of the high altitude if not acclimated to the Rocky Mountains; it can take an unexpected toll on a person.

☆ Rocky Mountain ☆
NATIONAL PARK
Hallett Peak

Sure, anyone can drive to the Continental Divide on Trail Ridge Road, but a person gets real satisfaction by hiking up to the backbone of our continent. In north-central Colorado's Rocky Mountain National Park, this hike to the broad summit of 12,324-foot Flattop Mountain begins at picturesque Bear Lake and requires no climbing skills at all. Just keep putting one foot in front of the other for 4.4 miles while ascending 2,849 feet. But stop often along the hike, anyway, to enjoy spectacular views of Longs Peak (the park's highest mountain at 14,259 feet) in the distance, with forested slopes, glacier-carved valleys, and alpine lakes nestled in between. Wildlife is plentiful. The rugged, pointed summit of 12,713-foot

☆ Crater Lake ☆
NATIONAL PARK
Mount Scott

Scenic views of Crater Lake are abundantly available to you in this Oregon park—an incredibly deep-blue lake set within the caldera (collapsed summit) of an ancient volcano that exploded 7,700 years ago. Quite naturally, one of the finest panoramas can be enjoyed from the 8,929-foot summit of Mount Scott, the park's highest point and a popular hiking destination. Not only does Crater Lake lie in the foreground below but the long-distance vista takes in Mount Shasta in California and, in Oregon, Mount Thielsen and the Three Sisters. There's a historic fire lookout station at the top, too, which is still manned. The alpine wildflower display below the summit can be spectacular in mid- to late July. The moderately strenuous trail to the top gradually climbs 1,479 feet in 2.5 miles, beginning at a trailhead on the eastern part of Rim Drive, which circles Crater Lake. A very snowy location, Crater Lake National Park may not be fully open until mid-July, and the high elevations may already be covered with snow by October.

> *The CCC men spent all week completing back breaking labor but still managed to complete great physical exertion on the weekends, "I went on a long hike. First to West Rim, then . . . to Angels Landing . . . The hike was at least 25 miles long round trip and we were tired."*

Area, a landscape showing the effects of Lassen Peak's violent May 22, 1915, eruption, which sent out massive amounts of ash, steam, and gas. Rising to 10,457 feet, Lassen Peak is one of the snowiest places in northern California, and most of the park's main roads may not open until July. The trail to the top of Lassen may be snow free for only three months or so.

☆ Lassen Volcanic ☆
NATIONAL PARK
Lassen Peak

There's plenty to see from roads and on short walks around this northern California national park, including four different types of volcanoes (plug dome volcano, composite, shield volcano, and cinder cone) and hydrothermal features such as hot springs, bubbling mud cauldrons, and steam vents. For a wonderful overview of the volcano-shaped landscape, though, it's a fairly simple matter, if acclimatized, to reach the top of Lassen Peak, ascending 2,000 feet over a distance of 2.5 miles. The largest plug-dome volcano in the world (one in which lava cooled and plugged the outlet vent), Lassen overlooks the rugged remains of an ancient volcanic peak called Mount Tehama, which collapsed hundreds of thousands of years ago. On a clear day, Mount Shasta, 75 miles to the northwest, is visible. Much nearer and to the northeast lies the Devastated

☆ Great Basin ☆
NATIONAL PARK
Wheeler Peak

The hike up to the glacier-carved summit of eastern Nevada's Wheeler Peak is no lazy stroll—it has an elevation gain of about 2,900 feet over 4.3 miles—but look on the bright side: It's a chance to stand atop a "thirteener" (Wheeler rises to 13,063 feet) after beginning your hike at the high starting point of 10,160 feet. The trail first snakes through aspen groves before climbing through meadows and stunted stands of Englemann spruce and limber pine and across an exposed ridgeline to the windswept summit beyond. Along the trail are excellent views of the Snake Range and the desert landscape of Great Basin below, with more mountain ranges off in the distance. The trailhead is reached via the paved, 12-mile Wheeler Peak Scenic Drive, which climbs steeply from the park's eastern boundary to Wheeler Peak Campground. The upper part of the road is usually closed by snow from November to May. While on Wheeler Peak, take the time to visit the groves of bristlecone pines, with some trees more than 3,000 years old, twisted and gnarled in picturesque shapes.

Gnarled and twisted by age and wind, bristlecone pines grow high atop Wheeler Peak in Great Basin National Park.

★ Zion ★
NATIONAL PARK
Angels Landing

Every year, thousands of people visiting this southern Utah park successfully make the 2.5-mile hike to Angels Landing to enjoy what may be the most spectacular view in one of America's most beautiful places. This adventure comes with serious cautions, though: The last half mile traverses a very narrow ridge (in geological terms, a sandstone fin) with sheer drops on both sides. Even though chains have been installed for safety, several people have fallen to their deaths here. The Angels Landing Trail begins at the Grotto and ascends 1,488 feet to its 5,785-foot end point, a small summit once described as so isolated that "only an angel could land on it." After a fairly easy 2 miles, the trail reaches Scout Landing, where many hikers decide not to continue; the last section is no place for those afraid of heights or for small children, and Scout Landing itself has a fine vista of Zion Canyon. Recalling their trip later, many visitors to Zion remember reaching Angels Landing as one of their most thrilling outdoor experiences. If you want to try this hike, you should keep its challenges in mind and start early in the day to avoid crowds.

canyon hikes

River-carved gorges inspiring awe and delight

The great canyons of the national parks are for most, drive-to jaw-droppers that lie below scenic drives and rim trails that lead to stunning overlooks. For some, though, canyons beg to be explored. Canyon hikes can be quite an undertaking—almost always a steep, dry descent and a climb back—but the sensory experience is worth it.

☆ Grand Canyon ☆
NATIONAL PARK
Hermit Trail

An out-and-back hike on the South Rim's Hermit Trail delivers the visceral impact of Arizona's Grand Canyon rim-to-rim epic without having to share it with hordes of fellow pilgrims. This lesser used trail provides awesome canyon views as it switchbacks down towering red-wall faces. Start at Hermits Rest off West Rim Drive and descend gradually through stands of piñon and juniper into a red-rock abyss as far as the heart desires. Backpackers can plunge 3,800 feet amid shale slopes and sandstone cliffs to lovely, cool Hermit Creek and a trail camp. Along the way stands evidence of this route's origins—a long-abandoned train track that served a tourist camp built by the Santa Fe Railroad. Set up camp and take a day hike down to Hermit Rapids on the Colorado River or on nearby portions of the Tonto Trail, which has superb river and canyon views. To simply make a day of it, follow the Hermit Trail to the Boucher Trail to Dripping Springs, hiking

beneath sheer 1,200-foot cliffs to a lovely spring nestled within an alcove of Coconino sandstone. The 7-mile round-trip drops "only" 1,700 feet and represents a grand cross section of canyon formations.

☆ Bryce Canyon ☆
NATIONAL PARK
Queen's Garden/Peekaboo Trails
and the Fairyland Loop

Only a thin red line divides fantasy from geology in Utah's Bryce Canyon. A hike amid the park's rococo hoodoos—sandstone spires arrayed in amazing mazes, fantastically animated forms shimmering in colors that Revlon can only covet—lends itself to true flights of fancy. The hoodoos rule. The Queens Garden/Peekaboo figure-eight loop (6.5 miles) is Bryce's signature hoodoo hike. Working clockwise from Sunrise Point, descend into Bryce Amphitheater on the Queens Garden Trail into hoodooland. Then pick up the Peekaboo Trail to crisscross a ridge rife with hoodoos, and climb out via Wall Street's towering sandstone spires. That's all warm-up for

Some two billion years of geologic history are writ in the sedimentary stone walls of the Grand Canyon.

Most canyon hikes are in arid Southwest parks where rangers always warn hikers to carry plenty of water—typically a gallon of water per person per day for wilderness hiking. Most people know that water is critical for survival, but it's common for hikers to compromise a bit, to carry less than what is recommended, or not to drink enough even if they are carrying plenty.

Those compromisers should consider some lessons conveyed by an early 20th-century researcher in a paper called "Desert Thirst as Disease." In it, W. J. McGee recounts the tale of prospector Pablo Valencia, who went without water for nearly a week in the Arizona desert. McGee came upon Valencia shortly before he would have died and describes the phases of (near) death by thirst in vivid detail.

Early on comes the cotton-mouth stage—"best relieved by water," McGee sagely opines. But soon enough, says McGee, "saliva ceases, and membrane-mucus dies into a collodionlike film which compresses and retracts the lips, tightens on the tongue until it numbs and deadens, shrivels the gums and starts them from the teeth, shrinks linings of nostrils and eyelids." Around this time, Valencia discarded his hat and shoes—clearly not a good idea, but apparently not uncommon. At this phase, the sufferer often begins to babble incessantly.

McGee goes on to describe "a progressive mummification of the initially living body, beginning with the extremities and slowly approaching the vital organs." Eventually the shrunken tongue swells and forces its way through the jaws, becoming "a reeking fungus on which flies . . . love to gather and dig busily." Luckily Señor Valencia survived, and so will you if you always carry the amount of water that park rangers suggest.

the 8-mile Fairyland Loop, which loses and gains 2,309 cumulative feet as it navigates first a hoodoo graveyard of stumpy towers, then a forest of tall hoodoos that rise to the canyon rim. The park's popular full-moon hikes—no flashlights permitted—drop into this same hoodoo fairyland.

☆ Death Valley ☆
NATIONAL PARK
Fall Canyon

California's Death Valley is really a park of canyons—slots and chasms and fluted corridors piercing the mountains that frame the valley. The one not to be missed is Fall Canyon, which can be reached from the Titus Canyon (a jeep road) trailhead: Proceed 3 miles up a wash surrounded by twisted striations of metamorphosed marble and dolomite to a dry waterfall, then another 3 miles through a narrow slot. Mosaic Canyon, near Stovepipe Wells, leads past walls of polished marble and ends at a dry waterfall 2 miles up. Golden Canyon is probably the most popular—an interpretive trail leads through the mile-long canyon, whose walls show tilted and twisted layers of rock that show the valley's faulting action, as well as mudstone deposits and ripple patterns that indicate an ancient lakeshore. At the head of the canyon is Red Cathedral's steep, rust-colored fluted cliffs.

☆ Glen Canyon ☆
NATIONAL RECREATION AREA
Cathedral Wash

True canyoneering is a technical craft that entails climbing, rappelling, and often swimming through slot canyons that can narrow down to a body squeeze, then drop off 40 or 50 feet into another slot. Cathedral Wash gives a sense of that adventure without the technical demands, though this 3-mile round-trip hike does require a bit of scrambling. The trailhead is on the Lees Ferry access road in Arizona, which curves around a prominent formation called Cathedral Rock. The hike leads through narrow passageways lined by cliffs of limestone and sandstone, smoothed and eroded into all manner of formations—arches, alcoves, overhangs, muddy pools, and dry waterfalls that are anything but dry when a flash flood courses through. This is obviously not a hike to make during or after a rain in the vicinity. In the heart of the canyon, hikers must make their way along ledges and ease themselves down drop-offs. Finally the trail opens up and reaches the Colorado River, which signals an about-face for the return hike.

✷ Black Canyon of the Gunnison ✷
NATIONAL PARK
North Vista Trail

Few canyons anywhere match Colorado's Black for its combination of sheer walls, narrow opening, and depth. It's 2,722 feet deep at its greatest depth, and in places its rim-to-rim opening is a mere 500 feet. Its name comes from the darkness of its gneiss and schist stone, but lack of direct sunlight contributes to the effect. No trails venture into the canyon, but determined scramblers can make their way down rock-filled gullies, as fly fishers occasionally do to cast in the gold-medal trout waters of the Gunnison. The return trip is arduous. Get guidance from park rangers before attempting a hike to the bottom. Otherwise, this is mainly a look-at, rather than a hike-into canyon, and the best look-at hike is probably the North Vista Trail, a 7.2-mile round-trip. It leads from the North Rim Ranger Station to Exclamation Point, for one great look at the canyon, and then to the top of Green Mountain, 867 feet higher, for a high view that takes in the rim as well as the canyon.

✷ Colorado ✷
NATIONAL MONUMENT
Monument Canyon Trail

As stunning as this Colorado monument's Rim Rock Drive is, it pales in comparison to a firsthand experience of the depths of Monument Canyon, where steep-walled gorges and naturally sculpted rock formations are a textbook of 1.7 billion years of geological history. Solitude and the singing of birds add to its pleasures. The signature hike is Monument Canyon Trail, which descends 600 feet in the first mile, then flattens out and continues another 5, passing some of the park's most striking landforms along the way. Note the layers of rock, from variegated sandstone and mudstone to dark reds of Kayenta and Wingate sandstones. About halfway down are three major formations—Pipe Organ, Praying Hands, and Independence Monument, the latter a remnant of a wall that once divided Monument Canyon from Wedding Canyon. But the hike isn't entirely made of stone—it also leads through piñon pine and juniper trees, and bighorn sheep might be spotted along the way.

✷ Canyon de Chelly ✷
NATIONAL MONUMENT
Bear Trail to Tunnel Trail

Canyon de Chelly National Monument lies within the Navajo Nation, some of whose people live and farm in the canyon. Hiking here, apart from one trail, has to be in the company of a professional Navajo guide. That's good, because local knowledge is necessary to navigate its hundred or so different trails, most of which are ancient, and many of which are extremely steep, "hand-and-toe" trails. Some are dangerous. Some require a notched log (ladder) to reach a goal. The guides know the safe routes, and, of course, know the cultural history of the canyon, which has been settled for more than 2,000 years. Hikes are always customized to suit the interest and fitness of the hikers. A typical hike would be along Bare Trail to Tunnel Trail, starting in Canyon del Muerto, ending in Canyon de Chelly, taking in at least a half dozen ancient Pueblo ruins and caves along the way. The one trail that can be hiked without a guide is White House Trail, a short hike to one of the monument's finest ruins. Any hike here is a walk through time. The park's website has a link to a list of certified local guides.

☆ Zion ☆
NATIONAL PARK
Angels Landing

The greatest hikes aren't only beautiful; they're an adventure. In southern Utah, Zion's Angels Landing hike is definitely both. It ascends a dramatic red sandstone formation that rises 1,488 feet from the middle of Zion Canyon, and hikers have no clue how

A Navajo guide speaks of an ancient battlefield in Canyon del Muerto, in Canyon de Chelly National Monument.

they'll get to the top until they do it. It begins innocently enough, skirting the Virgin River from a trailhead near the Grotto picnic area and slowly climbing through slopes dotted with piñon and juniper trees. Portions of it are paved. But soon enough, the real action begins in the form of Walter's Wiggles—21 crazy-steep, supertight, zigzagging switchbacks, like a spiral staircase carved right into the huge block of sandstone. The final leg is as steep as a trail can be, and the drop-offs are sheer, so hikers just might want to grab the handhold chains bolted into the cliff. That's the way to the top, to Scout Lookout. The view of the river and the Zion Canyon floor below looks like an aerial photograph, only there's no airplane.

> *When the Southern Pauite used to occupy this region, they referred to it as "u-map-wich," which translated to "the place where the rocks are sliding down constantly."*

☆ Cedar Breaks ☆
NATIONAL MONUMENT
Rattlesnake Creek Trail
and Two Short Rim Trails

Utah's early Natives called Cedar Breaks the "circle of painted cliffs." The circle is really a giant amphitheater whose floor is a maze of multicolored pinnacles, spires, fins, columns, and arches. It's a big commitment to walk to the depths of Cedar Breaks, but you can do it via Rattlesnake Creek Trail, a strenuous, 9-mile route that flirts with the northern boundary of the park and passes through Ashdown Gorge Wilderness Area. The trail drops 2,500 feet in 4 miles before it connects with Ashdown Creek, which can be followed into Cedar Breaks. Or, with a car shuttle, a hiker can continue 5 miles to Utah 14. Along the way stands Flanigan Arch, which rises 100 feet and spans 50 feet. This is a hike only for the fit and adventurous, although summer heat is far less a concern than in Grand Canyon because Cedar Break's rim is above 10,000 feet. Less intrepid visitors can enjoy two short rim hikes—Alpine Pond Trail leads to a great view at Chessman Overlook and to a spring-fed pond; Spectra Point/Ramparts Overlook Trail follows the south rim to a viewpoint before it passes through a stand of ancient bristlecone pines.

☆ Yellowstone ☆
NATIONAL PARK
Uncle Tom's Trail

Located in northwestern Wyoming, Yellowstone seems to contain every type of natural wonder on Earth, so it's no surprise that a magnificent canyon is among them. The 20-mile-long, 1,000-foot-deep, V-shaped Grand Canyon of the Yellowstone is both a thermal area and a river (the Yellowstone) canyon. It was at one time covered by rhyolite lava flows, and some geysers and hot springs are still evident here. An unusual trail leads to the bottom of the canyon at Lower Falls. Uncle Tom's Trail was built in 1898 as a tourist attraction— "Uncle" Tom Richardson built stairs and used rope ladders to get tourists down to the base of the waterfall. The trail is much improved, but still strenuous—it switchbacks steeply and uses more than 300 metal stairs in the course of a 500-foot drop that delivers hikers to the base of the roaring 308-foot waterfall. Distinct colors in the canyon walls indicate thermal spots where the rock has essentially rusted. The park's nominal yellow stone indicates the presence of iron.

winter sports

Frozen treats at America's national parks

National parks near peak capacity in summer—but what about winter? With many park services limited or closed and many roads blocked by snow, few head into these white, open spaces, so those who do have nearly exclusive access to snowshoe hikes, ice fishing, and alpine and cross-country skiing in wondrous landscapes.

☆ Glacier ☆
NATIONAL PARK
Cross-country Skiing and Snowshoeing

Although some stubborn glaciers are resisting the effects of global warming, winter activities here are focused more on cross-country skiing and snowshoeing rather than ice climbing and rappelling into a crevasse. Despite the towering presence of the north Rocky Mountains, many trails are low and level and are perfectly carved for cross-country skiing. Strap on the sticks and follow a glide path past meadows and woods of aspen and mixed conifers and around the shoreline of frozen lakes. Of course, this is a wilderness land which means alternate trails can display a more aggressive personality—and many do. In some cases the trails stretch as far north as the Canadian border, may remain unplowed and icy, and be far removed from the safety and shelter of park conveniences. The Going-to-the-Sun Road—the park's main east–west thoroughfare—is closed to vehicles (but open to cross-country skiers and snowshoers) due to snowfall beyond a certain point on each side of the park, so with the exception of the Lake MacDonald/Avalanche region, the established cross-country trails are concentrated along the edges of the park in the Apgar/West Glacier, Marias Pass, North Fork, St. Mary, and Two Medicine areas.

☆ Yosemite ☆
NATIONAL PARK
Snowshoeing and
Cross-country and Alpine Skiing

Following the first snowfalls, Yosemite slowly transforms into a winter wonderland of outdoor activities that would look at home in a Currier & Ives print. With the exception of ice-skating on an outdoor rink at Curry Village, the focus of the park shifts to surrounding areas where, on ranger-led hikes, the sound of frozen terrain crunching beneath snowshoes is echoed by heavy pants of breath. And on a variety of cross-country winter trails, snow is swishing beneath skis at Crane Flat, the Mariposa Grove of giant sequoias, and along Glacier Point Road where the paths are framed by heroic trees frosted with a cloak of snow and ice. More inclined toward inclines? Slide into the Badger Pass Ski Lodge *(209-372-8430)*, California's first alpine ski resort.

☆ Rocky Mountain ☆
NATIONAL PARK
Hiking, Sledding, Snowshoeing,
and Cross-country Skiing

The natural crease created by the north–south Rocky Mountains range leads to two distinct settings: To the west is an area of fluffy, powdery snow and, to the sheltered east side, harsh swatches of patchy frost, ice, and snow. No matter what conditions, the craggy rocks and towering peaks create a great American landscape worthy of winter sports being enjoyed in the shadow of either summit. The park's primary winter destination is Hidden Valley where kids, primarily, enjoy a fenced area where they get some action out of their saucers and sleds—beware, conditions can be fast and icy. Adults searching for the great outdoors minus the constraints of a fence will find a tangle of cross-country trails snaking across the park, primarily west of the Continental Divide. Sans skis, snowshoes can get you onto trails, with the easier paths on the east side of the

Cross-country skiers enjoy the wilds of Glacier National Park in wintertime.

park, and snowmobiles give riders a chance to rev it up on a 2-mile stretch of the North Supply Access Trail in the southwest corner of the park. Even hikers can get into the action: A good pair of waterproof boots is all that is needed to enjoy the lower elevation trails on the east side of the park, where snowfall is less.

> *Chainsaws are prohibited [in the national parks] except when being used to cut ice fishing holes.*

But even simple trails come with avalanche warnings, which extend to intermediate trails requiring climbs of up to 1,000 feet and long-distance slogs on advance-level paths that tie into the legendary hiking path, the Pacific Crest Trail.

☆ Crater Lake ☆
NATIONAL PARK
Ranger-guided Snowshoe Walks

Crater Lake National Park in southwest Oregon receives on average some 44 feet of snow in winter, more than many ski resorts, and between mid-December and late April it opens up a selection of the park for winter sports. The difference, however, is that Crater Lake does little to make life easy for winter sports enthusiasts. Perhaps the most easily accessible activity is snowshoeing, and on weekends the rangers lead guided snowshoe walks. Although the trek only covers about a mile, the experience lasts about 90 minutes—long enough to give participants a taste of how much effort is involved in the sport. Some of the sting of exertion is tempered, though, by lessons learned on the trail as rangers illustrate how the wildlife and vegetation adapt to survive the brutal winters. With some experience and determination, you can go off on your own on trails ranging from simple to serious, starting with loop trails along the Annie Creek Canyon and straight shots to overlooks of islands and Cascade volcanoes.

☆ Yellowstone ☆
NATIONAL PARK
Cross-country Skiing, Snowshoeing, and Snowmobiling

With a riot of geothermal activity taking place beneath the surface, Yellowstone, in northwestern Wyoming, is one of the more spectacular parks to see each winter. Working overtime underground are 60 percent of the world's active geysers that are creating hundreds of fumaroles, mud pots, hot pools, limestone terraces, and hot springs. So after a veil of white blankets the mountains and trees, some areas are punctured by heated steam and water that percolate through the ground. Where snow does manage to find a permanent home, between mid-December and mid-March you can tackle miles of trails on skis or snowshoes. Casual skiers will be pleased with groomed trails in close proximity to services; bolder outdoors enthusiasts disappear into backcountry treks that heighten the impact of the experience, knowing they'll need to be aware of changing weather, limited daylight, potentially aggressive wildlife, and the very real possibility of triggering an avalanche. Exploring by snowmobile or snowcoach is also permitted, but only when accompanied by a commercial guide (the park has a list of authorized operators that can provide guiding services and rentals if necessary). All in all, the winter sports here are as wild as Yellowstone.

☆ Mount Rainier ☆
NATIONAL PARK
Sledding, Snowshoeing, and Snowmobiles

Where there's a hill, there's a way. In winter at Mount Rainier, the hills are alive in the Paradise section of the park, where kids tackle the slopes on inner tubes and slippery flexible saucers. As they go slip-slidin' away, rangers are lacing up their snowshoes and trudging onto trails to lead you (in rented snowshoes) on educational outings that explore the secrets of survival in subzero temperatures. One active life-form that thrives on frigid temperatures is the snowmobiler, who is granted access to a 6.5-mile stretch of snow-covered roadway in the southwest section of Rainier; a 12-mile section of Wash. 410 in the north, from the park boundary to White River Campground; and the Stevens Canyon Road as far as Box Canyon in the southeast corner of the park. Overall, a generous snowfall averaging 680 inches a year is more than enough to set the stage for these and other winter activities at Washington's Mount Rainier.

☆ Cuyahoga Valley ☆
NATIONAL PARK
Alpine and Cross-country Skiing, Ice Fishing, Sledding, and Snowshoeing

At this Ohio park's winter-sports center based in a Depression-era, Civilian Conservation Corps–built building, you can rent equipment and get prepped for an array of winter sports. There are more than 125 miles of trails ranging from simple to challenging with paths running across open fields, through coniferous tree stands, past ponds, down steep hills, and even along a stretch of the Ohio & Erie Canal Towpath Trail. Cuyahoga offers a lineup of winter activities similar to other snowy national parks—sledding and snow tubing (particularly in the Kendall Hills), snowshoeing, and cross-country skiing (including a trek that leads along the Ledges Trail to the park's ice-covered rocks). There's even downhill skiing at the Boston Mills/Brandywine Ski Resorts, which together offer 17 trails. What adds a unique twist to Cuyahoga's lineup is ice fishing on Kendall Lake. When the ice is at least 7 inches thick (you'll have to be the judge of that), anglers can drop a line for largemouth bass, crappie, and bluegill.

☆ Hooked on Ice Fishing ☆

Not every national park supports ice fishing, but where it is offered novices find ice fishing a bit more challenging than standing on the shore and casting a line. If someone tried this approach in the middle of winter at Bighole Canyon or Curecanti or Cuyahoga or Voyageurs, the hook would just bounce off the ice. So be prepared. Rangers suggest bringing some essential equipment, namely a sled for transporting your gear, hot food, warm clothes, ice cleats for boots, and perhaps a sonar rig and flashlight to see what's beneath the surface. Also don't forget to pack an "ice spud" (a metal bar that helps keeps a person balanced while also testing the thickness of the ice) and then, to get through the surface, an ice auger (or drill). After drilling a hole, scoop out any floating ice chips that could cut the line, then bait the hook (worms, minnows, live shiners) and let it drop down near the bottom of the lake where the water's warmer and the fish are enjoying their ichthyological sauna. It may take a while but in time patient anglers may snag a walleye, pike, bass, trout, salmon, or perch, or whatever else lives in the lake. If not, there's probably a good seafood restaurant nearby.

☆ Great Basin ☆
NATIONAL PARK
Cross-country Skiing and Winter Camping

Great Basin in Nevada may not be the first park people think of when planning a winter excursion, and perhaps for good reason. During the park's long winter season, most guests are long gone and so are basic services like food. Still, the park does provide one of the more interesting slate of activities, because the people who come here really want to be here. They bring their own equipment (there are no outfitters here) and skiers won't just ski; in many cases they'll be going off marked routes and relying on orienteering skills to find their way on trails that loop through woods and around canyons. Trailheads that start at around 7,000 feet go up from there so the challenge isn't downhill skiing—it's knowing how to get up these unplowed, ungroomed trails; just as it takes skill to come down on trails that can be narrow, steep, and icy. But this demanding activity can actually seem like a day on the bunny slope compared to the challenge of winter camping at Lower Lehman Creek or the more remote backcountry.

☆ Acadia ☆
NATIONAL PARK
Cross-country Skiing, Ice Fishing, Snowshoeing, and Snowmobiling

Although the Northeast is one of the nation's most frigid regions, the winter activities of coastal Maine's Acadia are relatively limited. Limited, but not disappointing. The majority of the island's famed carriage roads, 45 miles of them created for nonmotorized vehicles, remain true to the cause as cross-country skiers hit the road. Sections groomed by volunteers are, of course, the most popular, and online maps and park guides direct you to the most popular areas. Skiers are also permitted to make tracks on unplowed park roads, which can be a bit more challenging since these same roads are also open to snowmobiles. Just steer clear of the high-revving vehicles and have a good time. Anglers willing to brave the cold can also ice fish in some of the park's lakes, weather permitting.

☆ Sleeping Bear Dunes ☆
NATIONAL LAKESHORE
Cross-country Skiing, Sledding, and Snowshoeing

Dozing on the Michigan shores of Lake Michigan are the towering sand dunes of Sleeping Bear. Already impressive in the summer, when winter arrives the snapping cold that hurtles across the Great Lake slams into this curving 35-mile lakeshore, decking it with snow and ice. Sand dunes are sprinkled with snow, scenic hiking trails are covered in white, and the land is primed and ready for winter activities including snowshoe hikes (taken with or without a ranger) across dunes and fields and forests, and many of the park's hiking trails are recycled for cross-country skiing, including the loops of Old Indian and Platte Plains Trails. Imagine a sledding excursion across the Sahara and you'll have an idea of what it's like when visitors take on the slopes at Dune Climb—the only place in the park where sledding is permitted—after the powder coats the sand.

accessible trails

Memorable park experiences available to all

Some of the finest aspects of America's national parks, from vistas to wildlife, can be enjoyed by all, even those with limited mobility. Scenic drives offer great opportunities, but trails provide more intimate experiences, with the sounds and smells of the natural world all around.

☆ Everglades ☆
NATIONAL PARK
Anhinga Trail

Encompassing the largest wilderness area in the United States east of the Mississippi River, Everglades National Park ranks as a World Heritage site, international biosphere reserve, and wetland of international importance for its nine distinct ecosystems and great biodiversity. Yet relatively few of this southern Florida park's most interesting features can be seen from through a windshield; you need to experience the area on a more personal level. One of the easiest ways to do this is at the 0.8-mile Anhinga Trail, a flat, easy, wheelchair-accessible loop that begins at the Royal Palm Visitor Center, 4 miles from the main park entrance. Named for a large, black, fish-eating bird, Anhinga Trail offers close views of alligators, turtles, and a variety of birds such as herons, egrets, gallinules, and—yes—anhingas. Part of the trail runs along land, while part is a boardwalk perched above a marshy wetland. All the animals are accustomed to humans,

so photography opportunities are excellent, even for normally skittish birds. For another accessible way to enjoy the Everglades, check the two-hour guided tram tour that departs from Shark Valley in the northern part of the park.

☆ Rocky Mountain ☆
NATIONAL PARK
Bear Lake Trail

There aren't many places in the United States where travelers can drive up to a true alpine mountain lake, and Bear Lake in Rocky Mountains National Park in Colorado is one of them. That fact, however, has good and bad points: good in that such a gorgeous site is accessible, and bad because even the large parking lot at Bear Lake can fill up at times. Even when the lot is full, though, a "park and ride" shuttle bus provides access from other parking areas back down Bear Lake Road. The 0.6-mile trail that encircles the small lake is not classed as completely accessible; some grades exceed the 8 percent steepness limit for such a ranking. Nonetheless, wheelchairs can make it around much of the lakeshore and traverse the full trail with assistance. The view over Bear Lake includes the stark profile of Hallett Peak looming on the Continental Divide, part of a scene of unforgettable beauty. Animals such as golden-mantled ground-squirrels, chipmunks, Steller's jays, and conspicuous Clark's nutcrackers are easily seen residents here.

✴ Shenandoah ✴
NATIONAL PARK
Limberlost Trail

This popular trail in one of America's most popular national parks takes its unusual name from a novel of the early 1900s—which was actually set in Indiana. Virginia's real-life Limberlost Trail is reached from a trailhead at milepost 43 of famed Skyline Drive, elevation 3,370 feet. The 1.3-mile loop leads into a forest of impressive red spruce trees, some of them very large and very old. Once, giant eastern hemlock trees loomed overhead, but an introduced insect called the hemlock woolly adelgid killed them, leaving bare trunks. Nevertheless, this rewarding trail reaches its peak of beauty when the mountain laurels display their masses of showy blossoms in June. At any time of year, the woodlands and wetlands of the Limberlost Trail create a great place to see wildlife. White-tailed deer are common, and even black bears are sometimes sighted. In early spring, the "drumming" courtship sounds of male ruffed grouse echo through the air. The 5-foot-wide crushed greenstone walkway includes only very

gentle grades as it makes a circuit through the Appalachian forest, a magical place of birdsong and the scent of conifers.

✴ Redwood ✴
NATIONAL AND STATE PARKS
Circle Trail

Among the tallest trees on Earth, coast redwoods once covered 2 million acres of the Pacific coast, but 96 percent of the original old-growth forest has been lost to logging. Newton B. Drury Scenic Parkway, about 40 miles north of Eureka, California, takes drivers on a 10-mile route through a magnificent stand of old-growth redwoods that escaped the loggers' saws. (Watch for Roosevelt elk along the way.) At milepost 128 of the drive is the Big Tree Wayside, a parking area with a very short trail leading to the aptly named Big Tree, a redwood more than 300 feet tall, 66 feet in circumference, and an estimated 1,500 years old. Beginning at the wayside, the 0.3-mile wheelchair-accessible Circle Trail provides an easy way to experience a mature grove of redwoods, one of the world's most distinctive ecosystems and an environment that can justly be called awe-inspiring. This site is actually located in Prairie Creek Redwoods State Park, part of an unusual partnership in which federal and California state lands are jointly administered. Few trails anywhere provide so much grandeur for so little effort.

✴ Kenai Fjords ✴
NATIONAL PARK
Exit Glacier Trail

Many activities at Kenai Fjords focus on boat trips into Resurrection Bay and the Gulf of Alaska, where wildlife ranges from orcas to rare seabirds. North of the town of Seward, Exit Glacier is the only part of the national park accessible by road. On the way

The National Park Service made the decision in 1979 to address issues of accessibility in a comprehensive manner rather than on a park-by-park basis. As part of the NPS plan, the agency partners with the National Center on Accessibility (www.ncaonline.org), an agency within Indiana University's School of Health, Physical Education, and Recreation. Over the years, NCA has studied issues ranging from the best surfaces for trails to accessibility guidelines for picnic areas and swimming pools. While the inherent nature of wild places means that not all visitors will be able to see all areas, good design allows people with disabilities to enjoy as much as possible of the national parks' beauty and wildlife.

to the parking area, note signs showing how the glacier has retreated more than a mile up the valley over the past century. Beginning at the nature center, a 1-mile loop trail, partially paved with the remainder compressed gravel, leads through a cottonwood forest to a viewpoint of Exit Glacier and the braided meltwater streams that crisscross its outwash plain; a telescope brings the massive "river of ice" closer. The glacier is born in the Harding Icefield, at more than 700 square miles the largest ice field lying entirely within the United States. As much as 800 inches of snow falls on the ice field annually, and it can take up to 50 years for snow to compress into the glacial ice that slowly flows downhill. Melting ice feeds the braided river flowing from the glacier's foot. The panoramic view from the observation point here takes in much of the wild beauty that typifies the Alaska wilderness, with the blue-tinged ice of Exit Glacier providing a subtle but striking bit of color to the scene.

☆ White Sands ☆
NATIONAL MONUMENT
Interdune Boardwalk Trail

Ranking among the most otherworldly landscapes in the United States, this New Mexico park protects a 115-square-mile area of sand dunes formed from the bright white mineral called gypsum, a type of calcium sulfate. Strong southwesterly winds continually reshape the dunes, moving them as much as 40 feet a year and creating a harsh environment where a surprising number of plants and animals manage to survive. Beginning at the wheelchair-accessible visitor center, the 8-mile (one way) Dunes Drive leads into the heart of the park. A trailhead 4.5 miles along the route marks the start of the fully accessible Interdune Boardwalk Trail, a 600-yard elevated path with interpretive signs explaining White Sands natural history. The trail is an excellent way to see wildflowers and other plants that have adapted to life in the lower, slightly wetter spots between the dunes. The boardwalk protects the interdune area, which is easily damaged by footprints. At times, animal tracks are visible in the sand beside the path. The trail features benches for rest stops and ends atop a dune with a scenic view of this unique terrain.

☆ Congaree ☆
NATIONAL PARK
Boardwalk Loop

The very factor that makes the bottomland hardwood forests of the southeastern United States so magnificent—the annual flooding that brings rich nutrients to renew the soil—also makes these swampy places hard to explore, at least on dry land. At Congaree National Park in South Carolina, all have a rare opportunity to enjoy this lush and diverse environment. Beginning at the park visitor center, a 2.4-mile elevated boardwalk, accessible to wheelchairs, loops through a dense hardwood floodplain to the edge of Weston Lake, an old oxbow of the Congaree River. Hurricane Hugo in 1989 toppled many of the park's tallest trees, but bald cypresses, oaks, hickories, tupelos, and loblolly pines still tower over the boardwalk. Congaree is home to many national and state champion trees; one survey found more than 150 trees in the park with a circumference of 12 feet or more. Visitors to the boardwalk might see river otters, bobcats, barred owls, wood ducks, cottonmouths, and green Carolina anoles (small lizards that can change color). A brochure available at the visitor center is keyed to stops along the way, interpreting the life of the Congaree forest.

☆ Yellowstone ☆
NATIONAL PARK
Upper Geyser Basin

Quite a few of the highlights of this famed park in northwestern Wyoming can be seen from roads and viewpoints, including the Upper and Lower Falls, parts of Mammoth Hot Springs, and some of Yellowstone's famed wildlife. Perhaps the best experience for persons with limited mobility or in wheelchairs can be found at the park's Upper Geyser Basin, which includes the iconic Old Faithful geyser. The visitor center and historic Old Faithful Inn are fully accessible, and a short trail leads to a viewing area of Old Faithful itself. This much publicized geyser is actually not that faithful: It varies in eruption frequency from 45 to 110 minutes. From Old Faithful, a hike/bike path accessible for

JANUARY 23 1932
New Mexico Gov. Arthur Seligman inaugurated the use of high-speed electric elevators, descending or rising 75 stories in a minute's time, at Carlsbad Caverns National Park, NM.

wheelchairs heads 1.5 miles north to Morning Glory Pool, named for its evocative colors. Along the way the path passes features such as Castle Geyser, so-called for the tall cone that has built up around the vent. Visitors with limited mobility will also enjoy nearby Firehole Lake Drive, with accessible viewpoints of thermal features such as Great Fountain Geyser, which sometimes sends steam and water up to 200 feet into the air.

☆ Carlsbad Caverns ☆
NATIONAL PARK
Big Room

Entering the underground wonderland of southeastern New Mexico's Carlsbad Caverns via the natural entrance requires a steep walk of 1.25 miles, descending 750 feet. Persons with limited mobility have another option, however: taking the elevator from the visitor center down to the Big Room. (The visitor center, including a theater and restaurant, is easily accessible from the parking lot.) The 1-mile Big Room Route is reached from the cave's underground rest area, and about two-thirds of that length is accessible to persons in wheelchairs with assistance; some sections are closed to wheelchairs because of steepness or narrowness of the trail. Visitors can rent the park's self-guiding audio program, which provides interpretation of some of the sights along the way. Among Carlsbad's famed cave formations and attractions visible along the wheelchair-accessible portion of the Big Room Route are the Hall of Giants, Temple of the Sun, the Caveman, Lower Cave Lookout, National Geographic Pit, Rock of Ages, and Crystal Springs Dome.

⭐ Grand Canyon ⭐
NATIONAL PARK
Rim Trail

The 12-mile-long trail along the South Rim of northern Arizona's Grand Canyon features magnificent views into one of the planet's greatest and most famous geological wonders. Not all the trail's length is accessible, but around 10 miles are paved, including the eastern and western stretches and sections around such views as Mather Point, Yavapai Point, and Pima Point. The entire length of the linear Rim Trail is served by wheelchair-accessible shuttle buses. Some paved sections slightly exceed grade requirements to meet accessibility standards; park rangers can provide advice on which parts are most wheelchair friendly. The westernmost section of the trail, 2.8 miles between Monument Creek Vista and Hermits Rest, is part of the Greenway Trail, 9 feet wide and paved. Use the park's shuttle bus, which stops at many points along the trail, to customize a visit to individual abilities and desires. The Rim Trail accesses Grand Canyon National Park's most popular area, the South Rim Village, which includes the main visitor center at Mather Point, the bookstore, the Market Plaza (with grocery store, bank, and post office), and many of the historic lodges.

Yellowstone National Park has more than 10,000 thermal features, including brilliantly colored hot springs.

day hikes with a twist

Strange and challenging routes, compelling surprises

The national parks are full of surprising hiking trails. Some routes, such as many in the western deserts, are positively bizarre. Others are challenging in strange ways, demanding fortitude, perseverance, or a tolerance for exposure, while others are ordinary hikes to extraordinary places. These hikes offer some of the most unusual experiences.

✳ Acadia ✳
NATIONAL PARK
Precipice Trail

A jolly sign in Maine's Acadia welcomes hikers to the start of the Precipice Trail: "Persons have fallen and died on this mountainside." Hikers shouldn't take the warning lightly, but also shouldn't let it dissuade them from doing this extraordinary hike/scramble/climb, so long as they're not averse to a bit of exposure. The "trail" is a vertiginously vertical route that scales a steep, 1,000-foot granitic dome on Champlain Mountain in less than a mile. Judiciously placed iron rungs and rings help hikers get up the dicier bits. Elsewhere a bit of boulder hopping and scrambling is necessary to reach the payoff viewpoint. And what a view: The entire east side of Mount Desert Island with its ponds, puddles, meadows, mountains, and cliffs, plus a smattering of offshore islets. The trail is generally closed late spring through midsummer to protect nesting peregrine falcons—which says a lot about what creatures are truly at home on this exposed summit.

✳ Death Valley ✳
NATIONAL PARK
The Salt Flats

One hike in western California's Death Valley is guaranteed to be one of the low points of a hiking career. It couldn't be more simple, nor more sensationally overpowering. The trail begins at the end of a boardwalk at Badwater, where the photo-op sign reads BADWATER: ELEV. −282 FT., and leads due west over the salt flats, the lowest terrain in the Western Hemisphere. The surreal flats look like a giant white jigsaw puzzle, and the footing is crunchy yet slightly resilient. Runoff from rains deposit minerals, mostly sodium chloride (salt) on the floor of the basin, and evaporation concentrates them. Expansion of the salt crystals creates the uplifted patterns. The trail—a broad expanse worn down by the footsteps of gone-by hikers—peters out as it stretches far from the boardwalk (most people walk out only ten minutes or so before turning back). Be sure to get out of the range of idling car engines so silence can reign supreme. Then turn around and look up. High on a sheer palisade of the Black Mountains a small sign reads: SEA LEVEL. The weight of the atmosphere is palpable. It's oddly pleasant.

☆ Everglades ☆

NATIONAL PARK

Slough Slogs:
Taylor and Shark River Sloughs

There's no better way to understand the Florida Everglades as a "river of grass" than to step right into that river on a slough slog—a toes-on experience of the essence of the glades. Rangers lead slogs into Taylor and Shark River Sloughs several times a week out of the visitor center in Shark Valley during December. High-tech equipment requirements: long trousers, socks, and a pair of old running shoes (sandals will get sucked into the muck). Slog participants slosh their way through crystal-clear water and dark black earth, out of which grow vast stands of sawgrass dotted with little carnivorous bladderworts. In water sometimes greater than knee-deep, sloggers will make their way to a cypress dome where cypress trees grow bright with bromeliads and orchids. Rangers will point out the odd gator hole or two along the way, but their creators aren't likely to be home during that time of year. Once a hiker gets

A hiker makes use of some well-placed iron rungs on the Precipice Trail to summit Acadia's Champlain Mountain.

the hang of slough slogging (like knowing where the snakes lurk), the world of the sloughs is open for exploration. The footing is dicey, the sawgrass sharp, the going slow, but these are the Everglades, up close and very personal. Remember to bring a change of pants.

★ Kenai Fjords ★
NATIONAL PARK
Harding Icefield Trail

Call it a staircase to the Ice Age. This stellar hike leads from the face of Exit Glacier, pretty cool in itself, to the stunning white vastness of the Harding Icefield on Alaska's Kenai Peninsula. The hike itself is not on snow, though some may be encountered near the top. The trail switchbacks steeply for nearly 4 miles and climbs 4,000 feet. Along the way a hiker might see some black bears indifferently grazing, and nimble mountain goats taunting his laborious approach. At the top, of course, is the ice field, a place that's more like the North Pole than the pole itself is—a 700-square-mile landscape of snow and ice, unbroken but for a few craggy peaks. If it sounds like too much effort, at least take the 1-mile Edge of Glacier Trail for an up close side-on view of the glacier's tall wall of blue ice.

★ Mojave ★
NATIONAL PRESERVE
Rings Loop Trail

At this California park, the Rings Loop Trail is as much playground as hiking trail as it makes its way around and through a Swiss-cheese rock formation known as Hole-in-the-Wall and down into

> [A]bout 300 mines were developed in what is now Joshua Tree National Park ... [T]he Lost Horse Mine ... produced 10,000 ounces of gold and 16,000 ounces of silver (worth approximately $5 million today) between 1894 and 1931.

Banshee Canyon. The 1.5-mile round-trip trail begins at the Hole-in-the-Wall picnic area; there's also a fine campground adjacent. The name refers to bolted-in metal rings that serve as handholds for the dicier sections. But the red rhyolite rock and its numerous holes—formed by crystallized lava—provides exceptional traction on its own. Some of the bigger holes form obvious frames for some photographic silliness. For a longer adventure, hikers can proceed north at the trail's junction with the Barber Peak Loop.

★ Yosemite ★
NATIONAL PARK
Half Dome Trail

It's mind-boggling to contemplate ascending any of the iconic rock faces in California's Yosemite National Park. When it comes to El Capitan, most of us will get no closer than sitting on a blanket in the meadow with binoculars watching world-class rock climbers at work. But anyone with will and determination can climb Half Dome. The long, challenging, 16-mile round-trip hike begins at the Happy Isles Nature Center on the Mist Trail, joins the John Muir Trail and then the Half Dome Trail, climbing 4,800 feet in the process. The last 900 vertical feet are on Half Dome itself. The crux is the last 400 feet, where strongly secured cables provide much needed assistance. Hang on, keep going. The view from the top is amazing. But for many hikers, besting the physical challenge of the hike and, perhaps, overcoming fears of exposure offer the greatest reward. (Check with the park on new permit requirements.)

✻ Joshua Tree ✻
NATIONAL PARK
Eagle Cliff Mine Loop

In California's Joshua Tree it is possible to create a route-finding and bushwhacking hiking adventure that takes in three old mines, a one-of-a-kind old dwelling, and great views. From Split Rock, a faint and rubbled trail leads steeply up the east side of some unnamed slopes, reaches a crest, and descends toward Eagle Cliff Mine. Near the crest is the hard-to-spot unusual dwelling: a multichambered cavity formed by huge rocks leaning against the face of a cliff. Miners filled cracks with crude stone walls and even put in a four-pane window—still intact, as are sundry implements, tin cans, and a cast-iron oven. From there forge a route to the ruins of Desert Queen Mine—a working gold mine until 1961—then to Elton Mine (nothing left but a few covered-over vertical shafts), and back to Split Rock. The hike is only 3 miles, but it feels utterly remote in time and space, and it's not easy. It's a 2-liter hike on even a cool day. Be sure to consult with park rangers before setting out.

✻ Haleakala ✻
NATIONAL PARK
Halemauu Trail

Park rangers at this Maui park get a little tired of the "like hiking on Mars" descriptions of the Halemauu Trail, which features a 1,400 plunge to the floor of Haleakala's volcanic crater. The crater is bereft of vegetation, striated with red and black cinder cones, and certainly has an otherworldly look. But there's a lot more life here than on Mars. The early part of the hike meanders through native scrub forest that looks exactly as it did 2,000 years ago—a rarity in Hawaii, which has been overrun by non-native species. Just before the big plunge into the volcano

☆ Nimble Footwear for Any Trail ☆

Heavy mountaineering boots are overkill for any purpose other than heavy mountaineering. Such boots can be tough to break in, and live up to the old adage that a pound on your feet is like five on your back. Happily, there are many lighter options that will exactly suit the type of hiking you enjoy.

For hikes that involve sloshing through a lot of water, such as the Zion Narrows hike, consider either a pair of water shoes—they're like light hiking shoes with perforated uppers for drainage—or sport sandals with a protective toepiece. For hiking on rocky trails with a small load on your back—say, the Harding Icefield Trail—look to day-hiking boots or shoes. Very often the same model comes in a hightop or lowcut version; the choice is a matter of how much ankle stability you need. Day hikers are usually nicely cushioned with EVA, the same stuff of running shoes, but augmented with a thin plate of plastic in the sole for extra stiffness and resistance to sharp rocks. Uppers are usually made of padded nylon mesh. If you hike frequently in wet conditions or rain, consider a Gore-Tex upper, but be warned—when it's not raining, Gore-Tex footwear can feel mighty hot.

For moving fast on smooth trails or rock, trail-running shoes or approach shoes are the ticket. Trail runners are tuned for moving fast on the trail, but they have sturdier uppers than do running shoes. The cushioning is ample, but it's sliced thin for a low center of gravity. It's easy for a hiker to turn an ankle wearing thick, cushy running shoes. Approach shoes are favorites with rock climbers and trail hikers—they often come with sticky rubber outsoles for great traction on rock, like on the Rings Loop Trail in Mojave National Preserve, and can also serve well for impromptu bouldering sessions.

stunning views of the Big Island and Maui's north shore open up. Deep inside the crater, is something nearly as alien as the landscape: astounding quiet. Holua Cabin makes a reasonable turnaround point for a 7.4-mile, six- to eight-hour hike.

✳ White Sands ✳
NATIONAL MONUMENT
Alkali Flat Trail

White Sands National Monument in New Mexico may be one of the most alien landscapes on Earth—massive piles of pure white gypsum sand, as far as the eye can see. For the sweet-toothed, they're like huge mounds of sugar, though the texture is much softer than sugar. Walk in 5 miles on the Alkali Flat Trail and soon all that seemingly exists are a few bleached earless lizards, miles of dunes, the azure sky, and framing mountains. Then come some bizarre apparitions: 50- to 60-foot "pedestal plants"—yuccas, sumac, or cottonwoods—that keep hoisting themselves higher to compensate for the departure of the dunes they originally called home, leaving these exposed, bizarrely elongated plants. You might get a bonus air show—the U.S. military tests its latest whiz-bang machinery out of the White Sands Missile Test Range immediately to the north.

✳ Zion ✳
NATIONAL PARK
Zion Narrows

Trail? What trail? Hiking this 2,000-foot-deep defile of fiery orange-red sandstone in this southern Utah park means sloshing right through the North Fork of the Virgin River in water that can be up to waist deep, making it a thoroughly sensual experience. (Late summer thunderstorms can create flash-flood conditions, so be sure to check with the visitor center before setting out.) Wear old tennies, seal valuables in Ziploc bags, and savor an entry into the deep and silent viscera of Mother Earth. The hike proceeds upstream from the Temple of Sinawava and continues as far as the heart and feet desire; every twist of the river reveals new subtleties of the vertical walls that frame it: sunset colors, striations of sedimentation, and plays of light. The slot canyon constricts in places to 20 feet. Look high above and see tributary streams tumbling down from side canyons. Hiking poles are highly recommended, because the river is a force to be reckoned with—sandy banks; rocky stretches that require boulder hopping; and cool, at times swift, water.

Hiking the Narrows in Zion National Park requires sure footing and a willingness to get wet.

serious summits
Top-of-the-world climbs

The western national parks contain most of the country's highest mountains, and certainly most of its most desirable summits—desirable, that is, to climbers, because no serious summit is easy. That, of course, is why they're so rewarding—challenge blends with beauty and with all the ineffable factors that compel climbers to climb.

☆ Denali ☆
NATIONAL PARK & PRESERVE
20,320-foot Mount McKinley/Denali:
West Buttress Route

The Athabascan Indians called the mountain that dominates Alaska "Denali"—the high one. The 20,320-foot summit is the tallest in North America. Although it was named Mount McKinley in 1897, the State of Alaska Board of Geographic Names has officially changed it back to Denali—but the federal government has not followed suit. Climbers call it Denali. By either name, it's a formidable mountain, with much greater vertical rise (17,000 feet) than Mount Everest. About 1,200 climbers attempt it annually, 90 percent of them via the West Buttress route, and about half succeed. It's a serious challenge that can take up to three weeks to accomplish. Climbers generally fly by ski plane from Talkeetna—where the park ranger station is the hub for all climbing activity—to the Kahiltna Glacier, where they camp at 7,800 feet, acclimate to the altitude, and begin to ferry loads to camps higher on the mountain. Most pull lightweight plastic sleds to haul supplies up the mountain. Cold, wind, thin air, and glacier crevasses all present dangers—in winter, Denali is one of the coldest places on Earth. Even in May, prime time for climbing, it's commonly minus 50°F at the 17,200-foot high camp. The summit is spectacular for its degree of exposure and steep drop-offs, and of course, for the view from the roof of North America. Guides: *www.nps.gov/dena/planyourvisit/*.

☆ Mount Rainier ☆
NATIONAL PARK
14,410-foot Mount Rainier

Mount Rainier lords over Washington State with such aloof dominance that it simply demands to be climbed, and 11,000 people or so per year rise to the challenge. Its 14,410 feet of perpetual snow and ice make it a proving ground for any mountaineer harboring Himalayan dreams, but it is also a trophy unto itself. The climbing season runs May through September. Most climbers go with a guide service and spend a day learning the necessary basics of mountaineering—cramponing, ice-ax arrest, rope travel, rest stepping, and pressure breathing—before a two-day ascent of the mountain. The standard Rainier route is up Muir Snowfield out of Paradise (5,400 feet) to Muir Camp at 10,000 feet. After dinner and a nap, you rise around midnight for a headlamp ascent of Cowlitz and Ingraham Glaciers, proceed up Disappointment Cleaver as the sun dawns, and dodge crevasses and bulges the last 1,200 feet. Then it's a short walk across the crater and up the crest. Mount Rainier is the hardest climb in the lower 48 states. Guides: *www.rmiguides.com.*

As the sun sets, a mountain climber pushes on to make a winter ascent of the Grand Teton.

☀ Olympic ☀
NATIONAL PARK
7,695-foot Mount Olympus:
Ascent via Blue Glacier

Mount Olympus (7,965 feet) has all the attributes of a trophy summit but one—extreme elevation, which is good news for anyone who has difficulty adjusting to lofty heights. It's one of the world's most challenging sub-8,000-foot peaks. Craggy Olympus serves up a long approach, climber-swallowing crevasses, snowfields that require crampons, and cold, unpredictable weather. The approach is 17.4 mostly gentle miles on the Hoh River Trail through pristine old-growth rain forest. Climbers then set up camp at Glacier Meadows, just below the alpine zone. The big day requires a wee-small-hours, headlamp-illuminated departure. Climbers ascend the icy moraine of Blue Glacier before traversing the glacier itself and climbing Snow Dome. Then it's a return to the upper part of the glacier, a narrow col, and a scramble up an exposed ridge to the summit, 3,765 feet above camp. In clear weather, the view is awesome: the Strait of Juan de Fuca, Vancouver Island, Mount Rainier, the distant snowy peaks of the Cascades, and a thousand surrounding shades of green. Guides: *www.mountainmadness.com.*

☀ Grand Teton ☀
NATIONAL PARK
13,770-foot Grand Teton:
Exum Ridge Route

There's a reason the Grand Teton in Wyoming is a symbol of North American mountaineering. The 13,770-foot summit is archetypally majestic—a sawtooth pinnacle overlooking the valley of the Snake River—and topping it requires climbing 13 highly exposed pitches. Still, with the commensurate knowledge, it's climbable by almost anyone with good fitness and preparation. Most climbers sign on for a preclimb ground school with local guide services, where they get ropework and climbing technique down pat. The mountain can be climbed in one long day, or from a base camp high on the mountain and an alpine (early) start. The most popular route is by the Exum Ridge—which, when first climbed by Glen Exum in 1931, required a leap across an exposed chimney, unroped. It and other routes require technical climbing—not difficult, but quite exposed. The reward is a summit view of the entire Greater Yellowstone ecosystem and 14 mountain ranges in four states. Guides: *www.exumguides.com, www.jhmg.com.*

✸ Rocky Mountain ✸
NATIONAL PARK
14,259-foot Longs Peak: Keyhole Route

Even in a realm of high mountains, Longs Peak (14,259 feet) dominates Colorado's Rocky Mountain National Park and intimidates would-be conquerors with its big-wall faces. Nonetheless, when the mountain is free of snow and ice, it's possible to simply hike to the summit. But it's not easy. For one, a very early start is needed in order to get off the summit by about 10 a.m. to avoid being above tree line during dangerous afternoon thunderstorms. The hike, known as the Keyhole Route, gains 4,850 feet. From the Longs Peak Ranger Station, hike 6 miles to the Boulderfield and scramble 1.5 miles through the Keyhole (follow the painted bull's-eyes) to the summit. There's also a couple mountaineering routes that

aren't too difficult. The Kieners Route is a classic that requires a 1,000-foot hike up the Lamb's Slide snow couloir, then a 1,000-foot traverse of the Broadway Ledge—and then the real climbing begins, but it's never more difficult than 5.3. The North Face, also called the Old Cables Route, starts at a little cirque called Chasm View. The view from the start is spectacular, and just keeps getting better.

✸ North Cascades ✸
NATIONAL PARK
8,815-foot Forbidden Peak

Some call the North Cascades "America's Alps." The strikingly beautiful North Cascades are renowned for their ruggedness and challenging approaches that often require glacier travel. The highest peak in the park is Goode Mountain, 9,200 feet, but its quintessential trophy is 8,815-foot Forbidden Peak, regarded as one of the 50 classic summits in North America. It and most of the other tallest mountains in the Washington park are in the South Unit. Access is from Cascade River Road by way of an old miners' trail. In typical North Cascades fashion the approach is a bit of grind, with detours and bushwhacks, but once above tree line it's gorgeous landscape. After some glacial moraine and a trudge up an unnamed glacier, the usual route proceeds to the stunning west ridge, with views of lakes, meadows, deep valleys, and jagged peaks and some enjoyable 5.7 climbing to the summit. Not enough of a challenge? Consider the Torment-Forbidden traverse, bagging Mount Torment (8,120 feet) first before traversing over to Forbidden. Guides: *www.ncmountainguides.com.*

☆ The First Time Is the Hardest ☆

Climbers who make the first ascent of a major mountain do so without benefit of a guide and route information, which is why they are so honored. They're pioneers, conquerors of the unknown.

Consider Hazard Stevens's account of the first ascent of Mount Rainier published in the *Atlantic Monthly* in 1876: "We gained a narrow ledge . . . and creeping along it, hugging close to the main rock on our right, laboriously and cautiously continued the ascent. The wind was blowing violently. We were now crawling along the face of the precipice almost in mid-air. On the right the rock towered far above us perpendicularly. On the left it fell sheer off, two thousand feet, into a vast abyss. A great glacier . . . stretched away for several miles, all seamed or wrinkled across with countless crevasses." At the summit they enjoyed a glorious view, but one tinged with apprehension: "On every side of the mountain were deep gorges falling off precipitously thousands of feet, and from these the thunderous sound of avalanches would rise occasionally."

Some first ascents are recounted in more understated fashion. John Boies Tileston was the first man up Mount Lyell in Yosemite, in 1871: "I was up early the next morning, toasted some bacon, boiled my tea, and was off at six. I climbed the mountain, and reached the top of the highest pinnacle ['inaccessible,' according to the State Geological Survey at the time], before eight. I came down the mountain, and reached camp before one, pretty tired."

☆ Sequoia ☆
NATIONAL PARK
14,494-foot Mount Whitney

Located in California, Mount Whitney (14,494 feet), the highest peak in the lower 48 states, looks like a castle tower of bare granite when viewed from below in the Owens Valley—and only gets more regal up close. Most climbers take the short way, from the east, choosing one of two routes—one a walk-up, the other a semitechnical way called the Mountaineers Route. The walk-up is an extremely popular challenge that can be done in one long day (with a predawn start). That option permits a light pack, but also means 6,100 feet of trudging with little chance for acclimating, and a 22-mile round-trip from the trailhead in Whitney Portal (8,361 feet). Two trail camps along the way can be used to break up the journey. Most of the hike is in Inyo National Forest, which issues a daily quota of permits. The Mountaineers Route is the way John Muir soloed Whitney in 1873. This way is far less busy, but calls for some scrambling and route finding. It's best done with a guide. Really serious climbers can ascend technical routes on Whitney's East Buttress. The reward for everyone is a soaring view of the Great Western Divide highlands and the Owens Valley lowlands. Guides: *www.sierramountaincenter.com*.

☆ Wrangell–St. Elias ☆
NATIONAL PARK & PRESERVE
18,008-foot Mount St. Elias: A Time-consuming Ascent

Although close to a whopping 2,300 feet shorter than Mount McKinley (Denali), 18,008-foot Mount St. Elias is the second highest peak in the United States, forming part of the coastal St. Elias Mountains of southern Alaska, on the Yukon Territory border. It rises above the Gulf Alaska with stunning vertical relief of more than 15,000 feet. St. Elias is rarely climbed in comparison with other parks' tallest summits. Logistics are challenging and expensive. The St. Elias Mountains get more than 100 inches of precipitation a year, meaning wintry storms that can cause delays, stalls, and avalanche danger at any time of year. Climbers take as long as four weeks to reach the top. Wrangell–St. Elias is a park of very serious summits; the fourth, fifth and sixth tallest peaks in the United States are also here, farther north in the Wrangell Range—Mount Bona (16,241 feet), Mount Blackburn (16,390 feet), and Mount Sanford (16,237 feet). Of the three, Mount Bona is relatively straightforward—doable for fit mountaineers with a guide and mountaineering experience. Guides: *www.steliasguides.com*.

> *Rocky Mountain is the highest national park in the US, with elevations from 7860' to 14,259'. More than one-third of the park is above treeline (11,200-11,500'), and tundra is a primary protected resource of the park.*

✫ Glacier ✫
NATIONAL PARK
10,466-foot Mount Cleveland

Glacier National Park in northwest Montana does not have a single trophy summit. Its highest peak is Mount Cleveland (10,466 feet), but it has dozens and dozens of spectacular mountains worthy of bragging rights, and all of them deliver an experience of mountain grandeur even greater than what motorists see from park roads. That said, some climbers do try to tick off the six peaks in the park taller than 10,000 feet, and of those, Mount Jackson (10,052 feet) is the most popular, largely due to its proximity to a hiking trail, versus long, difficult approaches for most of the other "ten-ers." The climb is not technical, but it's also not easy; it gains 6,052 feet

from the Gunsight Pass Trail. For something easier, try Reynolds Mountain (9,125), a distinctive horn-shaped summit visible from Going-to-the-Sun Road. The approach is short and the gain is only 2,500 feet. Rock in Glacier tends to be crumbly, and guide services aren't available, so be sure to get reliable route information for any climb in the park.

✫ Yosemite ✫
NATIONAL PARK
13,114-foot Mount Lyell

To many visitors, Yosemite National Park means Yosemite Valley. In truth, the valley is one percent of the park, and as many wonders lie in the California High Sierra as in the valley. Mount Lyell, in the southeast part of the park, is noteworthy for two reasons—it's the park's highest peak (13,114 feet) and holds its largest glacier. Lyell Glacier isn't huge (160 acres), but it's a remnant of the mighty Ice Age rivers of ice that carved the park's famous features. Climbers don't have to traverse the glacier to reach the top, but for the crampon-clad, it's something of a bonus. The climb is neither unknown nor extremely popular—a long approach keeps down the number of aspirants. Most approach it from Tuolumne Meadows, partly on the John Muir Trail through Lyell Canyon. The first several miles of the hike are easy, but total elevation gain is 4,500 feet. Then the route offers two choices: Either climb the glacier on the north flank or wind around to the southwest flank and stay on rock for a nontechnical scramble to the top. The view? Amazing, of course. Guides: *www.yosemitepark.com*.

hooting in the olympic woods

Author Robert Earle Howells's spotted owl search

You've got to be a nut or a biologist to voluntarily bushwhack the dense, boggy, ferny, slippery, fallen-log labyrinth that is the floor of Olympic National Park. I was the nut. I'd talked my way into a trip with a biologist on a spotted-owl census mission—though to our credit, we did enter the park on a designated trail. But even the Bogachiel River Trail was no walk in the woods. Every step was in a thick and consistent stew of mud.

The Bogachiel is one of five major river systems in the park's western lowlands. A constant, Pacific-born westward procession of supersaturated clouds, unimpeded until they collide with Mount Olympus, bestows staggering volumes of moisture upon this part of the park every year—something like 2 billion gallons of water per square mile. A little muck on the valley floor comes as no surprise.

THE LURE OF OLD GROWTH

Sure enough, it was raining steadily the morning I met wildlife biologist Scott Gremel at park headquarters in Port Angeles. But a high-pressure ridge moved in to quell the deluge just as we set off on the trail, though the forest was still plenty damp. Side streams flowed with spring-freshet exuberance. Every fern I brushed dumped a gallon or so of water onto my lower body. It was like walking in a drive-through car wash.

The first 1.5 miles of the Bogachiel trail run through second-growth spruce forest on Forest Service land. "Barred-owl habitat," sniffed the biologist, referring to a spotted-owl competitor that has

been displacing spotted owls in the region. Outside of park boundaries, much of the forest is secondary, but the park itself is a shrine for ancient temperate rain forest.

It was a desire to delve into some of these old-growth stands that drew me to Olympic. Since spotted owls are symbols of old-growth preservation—where old-growth habitat declines, so do the birds—I figured an owl researcher could lead me into some prime forest stands. Gremel has been participating in annual spotted-owl counts since 1994. The process requires deep forays into the backcountry.

After four or five gymnastic stream crossings over slick concatenations of stones, we set up camp between the river and a mélange of spruce, western hemlock, and vine maples swagged with moss. While we ate lunch, we watched an otter surface about 75 yards downstream from us, then dive and begin swimming upstream, only to emerge exactly at our feet. The critter showed its startled face for two seconds, then torpedoed back down the Bogie.

GETTING A BIRD

Time to get to work. We donned daypacks and began climbing up Indian Pass to a ridge where a pair of nesting owls had been observed in previous years. Our goal was to find out if they had returned. How do you spot spotted owls? You hoot for them. As we bushwhacked up a 70-degree slope, picking our way over and around huge fallen logs, Gremel would stop, swallow, and emit a staccato, four-note, *"Ooo. Oo-oo. Ooo."* He'd toss in an occasional James Brownian *"Ow!"* I finally dared a hoot series of my own. Gremel cautioned me to "Get the 'who' out of your hoot." Owls don't cotton to consonants.

Only by picking your way through its chaos do you get close to grasping the nature of an old-growth northwestern rain forest. It's characterized by a thousand shades of green and infinite degrees of rot. Forget any semblance of an ordinary forest floor. Between 200-foot western hemlock trees and 300-foot Douglas-firs are impassable thickets of huge ferns and innumerable fallen logs, and everything's so thickly furred with moss that shapes are just murky suggestions rather than clear outlines that would suggest a course of travel.

After a few minutes of hooting, we heard a soft whistle from downslope. "Contact whistle," Gremel whispered. "She's nearby." Scott pulled a 1-gallon coffee can from his pack, the can riddled with breathing holes for the white mice within. Gremel removed a mouse. Almost immediately, an owl soundlessly swooped to a branch 50 yards away. Gremel released the mouse on a log, and in seconds, the bird was on it. A red band on one leg identified her as a female. On a perch just 20 feet away, she proceeded to big-gulp the rodent, then froze, eyes fixed on us, hoping for another appetizer.

Amazing. Preposterous. Gremel estimates that the million-acre park holds just 229 pairs of the endangered owls, and here was one of them, playing stare-down with us. In owl-research parlance, we'd gotten a bird. We could head back to camp.

From our perch by the river, we watched a full moon rise. Groves

of budding alders across the river shone silver, and the Bogachiel looked like streaming tinsel.

A DREAM FULFILLED

We repeated the process for two more days, bushwhacking through ravines eight hours a day. No more birds. Perhaps this was consistent with the 3 to 4 percent annual decline in spotted-owl population since the mid-1990s. But we did turn up some cougar prints on the main trail, and from our campsite, we saw a bald eagle fly downstream. On the way out, we scared a herd of elk whose barnyard scent we'd caught a few minutes before. The mud remained tenacious.

Come here in July or August and the trail will probably be firm. Walk it in silence and listen for a four-note hoot. Or just imagine the sound, and follow it into the murky thickness of the rain forest's soul.

rock climbing

Walls and spires, domes and steep overhangs

Our national parks are home to some of the most fabled rock-climbing sites in the world. Even if you're not a climber, you can enjoy the theatrical thrill of watching climbers scale seemingly impossible rock faces. If you're intrigued, you can arrange for lessons or a guide at nearly every park that has great climbing.

☆ Yosemite ☆
NATIONAL PARK
El Capitan, World-Renowned
Walls and Spires, and Bouldering

Some of the most beautiful walls and spires in the world tower above eastern California's Yosemite Valley, the place where big-wall climbing was born, and where it has advanced beyond all possible dreams of the sport's pioneers. The accomplishments of climbers here are as humbling as the granite faces themselves. It used to take weeks to scale the famous Nose of El Capitan, but now it has been ascended in less than three hours. It has even been climbed by blind men (with sighted assistants) and soloed. El Cap remains the holy grail of Yosemite climbers, but the park has many other world-renowned routes, virtually all of them traditional, including Royal Arches, the Glacier Point Apron, Sentinel Rock, Snake Dike on Half Dome, and Cathedral Spire. Many are "only" 5.7 to 5.9, but these are long, long routes, and only one look at the tall, polished granite walls is needed to gauge their exposure. Climbers

looking for less daunting climbs should head to Tuolumne Meadows, which has a wealth of smaller slabs and domes—1 to 4 pitches versus 39 on the Nose. Yosemite also has dozens of bouldering areas, including several around Camp 4, the traditional hangout of Yosemite climbers. Guides and lessons: *www.yosemitepark.com*.

☆ New River Gorge ☆
NATIONAL RIVER
Nuttall and Bridge Buttress

The New River's superhard Nuttall sandstone cliffs are so revered by climbers that they'd just as soon call this West Virginia park New River Gorge National Cliffs. The cliffs stretch for 12 or so miles, range from 30 to 120 feet high, and are riddled with slabs, cracks, corners, steep overhangs, and vertical walls to the tune of more than 1,400 identified routes. That bomber rock—harder than most granite—and scores of elegant climbs make the New very popular. Many climbers favor Bridge Buttress, which stretches for 2 miles downstream from the New River Bridge. It's where New River climbing was pioneered in the 1970s, and where most of the park's moderate climbs are, mainly in the 35- to 75-foot range. Parkwide, most routes are 5.9-plus—but newbies can find plenty of easy routes—and sport climbs slightly outnumber trad routes. For sheer number of routes, look to Endless Wall—4 miles of cliffs, 675 routes, some as high as 150 feet. Across the river from Endless, the Kaymoor and South Nuttall areas feature sport climbs that require a longer hike in than other sites. Climbing is year-round. Guides and lessons: *www.newriver climbing.com.*

✳ Little River Canyon ✳
NATIONAL PRESERVE
Lizard Wall:
Towering Sandstone Cliffs

Little River in northeastern Alabama is the great secret of Southeast sport climbers, at least those with the mettle to tackle its predominantly difficult routes. The cleft's sandstone cliffs tower as high as 400 feet above the river, and most of them overhang. That means two things: First, challenge—most of the canyon's 400 or so routes are 5.11 to 5.14 in the 80-foot range, though there are some 5.8s and 5.10s. Second, many walls are climbable even when it's

In the New River Gorge, a rock climber scales to new heights on the Endless Wall via the 5.11 Leave it to Jesus route.

raining—overhangs like Lizard Wall work as a sandstone umbrella. Speaking of bonuses, a little-regarded climbing option are the thousands of boulders in the river itself. Climbers can challenge themselves and hop off into the cool river. You won't readily find guides or outfitters in the area; this is very much a word-of-mouth destination.

> Within [Joshua Tree] there are . . . ranges: the Little San Bernardino Mountains in the southwestern part; the Cottonwood, Hexie, and Pinto Mountains in the center; and the Eagle and Coxcomb Mountains in the eastern part.

✳ Joshua Tree ✳
NATIONAL PARK
Indian Cove and Hidden Tower

Anyone's who's scrambled for a line at a popular climbing site or queued up at the local rock gym to grab artificial nubs will celebrate the overwhelming abundance of superb rock in Joshua Tree National Park. It's amazing, grippier-than-Velcro stuff called quartz monzonite, so abrasive that a person can walk up or down a 70-degree slab in their tennies. Downside: It masticates city-slicker fingers within a couple of hours. Among the many delights of Joshua Tree is the bouldering. Opportunities are everywhere, and of all difficulty levels, so anyone can get into the action. Among the more than 8,000 climbs are Class 4 scrambles, scads of intermediate top-rope walk-off routes, and multipitch climbs that'll thump anyone's heart; many are found near campgrounds. The hotbeds are in the north, such as Real Hidden Valley, across the road from Hidden Valley Campground. A mile-long trail winds among some of the best climbs in the park including three rewarding 5.8 and 5.9 routes up Hidden Tower, a thick spire that dominates the valley—exposed,

vertical, but laced with the holds. Indian Cove is a great mixed-difficulty venue comprising crags, slabs, and cracks, with overtones of theater. From the comfort of a campsite chair, climbers can eyeball the day's challenges over coffee and celebrate them over a cool beverage. Guides and lessons: *www.vertical adventures.com.*

✳ Grand Teton ✳
NATIONAL PARK
Jenny Lake

Alpine climbing—climbing to reach a summit—has long ruled in northwest Wyoming's Teton Range, where the serrated peaks are beautiful and irresistible. But pure rock climbing on boulders, faces, slabs, and pinnacles is also superb in Grand Teton, and often the two merge—many of the best summiting routes entail rock climbing, and many students in Grand Teton's rock climbing courses are there to learn enough rock climbing and rope handling technique to scale the big mountains. The heart of the scene for either type of climber is Jenny Lake, where the ranger station serves as an information source for rock climbing in the park. Jenny Lake is also the site of three legendary boulders—Cutfinger Rock, Falling Ant Slab, and Red Cross. Symmetry Spire above Jenny Lake has great rock routes with a dash of alpine flair; an ice ax and crampons might be needed to reach its 5.6 to 5.9 climbs. Cascade Canyon is a rock-climbing hotbed, including the highly regarded Guide's Wall and its many variations, in the 5.7 to 5.9 range. Guides and lessons: *www.jhmg .com, www.exumguides.com.*

✵ Devils Tower ✵
NATIONAL MONUMENT
Durrante Route

There may be no more enticing climbing destination than the 867-foot granite monolith rising above the northeast Wyoming range. The routes tend to be long, 500 to 600 feet, and they require a serious rack; there's virtually no bolting on the tower. Trad rules here. The most popular way to the summit is the 5.7 Durrance Route, a six-pitch traditional crack climb (as most routes are here) of nonstop fun and awesome views—famed climber Todd Skinner free-soloed it in 18 minutes. The lower rock has plenty of sustained pitches, too. Climbing can be fine year-round, but the park encourages a moratorium in June, when Native Americans—who consider the tower sacred—often hold ceremonies. Also, some routes are closed in spring to protect nesting prairie falcons. Guides and lessons: *www.sylvanrocks.com*.

✵ City of Rocks ✵
NATIONAL RESERVE
Rye Crisp on Elephant Rock

Few places anywhere receive the kind of whispered reverence that City of Rocks inspires among climbers. The City is a collection of abruptly rising spires ranging from 30 to 300 feet in the Albion Mountains of south-central Idaho. The granite is sticky and the choices nearly endless, with hundreds of trad routes from 5.4 to 5.12, and plenty of 5.11-ish sport climbs, too. Formations tend to be highly featured, with lots of cracks, pockets, edges, and knobs, and many have unusual protruding flakes that are surprisingly solid. A classic example of the latter is Rye Crisp on Elephant Rock. Virtually every wall and feature has a mix of easy and difficult climbs, so it's almost always possible to find a choice line. Climbing starts as early as April and runs into October.

☆ Climbing Argot ☆

Free climbing: Climbing with ropes and hardware to protect in case of a fall, but not to help ascend.

Trad (traditional) climbing: Climbing placing own protection, rather than using bolted-in protection.

Sport climbing: Climbing using bolts fixed to the rock.

Aid climbing: Employing artificial devices to directly assist with upward progress.

Bouldering: Climbing on a large rock, usually without rope.

Yosemite Decimal System: Common difficulty-rating system in the United States. Class 5 climbing entails exposure, requires technical moves, and a fall results in severe injury or death. Ratings for technical climbs begin at 5.0 and progress to 5.14.

Pitch: A segment of a climb that can be accomplished with a single length of rope.

Top rope: A climb that is anchored from above.

Crack climbing: Following a crack in a rock by jamming a finger or a fist in and pulling upward.

Rack: A climber's collection of protective devices, slung around a shoulder on a climb.

Protection: Devices such as nuts and cams, placed in rock cracks to protect a climber in the event of a fall.

★ Acadia ★
NATIONAL PARK
Otter Cliffs

Coastal Maine's Acadia may not have a major climbing scene, but it has a little of everything—single-pitch, multipitch, trad, sport, and bouldering routes. The setting, of course, is stunning, especially when you climb Otter Cliffs' array of routes, 5.4 to 5.12, and savor the heady sensation of climbing right over the water. South Bubble, overlooking Jordan Pond, is less exposed—great for reassuring routes and bomber holds. But a Champlain Mountain venue called South Wall, accessible by a faint climbers' trail a few hundred feet south of the Precipice Trail trailhead, is where experienced climbers muster. There they find multipitch routes 60 to 100 feet high and a selection of laybacks, hand cracks, and some very fun and long finger cracks. The wall's ledge system allows climbers to climb, rest, traverse, and keep on going to the next ledge—and the next. Guides and lessons: *www.acadiamountainguides.com.*

★ Zion ★
NATIONAL PARK
Moonlight Buttress on Angel's Landing

In southern Utah, Zion's soaring walls of red Navajo sandstone are host to some of the world's most aesthetic big-wall climbs—hundreds of them, 800 to 2,000 feet high. Climbing here is like nowhere else, so even experienced climbers need to respect the uniqueness of the sandstone and the nature of the climbs. Climbers need excellent crack-climbing skills and need to place a lot of protection—all climbing here is traditional—given the relative softness of the rock. Routes are long and often the higher rock transitions to crumbly white sandstone, so an aesthetic wall might not be an aesthetic climb; the services of a guide are almost mandatory for first-time visitors. Virtually every wall on every grand formation has climbing routes. Probably the most famous is Moonlight Buttress on Angels Landing—a steep 5.12 multipitch that has a stretch of 600 feet of continuous vertical and overhanging cracks. Other legendary routes are on Cerberus Gendarme and the Temple of Sinawava. Those are just a few of hundreds, virtually all of them difficult but lovely. Many formations are closed when falcons and other raptors are nesting. Guides and lessons: *www.zionadventures.com.*

★ Rocky Mountain ★
NATIONAL PARK
Longs Peak Cirque and Mummy Range

Colorado's Rocky Mountain features great climbs on both sides of the Continental Divide, but the most popular climbing areas are on the east side, namely the Longs Peak cirque, Glacier Gorge, Loch Vale, Tindall Gorge, Odessa, and Mummy Range. Routes tend to be clean, on firm granite, with wonderful views. Most are multipitch, which climbers appreciate, given that they need to hike 2 to 6 miles just to start. At Loch Vale is Petit Grepon, listed as one of the 50 classic climbs in North America in the book of the same name. The south face is the most famous way up—a 5.8 climb with eight exposed pitches to an extraordinarily small summit. Spearhead at Glacier Gorge is every bit as classic and just one of several stunning formations there, where crack climbs range from 5.6 to impossible. And the famous Diamond face of Longs Peak is gorgeous, if difficult; even the so-called Casual Route is 5.10. Guides and lessons: *www.totalclimbing.com.*

backpacking: epic hikes

Walk, don't run

For independent spirits who prefer to trek for days and cover tens, if not hundreds, of miles, the parks offer a bonanza of great opportunities. From the spine of the Appalachians to the crest of the Continental Divide, these trails allow a hiker to become immersed in nature and do something few of us accomplish—experience America.

✷ Yosemite ✷
NATIONAL PARK
215-mile John Muir Trail

The time invested on California's John Muir Trail rewards hikers with what may be the most memorable month of their lives. With the trailhead within Yosemite National Park, the 215-mile trek ties in the Ansel Adams Wilderness and Sequoia and Kings Canyon National Parks before coming to a close at Mount Whitney, the highest peak in the lower 48 states. Backed by plenty of time and loads of stamina, journeys can be accented with an ascent. The route follows the Sierra Nevada, ascending and descending some 50,000 feet as hikers pass, ford, and scale over, around, or near legendary sites such as subalpine Tuolumne Meadows, Merced River, Half Dome, Cathedral Lake, and the Lyell Canyon and Glacier. Keep walking and the scenery includes Jeffrey pines, fir trees, blue spruce, azaleas, ferns, violets, and fields of wildflowers. There are creeks and peaks, butterflies and waterfalls, cascading rivers, narrow canyons, grouse, deer, bear, and lakes.

✷ Rocky Mountain ✷
NATIONAL PARK
40-mile Colorado Grand Loop

Since this loop hike in Colorado clears the Continental Divide, consider it the rare cross-country hike that'll only take a week, traveling west to east and back again in just 40 miles. Kicking off with a half-mile ascent from the Bear Lake Trailhead to Flattop Mountain (elevation 12,324 feet), short but intense stretches lead to much-appreciated campsites. After crossing the 12,061-foot Boulder-Grand Pass, the trail climbs below Longs Peak's south face and eventually reaches the base of the Palisades cliffs and then affords great views from the summit of Longs Peak; afterward, a well-deserved downhill hike drops nearly 1 mile over the course of 10. Hikers get a bird's-eye view of the American West with panoramas of wildflowers, purple mountains majesty, and the occasional elk. If planning to hike in the fall or late spring shoulder seasons, though, hikers should add something else to the pack: an ice ax and crampons.

Mount Rainier's glaciers gleam at daybreak as the early morning fog begins to dissipate.

☆ Grand Canyon ☆
NATIONAL PARK
34-mile Royal Arch Loop

Descending into Arizona's Grand Canyon is an adventure no matter how it is achieved—by mule or foot. But for experienced hikers wanting to truly experience the grandeur and quiet of the canyon, the challenging 34-mile Royal Arch Loop hike delivers everything one would expect, from cliffs and rock climbs to the incredible sensation of being dwarfed by towering sandstone buttes. There are gorgeous gorges and evenings camped out beside the rushing Colorado River, steep drops into Bass Canyon, and further descents of nearly half a mile over the course of about 2.5 miles. The trail also leads to a lovely open plateau campsite beneath the majestic presence of the Tyndall Dome, a 4,800-foot red-rock wall. Over the next several days, hikers can camp on the sands of Toltec Beach and embark on a there-and-back hike into Elves Chasm for a visit to the hidden waterfalls and grottoes at the mouth of Royal Arch Creek. Some steep walls will require some climbing rope and carabiners (or a chance to rappel if the trail is done in reverse), but the preparation pays off when the trail reaches Royal Arch, the largest natural rock bridge in the Grand Canyon.

☆ Mount Rainier ☆
NATIONAL PARK
93-mile Wonderland Trail:
A Slice of the Pacific Northwest

Pacific Northwest scenery such as displayed on post-cards and calendars and bookmarks is what inspires hikers to take on the Wonderland Trail. Clocking in at just under a century, the 93-mile trail is resplendent with glaciers and volcanoes and swatches of high-altitude wildflowers and towering cedar and fir trees, all of which will be revealed from a repeated series of crests slicing across Washington State's Mount Rainier. A range of wildlife includes elk and deer and bears (beware), but perhaps even more challenging are sections of the trails that, when not conveniently flat, are rising and falling a collective 23,000 feet and areas where hikers are expected to ford streams that may or may not be traversed by a bridge or fallen tree.

☆ Glen Canyon ☆
NATIONAL RECREATION AREA
30-mile Rainbow Trail

The spectacular Rainbow Trail winds for nearly 30 miles around the footprint of Navajo Mountain; because much of the trail falls within the Navajo Reservation, this five-day hike will require a permit issued from the Navajo Nation Parks and Recreation Department (928-871-6647, www.navajonation parks.org). Setting off through a scrub forest, the path slips into First Canyon then crosses the state line from Arizona into Utah. After following a dry creek bed in Horse Canyon, the trail starts its drop of nearly 2,000 feet into Cliff Canyon. Sunset Pass provides spectacular views, and later, hikers encounter a Navajo hogan and have the chance to camp out beside Rainbow Bridge, the world's largest natural bridge. A sacred site to the Navajo (don't

walk beneath it), the bridge stands 290 feet high and spans an incredible 275 feet. The trail next snakes past the crimson shades of Super Dome, campsites near Owl Bridge and Bald Rock Canyon, and glimpses of centuries-old rock art created by ancient tribes. The entire journey? A masterpiece.

☆ Chesapeake & Ohio Canal ☆
NATIONAL HISTORICAL PARK
184.5-mile Towpath

When is an epic hike not an epic hike? When it's a 184.5-mile stroll through a national park beside the remnants of a historic canal. Actually, this may be a

☆ Pacific Crest Trail ☆

For hikers who've the fortitude and the time, maybe about six months, it may be tempting to tackle the entire 2,650 miles of the Pacific Crest Trail, a path that runs from Canada to Mexico (or vice versa) via California, Oregon, and Washington. If this seems too much (and it more than likely is), slice off a 200-mile section of the trail—Section 20—which leads into and out of three national parks: Sequoia, Kings Canyon, and Yosemite. While on the move for several weeks, hikers make their way to or near Mount Whitney via the adjoining John Muir Trail, into Tuolumne Meadows in Yosemite's eastern side, and to nice views of the high-elevation desert of the Owens Valley, located within distance of a hitch into the town of Lone Pine for supplies. In addition to views of canyons and meadows, other rewards include a refreshing encounter with Chicken Springs Lake or beautiful alpine-like Guitar Lake, and much appreciated arrivals of campgrounds featuring small diners and well-stocked stores. It's wild. It's the West.

good way to test the waters of hiking by keeping one foot on the trail and one close to conveniences between Point A (Georgetown) and Point B (Cumberland) along a towpath that parallels the north bank of the fabled Potomac River. Out of commission for nearly a century, the canal now serves a greater purpose, providing Washingtonians with a convenient path for jogging, biking, and walking. While most of the trail's three million recorded annual visitors stick relatively close to D.C., others opt for a "thru-hike" that passes towns followed by long stretches of solitude and areas where the once flowing canal has been reclaimed by vegetation. It's adventure without the drama, and an opportunity to hike past locks, dams, and tunnels and historic sites like Harpers Ferry.

✳ Canyonlands ✳
NATIONAL PARK
7–20-mile Trails:
Sky, Needles and Maze Districts

Endowed with hundreds of miles of independent and interconnecting trails, Utah's Canyonlands National Park is a hiker's dream park. There is no major long-distance trail, but the trails in the Island in the Sky, Needles, or more primitive Maze Districts offer a grab bag of short and long runs that can be patched together into an epic journey, such as completing the Syncline Loop Trail in the Island in the Sky District and then heading to the nearby Whale Rock or Alcove Spring Trails. Ranging from around 7 to 20-some miles, collectively the trails to be tackled are challenging, with steep passes, alarming drop-offs, sections where climbing

---

> **AUGUST 14 1937**
> *The last mile of the Appalachian Trail was opened on Mount Sugarloaf, Maine . . . [T]he footpath was officially designated the Appalachian National Scenic Trail in 1968*

---

skills are just as important as stamina, and a sobering absence of water. In some places, the remote Maze area especially, it's easy for a hiker to lose the trail if they fail to spy the small route-marking cairns (rock piles). For those still prepared to hike the trails back to back, there are scenic expanses of desert grass, sandstone spires, opportunities to navigate canyon bottoms, and, on a 22-mile one-way trek through Salt Creek Canyon (in the Needles District), dense vegetation and the pure joy of being in the wilderness, off the beaten path, and disconnected from the electronic shackles of everyday life.

✳ Appalachian National Scenic Trail ✳
MAINE—GEORGIA
2,175-mile Maine to Georgia Trail

Along with "thru-hikes" on the long-distance Pacific Crest Trail and Continental Divide Trail, accomplishing a similarly straight shot on the fabled Appalachian Trail completes the "Triple Crown of American Hiking." Although some hikers have completed the 2,175 miles from Maine to Georgia in as little as 48 days, allot at least six months for the expedition—while adding a few more years just to plan and train for it. By the time someone's walked from Springer Mountain, Georgia, to Mount Katahdin, Maine, they've hiked through 14 states and balanced along the ridge crests and ventured into the valleys of the Appalachian Mountains to see national parks, national forests, state parks, historic sites like Harpers Ferry and the Bear Mountain Bridge, then the Adirondacks, Blue Ridge, Catoctin, Piedmont . . . the list and the views go on.

✶ Wrangell–St. Elias ✶
NATIONAL PARK & PRESERVE
45-mile Tebay Lakes to Bremner

According to experienced hikers, this epic Alaska trek from Tebay Lakes to the wreckage of the gold rush town of Bremner is tougher than most, and the fact that it will take nearly two weeks to trudge less than 100 miles attests to its difficulty and may even encourage participants to consider an easier hike to the North Pole instead. Hikers can tell they are making progress by checking off what they'll encounter: a few dozen frigid streams that need to be waded across; two glaciers (which, hopefully, will still be there); a half dozen ice fields; and nine icy and challenging passes. The trail is steep, overgrown, and the footing can be tricky, but it places the adventurer in the middle of 24 million acres of wilderness—the combined acreage of the park and Canada's adjacent Klune National Park, form the largest protected swath of wilderness on Earth. Tough it out if possible and be one of the few people on Earth to return home with visions of rivers, lakes, glaciers, and heroic mountains rarely seen by human eyes.

✶ Voyageurs ✶
NATIONAL PARK
30-mile Kab-Ash Trail

In the remote and untrammeled Minnesota North Woods, Voyageurs' Kab-Ash Trail is a popular year-round draw. Although it is less than 30 miles east to west, it will still take a few days to complete. In wintertime, cross-country skiers take to the trail for adventure in the snow-hushed woods. When the snows melt (in the few brief summer months), the rough country trail provides firm footing for hikers, meandering through a mix of backcountry forests of pines and rock ridges and wetlands that connects the Kabetogama and Ash River communities on the southern edge of the national park. On the west, the trail literally begins where the road (Salmi Road) ends and the wilderness begins, home to bald eagles, white-tailed deer, and black bears. From here the path snakes east and south and then north and, midway through, spins into loop trails and eventually hooks into new paths that venture to the shores of Kabetogama Lake, Sullivan Bay, and the Ash River. Where the trail crosses the road to the Ash River Visitor Center, stop at the Beaver Pond Overlook to see the creatures at work.

America's most celebrated long-distance trail, the Appalachian Trail covers 2,175 miles.

4x4 trips

Remote backcountry via dirt, rock, and gravel roads

National parks preserve a unique beauty that ignites a sense of freedom—and that feeling is magnified when drivers discover the roads less traveled. Namely the thousands of miles of unpaved dirt, rock, and gravel traversable only by 4x4 vehicles— freeing people to explore remote stretches of backcountry that lead to rarely seen vistas.

☆ Canyonlands ☆
NATIONAL PARK
White Rim Road Loop
and Remote Backcountry Tracts

Considering that just two paved roads lead into Canyonlands, it doesn't take much to understand that this is a destination designed for 4x4 adventures. This central Utah park has so much remote backcountry that deciding where to go will be the hardest part of the journey. In the Needles and Maze Districts in the southeast and southwest portions of the park, extremely technical and treacherous routes are best tackled by skilled drivers. For everyone else, a somewhat easier alternative is sticking with the 100 miles of unpaved fun on the White Rim Road Loop that encircles the canyon in the Islands of the Sky section of the park. It can be rugged, rocky, and, at times, spookily dangerous with sheer drop-offs that, with a slip of the wheel, could turn a truck into tinfoil. All around are spectacular views of buttes and mesas and wide-open skies, while far, far, far below, the Green and Colorado Rivers wind sinuously through their respective canyons. Campgrounds dot the loop, so it is possible to turn a day trip into a leisurely exploration, allowing time to soak in the majesty of the red-rock country.

☆ Great Sand Dunes ☆
NATIONAL PARK & PRESERVE
Medano Pass Primitive Road

Drivers could motor from Maine to California and never spy sand dunes as majestic as the ones within this park (some surpass 700 feet), and that's reason enough for 4x4 owners to make tracks for Colorado. Even though the dunes are off-limits to motorized vehicles, the Medano Pass Primitive Road more than provides an eventful experience in the shadow of the dunes. The road begins at the ominously named Point of No Return parking area, beyond which two-wheel vehicles are forbidden and a high clearance is required. The road threads the land between the dunes and follows Medano Creek up into the Sangre de Cristo Mountains, stretching 22 miles from Great Sand Dunes to Colo. 69 on the east

Drivers willing to withstand the lurching and bucking of unpaved roads can explore America's much less traveled wilds.

side of the mountains. Over the dozen miles to 9,982-foot Medano Pass, drivers must tackle soft, deep sand for a couple miles; inch up the mountains, fording nine streams; and contend with a rocky roadbed on the approach to the pass. At the pass, the road exits the national park and preserve and heads down 10 miles through the San Isabel National Forest. Now named Forest Service Road 559, the road enters the Wet Mountain Valley and intersects with Colo. 69, a paved road that can turn this into a daylong loop ride. Drivers should expect to travel only 5 to 10 miles an hour. The road is usually open between May and November, weather permitting.

☆ Padre Island ☆
NATIONAL SEASHORE
A 60-mile Stretch of Beach

Arched like a bow sandwiched between the Gulf of Mexico and the Intracoastal Waterway, the longest stretch of undeveloped barrier island in the world is custom designed for four-wheel touring. From the park's north entrance, a paved road parallels Malaquite Beach for about 5 miles then terminates at the beach vehicle barrier, after which 60 miles of beach stretch south, which in Texas means 60 miles of public highway, complete with posted speed limits. While a two-wheel vehicle can travel down the first 5 miles or so, along South Beach, a 4x4 is necessary to continue down Little Shell and then Big Shell Beaches to the end point at Mansfield Channel, within sight of South Padre Island. From about milepost 20 to 40 vehicles will encounter soft and/or deep sands. And some stretches of beach can become particularly tricky when affected by weather, wind, and tides. The farther south one

> *Did You Know?*
> *The beaches in Texas are considered public highways?*

goes, the more remote and tranquil the scenery, with Gulf waters lapping the shore to the east and dunes, grasslands, and mudflats (all three habitats off-limits to vehicles) to the west, backing the beach. The park has plenty of primitive campsites for those who desire to camp out on a piece of land that hardly ever sees a human.

☆ Mojave ☆
NATIONAL PRESERVE
Off Mojave Road

The map of California's Mojave shows a network of dashed lines, indicating a tantalizingly wide range of 4x4 roads. Yet it can also be intimidating: The deeper one goes into the 1.6-million-acre wilderness, the farther one is from civilization and a lifeline. The park's main thoroughfare—the east–west Mojave Road—stretches from border to border and, aside from a paved stretch near the middle of the park, is as rocky and sandy as it was when Indians, cavalry soldiers, and pioneers were blazing the trail in the 1800s (traces of their existence can still be see at ruins including Fort Piute, one of their military outposts). There's much to explore here—abandoned mines, railroad depots, and ghost towns—courtesy of the numerous primitive dirt roads that branch off the Mojave Road.

☆ Cape Hatteras ☆
NATIONAL SEASHORE
50-mile Atlantic Shoreline Beaches

The 50-plus miles of beautiful Atlantic shoreline in North Carolina's Cape Hatteras are a magnet for off-road aficionados. However, national parks must frequently balance the desires of visitors with the needs of nature, and at Cape Hatteras that means periodically imposing beach closures or driving restrictions in order to protect the nesting grounds of endangered sea turtles and a wide range of birds, especially between mid-March and early November. That may sound limiting but the amount of protected shoreline usually fluctuates, so a generous number of miles should always be accessible. The barrier island beaches can be challenging—savvy four-wheelers deflate their tires to about 18–25 psi to get a wider grip and reduce demand on the transmission. In addition to the sea oats and sand and wonderfully picturesque Atlantic Ocean and Pamlico Sound (also accessible by off-road vehicle), the seashore is also home to the tallest brick beacon in the United States, 208-foot-tall Cape Hatteras Lighthouse.

☆ Rocky Mountain ☆
NATIONAL PARK
Old Fall River Road

Most visitors to Colorado's Rocky Mountain National Park are content with the miles of paved roads tangled up in the park's 266,000 acres, and in fact the park is off-limits to 4x4s. But those who want a more intimate experience with nature head for the manageable dirt and gravel Old Fall River Road, a seasonal one-way tract on the east side of the park. Open from roughly early July to when the snows arrive in September or October, Old Fall River Road is an entry-level off-road excursion. In the 11 miles between the start of the road at Horseshoe Park and the Alpine Visitor Center at 11,796 feet, drivers proceeding at a cautious 15 miles an hour will pass large boulders and tall trees and deep valleys and have a chance to stop at pullouts for scenic views and perhaps even spy elk, deer, and bighorn sheep. One of the most impressive sights is the road itself, the first route to clear the Continental Divide, in 1921.

The narrow road does feature some tricky switchbacks, but those moments are more than compensated with views of alpine tundra and wildflowers and valleys and mountains.

☆ Grand Canyon ☆
NATIONAL PARK
Kaibab Plateau

Unfortunately for four-wheel drivers in Arizona's Grand Canyon National Park, mules have the advantage in navigating the *depths* of the canyon. Where drivers do have the advantage is on roads where they're given free rein to explore portions of the backcountry that frames the chasm, primarily near the North Rim. Those who travel with a sense of adventure will find miles of unpaved roads at the end of Ariz. 67 on the subalpine Kaibab Plateau, although North Rim services are only open between snow's departure and its return, mid-May through mid-October. Among the routes for 4x4s are primitive roads leading through canyons and to lookout points. One of the most popular routes (a relative term here) is the 17-mile tract of dirt and gravel that leads west through a lush forest of spruce, pine, fir, and oak. Along the way, rocks crush and grind under tires as the road alternates between roughly smooth and seriously bumpy. The payoff is the road's end point, Point Sublime. Here the view is as majestic as any afforded by the South Rim—except here one is likely to have the Grand Canyon all to oneself.

✶ Death Valley ✶
NATIONAL PARK
Off-track Adventures with Sheer Drop-offs,
River Crossings, and Washboarded Roads

Just crossing California's Death Valley via paved Calif. 190 is a demanding experience, requiring scaling the Inyo Mountains before tackling the challenge of a long and lonely trek across the valley floor. But it's a peaceful Sunday drive compared to going off road in the park, where anxiety runs high on trails of soft sand and loose gravel and large boulders and washouts. Threading through Death Valley's 3-million-plus acres is a potpourri of 4x4 roads. In total, there are more than 1,000 miles of roads to explore, of which the majority are unpaved. More than 80 wilderness avenues test driving skills and nerves with sheer drop-offs, river crossings, and washboarded roads. These roads lead to desolate places and sights the vast majority of park visitors have never seen, nor ever will: strange geological formations, hidden canyons, and the ruins of mining camps and cabins. Titus Canyon Road is the most popular backcountry road (a high-clearance two-wheel vehicle is sufficient). Tips: Bring spare gas and water, and come between October and April to avoid summer temperatures that can clear 120°F.

Canyonland's White Rim Road provides one of the most stunning 4x4 adventures in the United States.

☆ Joshua Tree ☆
NATIONAL PARK
Covington Flats Area
and the Geology Tour Road

Stark and spare, the landscape in California's Joshua Tree is well suited for 4x4s, with a limited but far-reaching series of dead-end and loop roads that lead out into the wilderness to follow historic paths down old mining roads, across dry washes, and into canyons; others bump along rocks and around boulders while demanding extra traction to summit steep hills leading to panoramic views. The dirt roads in the Covington Flats area access the most verdant area of the park and some of the park's largest Joshua trees; an overlook at Eureka Peak provides a view of the neighboring community of Palm Springs and the Morongo Basin. The 18-mile Geology Tour Road, on the other hand, delivers adventure in the form of rock piles, boulders, parched ravines, and a dam created by ranchers more than a century ago to water their cattle. There will also be remnants and ruins of a long-gone industry seen in an assortment of cyanide vats and abandoned mines and dangerous shafts that should pique anybody's curiosity—and sense of caution.

☆ Capitol Reef ☆
NATIONAL PARK
Cathedral Valley Loop

The 58-mile Cathedral Valley Loop in Utah's Capitol Reef is a feast for the eyes and a challenge to drive. Two-wheel drives with high clearance can travel this road, but the extra traction of a 4x4 can be much more comforting when weather tangles with this unpaved trail of rock, sand, and dirt that snakes through the mountains. The access point is on Utah 24, about 12 miles east of the park's visitor center (with another entry point found about

☆ 4x4 Adventures: Be Prepared ☆

Outside many national parks where 4x4s are permitted, a fleet of vendors are usually geared up to lead off-road tours. In addition to having the right equipment, they usually have an understanding of the area's history and terrain to reach the region's most beautiful and intriguing destinations. Not only that, if a jagged boulder rips open the undercarriage of their truck, they'll call their insurance company—not yours. But if you insist on traveling solo in your own 4x4, do so with the understanding that while it can be fun, it's not a game. Often you'll be traveling outside cell phone range and beyond the reach of park services and rangers, so if your vehicle gets stuck, breaks down, or someone is injured, you're essentially on your own. Take precautions. Have your vehicle inspected before setting out, talk with rangers about road closures, pack current maps and a GPS, and carry plenty of water, extra fuel, and all manner of vehicle fluids. Stow a tool kit, spare tire(s), towrope, shovel, and high-lift jack. If this seems too much preparation, consider the rewards that await you: rarely seen vistas away from the maddening crowds.

8 miles past that), outside the park. The loop is created by stitching together Utah 24 and the dirt Hartnet and Cathedral Roads. Most visitors begin the loop on Hartnet Road, which requires a ford of the Fremont River shortly after turning off Utah 24. The road leads to remote regions and geological curiosities, including spectacular multicolored mesas, spires, and other rock formations. The road is usually closed from mid-November to mid-March, when not even the most skilled drivers and sturdiest 4x4s can navigate the road.

trail runs

The place to set your pace in the parks

Whether the jogging path is in the heart of a high desert or a refreshing run on a New England trail shaded by sycamores and elms, there are thousands of terrific trails. Due to the nature of the activity, runners love getting out to enjoy the great outdoors—which makes their sport and America's national parks a perfect match.

⁂ Lake Mead ⁂
NATIONAL RECREATION AREA
Lakeshore Drive
and Northshore Road

At Arizona's Lake Mead, hard-core runners looking for places to test their endurance will find plenty of trails leading into fantastic canyons. Most casual runners, however, are attracted to the popular area surrounding the southwest shores of sinuous Lake Mead. As a natural energizer, 11-mile Lakeshore Drive and the southern portion of Northshore Road offer pavement for firm footing as well as a perpetually scenic panorama of the lake's clear blue waters framed against colorful distant hills and mountains. There's no separate jogging lane, so stretch out and keep one eye on traffic from Boulder Beach along long, loping blacktop that continues into the hills or down to the shore. Considering the heat of the Mojave Desert can bake this national recreation area (desert temperatures can reach 120°F in the shade), this may be a run better saved for fall or spring when the mercury drops into the comfortable 50s and 60s.

⁂ Rock Creek ⁂
PARK
Western Ridge Trail
and Valley Trail

Washington, D.C., isn't just for politicians. Runners, too, can find much to enjoy, including several choice trails in Rock Creek Park, one of the oldest federal parks (established 1890). At just over 1,700 acres (twice that of Central Park), Rock Creek Park packs in an impressive 20 miles of dirt trails that usher runners into an assortment of tree-lined paths along wooded hillsides, ridges, and valleys that are perfect for easy hiking or a gentle jog. The blaze-marked single-track Western Ridge Trail and Valley Trails are both well suited for runners ready for a moderate workout, not a marathon. For a little more elbow-room, trot onto one of the wider trails that double as equestrian trails (so watch your step), or drop down to the paved multipurpose path that parallels the park's eponymous stream. By using connector trails and roads, it is possible to make short and large loop runs. In addition, many trails branch out of the park into nearby D.C. neighborhoods, such as Dumbarton Oaks and Palisades Park, as well as into the Maryland suburbs.

✳ Golden Gate ✳
NATIONAL RECREATION AREA
Marin Headlands

With the twin icons of San Francisco and the Golden Gate Bridge providing inspiration (and a water bottle providing hydration), the maze of trails in the Marin Headlands is a trail runner's delight, offering myriad runs. One option is to scale a solid section of the Coastal Trail from Rodeo Beach, climbing into the headlands and cresting out along Wolf Ridge, then descend on the Miwok Trail to find a way through the Tennessee Valley. Another option from Rodeo Beach is to head south around Rodeo Lagoon and capture sections of the coast en route to water's edge at the Point Bonita Lighthouse. Both runs are out-and-back routes, but with a map it is possible to create any number of loops, and of any distance one could possibly desire. If the body's running on autopilot, try to take in the setting's spectacular remoteness, the hills and fields that accent windswept cliffs overlooking the grand Pacific Ocean. It's worth the time spent training.

Golden Gate Bridge seen from the Marin Headlands

☆ Channel Islands ☆
NATIONAL PARK
Island Trails

A quintet of islands (Anacapa, Santa Cruz, Santa Rosa, San Miguel, and Santa Barbara) make up the Channel Islands National Park, and each is proud to promote hiking trails that alternate between smooth and steady and rough and rugged. For runners, this means the trails are more suited to experienced cross-country runners, surefooted and well-balanced runners who can negotiate the trails at a steady clip. Most of the islands have trails that range from easy to strenuous, with the easy ones sticking to coastal areas and the strenuous ones often venturing into the mountainous interiors. As an added bonus, coastal trails offer the opportunity to see marine wildlife. Trails range between 2 and 20 miles, and on the largest of the five islands, 62,000-acre Santa Cruz, several trails on the northern coast provide views of beaches, ocean, mountains, and cliffs that create a classic California backdrop. It is only possible to reach the islands via boat or plane; the trip can take one to three hours.

☆ Great Trail Running Gear ☆

The most important piece of gear that you'll need are shoes. Trail shoes—designed with shock-absorbent cushioning, waterproof uppers, a lower, more stable profile to help prevent ankle rolling, and maximum traction—provide an advantage when it comes to negotiating slippery rocks, uneven terrain, and root- and rock-strewn paths. When choosing your trail shoe, you'll need to find a model that suits your foot and gait type. If you're not sure, the salespeople at a good running store can help you out. *Runner's World* magazine annually rates the top trail shoes (www.runnersworld.com).

Gators are available to help protect your shoes from getting muddy. Double-layer socks protect against blistering. And consider longer shorts or tights to protect from trailside branches. Be sure to carry water and/or an electrolyte drink in a belt around your waist or in a CamelBak. You should also bring along energy food, such as GU Energy Gel or energy bars.

A GPS isn't a bad idea, either.

☆ Valley Forge ☆
NATIONAL HISTORICAL PARK
Outer Line Drive Multipurpose Path

There's not only history at Pennsylvania's Valley Forge, but an opportunity for a pleasing run along a wonderful loop road. The scenery protected within the boundaries of Valley Forge—from the cannon and monuments to the restored headquarters of George Washington—is so impressive and this land so bucolic that it's a challenge to picture the grounds as they were in the winter of 1777–78, when George Washington and his Continental Army toughed it out for several harsh winter months. Starting near the visitor center, the 6.6-mile Joseph P. Martin Trail, a wide, paved multipurpose path, parallels the scenic North and South Outer Line Drives, providing a perfect avenue for bicyclists and joggers. Sweeping across rolling hills and past re-creations of cabins troops constructed to shelter themselves from the snow and sleet, the path stretches from the visitor center past the magnificent National Memorial Arch and on to Knox's Quarters. The trail connects with other trails to make a loop of the park's windswept fields, filled with deer and birdsong.

✵ Muir Woods ✵
NATIONAL MONUMENT
Dipsea Trail

When even motorcyclists find this coast region's paved roads challenging, imagine what joggers feel when they take on the jittery single-track trails of Muir Woods. Snaking in and out of the national monument, the Dipsea Trail is one of the most challenging trails in the nation. Each year the single-track terror attracts hundreds of contestants to a century-old race famed for its utter punishment of runners. With a vertical ascent of more than 2,200 feet over its 7.1-mile length from the town of Mill Valley to Stinson Beach, prepare for demanding climbs—including three sets of stairs, together numbering more than 600 steps— and the obstacles of rocks and roots and branches and slopes that are alternately grueling and, when conquered, rewarding. Runners should pace themselves and enjoy the scenery (walk if need be; many runners do in places); focus on the cooling pleasures of the old-growth coastal redwood forest— the only one in the San Francisco Bay area—and soak in the awe-inspiring Pacific Ocean views at Stinson Beach.

✵ Cape Hatteras ✵
NATIONAL SEASHORE
Lighthouse Beach

The coastline of North Carolina's Outer Banks is a natural jogging trail for runners. Finding the optimal stretch of strand to sample would be difficult were it not for the Cape Hatteras Lighthouse. At 198 feet this beacon, one of three within the park boundaries, is the tallest lighthouse in the United States. An iconic image, the chance to run in its shadow is the "OBX" (Outer Banks) equivalent of a Paris jog around the Eiffel Tower. Although eroding

Trail runners love to pound the trails threading through California's stately coast redwood forests.

sands necessitated its move a quarter-mile inland in 2000, the shoreline is still close enough to start the day with a sunrise beach run here . . . or perhaps return at dusk for a brisk shoreline jog in the pulsing glow of its powerful light.

✵ Rocky Mountain ✵
NATIONAL PARK
Loch Vale

The thrill of running in the Colorado Rockies is not only in the sights, but in the challenge. The 6-mile round-trip run around the Loch Vale begins at the already thin-air altitude of 9,240 feet before scampering as high as 10,210 feet. The reward, of course, is the pure joy of being here, where the waters of Andrews Creek and Icy Brook flow from Andrews Glacier and Taylor Glacier into the Loch, a subalpine lake as picturesque as one can imagine, with emerald green aspens and evergreens framing the sapphire blue lake. From the Glacier Gorge Trailhead the moderately difficult trail climbs past Alberta Falls through a gorge to Glacier Junction where, incredibly, two glacial valleys have converged. The trail then clears Icy Brook and springs ahead through a series of switchbacks that climb up through the Loch Vale toward the waters of the Loch. The ultimate reward: even more spectacular views of an unspoiled American wilderness.

✳ Lewis and Clark ✳
NATIONAL HISTORIC PARK
Fort to Sea Trail:
In the Footsteps of the Corps of Discovery:

It was quite a challenge for 28-year-old Meriwether Lewis and 32-year-old William Clark to cross the country and reach the Pacific in December 1805, but a run in this historic park that honors their achievement is nowhere near as exhausting. This national park shares the accomplishments of the explorers with nearby state parks and preserves in both Oregon and Washington, so options are not limited to these trails alone. In Oregon, the Fort to Sea Trail runs between Fort Clatsop, the winter encampment for the Corps of Discovery, and Sunset Beach on the Pacific coast. On the gentle 6.5-mile trail, one appreciates the beauty of the Pacific

> *In 2007 Golden Gate hosted . . . 101 major races, walks and biking events, including Escape from Alcatraz Triathlon, Nike Women's Marathon, Avon Breast Cancer Awareness Walk, and the Cystic Fibrosis Walkathon.*

Northwest, particularly in trees that seem heroically large and landscapes and woods and water that are each consistently impressive. The misty forests, coastal streams, dunes, and the endless sea are very much as they were in the time of Lewis and Clark. The Lewis and Clark River Trail connects to the Fort to Sea Trail at Fort Clatsop. It runs 1.5 miles to Netul Landing, the expedition's canoe landing on today's Lewis and Clark River, up which the Corps paddled to reach their winter campsite.

✳ Acadia ✳
NATIONAL PARK
Carriage Roads
45-Miles Encircling Island

In 1919, a group of "Rusticators"—extremely wealthy families who summered in fabulous mansions on Mount Desert Island—donated a substantial 30,000-plus acres of mountains, lakes, and seashore to the federal government to help create Acadia in Maine, the first national park east of the Mississippi. In addition to this generous gesture, John D. Rockefeller, Jr., advanced the design of 45 miles of carriage roads that encircle the isle. These roads now serve in part as excellent running trails. One pleasing stretch of about 3 miles wraps around Witch Hole Pond and offers a splendid path through eastern deciduous trees, including oak, maple, beech, and other hardwoods. Try to come during the fall, because in a region known for its fiery burst of changing leaves, autumn trail running in Acadia can seem, in the words of one runner, "As if you're running through a painting."

mountain-bike rides

Over hill, over dale

Sporting scraped elbows, bloody knees, and big smiles, mountain bikers appear as rugged as the trails they tackle. Steep passes and deep woods are no obstacle in their pursuit of fire roads, back roads, and coveted single-tracks—narrow paths that slice across deserts, rocks, and forests—set against the backdrop of beautiful national parks.

☆ Mammoth Cave ☆
NATIONAL PARK
Ferry Loop, Sal Hollow Trail, and the
Mammoth Cave Railroad Bike and Hike Trail

Granted the main attraction at this Kentucky park is a hole in the ground, but there are plenty of above-ground thrills as well, including a set of trails and loop mountain-bike rides that either dive into the forest, follow a paved path, or provide a grab bag of dirt and gravel. For a surf-and-turf ride, mountain bikers have dubbed one route the Ferry Loop, as the 32-mile long-distance run includes a ferry trip across the Green River; the route sticks to roads, including 6 miles of gravel roads. Kicking off from the Maple Springs Trailhead, the 9-mile one-way Sal Hollow Trail cuts through the center of the park; the single-track is best suited to intermediate riders. (Plans are in motion to replace this portion of the route, so check with the park.) South of the Green River the Mammoth Cave Railroad Bike and Hike Trail is another 9-mile run that parallels a historic railroad bed from the visitor center to the park's southern boundary at Park City. For mountain bikers that would like to expand their range, plan on a return trip—new trails are always being considered and the old improved.

☆ Whiskeytown ☆
NATIONAL RECREATION AREA
Mount Shasta Mine Loop

In California's Whiskeytown, nestled in the Klamath Mountains, bicycles are welcome on nearly all trails. Adding in the numerous trails found in the surrounding national forest lands, you can be assured of enough trails and single-track to deliver exciting rides on stretches that provide steady handling on hard-packed clay while adding the challenging obstacles of gravel and leaves and washed out gullies and exposed roots capable of laying flat a rider. At times riders have to put on the brakes and clutch their bike when fording a stream, but in the wilds of Whiskeytown that's part of the appeal. The 3-mile Mount Shasta Mine Loop winds past the mine and then climbs steadily to views of surrounding peaks, before descending via a forest access road.

⋆ Big South Fork ⋆
NATIONAL RIVER & RECREATION AREA
Collier Ridge Loop Grand Gap Loop Trail

In Kentucky's Big South Fork, mountain bikers have the best of all worlds: access to horse trails, back-country roads, and single-track trails like the 8.4-mile Collier Ridge Loop with its repeated climbs and exciting descents. Of special note, Monday through Friday rangers open the Grand Gap Loop to bikes, so riders can take on a single-track that rips into some serious wilderness that challenges riders with dense southern forest and drop-offs, ridges and creeks, and a track that includes tight switchbacks then swirls across the land past a lumberyard of felled trees mingled with boulders and rocks and dirt and mud. Bikes bounce off small boulders, ricochet over roots, and negotiate narrow board bridges that make this a challenging run for any rider.

⋆ Big Bend ⋆
NATIONAL PARK
Old Ore Road

Although Big Bend is located in one of the hardest to reach sections of the nation—southwest Texas, on the Rio Grande—when riders reach the middle of mile after mile of mountain-biking roads, they

Canyonlands National Park is a mecca for mountain bikers, enticed by its challenging terrain and gorgeous scenery.

don't mind the drive. The relatively untouched roads make this a prime destination for mountain bikers. For those who like things slow and smooth, there are roughly 100 miles of paved roads while riders that prefer a fast and furious outdoor adventure can choose from more than 150 miles of backcountry roads that provide a grab bag of challenges atop dirt and gravel trails. Rangers and riders praise the merits of the Old Ore Road, a bumpy and rocky 26-mile one-way unpaved 4x4 road that reveals views of the Chisos Mountains. Another recommended ride is the 20-mile out-and-back from Panther Junction to Chisos Basin, which requires peak physical condition. The good news is that after conquering the narrow, steep, and curvy road—often working through 15-degree grades—once a rider hits the heights, the downhill run is a blast.

> *To encourage prospectors [for uranium in the 1950s], the Atomic Energy Commission offered monetary incentives and built almost 1,000 miles of road in southeast Utah. In Canyonlands, these roads include the . . . White Rim Road.*

✳ Canyonlands ✳
NATIONAL PARK
White Rim Loop

It may not be trailblazing, but a ride along the White Rim Road in Utah's Canyonlands will be trail *amazing*. Jeeps have already made this a popular ride, and even though it's not single-track, mountain bikers still enjoy the wide road's rough tread and the chance to pedal around the rim of the sandstone cliffs and canyons. Located in the Island in the Sky District, the road kicks off with a sharp descent down a cattle trail turned road called the Shaffer Trail, switchbacking down to the White Rim Road for the majority of the ride; at the end of the White Rim, riders pick up Mineral Road, which leads to Utah 313 and back to the starting point at Red Sea Flat. When not gasping for breath, riders stop to catch their breath at photo ops of White Rim Canyon. While some claim that hard-core riders can conquer the 100-mile loop in one long, bone-bouncing day, an ordinary person who has a goal to complete the circuit should allot at least two or three days. Campgrounds and rustic restrooms are tacked around the entire loop; bring plenty of water. If the route is ridden counterclockwise, riders face a 1,000-foot ascent up switchbacks, so a vehicle stationed near the finish is a convenient way to get bailed out of the park.

✳ Point Reyes ✳
NATIONAL SEASHORE
Tomales Point

A sampler of coastal habitats and terrains helps deliver a splendid range of mountain-biking options in this California park, with trails that rip through evergreen forests and skim across coastal scrubs and beside estuaries. While mountain bikers can't enter protected wilderness areas, they do have access to all paved roads as well as fire roads, horse trails (equines have the right of way), and a handful of single-track trails. The off-road trails are generally narrow and winding and grant riders admission to beaches and bays and atop mountain crests. Explore the northern reaches of Tomales Point or concentrate on a flurry of trails in the heart of the park or cross the border to pedal outside of Point Reyes and into the neighboring Golden Gate National Recreational Area.

☆ New River Gorge ☆
NATIONAL RIVER
Cunard-Kaymoor Trail

Bungee jumping commands the lion's share of attention at New River Gorge; however, more practical outdoor adventurers are content to make use of the dynamic and dramatic hills and woods and single-track trails cleaved into this densely wooded and highly challenging landscape in southern West Virginia. On the Cunard-Kaymoor Trail, the track descends into a gorge and then gradually climbs to the site of the abandoned Kaymoor Mine (the trail continues, but bikes are not permitted past the mine), while the relatively easier 3.2-mile Thurmond-Minden Trail is on the level as it follows a branch of the old Chesapeake & Ohio Railway, crossing five trestles en route. Shaded by a canopy of trees, the moderate 6-mile Brooklyn–Southside Junction Trail follows an abandoned railway line and the flow of the New River visible ten stories below the trail.

☆ NPS & IMBA ☆

Some could argue that our national parks face more serious threats than a contingent of outdoor enthusiasts who like riding bicycles, but it took years for the International Mountain Bicycling Association (IMBA) to convince the National Park Service (NPS) that mountain bikers deserved a chance—and a place—to pedal their wares. Founded in 1988, the IMBA lobbied for years that mountain bikers would be good stewards of the land, and in 2002, it displayed an admirable level of persistence and prescience when it partnered with the Rivers, Trails and Conservation Assistance program of the NPS. This step affirmed its larger view that both organizations were committed to encouraging more active exploration of national parks. By 2005 the NPS reached the same conclusion and, in the words of the IMBA, "formally recognized mountain biking as a positive activity, compatible with the values of our National Park System." The NPS began, on a case-by-case basis, to open mountain-bike trails in national parks, starting with pilot projects on dirt roads and later introducing single-track trails. The IMBA pledged to assist in the care, maintenance, design, and development of the trails.

☆ Hawaii Volcanoes ☆
NATIONAL PARK
Escape Road and Crater Rim Drive

Perhaps no park serves as the perfect backdrop for a commercial on the joys of mountain biking more than Hawaii Volcanoes on the Big Island. The fact that motorists dominate the two-lane paved roads makes mountain bikers more desirous to reach the dirt and gravel paths that release them to more remote regions of the park, where adventure and vegetation are found in abundance. Beyond the obvious appeal of volcanic landscapes, the park also frees riders to immerse themselves in a multitude of environments including deserts and rain forests, but when the craters call, a few paths command the most attention. Launching from just below 4,000 feet at the Thurston Lava Tubes, the Escape Road is really that—an escape route for locals and visitors should the lava start to spew. According to a ranger, the gravel and rock trail is a "crazy insane steep downhill" and a "way challenging uphill" enveloped within a forest of ferns. Near the park entrance, Escape Road intersects with the park's premier route, Crater Rim Drive. Here cars are restricted to the pavement, while mountain bikers can look for the drive's parallel gravel and cinder path perched above the steaming caldera floor. Cooled lava has closed the drive to a complete circle tour, so at some point riders have to double back. Riders need to exercise caution on the narrow drive, not only looking out for cars but also steering clear of the crater.

✶ Redwood ✶
NATIONAL AND STATE PARKS
Trails Along U.S. 101

Aware that conservationists had to work overtime to protect the redwoods that remained after many had been felled by axmen, rangers at Redwood have been intent on safeguarding the environment by limiting the access of mountain bikers to backcountry trails. Six designated bicycling routes, often on rehabilitated logging roads, range from 3 to 11 miles in length and from easy and level to steep and difficult. Many of the trails interconnect with each other and with U.S. 101, allowing for lengthier loop rides and providing a variety of habitats in one ride, from coastal scrub and ocean views to ancient and second-growth coastal redwoods, conifers, and Sitka spruce forest to open prairie. Some terrific single-tracks and vegetation plucked from the set of *Jurassic Park* make this park one of the finest for riders.

✶ Saguaro ✶
NATIONAL PARK
Cactus Forest Trail

With its close proximity to Tucson (the Rincon and Tucson Units sandwich the east and west sides respectively), Saguaro is also one of the most easily accessible parks for urban mountain bikers. Even if Rincon offers only one multiuse trail for riders, according to a spokesman for the International Mountain Bicycling Association (IMBA), this route is one of the first meaningful mountain-bike

Standing like sentinels, saguaro cacti add flavor to a mountain bike ride through the hills near Tucson.

trails at a national park. The Cactus Forest Trail is a gritty, hard-packed single-track run that rolls past desert scrub and grassland and sagebrush, flashing across dusty and nostalgic scenes reminiscent of serial Westerns where the low hills and ubiquitous saguaros stand sentinel. Although the surrounding elevations rise from about 2,700 to 8,700 feet, the path is rated easy to moderate so riders won't have to worry about losing control on a precarious descent. Just keep an eye out for the black bears and king rattlesnakes that call this land home. By combining the 2.5-mile trail with the Cactus Forest Loop Road, riders can make a loop of about 8.5 miles.

chapter three

by sea, lake, & river

ten best parks
fly-fishing spots
Angling with the light-handed touch of a fly rod

National Park System properties protect entire functioning ecosystems. That includes fish. Although many parks allow fishing (a permit is always required), regulations are strict and the fishing is primarily catch-and-release. These places are for people who love where they fish more than what they catch.

☆ Yellowstone ☆
NATIONAL PARK
Firehole River:
Brown and Rainbow Trout

Northwest Wyoming's Firehole River—the length of which is entirely within Yellowstone National Park—must be the strangest fly-fishing stream in the world, but in the best of ways. If you fish in the fall (the best season) in the early morning (the best time of day), you might think you've stepped into a different world. Gone down the rabbit hole, as it were. Mists from hot springs fill the valley. You can hear the thumping and wheezing of fumaroles and boiling water, perhaps the hiss of a geyser. Hulking bison grunt from the meadows, or loom ominously in the sulfur-smelling fog. The air is cold but the river is warm, heated a few degrees by the biggest concentration of geysers and hot springs in the world. During summer, the Firehole can be too warm for trout. They escape into cooler side streams. But in autumn and spring, the river is a lush buffet of aquatic foods, making it one of the

world's premier fly-fishing waters for brown and rainbow trout. Yellowstone was among the first to institute low-impact fishing regulations. The Firehole has been a fly-fishing–only stream since 1968 and is now catch-and-release only.

☆ Glen Canyon ☆
NATIONAL RECREATION AREA
Glen Canyon Dam Tailwaters:
Rainbow Trout

The Colorado starts out as a clear, alpine stream high in the Rocky Mountains, a happy home for trout. But when it enters the red-rock country of Utah, it picks up a heavy load of sand and clay, and turns as red as the name given to it by Spanish explorers. Its native fish include the likes of humpback chubs and razorback suckers, warm-water species protected throughout the Grand Canyon because they're having trouble surviving. What changed? Both the Boulder Dam near Las Vegas and the Glen Canyon Dam altered the river and its biota in ways that are still not fully understood or measured. Yet some impacts are clear. The water that enters Lake Powell warmed by the sun and sometimes as thick as paint, leaves it below the dam icy cold, rivaling spring water for clarity, and making an exceptional habitat for big rainbow trout. From the dam to the boat ramp at Lees Ferry is 15.5 miles. There is limited access by walking upstream. For full access you have to motor against the current. As with most great trout fisheries, use only barbless hooks; release all fish over 12 inches.

✯ Great Smoky Mountains ✯
NATIONAL PARK
Headwaters Streams: Brook Trout

Headwaters streams above 3,000 feet in elevation are home to tiny brook trout as beautiful as warblers, and a big surprise if you think American freshwater fish can't put on the flash of their bright cousins in tropical waters. Red speckles ringed with blue spangle their green backs. Their bellies are orange, and their fins sport jaunty black and white stripes. These are gorgeous native fish living in their native place. The story of brookies in the Great Smoky Mountains is an unexpectedly happy one. As in many other places around the country, the introduction of non-native trout (in this case rainbows), along with habitat destruction before the park was established, decimated the native population. But a restoration effort came to the rescue. By removing non-natives from sections of streams

> *Nearly 300 different species of fish are known to inhabit the freshwater marshes and marine coastline of Everglades National Park.*

protected by natural obstacles—like waterfalls—the park gave brookies a chance to thrive without competition. In 2006, after 30 years of strict limitation, the park opened virtually all streams for brook trout fishing. Among the best is Raven Fork, along the Enloe Creek Trail; also the East Prong of the Little River, along the trail from Elkmont Campground.

✯ Everglades ✯
NATIONAL PARK
10,000 Islands: Tarpon and Redfish

It's a far cry from little brook trout in mountain streams to 100-pound tarpon in the coastal waters of South Florida. The 10,000 Islands area near Everglades City on the Gulf Coast is prime water—a big place of open shallows, mangrove swamps, hidden backcountry inlets, lagoons, and beaches. Fishers typically use shallow-draft boats with motors to reach their fishing grounds but switch to quiet poling when they get close. Fishing from the shore is generally not practical. They call it sight fishing because you look for the fish before casting. You can see tarpon hanging in shallow water as if asleep, but they can be stirred to action by a well-placed fly tossed from a distance of about 60 feet. Snook prefer the cover of mangroves, where they lie waiting in ambush for smaller fish. Redfish, also called channel bass, red drum, and other names, are found in very shallow water, sometimes so shallow you see their dorsal fins. When taking a fly, they do it with speed and ferocity. This is not easy fishing. Searching is a challenge, and bugs do a lot of the biting, but those who experience Everglades fishing become passionate repeat visitors.

✱ Grand Teton ✱
NATIONAL PARK
Snake River: Cutthroat Trout

The best fishing always seems to be in beautiful places. This is partly because natural habitat and clean water are the best protection for wild fish. But it might also depend on the meaning of the word "best." Catching a lot of fish (something that is almost never common) is less important than where you make your attempt. For many, wetting a line is merely an excuse to be outside in the happy embrace of nature. Beautiful water, good companions, a smoothly floating boat, and great craggy peaks in the background could be enough without the fish. But fish there are, in this most beautiful of alpine settings in northwest Wyoming. The Snake hurries out of Yellowstone, tarries for a while in Jackson Lake, and then runs fast over a stony bed through Jackson Hole. Most fishers float in rafts or drift boats. Some bank fishing is possible. You fish the river by drifting the bank, tossing flies as close to overhanging vegetation as possible, or by pulling out on a gravel bar and letting wet flies swing in the deep pools. The fish are Snake River cutthroats, which see an awful lot of fishers in a season and tend to be savvy. A good day for most people is to catch (and release) three or four fish, and to bask in the grand scenery.

✱ Rocky Mountain ✱
NATIONAL PARK
Roaring River: Greenback Trout

Fishing for greenback trout in the waters of Rocky Mountain National Park is a bit like searching for willow flycatchers in Arizona—a rare species, a special sighting. Greenbacks, a subspecies of cutthroat, sport prominent speckles, red lateral stripes, bright red cheek patches, and yes, a green back. Once widespread, they were displaced by planted exotics including brook, brown, rainbow, and Yellowstone cutthroat trout. In the 1930s, they were thought to be extinct, but in 1957 a small remnant population was found in the Big Thompson River. For several decades, the park and the state of Colorado have worked to restore greenbacks to their native habitat. The effort has seen some success. Put on the endangered list in 1978, they are now listed as threatened. In the park, restored populations of greenbacks (and their cousins, Colorado cutthroat) can be fished in specific lakes and streams using barbless hooks, but never kept. Roaring River and Lawn Lake are a center of interest for greenback fishers.

An angler casts for brook trout in a clear mountain stream in Great Smoky Mountains National Park.

✵ Katmai ✵
NATIONAL PARK & PRESERVE
Brooks River: Sockeye Salmon

To catch wild sockeye salmon and to do it in the company of fish-catching brown bears holds a special cachet for fly fishers. There are few places in the park system where such an experience is possible—and Katmai, at the head of the Alaska Peninsula, is one of them. Most people venture here to watch the bears, who do their fishing without benefit of tackle. Bears concentrate at Brooks Falls but prowl all of the short length of river between Brooks and Naknek Lakes. For human fishers, the river is fly-fishing only, and catch-and-release; the bears get to catch-and-eat on the spot. Access is by floatplane only, via Anchorage. Stay at Brooks Lake Lodge or in the adjacent campground; plan well in advance.

☆ Tenkara ☆

With the purity of Japanese calligraphy, Tenkara is fly-fishing reduced to its simplest form. The telescoping rod measures about 14 inches until a flick of the wrist opens it to a gracefully tapered length of 10 feet. At the tip of the last section, built into the carbon fibers, is a small loop of braided cord. Attached to the loop is all the line you need, a tapered length of monofilament a little longer than the rod. No reel, no line guides, no heavy shooting line. You don't normally touch the line at all. Casting is an artful twitch of the rod. Because the line is short, the fly stays close—a good thing on small streams. Raising or lowering the rod tip easily controls the floating line so that the fish, when it comes, is felt instantly. Perhaps 3,000 years old, the Tenkara method is about presentation—the light, expressive touch of a calligrapher's hand on water.

✵ Shenandoah ✵
NATIONAL PARK
Rapidan River: Brook Trout

When, in 1929, President Herbert Hoover decided to build a retreat far from the Washington scene but near enough for quick weekend visits, he specified that it be in Virginia's Blue Ridge Mountains near a first-rate trout stream. He chose a spot where two streams merge to form the scenic, boulder-strewn Rapidan River, in the newly authorized (but not yet formally established) Shenandoah National Park, saying, "Fishing is an excuse . . . for temporary retreat from our busy world." So it is, and the Rapidan remains a fine place to float dry flies for native brook trout. It's catch-and-release only, as are most waters in the park. There is no road access. Mill Prong Trail leads 2 miles from Skyline Drive to Hoover's Rapidan Camp on the river.

✵ Yosemite ✵
NATIONAL PARK
Tuolumne River: Brown and Brook Trout

Nestled high in the Sierra Nevada peaks of eastern California, Yosemite National Park's Tuolumne Meadows is the upcountry opposite of the park's Yosemite Valley. Here, the mountains step back, the streams meander, and it's easy to understand what John Muir meant when he wrote "Oh, these vast, calm, measureless mountain days, inciting at once to work and rest!" The work is easy if anglers stay in the meadows, and not much harder if they walk up Lyell Fork beside the peacefully winding stream. It comes out of a steep-sided canyon with a nearly level floor—good waters for brown trout and for brookies higher up, if fishers backpack in and camp at least one night. The Dana Fork (which joins the Lyell to form the Tuolumne River) is smaller,

Cool and enticing, rivers in Yosemite National Park lure anglers with the promise of wild trout.

more accessible, and faster moving. Think rainbows and, in the deeper pools, browns. The Tioga Pass Road parallels Dana Fork for about 5 miles. Road traffic might be heavy, but fishing pressure can be surprisingly light.

☆ Chattahoochee River ☆
NATIONAL RECREATION AREA
"The Hooch": Brown and Rainbow Trout

Buford Dam holds back Lake Sidney Lanier just outside of Atlanta, Georgia. It also provides what some anglers consider to be the best trout fishing in the South. Purists, however, like to point out that almost all of the browns and rainbows along this 48-mile stretch of the Chattahoochee River below the dam come from hatcheries, and that the river needs continual habitat improvement to become a wild fishery. On the other hand, the river's proximity to Atlanta makes it a much-loved urban asset, commonly referred to as "the Hooch." As with most hydropower tailwaters, river flow here can change dramatically—as low as 700 cubic feet per second to more than 10,000—which requires some planning for wading or boating. Fluctuation is less extreme during the cool months, when peak power demands diminish. In addition to trout, a number of other species can be found in the Hooch's cool waters, including bass and catfish. The park can provide a list of authorized fishing guide outfitters for both float and wade fishing as well as fly-fishing lessons.

lake fishing

Beneath still waters

Drift along the shore. Anchor in a bay. Probe the inlets and narrow channels. Or find a pleasant spot on land to relax in a folding chair while you keep an eye on a bobber. Use anything from flies to spinning lures to live bait. Lake fishing can be as energetic or lazy as you like. Permits—from the state, park, or both—are required in all jurisdictions.

☆ Glen Canyon ☆
NATIONAL RECREATION AREA
Lake Powell: Channel Catfish, Black Crappie, Walleye, and Bass

Imagine a gently sloping beach made not of sand but of smooth sandstone. Walk down to the water. You can see the stone slanting down into water of startling clarity before it gives way to a deep mid-ocean blue. Really deep. It's almost hard to fathom how deep that water is. You can get a sense of it by visiting the 710-foot-high Glen Canyon Dam. Lake Powell is on one side. On the other, the vertical walls of Marble Canyon drop away, far below, to the Colorado River. Then imagine walls that curve, that overhang like vast egg shells, pierced by arches and pinnacles and slot canyons, and you get a picture of the precipitous landscape that lies beneath the waves. With more than 2,000 miles of shoreline (depending on water level) the lake surface is a delightful maze of channels and canyons. Stone beaches alternate with sand beaches and towering vertical cliffs. Fish love it, and so do campers,

boaters, and anglers who come looking for channel cats, black crappie, walleye, and bass (striped, large-mouth, and smallmouth).

☆ Lake Mead ☆
NATIONAL RECREATION AREA
Lake Mead: Striped and Largemouth Bass
Lake Mohave: Rainbow Trout

The park straddling the Nevada–Arizona border includes two lakes, both on the Colorado River, both created by dams. Lake Mead, behind Hoover Dam, is the larger. Lake Mohave, the product of Davis Dam, lies not far downstream, partially confined within the walls of Black Canyon. Together, they offer some of the best sportfishing in the country set in a rugged desert landscape. More open and less sculpted than Lake Powell, Lake Mead is better suited to motorboats (and well traveled by them) than hand-powered craft. Striped and largemouth bass are found throughout the lake, stripers being the stars, sometimes weighing more than 40 pounds. Anglers will find rainbow trout in Lake Mohave.

★ Grand Teton ★
NATIONAL PARK
Jackson Lake: Lake and Other Trout

Carved out by glaciers, then enlarged by a dam built at its outlet in 1911 (and replaced by a newer structure since then) before Grand Teton National Park was established, Jackson Lake can be an outstanding experience both for its location at the base of northwest Wyoming's spectacular Teton Range and for its excellent fishing. Jackson is a big lake when full, about 40 square miles and 438 feet deep at its deepest point. The water, coming out of Yellowstone National Park through the Snake River, or pouring directly off the Tetons, is as clear and enticing as mountain water can be. Lake trout (Mackinaw) are the top draw for fishermen, but they share billing with brook, brown, and native Snake River cutthroat trout. While the best fishing may be June through September, the lake is open for fishing all year except for October to protect lake trout during their spawning season. Ice fishing is the local angler's secret; it begins usually in January, when the ice gets thick enough to be safe. The other prime time happens in the spring, just after iceout, when lake trout prowl shallow waters along the shore for prey, making them easy targets for bank fishing. After that they go deep, and anglers pursue them with trolling rigs. Access is easy, with many marinas, parking areas, and trailheads scattered around the lakeshore.

Marinas line the shores of Lake Mead National Recreation Area, catering to thousands of sportsfishers in search of bass.

✦ Amistad ✦
NATIONAL RECREATION AREA
Amistad Reservoir: Largemouth Bass

Amistad means friendship. The reservoir that carries its name, located at the confluence of the Rio Grande, Pecos, and Devils Rivers in Texas, shares its basin with Mexico. The lake has 850 miles of shoreline and strikingly clear water thanks to the quality of its contributing rivers, but also to its clean limestone bedrock and two large springs. This aspect of the lake attracts snorkelers and scuba divers, the most skilled of whom explore deep underwater caves in the limestone. No doubt they also come face to fin with the lake's famous largemouth bass, the fish most anglers here desire. Bass do well around the ledges and submerged cliffs of the long rocky shoreline. The lake also has smallmouth, striped, and white bass; and channel and blue catfish. A cliffy shoreline riddled with canyons, coves, and protected inlets provides good camping spots and enough variety to please even nonmotorized boaters.

✦ Lake Meredith ✦
NATIONAL RECREATION AREA
Lake Meredith: Walleye

Walleyes are the main quarry for anglers in this Texas Panhandle lake, but also bass, catfish, crappie, and trout. Formed by the Sanford Dam, and filled by the Canadian River, Lake Meredith seems all the more precious because of its arid, mostly treeless surroundings. The walleye population is naturally reproducing, with big fish running 6 to 8 pounds. From April to June, the lake provides the best walleye fishing in Texas. Fishers do best at night with minnows and night crawlers drifted slowly past cliffs and rocky outcrops. Summer and fall is the time for white bass, which along with smallmouth bass find good habitat in the lake's rocky basin. Drought alert: This area is currently experiencing a drought, and the lake could possibly dry if the conditions do not change.

✦ Yellowstone ✦
NATIONAL PARK
Yellowstone Lake: Cutthroat and Lake Trout

For anyone who cares about fish and natural habitats, the case of Yellowstone Lake represents a heartbreak. Its native cutthroat trout—pure and unhybridized—are the core of a vibrant ecosystem that ties together the lives of fish, grizzly bears, osprey, cormorants, white pelicans, river otters, bald eagles, and a range of associated creatures. This northwest Wyoming lake and its tributaries perhaps once held the world's largest inland population of cutthroat. Lake trout, fierce predators that feed

---

☆ Transcontinental Trout ☆

If bluebirds can fly over the rainbow, can trout swim over the Continental Divide? The seemingly impossible could happen at Two Ocean Plateau south of Yellowstone. Here, Two Ocean Creek splits at the edge of a marshy meadow: Pacific Creek heads west through the Snake River to the Pacific Ocean; the Atlantic Creek flows east through the Missouri River to the Atlantic. When water levels are high, as in the spring snowmelt, trout with a nomadic urge could make the crossing. Mountain man Osborne Russell wrote about the "parting of waters and fish crossing mountains" in the 1830s. "Here a trout of 12 inches in length may cross the mountains in safety."

on young cutthroat, were illegally introduced over several years beginning in the late 1980s. Since then, despite urgent efforts by management, they have proliferated. Making it worse, the often fatal whirling disease recently appeared in the lake basin. Cutthroat numbers have fallen drastically. Spawning runs in tributary streams—once an important food source for bears and other fish-eating predators, have nearly disappeared. Lake trout, in contrast, spawn on the lake bottom. Because they live at depth, they are not available as a substitute food source for predators. It's a bad situation, but not a hopeless one. Gill nets, set deep, catch lake trout but not cutts. Efforts to target lake trout spawning areas show some promise. If lake trout numbers can be kept in check, cutthroat arc likely to survive, albeit in reduced numbers. For anglers, this is a chance to fish for a higher purpose. The park requires that all lakers caught must be kept or killed. Catch all you can. Do it for the ecosystem.

> There are 2,261,274 acres of lakes and reservoirs in the National Park System, and roughly 3 million acres of oceans and estuaries in the National Park System. That's . . . nearly the size of Massachusetts.

✴ Voyageurs ✴
NATIONAL PARK
Interconnecting Lakes and Waterways:
Walleye and Many Other Freshwater Species

The Canadian Shield makes for the finest lake country on the planet. Ancient Precambrian rock, smoothed by the great glaciers of the Ice Age, creates a wonderland of interconnecting lakes and waterways. Beginning in the late 17th century, French-Canadian voyageurs traveled the water highways carrying trade goods to the interior and paddling back with furs. Voyageurs, in the heart of Minnesota's North Woods, protects a generous sample of the countryside the legendary canoeists traversed. The park is perfect for exploring with a boat and fishing gear. The piscine list is long and distinguished: walleye, sauger, northern pike, smallmouth and largemouth bass, yellow perch, sturgeon, lake trout, and the champion of northern fish, the muskie. Fishing here, especially at dawn or dusk, can be an idyllic experience. The plunk of spinning lures hitting the water, the gentle splash of ripples against the canoe, and the haunting cry of loons make powerful music.

✴ Isle Royale ✴
NATIONAL PARK
Lake Superior: Lake Trout and Salmon
Inland Lakes: Walleye and Yellow Perch

Unlike lakes surrounded by a park, this is a park surrounded by a lake. Lake Superior is the world's biggest freshwater lake measured by surface area, and third largest if measured by volume. Michigan's Isle Royale is an archipelago consisting of one long narrow island and more than 450 small ones. Bays, inlets, open water, and inland lakes offer variety for the angler. In Lake Superior, lake trout and salmon take top honors. Walleye, yellow perch, and northern pike swim the inland lakes. Visiting the island is a wilderness experience and not a casual trip. Ferry services operate from mainland ports in Minnesota and Michigan, and will carry a limited number of canoes and kayaks.

The *Ranger III,* sailing from Houghton, Michigan, six hours away,

can carry motorboats up to 20 feet. Canoes and kayaks can be rented on the island at Rock Harbor Lodge, on the park's south side, the only lodging other than campsites (reserve well in advance for either). Lake Superior can be a dangerous place for small craft; the park advises canoers and kayakers to stay on protected inland waters.

✴ Everglades ✴
NATIONAL PARK
River of Grass: Largemouth Bass

Everglades National Park is renowned for the saltwater fishing in its bays and mangrove swamps, but the park's inland waters deserve equal attention. Largemouth bass are king, with big ones commonly weighing in at around 5 pounds. Locals like to call them

An air boat navigates the grass-filled waterways of Everglades National Park.

"hawgs." Fishers also go for alligator gar, oscars, bluegills, and a feisty, brightly colored fish called peacock bass. Not a bass at all, it's a cichlid native to South America, introduced in southern Florida in 1984. The park has so much water—one-third of its 1.5 million acres is navigable water—and so much soggy ground mixed up with it, that it can be hard to distinguish particular lakes. Getting around requires the right sort of boat. Bank-fishing options are extremely limited. Route finding is also a challenge. Winter months, when water levels drop, are best for fishing. Going with a local guide, at least for an introduction, is a prudent move both to find your way and to find the fish. Paddlers might consider a designated canoe trail, like Nine Mile Pond or West Lake.

✴ Lake Clark ✴
NATIONAL PARK & PRESERVE
Lake Clark: Grayling, Dolly Varden,
Lake Trout, Red Salmon, and Northern Pike

Among the most pristine fish habitats in all the national parks, Alaska's Lake Clark represents a high ideal in conservation. The park protects the upper Kvichak River watershed, from its glacier origins through the park's 50-mile-long namesake lake. For sockeye salmon, the Kvichak is of paramount importance as a spawning ground that provides a third of the annual total U.S. sockeye catch. From the park's ecological rather than commercial perspective, sockeye are a keystone species, a primary element in the park's biotic health—a larger picture that includes the full catalog of subarctic wildlife. Lake Clark itself is not the only lake by any means, just the largest. In its waters, sport anglers toss lines for grayling, Dolly varden, lake trout, red salmon, and northern pike. Access is by floatplane. Lodges provide services on several lakes; all camping is primitive, meaning naturally splendid.

ten best parks
float trips

Gliding down America's wilderness rivers

Make your home on the river for a while during a long and languid float trip down some of America's wildest and most scenic rivers. Savor the solitude on your own or in the hands of an experienced outfitter that knows every sandbar and current. But whether you raft, canoe, or kayak, proper planning is imperative.

☆ Alagnak ☆
WILD RIVER
Alagnak River

The Alagnak packs a lot of punch into its 79 miles: white water and wildlife, seclusion and incredible tundra and spruce forest scenery. From its source in Katmai National Preserve, the river flows west across the Alaska Peninsula before poring into Bristol Bay. The incredible quantity and quality of game fish makes the Alagnak one of Alaska's most renowned sportfishing rivers and a popular venue for fly-fishing float trips. Rainbow trout, char, grayling, northern pike, and five different types of salmon inhabit the river. But boating or fishing the park is no easy matter: A complete lack of roads means you need to hop a floatplane to Kukaklek or Nonvianuk Lakes near the river's headwaters. You should ask your pilot to do a flyover of the river beforehand to check overall river conditions and potential hazards. Vast stretches of the Alagnak flow free and easy, but a narrow gorge in the upper section churns up Class III rapids. It takes about six days to float the river at a leisurely pace. Katmailand (*www.katmailand.com*) outfits unguided float and fishing trips down the Alagnak from June to September, including floatplane transport and rubber raft.

☆ Big Bend ☆
NATIONAL PARK
Rio Grande Wild & Scenic River

If West Texas is no country for old men, then the Rio Grande is no river for the squeamish of any age or gender, a mighty watercourse that separates the United States and Mexico and that marks the southern boundary of Big Bend National Park. Roughly 70 miles of the river flow through the park, the upper section of a 196-mile protected corridor called Rio Grande Wild and Scenic River, jointly managed by the Park Service and the U.S. Bureau of Land Management. Float trips along the river can range from a few hours to several weeks through some of the wildest country in the Southwest. One of the more popular day trips is the 10-mile float

Canoers lazily paddle down a calm stretch of the Rio Grande river running through Big Bend.

between Talley and Solis Landing, the highlight of which is the 6 miles through Mariscal Canyon; 1,400-foot cliffs and Class II–III rapids make this journey spectacular. It takes two or three days to run Boquillas Canyon, but the lack of serious rapids makes this a great float trip for beginners. The Lower Canyons just outside the national park are another matter, a five- to ten-day journey through deep canyons and desert wilderness nearly devoid of human impact. Several outfitters run float trips along the Rio Grande, including Big Bend River Tours *(www.bigbendrivertours.com)* in Terlingua.

☆ Buffalo ☆
NATIONAL RIVER
Buffalo River

Proving that it's not just wildlife that can be rare and endangered, the Buffalo is one of a few rivers in the lower 48 states without dams, reservoirs, or other impediments to its flow. This fact was recognized in 1972, when the Buffalo became the nation's first national river. It meanders west to east across northern Arkansas before a rendezvous with the White River near Buffalo City. About 135 miles of the river corridor is designated parkland, an Ozark wilderness that shelters myriad wonders, from waterfalls to sinkholes to elk herds and 300 different types of aquatic creatures. Rangers lead guided float trips in the lower district between Buffalo Point and Rush Landing, a journey that takes five to seven hours with a mid-river lunch stop. Independent outfitters, like the Buffalo Outdoor Center *(www.buffaloriver.com)*, organize much more substantial floats, including multiday trips between Ponca and Woolum.

✶ Canyonlands ✶
NATIONAL PARK
Colorado and Green Rivers

Brown Betty Rapids and the Doll House are just two of the many landmarks well known to river runners in southern Utah's Canyonlands. This red-rock park affords the rare opportunity of floating two legendary rivers—the Colorado and the Green—through a deeply eroded desert landscape every bit as stunning as the Grand Canyon downstream. Both rivers are smooth as silk above their meeting, but then the combined flow churns through Cataract Canyon, kicking up world-class rapids on a wild ride down to Lake Powell. The town of Moab is the staging point for nearly all river trips. Short journeys through the park run two to three days, the longest more than a week. Visitors can easily arrange their own flat-water trips down to the confluence or Spanish Bottom, over-nighting at primitive riverside campsites; however, there is no road access to either point, so boaters must either paddle back upstream or arrange a boat shuttle back to Moab. Owing to Class V rapids and fluctuating water levels, only the most experienced boaters should try to run the 14 miles of Cataract Canyon on their own. Many outfitters offer guided trips along both rivers, including Tag-A-Long Expeditions *(www.tagalong.com)*, NAVTEC Expeditions *(www.navtec.com)*, and Adrift Adventures *(www.adrift.net)*.

✶ Gates of the Arctic ✶
NATIONAL PARK & PRESERVE
Arctic Circle Rivers

It's not so much another state as a different planet—the endless tundra on the north slope of the Brooks Range is in a part of Alaska that even most state residents have never seen. The entire park lies north of the Arctic Circle, and within its boundaries are six national wild and scenic rivers and half a dozen other large waterways that are eminently floatable, including the Nigu and Kobuk. A float trip here is edge of the envelope boating: Take everything with you and hope nothing goes wrong, because help is far away. But the rush along these rivers is unparalleled: herds of caribou thundering across the frozen plains, grizzlies fishing downstream (and hopefully down-wind) from your campsite, tramping across ancient Inuit hunting grounds. Arctic Wild *(www.arcticwild.com)* runs six- to nine-day float trips between June to August on several of the park's rivers.

✶ Glen Canyon ✶
NATIONAL RECREATION AREA
San Juan River

Although the recreation area revolves around Lake Powell, the park also includes the lower reaches of the wild and rugged San Juan River. One of the most remote corners of the American Southwest, the stretch of river between Goosenecks State Park and Clay Hills Crossing skirts the northern edge of the Navajo Indian Reservation and is only reachable by boat. The river runs fairly gentle, with nothing more than Class II rapids to raise your heartbeat. It's wilderness camping all the way, mostly on beaches tucked beneath soaring red-rock walls. O.A.R.S. *(www.oars.com)* is one of the few outfitters to organize guided floats along the San Juan, trips that range from 2.5 to 6 days in length.

☆ Floatplanes ☆

Many floatable rivers can only be reached by float-plane, small aircraft mounted with pontoons that can land on lakes, rivers, and even glaciers.

They were originally developed for naval use during World War I. Afterward, pilots soon realized their value to commercial aviation, especially in remote places like Alaska and northern Minnesota, where there was a lack of airstrips but abundant flat water.

Floatplanes appeared as early as the 1920s in many places that now fall within the National Park System, especially Alaska units like Lake Clark, Katmai, and Gates of the Arctic, where they continue to perform vital passenger, cargo, and public safety duties. They are also a part of the landscape in lower 48 parks like North Cascades, Isle Royale, and Voyageurs.

The "muscle cars" of the floatplane world are the Canadian-made de Havilland planes—the DHC-2 Beaver and the DHC-3 Otter—single engine, pro-peller-driven aircraft with short takeoff and landing capability. With their powerful engines and deep roar, both aircraft seem more like wild beasts than something man-made.

The Beaver has been around since 1947, the Otter since 1951, and although manufacture of the original models stopped long ago, hundreds of the planes are still in service and much loved by their pilots.

☆ Grand Canyon ☆
NATIONAL PARK
Colorado River

The granddaddy of all float trips follows the roller-coaster Colorado River through the bottom of Arizona's big ditch. John Wesley Powell famously pioneered the route during a daredevil 1869 expedition to survey the length of the river. Powell and his men ran the Colorado in doubled-ribbed oak boats with water-tight compartments to prevent sinking; nowadays the float is undertaken in neoprene rafts, plastic kayaks, and throwback wooden dories that come the closest to replicating Powell's wild ride through the canyon. Between the main put-in at Lee's Ferry and the westernmost haul-out at Diamond Creek, the river throws up 42 rapids rated Class V or higher. That's an awful lot of white water. But floating the Grand Canyon is more than adrenalin. Side hikes lead to fern-covered gullies and Pueblo ruins. Wildlife along the river ranges from rattlesnakes to desert bighorn sheep. There are quiet places to swim or contemplate, and beach parties after dark. A number of outfitters offer guided float trips of anywhere from 1 to 18 days in length, including Wilderness River Adventures *(www.riveradventures.com),* Hatch River Expeditions *(www.hatchriverexpeditions.com),* and Grand Canyon Expeditions *(www.gcex.com).* Self-guided floats of the heart of the canyon are also allowed, but each group must have at least one member with river skills that match the demanding Park Service criteria. Permits for private trips are obtained via lottery.

☆ Lake Clark ☆
NATIONAL PARK & PRESERVE
Three National Wild Rivers

Three national wild rivers shoot through this vast Alaska park: the Tlikakila, the Chilikadrotna, and the Mulchatna. Each has a distinct personality, and all of them are ideal for float trips of up to a week in length. The Tlikakila is probably the roughest of the three, a glacier-fed waterway that rages with Class III and IV rapids. It flows entirely inside the park and tumbles into the east end of Lake Clark. With float trips that can range up to 230 miles, the Mulchatna is the longest, although most of the river meanders outside the national park. The Chilikadrotna lies somewhere between the two in location and mood, a swift and sometimes treacherous river that intersects with the Mulchatna in the upland forest west of Lake Clark. Floatplane is the only way to reach the headwaters of all three rivers. The season generally runs June to September, although the Tlikakila, at a slightly higher elevation, might not be runable until early July. Go Alaska Tours *(www.goalaskatours.com)* can organize guided or individual float trips on all three rivers.

★ St. Croix ★
NATIONAL SCENIC RIVERWAY
Namekagon River and the
Upper Reaches of the St. Croix River

The lower St. Croix between Wisconsin and Minnesota may be hard-core houseboat country, but the upper reaches of the river and its Namekagon tributary are more float-trip friendly, and near ideal for canoeists. It takes about six days to float the 100-odd miles of the Namekagon between the eponymous lake and Riverside Landing near its confluence with the St. Croix. There are numerous primitive campsites and put-in points, which means that floaters can easily chop the journey into shorter sections. The Namekagon is slender and serene, flanked by

> There are 84,271 miles of perennial rivers and streams in the National Park System—enough river and stream mileage to encircle the earth over 3 times.

thick northern Wisconsin woods and interrupted every so often by minor rapids and small dams that require a short portage. Similar characteristics prevail along the 100 miles of upper St. Croix between Gordon Dam and Taylors Falls (home of the St. Croix River Visitor Center), a trip that takes six or seven days. Wild River Outfitters *(www.wildriver paddling.com)* in Grantsburg, Wisconsin, is one of many outfitters that provides canoes and kayaks for float trips, as well as maps and shuttle service.

★ Wrangell–St. Elias ★
NATIONAL PARK & PRESERVE
Copper and Chitina Rivers

America's largest national park offers plenty of big rivers fed by glaciers and spring rain, and damless along their entire length, including the Copper and Chitina. The Copper forms the western boundary of the national park as it shoots through a mighty gap in the Chugach Range on its way to the Gulf of Alaska. Although it's a tributary of the Copper, the Chitina is just as mighty, a meandering river with many islands and channels that runs right through the heart of the giant park. Smaller rivers in the park like the Nabesna and White are also floatable. It's not unusual to go days along these rivers without seeing another boat or human being; however, waterfront wildlife is plentiful: grizzly and black bear, moose and elk, bald eagles and more game fish than you could catch in a lifetime. Copper Oar *(www.copperoar .com)* runs six-day guided floats along its namesake Copper River and a four-day trip that includes the Kennicott, Nizina, and Chitina Rivers between McCarthy and Chitina Ranger Station.

paddling the channel islands

Author Joe Yogerst's Santa Cruz Island kayaking sojourn

"They're kind of what California was like 150 years ago," says skipper Randy Davis as he guides us in his Island Packers ferry toward Channel Islands National Park. "Not a day goes by when we don't see something spectacular out here in terms of nature—sea lions, dolphins, different types of whales, and even the occasional sea otter. It makes you think about the fact that all of California used to be this way, a huge paradise for wildlife."

Often called the "Galápagos of North America" because of its profuse wildlife, the national park comprises five islands—Santa Barbara, Santa Rosa, San Miguel, Santa Cruz, and Anacapa—easily reached by boat from Santa Barbara or Ventura on the southern California mainland. The park is also a haven for water sports, from scuba diving and snorkeling the offshore canyons and kelp beds to board surfing, beachcombing, sailing, and sea kayaking.

Separated from the mainland by broad channels, the islands are the peaks of an uplifted volcanic mountain range that perches on the edge of the continental shelf. Although Anacapa and Santa Barbara have been federally protected

since 1938, it was only in 1980 that Channel Islands National Park and its companion national marine sanctuary came into being. Further protection has been added with the creation of 11 marine reserves where fishing and harvesting is prohibited.

The journey out and back is part of the adventure, a chance to see animals that one normally only sees in wildlife documentaries. The waters around the national

park attract about a third of the world's cetacean species—27 different types of whales, dolphins, and porpoises. More than 50,000 seals and other fin-footed mammals—one of the world's greatest concentrations of pinnipeds— gather in these islands to mate and raise their pups. And the kelp forests offshore are magnets for hundreds of fish species, including California's state fish, the bright orange garibaldi.

Soon the ferry pulls into Scorpion Bay on the leeward side of Santa Cruz, largest of the national park isles. Backpack, tent, and sleeping bag in tow, I trudge down the gangplank and onto a cobblestone beach at the bottom of a breezy coastal valley that contains both the campground where I intend to stay and trailheads to other parts of the island where I can swim, snorkel, or laze along a beach over the next three days.

My primary reason for venturing to Santa Cruz is kayaking, a chance to explore some of the richest waters and largest sea caves on the West Coast. Paddling is an ancient tradition in the archipelago, the means by which the indigenous Chumash and Gabrielino people got around the islands before the Spanish appeared. "The Indians moved freely and swiftly between the islands in plank wood canoes," ranger Gail Narkevic had told me at the park visitor center in Ventura. "They were active traders and expressive artisans and very resourceful at harvesting the bounty of the surrounding sea."

Nowadays, no one knows these waters better than Tony Chapman. His experience in the islands stretches back nearly five decades. Over those years he slowly but surely morphed from being a marine researcher for the University of California at Santa Barbara into a highly experienced paddle guide for Ventura-based Aquasport, the park's leading kayak outfitter.

"Wind and tide permitting, we're going to explore about half

a dozen caves," Chapman tells a group of eight eager paddlers as we launch our kayaks into the surf at Scorpion Bay. Our first goal is The Elephant, a sea cave chiseled into the base of a huge rock formation that resembles a pachyderm's trunk. Water surges in and out of the cavern, ferociously breaking on the rocky walls within. But Chapman doesn't bat an eye. He disappears into the dark chasm for a few breathless seconds and then pops out at the other end with an enthusiastic thumbs-up—indicating that it's safe for everyone to take a shot at The Elephant.

"You've gotta time it just right," Chapman yells over the sound of the crashing surf. "Run the cave between waves, when the water is at its lowest. Keep yourself off the rocks with the tips of your paddles. And no matter what happens, never ever leave your kayak!"

The task looks daunting if not downright frightening. But everyone makes it through. Then it's on to other water-filled apertures—Shipwreck Cave with its rusty metal wreck and Seal Cave with its resident pinnipeds—along a shoreline that boasts more than 300 sea caves and sea arches in total. I'm thoroughly exhausted by the time we pull our kayaks back up on the beach at Scorpion Bay.

After our paddle, Chapman tells me about some of his adventures in the Channel Islands. The most remarkable thing he's seen took place right here in Scorpion Bay. "A mama orca (killer whale) teaching its baby how to hunt harbor seals," says Chapman. "The mother kept breaching and falling on a poor seal. *Blam! Blam! Blam!* But junior could never get the hang of it and eventually the seal got away."

At the end of my Santa Cruz sojourn, on the ferry back to the mainland, I have my own close encounter of the whale kind. Three humpbacks. Two females and a youngster, cruising along the surface, their backs glistening in the California sun, unfazed by the sudden appearance of a boat full of pointing, shouting, camera-clicking humans. For a good 15 minutes we trail in their wake before the whales literally turn tail and dive. A magic moment in a magical place.

white-water thrill rides

Rivers that run wild and fast

Rapids, whirlpools, and risky currents transform some national park rivers into raging infernos and white water. Rafts and kayaks are the best ways to experience the big thrills and spills. Most of these routes can be run in a half or single day, although some are a ripe two days of adventure with a much needed breather in between.

☀ Black Canyon of the Gunnison ☀
NATIONAL PARK
Gunnison River

The only thing you need to know about rafting or kayaking the Gunnison River through the notorious Black Canyon is the fact that no commercial operator makes the trip. That tells you how extreme this river is, one of the most dangerous in North America and one of the most rewarding for skilled river runners. This is Class V water all the way, with some sections that even the best kayakers cannot negotiate safely. Attaching a parachute to your kayak is not as farfetched as it may sound. The Colorado River through the Grand Canyon falls an average of 7.5 feet per mile; by comparison, the Gunnison River through the Black Canyon plummets 95 feet per mile. That's big air. But that doesn't mean that mere mortals can't experience one of Colorado's foremost natural wonders. The spectacular Gunnison Gorge downstream from the park is tamer but still wild enough to get your knuckles white and your heart thumping. Preserving the gorge's

solitude, only two rafting groups (of no more than 12 people per group) each day are allowed to make the journey. Boulder Outdoor Center *(http://boc123.com)* and Dvorak Expeditions *(www.dvorakexpeditions.com)* offer guided trips between May and September.

☀ Denali ☀
NATIONAL PARK & PRESERVE
Nenana River Canyon

Born of snow, sleet, and glaciers in the mighty Alaska Range, the Nenana River runs a swift course down the east side of Denali National Park before pouring into the Tanana River near Fairbanks. It's a wild one, especially through the narrow Nenana River Canyon near the park visitor center, a stretch that features wicked Class III and IV rapids like the Coffee Grinder, Royal Flush, and Razorback. The dozen miles of river between the visitor center and the put-out point near the town of Healey takes around two hours. And don't try it without a dry suit; even on the hottest summer days, Nenana's waters are just above freezing. Denali Outdoor Center *(www.denalioutdoorcenter.com)* runs white-water trips through the canyon and along milder stretches of the Nenana.

✫ Glacier ✫
NATIONAL PARK

North and Middle Forks
of the Flathead River

The long and twisty Flathead River forms the western boundary of Montana's Glacier National Park, separating the national park from national forest on the opposite shore. The entire length of the watercourse alongside Glacier has been designated a national wild and scenic river. The North Fork of the Flathead takes three or four days to run. But parts of the Middle Fork between Walton and West Glacier can be rafted in a single day. The portion through narrow John Stevens Canyon features challenging Class III and IV rapids, especially hairy during the early summer when water flow on the Flathead peaks. But there's also plenty of time to eye the scenery—snowcapped peaks rising on either side, thick forest along the shoreline, and maybe even a glimpse of bear, moose, or wolves. The Middle Fork also has Hollywood cachet: Parts of the 1994 movie *The River Wild* with Meryl Streep and Kevin Bacon were shot on location here. The locally based Glacier Raft Company *(www.glacierraftco.com)* offers single and multiday trips on both forks of the Flathead in

Rafters come face to wave with the Bone Crusher Rapids of Montana's Middle Fork of the Flathead River.

rafts and inflatable kayaks. GRC also rents equipment and provides shuttle service for those who wish to run the river themselves.

✵ Dinosaur ✵
NATIONAL MONUMENT
Yampa and Green Rivers

River rats know there's more to Dinosaur than old bones. This national monument straddling the Colorado–Utah border also boasts some of the best white water in the West. The park's rivers churn up nasty rapids and whirlpools. The Yampa and the Gates of Lodore on the Green are best done as multiday white-water trips with experienced guides. But a less intense stretch of the Green River through Split Mountain Canyon can be run in a single day. Class III rapids give the Green enough oomph for a mild adrenalin rush, but not enough to preclude kids as young as seven from testing their mettle on the river. The upstream access point is Rainbow

Park, not far from the McKee Springs Petroglyphs. Downstream you can exit at several points along Cub Creek Road. Several local outfitters run Split Mountain trips, including Adrift Adventures *(www .whitewater.net)* and Don Hatch River Expeditions *(www.donhatchrivertrips.com)*. The season runs May to September.

✵ Grand Teton ✵
NATIONAL PARK
Snake River

Only a small portion of the 1,000-mile Snake River flows through the Tetons, but it's about as gorgeous as a river can get, ribbons of water set against jagged, snow-covered summits. But that handsome face hides a mean temper, a Wyoming river that should never be taken for granted. Advanced white-water skills are necessary for several sections of the Snake, in particular a stretch of white water in the Rockefeller Parkway between Southgate and Flagg Ranch. Despite a lack of rapids and whirlpools, the river south from Deadman's Bar can also get pretty nasty, thanks to tricky currents and logjams. Snake River Canyon south of Jackson Hole tenders a much longer stretch of white water. At least half a dozen outfitters in Jackson Hole offer half- and one-day trips along the Snake.

✵ Harpers Ferry ✵
NATIONAL HISTORICAL PARK
Shenandoah and Potomac Rivers

Harpers Ferry might be an icon of American history, but the park at the confluence of the Potomac and Shenandoah Rivers is also a hub for rafting, kayaking, and tubing. As they tumble down from the Appalachians, both rivers churn up considerable white water upstream from Harpers Ferry. Renowned rapids include the White Horse on the

---

☆ Gauley Fest ☆

America's premier white-water festival is the annual Gauley Fest, which takes place over the third weekend in September in Summersville, West Virginia. In addition to rafting and kayaking the nearby **Gauley River National Recreation Area** and **New River Gorge National River,** the event includes live Appalachian-flavored music, a white-water gear and equipment market, and close encounters with the nation's top river runners. The fest kicked off in 1983 as a way for paddlers and environmentalists to celebrate their successful battle against a hydroelectric scheme that would have severely impacted white water on the Gauley. Low-cost camping is available on the festival grounds during the entire four-day event.

Potomac and the mile-long Staircase on the Shenandoah. No matter which river is run, the trip eventually flows through the middle of the national historical park and the famous water gap at Harpers Ferry. Formed 360 million years ago when the Potomac cut through the Blue Ridge, the dramatic breach is one of the natural wonders of the mid-Atlantic region, a spot where three states (Maryland, Virginia, and West Virginia) collide in a mosaic of water, stone, and forest. Thomas Jefferson called it "one of the most stupendous scenes in Nature . . . This scene is worth a voyage across the Atlantic." Local companies that offer guided trips on both rivers, as well as equipment rentals, include River & Trail Outfitters (*www.rivertrail.com*), BTI Whitewater (*www.bti whitewater.com*), and River Riders (*www.riverriders .com*). Trips are offered March through November, although river runners in spring and fall should probably invest in a good wet or dry suit.

> *The National Park Service is responsible for 38 rivers under the Wild and Scenic Rivers Act flowing more than 2,800 miles throughout the United States. (2009)*

☆ Olympic ☆
NATIONAL PARK
Elwha, Hoh, and Sol Duc Rivers

Rivers radiate from Washington State's Mount Olympus likes spokes on a wheel, and at least two of them afford trips that combine white-water adventure and the park's Pacific Northwest woods. The most popular trip is the Elwha River through the heart of the park, a waterway that combines gentle stretches and mild rapids, good for families or for people who would rather watch the scenery than constantly battle for survival. The secluded Hoh River is another possibility, a voyage through Oxbow Canyon and the lush rain forest that carpets the park's western fringe. Olympic's best white water is the Sol Duc River, where the Class III rapids can get a little daunting as it passes out of the park and into Olympic National Forest. But there's only enough water in the Sol Duc during the winter months, which means rafting and kayaking is limited to November through March. And the water is most definitely cold. The only water outfitter licensed to operate inside the national park, Olympic Raft and Kayak (*www.raftand kayak.com*) runs trips on all three rivers.

☆ Sequoia ☆
NATIONAL PARK
Kaweah River

California's southern Sierra park has lots of rivers, but few of them deep or wide enough for boating. The exception to that rule is the Kaweah River, a short but turbulent waterway that starts as several forks inside the park before coming together in a single channel. The Middle Fork is navigable starting just outside the park, 2 miles down the road from Ash Mountain entrance gate. The scenery is more California foothills than High Sierra, golden hillsides speckled with oaks and wildflowers. The season is early, April through June, and highly dependent on Sierra snowmelt. All-Outdoors Rafting (*www.aorafting.com*) organizes one- and two-day guided trips on the Kaweah.

The turbulent Gauley River provides rafters with autumnal white-water thrills and chills.

✴ Gauley River ✴
NATIONAL RECREATION AREA
Gauley River

The turbulent Gauley charging through the mountains of West Virginia is the wicked river of the East. The numbers tell a tale of lurking danger: a drop of 668 vertical feet in 28 miles; a watercourse strewn with more than a hundred rapids, some of them gnarly Class V raft-eaters. That translates into fast, steep, rocky, and wild, a river that demands constant attention and a high degree of technical skill. Rapids like Shipwreck, Suckers Go Right, and Pure Screaming Hell earn their names from reputation rather than whim. The upper Gauley is often ranked as one of the world's top ten white-water runs. But the river does have a kinder, gentler side: The lower Gauley is less rigorous and open to rafters as young as 12 years of age. Needless to say, it's best to run this river with experienced local outfitters like Songer Whitewater in Hico *(www.songerwhitewater.com)*, which offers both overnight and one-day trips along both the upper and lower sections. Unlike the rest of the white-water world, summer is not the season for rafting. The Gauley is only open over six weekends in September and October, when water is released from upstream Summersville reservoir.

✴ Big South Fork ✴
NATIONAL RIVER & RECREATION AREA
Big South Fork of the Cumberland River

Paddlers can hear the banjos dueling in their heads as they set off along the water of this backcountry park, a slice of the South that seems little changed since the days when this neck of the Kentucky and Tennessee woods was the stomping ground of frontiersmen like Daniel Boone. The Big South Fork of the Cumberland River and at least three of its tributaries beckon white-water paddlers to a world of thick woods, abundant wildlife, and the occasional Class IV rapid. River conditions vary greatly, with some streams as quiet as a field mouse while others roar like the black bears that still live in these hills. Some waterways are best in summer, others only runable after winter and spring rains. The toughest run is the 11 miles of the Big South Fork between Burnt Mill Bridge and Leatherwood Ford, where serious rapids are flanked by soaring sandstone cliffs. The section from Leatherwood down to Blue Heron Mine is also risky business, in particular Angel Falls and Devil's Jump. Sheltowee Trace Outfitters *(www.ky-rafting.com)* organizes guided raft and unguided canoe trips in the park.

flat-water trips

Canoeing and kayaking into nature, history, and solitude

The nation's oldest boating tradition is the canoe, a craft used by both Native Americans and early Europeans as a means of transport, trade, and exploration. National parks preserve that heritage with canoe and kayak routes little changed from the days when the boats were made from birch bark rather than aluminum or plastic.

⁂ Big Thicket ⁂
NATIONAL PRESERVE
Neches River and Village Creek

The name alone is enough to conjure images of paddling through primeval woodland or swamp. And that's exactly what Big Thicket is: six water corridors and nine land units protecting more than 105,000 acres of east Texas wilderness encompassing several ecological zones, among them longleaf pine forest, southern swamp, and midwestern prairie. The park has enough size and scope to accommodate paddles from a couple of hours to a couple of days. The waterways are mostly slow flowing, with plenty of campsites and sandbars, and shorelines rich with indigenous flora and fauna. The Neches River on the park's eastern fringe presents the longest, wildest path for kayaks and canoes, winding through tall bluffs and dense vegetation. Paddlers can explore numerous lakes and bayous off the river, or keep following the Neches south of the park all the way to the Gulf of Mexico. The park's other great paddle route is Village Creek between the Big Ticket Visitor Center and its confluence with the Neches near Lumberton. Eastex Canoe Trails (*www.eastexcanoes.com*) and Piney Woods Canoe Outfitters (*www.canoetexas.com*) rent canoes to those who want to explore the Big Thicket on their own, and offer guided canoe trips of various lengths on both the Neches and Village Creek.

⁂ Chattahoochee River ⁂
NATIONAL RECREATION AREA
Chattahoochee River

Country superstar Alan Jackson immortalized this waterway with his 1993 hit "Way Down Yonder on the Chattahoochee." But the river's repute stretches back to antebellum days, when local poets were writing odes to the fluid corridor. The northern Georgia park includes 48 miles of the Chattahoochee between Lake Sidney Lanier (named after one of those bygone poets) to Paces Mill on the outskirts of Atlanta. Conditions range from absolutely dead flat to Class I and II rapids depending on how much water is released on any given day from Buford Dam. Depending on your speed, it can take anywhere from 17 to 26 hours to paddle the entire length of the river inside the park. Given the fact there are no campgrounds and the park is not open overnight, the paddle will certainly have to stretch over several days. Morgan Falls Dam presents a formidable barrier 35 miles downstream from Lake Lanier, making it impossible to continue southward without portage between Chattahoochee River Park and Morgan Falls Park. Canoes and kayaks can be rented from several vendors in the area including Up the River Outfitters *(www.uptheriver outfitters.com),* Chattahoochee Outfitters *(www .shootthehooch.com),* and RiverEcoLogic *(www.river ecologic.com).*

✶ Voyageurs ✶
NATIONAL PARK
Labyrinth of Lakes,
Rivers, Channels, and Ponds

Named after the French trappers and traders who roamed the North American interior in the late 17th and 18th centuries, Voyageurs is still the crème de la crème of backwoods canoeing and kayaking. This watery wilderness in northern Minnesota boasts more than 500 islands scattered across a vast labyrinth of lakes, rivers, channels, and ponds. The international boundary between the United States and Canada closely follows the classic voyageur route along the park's northern fringe, but there are hundreds of other paddling paths that take anywhere

A canoeing haven, Voyageurs' myriad interconnected lakes are dotted with isles perfect for solitary camping.

from a few hours to more than a week. Further adding to the park's canoe/kayak cachet is the fact that boat is the only way to reach the 200-plus campsites. Numerous outfitters along the park's southern border rent boats and camping equipment; check with the park for a list of authorized companies. Visitors without their own boats can join short ranger-led paddles that depart from the park's visitor centers during the summer months, including a voyage back in time on a 26-foot North Canoe and basic introduction to paddling called Explore by Canoe.

☆ Congaree ☆
NATIONAL PARK
Congaree River and Cedar Creek

Make like a "swamp fox" and paddle the Congaree River region of South Carolina. It was amid these watery woods that Continental Army general Francis Marion (nicknamed the "Swamp Fox") hid from the Redcoats during the American Revolution. The riparian scenery hasn't changed much in the years since. Nowadays, Congaree is the nation's largest remaining old-growth floodplain forest and home to some of the tallest, biggest trees in the eastern United States. The wide Congaree River runs roughly 25 miles along the park's southern boundary. But the most popular paddling ground is the Cedar Creek Canoe Trail through a gauntlet of huge cypress trees. Rangers lead guided paddles along Cedar Creek on weekends. Otherwise, visitors must provide their own boats. The canoe trail runs 7 miles between Bannister's Bridge and Cedar Creek Landing and is easily paddled in four to six hours. More ambitious paddlers can pick up a backcountry camping permit at the visitor center and venture all the way down Cedar Creek to the Congaree River and a put-out point at the U.S. 601 bridge, a distance of around 20 miles.

☆ Epic Canoe Voyages ☆

The bygone voyageurs may have pioneered the North American interior with birchbark canoes, but they weren't the greatest paddlers of all time. Most of the records are fairly recent.

In April 1936, Geoffrey Pope and Sheldon Taylor launched a canoe at the foot of 42nd Street in Manhattan and headed up the Hudson River. Sixteen months later they arrived in Nome, Alaska, after paddling thousands of miles through the Great Lakes region and western Canada.

Verlen Kruger and Steve Landick topped that in 1980–83, when they paddled 28,000 miles around North America, including the eastern seaboard, the Pacific Coast, the Arctic Ocean, and Alaska, as well as the Missouri, Mississippi, and Colorado Rivers and the Great Lakes.

More recently, British lads Chris Maguire and Neil Armstrong paddled from Canada to the Amazon Basin in 1993–96, a 13,000-mile odyssey that took them all the way down the Mississippi River and along the Texas coast.

☆ Delaware Water Gap ☆
NATIONAL RECREATION AREA
Delaware River between
Milford Beach and Kittatinny Point

New Jersey's other "shore" is the Delaware River, which divides the Garden State from Pennsylvania. The lower reaches of the river around Philadelphia might be highly urbanized, but the upstream portions are surprisingly pristine, especially the 40 miles of calm water that compose Delaware Water Gap National Recreation Area. Canoe camping is one of the more popular ways to explore the park, with three days about average for paddling the full length of the river between Milford Beach and Kittatinny

Point. The route meanders through farmland and forests, past towering palisades and tumbling waterfalls, a landscape little changed from colonial times. Boat-only campsites are spread along the river's length, some on islands and others on the main bank. They are first come, first served; no reservations or fees are required.

☆ Missouri ☆
NATIONAL RECREATIONAL RIVER
Missouri River

The Big Muddy may look slow and placid as it flows through South Dakota and Nebraska, but America's longest river is one of its most challenging. Among its dangers and annoyances are submerged sandbars, waterlogged trees, floating debris, swirling eddies, and tricky currents. Careful preparation and caution is imperative. The park is divided into two units on either side of Lewis and Clark Lake. The 39-mile upstream portion threads its way through the Karl Mundt National Wildlife Refuge and Yankton Sioux Indian Reservation before tumbling into the lake. The 59-mile downstream section runs through ranch and farm country between Gavins Point Dam on the Nebraska–South Dakota border and Ponca State Park, Nebraska. There are numerous put-in places along the length of the park, but only a few campgrounds because so much of the shoreline is private property. Primitive camping is allowed on many islands and sandbars. Missouri River Expeditions *(www.missriverexp.com)* in Sioux Falls, South Dakota, offers fully guided kayak expeditions in both portions of the park.

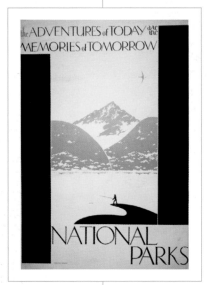

☆ Mammoth Cave ☆
NATIONAL PARK
Green and Nolin Rivers

It's not just about the cave at this central Kentucky park. There is plenty to do *above* ground, like paddling the park's slow-flowing Green and Nolin Rivers through floodplain forest replete with beach, maple, and sycamore trees, as well as deer, raccoon, bobcat, and many other species. Both streams can flow quickly at times, but with an average speed of 5 miles an hour or less, absolutely no white water, shallow depth, and lots of places to beach, both watercourses are ideal for family or novice canoeing and kayaking. There are three places to launch boats along the Green River. The longest paddle inside the park is the 20-mile stretch between Dennison Ferry and Houchins Ferry, although it is possible to undertake a 42-mile downstream journey by launching from Munfordville to the east of the park. Houchins boasts the park's only riverside campground. The best place to put in on the Nolin River is at the U.S. Army Corps of Engineers–managed Tailwaters Recreation Area just below Nolin River Dam, just outside the northwest corner of Mammoth Cave National Park.

☆ Mississippi ☆
NATIONAL RIVER & RECREATION AREA
Mississippi River

Spread along 72 miles of the Mississippi River on either side of Minneapolis–St. Paul, this eclectic park protects the upper reaches of America's most celebrated waterway. The Park Service manages the riparian trail in partnership with numerous local entities including counties, towns, nonprofits, and private landowners. The 40 miles of river upstream from Minneapolis is too shallow for large craft, but perfect for canoes and kayaks, an interesting blend of rural and urban landscapes that includes more than a dozen bald eagle nests. Numerous public boat ramps provide access to the river for those who have their own boats. Those who wish to paddle the entire length of the park must navigate through four locks. Clear Waters Outfitting *(www.clear watersoutfittingco.com)* can set you up with canoes, kayaks, and other equipment to undertake a Mississippi River paddle between St. Cloud and Minneapolis–St. Paul.

along the river. The usual boating season runs mid-April to mid-October. Outfitters in the nearby towns of Valentine and Sparks rent canoes and camping equipment, including Dryland Aquatics *(www .drylandaquatics.com)*, Little Outlaw *(www.outlawcanoe .com)*, and Brewers *(www.brewerscanoers.com)*.

☆ Niobrara ☆
NATIONAL SCENIC RIVER
Niobrara River

A watery wedge between Nebraska's Sand Hills and the wide-open prairie, the Niobrara River offers an environment little changed from the days when the Pawnee, Lakota, and bison were masters of the surrounding plains. The park protects a 76-mile stretch of the river as it slices through the Great Plains. While the river's lower stretches (below Meadville) are wide and calm, the upper reaches generate numerous rapids, including the Norden Chute (Class IV) and Rocky Ford (Class III). This western section is bounded by sandstone cliffs riddled with fossil beds and more than 200 waterfalls, including 63-foot Smith Falls, the highest in Nebraska. Paddlers can overnight at any of ten campgrounds

☆ Ozark ☆
NATIONAL SCENIC RIVERWAYS
Current and Jacks Fork Rivers

Dedicated in 1971, Ozark was the first U.S. national park dedicated to protect a wild river system. The plural in the name derives from the fact that the park embraces two major waterways: 105 miles of the Current River and 41 miles of the tributary Jacks Fork in southern Missouri. Float trips are popular on both waterways, especially during the sultry summer months. The lush scenery is enough of a draw on its own, a mosaic of maples, cottonwoods, sycamores, and willows that provides habitat for hundreds of bird, reptile, and mammal species. But the park also contains more than 300 caves and sinkholes, the world's largest assemblage of first-magnitude springs, and historic waterfront buildings like the 1894 Alley Mill. Paddlers can put in at two dozen spots, most of them equipped with campsites and picnic areas. Canoe liveries can be found at Van Buren, Salem, Eminence, and Akers Ferry.

ten best parks
houseboating trips
Home away from home on the water

Cruising into the wild blue yonder on a houseboat is one of the more relaxing ways to explore many of the units in the National Park System. Some parks offer boat ramps and marina facilities for those who have their own houseboats; others offer rentals by the hour, day, week, or month.

✳ Glen Canyon ✳
NATIONAL RECREATION AREA
Lake Powell

Although the recreation area is named after its iconic dam, Lake Powell is the raison d'être for a visually stunning park that blends orange rock, golden cliffs, sapphire sky, and turquoise water. Stretching nearly 200 miles across northern Arizona and southern Utah, the lake whisks house-boaters into the heart of the American Southwest, a landscape of sheer sandstone walls, slot canyons, and hanging desert gardens that has served as the backdrop for dozens of movies. Although Lake Mead holds more water, deeply indented Lake Powell has almost four times as much shoreline— around 2,000 miles total, or more than the entire U.S. West Coast. Houseboats can sojourn in 96 major canyons and hundreds of isolated beaches. Boating is the only way to reach park landmarks like Rainbow Bridge National Monument, Cathedral in the Desert, Defiance House pueblo, and Tapestry Wall. Private boats can be launched at four marinas

scattered around the lakeshore. Houseboats can be rented at Antelope Point (*www.antelopepointrentals.com*) and Wahweap (*www.lakepowell.com*) at the southern end of the park near Page, Arizona, as well as at Bullfrog Marina (*www.lakepowell.com*) in southern Utah.

✳ Lake Mead ✳
NATIONAL RECREATION AREA
Jimbilnan Wilderness and Gypsum Reefs

The biggest thrill of piloting a houseboat on Lake Mead is a chance to cruise into the flooded far western end of the Grand Canyon, lying on your back on the vessel's roof, staring up at the incredible red-rock walls with nothing but the sound of the wind in your ears. With 550 miles of shoreline, Lake Mead is the nation's largest reservoir. Areas close to Las Vegas are rife with watercraft, especially on holidays and summer weekends. But houseboats give the option of getting far away from the motorized crowds, to less visited shores like the Jimbilnan Wilderness, Gypsum Reefs, and the drop-dead-gorgeous Temple

Basin. Houseboats are available for rent in the marinas at Callville Bay *(www.callvillebay.com)* and Temple Bar *(www.templebarlakemead.com)* on Lake Mead. Houseboating is also popular on Lake Mohave in the park's southern extension, with rentals at Cottonwood Cove *(www.cottonwoodcoveresort.com)* and Katherine Landing *(www.sevencrown.com)*.

⭑ Lake Meredith ⭑
NATIONAL RECREATION AREA
Canadian River's Lake Meredith

Even by Texas standards, Lake Meredith is secluded, tucked up on the high plains north of Amarillo in an area once afflicted by the Dust Bowl. Nowadays it's a water-sports paradise. Formed in the 1960s by the construction of Sanford Dam across the Canadian River, Lake Meredith is open year-round for houseboating and other aquatic activities, but it is especially inviting during the Texas Panhandle's triple-digit summers, when the cool water offers respite from the sweltering heat. The concession marina at Sanford-Yake has a ramp for getting houseboats easily into and out of the water, and rents slips by the month for those who want to stay longer. There's another public boat ramp at Fritch Fortress. All watercraft must obtain a boating permit from the park visitor center, marina, or local bait shops before entering the lake. Houseboats are allowed to anchor overnight (at no charge) anywhere they like on Meredith.

With its many nooks and crannies and sheer canyon walls, Lake Powell in Glen Canyon is a great houseboating lake.

☆ Lake Roosevelt ☆
NATIONAL RECREATION AREA
Crescent Bay or China Bend

One of the landmark public works projects of FDR's Presidency, Grand Coulee Dam created a massive reservoir named after the man who made it all possible. Lake Roosevelt, which stretches more than 150 miles along the Columbia River in eastern Washington, is one of the most popular houseboating venues in the Pacific Northwest. The lake's manifold attractions include wildlife (moose, bear, deer), copious fishing (30 different types of fish), and a dramatic change of scenery from the arid grasslands around the dam to the forested slopes upstream. Skippers can launch their craft from 22 public boat ramps, from Crescent Bay right behind the dam to China Bend near Northport. Houseboats are free to overnight anywhere on the lake or anchor at boat-in campsites like Barnaby Island or Sterling Point. Park Service boat launch permits are required for all vessels going into the water. Kettle Falls Marina (www.lakeroosevelt.com) and Seven Bays Marina (www.dakotacolumbia.com) both rent houseboats for periods of three to seven days; the season runs mid-spring to mid-autumn.

☆ Cape Lookout ☆
NATIONAL SEASHORE
Core Sound, Back Sound, and Barden Inlet

Boats are the only way to reach this park unit off North Carolina's coast, and houseboats are one of the more relaxing ways to explore the national seashore's more remote areas. Core Sound, Back Sound, and Barden Inlet on the inside of the barrier islands offer ideal houseboating terrain: calm water, superb scenery, secluded coves, and myriad small islands. Given the often shallow water, NOAA navigation charts are highly recommended, especially for skippers not familiar with the area. Houseboats can anchor overnight just about anywhere in the park, but they are subject to the same regulations as land campers including a limit of 14 consecutive days inside the park. Two of the more popular places for houseboat "camping" are Cape Lookout Bight and the inside of Shackleford Banks between Wades Shore and Whale Creek.

☆ Amistad ☆
NATIONAL RECREATION AREA
Indian Springs and Box Canyon

Flit back and forth across the international border on Lake Amistad in southern Texas. Formed by the massive Amistad (Friendship) Dam on the Rio Grande, the lake offers warm water and clear skies throughout the year, although winters can get a little breezy. Houseboats provide a perfect platform for fishing (for three different kinds of

---

☆ "Rolls Royce" Houseboats ☆

Long gone are the days when houseboats came with little more than steel-frame bunks, a claustrophobic galley, and a pit toilet. Today's luxury models literally have all the comforts of home: central heating and air-conditioning, wet bars and gas fireplaces, waterslides and Jacuzzi tubs, satellite TV, compact disc players, and surround-sound music systems. Master bedrooms with queen beds, vanity tables, mirrors, and lots of storage space. Kitchens outfitted with dishwashers, microwaves, and trash compactor. Bridges equipped with GPS units, depth finders, and back-up cameras. Brand-new vessels with these amenities cost upward of $400,000. But that isn't even close to the most expensive houseboat of all time: a $1.5-million designer craft moored along the Thames River in England.

bass), swimming, and even scuba diving this rugged desert lake. In addition, boating is the only means to reach some of the park's more secluded attractions like Indian Springs, Box Canyon, and the waterfront Panther and Parida caves archaeological sites with their ancient rock art. While the national recreation area hugs the U.S. shore, houseboaters are also free to explore Mexican landmarks like Cañon del Zorro on the southern side of the Rio Grande Valley. U.S. houseboats can anchor and overnight on the Mexican side. However, U.S. boaters are not allowed to beach their boat or otherwise land on the Mexican shore, and anyone who angles south-of-the-border requires a Mexican fishing permit. Visitors without their own houseboat can rent one at Lake Amistad Resort and Marina in Diablo East *(www.lakeumistad resort.com)*, but know that rental boats are not allowed in Mexican waters and come with restrictions on how far you can navigate up the Rio Grande.

> *One of the [CCC] wildlife camps occasioned national interest. This was the "Arkansas floating camp," whose enrollees lived on a fleet of houseboats while developing waterfowl refuges in streams, swamps, and bayous. They were given "shore leave" on weekends. (1934)*

✵ St. Croix ✵
NATIONAL SCENIC RIVERWAY
Namekagon River

This elongated park runs all the way from Chequamegon–Nicolet National Forest in northern Wisconsin to the Mississippi River near St. Paul, Minnesota, a watery path through wilderness and bucolic countryside that is often ideal for houseboats. Although the St. Croix River (dividing Minnesota and Wisconsin) lies at the heart of the park, a good deal of the Namekagon River also falls within its boundaries. Patches of shallow water and the zebra mussel access control point near Somerset make it impossible to navigate the entire length of the park in a single trip. The best sections for houseboating are the 28.5-mile stretch between Somerset and the St. Croix's confluence with the Mississippi, and the 10-mile stretch between Taylors Falls and Nevers Dam. There are numerous public boat ramps along the length of the riverway. Beanie's *(www.boatingatbeanies.com)* at Maui's Landing in Lakeland, Minnesota, rents houseboats for use on the lower St. Croix and nearby Mississippi.

✵ Voyageurs ✵
NATIONAL PARK
Voyageurs' Waterways

Northern Minnesota's watery wilderness may have earned its repute on birchbark canoes, but this watery expanse along the U.S.–Canada border is pretty near perfect for houseboats too. Comprising four large lakes linked by narrow portage channels, this North Woods park offers countless places to float off the beaten track. The water might be a little chilly for swimming (even at the height of summer), but houseboaters can while away the days plenty of other ways: berry picking and bird-watching, fishing and stargazing, photographing the great northern forest or popping into the historic Kettle Falls Hotel for a game of pool and a cold brew. There are dozens of designated overnight mooring sites throughout the park, in secluded coves, at small remote islands, and more. Skippers with their own craft can slide their houseboats into the water at public ramps near the park's three visitor centers. Among the outfitters that rent fully equipped vessels is Ebel's Voyageur Houseboats *(www.ebels.com)* in Ash River.

☀ Whiskeytown ☀
NATIONAL RECREATION AREA
Lake Shasta

Four lakes compose this far-flung three-unit national recreation area in northern California, sitting at the ecological crossroads of the Sacramento Valley and the Cascade, Coast, and Klamath mountains. This recreation area is one of the few jointly managed by the National Park Service and the U.S. Forest Service; the interagency marriage has lasted since 1963, when President John F. Kennedy dedicated the park. The Whiskeytown Unit, containing its eponymous reservoir, is the only one exclusively managed by the Park Service. Small houseboats (maximum length 35 feet) are allowed on the lake and can be slipped into the water at three public boat ramps. Houseboats (and other vessels) cannot be moored overnight on Whiskeytown, which means you will have to dock from dusk till dawn at Oak Bottom Marina *(www.whiskeytownmarinas .com)*. Lake Shasta is the recreation area's houseboating hub, a massive body of water larger than San Francisco Bay. Most of the 370 miles of shoreline is pristine national forest set against a backdrop of frequently snowcapped Mount Shasta. Seven public boat ramps and ten marinas provide access to the lake for houseboats and other vessels. A number of outfitters rent houseboats, including Shasta Marina Resort *(www.shastalake.net)*.

☀ Timucuan ☀
ECOLOGICAL & HISTORIC PRESERVE
Sisters Creek, Nassau River,
St. Johns River and Waterways

A labyrinth of subtropical waterways, wetlands, and woodland in northeastern Florida, Timucuan explores human interaction with nature over a 500-year span. It's also one of the few national parks astride the Intracoastal Waterway, an excellent venue for all sorts of boating, including the house variety. Sisters Creek Marina in the heart of the park is the best place to put your boat in, but it's also possible to cruise down from Amelia Island or up from St. Augustine. Some of Timucuan's more secluded waterways are too shallow or narrow for houseboats, but there's still plenty of liquid to float along, including Sisters Creek, the Nassau River, and the broad St. Johns River. The park's major historical landmarks are both served by public docks: 16th-century Fort Caroline and the 18th-century Kingsley Plantation. Houseboats (and other vessels) are not allowed to anchor overnight in plantation-house waters.

Bearded cypress trees and cabbage palms tower above a houseboat on Florida's coastal waterways.

ten best parks
swimming holes
Soothing waters and chilly dips

As the words of 19th-century naturalist John Muir so often remind us, national parks are also places to cleanse our bodies, minds, and souls. This is especially true of the springs, natural pools, and swimming holes found at many parks. The waters—some hot, some cold—refresh and reinvigorate under the guise of recreation.

☆ Big Bend ☆
NATIONAL PARK
Hot Springs Historic District

Down beside the Rio Grande, the Hot Springs Historic District of Big Bend preserves the remnants of an early 20th-century bathhouse that drew health seekers to this remote corner of Texas. J. O. Langford homesteaded the riverside patch in 1909 with visions of transforming the area into a Western version of Hot Springs, Arkansas. Dubbing it the "Fountain of Youth that Ponce de Leon Failed to Find," Langford charged ten cents a day or $2 for a three-week treatment in waters that could allegedly cure anything that ailed you. The resort endured until the 1930s, when a series of floods destroyed the bathhouse. Modern-day bathers will find that it's a 2-mile drive down a gravel road and then a half-mile hike from the parking area to the stone ruins and a 105°F pool on the river's north bank. It's not a huge pool, but the views are sublime looking across the Rio Grande to the rugged mountains of Mexico, and the water soothing after a day of hiking in the park.

☆ Chickasaw ☆
NATIONAL RECREATION AREA
Freshwater Springs, Pools, Creeks, and Lakes

Swimming holes are what Chickasaw is all about, a cluster of freshwater springs, pools, creeks, and lakes in south-central Oklahoma. The water gushes up from the 500-square-mile Arbuckle-Simpson Aquifer that underlies the region, rising through porous limestone and dolomite to reach the surface. One of the oldest national parks, the spread was originally called Sulphur Springs Reservation, created in 1902 to protect the plentiful mineral springs along Travertine Creek near the town of Sulphur. Within a couple of years it had been renamed Platt National Park, a moniker that lives on in the park's Platt Historic District, where most of the best swimming holes are located. The most popular of these is Little Niagara, but it is also the most crowded. To find more secluded spots follow Travertine Creek farther east of Niagara. As part of the park's interpretive program, rangers lead creek

In Haleakala National Park, the freshwater Seven Sacred Pools step down to the Pacific Ocean.

hundred different shades of green. Oheo Gulch tumbles down from the highlands, a volcanic-rock ravine that channels its stream into the Seven Sacred Pools. Trails lead down from the Kipahulu Visitor Center to a string of freshwater ponds divided by stone ledges and short waterfalls. The lowest is just yards away from the raging Pacific. A number of creatures inhabit the pools, including tiny shrimp and rock-climbing goby fish. The 2-mile Pipiwai Trail leads up the gulch to 400-foot-high Waimoku Falls. The Seven Sacred Pools are prone to flash floods; injuries and deaths have occurred here. So it's wise to keep an eye on the weather and streambed conditions at all times. Rugged terrain makes the Kipahulu area inaccessible from the rest of the national park. The only way to reach the coast is driving around the east end of Maui (via the tough, curvy Hana) or south around the park on the rough (but gorgeous) unpaved road that goes through Kaupo.

☆ Gila Cliff Dwellings ☆
NATIONAL MONUMENT
Lightfeather and Jordan Hot Springs

The Gila River flows through desert along most of its length, but its headwaters are high in the mountains of western New Mexico, the flow stoked by snowmelt and natural springs. Several remote thermal areas are found around the ancient Gila Cliff Dwellings. Lightfeather Hot Springs lies only 20 minutes by foot from the visitor center, but the journey entails two crossings of the Middle Fork of the Gila River. The spring exits the ground at a scalding 130°F, but then mixes with cooler river water in rock-lined pools to create comfy lukewarm baths. Jordan Hot Springs in the Gila Wilderness is much more remote, but the water temperature is a very comfortable 94°F in a pool that reaches

and spring hikes, explaining Chickasaw's watery wonders. Chickasaw's 1930s Civilian Conservation Corps architecture is another draw. There are plenty of campgrounds for those who want to stretch their swimming over multiple days.

☆ Haleakala ☆
NATIONAL PARK
Seven Sacred Pools

On the Hawaiian island of Maui, in stark contrast to its upcountry desert-like volcanic landscapes, Haleakala's coastal portion offers a tropical mosaic of waterfalls, wave-splashed bays, and foliage a about 3 feet in depth. There are two ways to trek there: 6 miles up Little Bear Canyon or 8 miles up the Middle Fork route, past the Lightfeather Hot Springs.

☆ Olympic ☆
NATIONAL PARK
Sol Duc Hot Springs

Native American legend says the Sol Duc Hot Springs of Washington State's Olympic Peninsula are fed by the tears of dragons living in nearby caves. Located in the park's northwest region not far from Crescent Lake, the springs lie amid old-growth evergreen forest alongside a wild river renowned as a coho salmon spawning ground. The rustic hot springs resort offers three mineral pools and a freshwater swimming pool, as well as cabins for overnight stays. The water temperatures vary between 50°F and 104°F depending on the pool and the season. Adding to the spa-like ambience, the resort also offers massage service. The resort is closed in winter, but during the spring and fall the hot pools are open during twilight hours to expedite a sublime combination of soaking and stargazing. The local Quileute Indians frequented the springs long before European settlers discovered their curative powers. A huge lodge was developed around the pools in 1912, but it was destroyed by fire four years later and never rebuilt.

☆ Sequoia ☆
NATIONAL PARK
Kern Hot Springs

It takes several days of steady hiking along the High Sierra Trail to reach Kern Hot Springs in the backcountry of eastern California's Sequoia. But the effort isn't wasted, as a soaking spot secluded in a deep valley surrounded by Jeffrey pine, incense

☆ Tide-pooling ☆

Exploring seaside tide pools is a popular pastime in several parks. The name derives from the fact that the rocky depressions—and their inhabitants—are only exposed at low tide. Life in a tide pool is fragile, so the rule at national park tide pools is look-and-don't-touch when it comes to marine creatures.

Although its primary function is history, **Cabrillo National Monument** in San Diego boasts excellent tide pools along the western shore of Point Loma. With an underwater kelp forest just offshore, the animal life of Cabrillo's tide pools is especially rich and diverse—sea stars, sea urchins, and anemones, limpets and chitons, crabs and young lobsters, octopuses and small fish trapped by the outgoing tide. Rangers are often on duty to answer questions about the pools and their inhabitants.

Farther north along the West Coast, four of the islands in **Channel Islands National Park** have great tide-pooling sites. In each case, you need to travel by ferry or private boat from Ventura or Santa Barbara on the mainland, and then hike varying distances to the tide pools.

Over on the other side of the nation, Maine's **Acadia National Park** is also well endowed with tide-pool sites. The most popular include the gravel isthmus that connects Bar Island and Mount Desert Island at low tide, as well as Wonderland and Ship Harbor on the island's southern flank, near Bass Harbor Head Lighthouse. The ranger-led Tidepool School interpretive program takes place at various locations around Acadia from June to October.

cedar, and soaring granite faces awaits. The main pool is a scorching 115°F, but the runoff mixes with cold water from the nearby Kern River to create a sublimely warm pool that's just right for dipping. Clothing optional? Of course, this far off the beaten track—although a crude wooden fence around the hottest pool provides some privacy. Those who want to linger can stay at the primitive campsite near the springs. But it's first come, first served and very popular with backpackers trekking between Giant Forest Village and Mount Whitney. For those who enjoy ice-cold water, many of the tarns along the High Sierra Trail are definitely swimmable, including Upper Hamilton Lake and Precipice Lake.

> *Nationwide, the CCC operated 4,500 camps in national parks and forests . . . More than three million men enrolled between 1933 and 1942, planting three billion trees, protecting 20 million acres from soil erosion, and aiding in the establishment of 800 state parks.*

☆ Death Valley ☆
NATIONAL PARK
Saline Valley Warm Springs

A former flower power hangout that was later invaded by New Agers, Saline Valley Warm Springs is a quintessential California desert escape. Visitors can reach the Saline Valley from Calif. 190 near the park's western entrance, but the easiest access is probably from Big Pine Road in the north. Visitors can also fly into the valley's primitive desert airstrip. The springs are located 7 miles down a dirt track off Saline Valley Road. Three pools have been developed for soaking—Sunrise, Wizard, and Volcano—the latter two surrounded by palm trees, grass, and shrubs in oasis-like settings. Clothing is most definitely optional. Camping is allowed in designated sites around the springs, and some soakers stay for weeks at a time. Over the years much counterculture artwork (including many bat motifs) has accumulated in the hot springs area. There's also an impromptu lending library on wooden shelves near one of the pools. Some pretty out-there happenings still go on at Saline (among the Park Service rules: birthing or attempting to give birth in the springs is prohibited). Go with an open mind, and extra sunscreen for body parts that rarely see the light of day.

☆ Point Reyes ☆
NATIONAL SEASHORE
Bass Lake

The park is technically a national seashore, but the freshwater swimming is also superb at Point Reyes in northern California. The peninsula that Sir Francis Drake most likely set foot on 500 years ago is riddled with small ponds and lakes that make for great wading, floating, or even a vigorous backstroke if you are so inclined. Bass Lake at the southern end of the park is generally considered the best inland swimming. It's about 3 miles up the Coast Trail from Palomarin Trailhead near the town of Bolinas. Bring your own lunch and picnic beneath the shoreline evergreens or browse for thimbleberries and salmonberries in the lakeside vegetation during the summer months. There's a "Tarzan rope" for swinging over the water and many regulars bring blow-up floats to laze away the day on the lake. Bass has long been one of the San Francisco Bay Area's favorite skinny-dipping spots, so bathing suits are optional. The Point Reyes "lake district" includes four other small water bodies, but none of them are especially swimmer friendly.

✴ Shenandoah ✴
NATIONAL PARK
Big Rock Falls

Virginia's long, leafy national park is rife with swimming holes, most of them located far off the beaten track and accessible only to those who are willing to hike for a cool dip. Many of the trailheads are on Skyline Drive along the crest of the Blue Ridge. One of the easiest to reach is Big Rock Falls near the Byrd Visitor Center, a round-trip hike of roughly 3 miles. The trail leads downhill from the Milam Gap parking area toward Mill Prong Creek and a wilderness camp where President Herbert Hoover once stayed. The Moormans River in the park's deep south is another great place to get wet, reached via trails that start from the Wildcat Ridge parking area on Skyline Drive. Both the South Fork and North Fork of the Moormans have a number of swimming holes, but the best camping is found along the north branch, which also offers a side trail to lovely Big Branch Falls. White Oak Canyon in the park's central section, north of the Byrd Visitor Center, offers natural swimming pools at the bottom of several waterfalls, reached on a steep downhill trail from either the White Oak or Limberlost parking areas off Skyline. On the other hand, some pools are more easily accessed via roads and parking areas along the park fringe. For instance, Nicholson Hollow and its excellent Hughes River swimming holes are best approached from the Old Rag parking area at the top of Va. 600 out of the town of Nethers.

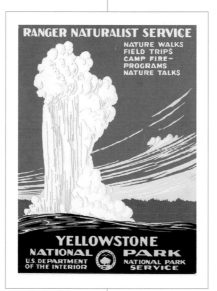

✴ Yellowstone ✴
NATIONAL PARK
Boiling River

"Hot-potting" is the slang term for taking a dip in one of Yellowstone's celebrated thermal features. The practice used to be widespread, especially among park employees, who would slink off after work for hot-potting parties at various natural pools around Old Faithful and other geyser fields. But nowadays it's forbidden at all but one spot in the vast park—Boiling River near Mammoth Hot Springs. The spring flows into the Gardner River and is closed when the river runs too high. The waters mix in the pools along the river's edge, so some spots may be warmer than others. The area is closed between dusk and dawn, and bathing suits are mandatory. The spring also has its quirky history. In the early 1870s, right before Yellowstone was designated a national park, McGuirk's Medicinal Springs (as it was then called) attracted people suffering from various ailments including rheumatism. Park surveyor F. V. Hayden described the scene as a "party of invalids, who were living in tents, and their praises were enthusiastic in favor of the sanitary effects of the springs. Some of them were used for drinking and others for bathing purposes." Boiling River lies 2 miles north of Mammoth along the highway to the North Entrance and the town of Gardiner. Bathers park in the small lot on the east side of the road (near the Wyoming–Montana state border sign and a sign marking the 45th parallel) and walk a half-mile trail to the pools.

sea kayaking spots

Sleek paddling in wilderness waters

Long, low, sleek, and lightweight, kayaks are ideally suited for water-based touring, especially when there's no current working to your advantage. You might see a few canoes in a few of the waters described here, but by and large, these are made-to-order kayak trips that ply some of the country's most magical coastal and inland waters.

✹ Everglades ✹
NATIONAL PARK
Wilderness Waterway

Meet Florida at its wildest and wilderness kayaking at its finest: the 99-mile Wilderness Waterway of Everglades National Park. The route courses narrow, mangrove-lined rivers and streams and winds around thousands of mangrove islands from Everglades City to Flamingo. Supreme serenity is certain, and sightings of manatees and dolphins are likely. The route is well marked, but it also invites variations—with the proper charts and a copy of *Guide to the Wilderness Waterway of the Everglades National Park,* all available at the Gulf Coast Visitor Center in Everglades City, you can fashion your own itinerary using the waterway as an organizing structure. For example, you can form open loops by choosing a river, paddling it out to the Gulf of Mexico, camping on an island, then following a different waterway back into the mangrove maze. Your course, though, has to be cleared with rangers at the Gulf Coast Visitor Center so that you can

be assured of campsites, either on beaches or on the park's camping platforms called chickees. The full waterway takes about ten days to paddle, but you can also make a shorter loop trip out of Everglades City without retracing your paddle strokes and still have a full-on experience of the Everglades wilderness.

✹ Kenai Fjords ✹
NATIONAL PARK
Resurrection Bay, Aialik Bay, and Northwestern Lagoon

The vast fjords of Alaska's Kenai Peninsula offer superb kayaking in the face of towering tidewater glaciers amid drifting icebergs and harbor seals. If your time is limited, spend a day paddling in Resurrection Bay right from park headquarters. You'll see hanging glaciers hundreds of feet high above the water, you'll paddle by the base of cascading waterfalls, and you're likely to see sea otters, porpoises, and seabirds such as auks and puffins. A more ambitious day requires a 42-mile motorboat ride to Aialik

A sea kayaker paddles through the icy clutch of Bear Cove, off Ailik Bay, in Kenai Fjords National Park.

If you dig deep into the **Gulf Islands National Seashore** archives, you might come across this curious tidbit about Cat Island, one of the kayaking destinations described here: "During World War II the island was used by the U.S. Army Signal Corps to train service dogs for the military."

The call to press dogs into service came not long after Pearl Harbor, as concerns about enemy intrusion and sabotage grew. Dogs were considered valuable as sentries at critical installations. Thus the War Dog Program, more commonly called the K-9 Corps, was born and the Cat Island War Dog Reception and Training Center established. The island was quiet and secluded for the hush-hush work, plus it was densely vegetated and humid—similar to the tropical jungle in the Pacific theater. Sentry dogs were trained in about eight weeks and put to work guarding shorelines where submarine attacks were a concern. As the war progressed, dogs learned to perform reconnaissance, to detect mines, and to deliver messages. As scouts, they warned against enemy ambushes. Nearly 2,000 dogs served nobly in all these regards in both theaters of the war.

There's a strange footnote to the Cat Island training. Recently discovered and declassified documents indicate that the facility's civilian director brought Japanese Americans from Hawaii to Cat Island in 1943 in an attempt to train dogs to seek out and attack enemy soldiers. The human-bait experiment lasted 90 days. It was unsuccessful.

Bay, which distills all the glacial glories of Kenai Fjords, including the frequently calving, 800-foot face of Aialik Glacier. In the icy waters you might see humpback whales, orcas, and fin whales—and harbor seals catching a rest on the icebergs. With more time, venture to Northwestern Lagoon, a similar environment where one could paddle for hours or even days and not see another soul, and camp in solitary splendor. The park maintains a list of authorized outfitters that organize guided kayak trips.

☆ Glacier Bay ☆
NATIONAL PARK & PRESERVE
West Arm Inlets

The primordial majesty of Alaska's Glacier Bay has to be seen close up and in solitude to be truly appreciated. A paddle around the narrow inlets of the West Arm in a sea kayak, weaving around just-calved icebergs, feels like the beginning of time. The 15,000-foot summits of the Fairweather Range tower overhead. Glaciers seem to flow from their every crevice. The sounds are as impressive: water flowing beneath the glaciers, water tumbling from mountain streams, the crackling and gurgling ice, and the "white thunder," as the locals called the calving of tidewater glaciers. For a perfect three- to five-day trip, pick up a rental kayak at Glacier Bay Sea Kayaks *(www.glacierbayseakayaks.com)* in Bartlett Cove, hop the lodge's sightseeing boat to Queen Inlet, and start paddling west to see massive Grand Pacific Glacier. Once past the glacier and the cruise ships, solitude can be found in Johns Hopkins Inlet at the mouths of Lamplugh and Reid Glaciers, where you can camp before making the open-water paddle back to Queen Inlet. Glacier Bay's waters are quite protected, but glaciers come with their own weather systems—beware of strong winds coming off them, and, of course, the surge that accompanies calving.

☆ Gulf Islands ☆
NATIONAL SEASHORE
Cat Island

The jewel among jewels of the Gulf Coast barrier islands stretching across Mississippi and the Florida Panhandle is 2,100-acre Cat Island, a gorgeous and fascinating goal at the end of a 6-mile paddle from Gulfport, Mississippi. The island rises higher and has more vegetation than the rest of the other park islands, and it's ringed by 50 miles of white-sand shoreline. (Parts of the island are private inholdings; heed posted signs.) Like the rest of the national seashore, Cat was affected by the 2010 Gulf oil spill. It will continue to require cleanup—simply a fact of life in the post-spill era—but it's still a glorious paddling destination. En route you might be escorted by jumping mullet or pods of bottlenose dolphins. Ashore, solitary camping (no facilities; bring your own drinking water) is allowed just above the high-tide line. Inland highlights include marshes (watch for gators), and forests of pines, palmettos, and live oaks dripping with garlands of Spanish moss. Fall is the best time to go; the humidity has subsided, thunderstorms unlikely, and the seawater remains pleasantly warm.

☆ Glen Canyon ☆
NATIONAL RECREATION AREA
Lake Powell's Side Canyons
and Slot Canyons

When the Glen Canyon Dam on the Colorado River was built a generation ago, the world lost a magnificent canyon but gained a stellar freshwater kayaking destination. The main watercourse of Lake Powell, 180 miles long, reaches into some 94 side canyons, many of which narrow down to almost nothing, but their Navajo sandstone walls soar 500 feet. With a kayak and a day or two, a paddler can put in near

A kayaker paddles in Anasazi Canyon, a side canyon flooded by the waters of Lake Powell in Glen Canyon.

Page, Arizona, and oar to Antelope or Lone Rock Canyon, set up camp, and gain a taste of Glen Canyon's hidden wonders. But the more compelling paddling is farther along and requires some motorized assistance and knowledge of the many-tentacled lake. Going with an outfitter is perhaps the best way to get into deep slot canyons like Cascade, Driftwood, and Rainbow—the latter is the gateway to a massive natural arch, Rainbow Bridge. Spring and fall are the best times to avoid the swarms of speedboats and Jet Skis in the main channel. The water is chilly in spring, but the warm water of summer lingers into fall.

✷ Cape Lookout ✷
NATIONAL SEASHORE
Black Sound

The North Carolina barrier islands of Cape Lookout stretch 112 miles, yet lie just 3 miles offshore and are without roads or facilities, making them an ideal place for secluded, protected paddling in shallow water. The island waters are also a mecca for kayak-based fly-fishing for false albacore. Camping is permitted everywhere; there are no designated spots on the long, unspoiled beaches. You can build a fire, swim, fish, clam, crab, bird-watch, and watch for humpback whales and four types of sea turtles—loggerhead turtles nest here in the summer months—and even play in the surf on the windward side. For an easy, short trip, put in at Harkers Island on Black Sound, site of the park visitor center, and paddle over to Shackleford Banks on Onslow Bay, where 140 or so wild ponies roam, as they have for hundreds of years. It's best to paddle early, before the wind picks up, and be sure to pick up a tide chart so you can avoid paddling against a surging current.

✷ Pictured Rocks ✷
NATIONAL LAKESHORE
Lake Superior's Southern Shoreline

The colorful rocks of the park's name are just one highlight of a wild 42-mile shoreline that rivals the Apostle Islands as one of the finest kayak destinations on Lake Superior. The 50- to 200-foot multihued sandstone cliffs, striped and colored by seeping, mineral-filled water, stretch for 15 miles

along the west end of the park. The 500-million-year-old rocks have been carved into arches, spires, and caves that are a delight to explore by kayak. They begin just upcoast from Sand Point; day trippers can put in here or at Miners Castle. Touring kayakers can proceed beyond and camp in any of eight backcountry campsites, plus two more that are also car accessible. Beyond the rocks is Twelvemile Beach, a long stretch of white sand crowned by a backdrop of wild North Woods. Beyond the Twelvemile Beach campground is Au Sable Point and its 1874 lighthouse, still active, and the Grand Sable Dunes, perched atop the 300-foot-high Grand Sable Banks. Guided trips: *www.northern waters.com*.

✷ Apostle Islands ✷
NATIONAL LAKESHORE
Lakeshore Trail

With 21 islands scattered in the waters of Lake Superior off the tip of Wisconsin's Bayfield Peninsula, plus 12 miles of mainland shoreline, the Apostles are ideally suited for all sorts of kayak touring, from day trips exploring cliffs and sea caves to multiday excursions to the outer islands. For a day trip or a simple overnighter, put in at Meyers Beach and paddle north along the mainland's Lakeshore Trail, where red sandstone cliffs tower above and sea caves and arches make for great paddling. Eighteen of the 21 islands permit camping, so options for longer trips abound. Sand Island, for example, is less than an hour's paddle across open water—skirt the circumference, explore the sea caves at Swallow Point, and tour its lighthouse before setting up camp. With more time,

RANGER NATURALIST SERVICE
ENJOY BOAT CRUISES TO OFFSHORE ISLANDS
VISIT THE ISLESFORD HISTORICAL MUSEUM
EXPLORE CADILLAC MOUNTAIN

ACADIA
NATIONAL PARK
U.S. DEPARTMENT
OF THE INTERIOR
NATIONAL PARK
SERVICE

continue on to Oak Island, put ashore, and hike to the overlook for a great view of all the Apostles. More ambitious paddlers can focus on notching up lighthouses—six in all—or aim to reach Outer Island, the park's most remote spot, for more amazing views and a wonderful sense of solitude. Heed the Park Service warnings that Lake Superior is cold and lake conditions can turn rough. Wetsuits are recommended, as are guide services. The park's website has a link to a list of authorized outfitters.

> *Painted Cave on Santa Cruz Island is one of the world's largest known sea caves. The cave measures 1215 feet in length (the size of more than four football fields), has a 160 foot entrance, and is almost 100 feet wide.*

☆ Channel Islands ☆
NATIONAL PARK
Santa Cruz Island

The 300-foot north-facing cliffs of the east end of Santa Cruz Island, largest of the Channel Islands, have the appearance of Swiss cheese, pocked as they are with some of the world's largest sea caves. Dark, mysterious, and thrilling to explore—ideally in a superbuoyant sit-on-top kayak with a guide—the caves are numerous, long, and subject to seasonal variations, so local knowledge is vital. And always wear a helmet—surges of tides and waves can quickly make a big cave turn small. As one outfitter puts it, it's a low-rigor but high-adventure outing. It can be done in a day—or camp on the island and make a long weekend of it. Most tours begin at Potato Harbor, where guides will start off with some easy pass-through caves. One, Surging T Cave, is 354 feet long. Of the island's 100-plus caves, 72 are more than 200 feet long. Some are huge and vaulted, like the immense Painted Cave. Others are best avoided by claustrophobes. Seal Canyon Cave, for instance, winds 600 feet into oblivion and is so narrow that kayakers have to back in, then shoot out—and surge occasionally cuts off that reassuring light at the end of the tunnel. Watch for blowholes in the cliffs that spray out a sudden *ptooey* of foam, and watch for harbor seals everywhere. The park has a list of authorized outfitters, including Aquasports (*www.islandkayaking.com*).

☆ Acadia ☆
NATIONAL PARK
Blue Hill and Western Bays

Technically speaking, the Atlantic coastal waters surrounding much of Maine's Acadia are not actually in the park. But kayaking is nonetheless a great way to gain perspective on the stunning scenery of Acadia, to poke around its surrounding islands (most are in private hands), and to see wildlife up close. The best kayaking is on the quiet west side of Mount Desert Island, where it's preferable to go with an outfitter (*www.nationalparkkayak.com*); they can run one-way trips so paddlers don't have to backtrack against the wind or tides, or search for parking. Blue Hill Bay and Western Bay are well away from cruise ships, ferries, and whale-watching boats, so the experience is quiet and you get to paddle by seal rookeries on uninhabited islands and see lots of porpoises and birds—loons, terns, black-backed and herring gulls, guillemots, and occasional bald eagles. All the while Acadia's mountains—Bernard, Mansell, even Cadillac—loom above or in the distance. Intrepid paddlers can brave the busier waters of Frenchman Bay out of Bar Harbor to the national park's Porcupine Islands (*www.acadiafun.com, www.treknraft.com*).

scuba & snorkeling sites

Underwater adventures in lakes, lagoons, and bays

Whether you're a veteran diver or a novice with mask and snorkel, a cold-water devotee or a tropical lagoon aficionado, the National Park System offers numerous locations where you can get your (fin) kicks in the water. Delights to be found include shipwrecks, coral reefs, colorful fish, and underwater heritage trails.

☆ Biscayne ☆
NATIONAL PARK
Long Reef

Although just about any place in this South Florida park is ripe for scuba, the best underwater terrain is a chain of six wrecks on the park's far eastern fringe. Part of a new maritime heritage trail, the wrecks run the gamut from 19th-century sailing vessels like the triple-masted *Erl King* (sank 1891) to early 20th-century iron-hulled steamships like the *Lugano* (sank 1913). The only way to reach the secluded sites is by boat, tying up at mooring buoys poised above the wrecks. Five of the sites are too deep to preclude anything but diving. However, the remains of the *Mandalay* are in waters shallow enough for snorkeling. Dubbed the "red carpet ship of the Windjammer fleet," the super-chic steel-hulled schooner smashed onto Long Reef on New Year's Day of 1966 on an overnight run between the Bahamas and Miami. The National Park Service is in the process of producing maps and waterproof information cards on each of the wrecks.

☆ Buck Island Reef ☆
NATIONAL MONUMENT
Underwater Trail
U.S. Virgin Islands

One of the few dedicated marine units in the park system, Buck Island protects an astonishing coral garden and underwater habitat near St. Croix in the U.S. Virgin Islands. Snorkelers flock to the island's east end for a renowned underwater trail through warm, translucent water that never reaches more than 12 feet in depth. Submerged signs describe a reef ecosystem rife with brain, star, and elkhorn coral, as well as sponges and soft corals. Sea turtles, rays, and reef sharks are among the larger species that frequent the lagoon; overall the park protects more than 250 fish marine species. Diving is limited to two scuba moorings in about 30 to 40 feet of water above an elkhorn reef. Visitors who crave a break from the water can hike, picnic, sunbathe, or take a siesta on 176-acre Buck Island. Access to the park is by boat only. Concessionaires operate out of Christiansted or Green Cay Marina on St. Croix.

⭑ Virgin Islands Coral Reef ⭑
NATIONAL MONUMENT
Hurricane Hole

The only unit of the National Park System that does not include any dry land, this Caribbean preserve protects 12,708 acres of pristine marine habitat around St. John Island in the U.S. Virgin Islands. In one of his last acts in the White House, Bill Clinton created the park by presidential proclamation in January 2001 to protect the waters of Virgin Islands National Park. Only one of the monument's four segments touches shore, a slice of Hurricane Hole, Coral Bay, and Round Bay that includes mangrove swamps and shoreline coral reef. Other than Hurricane Hole—which can be accessed on U.S.V.I. 10 from Coral Bay village at the east end of St. John—the park is difficult to explore without a boat. Further complicating access is the fact that anchoring is forbidden throughout the park in order to protect the fragile tropical marine ecosystems. The national monument is jointly administered with the national park and shares the visitor center at Cruz Bay at the western end of St. John. Two of the park's more popular activities are fishing the open ocean south of St. John and snorkeling the Hurricane Hole mangroves in search of fish and marine invertebrates.

Snorkelers examine the tropical undersea world of St. John, U.S. Virgin Islands, filled with colorful fish and corals.

✷ Channel Islands ✷
NATIONAL PARK
Santa Barbara and Anacapa
Kelp Forests

Ethereal kelp forests, spooky sea caves, and a multitude of large animals are just three of the factors that make these southern California islands an incredible place to dive or snorkel. The best conditions are found off Santa Barbara and Anacapa Islands, as well as the east end of Santa Cruz. Kelp forests are known to harbor as many as a thousand different species, from sea urchins, sea cucumbers, and delicate sea stars to moray eels, sheephead, and bright orange garibaldi (the California state fish). Santa Cruz is especially rich in sea caves, some of them among Earth's largest, but they should always be approached with caution. Harbor seals, sea lions, and dolphins are Channel Islands regulars, and there is always a chance of spotting gray, humpback, and minke whales—and occasionally orcas—in the open waters around the islands. There are even wrecks, like the remains of the Pacific Mail steamer *Winfield Scott* that went down off Anacapa in 1853.

☆ Famous Wrecks ☆

Some of the most renowned shipwrecks in American history took place in and around national parks. The U.S.S. *Monitor* lies in 230 feet of water about 16 miles off **Cape Hatteras National Seashore.** The famed Civil War ironclad went down during an 1862 storm only nine months after her epic fight in Hampton Roads. In April 1554, three Spanish galleons ran aground in a storm along the shore of today's **Padre Island National Seashore.** Some of the survivors eventually made their way back to the Mexican port of Veracruz, but more than 300 passengers and crew perished in the disaster, one of the worst in Spanish colonial history. The wrecks weren't relocated until 1967 and remains occasionally still wash up on Texas beaches. In terms of sheer numbers, **Cape Cod National Seashore** is the clear winner—more than 3,000 ships have wrecked on the peninsula's outer side. Among them was the British man-of-war H.M.S. *Somerset III*, which survived combat in the Seven Years War and the early part of the American Revolution, but not a horrific storm off Cape Cod in November 1778.

✷ National Park of American Samoa ✷
NATIONAL PARK
Olosega and
Ofo Island Reefs

Warm, clear tropical Pacific waters make American Samoa a natural for scuba diving and snorkeling. Spread across four different islands, the territory's namesake national park encompasses lagoons and coves protected by offshore reefs. More than 200 types of coral and nearly 1,000 fish species have been spotted in waters in and around the park, including moray eels, eagle rays, Moorish idols and mantas, lionfish, stonefish, puffers, and reef sharks. Larger animals like humpback and sperm whales are sometimes seen farther from shore. From poisonous sea snakes to sea turtles, marine reptiles are also present. The park's largest section sprawls across the remote northern shore of Tutuila Island, home of territorial capital Pago Pago. But most of this area is impossible to explore without your own boat. Far better to hop a puddle jumper to the twin islands of Olosega and Ofu in the Manu'a Archipelago, where the reefs and lagoons are far easier to reach. Pago Pago Marine Charters (*http://pagopagomarine charters.com*) offers diving equipment rental as well as crewed boats to scuba and snorkel spots in the park.

☀ Isle Royale ☀
NATIONAL PARK
Lake Superior Shipwrecks

As Gordon Lightfoot sang in "The Wreck of the Edmund Fitzgerald," Lake Superior's fickle weather has taken more than its fair share of ships to the bottom. A good number went down around Michigan's Isle Royale and are now protected by the National Park Service. Superior's cold water has helped preserve their remains, and the lake's clarity makes them easy to explore. The 532-foot-long *Chester Congdon* is the largest of the park's wrecks, a bulk freighter that sank in 1918; the pilothouse, bow, and stern are still intact. Another bulk freighter, the *Emperor* (sank 1947), is the most intact wreck, retaining its engine room and various cabins. All divers must register beforehand at one of the park's visitor centers. With water temperatures between 34°F and 55°F, a full wet suit or dry suit is highly recommended. Three outfitters are licensed to run scuba trips in park waters: Superior Trips *(www.superiortrips.com)*, MN-Blackdog Diving *(www.mn-blackdogdiving.com)*, and Isle Royale Charters *(www.isleroyalecharters.com)*. The scuba season runs mid-June to early September.

☀ Sleeping Bear Dunes ☀
NATIONAL LAKESHORE
Manitou Passage Underwater Preserve

Located in the channels that separate the mainland and island portions of this Michigan national lakeshore, the Manitou Passage Underwater Preserve offers sunken docks, shipwrecks, and natural submarine landscapes. Several wrecks lie in shallow water, which makes them ideal for novice divers and even snorkelers. The remains of the three-masted schooner *Flying Cloud* (sank 1853) and the wooden brig *James McBride* (sank 1857) can be accessed directly from the mainland. Other wrecks lie scattered around North and South Manitou Islands and will require a boat or a combination of ferry passage (from Leland) and hiking to the shoreline wade-in points. Manitou Island Transit *(www.leelanau.com/manitou)* makes the 90-minute crossing daily between May and October; divers can choose to return the same day or camp overnight on either island. South Manitou's wrecks include the package freighter *Francisco Morazan* (sank 1960), the wooden steamer *Walter L. Frost* (sank 1905), and the steam barge *Three Brothers* (sank 1911).

☀ War in the Pacific ☀
NATIONAL HISTORICAL PARK
Agat and Asan Reefs, and Lagoons

Although dedicated to the memory of soldiers and civilians from all nations who lost their lives in the War in the Pacific, the national park also safeguards a fair amount of Guam nature, including beaches, coral reefs, and lagoons. More than 3,500 marine species have been seen inside the park. U.S. Marines kicked off the Allied invasion of Guam by storming ashore at Agat and Asan beaches in July 1944. Nowadays, the warm tropical waters off both of these strands are prime places for snorkel and scuba. Asan Beach Unit features two designated scuba areas at the west and east ends of the beach, as well as a snorkel area at Adelup Point. The Agat unit has four scuba areas as well as a snorkel area at both Apaca Point and Ga'an Point. Waters near the national park shelter the remains of many ships and airplanes that went down during two wars. The artifacts range from a World War I German cruiser called the *Cormoran* to a Japanese Aichi D3A "Val" bomber from World War II. As many as four of these wrecks can be dived in one day. The Guam branch of the Micronesia Divers Association *(www.mdaguam .com)* offers shore dives at Agat and Asan.

✴ Crater Lake ✴
NATIONAL PARK
Cleetwood Trail

Oregon's flooded caldera offers scuba divers a chance to explore the deepest lake in the United States (1,943 feet) and one of the world's clearest freshwater lakes. Completely cut off from surrounding watersheds, Crater Lake never had a native fish population, but the water body was once stocked with rainbow trout and kokanee salmon, the largest denizens that divers will come across. Other residents include phytoplankton, zooplankton, algae, and moss. Underwater geological features include volcanic cones, landslides and talus slopes. There are only two scuba put-in points. Divers need to carry all of their equipment—tanks, weights, and more—down the 1.1-mile Cleetwood Trail, a vertical descent of 700 feet. And do the same back up after the dive. Once at the bottom, divers can enter the water from the Cleetwood Cove dock or hop a concessionaire-operated boat tour to Wizard Island. All divers must obtain a permit from park headquarters before entering the lake and wear a good-quality wet suit or dry suit. Summer surface temperatures range between 50°F and 58°F, but quickly drop below 40°F. Severe winter weather and snow limits the lake's diving season to summer and very early fall.

✴ Amistad ✴
NATIONAL RECREATION AREA
Indian Springs Underwater Cliffs

Diving in the desert may seem like an oxymoron, but scuba is a major draw at Lake Amistad in southern Texas. The 65,000-acre reservoir was created in 1969 by the building of the Amistad Dam near the confluence of the Rio Grande and Devils River. The submarine scenery includes sunken boats, underwater cliffs, and a ranch house submerged by the rising lake. One popular site is Indian Springs, a spring up the Devils River arm that raises the surrounding water temperature to 72°F. Animal life includes catfish and three types of bass; spearfishing (with a license) is allowed in four areas around the lake. Although the lake is colder in winter, the underwater visibility is much better between November and April, often reaching beyond 35 feet. Amistad Aqua Adventures *(www .amistad-aqua-adventures.com)* offers scheduled lake dives and rents small speedboats for private dives.

beaches

Secluded surf, sun, and sand

From the coconut palm-fringed bays of the Virgin Islands to the chilly wind and wave-carved Olympic Peninsula coast, some of America's best beaches are protected within the confines of the park system. They tread a delicate balancing act between recreation and conservation of fragile shoreline ecosystems that nourish billions of creatures.

☀ Assateague Island ☀
NATIONAL SEASHORE
Atlantic Coast, Maryland and Virginia

Sprawling across a barrier island shared by Maryland and Virginia, this national seashore boasts 37 miles of white-sand strand within easy driving distance of several of the eastern seaboard's largest cities. Only a small part of Assateague's beaches are accessible by paved road, which means that sunseekers must either hike to their favorite patch of sand or obtain an over-sand vehicle permit from the park service and cruise down the 12 miles of beach on the Maryland side, where driving is allowed. The Maryland side also sports several beachfront campsites, but you may have to share your secluded camp with the island's wild horses. Surf fishing has long been popular along the Assateague coast; crabbing and clamming are possible in the shallow bays on the island's leeward side. The seashore is also one of the best places along the mid-Atlantic to board surf, with consistent surf throughout the year and fairly warm water in summer thanks to the Gulf Stream.

☀ Cape Cod ☀
NATIONAL SEASHORE
Duck Harbor, Nauset, Marconi Beach

To naturalist Henry David Thoreau, who made four visits to Cape Cod between 1849 and 1857, the cape was a coastal version of Walden Pond, a place to discover and escape back into nature. The cape is still that way today, a wild thing on the eastern edge of Massachusetts that continues to rebuff civilization. The national seashore portion includes 40 miles of strand, much of it backed by rolling dunes, with 15 different beaches, some town managed and others under the auspices of the Park Service. They range from the placid bayside sands of Duck Harbor to untamed Atlantic strands like Nauset to historical shores like Marconi Beach, where, in 1903, Italian inventor Guglielmo Marconi sent the first successful transatlantic wireless radio message between the United States and Britain. The long stretch of sand between Race Point and Head of the Meadow is open to off-road vehicles with a park permit. The only camping within the national seashore is self-contained vehicle camping at Race Point; tents and camping trailers are not allowed. The nearest other camping is in Nickerson State Park near Orleans.

✷ Virgin Islands ✷
NATIONAL PARK
Hawksnest Bay, Trunk Bay,
and Cinnamon Bay

Turquoise water, talcum-powder-fine sand, palm trees swaying in a gentle breeze: What's not to love about the beaches in this Caribbean national park? The more renowned beaches are on the north shore of St. John Island, a chain of pearly white strands that includes Hawksnest Bay, Trunk Bay, and Cinnamon Bay. Trunk Bay boasts a snack bar and an offshore snorkel trail through coral gardens. Cinnamon has a beachfront campground and cottages, and a water-sports shack where various boards and boats are rented. Farther east, gorgeous Maho Bay is home to a luxury tented camp on a sliver of private land between two park sections. Those who crave more seclusion can hoof it to isolated strands on the south shore of St. John and the park's Anneberg sector. The beach at Brown Bay looks out across Sir Francis Drake Channel to the British Virgin Islands.

Pearly white sands, turquoise waters, and soft Caribbean breezes make the strand at St. John's Trunk Bay near perfect.

The 1-mile Ram Head Trail leads to an unusual (and normally empty) blue cobblestone beach. The park's most isolated beach, located at Reef Bay, requires a 2.23-mile hike along a trail of the same name.

Barrett Beach/Talisman is one of the narrowest parts of 32-mile-long Fire Island. You can easily walk from one side of the island to the other—bay to ocean— in 5 minutes or less.

⋆ Cape Lookout ⋆
NATIONAL SEASHORE
Shackleford Banks

The main advantage of Cape Lookout over its much more visited northern neighbor (Cape Hatteras) is the remoteness, a solitude born of a lack of bridges to the mainland: A boat is the only way to reach these unsullied North Carolina barrier island beaches. And advance planning is necessary, because other than the five ferry landings, the islands are completely wild. Swimming, surf fishing, and beachcombing for shells are three ways to while away a lazy Cape Lookout day. The surfing isn't half bad, either, especially along Shackleford Banks and Cape Point. With so little development, wildlife thrives inside the national seashore, in particular shore and migratory birds, and the harems of wild horses that roam the Shackleford Banks. Primitive camping is allowed along the beaches, and there are two sets of rustic cabins at Great Island and Long Point.

⋆ Fire Island ⋆
NATIONAL SEASHORE
Watch Hill and Sailors Haven

The best thing about Fire Island—other than the quantity of so much pristine coastline so close to one of the planet's largest urban areas, greater New York City—is the fact that a ferry ride is needed to reach the park's choicest beach areas. Regular boat service operates from Sayville and Patchogue on Long Island May to October. The rest of the year it's a long hike to those lonely beaches from car-accessible Fire Island Lighthouse in the west and Wilderness Visitor Center in the east. Lifeguards are on duty throughout the summer at Watch Hill and Sailors Haven, the two ferry-accessed beaches in the heart of the park. Besides sunning and swimming, the barrier island's shoreline offers plenty of other activities, including surf fishing, waterfront nature walks, bird-watching, and beachcombing (you are allowed to take away 2 quarts of empty seashells per day). Watch Hill's campground is open May to October; year-round backcountry camping is allowed in the Otis Pike Fire Island High Dune Wilderness area at the park's eastern end.

⋆ Golden Gate ⋆
NATIONAL RECREATION AREA
Baker, Muir, and Rodeo Beaches and Crissy Field

There's an argument to be made that Golden Gate offers a greater variety of beaches than any other unit of the National Park System. Beaches in the San Francisco Bay Area park range from tiny urban slivers popular with early morning swimmers (Aquatic Park) to massive strands that can accommodate as many as a million people on summer holiday weekends (Ocean Beach) to secluded wilderness beaches that can only be reached by foot (Tennessee Cove). Boulder-strewn Baker Beach offers unsurpassed views of the nearby Golden Gate Bridge. The thin strip of sand at Crissy Field is a popular launching pad for windsurfers and kiteboarders. Muir Beach is home to a Zen meditation center, a popular English pub (the Pelican Inn), and a Monterey pine grove where monarch butterflies often winter. Rodeo Beach shares its magnificent stretch of coast with a wildlife rich lagoon, and Marin Headlands, on the north side of the Golden Gate, houses vintage World War II Army buildings and a Cold War–era Nike missile site. The park offers three waterfront campgrounds, all of them in the Marin Headlands section.

☆ Indiana Dunes ☆
NATIONAL LAKESHORE
Lake Michigan Shore

Anyone's first visit to Lake Michigan's Indiana Dunes is a mind-blowing experience: a pristine lakeshore set against a backdrop of smokestacks, cranes, and other bleak industrial architecture. But that is what is so special about this park, the fact that it shares space with steel mills and port facilities. Conservationists kicked off the campaign to save the nearly 200-foot-tall dunes more than a century ago, but it wasn't until the 1960s that their dream became reality. The park extends along roughly 20 miles of lakeshore just east of Chicago, a stretch that also includes Indiana Dunes State Park and a number of private holdings. Swimming is allowed between 7 a.m. and dusk, but bathers should recognize that a freshwater body as large as Lake Michigan can be just as hazardous as the open ocean, including rip tides, large waves, and ice in winter. Hikers and bikers can enter the park an hour earlier. Visitors can overnight at Dunewood Campground or at a site inside the state park.

☆ Olympic ☆
NATIONAL PARK
Kalaloch, Rialto, and Ozette Beaches

Dramatic, windswept strands define the western edge of Washington State's Olympic National Park, a place where you can always find an empty beach even at the height of the summer season. The 73 miles of park coastline feature soaring cliffs and sea stacks, sandy beaches and rocky shores, chromatic tide pools and rocky offshore islands where millions of seabirds nest. Kalaloch is the most user-friendly, a wide and sandy strand with a lodge and two campgrounds. The only other drive-up sand is rough and tumble Rialto Beach, adjacent to the Quileute Indian Reservation. Even farther north, the refreshingly remote Ozette beaches are reached via 3-mile boardwalk trails from the parking lot at Ozette ranger station. Dozens of remote beaches bask in the park's Olympic Wilderness Coast. Some are accessible by walking along the shore at low tide; others involve hiking along various coastal paths like the Oil City Trail, Shi Shi Beach Trail, and the lengthy North Coast Route. Camping is permitted along wilderness beaches with a park permit. To avoid getting trapped by the incoming tide, rangers recommend that anyone hiking the Olympic coast always carry a current tide chart and topographic map.

☆ Padre Island ☆
NATIONAL SEASHORE
North Padre Barrier Island

Texas' quiet North Padre Island remains virtually unchanged from when Spanish explorers first probed its long crescent shore 500 years ago. Eons of waves, tides, and hurricanes created the 70-mile-long landfall and its wilderness beaches, the longest stretch of undeveloped barrier island on the entire planet, and likely to remain so given its Park Service protection. Five species of sea turtles lay their eggs along local beaches, and given that it's located on the central flyway between North and South America, the island offers rich pickings for bird-watchers. Recreation opportunities also abound: swimming and surf fishing on the Gulf shore, windsurfing and kayaking on the lagoon side. The national seashore's only vehicular entrance is in the north, near Corpus Christi. Paved road extends only a few miles into the park; south of the Malaquite Visitor Center, the only way to transit the strand is by hiking, biking, or driving on top of the sand. Vehicles are allowed on the beach all the way down to the park's southern tip; four-wheel drive is highly recommended.

☆ Pictured Rocks ☆
NATIONAL LAKESHORE
Twelvemile and Sand Point Beaches

It seems counterintuitive that some of the nation's best beaches should be so far away from the sea. However, the Great Lakes aren't exactly ponds and many a coastal resort would love to have the kind of beaches lining Michigan's Pictured Rocks. The park name derives from the sandstone cliffs that etch much of this Upper Peninsula shoreline. Wildly scenic beaches flank the multicolored palisades. Sand Point's placid pocket-size beach is protected within the confines of South Bay, whereas Twelvemile Beach opens straight onto Lake Superior with views that seem to stretch to Canada. The small beaches at Chapel Rock and Miners Castle are named after nearby rock formations. At the far end of the park are the Grand Sable Banks and Dunes, which plunge 300 feet to the lake. Only the hardy go for a dip in chilly Lake Superior (also known for its rip currents), but the Pictured Rocks beaches make for great walking, camping, and just contemplating.

☆ Best Beach Camping ☆

Bechers Bay (Channel Islands National Park, California): Steinbeck's California come to life; waterfront camping on uninhabited Santa Rosa Island.

Cinnamon Bay (Virgin Islands National Park, U.S. Virgin Islands): The quintessential Caribbean campground; cook cheeseburgers in paradise.

Garden Key (Dry Tortugas National Park, Florida): Sack out beneath coconut palms on the same island as historic Fort Jefferson.

Holgate Beach (Kenai Fjords National Park, Alaska): Were those grizzly bear tracks outside your tent this morning? You betcha.

Kalaloch (Olympic National Park, Washington): RV and tent campsites with views of the wild Pacific coast; ranger campfire talks at night.

Ocracoke (Cape Hatteras National Seashore, North Carolina): Wild ponies, rolling dunes, and seafood barbecues; the Outer Banks doesn't get any better.

Sea Camp (Cumberland Island National Seashore, Georgia): Splendid isolation in a cool grove of trees; wild horses and armadillos keep you company.

Twelvemile Beach (Pictured Rocks National Lakeshore, Michigan): Secreted in a grove of white birches on a bluff overlooking Lake Superior.

Watch Hill (Fire Island National Seashore, New York): An oceanfront campground with marina, restaurant, and tiki bar? Hey, it's Long Island.

Wildcat Beach (Point Reyes National Seashore, California): Bluff-top campground near beachfront Alamere Falls; site No. 7 has the best ocean views.

wind sport locales

Parks where wind and water collide

The breeze blows strong and steady in several national parks that lend themselves perfectly to wind sports like sailing, kiteboarding, and windsurfing. Seaside locations might be expected, but this top ten also features inland waters where wind sports fans will find great recreational opportunities amid stunning scenery.

✳ Golden Gate ✳
NATIONAL RECREATION AREA
Crissy Field, Rodeo, Muir, and Ocean Beaches

Home port of the current America's Cup yachting champs, San Francisco Bay provides one of the world's most dazzling places to sail. The twin arms of Golden Gate National Recreation Area separate the (sometimes) calmer bay waters from the often turbulent open Pacific. Crissy Field Beach on the south shore is the most popular place for kiteboarding, a spectacular new sport that combines surfboard and parachute. The same beach is also a great place to launch Windsurfers for a cruise beneath the Golden Gate Bridge or a quick whip around Alcatraz. Rodeo Beach and Muir Beach in the Marin Headlands and Ocean Beach in San Francisco are other awesome windsurfing and kiteboarding spots. While most sailors set out from marinas outside the park, Golden Gate does have its own facility—Travis Marina (aka Presidio Yacht Club) on Horseshoe Cove in the Fort Baker section in Marin County. A holdover from when Fort Baker was occupied by the military, the Air Force–operated marina offers sailing lessons and rentals to both military families and the general public *(www.travisfss.com/marina.html)*.

✳ Padre Island ✳
NATIONAL SEASHORE
Bird Island Basin

With miles of flat water and a shallow, sandy bottom, Laguna Madre on the western flank of Texas' Padre Island is considered a prime place to learn and practice windsurfing. Bird Island Basin—not far from the entrance gate and the Malaquite Visitor Center—is the park's windsurfing hub and the only developed launch area. With an average annual wind speed of 18 miles an hour and some sort of breeze nearly every day, *Windsurfing Magazine* ranks "BIB" as the best flat-water sailing in the lower 48. The season runs early spring to late fall, although midsummer can be scorching hot and humid. A private outfitter called Worldwinds *(www.worldwinds.net)* operates a windsurfing school and rental center right on the beach at Bird Island. Their

With their spinnakers filled with Pacific breezes, sloops colorfully sail under the Golden Gate Bridge.

A four-masted schooner in full sail rounds the coastal headlands of Acadia National Park.

instruction runs from group beginners classes and kids camps to private lessons in deepwater starts, jibe footwork, and other advanced skills.

⭐ Gateway ⭐
NATIONAL RECREATION AREA
Jamaica Bay and Sandy Hook

What do Brooklyn and the Jersey Shore have in common besides beach boardwalks and minor league baseball? Great sailing. A multiunit park flanking the entrance to New York Harbor, Gateway National Recreation Area includes wild and untamed Jamaica Bay on the back end of Brooklyn and the Sandy Hook Peninsula in northern New Jersey. During the summer at Jamaica Bay, the Park Service offers basic sailing instruction, youth group sailing classes, and ranger-led interpretive sails out of Gateway Marina on Flatbush Avenue. Private outfitters like Brooklyn's Sebago Canoe Club (*www.sebagocanoeclub .org*) also have sailing clinics and flotilla cruises on Jamaica Bay. On the Jersey Shore, the calm waters of Sandy Hook Bay are ideal for Hobie Cats and other small, nonmotorized sailboats, which can be launched at Horseshoe Cove. The best conditions for windsurfing and kiteboarding are found on the bay side of the peninsula near Beach Area C.

✳ Virgin Islands ✳
NATIONAL PARK
Caribbean Waters and
Cinnamon Bay

A favorite with both first-time sailors and experienced yachtsmen, the Virgin Islands have everything that makes Caribbean sailing compelling: blue skies, warm weather, and a steady but gentle breeze, as well as great tunes, delicious seafood, and coves that never seem to get too crowded. Virgin Islands National Park sits at the heart of the action, easternmost of the American isles and just across the Sir Francis Drake Channel from the British portion. Many people bring their own boats down from the U.S. eastern seaboard or arrange bareboat charters from adjacent islands like Tortola and St. Thomas. The park provides plenty of safe anchorages and pristine waters in which to swim, snorkel, or scuba dive off the back end of a boat. The town of Cruz Bay is home to both the park visitor center and provision stores where sailors can stock their galleys. Several local outfitters offer crewed charters and catamaran cruises in national park waters, including Radio Flyer *(www.radioflyercatamarancharters.com)* and Cruz Bay Watersports *(www.divestjohn.com)*. Small sailboats and Windsurfers can also be rented on the beach at Cinnamon Bay inside the park. The height of the local yachting season is December to March, but fall and spring are also pleasant. Avoid the June–November hurricane season.

✳ Biscayne ✳
NATIONAL PARK
South Florida Waters

"Sailing again in Margaritaville" could easily be the theme of this laid-back tropical park at the southern end of Florida. Stretching between South Miami and Key Largo, Biscayne embraces more than 200 square miles of sultry sea and sandy islands. Needless to say, boating is the only way to explore much of the park. Most people cruise down from the Miami metro area, but boats can also be put in the water via ramps at three county parks (Homestead Bayfront, Black Point, and Matheson Hammock) adjacent to the federal reserve. Broad, shallow Biscayne Bay separates the mainland park from insular portions like Boca Chita and elongated Elliott Key with their picnic areas and primitive campgrounds. A maritime heritage trail along the eastern edge of the park connects a string of six shipwrecks spanning a hundred years of local maritime history. Windsurfing is also popular, especially along the park's mainland coast, where the calm waters are ideal for novices. Owing to numerous reefs and shoals, National Ocean Service (NOS) navigation charts are highly recommended.

✳ Acadia ✳
NATIONAL PARK
Mount Desert Island Lakes, Somes Sound,
and Frenchman Bay

With a maritime heritage that stretches back more than 400 years, Maine is a cornerstone of American sailing and Acadia one of the few national parks that offers both lake and ocean boating. Small nonmotorized craft can take to the waters of 24 lakes and ponds in the park's Mount Desert Island portion. These range from relatively large bodies of water like Long Pond to the cozy confines of The Tarn near the park's Nature Center. Saltwater sailors also have plenty of scope, from the calm waters of the Somes Sound fjord and Frenchman Bay to the blustery open Atlantic between Mount Desert and Isle au Haut. A number of Acadia's smaller islands are closed during the eagle and seabird nesting seasons; boats can anchor at or circumnavigate the islands

then, but stepping ashore is not permitted. The town of Bar Harbor on the park's eastern flank is a huge sailing center, with numerous marinas and sailing outfitters. Downeast Sailing Adventures (*www.downeastsail.com*) specializes in family-oriented cruises of Somes Sound and the Cranberry Islands on the two-masted schooner *Rachel B. Jackson*. Mansell Boat Rental Company (*www.mansellboatrentals.com*) in Manset village on the south shore of Mount Desert Island offers sailing lessons, personalized sailing tours around Acadia, and 19-foot sailboat rentals.

☆ Apostle Islands ☆
NATIONAL LAKESHORE
Lake Superior Archipelago

A labyrinth of sea caves, hiking trails, empty beaches, and pristine wildlife habitats, Lake Superior's Apostle archipelago offers a rare glimpse of the long-ago Great Lakes. Boating is the only way to explore the islands of this Wisconsin park, especially the smaller and more far-flung landfalls. Thirteen of the islands boast docks where boaters can tie up for the day or overnight, and 13 offer campgrounds for those who want to sleep ashore (some campgrounds are on islands without docks). Sailors can launch their craft from the National Park Service ramp at Little Sand Bay or more than half a dozen locations just outside the park boundaries, including the towns of Bayfield, Ashland, and

Red Cliff. Overnight docking fees on the islands vary from $10 to $20 depending on the length of boat; alternatively, boats can be anchored offshore for free. While sunny days predominate during the boating season, Lake Superior is famous for dramatic shifts in weather including thick fog and violent squalls. For those who don't have their own vessel, Dreamcatcher Sailing (*www.dreamcatcher-sailing.com/apostleislands.htm*) in Bayfield offers day trips and overnight live-aboard cruises.

☆ Cape Hatteras ☆
NATIONAL SEASHORE
Salvo and Haulover on Hatteras Island

"Radical" is the word that veteran windsurfers use to describe the conditions at Cape Hatteras, known for its big waves and big breeze even when its not hurricane season. Newbies (and anyone with any sense) should stick to the calm Pamlico Sound along the western edge of the barrier islands. Those who want to ratchet up their heart rates and adrenalin flow should head for the open ocean side. Maybe even more than for the Wright brothers, the North Carolina seashore is renowned for its capricious weather. One day it's board shorts and sunscreen, the next day dry suit and hood are de rigueur. Even during summer windsurfers should pack for extreme weather shifts. Salvo and Haulover on Hatteras Island are two of the more popular spots to put in, especially when there's good wind blowing from the northeast. Booties are recommended to safeguard feet from sharp, broken shells on the shallow seafloor.

☆ Curecanti ☆
NATIONAL RECREATION AREA
Bay of Chickens and Iola Basin

Don't be fooled by the fowl name: The Bay of Chickens is Colorado's coolest place to windsurf and just one of several where you can "bump and jump" in Curecanti. Strung out along 40 miles of the Gunnison River on the western flank of the Rockies, the recreation area comprises three remote reservoirs. Blue Mesa is the largest of these, home to both the Bay of Chickens and another popular windsurfing spot called the Iola Basin. The former is on the north shore between Dry Gulch Campground and the park's Elk Creek Visitor Center. Iola Basin is farther east, a broad stretch of water that is best accessed from the boat ramp at Stevens Creek Campground. Breezes barreling down through the park's steep, narrow semidesert canyons can present quite a challenge, even for experienced windsurfers. Water temperatures in July and August can reach comfortable levels, but the rest of the year a wet or dry suit is highly recommended.

☆ Yellowstone ☆
NATIONAL PARK
Yellowstone Lake: Volcanic Crater

America's oldest national park may not seem the most obvious place to set sail, but with its steady breeze, wide-open waters, and dazzling scenery, the park's Yellowstone Lake offers an ideal venue for wind sports. In fact, the first European-style craft to grace the lake was a sail-fitted rowboat called *Annie,* part of the 1871 Hayden Survey of the region. Perched at more than 7,000 feet, this is the nation's largest high-altitude lake—as much as 20 miles from north to south and 14 miles from east to west. Bridge Bay Marina on the north shore is the best place to launch sailboats, but all craft should have collapsible masts in order to clear the highway bridge across the harbor mouth. Windsurfers are best launched from Grant Village Marina on the west side, where floating docks and a cement slip provide quick access to the lake. Sailors and surfers must obtain a boating permit ($5 for seven days) from a ranger station before going onto the water. Secluded "boat party" campsites are located along South Arm and Southeast Arm along the lake's roadless southern shore.

☆ Go Fly a Kite ☆

While it might be cool to honor the legacy of Ben Franklin by flying a kite at Independence National Historical Park in Philadelphia, other units of the park system are much more apropos for aerial artistry.

San Juan National Historic Site in Puerto Rico stages a Kite Flying Festival each March on the grounds of El Morro castle, an event that includes kitemaking classes, competitions, and educational talks.

The annual Salem Maritime Festival at **Salem Maritime National Historic Site** in Massachusetts includes kite-flying sessions and lessons, as well as sea chantey sing-alongs and model-boat building.

Kids can relive the world's most famous flight during kite-flying demonstrations and kitemaking workshops at **Wright Brothers National Memorial** in North Carolina.

Children of all ages can design, assemble, and fly kites during summer kite-flying sessions on the Canarsie Pier in **Gateway National Recreation Area,** New York.

chapter four

seasonal enjoyment

wildflower blooms

Enjoying the colors of nature's own palette

Mountains may be spectacular, and waterfalls may be awe-inspiring, but wildflowers in many of our national parks can be unmatched in their display of nature's beauty and variety. Peak seasons vary from year to year depending on rainfall and other factors, so check with rangers before planning a bloom-viewing trip.

Mount Rainier
NATIONAL PARK
Salmonberry to Bunchberry

When it comes to volcanoes, there's bad news and good news: The bad news is that they sometimes create havoc for humankind and nature alike; the good news is that the ash they scatter acts as rich fertilizer, creating lush growing conditions for plants. After millennia of eruptions, the slopes of Washington's Mount Rainier constitute a naturally tended garden of wildflowers. In fact, the park's most popular area was given its name "Paradise" in 1885, when a settler saw a glimpse of heaven in the panorama of Rainier's peak rising above a field of wildflowers. From salmonberry to paintbrush, from lupine to penstemon, from phlox to bunchberry, Mount Rainier offers a never-ending display from late spring through summer, when the meadows of Paradise are a sea of purples, blues, reds, and yellows in all shades. Note that the road to Paradise may not open until late May, depending on weather, and the peak of bloom for subalpine flowers is brief.

Great Smoky Mountains
NATIONAL PARK
1,600 Blooming Plants

The list of 1,600-plus species of flowering plants in Great Smoky Mountains tops that of any other North American national park—the park's own biologists refer to it as "Wildflower National Park"—and in fact, this Appalachian site boasts the greatest biodiversity of any site of similar size on Earth outside the tropics. One major reason is the stability of the landscape: The Great Smoky Mountains are among the planet's oldest ranges, and have been relatively untouched by major geological forces for more than a million years, giving life-forms time to diversify. Elevations in the park range from 875 to 6,643 feet, making it possible to (figuratively) travel from the Southeast to Canada within the park's boundaries. The wildflower show at Great Smoky Mountains begins with spring blooms such as trilliums, lady's slipper orchids, and violets, continues with summer species such as cardinal flower and butterflyweed, and finishes in fall with composites such as goldenrod and coneflowers. Each April the park holds a Spring Wildflower Pilgrimage, a weeklong series of guided walks and programs spotlighting its varied and colorful flora.

✴ Big Bend ✴
NATIONAL PARK
Cacti and Bluebonnet

The words "desert" and "diversity" might seem mutually exclusive to some, but in fact the Chihuahuan Desert of the southwestern United States and Mexico is among the wettest and most biologically varied deserts on Earth. Big Bend serves as the premier showcase of Chihuahuan Desert ecology, with more types of cacti (around 60) than any other national park, and has been honored as a World Heritage site for its globally significant biodiversity. As is the case in all deserts, the wildflower bloom at Big Bend is highly dependent on winter and early spring rains, but in most years it's striking, and in wet years it can be truly spectacular. Not only do cacti such as claret cup and prickly pear provide color, but the park lowlands can be a virtual carpet of wildflowers such as bluebonnet,

Summer blooms add a splash of color to Great Smoky Mountains National Park.

desert baileya, globemallow, cowpen daisy, desert marigold, Chisos prickly poppy, and cenizo, to name only a few of the scores of species. One of Big Bend's most spectacular blooms is displayed by a plant hardly regarded as a wildflower: the Harvard agave or century plant, which features a stalk up to 20 feet high loaded with yellow flowers, blooming just once before it dies.

Although it is native to the Blue Ridge Mountains, much of the beautiful mountain laurel you see blooming along Shenandoah National Park's Skyline Drive in June was planted by the [CCC] in the 1930s.

✻ Indiana Dunes ✻
NATIONAL LAKESHORE
Moss Pink, Blue Flag Iris, and Cardinal Flowers

Best known as a beach getaway for the Chicago metropolitan area, Indiana Dunes surprisingly ranks among the top ten most biologically diverse National Park Service sites, with more than 1,100 flowering plants and ferns. The impetus for the park's creation, in fact, was not recreation but biology—dating back to 1899, when a local biologist wrote a scientific paper describing the site's varied ecosystems. Wildflower diversity is boosted by the presence not only of dunes but of oak savannas, swamps, bogs, marshes, prairies, and forest. Hikers can enjoy blooms such as moss pink, blue flag iris, Dutchman's breeches, cardinal flower, columbine, lupine, pitcher plant, and more than two dozen species of orchids.

✻ Shenandoah ✻
NATIONAL PARK
Bellwort to Toothwort

The ancient Appalachian Mountains are renowned for their biodiversity, a circumstance owing in part to their varied terrain and elevations, as well as their abundant moisture. President Theodore Roosevelt, an ardent nature lover and conservationist, once referred to the Appalachians' "marvelous variety and richness of plant growth." Spanning more than 70 miles north to south, with an elevation range of around 3,500 feet, Shenandoah National Park in Virginia reflects that variety: It's home to more than 1,300 species of plants. Wildflower blooms generally begin in late March and continue through fall; the second weekend in May is the date of the park's annual Wildflower Weekend, when guided field trips help beginners learn colorful species such as bellwort, toothwort, lady's slipper orchid, Solomon's seal, wild ginger, sweet cicely, and various violets.

✻ Rocky Mountain ✻
NATIONAL PARK
Lower Elevation Miner's Candle to Alpine Zone Tundra Blooms

The vast and magnificent peaks of this Colorado park extend the wildflower season for visitors, with displays appearing in spring in the drier montane zone below 6,000 feet, while some species may not bloom on the tundra above tree line until June or even July. In the lower habitat dominated by ponderosa pine, look for geranium, mariposa lily, miner's candle, lupine, and tall penstemon. Higher up in elevation thrive calypso orchid, twinflower, pipsissewa, and the gorgeous blue columbine, the Colorado state flower. But the truly special wildflowers of Rocky Mountain occur in the alpine zone from around 11,000 feet up to more then 14,000, where the growing season is a brief few weeks and harsh conditions mean plants hug the ground to escape the worst of the bitter winds. Plants found here include alpine sunflower, primrose, bistort, avens, mountain dryad, alplily, moss campion, snow buttercup, and sky pilot. Trail Ridge Road provides easy access to this tundra flower garden, but hikers should take special care not to destroy plants with careless footsteps: A small plant may actually be decades old, and revegetation may take even longer.

☆ Yosemite ☆
NATIONAL PARK
Western Wallflowers and California Poppies

Mountains, waterfalls, and giant sequoia trees get the headlines at Yosemite, but many wildflower lovers rank the park among their favorite places for its colorful array of blooms. Habitats range from the foothill-woodland zone at around 1,800 feet up through montane and subalpine forests to the alpine zone above 9,500 feet. As spring and summer progress up the slopes, so do Yosemite's wildflowers change from week to week. Some of the most colorful blooms are western wallflower, blue flag iris, fire pink, leopard lily, shooting star, Lewis's monkeyflower, marsh marigold, fiddleneck, California poppy, and crimson columbine—although this list barely scratches the surface of Yosemite's diversity. To experience the full range of park wildflowers in summer, drive from the Arch Rock entrance on El Portal Road to Crane Flat and then up Tioga Road through Tuolumne Meadows to 9,945-foot Tioga Pass.

☆ Buffalo ☆
NATIONAL RIVER
Spring-blooming May Apple

America's first national river, the Buffalo is famed for crystal-clear water, high bluffs, and canoeing suitable for boaters of all abilities. The Arkansas Ozark Plateau also boasts a splendid diversity of flora, especially in the moist, steep-sided valleys locally called "hollers." Blooming begins as early as February, when the leaves have yet to appear on trees. Hepatica, bloodroot, toothwort, rue anemone, wild ginger, trout lily, and various violets are among the first to appear, followed by trilliums, May apple, jack-in-the-pulpit, green dragon, Solomon's seal, columbine, phlox, and many others. The easy trail in Lost Valley, near Ponca, is a good place to start enjoying Buffalo River wildflowers, but visiting a variety of habitats, from streamsides to clearings to rocky ledges, will bring the greatest species total. Trails near Pruitt and the ghost town of Rush, once a thriving mining community, are other good places to explore.

☆ Wildflower Identification ☆

Think it's impossible to tell one wildflower from another? If so, it's probably just because you haven't tried. Most parks have bookstores with field guides ranging from booklets covering the most common local wildflowers to comprehensive regional guides. Some wildflower books are  arranged by color and season, making it even easier to attach a name to an unknown bloom, or check at the visitor center to see if any wildflower hikes are being offered. If you're carrying a digital camera, snap a photo of that mystery plant and show it to staff; they are often very knowledgeable about the blooms in their park and can at least provide the species common name or place it in a family. Pretty soon you'll know a larkspur from a lily, and you'll enjoy your outdoor adventures even more.

☆ Tallgrass Prairie ☆
NATIONAL PRESERVE
Milkweeds, Prairie Clover, and
Native Bluestem

When Europeans first arrived on the shores of North America, tallgrass prairie covered 140 million acres of the continent, supporting spectacular gatherings of wildlife, from bison to elk to wolves to prairie-chickens. Today, only about 4 million acres of this habitat remains, most of it in scattered patches too small to serve as functioning ecosystems. Tallgrass Prairie National Preserve, in the Flint Hills of eastern Kansas, protects a sizable tract of the grassland that once blanketed much of the Great Plains. The 500 species of plants occurring on the 10,894 acres here include butterflyweed and other milkweeds, wild indigo, Indian blanket, liatris, beebalm, prairie clover, coneflower, compass plant, coreopsis, aster, and leadplant. The Southwind Nature Trail and the Bottomland Trail both offer up close looks at prairie wildflowers, as well as native grasses such as big bluestem, Indian grass, and switchgrass growing to heights of 8 feet or more.

☆ Joshua Tree ☆
NATIONAL PARK
Joshua Trees to Fan Palms

This vast park (covering 789,745 acres) in southern California is a favorite destination for travelers who enjoy seeing and photographing wildflowers. Joshua Tree lies at the meeting point of the Colorado and Mojave deserts, two ecosystems quite different in the composition of their vegetation. The Colorado Desert, in the eastern part of the park, is both hotter and drier than the Mojave Desert in the west. The plant for which the park is named, the Joshua tree (a species of yucca), grows in the latter habitat, blooming profusely in spring. The park also includes part

Joshua Tree is home to 813 vascular plant species, including several species of cholla cactus.

of the Little San Bernardino Mountains, dominated by juniper and pinyon pine, and several oases where fan palms grow. Wildflower season begins in early spring in the southern part of Joshua Tree, progressing through the year to blooms in the highest mountains in June. Some of the herbs and shrubs growing here include desert dandelion, desert gold poppy, chuparosa, ocotillo, Arizona lupine, paperbag bush, mariposa lily, desert senna, indigo bush, brittlebush, chia, fiddleneck, and several types of cactus. How diverse is the vegetation in Joshua Tree National Park? When conservationists proposed saving this area in the 1930s, one suggested name was Desert Plants National Park.

fall foliage

Great destinations for traveling leaf-peepers

Each autumn, nature puts on its own display of artistic creation, as hardwood trees from oaks to aspen change color as the tree gets ready for winter, delighting us with blazing reds and yellows, subtle earth tones, and nearly every shade in between. The following national parks offer some of the best fall color to be found in the United States.

☆ Blue Ridge ☆
PARKWAY
Maples in Shenandoah and Great Smokies

Timing is everything in viewing fall foliage, as environmental factors can cause peak color to vary from year to year at any one spot. Stretching 469 miles mostly north to south through Virginia and North Carolina, the Blue Ridge Parkway offers travelers assurance that they'll run into the best colors somewhere along the way, as autumn (figuratively speaking) moves south across the eastern United States, and specifically across the Blue Ridge Range of the Appalachian Mountains. In addition, the parkway links two of our best fall-foliage national parks: Shenandoah and Great Smoky Mountains, each worth exploration by road and trail. Maples are the stars of the scenic show along the drive, with a supporting cast of oak, poplar, birch, blackgum, sassafras, tulip-poplar (a species of magnolia that grows very tall in these mountains), sumac, and other hardwoods. The great elevation differences along the Blue Ridge Parkway and in the two national parks

means that different areas reach top color at different times, adding to the likelihood that a visitor will find eye-popping hues. Peak color usually arrives at Shenandoah National Park in mid-October, with Great Smoky Mountains National Park typically a little later.

☆ Acadia ☆
NATIONAL PARK
Coastal Birch, Aspens, Poplars, and Maples

Much of the fabulous fall color of this national park on the Maine coast is owed to a disaster of more than a half century ago. The autumn of 1947 brought the driest conditions ever recorded to Mount Desert Island, location of most of Acadia National Park's expanse. A fire broke out in mid-October and raged for ten days, burning 17,188 acres, including 10,000 acres in the park. Mature spruce and fir forest was destroyed, replaced by fast-growing hardwoods such as birch, aspen, poplar, and maple. Instead of the uniform year-round green of conifers, once

In autumn, the Blue Ridge Parkway's forests dazzle in reds, yellows, and browns.

devastated parts of Acadia now display reds, oranges, and yellows in fall, delighting those who drive its scenic loop or hike or bike along its historic unpaved carriage roads, from which motorized vehicles are banned. A map of Mount Desert Island

> *Indian legend has it that celestial hunters killed the Great Bear and the blood splattered some trees red. When the bear was cooked, its fat splattered other trees yellow.*

is often described as looking like a lobster claw; the burned area is located on the central part of the eastern half of the "claw."

✳ Guadalupe Mountains ✳
NATIONAL PARK
Maples, Oaks, and Walnuts
in McKittrick Canyon

How in this western Texas park do the words "fall foliage" and "Guadalupe Mountains" possibly go together? The stark Chihuahuan Desert landscape seems too harsh for any but the hardiest plants, and the highest slopes are covered with ponderosa pines and Douglas-fir, green year-round. Yet there's a special spot in this national park that attracts thousands of leaf-peepers each fall and in fact has been called, with plenty of justification, "the most beautiful place in Texas." It's McKittrick Canyon, in the northeastern part of the park, a chasm known for both its geology and its flora. Here, bigtooth maples, oaks, walnuts, and other hardwood trees and shrubs turn shades of yellow, red, and orange each fall, creating a scene so striking that crowds sometimes cause park managers to limit entry to prevent damage to the natural resources. Late October through mid-November is the usual period for peak leaf color in this riparian oasis, where hiking trails of various lengths offer the chance to see the show up close. Be sure to take note of the unusual geology here: These massive mountains

actually began as reefs under an ancient warm ocean. The same limestone has been hollowed out underground just north of here to form the network of caves at Carlsbad Caverns National Park. The canyon is designated for day use only, but a drive-in campground is within distance for those people who'd like to spend more time exploring this canyon during the cooler days of fall.

✳ Rocky Mountain ✳
NATIONAL PARK
Quaking Aspen
Along Trail Ridge Road

One species of tree dominates the fall foliage at this central Colorado park: quaking aspen *(Populus tremuloides)*. But this deciduous tree's stunning colors of greenish yellow to glittering gold make it worthy of a visit all by itself. Beginning in mid-September, aspens start to change their hues, continuing into October before the harsh Rocky Mountain winter strips the leaves from the branches. Aspens grow where fire or past logging has removed the dominant conifer forest and are found up to 10,000 feet on mountainsides. They often grow in clumps or groves and can reach heights of up to 100 feet. These trees "quake" because the leaf petiole (stem) is flat instead of round as in most trees, causing the leaves to quiver in the slightest breeze and adding to the attractiveness of the golden masses; in addition, when the aspens quake, they make a delightful soft rustling sound unlike any other tree ruffled by the wind. Large areas of aspen grow throughout Rocky Mountain National Park, easily seen from Trail Ridge Road, Bear Lake Road, and many other park locations.

✵ Cuyahoga Valley ✵
NATIONAL PARK
Oak, Hickory, Maple, Beech, and Sycamore
Beside the Ohio & Erie Canal

Covering more than 51 square miles along 22 miles of the Cuyahoga River between Cleveland and Akron, Ohio, this diverse, quasi-urban park protects some of the region's most attractive woodlands. Though perhaps best known for its Towpath Trail and waterfalls, Cuyahoga Valley provides fall foliage in areas of mixed hardwood forest comprising oak, hickory, maple, beech, and sycamore. Fall color usually peaks in October. The Ohio & Erie Canalway Scenic Byway runs through the center of the park, but for an unusual way to admire the autumn color, buy a ticket on the Cuyahoga Valley Scenic Railroad, sit back, and watch the forest pass outside the train window.

✵ Zion ✵
NATIONAL PARK
Virgin River's
Freemont Cottonwoods

Best known for its spectacular geological formations and slot canyons, this southwestern Utah park is also well known regionally for the fall foliage of its hardwoods. In riparian areas along the Virgin River and other streams grow Fremont cottonwoods, which turn a beautiful shade of pale gold in autumn, while bigtooth maple, box elder (another type of maple), birch, oak, and hackberry add their hues, as well. In both streamside locations and higher on slopes, quaking aspens turn a more brilliant gold. Because Zion National Park encompasses a large elevation range, the period of fall color extends from September (in the high mountains) well into November (in the lowlands). When sunrise or sunset light turns Zion's rocks a gold-red color and the leaves add their spectacle, few parks can match it for sheer visual impact.

✵ Buffalo ✵
NATIONAL RIVER
Oak and Hickory of the Ozark Plateau

While less celebrated, fall color in the highlands of the Ozark Plateau in northern Arkansas and southern Missouri can match that of the Appalachian mountain ranges. Beginning in late October and peaking sometime in November, the spectacle here can be breathtaking. Many species of oaks and hickories dominate the forest, with maples, sassafras, sweet gum, blackgum, beech, sumac, and dogwood adding to the fall spectrum. It all starts with the bright crimson of blackgum (also known as black tupelo) in early September, continuing well into November

In the fall, the white bark and bright yellow leaves of quaking aspen make for a spectacular display.

The setting sun highlights Zion National Park's autumnal colors and its red-rock walls.

with oak leaves in shades of yellow and rust. The topography is an attraction in itself: Millennia of erosion have cut steep-sided canyons throughout the region, creating some of the most rugged landscape between the Appalachians and the Rockies. Arkansas 21 near Boxley, Ark. 74 between Ponca and Jasper, and U.S. 65 near Marshall are all fine driving routes to see Ozarks fall color. The lower stretches of Buffalo National River can be paddled in a canoe or raft in fall as well, and many miles of trails are available to hikers. Try the short, easy Lost Valley Trail for a good introduction to the Buffalo River area, or drive down the switchbacks to the Steel Creek area to see beautiful foliage against a background of the tall riverside bluffs for which the Buffalo is famous.

✴ Delaware Water Gap ✴
NATIONAL RECREATION AREA
Delaware River Oak

Set in the Delaware River Valley of Pennsylvania and New Jersey, this park includes historic villages, farmland, and grassland, but it's mostly covered by a maturing hardwood forest, slowly growing back from periods of logging in previous centuries. Extensive tracts of various oaks offer a range of fall colors from dull yellow to red-orange. Other hardwoods showing beautiful fall colors include maple, birch, hickory, dogwood, beech, and sycamore. More than 200 miles of roads wind through Delaware Water Gap; some good ones to explore include Old Mine Road in New Jersey and U.S. 209 and River Road in Pennsylvania. Three scenic overlooks along Pa. 611 provide great views of the Delaware River as it passes through the Water Gap, an eroded low point in Kittatinny Ridge. For a closer view of the park's forest, hike some of the 27 miles of the Appalachian National Scenic Trail running through the area.

☆ Little River Canyon ☆
NATIONAL PRESERVE
Southern Hardwoods Along Canyon Rim

This little-known park in northeastern Alabama combines tree species of the Appalachians with those of Deep South hardwood forests for a diversity that adds to the color palette in fall. Take the Canyon Rim scenic drive off Ala. 35 along Little River Canyon for a fine overview of the environment. Several overlooks include one at beautiful Little River Falls, where the river cascades over rock ledges beneath tree-covered hillsides. Maples, oaks, hickories, sweet gum, black-gum, and tulip-poplar span the color range from pale yellow to vivid orange. The gorge, one of the deepest in the country east of the Mississippi River, looks especially stunning at the peak of color, usually from mid-October through early November.

☆ Effigy Mounds ☆
NATIONAL MONUMENT
Mississippi Bluffs Aspens and Walnuts

Iowa is not all flat—as evidenced by this park in the extreme northeastern corner of the state, where 400-foot-high bluffs loom over the Mississippi River. Neither is the state all farmland and prairie; for proof, just walk some of the 14 miles of trails in Effigy Mounds National Monument through upland forests of oak, sugar, maple, hickory, aspen, walnut, Kentucky coffee tree, and basswood, all of which show beautiful colors in a brief blaze of glory, late September through early October. The national monument was set aside to protect more than 200 American Indian ceremonial mounds (including 31 in the shape of animals such as birds, bear, and deer), but the park designation had the side effect of preserving woodlands, wetlands, and 81 acres of native tallgrass prairie. In all, the natural features of this historical park make it one of the most diverse sites in the upper Midwest for everyone from bird-watchers to hikers to weekend scenery oglers.

☆ Fall Foliage Watch ☆

Predicting peak autumn color for a particular location is a tricky business. Though some general assumptions can be made, the exact period of brightest shades varies annually depending on factors such as rainfall, temperature, and amount of sunshine. So what's a would-be leaf-peeper to do? Increasingly, state and local tourism agencies as well as weathermen are providing up-to-the-moment reports on fall foliage, allowing travelers to make last-minute plans to see those flaming maples. Check the websites of tourism departments for foliage status reports or local toll-free numbers providing information on when and where to travel for the best leaf color.

night skies

Where stars shine brilliantly against a dark backdrop

Just as the parks are dedicated to preserving landscapes, cultural sites, and habitat for wildlife, so are they concerned about overhead resources—particularly the kind of dark skies that reveal the beauty of the nighttime firmament. A major component of the parks' night-sky programs is to guide visitors toward an appreciation of dark skies.

✴ Bryce Canyon ✴
NATIONAL PARK
Andromeda Galaxy

Bryce has long staged one of the most popular night-sky shows in the national parks—so much so that the program consists of two shows, one at Bryce Canyon Lodge, the other at the park visitor center, on Tuesdays, Thursdays, and Saturdays in summer and fall. (Be sure to confirm the schedule with the park.) After the shows, everyone moves outdoors to view the sky through dozens of telescopes provided by the park and volunteers. And what a sky—so dark and clear that the Andromeda galaxy can be seen with the naked eye, a claim astronomers don't believe until they come to Bryce and see it. While program participants wait for a scope session, they can see the Milky Way arcing across the sky from horizon to horizon. So dark is the sky here that Jupiter and Venus throw shadows, and if the moon is out, a third shadow might be cast by the heavens. If the moon is full the star show is diminished, but the park then leads full-moon hikes.

✴ Natural Bridges ✴
NATIONAL MONUMENT
Milky Way

Remote Natural Bridges is about as close as you can come to experiencing the night sky as it was before human lights trespassed upon it. The monument's dark sky is rated a Bortle Class 2, Class 1 being the sky as it would be before the invention of the light bulb. In fact, a look out over the horizon from the parking lot reveals no artificial lights. The monument's arid climate and elevation (6,500 feet) contribute as well. Little wonder, then, that Natural Bridges was named the world's first International Dark-sky Park by the International Dark-sky Association. The park runs a weekly program from spring through fall that starts with a lecture and a naked-eye guided tour of the Milky Way's intricately interwoven stars and clouds of dust and gas, vivid without the aid of optics, followed by viewing sessions through an 11-inch Celestron telescope. The park astronomer often shares his own powerful personal custom optics.

✶ Chaco Culture ✶
NATIONAL HISTORICAL PARK
Supernovas and Asteroids

How valued is Chaco Culture's night sky? It's the only unit in the National Park System with its own observatory. Thanks to a private donation, the park, researchers, and the public have a 25-inch Dobsonian telescope at their disposal, a powerful scope whose specialty is deep-space viewing. In tandem with a digital imaging system, the scope is able to track and photograph changes in the heavens, such as supernovas and asteroids. Many of its thousands of images are incorporated in the park's frequent night-sky programs. Those programs, held Tuesday, Friday, and Saturday evenings in an outdoor amphitheater, include the opportunity to view the heavens directly through the big Dobsonian, as well as a number of smaller but still very powerful telescopes and others provided by volunteers. Of course, this being a historic park, cultural connections are also part of the presentation, which illustrates how certain doorways and structures built by the Chaco people receive the rays of the sun at the time of the solstices. Full moon? No problem. That's when the park conducts special full-moon tours of some of the ancient Chacoan structures.

The Milky Way galaxy stretches across the night sky above Owachomo Bridge in Natural Bridges National Monument.

In a rare conjunction, the moon, Venus, and Jupiter hang above the lava fields of Hawaii Volcanoes.

✳ Hawaii Volcanoes ✳
NATIONAL PARK
Southern Cross Constellation

Hawaii Volcanoes shares some of the conditions that make nearby Mauna Kea one of the world's great observatories—namely, distance from cities and an islandwide lighting ordinance that ensures dark skies. The park adds two bonuses—a certain volcano and programs that pay cultural homage to the Polynesians, who were amazing celestial navigators. You can gather on the back deck of the park's Jagger Museum at dusk and look down into the Halemaumau Crater, with its orange-glowing lava lake churning 300 feet below. As dark falls and the stars emerge, a ranger will bring out a spotting scope to train on the skies, so you get two shows in one. Afterward, driving down Chain of Craters Road, claim a pullout for an astounding, open-horizon view out over the lava fields beneath the Southern Cross constellation.

✳ Sleeping Bear Dunes ✳
NATIONAL LAKESHORE
North Star and Milky Way

Sleeping Bear Dunes has one of the darkest skies in the Midwest; one just has to be willing to stay up late to see it. The park is on the western edge of the eastern time zone, so dark doesn't fall in summer until 10 or 10:30 p.m. When it does, it's really dark—Lake Michigan to the west is an utter void, and the nearest town of any size is more than 30 miles away. While waiting for the appearance of the Milky Way, you can attend a ranger talk on the night sky, watch for the occasional green flash that accompanies sunset, and possibly enjoy the moonset over the lake. Later in the year, the northern lights often appear. At dark, head for the beach at the mouth of the Platte River, or the Lake Michigan overlook on the park's scenic drive, or simply burrow into a sand dune and practice what you learned in the ranger show—celestial navigation, measuring latitude by the North Star, or grab some binoculars and behold sights like the Lagoon Nebula in Sagittarius.

✳ Haleakala ✳
NATIONAL PARK
Jupiter's Moons

An ancient Hawaiian tradition says that day begins at sunset. Haleakala is a great place to begin your day. The 10,000-foot volcano has consistently clear, dark skies—so dark that visitors familiar with constellations get disoriented when there's little or no moon out. High on the mountain, with clouds sealing out light from below, they become confused by the amazing profusion of stars. Check with the park regarding its schedule of night-sky programs, which take place at Hosmer Grove Campground. The programs are often about the stargazing prowess and stories of the early Hawaiians. If there's no program, pick up a star map at the visitor center and proceed to the top of the mountain or one of the overlooks en route. Dress for the chill. It's a great show even without optical aid. With just average binoculars, the Galilean moons of Jupiter are visible.

☆ Acadia ☆
NATIONAL PARK
Milky Way

Because Acadia is largely surrounded by ocean and its nearby communities honor dark-sky ordinances, the park has by far the darkest sky in the eastern United States. During Summer on Sand Beach sessions, you lie on your backs in the sand while a ranger stages a guided tour of the night sky, and afterward view the sky through telescopes provided by the park and volunteers. The park also stages regular nighttime hikes to illustrate how humans can easily adapt to the dark. The annual Night Sky Festival in September (*www.nightskyfestival.org*) is a time of lectures, star parties, and viewing the Milky Way through telescopes. On your own, Cadillac Mountain is a great place for a 360-degree dark-sky view, but be prepared for a cold and windy session.

☆ Great Basin ☆
NATIONAL PARK
Hercules and Albireo

Nevada may be synonymous with bright lights for some, but Great Basin, with its isolated setting near the Utah border, is hardly on the same planet as Las

☆ Shining Light on Dark Skies ☆

In dark-sky national parks, rangers urge visitors to try going without any light at all at night—stars and moon provide plenty of illumination in these parks, and being dark adapted is the best way to enjoy the night sky. To read a star chart in the field, rangers recommend a small red-bulb flashlight. The National Park Service's Night Sky Team is attempting to raise this kind of consciousness among park visitors and employees alike.

Light pollution has more than an aesthetic effect. It also confuses and harms nocturnal animals: It affects their ability to prey, causes bird–building collisions, and disrupts migration patterns. And it's common knowledge how deer react to headlights. A modest triumph for the Night Sky Team, many parks now use "down lighting" that directs outdoor lights to where they're needed—down. Lights that shine upward are a waste of electricity and a major cause of light pollution.

The team monitors light pollution in 30 parks nationwide, which is how Natural Bridges National Monument won the title of darkest sky in the parks. Even in the lower parts of the Grand Canyon, the glow of lights from Las Vegas, 175 miles away, shimmers on the horizon. But in Natural Bridges, Bryce Canyon, and so many other parks, it is still possible to sleep under the stars and experience the awe that Galileo must have known back when all night skies were dark.

Vegas or Reno. The park is blessed with exceptionally dark skies and, outside of its high forested sections, a nearly 360-degree view of the horizon, where the Milky Way takes center stage on summer nights. Weekly programs at the Lehman Caves Visitor Center stress the importance of dark skies and the impact of light pollution (check with the park for schedule and for details on the annual August Astronomy Festival). Then everyone steps outside for a telescope viewing session of such distant objects as the Hercules globular star cluster and the binary star Albireo, and naked-eye views of the dramatic galactic center of the Milky Way. The park also stages regular walks on moonlit nights, often among the bristlecone pines high on Wheeler Peak.

✶ Capitol Reef ✶
NATIONAL PARK
Saturn, Mars, and
Dumbbell Nebula

Distant from cities and a mile high, Capitol Reef has what astronomers call magnitude 7 skies, meaning one can see magnitude 7—very, very distant—objects with the naked eye. Which means the unpolluted sky is very, very dark and the star show is amazing. After the regular evening ranger presentations, rangers bring out the park's Meade telescope and the star party starts around 10 p.m. with dazzlers like Saturn and Mars just before they fall below the horizon. Then come more distant showpieces and their accompanying stories, like the Dumbbell Nebula, revealing amazing detail—its spiral arms, its tidal interactions with neighbors,

> *Interpretations of the celestial bodies varied widely among cultures, but often the sky was considered the abode of gods, a place humans could never touch.*

the Lagoon Nebula and the Triffid Nebula—9,000 light-years away in Sagittarius. Naked-eye viewing is also dazzling—Mizar and Alcor, binary stars in the Big Dipper, and Albireo, which appears to be one bright star until the Meade reveals its companion. Unless a midsummer monsoonal flow clouds the skies, viewing is superb throughout the park, but nowhere more dramatic than from Panorama Point.

✶ Big Bend ✶
NATIONAL PARK
Andromeda Galaxy or
Moonless Sky

It's no surprise that arid, remote Big Bend, 225 miles from the nearest city, has night skies among the darkest in the national parks. You are frequently startled by the darkness of the sky—Big Bend is considered to be the least light-polluted national park in the lower 48 states—and the abundance of stars. At least 2,000 stars are visible to the naked eye on a clear moonless night, as well as planets and shooting stars. A broad, 250-mile-distant horizon helps too, as does new night-sky–friendly lighting around the main visitor centers at headquarters and Chisos Basin. Both centers stage occasional outdoor night-sky viewing sessions, with park telescopes. On a clear night, the telescopes can see as far as 2 million light-years away to the Andromeda galaxy. Check with the park for the current schedule. Winter brings the darkest and cleanest skies—in part due to low humidity and infrequent cloud cover—and there's no particular "best" place in the park to view them. Just look up.

ten best parks
sunrise/sunset points

Nature's take on *Good Morning America* and *The Tonight Show*

Although it happens twice a day, more often than not the natural phenomenon of the rising and setting sun is overlooked. Where this event does command a lot of attention is at national parks, where perhaps an extraordinary landscape or a prominent feature accentuates this important and extraordinarily beautiful event.

☆ Acadia ☆
NATIONAL PARK
Sunrise From Cadillac Mountain

Long before early risers are up for their doughnuts and coffee, earlier risers are up at Acadia National Park in time to catch America's first sunrise. Between October and March, the first light of day to fall upon the United States shines upon 1,528-foot Cadillac Mountain in the heart of Acadia, on Maine's coast. It's a wonderful sensation to feel the warmth of the sun without having to share it with 300 million others, and that experience is heightened by spectacular panoramic views from an overlook at the peak. The sun rises above the Atlantic Ocean's horizon and casts streaks of color—oranges, reds, pinks, depending on atmospheric conditions—upon the water, while in the foreground the exposed rock of the mountains glows warmly in the sun's glow. From the parking lot walk to the Summit Trail and find a spot (out of the wind) facing east. Plan this ascent. Gates are open 24 hours at the park, but due to weather conditions, the road to the top of Cadillac Mountain is closed between December 1 and April 14. Sunrise occurs around 6:30 a.m. in October, about a half hour later in November. Dress for the weather, bring along a camera, some snacks, and something warm to drink while waiting for the start of the daily show.

☆ Yosemite ☆
NATIONAL PARK
Sunset Views of Half Dome

Nature photographers will never lack for an amazing image as long as there are sunsets and Half Dome. Near the end of each clear day, the usually harsh sun softens to cast an even and gentle glow throughout the eastern end of Yosemite Valley, deep within this California national park. Within minutes, the exposed northwest face of Half Dome begins to change hues with the setting sun and, depending on the season, the scene may vary between a brilliant reddish orange and a soft wintery gray. Other mountains are being illuminated across America, certainly, but Half Dome's broad wall of granite seems to scoop up every ray of the setting sun, creating an inspiring glow across what could be the world's largest sundial.

☆ Canaveral ☆
NATIONAL SEASHORE
Sunrise Over
Klondike Beach

In the 1950s, the government determined that the scientists, engineers, and astronauts working on America's space program on the southern end of Cape Canaveral needed some privacy. To protect the cape from further development while ensuring privacy, in 1975 Congress preserved 58,000 acres of seashore, land, and lagoons along with 24 miles of protected coastline to create the longest undeveloped beach on Florida's Atlantic coast. Arrive here for sunrise and infinity lies to the east. The barrier island beaches—Apollo, Klondike, and Playalinda—are largely absent of people so this will reveal a Florida sunrise in its natural state, an experience that is a pure pleasure and one that can be savored minus the din of highway traffic and far from the sight of 20-story condos. This is especially true of Klondike beach, sandwiched between the two others and accessible only by foot; Klondike has been designated

The Bass Harbor Lighthouse provides a perfect setting for watching the sun set at Acadia National Park.

a backcountry beach, and the park restricts the number of visitors to its wave-lapped sands. Bring a beach chair, set up on the sands, and at daybreak the music of nature begins. Here comes the sun.

☆ National Mall ☆
WASHINGTON, D.C.
Sunrise & Sunset Beyond
Capitol Building and the Lincoln Memorial

With national icons framing each end of the east-west National Mall in Washington, D.C., dawn and dusk softly and gradually illuminate silent sentinels of American history. When the crisp blue and orange sky breaks in the east, the gleaming white Capitol dome topped by the Statue of Freedom is bathed in the refreshing rays of daybreak, and the effect elicits a natural sense of optimism. At dusk, try to find a spot on or near the steps on the west front of the Capitol building. The Mall is adorned in the comforting rays of sunset that first descend behind the Washington Monument before backlighting the Lincoln Memorial. Once again, that sense of hope and optimism returns, knowing that now and for the next several hours it will shine from here to the Pacific as it falls across 3,000 miles of America.

☆ Joshua Tree ☆
NATIONAL PARK
Sunset of Joshua Trees Along Park Roads

As the afternoon fades into evening over Joshua Tree's cactus and pinyon, cool clouds fingerpaint the sky above this southern California desert park. Adding an aural layer to the vivid spectacle of sunset is the distinct bay of howling coyotes. Roads and ridges that run north and south persuade travelers to reach peaks that provide an ever changing vista as the world turns. Should a vehicle be able to negotiate off-road trails, views can improve through access to

☆ Native American Sky-watchers ☆

With instant access nowadays to information about weather and tides, sunrises and sunsets, phases of the moon and seasonal changes, it's easy to assume we hold a monopoly on understanding the cycles of nature. Not necessarily. A few hundred—or a few thousand—years ago Native Americans, primarily in the Southwest, were capable of observing celestial bodies and tracking the seasons to predict with amazing accuracy the cycles of the sun. On summer solstice, winter solstice, and the vernal equinox, petroglyphs at Arizona's **Petrified Forest National Park** highlight the relation between Earth and the sun. In New Mexico, in the remote Chaco Canyon at the **Chaco Culture National Historic Park,** shafts of light called "sun daggers" similarly pierce spiral petroglyphs on Fajada Butte. Although off-limits to park guests to protect its integrity, this and other examples of archaeoastronomy are displayed at national parks.

little-visited areas populated by cacti and junipers and yuccas, and silhouetted against the horizon, the most special part of sunset, the park's eponymous Joshua trees. Framed by bands of color, darker above and brighter below, these otherworldly plants appear as inky black splotches against the sky.

☆ Badlands ☆
NATIONAL PARK
Sunrise & Sunset From
Eastern Overlooks and North–South Ridges

The cliché image of a cowboy riding into a beautiful sunset magnifies the cowboy's independence as well as nature's power. That feeling still exists in South Dakota's Badlands National Park, where a lack of development leads to a refreshing sense of solitude. In the eastern reaches of the park, a series of overlooks are carved out from the colorful buttes for a perfect vantage point and sanctuary, where the lonely wide-open prairie, protected in the adjoining Buffalo Gap National Grassland, leads to a feeling of oneness with nature. From atop a north-south ridge are commanding views at dawn and dusk, and after the sun disappears in a swirl of pink and orange clouds the night sky is soon aglow with a shimmering sheath of stars.

> *After sunset [in Arches], the ground rapidly loses heat to the night sky and ambient air temperatures may drop significantly before dawn. Temperature fluctuations of over 40 degrees in a 24-hour period are not uncommon.*

✴ Death Valley ✴
NATIONAL PARK
Sunrise and Sunset at
Zabriskie Point and the Sand Dunes

Two areas in this western California national park offer near-ideal settings for watching the sun rise or set. Zabriskie Point is encircled by a colorful montage of mountains and valleys, and here the line of sight will sweep up to the summit of Telescope Peak and, in the distance, down again into the depths of a smidgen of 156-mile-long Death Valley. Of the 2,600 square miles contained within the park, this vantage point near Furnace Creek is considered the premium overlook for both sunrise and sunset. Just off Calif. 190, this viewpoint is easily accessible by vehicle; a paved trail leads to a popular observation deck while a little-noticed path leads a short distance north to present the landscape from a slightly higher elevation. With this advantage, the soft red-violet glow of sunrise adds shadows and depth to the surreal landscape of the peaks and ridges once hidden by a prehistoric sea. The Eureka and Mesquite Flat Sand

Dunes offer a no less spectacular sunrise or sunset, just a different one. Here at dawn or dusk the low-angled rays of the sun rake across the dunes, burnishing the sand to a high glow and highlighting ripples and ridges and animal tracks.

✴ Arches ✴
NATIONAL PARK
Dusk at Delicate Arch

At sunset in Utah's Arches National Park, Delicate Arch seems to ignite with the flare and fire of the desert sun, its iconic image symbolizing the American Southwest. It's roughly 1.5 miles from Wolfe Ranch to the arch via the Delicate Arch Trail, so time your hike to arrive at least 30 minutes before sunset and simply follow the cairns that mark the route. The trail pitches up and around the final corner where, pierced by wind and sand, the center of the "sandstone fin" has created a 46-foot arch that, at sunset, changes like a desert chameleon, filtering sunset through a color wheel of red and orange and crimson and gold.

✴ Petrified Forest ✴
NATIONAL PARK
Summer Solstice Sunrise

With Arizona's Petrified Forest National Park an already magical setting for a great American sunrise, one day in particular may influence anyone's travel schedule. With the sun's rays tracking a slightly different path throughout the year, for ten days before and after June 21 (with the highlight being on the summer solstice), the Earth's alignment with the sun impacts more than a dozen "solar calendars" left throughout the park by prehistoric peoples, with the spiral and circular petroglyphs being intersected by or interacting with the sun's rising rays. Ancient tribes took time to place them here. Take time to marvel at their confluence of ancient science and nature.

☆ Saguaro ☆

NATIONAL PARK

Sunset Silhouettes of Saguaro
Along Cactus Forest Drive

Any diorama of the Old West includes the striking silhouettes of Arizona saguaro cactus, the towering icon recognized by its barrel trunk and upraised arms. These alone are worth the visit to the two areas of this national park that bookend the city of Tucson. The eastern Rincon Mountain District is the larger of the two, with ancient saguaros sharing the land with other varieties of cactus including prickly pear and ocotillo. There's a greater density of saguaro in the western region, but the eastern side features Cactus Forest Drive, a popular loop road across the flatland that provides easy access to saguaro views. These sunsets may not be the most spectacular in America, but seeing a Southwest icon framed in silhouette is a vision not to be missed, especially as twilight falls and bands of color are squeezed on the horizon beneath a velvety dark blue night sky.

Sunset views across the badlands of the eponymous national park reveal wide-open skies ablaze with color.

ten best parks
picnic spots
Places that make outdoor dining an event

Apicnic shouldn't be just a meal quickly swallowed on the way to something else—it should also be an opportunity to savor time and place. The following picnic spots in the national parks make even a simple sandwich outside a real occasion, with scenery, atmosphere, and recreation all important parts of the experience.

☆ White Sands ☆
NATIONAL MONUMENT
Lyle Bennett Picnic Shelters
Along Dunes Drive

For a dramatic change in surroundings from the lush, shaded sites of Shenandoah and Whiskeytown, try picnicking in the American Southwest at White Sands National Monument in New Mexico. Brilliantly white under a strong sun, 275 square miles of sand dunes form an expanse that's starkly beautiful and constantly shifting as wind blows the malleable terrain. In the very heart of the dunes, off Dunes Drive, are picnic areas with individual picnic shelters scattered through the sands. These shelters were crafted by architect Lyle Bennett to reflect the architectural style of Frank Lloyd Wright, and are designed to shade visitors from the sun. Those picnicking under one of these shelters are guaranteed a truly memorable experience: Looking out over the dazzling expanse of gypsum dunes while enjoying their meal, alfresco diners feel alone and very small, and set adrift in the vast sea of sand. It's

an interesting and unusual place to enjoy a picnic lunch, but here's the one hitch: Picnickers need to be prepared to do whatever possible to keep sand out of their food. And don't forget sunglasses!

☆ Pictured Rocks ☆
NATIONAL LAKESHORE
Miners Castle and Miners Beach

The colorful variegated sandstone cliffs of Pictured Rocks National Lakeshore are a stunning setting for picnicking. Water and wind chiseled sandstone into striking, irregular cliff formations that tower above Lake Superior on Michigan's Upper Peninsula, and nowhere is this phenomenon better witnessed than at Miners Castle, one of the best known features in the park. There's a beautifully constructed picnic site at the head of a trail that leads down to an overlook of Miners Castle, and it's the perfect spot to bring a basket lunch and fuel up before ambling down to the overlook, taking in sweeping views of Lake Superior and Grand Island on the way. Miners Beach, about 6 miles north of Miners Castle,

Sheltered picnic tables appear otherworldly against the sugar white backdrop of White Sands National Monument.

is another idyllic—and more secluded—spot for a picnic. Here gorgeous beaches stretch for a mile along the lakeshore, where picnickers can spread a blanket and enjoy a meal to the sound of gentle waves rolling in off the lake. To speed digestion afterward, take a lazy walk up the shore.

✻ Whiskeytown ✻
NATIONAL RECREATION AREA
Crystal Creek Falls and
Brandy Creek and Oak Bottom

For a picnicking experience that's a bit farther off the beaten track than California's larger, well-trodden national parks, but that still offers lovely views and chances to spot wildlife, head to Whiskeytown National Recreation Area. It has several nice picnic grounds, all beautifully maintained by the Park Service. There are impressive views of the 50-foot cascade of Crystal Creek Falls from two of the picnic areas, and at the Brandy Creek and Oak Bottom areas of the park, other picnic grounds are invitingly shaded by Douglas-firs, canyon live oak, and ponderosa pines. These latter two areas are wheelchair accessible and there's access to the beach, fishing piers, and hiking trails from them. All of the national recreation area picnic sites have tables, grills, and restrooms, as well as offer the occasional wildlife sighting. Whiskeytown—at the ecologically rich junction of the Klamath, Cascade, and Coast Mountains—is home to, among other creatures, bald eagles and black-tailed deer. But picnics are not to be shared with the animals; do not feed them.

☆ Picnics Are for People ☆

Want to make sure your much anticipated grizzly sighting doesn't occur at close range as you're getting ready to bite into your turkey sandwich? You're not likely to be interrupted by one, but the National Park Service has done a lot of research on grizzly bears over the years and discovered that grizzlies engage in reward-reinforced behavior when it comes to food. In layman's terms, that means that if a grizzly starts realizing it can come by an easy bite to eat in a certain place, that incentive will begin to override its innate tendency to avoid people. This applies not only to bears, but to deer, raccoons, skunks, squirrels, and many other animals. That means picnickers need to clean up and dispose of refuse food intelligently when they leave the grounds. The parks usually have specific instructions for food storage and disposal in places where animals are likely to look for leftovers, and it's always illegal to feed wildlife. So follow the rules and be tidy—the reward is the full benefit of an outdoor meal in a beautiful, unspoiled setting.

✻ John Day Fossil Beds ✻
NATIONAL MONUMENT
Painted Hills

Oregon's John Day Fossil Beds National Monument, which protects one of the most comprehensive fossil records of ancient life in North America, is a fascinating place for a lesson in natural history and geology, but it's also a great place to have a picnic. The Painted Hills Unit of the park is a particularly striking place to bring a basket lunch—the landscape is dominated by bluffs with colorful ash layers in shades of yellow, red, gold, and black that chronicle ancient volcanic activity. An attractively landscaped picnic area at Painted Hills has shaded picnic tables, restrooms, and outdoor exhibits on the region's history. The vividly colored striations of the hills are best seen in the afternoon, so plan for a late lunch if possible, or stop by for a mid-afternoon snack. The area is also celebrated for its wildflower blooms in the spring, so picnicking here in late April or early May is all the better for the added profusion of color. After lunching, be sure to take advantage of one of the short scenic trails that begin in the vicinity of the picnic area and lead to beautiful overlooks of the Painted Hills.

> *Lyle Bennett, the principal architect for the White Sands Visitor Center … also designed the Painted Desert Inn at Petrified Forest National Park … and buildings at Carlsbad Caverns and Mesa Verde National Parks.*

✫ Shenandoah ✫
NATIONAL PARK
Skyline Drive Picnic Sites

Shenandoah National Park, which runs in a long, narrow swath along the Blue Ridge from Front Royal, Virginia, to Rockfish Gap and the northern entrance of the Blue Ridge Parkway, has several large, scenic picnic areas that are most stunning in the fall when the leaves take on vibrant autumn hues, creating a canopy of brilliant reds, yellows, and browns. These picnic grounds are the perfect place for a large outdoor gathering like a family reunion or cookout with friends. All the picnic areas in Shenandoah have tables and grills and restrooms in the vicinity, and several of these picnicking sites are also within easy reach of hiking trails that lead to lovely mountain scenery and overlooks of the broad Shenandoah Valley. The national park's most famous attraction, Skyline Drive, runs along the crest of the mountains through the entire length of the park, and all the picnic areas are accessible along it. The Dickey Ridge picnic area, at milepost 4.7, provides access to three short, easy trails—Dickey Ridge, Fox Hollow, and Snead Farm—that meander past streams, old orchards, a cemetery, and fields.

From the Big Meadows picnic area (milepost 51.2), the Lewis Falls Trail—a steeper hike—leads down to an observation point of the 81-foot-tall cascade. There's also a moderately strenuous 2.6-mile round-trip hike from the South River picnic area (milepost 62.8) that leads to a view of the 83-foot-high South River Falls.

✫ Castillo de San Marcos ✫
NATIONAL MONUMENT
Sloping Green
of the 17th-Century Spanish Fort

If you are looking for a picnic site to complement a cultural activity, a visit to Castillo de San Marcos National Monument in St. Augustine, Florida, is one great option. The old fort is a historical and architectural gem—it was built in the 17th century by the Spaniards then occupying Florida and is now the oldest masonry fort remaining in the United States. Take a tour, which includes weapons demonstrations and reenactments by period-clad guides, before heading out onto the fort's beautiful grounds to refuel with a picnic lunch. On the gently sloping green, picnickers can take refuge under the shade of palm trees, enjoy the waterfront views and passing boats, and imagine life in the 1600s. Be sure to bring a blanket to spread the meal out on, and afterward, something to put trash in—there aren't picnic tables or many trash cans on the fort's green.

✴ Wolf Trap ✴
NATIONAL PARK FOR THE PERFORMING ARTS
Lawns of the Filene Center

There aren't many places where one can combine a world-class performance with open-air seating, a picnic, and a glass of red wine, but the Filene Center in Wolf Trap National Park in Virginia offers the chance to do just that. The Filene Center's elegant outdoor amphitheater hosts more than 90 performances between late May and early September, and these range in genre from musical acts to dance and theater productions. Audience members who watch from the sloping lawn are encouraged to pack their own basket of food and bring a bottle of wine or six-pack to savor during the show. Picnicking isn't allowed in the fixed, covered seating areas along the stage, so many seat holders come early to picnic on the lawn before the show begins. For those attendees who'd rather not pack a picnic basket, Wolf Trap's Official Picnic Caterer, Capital Restaurants Concepts *(www.mealsbeneaththemoon.com)*, takes orders the day before and will have the picnic ready for pick up before the show. Try to arrive early as the lawn can soon become a sea of blankets. Watching an entertaining performance alfresco under the stars is a pretty incredible way to enjoy a picnic.

Picnics are for humans. Always follow a park's rules regarding food storage and disposal. Never feed the wildlife.

✮ Puuhonua o Honaunau ✮
NATIONAL HISTORICAL PARK
Beachside Picnic Grounds

It's hard to improve upon Hawaii's gorgeous coastlines and halcyon weather, but you can add a flourish to the outing by packing a picnic to enjoy under the shade of coconut trees near the shore. The picnic area at Puuhonua o Honaunau National Historical Park on the Big Island has gorgeous views of the ocean, beaches, and palm tree groves, all backed by clear blue skies. In the tide pools near the picnic grounds, look for colorful native fish swimming amid coral and seaweed. The picnic grounds are at the back of the park, right on the water, and are shaded enough to be comfortable during the day. Or come in the evening for a stunning view of the sunset; the park closes at 8 p.m., however, so plan accordingly. The picnic grounds have tables and barbecue pits, but there's no food to purchase in the park, so it is best to arrive fully provisioned. If necessary, stock up at a store along Hawaii 11 before heading into the park.

✮ Cumberland Gap ✮
NATIONAL HISTORICAL PARK
Bartlett Park and Others

The Appalachian Mountains—celebrated today for their beauty, variety of wildlife, and potential for recreation—were actually a major impediment to the exploration and settlement of the West, until Cumberland Gap was discovered to be a point of passage. Today, Cumberland Gap National Historical Park straddles the boundaries of Kentucky, Tennessee, and Virginia. The park is beautiful and boasts a wealth of attractions—caves, historic trails, settlements, and overlooks with thrilling views of the area. The park has several picnic areas—at Bartlett Park, Sugar Run, near the Pinnacle Overlook, Wilderness Road, and Skylight Cave—and any of these are a wonderful place to eat outdoors. They are all set in beautiful landscape, within easy reach of stunning natural features, and most have shaded picnic tables, water fountains, and even covered shelters for larger groups. Plan to eat a hearty meal—much of the park is accessible only by hiking its 50-some miles of trails.

✮ Mount Rainier ✮
NATIONAL PARK
Sunrise Visitor Center Area

At 14,410 feet, Mount Rainier is the highest point in Washington State, and the picnic area at Sunrise Visitor Center, at 6,400 feet, is the highest place in the national park (and actually in the state) that is accessible by car. The picnic area is located in a unique and beautiful setting—in addition to lovely views of glacier-draped Mount Rainier across a large scenic valley, the site is surrounded by the intriguing spectacle of gnarled, stunted trees, whose growth has been impeded by frigid winter gales. A picnic here affords not only the enjoyment of eating outside in a stunning setting—grills are available if a barbecue is on the menu—but also easy access to the restrooms and exhibitions of the visitor center. The center's displays on the volcano's history and the area's flora and fauna will make an invigorating post-lunch hike on one of the many trails that originate here all the more meaningful.

ten best parks
sounds of nature
Concert halls for the planet's own music

One of the most appealing aspects of a park getaway is the chance to trade honking horns and ringing phones for the infinite variety of natural sounds. The wind in the pines soothes campers to sleep, birdsong serves as a gentle alarm clock, and a rushing creek creates background music for a streamside picnic.

✷ Yellowstone ✷
NATIONAL PARK
Howling Wolves

Is there a sound more thrilling for a nature lover than the howling of wolves? An audio icon of wilderness, a wolf's call symbolizes nature's endurance against habitat loss and persecution, as well as the resilience of ecosystems that are allowed to function naturally. Though gray wolves are most abundant north of the lower 48 states, for most travelers they're easiest to see and hear in Wyoming's Yellowstone National Park, where they were reintroduced in 1995 after being extirpated in the 1920s. Thousands of people see them annually in Yellowstone, primarily in Lamar Valley in the northeastern part of the park. But exciting as seeing a wolf may be, there's nothing quite like hearing a wolf's howl, and hopefully an answering call, to thrill the senses. Hearing a wolf howl is most likely to occur at dusk or early in the morning, and fall through spring is usually the best time to experience the sounds of this predator.

Wolves howl for many reasons, including communication within the pack and as a way to find mates. They may also howl during a hunt; in Yellowstone, elk constitute more than 80 percent of wolves' diet. On a still night, the long, shrill tones of a wolf pack can send a chill down the spine, as we feel a mixture of apprehension, respect, admiration, and gratitude for sharing such a wondrous moment in nature.

✷ Point Reyes ✷
NATIONAL SEASHORE
Trumpeting Elephant Seals

Despite being nearly wiped out by hunting in the early 20th century, elephant seals have made a good comeback and now number more than 1,500 at Point Reyes on the central California coast, and the population is growing at a dramatic rate. They can be observed easily from December through March at Chimney Rock above Drakes Bay, where they come ashore to breed. And while the sight of these marine mammals is impressive (males can weigh more than 2 tons), their sound is just as awe-inspiring: The males' powerful trumpeting can be heard for more than a mile. The raucous noise heard on the approach to the national seashore's overlook at Chimney Rock reveals the seals' presence long before they come into view. In addition to the trumpeting, you will hear a veritable symphony—grunts, snorts, belches, whimpers, squeaks, and squeals. Seeing the teeming mass of animals and their interactions—mothers raising pups, males challenging each other for dominance—and hearing the commotion evokes the wonder of the life of the ocean.

✳ Rocky Mountain ✳
NATIONAL PARK
Bugling Elk

In many parts of the country, one of the most telling signs of fall's approach is the "bugling" of elk during the rut, or mating season, as the males attempt to gather or increase their harem of females. Though the call is commonly known as bugling, it's really more of a screech or whistle—one that starts off deep and resonant and then fades to a high-pitched squeal, ending with a series of grunts. However it is perceived, the bugling is as much a part of autumn as the quaking aspen leaves turning gold. Older

A female wolf raises its head and howls to its pack or mate, making the quintessential sound of the wild.

males have stronger calls than do young animals, which helps their mating success. Elk are common in several national parks, but there's no better place to enjoy their bugling than Rocky Mountain National Park, with a backdrop of the rugged peaks of central Colorado's Continental Divide.

> *The call of an adult wolf differs from that of a coyote or dog—the howl is long and clear, uninterrupted by short yaps or barks.*

☆ Everglades ☆
NATIONAL PARK
Roaring Alligators

Alligators are always impressive—even more so when a big male raises its head and tail above the water, inflates its throat, and gives forth with the deep, rumbling growl that's often called bellowing. Head to Florida's Everglades National Park in the early spring mating season, find a spot where gators have congregated and are trying to attract mates while scaring away rivals, and just listen. It's probably the closest humans will come to experiencing a dinosaur in action, or at least it's easy to think so. A gator's size influences the tone and intensity of its bellow. At times several individuals roar in a chorus, seeming to encourage each other in a wild concert that can last several minutes and travel great distances across the water.

☆ Mojave ☆
NATIONAL PRESERVE
Singing Sands

Travelers in desert country have long observed that sand dunes sometimes make a long, low booming or "singing" noise when some disturbance (like a person sliding on them) creates a mini-avalanche of sand down a slope. The phenomenon has baffled scientists, with the best guess on the source being friction between individual grains of sand. Lately, though, a theory speculates that the sound really originates in a sort of echo between dry sand on the surface and a layer of wet, hard-packed sand beneath. Whatever the reason, it's fun to play on sand dunes and, when conditions are right, cause them to "sing." A good place to try this is the Kelso Dunes area within southern California's Mojave National Preserve. Located far off the beaten path, about 42 miles southeast of Baker, the dunes rise to 700 feet high and cover more than 45 square miles. Check with a park ranger about conditions before setting out along the backcountry roads for the Kelso Dunes—and once there, try running down a dune to set the sand in motion.

☆ Glacier Bay ☆
NATIONAL PARK & PRESERVE
Calving Glaciers

This Alaska Panhandle park is known for having one of the finest guided boat tours within the National Parks System, a nine-hour, 130-mile cruise around Glacier Bay to see wildlife and, of course, glaciers. Often, passengers get to witness the sight and sound spectacle of a glacier "calving" an iceberg, losing a portion of the glacier to the water. When stress where the river of ice meets the water causes a massive chunk of ice to break off, it does so with a loud crack like a rifle shot amplified many times, crashing into the water with a huge splash and sending spray and waves in all directions. As the tour boat approaches the park's tidewater glaciers (those that reach water rather than ending on land), icebergs drift through the bay, and the boat pauses for up to a half hour to increase the chances of seeing calving. For those who experience the birth of a new iceberg, it's a sight—and sound—they'll long remember.

☆ Voyageurs ☆

One of the essential delights of the North Woods, the call of the male common loon is probably best heard at dawn, echoing over a tree-fringed lake when the air is still enough that the water reflects dawn like a mirror. (The smell of bacon frying in a skillet helps, too.) Sometimes called "laughter," the sound is something like a falsetto yodel—and the inspiration for the expression "crazy as a loon." Breeding loons are common at northern Minnesota's Voyageurs National Park, building their nests along the shores of lakes both large and small. These black-and-white birds superficially resemble ducks, but they are not related to waterfowl. Loons are designed for efficient diving, with legs set so far back on their bodies that they are unable to walk on land and must push themselves along on their chests. Listen for them when they return from their wintering grounds in May, and throughout the summer nesting season.

☆ Acadia ☆
NATIONAL PARK
Crashing Waves

The sound of crashing ocean waves is one of the most stirring in nature. The strikingly rugged coast of Maine ranks among the best places to enjoy surf sounds, with the added bonus of a special location in Acadia National Park that provides a variation on the theme. At Thunder Hole, located along the park's scenic Loop Road just beyond Sand Beach, a crack in the pinkish granite rock has been widened over millennia to a long rectangular opening; heavy waves compress air within this chamber, causing a low, resonating boom like distant thunder. The thunderous *whoomp* doesn't occur on calm days, and even at times of high waves you sometimes have to wait a few minutes for the right conditions. For a more soothing sound, head to the lovely pebbled beach nearby, where multicolored cobblestones make a pleasant rattling noise when the waves go in and out. All in all, the sounds here enhance a visit to one of the most picturesque coastlines in North America.

With a loud crack, then a deafening crash as it hits the water, a chunk of ice calves off a glacier.

☆ Tallgrass Prairie ☆
NATIONAL PRESERVE
Booming
Greater Prairie-Chickens

One of the oddest sounds in the bird world is given out during one of the oddest rituals in the bird world, and both can be experienced at Tallgrass Prairie National Preserve in eastern Kansas in early spring. Greater prairie-chickens—which do indeed resemble large brown chickens—gather at courting sites called leks, where males perform a foot-stomping "dance" while females watch from the sidelines, rating the dancers and choosing which ones they will mate with. (So intriguing are prairie-chicken displays that they inspired the ceremonial dances of some Plains Indian tribes.) As part of their performance, males inflate orange air sacs on their necks, which amplify a bizarre call often referred to as "booming," although it sounds more like blowing air over the opening of a large bottle. The "boom" can sometimes be heard well over 2 miles away. The females apparently use the quality of booming, as well as dancing, to judge males in what might be seen as a courtship song-and-dance talent contest. Those who wish to hear booming prairie-chickens should arrive before dawn and take care not to get too close to leks, as disturbance will cause the birds to leave the area. Speak to a park ranger about ways to enjoy the dancing birds without interfering with their love lives.

☆ Mammoth Cave ☆
NATIONAL PARK
Sound of Silence

You may think you've experienced silence—in a remote forest, camping in the desert, in an empty basement—but have you, really? Wasn't there a slight breeze, a distant bird chirping, the subtle hum of a man-made device? To experience true, absolute silence, visit Mammoth Cave National Park in Kentucky, renowned for its quiet even in the context of caves. Mammoth differs from many caves in that portions of it are extremely dry. A layer of sandstone and shale above the limestone of the cavern keeps water from seeping down, which means it has none of the slow dripping sounds of drops splashing into underground pools or striking stalagmites. When it's quiet in Mammoth Cave, it's truly quiet—so much so that it can be startling for people experiencing it for the first time. Famed naturalist John Burroughs wrote of Mammoth: "When no word is spoken, the silence is of a kind never experienced on the surface of the earth, it is so profound and abysmal . . . [T]he sense of hearing is inverted, and reports only the murmurs from within."

☆ Noise-free Parks ☆

The sounds of traffic and aircraft (such as flightseeing rides over the Grand Canyon) can intrude on natural sounds in parks, lessening the wilderness experience for visitors. One organization addressing this issue, One Square Inch (*www.onesquareinch.org*), works to raise awareness of the natural soundscape in Washington's Olympic National Park. Olympic was chosen because it so far has suffered less from noise intrusion than have most other parks. The group's members hope to influence land managers to consider soundscape management and prevent noise pollution just as they do water pollution, invasive species, and other threats to parks.

32 USA

Grand Canyon National Park 1919

scenic drives

Lots of "wow" without leaving your car

There is no substitute for getting out and seeing a national park up close, whether on foot, on horseback, on a bicycle, or in a canoe. But it's also fun, and certainly less exhausting, to be presented with one superlative view after another in a relatively short time, as is the case with our most spectacular scenic drives.

✷ Glacier ✷
NATIONAL PARK
Going-to-the-Sun Road

"One of the world's most spectacular highways" is the park's own description of Going-to-the-Sun Road, and no one who has traveled this 50-mile mountain route between the park's east and west entrances over the Continental Divide in northwestern Montana would argue. The glacier-carved Rocky Mountain scenery along the way provides countless eye-filling vistas, roadside overlooks, waterfalls, and access to short trails. Dedicated in 1933, the drive was named for nearby Going-to-the-Sun Mountain. How the mountain got its name is uncertain—some say from an ancient Indian legend, while others say the "legend" was created by an explorer in the 1880s. The route, open seasonally, reaches its literal high point at 6,646-foot Logan Pass, where, in addition to knife-edged ridges, sheer cliffs, and sharp-pointed peaks, there may be mountain goats and bighorn sheep within sight. East of Logan Pass there's a view to the south of Jackson Glacier, one of the few glaciers in the park visible from a road. Lesser snowfall on the eastern side means Going-to-the-Sun Road stays open longer and higher in fall here than it does on the western slope.

✷ Yosemite ✷
NATIONAL PARK
Yosemite Valley Loop Road,
Glacier Point Road, and Tioga Road

These three separate roads in Yosemite are close enough together that all can be traversed in five hours or so, if one was so inclined. Yosemite Valley, 195 miles southeast of San Francisco, boasts far more than its share of natural icons visible from the road: Highlights include 620-foot Bridalveil Fall, the massive granite monolith of El Capitan, 1,000-foot Horsetail Falls, Yosemite Falls (three falls totaling 2,425 feet), and Half Dome. The famed overlook Tunnel View, on the road out of Yosemite Valley toward Wawona, offers what is perhaps the park's single most famous vista. To the south, Glacier Point Road climbs up to Glacier Point, 3,200 feet above

Yosemite Valley, another awesome panorama of the valley, peaks, and waterfalls. Bisecting the park to the north of the valley, Tioga Road runs west-east to cross the Sierra Nevada via 9,945-foot Tioga Pass. Originally a wagon road built in 1883, Tioga Road ascends into an alpine world of snowy peaks, crystal lakes, and meadows bright with wildflowers.

☆ Rocky Mountain ☆
NATIONAL PARK
Trail Ridge Road

Just before Trail Ridge Road was completed in 1932, the director of the Park Service described its appeal: "You will have the whole sweep of the Rockies before you in all directions." Winding for 48 miles to cross the Continental Divide between Estes Park and Grand Lake, Colorado, this scenic route 60 miles northwest of Denver rises to a high point of 12,183 feet, making it the highest continuous road in the United States. It takes drivers from ponderosa pine forest through the zone of spruce and fir to the open tundra, with magnificent views of valleys, lakes, rivers, and mountains, including 14,259-foot Longs Peak, the park's highest summit. Overlooks such as Many Parks Curve, Rainbow Curve, and Rock Cut provide panoramas that truly give you the impression of being on top of the world. People with difficulty breathing should beware the thin air. At Fall River Pass, a visitor center offers exhibits interpreting the harsh environment above tree line, where only the hardiest plants and animals can survive. Heavy snow may close Trail Ridge from mid-October until late May.

☆ Shenandoah ☆
NATIONAL PARK
Blue Ridge Parkway and Skyline Drive

These two routes in western North Carolina and western Virginia are administered by two different National Park Service units. It makes sense to treat them as one route, though: The northern terminus of the 469-mile Blue Ridge Parkway links with the southern end of 105-mile Skyline Drive (part of Shenandoah National Park) at Rockfish Gap, Virginia, creating a 574-mile drive that takes in some of the most beautiful scenery of the central Appalachian Mountains. In addition to dozens of overlooks providing views of forested ridges and valleys, attractions along the combined drives (many open only seasonally) include visitor centers, lodges, campgrounds, restaurants, the North Carolina Folk Art Center, the North Carolina Minerals Museum, the historic Skyland Resort in Virginia, and hiking trails leading to mountain summits, waterfalls, and other natural features. Both drives are well marked with mileposts, making it easy for travelers to keep up with location and find sites. With limited entrances and exits, no billboards, and speed limits of 45 miles an hour on the Blue Ridge Parkway and 35 on Skyline Drive, this combined route offers an experience as relaxing as it is beautiful.

☆ Crater Lake ☆
NATIONAL PARK
Rim Drive

Rangers at southwestern Oregon's Crater Lake are occasionally asked, "What do you put in the water to make it so blue?" The truth is that the striking deep blue color is completely natural, a result of the purity of the water and its stupendous depth: 1,943 feet deep, Crater Lake is the deepest lake in the United

As Yosemite's Glacier Point Road winds to a high point above Yosemite Valley, it offers glimpses of iconic Half Dome.

States and one of the ten deepest in the world. The lake is actually a caldera, a crater formed after a massive volcanic explosion 7,700 years ago. The park's Rim Drive *(open early July–mid-Oct.)* winds for 33 miles around Crater Lake, with more than 30 scenic overlooks offering an ever changing perspective. Must-see stops include Watchman Overlook, with a great view of Wizard Island, a cinder cone rising in the lake; Phantom Ship Overlook, where a small island resembling a ship is visible; the spur road to the Pinnacles, a collection of 100-foot-tall spires; and Vidae Falls, where a creek drops 100 feet over a series of ledges.

☆ Acadia ☆
NATIONAL PARK
Park Loop Road

Maine is justly famous for its ruggedly beautiful rocky shoreline, where waves continuously crash into reddish granite ledges while the boats of lobstermen cruise by. An especially striking section of this coast is a highlight of Acadia's National Park's 27-mile Park Loop Road, which winds around the eastern section of Mount Desert Island, south of the town of Bar Harbor. Open from about April 15 through November, the road provides access not only to the coast but also to lush forests, lakes, the park's famed carriage roads—broad paths suitable for hiking or biking—and a road leading to the top of 1,530-foot Cadillac Mountain, the tallest summit on the East Coast. Coastal sites reached by the scenic drive include Sand Beach, where those who can tolerate 55-degree water swim; Thunder Hole, where heavy surf compresses air in a hole in the rocks, causing a low booming sound; and Otter Cliffs, one of the most picturesque sections of rocky coast.

✶ Wrangell–St. Elias ✶
NATIONAL PARK & PRESERVE
McCarthy Road

This 60-mile dead-end road into Alaska's Wrangell–St. Elias National Park and Preserve isn't for everybody. A converted railroad right-of-way, it's narrow,

---

☆ Building the Roads ☆

The stories behind the construction of some of the parks' scenic drives are almost as fascinating as the natural wonders surrounding them. Shenandoah's Skyline Drive was begun in 1931, during the Great Depression. The original construction crews included out-of-work farmers and apple pickers. In 1933, workers of the newly formed Civilian Conservation Corps arrived; eventually, ten camps of "CCC boys" helped complete Skyline. Glacier's Going-to-the-Sun Road was finished in 1932; it took 11 years to build the 50-mile-long road. The drive is still considered a major engineering feat and is listed as a national historic landmark. The initial three-month survey work for the road was so challenging that the crew had a 300 percent turnover.

---

rocky, and winding, and passes over historic trestles that are high and narrow enough to make some drivers nervous. The park estimates average driving time to be three hours, which says something about McCarthy Road's condition. The reward for taking on this challenge is an intimate look at America's largest national park: four rivers (Copper, Kuskulana, Gilahina, and Kennicott), lakes, forest, snow-capped mountains, wildlife, an old mining town (McCarthy), and Kennecott Mines National Historic Landmark, which once produced vast amounts of copper. Before heading down McCarthy Road, get advice from park staff at the Chitina Ranger Station (at the western terminus of the route)—and make sure your spare tire has air.

✶ Canyon de Chelly ✶
NATIONAL MONUMENT
North and South Rim Drives

Much of the landscape in northeastern Arizona is dominated by reddish sandstone. At Canyon de Chelly, the sandstone began as desert dunes more than 230 million years ago. Rivers cut down into the rock rising with the uplift of the Colorado Plateau, resulting in the spectacular sheer walls seen today looming hundreds of feet above valley floors. Ruins of ancient dwellings can be seen along ledges on the cliffs, while elsewhere in the park dozens of modern Navajo families still live and farm. (The park is operated in cooperation with the Navajo Nation.) Canyon del Muerto and Canyon de Chelly come together as a V pointing west, with the park visitor center at the junction. The 17-mile North Rim Drive and the 18-mile South Rim Drive wind above the canyons, with a total of ten overlooks offering awe-inspiring views. Near the beginning of South Rim Drive, Junction Overlook provides a viewpoint of the confluence of the two canyons. This drive ends at the amazing spectacle of Spider Rock, an eroded pinnacle rising 800 feet above the canyon floor. Side roads along the North Rim Drive lead to views of several ruins, including Mummy Cave Ruin, one of the park's largest structures, with dwellings and ceremonial buildings flanking a central tower, all beneath an overhanging bluff. Nearby is Massacre Cave, where in 1805 Spanish soldiers killed 115 Navajo trapped on a ledge on the canyon wall.

✳ Capitol Reef ✳
NATIONAL PARK
Cathedral Valley Loop

Located in southern Utah, Capitol Reef encompasses striking rock formations typical of the Colorado Plateau, intriguing historic sites, and a wonderland of canyons, buttes, washes, and back roads to explore. The word "reef" in the park's name has nothing to do with coral reefs found in oceans; it was applied by early pioneers to any long ridge that was a barrier to travel. "Capitol" came from the resemblance of high, white sandstone domes in the area to the domes of capitol buildings. Capitol Reef's Cathedral Valley Loop Drive covers 58 miles of rough, unpaved road that can be impassable at times. Check with the park visitor center on Utah 24 before setting out. The route begins with a ford of the Fremont River that is passable most of the time, except during high water after storms and for more extended periods during spring runoff. The road continues to pass alongside dramatically beautiful, multicolored mesas, spires, and other rock formations with names such as Walls of Jericho and the Temple of the Moon. Quite visible in many places are black boulders that look different from the rest of the landscape. Remnants of lava flows that capped nearby mountains about 20 million years ago, they were eroded and later moved to lower locations by various processes including glacial melting. After heading northwest, the loop turns back southeast on Caineville Wash Road. There are several panoramic vistas along the route, which returns to Utah 24 at the community of Caineville.

✳ Organ Pipe Cactus ✳
NATIONAL MONUMENT
Ajo Mountain Drive

Located 120 miles southwest of Tucson, Organ Pipe Cactus rewards travelers with a beautifully rugged volcanic landscape and an environment so biodiverse that the area was named an international biosphere reserve in 1976. The 21-mile Ajo Mountain Drive loops east of Ariz. 85, circling the Diablo Mountains to skirt the Ajo Range, providing a good overview of the park. The route is unpaved, but the gravel road is suitable for all vehicles. Much of the breathtaking scenery is composed of rhyolite, rock formed by lava cooling on the earth's surface. In many places, cliffs display bands of dark rhyolite paralleling lighter bands of tuff, volcanic ash compressed and "welded" into rock. Among the plants visible in the desert are organ pipe cactus, elephant tree, and the saguaro cactus, symbol of the Sonoran Desert. Nine miles into the loop, a natural rock arch 90 feet wide appears on a cliff above the road. In higher elevations the desert gives way to a landscape of oaks, junipers, and jojoba, a shrub favored by bighorn sheep, which might be spotted here.

chapter five

wildlife

ten best parks
bird-watching sites
Where to go to make your life list grow

The diverse range of habitats within our national parks, from deserts to seashores to alpine peaks, means a correspondingly high diversity of birds. Some species are confined to small areas, while others can be found across large swathes of land. These parks offer a superb selection of environments to tempt traveling birders.

⁂ Big Bend ⁂
NATIONAL PARK
Colima Warbler

More bird species have been spotted in Big Bend National Park than in any other National Park System unit except for Point Reyes National Seashore. Big Bend's number of specialty birds, however, gives this out-of-the-way site in western Texas the top spot on the bird-watching ranking. The park's list of more than 450 bird species owes its length in part to the fact that Big Bend is often described as "three parks in one": lush riparian vegetation along the Rio Grande, a vast area of Chihuahuan Desert, and the Chisos Mountains, rising to more than 7,800 feet in the center of the park. The star attraction is the little Colima warbler, which nests nowhere else in the United States. It takes some effort (and a little bit of luck) to find such species as flammulated owl and black-capped vireo; more common and conspicuous are the colorful acorn woodpecker, Mexican jay, pyrrhuloxia, and Scott's oriole. The secret to finding a lot of bird species is

visiting the park's many different habitats, spending time in places such as Hot Springs Village on the Rio Grande, lower Green Gulch in the desert, and Boot Canyon in the mountains.

⁂ Point Reyes ⁂
NATIONAL SEASHORE
Endangered Northern Spotted Owl

Around 490 species of birds have been seen at California's Point Reyes, which represents more than 40 percent of the total for North America. Many of those species are extreme rarities—birds that lost their way and ended up at this Pacific Coast peninsula, an hour north of San Francisco. Combining seabirds with birds of shore, grassland, scrubland, and forest, Point Reyes offers year-round interesting birding. Visitors to Bear Valley, Limantour, Abbotts Lagoon, and the cliffs around the lighthouse will possibly see such species as sooty shearwater, brown pelican, Brandt's cormorant, pelagic cormorant, osprey, California quail, black oystercatcher, common murre, rhinoceros auklet, tufted puffin,

Allen's hummingbird, Nuttall's woodpecker, Pacific-slope flycatcher, Hutton's vireo, chestnut-backed chickadee, wrentit, and California towhee. Point Reyes is also home to the endangered northern spotted owl (rare here) and the threatened snowy plover, which nests on park beaches. Peregrine falcons sometimes cruise along beaches and mudflats, looking for prey. But the real magic of Point Reyes is simply the fact that anything can show up here, anytime, making every birding visit an adventure.

✷ Dry Tortugas ✷
NATIONAL PARK
Sooty Terns and Brown Noddies

For a few weeks each spring, this tiny island park—a few specks of land in the Gulf of Mexico, 70 miles west of Key West, Florida—provides an unparalleled spectacle. Thousands of birds flying northward from their wintering grounds in Latin America to nesting areas in the United States and Canada, tired and hungry after crossing the Gulf of Mexico, drop out of the sky at Garden Key (the main Dry Tortugas island), covering shrubs, buildings, and even the lawn, so unwary that they can be approached closely. There's no predicting what might show up at any given moment. In addition, thousands of sooty terns and brown noddies (also a type of tern) nest on Bush Key, just 200 or so yards from Garden Key. Magnificent frigatebird, brown booby, masked booby, and white-tailed tropicbird are among other seabirds that might be spotted here, and for the lucky, a black noddy might be found perched on the old coaling docks. For birders there's nothing like Dry Tortugas in spring.

✷ Cape Hatteras ✷
NATIONAL SEASHORE
Wintering Waterfowl and Migrant Raptors

America's first national seashore (established 1953), Cape Hatteras protects 70 miles of barrier islands on the North Carolina coast. Bird-watchers know it as a place of wintering waterfowl and migrant raptors and shorebirds, often in significant numbers and variety. Contained within the national seashore is Pea Island National Wildlife Refuge *(252-987-2394, www.fws.gov/peaisland)*, where marshes and impoundments can host swans, geese, ducks, herons, ibises, rails, and shorebirds. Groves of trees, such as Buxton Woods, provide shelter for migrant songbirds in fall, when hawks and falcons appear, heading south along beaches. (October is a good time to see the magnificent peregrine falcon.) Nesting birds include the threatened piping plover, American oystercatcher, least tern, and black skimmer. The famed Cape Hatteras lighthouse is a good place from which to scan the Atlantic Ocean for northern gannets, shearwaters, jaegers, and gulls.

✷ Rocky Mountain ✷
NATIONAL PARK
White-tailed Ptarmigan and Brown-capped Rosy-finch

Spanning the Continental Divide in northern Colorado, this park is home to a delightful variety of Rocky Mountain foothill and high-elevation birds. Driving Trail Ridge Road across the park means ascending to more than 12,000 feet, with amazing vistas of mountain peaks in all directions. Simply stopping along the way can bring sightings of birds such as Steller's jay, gray jay, Clark's nutcracker, pygmy nuthatch, Townsend's solitaire, and western tanager. Above tree line, lucky birders might find white-tailed ptarmigan or brown-capped rosy-finch. It usually takes a bit of exploring to find species such as dusky grouse, northern pygmy-owl, three-toed woodpecker, Williamson's sapsucker, Cassin's finch, and pine grosbeak. Look along streams for American dipper, and at blooming flowers for broad-tailed hummingbird. The beautiful mountain bluebird frequents open areas at lower elevations. There may be no park in North America that combines such rewarding birding with such spectacularly accessible scenery.

✴ Everglades ✴
NATIONAL PARK
Greater Flamingo

Geographically speaking, it's no surprise Everglades National Park hosts a distinctive set of birds: It's located at the southern tip of peninsular Florida, just 120 miles from the tropics. Bird-watchers come here in search of the short-tailed hawk, limpkin, white-crowned pigeon, mangrove cuckoo, gray kingbird, and black-whiskered vireo. Much more obvious, though, are flocks of herons, egrets, ibises, roseate spoonbills, and wood storks. These species may appear abundant at times, but in fact the southern Florida population of wading birds has dropped as much as 90 percent over the past century because of development and disruption of water flow through the "river of grass." The Everglades is the only place in the United States where greater flamingo

can be found with regularity (check at the end of Snake Bight Trail). Shark Valley is a good spot to look for snail kite, a raptor that feeds almost entirely on large snails. Along the Anhinga Trail, at the Royal Palm Visitor Center, birders can get excellent close-up views of numerous species—including anhingas.

✴ Chiricahua ✴
NATIONAL MONUMENT
Zone-tailed Hawk
and Anna's Hummingbird

Southeastern Arizona undoubtedly rates among America's two or three most popular birding destinations, and within that region the Chiricahua Mountains rank among the very best sites. One of several mountain ranges popularly called "sky islands," the Chiricahuas rise up from the surrounding arid lowlands, cloaked in dense forest like an oasis in the desert. Chiricahua National Monument is best known for its spectacularly varied rock formations, eroded from 27-million-year-old volcanic material called rhyolite. It's also home to many southeastern Arizona specialty birds, from the aptly named Arizona woodpecker to the beautiful and graceful painted redstart. The 8-mile scenic Bonita Canyon Drive leads up to 6,870-foot Massai Point, passing through forests of pine, spruce, sycamore, Douglas-fir, Arizona cypress, and oak. Bird-watchers search along the road and on hiking trails for zone-tailed hawk, Anna's hummingbird, white-throated swift, dusky-capped flycatcher, Mexican chickadee, bridled titmouse, Mexican jay, black-throated gray warbler, and Scott's oriole. Most birders combine a trip to the national monument with a drive up Pinery Canyon Road to visit the adjacent Coronado National Forest, home to even more regional specialties.

☆ Blue Ridge Parkway ☆
NATIONAL PARK
Blackburnian Warbler

The late Ludlow Griscom, one of the original gurus of American bird-watching, once said, "Be near Asheville, North Carolina, the third week in April and you will see warblers pour across the mountains." Certainly spring migration is a wonderful time to be in the southern Appalachians, but these mountains are also known for a diverse collection of breeding birds more reminiscent of Canada than of the American Southeast. With elevations up to 6,684-foot Mount Mitchell (the highest U.S. point east of the Mississippi River), the southern Appalachians are home to coniferous forests that mimic habitats far to the north. So, too, does the bird fauna seem more like Quebec than North Carolina or Virginia. Birds found on Appalachian ridges include ruffed grouse, saw-whet owl, yellow-bellied sapsucker, common raven, red-breasted nuthatch, brown creeper, golden-crowned kinglet, veery, black-throated blue warbler, Blackburnian warbler, Canada warbler, dark-eyed junco, and red crossbill. Many excellent sites for seeing these and other birds can be accessed along the 469-mile Blue Ridge Parkway, a scenic drive administered by the National Park Service. Overlooks, picnic sites, and trails offer chances to leave vehicles and enjoy the varied birdlife.

☆ Hawaiian Birds ☆

The rarest birds in the National Park System are probably found in **Haleakala National Park,** on the Hawaiian island of Maui. Native Hawaiian species have suffered severe declines due to habitat loss and introduced species. Among them are many species of Hawaiian honeycreepers: small, colorful birds once common across the islands. Some have already become extinct, while others are threatened or critically endangered. Haleakala provides a refuge for *akohekohe* (crested honeycreeper), Maui parrotbill, and *alauahio* (Maui creeper). The *nukupuu*, believed extinct, may yet survive. The major stronghold for these birds is Haleakala's restricted Kipahulu Scientific Reserve, fenced to keep out goats and other non-native species.

USA 32
Crested Honeycreeper

☆ Glacier ☆
NATIONAL PARK
Calliope Hummingbird and Pine Siskin

Northern Montana's Glacier National Park combines dense forest, meadows, lakes, streams, cliffs, and tundra above tree line to create one of the region's best birding destinations. The fabulously scenic Going-to-the-Sun Road crosses the park from west to east, reaching its highest point at 6,646-foot Logan Pass. Some of the species that can be seen at overlooks, picnic areas, campgrounds, and trails along the road are dusky grouse, three-toed woodpecker, red-naped sapsucker, calliope hummingbird, Hammond's flycatcher, gray jay, Clark's nutcracker, boreal chickadee, hermit thrush, varied thrush, Townsend's warbler, evening grosbeak, Brewer's sparrow, red crossbill, and pine siskin. Birds found near the park's lakes and streams include harlequin duck, Barrow's goldeneye, bald eagle, osprey, and American dipper. Both Vaux's swift and the elusive black swift nest on cliffs, while

A calliope hummingbird, common in Glacier National Park's mountain meadows in the summertime, feeds on a flower.

white-tailed ptarmigan and gray-crowned rosy-finch nest on the highest peaks, above timberline. Glacier's list of 12 owl species is notable, although many of them are rare and seldom observed.

✷ Gateway ✷
NATIONAL RECREATION AREA
325 Species Including Curlew Sandpiper

This multi-unit park encompasses 26,000 acres around the entrance to New York Harbor. Unlikely as it may seem, this area near the nation's largest metropolis includes two excellent birding destinations. Sandy Hook, a 5-mile-long peninsula on the eastern New Jersey shore, is famed among birders mostly for spring and fall migration, when raptors, shorebirds, and songbirds pass through in great numbers. In winter, waterfowl and seabirds can be observed in the bay to the west and in the Atlantic Ocean to the east. Gateway's Jamaica Bay Unit in Brooklyn and Queens encompasses Jamaica Bay National Wildlife Refuge, where the major birds of note include waterfowl, waders, and shorebirds. Eagle-eyed birders have seen a large number of rarities over the years. Curlew sandpiper, for example, an Old World species, is found at Jamaica almost every year. Black-crowned night-heron, yellow-crowned night-heron, osprey, American oyster-catcher, glossy ibis, and barn owl are among the breeding birds here. More than 325 species have been recorded at Jamaica Bay in total.

ten best parks
quirky critters

You don't have to be as big as a bison to be interesting

When it comes to wildlife, the big guys get most of the attention. Visitors generally want to see bears, elk, moose, alligators, and other species of photo-friendly large animals. Yet such an attitude ignores a whole range of wildlife that, though smaller in size, can be just as fascinating in appearance, lifestyle, oddity, and charm.

⭑ Carlsbad Caverns ⭑
NATIONAL PARK
Brazilian Free-tailed Bat

From spring through October, there's more inside this famous southern New Mexico cave than spectacular formations: Hundreds of thousands of Brazilian free-tailed bats roost in cave passages by day, leaving each evening shortly after sunset, with their exit flight continuing for up to three hours. For reasons that are not understood, the bats always spiral out of the cave in a counterclockwise direction. Visitors gather at a natural amphitheater at the cave's entrance to watch this spectacle, with park rangers providing commentary from Memorial Day weekend through mid-October. The best bat flights occur in July and August, when newborn bats join their parents to swell the numbers leaving the cave, spending the night searching the sky for miles around to feed on insects. So large are the bat flights that visitors below can hear the sound of the mammals' wings (around 11 inches from tip to tip) and even smell them (not all species of bats have an odor). The bats' return to the cave at dawn is also an exciting sight, with the bats performing zooming dives from hundreds of feet in the air. Like many species of birds, the Carlsbad Caverns bats migrate south for the winter, spending the season in caves in Mexico.

⭑ Great Smoky Mountains ⭑
NATIONAL PARK
Synchronous Firefly

The cool yellow flashing of fireflies is one of the joys of a summer evening, and this park on the Tennessee–North Carolina border offers a special twist on the theme: One species of "lightning bug" here is famed for flashing synchronously, with hundreds of individuals blinking together to create an amazing effect on wooded hillsides. Though there are more than a dozen types of firefly in Great Smoky Mountains National Park, the synchronous firefly (*Photinus carolinus*) is the only species in North America that can synchronize its flashing patterns. The peak period for this display occurs during a two-week period, usually in mid-June.

Hundreds of thousands of Brazilian free tailed bats swarm out of Carlsbad for nightly feedings spring through fall.

Viewing the synchronized flashing has become so popular that the park has instituted controls on visitation, trying to assure that traffic, headlights, and noise won't detract from the visual experience. And there's another reason Great Smoky Mountains ranks with the "quirky critter" parks: These mountains have been called the "salamander capital of the world," with 30 varieties found in the park. Not easy to see, salamanders are amphibians showing a spectrum of beautiful glossy colors. Many of those here are lungless salamanders that breathe through the walls of blood vessels in their skin and in the linings of their mouth and throat. A patient visitor can observe salamanders by going out at night with a flashlight after rain or by carefully watching for ground movement in moist areas.

In 1901, scientists surveyed a single Texas "dog town" that covered an area of 25,000 square miles and contained an estimated 400,000,000 prairie dogs. But this town and others were already under sentences of death.

☆ Rocky Mountain ☆
NATIONAL PARK
Members of the Squirrel Family

Though some varieties can be a nuisance in suburban yards, there's something that's undeniably appealing about the active little animals of the squirrel family. Their sleek forms and frenetic, inquisitive behavior often make them seem as though they have some urgent business to attend to. They're fun to watch—and easily so, too, which can't be said for some mammals such as elusive weasels and shy foxes. Rocky Mountain National Park in north-central Colorado is one of the best places in the country to enjoy a variety of small mammals, from the diminutive least chipmunk to the noisy chickaree (or red squirrel) to the chubby yellow-bellied marmot, which often greets hikers on mountain summits, sunning itself and occasionally giving a loud whistle. Most appealing of all is the tassel-eared or Abert's squirrel, which with its long tufts of ear fur seems like a cross between a rabbit and a squirrel. Many types of squirrels will approach visitors to beg for food, but of course feeding animals in a national park is prohibited.

☆ Theodore Roosevelt ☆
NATIONAL PARK
Prairie Dog

Theodore Roosevelt described prairie dogs as "the most noisy and inquisitive animals imaginable," and Lewis and Clark wrote that they found the animals "in infinite numbers" on their 1804–1806 western expedition. Prairie dogs are still noisy and inquisitive, but their numbers have been greatly decreased by persecution over the past century or so. One good place to observe these animals—which were called "dogs" by early explorers for their barking call, but are in fact squirrels—is Theodore Roosevelt National Park in western North Dakota. Their "towns" of interconnected burrows can be seen along the South Unit's scenic Loop Drive, as well as other places in the park. Highly social, prairie dogs live in family units called coteries, greeting each other with what looks like a quick kiss and hopping up to give a comic *jump-yip* call that tells others that no predators are within sight. A visitor who sits watching quietly and inconspicuously can be entertained for quite a while by the endless antics of these engaging little mammals.

✷ Fire Island ✷
NATIONAL SEASHORE
Horseshoe Crab

One of the oddest creatures found on the shores of North America, the horseshoe crab looks like the offspring of a sting ray and a motorcycle helmet, its fearsomely spiky appearance causing unease among some people who encounter one on a beach. Nonetheless, this animal—not really a crab but more closely related to spiders and scorpions—is harmless. Its vast numbers of eggs provide essential food for fish and migratory birds, and horseshoe crabs have been used in important medical research. Fire Island National Seashore on New York's Long Island is a good place to see and learn about horseshoe crabs when they come ashore to mate and lay eggs during evening high tides in May and June. Check with the park for times to attend a ranger walk to observe this bizarre yet intriguing animal.

✷ Saguaro ✷
NATIONAL PARK
Desert Iguana and Gila Monster

Not nearly as common as bird-watchers or wildflower lovers, reptile enthusiasts have learned to love the amazing variety and beauty of turtles, lizards, and—yes, it's true—snakes. Hot places host many more reptiles than do temperate areas, so it stands to reason that southern Arizona's Saguaro National Park would be one of the best places to observe reptiles. With around 50 species in its two geographic divisions east and west of Tucson, Saguaro provides a home for scaly critters such as the threatened desert tortoise; desert iguana; regal horned lizard, a variety of horned toad; Gila monster, one of only two poisonous lizards in the world; Sonoran mountain kingsnake; and six species of rattlesnakes, including sidewinder and the very dangerous Mojave rattlesnake. The best time to see reptiles is at dusk or dawn during the summer "monsoon" rains of July and August.

✷ Cape Lookout ✷
NATIONAL SEASHORE
Seashells

If you're looking for the beauty of form, symmetry, and color, little in nature can match seashells. Collecting shells has been popular throughout human history (and in some places shells have even served as money). If done properly—never taking a shell with a live animal inside, for example—shelling does little or no harm to the environment. Most

Common in alpine tundra, a yellow-bellied marmot suns itself in Rocky Mountain National Park.

Nearly extirpated in the 1990s, the Channel Islands' endemic island fox population is showing signs of recovery.

national parks allow collecting reasonable amounts of shells (often 2–5 gallons daily) for noncommercial purposes. Gulf Coast beaches such as those at Gulf Islands and Padre Island National Seashores are excellent, but many collectors rank the beaches at North Carolina's Cape Lookout National Seashore even higher, especially those on relatively undeveloped Ocracoke Island. Shells such as lettered olive, lightning whelk, and slipper shell are common, but one prized find is the Scotch bonnet, the state shell of North Carolina. Mornings after winter storms at low tide are best for finding good shells.

✸ Channel Islands ✸
NATIONAL PARK
Island Fox and Island Night Lizard

The word "endemic" indicates a species found in only one place in the world. That place might be a country, a mountain range, or even a small island. The Channel Islands, off the coast of southern California, have been called the "Galápagos of North America," in part because they host more than 150 endemic species. Some are very rare and hard to see, while others might be spotted by travelers who make the boat or seaplane trip to this relatively little-visited national park. Many bird-watchers hope to spot the rare island scrub-jay, searching for it on Santa Cruz Island. Another special animal is the island fox, a smaller relative of the gray fox found across North and South America. After a population decline of more than 90 percent in the 1990s, the island fox has seen a good recovery on the six islands where it lives, and lucky park visitors may spot the cat-size mammal hunting for insects, mice, or crabs; it's more active in the daytime than most foxes. The island night lizard is found only on Santa Barbara Island in the park and two small islands owned by the U.S. Navy. These reptiles can live more than 20 years in a range of less than 200 square feet. Any park visitor seeing one of these animals can feel privileged, for each is unique to this single spot.

☆ White Sands ☆
NATIONAL MONUMENT
Pocket Mice and Darkling Beetle

In most places the world of nocturnal creatures remains virtually unknown to wildlife-watchers. The comings and goings of night-active mammals, reptiles, and invertebrates might as well be happening on the moon, so seldom are they noted. At White Sands National Monument in southern New Mexico, however, where the fine material of the gypsum sand dunes records the surprising variety of nocturnal residents, their tracks are like an open book that can be read by interested visitors. If there has been little wind to disturb the dunes overnight, an early morning observer might see the X marks of roadrunner feet, the large prints of a kit fox, the neat claw marks of lizards, the treadlike evidence of a centipede, the paired dots of pocket mice, the parallel depressions of a darkling beetle, or dozens of other types of prints. The Dune Life Nature Trail is a good place to test your footprint identifications skills.

☆ Big Bend ☆
NATIONAL PARK
Orange-Barred Sulphur Butterfly

In recent years ever growing numbers of people have taken up butterfly-watching, using close-focus binoculars to enjoy the brilliant colors and intricate patterns of these "flying jewels." Big Bend, in western Texas, has long been known for its birds, but its butterflies are equally diverse. In fact, the park list of more than 170 species is higher than the totals of most states. Such striking species as variegated fritillary, southern dogface, Texan crescent, California sister, and queen are common, and a lucky observer might spot such uncommon and beautiful butterflies as orange-barred sulphur, Sandia hairstreak, theona checkerspot, and Chisos metalmark.

☆ Banana Slug ☆

In the running for quirkiest critter in our national parks, the banana slug is a mollusk (like a snail) with no shell: an elongated, bright yellow, slimy blob whose oddness has made it an animal celebrity in the Pacific Northwest. It's the official school mascot of the University of California at Santa Cruz and the designated California state mollusk, and its form decorates countless T-shirts taken home as souvenirs by visitors to the region. Especially in the rainy season, banana slugs are easy to find (and admire?) at several parks, from Muir Woods National Monument in California north through Olympic National Park and north and onward toward the Panhandle of Alaska.

wildlife-viewing tips

Words of wisdom from Yellowstone's Al Nash

Whether it's prairie dogs popping up from their burrows on the Great Plains, eagles nesting on a Minnesota lake, or brown bears fishing in an Alaska river, wildlife is an essential part of many of our national parks. Millions of visitors drive or hike through parks annually, hoping to observe some of the animals that make the parks their homes—and no park may be more popular for wildlife viewing than Yellowstone National Park.

Getting a look at a bear, elk, or other creature can be a thrill, but park visitors should always keep in mind that wild animals are indeed wild, not displayed behind bars in a zoo. Knowing the best ways to observe wildlife will bring exciting moments of discovery for visitors while protecting the safety of both the watchers and the watched.

KEEP YOUR DISTANCE

"Yellowstone National Park is a great place to see wildlife," says park spokesperson Al Nash. Bison, grizzly and black bears, elk, moose, mule deer, pronghorn, gray wolves, coyotes, mountain lions, and bighorn sheep are among the large mammals found in Yellowstone. All should be treated with respect.

"Visitors get lulled into a bit of complacency because an animal's immediate behavior may not appear threatening," Nash says. "People just get excited and don't realize how close they may be approaching. We remind visitors that you need to stay at least 25 yards away from all big animals, and 100 yards—a football field length—away from bears and wolves."

There are occasions when wildlife-watchers should stay even farther away, Nash says.

"We use those distances as good guidelines, but if for whatever reason an animal reacts to your presence, that means you're too close and you need to back up. I've certainly seen incidents in the park when visitors may be 25 yards away from something like an elk, but all of a sudden there's a large group of people encircling the animal, which then feels trapped.

"I always tell visitors that the most important things to bring for wildlife viewing in this park are binoculars and a zoom lens. Don't get too close."

Though many people are aware of the dangers of bears and

mountain lions, bison can pose just as much of a threat. These massive animals look sluggish as they graze calmly in a pasture, but their behavior can change quickly. Photographers tempted to approach a bison for that perfect picture may learn the hard way why this species is often described as "unpredictable."

"A bull bison can literally weigh a ton," Nash says. "He can get under way quickly and move at 30 miles an hour. And that big hump behind their head is all muscle, so they're very strong."

DON'T FEED THE ANIMALS

It should go without saying that feeding wild animals is a very bad idea, for several reasons. First and foremost, it habituates animals to human presence, causing them to associate people with food and making them more likely to approach humans. In many cases, such habituation results in individual animals having to be relocated or even destroyed. Visitor safety is another reason why feeding animals is prohibited in parks. Visitors have been seriously injured in Everglades National Park, for example, while trying to feed alligators—another species that, like the bison, is far faster than its usual lethargic behavior would indicate.

"We have a really good track record here at Yellowstone about animals and food," Nash says. "Not only have we worked for decades to educate visitors and to deal with the issues of food storage and properly taking care of garbage, but we continue to reinforce that with people who come to the park."

STUDY ANIMAL BEHAVIOR

With common sense and respect for animals' behavior, travelers can experience one of the great natural spectacles of the continent in the grasslands, forests, and wetlands of Yellowstone. There's something to see any time, any day, in the park, but planning and preparation will bring bigger rewards.

"Getting to know a little bit about the animals, where they live and how they live, makes you more successful at trying to spot them," Nash says. "A lot of our animals are active in the early morning and at dusk. So if you're looking for

something like a bear in the park, the heat of the day is not the most likely time to see one. If you were wearing a fur coat and it was over 70 degrees outside, you'd probably not be romping around in the open sunshine either."

As well as the time of day, the season can make a big difference in successful wildlife spotting.

"Typically, many animals are a little lower in elevation, which means closer to roadways, in the spring and fall," Nash says. "Fresh food such as berries or new grass grows at lower elevations in the spring, and then the animals follow the progression of the food, as well as the cooler temperatures, up the mountains as summer arrives. As seasons change, often they come back down to lower elevations. They start to sense winter's coming even before we do."

In addition, animals wander at will, so up-to-date information on their whereabouts is invaluable.

"I tell visitors, if you're looking for animals, go to the nearest visitor center," Nash says. "Ask them what they've heard from park staff and from other visitors. They have current information.

"You need some patience. And if you can plan your trip outside that hot July and August time frame, there are animals you may be a little more likely to spot, too."

charismatic megafauna

Where the (big) wild things are

Park managers call them "charismatic megafauna": large animals that all visitors want to see, from bears to bison. Rangers are quick to point out that national parks aren't zoos—animals go where they want to go and sightings aren't guaranteed—but these sites offer opportunities to observe some of North America's most impressive wildlife.

✳ Yellowstone ✳
NATIONAL PARK
Grizzlies and Pronghorns

Sometimes called the "American Serengeti"—a comparison with eastern Africa's famed wildlife-rich plains—Yellowstone, in northwestern Wyoming, hosts the largest concentration of mammals in the lower 48 states. A very lucky visitor might see grizzly and black bears, bison, elk, moose, mule deer, bighorn sheep, pronghorn, gray wolves, and coyotes, to list only the largest of Yellowstone's 67 species of mammals. The best places to look for the park's wildlife are Hayden Valley, along the Yellowstone River between Canyon Village and Fishing Bridge, and Lamar Valley, in the northeastern part of the park. Hayden Valley is also a good place to see big birds, including sandhill cranes, white pelicans, trumpeter swans, and bald eagles. Lamar Valley is probably the most likely spot for gray wolves. Two other top wildlife-watching spots are the Blacktail Plateau Drive and the northern entrance to Yellowstone; look for bighorn sheep and pronghorn in the latter area.

✳ Katmai ✳
NATIONAL PARK & PRESERVE
Brown Bears Feeding on Salmon

This huge park in Alaska gets the number-two ranking on our list essentially for one animal—but what an animal it is, and what a spectacle it provides. At Katmai, you get up-close looks at brown bears as they feed on salmon, sometimes with dozens of bears visible simultaneously. The park has built special bear-viewing platforms at falls on the Brooks River near its mouth at Naknek Lake (the largest lake within any unit of the National Park Service), where bear numbers peak in July and September. No roads lead from the outside world into Katmai. Most park visitors fly to the community of King Salmon, then travel by floatplane or boat to Brooks Camp. Arranging a visit isn't hard, though, since more than a hundred authorized outfitters operate trips in the Katmai area. Backpackers and canoeists who venture into the park's backcountry may find moose, caribou, gray wolves, wolverines, and lynx in addition to brown bears.

A brown bear patrols the shores of Nonvianuk Lake in Katmai National Park and Preserve.

✳ Grand Teton ✳
NATIONAL PARK
Elk and Coyotes

This near neighbor to Yellowstone hosts much of the same megafauna, but the abundance and variety are different enough to earn it its own spot on the Top Ten list. As is the case with Yellowstone, there are good wildlife-viewing opportunities from roads at Grand Teton. Simply driving along Teton Park Road will probably bring sightings of pronghorn, elk, bison, coyotes, and mule deer. Other good spots to check from the side of a road include Blacktail Ponds, just north of Moose Junction, for moose and elk; the meandering Snake River for bison, moose, and bald eagles; and Oxbow Bend, for moose, elk, white pelicans, and river otters. In winter, thousands of elk gather in the Jackson Hole area, many on the National Elk Refuge (*www.fws.gov/nationalelk refuge*) adjacent to the national park. Viewing opportunities here include winter sleigh rides to see elk and the drive to Miller Butte to see wintering bighorn sheep.

✳ Wind Cave ✳
NATIONAL PARK
Bison and Pronghorn Herds

Located in southwestern South Dakota, this national park in 1903 became the first in the world created specifically to protect a cave—currently the fourth longest on Earth. But it's what's above ground that attracts wildlife-watchers to this underappreciated park: easily visible herds of bison and pronghorn, as well as elk, mule deer, white-tailed deer, and coyote. Fourteen bison were reintroduced

DON'T KILL OUR WILD LIFE
DEPARTMENT OF THE INTERIOR NATIONAL PARK SERVICE

to Wind Cave in 1913, and six more in 1916. All were believed to be descended from true wild bison, with no cattle genes intermingled from crossbreeding. Disease-free, and with good genetic makeup, Wind Cave's bison population is an important factor in the continued survival of this iconic American mammal. Pronghorn (often called antelope although this North American mammal is not related to true Old World antelopes) are regularly seen at Wind Cave. Most visitors to Wind Cave National Park also take time to visit adjacent Custer State Park. The 1,500-strong bison herd here is one of the largest in the world.

✳ Denali ✳
NATIONAL PARK & PRESERVE
Dall Sheep

Alaska's Denali protects the tallest mountain in North America, 20,320-foot Mount McKinley—also known by its native Athabaskan name Denali, or "the high one." Only one road leads into the park's vast heart, a 91-mile, mostly unpaved route from which private vehicles are banned beyond the first 15 miles. Most people take one of the several types of shuttle buses to enjoy the scenery and the park's legendary wildlife: grizzly and black bears, moose, gray wolves, caribou, Dall sheep, lynx, wolverines, coyotes, porcupines, and hoary marmots. Protected from gawking tourists who leave their vehicles and approach too closely to get that "perfect" photograph, Denali's animals often stay put when buses pass or stop for observation, allowing excellent viewing through binoculars and photography using telephoto lenses. Bus drivers on interpretive tours are experienced in identifying wildlife and providing descriptions and commentary.

☆ Theodore Roosevelt ☆
NATIONAL PARK
Feral Horses and Longhorn Cattle

The badlands of southwestern North Dakota played a big part in Theodore Roosevelt's life, not least because his experiences while hunting and ranching here turned the future President into an ardent conservationist. Today, the park named in his honor, made up of two units, ranks among the best places in the Great Plains to observe wildlife. Reintroduced in 1956, bison now number several hundred in the park, and often are observed at very close range along roads. The speedy pronghorn wanders the park, as well, though it's seldom seen in the North Unit. Mule and white-tailed deer occupy both units, while elk are found only in the South Unit (look for them in the Buck Hill area). Wild (feral) horses are maintained as part of the historical setting in the South Unit only; Theodore Roosevelt National Park is one of the few areas in the West where free-roaming horses can be observed. Also in the quasi-domestic category are the park's longhorn cattle, residing in the North Unit.

☆ Glacier ☆
NATIONAL PARK
Lynx, Bison, Caribou, and Grizzly Bears

Northwest Montana's Glacier National Park is home to 62 species of mammals, but it's even more impressive to learn that, of the large mammals present hundreds of years ago, only two species are no longer found in the park: bison and caribou. You have a chance to see lynx, mountain lion, black and grizzly bears, gray wolf, wolverine, white-tailed and

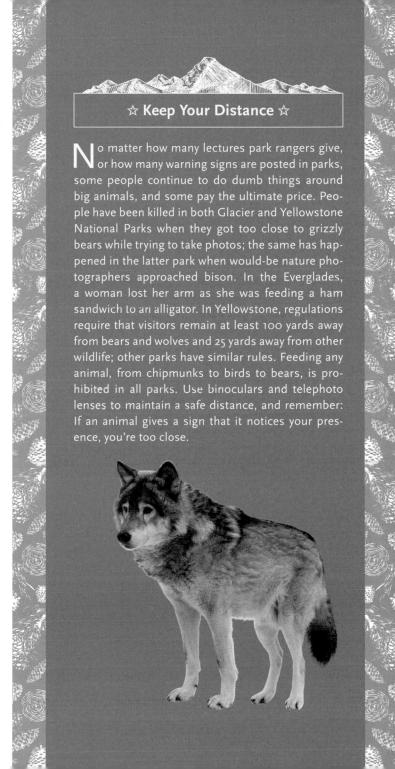

☆ Keep Your Distance ☆

No matter how many lectures park rangers give, or how many warning signs are posted in parks, some people continue to do dumb things around big animals, and some pay the ultimate price. People have been killed in both Glacier and Yellowstone National Parks when they got too close to grizzly bears while trying to take photos; the same has happened in the latter park when would-be nature photographers approached bison. In the Everglades, a woman lost her arm as she was feeding a ham sandwich to an alligator. In Yellowstone, regulations require that visitors remain at least 100 yards away from bears and wolves and 25 yards away from other wildlife; other parks have similar rules. Feeding any animal, from chipmunks to birds to bears, is prohibited in all parks. Use binoculars and telephoto lenses to maintain a safe distance, and remember: If an animal gives a sign that it notices your presence, you're too close.

Great Smoky Mountains National Park's Cades Cove is home to both domesticated and wild animals.

mule deer, elk, moose, bighorn sheep, and mountain goat, to name only the largest species. Glacier's mammal list is unique in the lower 48 states. The park provides a sanctuary for the largest remaining population of grizzly bears south of the Canadian border, considered to number slightly more than 300 individuals. One of the best ways to see Glacier wildlife is simply to find a spot in the alpine habitat, such as along a trail near 6,646-foot Logan Pass, and scan the landscape with binoculars. Mountain goats and bighorn sheep are often seen this way, and if lucky, you might also spot a wandering bear.

☆ Rocky Mountain ☆
NATIONAL PARK
Bighorn Sheep

Colorado's scenic showplace park of the central Rockies is a great place to enjoy characteristic wildlife of the region. In fall, elk come down from the high mountains to open, grassy areas for breeding season, and the "bugling" calls of males echo around valleys. Herds can be seen often in places such as Moraine Park, Kawuneeche Valley, and Horseshoe Park. Bighorn sheep have made a comeback in the park and now number around 600. They're most easily seen in early summer at Horseshoe Park, where they come to obtain minerals. In late summer, a hike to The Crater site may bring sightings of bighorn. Moose are seen most often on the west side of Rocky Mountain National Park, in wetlands of the Colorado River Valley where they browse on willows. Mule deer and coyotes are common in the park. Black bear and mountain lion are seldom seen, but hikers need to be aware of their presence, however, and know what to do if one is encountered along a trail.

> *No one knows how many bison there were, but the naturalist, Ernest Thompson Seton, estimated their numbers at sixty million when Columbus landed. They were part of the largest community of wild animals that the world has ever known.*

✵ Great Smoky Mountains ✵
NATIONAL PARK
Black Bears and Mountain Lions

The advance of settlement across the eastern United States in the 18th and 19th centuries led to the extirpation of bison, elk, mountain lions, black bears, and even white-tailed deer over large areas east of the Mississippi River. As a result, travelers who want to enjoy such creatures usually head to parks out West. But at Great Smoky Mountains National Park, on the Tennessee–North Carolina border, you can experience a little of what eastern North America was like before European settlement. The park's most famous wild inhabitant is the black bear, which thrives here in one of the lushest and most diverse environments on the continent. Around 1,500 bears live in the park (around two per square mile), which means that the odds of seeing one are good. Elk disappeared from this region in the mid-1800s, but beginning in 2001 several dozen have been reintroduced into the park. The best place to look for these animals is the Cataloochee area in the southeastern section of the park, with dawn and dusk the best times. White-tailed deer are common in Great Smoky Mountains National Park. While visitors sometimes report seeing mountain lions, no hard evidence has been found that they have returned to the area.

✵ Everglades ✵
NATIONAL PARK
Alligators and Crocodiles

People have different definitions of "charismatic," but there's no doubt that nearly everyone who visits this expansive national park in southern Florida wants to see alligators. These reptiles and their crocodilian kin are the closest we can come in modern times to seeing a dinosaur, and their sheer size makes sighting one a memorable event. Gators are easily seen at freshwater locations including Shark Valley, the Anhinga Trail at Royal Palm, and Eco Pond near Flamingo—although they're likely to be seen in any roadside pond, creek, or ditch. In the dry season *(Nov.–May)* alligators may be seen in great concentrations at shrinking ponds. It's not so easy to see an American crocodile, an endangered species that has made an encouraging comeback in Florida in recent years. Crocs inhabit salt water, and are sometimes seen around Flamingo.

ten best parks
ocean life

Enjoying the marine world from whales to barnacles

Some of the country's finest natural areas are located around our seacoasts and on islands, where habitats range from rocky shores to salt marsh to sandy beach to coral reefs. Viewing animals here isn't always as easy as watching elk graze in a meadow, but the diversity of life found in the sea makes the effort worthwhile.

☆ Kenai Fjords ☆
NATIONAL PARK
Resurrection Bay and the Gulf of Alaska

Though this park 125 miles south of Anchorage, Alaska, covers more than 1,000 square miles, most of it is inaccessible to the average visitor: A massive ice field makes up much of the area, and only one short road enters the park. For many the highlight of a trip to Kenai Fjords is a boat trip into Resurrection Bay and the Gulf of Alaska to explore the fjords, experience tidewater glaciers (glaciers that meet the sea), and see wildlife. Tours leave from the town of Seward; some ships feature national park rangers to provide narration and identify wildlife. All-day trips make a cruise of more than 100 miles to Aialik Bay, and some travel past the Chiswell Islands, part of Alaska Maritime National Wildlife Refuge. Marine mammals often seen on cruises include humpback whales, orcas (also called killer whales, though they are dolphins), harbor seals, Steller sea lions, Dall's porpoises, and sea otters. Depending on the season, a cruise might also bring sightings of minke,

humpback, or fin whales. In few places are so many varieties of marine life so enjoyably available as at Kenai Fjords.

☆ Virgin Islands ☆
NATIONAL PARK
Trunk Bay Underwater Interpretive Trail

Many naturalists have compared coral reefs to rain forests for the great variety and beauty of life they host; however, the diversity of a coral reef is usually much more easily visible. A snorkel mask is all it takes to enjoy the array of fish and invertebrates of a reef. Virgin Islands National Park in the Caribbean provides a marine highlight just offshore from the island of St. John. At Trunk Bay, often called one of the world's most beautiful beaches, snorkelers will find a 225-yard-long underwater interpretive trail featuring signs identifying many elements of undersea life. To protect even more of the local reef system, Virgin Islands Coral Reef National Monument encompasses nearly 20 square miles of Caribbean Sea off St. John. Many local firms offer snorkel and scuba trips to nearby reef sites. Travelers should also consider Buck Island Reef National Monument, located less than 2 miles offshore from the island of St. Croix. A marked undersea trail at a lagoon here features interpretive signs, and scuba diving is allowed at two mooring sites.

✳ Channel Islands ✳
NATIONAL PARK
Channel Islands National Marine Sanctuary

There's a reason these five islands off the coast of southern California are often called the "Galápagos of North America": They boast a unique and fascinating natural history, including more than 150 endemic species and the largest breeding colonies of seabirds in southern California. In addition, the ocean within 6 nautical miles of the islands is protected as Channel Islands National Marine Sanctuary, including a vast undersea "forest" of kelp. The sanctuary is home to seals, sea lions, sea otters, more than two dozen species of whales and dolphins, and hundreds of species of fish and invertebrates. Most reach the islands by way of boat tour companies, while a few travel on a short commercial airplane flight. Park rangers and volunteers conduct a variety of guided programs, including tide-pool walks to view creatures

A sea lion frolics in one of the many kelp forests ringing the isles of Channel Islands National Park.

such as anemones, sea stars, sea urchins, limpets, periwinkles, chitons, barnacles, and mussels. A summer program at Anacapa Island features park rangers diving into the Pacific Ocean with video cameras, allowing those on dry land to see undersea life including sea stars, colorful fish, and the occasional mammal. You can ask questions of the rangers via a communications system.

☆ Glacier Bay ☆
NATIONAL PARK & PRESERVE
Glacier Bay

Wildlife abounds at this beautiful park 50 miles west of Juneau, Alaska, with many species readily seen during boat trips. Glacier Bay is accessible only by air or sea; no roads reach the adjacent town of Gustavus. The spectacular scene here appeared very different 250 years ago, when a massive glacier filled the entire bay. Since then, glaciers have

☆ Sea Otter ☆

The appealingly cute sea otter, the largest member of the weasel family (males can weigh up to 100 pounds), once numbered in the hundreds of thousands in the northern Pacific Ocean. Unlike blubber-insulated whales, sea otters possess extremely dense fur to protect themselves from frigid ocean water. That fur made them targets of relentless hunting, and by the early 1900s the world's population is thought to have totaled fewer than 2,000. Thanks to various conservation measures, some sea otter populations have made a comeback, and national parks have provided important refuges. These mammals can be seen at Kenai Fjords and Glacier Bay National Parks in Alaska and Olympic National Park in Washington.

steadily retreated, exposing "new" land that has slowly revegetated. For many the most rewarding activity is the daily boat tour, a seven-hour, 130-mile trip around the bay. A park ranger is aboard to help see and identify wildlife and to provide information on natural history and geology. Among the marine mammals often sighted are humpback and Minke whales, orcas (killer whales), harbor and Dall's porpoises, Steller sea lions, harbor seals, and sea otters—not to mention seabirds such as tufted and horned puffins, common murres, double-crested cormorants, and black-legged kittiwakes (a small gull). A common highlight is the chance to see a glacier "calve" an iceberg into the bay with a sound like a cannon shot and a huge splash. For those who want a more intimate experience, kayaks can be rented for quiet paddling trips.

☆ Biscayne ☆
NATIONAL PARK
Biscayne Bay and the Atlantic Ocean

Marine life dominates the ecosystem at this national park south of Miami, Florida—and with good reason. Ninety-five percent of the park's acreage is made up of the waters of Biscayne Bay and the nearby Atlantic Ocean. A quarter-mile trail on the mainland at Convoy Point offers a glimpse of the above-water world of Biscayne, but to truly experience the park requires taking a boat trip. The park concessionaire *(305-230-1100, www.biscayneunderwater .com)* offers various excursions. One popular activity is a three-hour trip on a glass-bottom boat, during which you can see some of the 512 species of fish that frequent the park, and possibly sea turtles, moray eels, and dolphins as well. The concessionaire also offers scuba and snorkeling trips. (All boat trips require a fee and are weather dependent.) Biscayne National Park encompasses the northernmost islands of the Florida Keys and the northernmost section of the world's third largest coral reef, in the Atlantic Ocean just beyond the keys. Among the creatures that might be seen around the coral reefs are spiny lobsters, sea cucumbers, Christmas tree worms, sponges, and fish including such colorful species as butterfly fish, parrot fish, damselfish, wrasses, angelfish, gobies, and barracuda.

☆ Olympic ☆
NATIONAL PARK
Olympic Coast National Marine Sanctuary

While this national park in northwestern Washington is best known for its glacier-capped mountains, rushing rivers, and incomparably lush temperate rain forests, it also encompasses 73 linear miles of Pacific coastline. Sandy in places, in other areas featuring spectacular rock formations, the Olympic coast has in large part been designated a federal wilderness area. In recognition of the rich marine life here, some 3,310 square miles of ocean—extending 25 to 50 miles from shore—have been designated Olympic Coast National Marine Sanctuary; the offshore islands and seastacks, with colonies of nesting seabirds, form part of Washington Maritime National Wildlife Refuge Complex. Some 29 species of marine mammals have been recorded in the sanctuary. Gray whales migrate northward to their summer range from March into May. Other mammals seen with some regularity include sea otters, harbor seals, northern fur seals, Steller sea lions, and California sea lions. For sheer diversity, though, nothing beats a trip to examine a tide pool, where there may be dozens of species living in an area of just a few square yards. Park rangers lead regular beach walks and tide-pool explorations at sites such as Mora and Kalaloch.

Spectacular rock formations line Shi Shi Beach, Olympic National Park's northernmost beach.

☆ National Park of American Samoa ☆
NATIONAL PARK
Offshore Ofu and Olosega Islands

On September 29, 2009, an earthquake-caused tsunami struck the southern Pacific islands of American Samoa, killing more than 30 people and destroying the visitor center of the National Park of American Samoa. Despite this tragedy, the park soon reopened with a temporary visitor center in the village of Ottoville, on the island of Tutuila. The natural features that made this property unique within the National Park System—rain forest and coral reef ecosystems—survived the tsunami mostly unharmed. Only a few hundred visitors a year explore American Samoa, one of the most remote U.S. national park units. Those people who do find some of the world's most beautiful beaches and coral reefs that are home to more than 800 native species of tropical fish, such as moray eels, groupers, cardinalfish, butterfly fish, angelfish, wrasses, parrot fish, stargazers, puffers, and gobies. With giant clams, hawksbill and green sea turtles, and more than 200 species of coral, the reefs are home to the greatest marine biodiversity of any site in the United States and its possessions. The islands of Ofu and Olosega have excellent coral reefs and offer the best snorkeling.

> *The National Parks contain more than 5,100 miles of beaches, coral reefs, kelp forests, wetlands, historic shipwrecks and forts, and other features.*

✳ Point Reyes ✳
NATIONAL SEASHORE
Central California Coast
Biosphere Reserve

It's a measure of the ecological importance of this park 30 miles north of San Francisco that it has been recognized by the United Nations as an International Biosphere Reserve, known as the Central California Coast Biosphere Reserve. Those interested in marine life will find rich biodiversity here, thanks in part to the upwelling of cold, oxygen-rich ocean water offshore, supporting animals from tiny invertebrates to whales. In addition, Point Reyes's marine habitats include lagoons, estuaries, tide pools, marshes, and beaches. A good place to begin learning is the Kenneth C. Patrick Visitor Center, featuring exhibits on maritime exploration, marine fossils, and ocean environments. Cliffs near the 1870 Point Reyes Lighthouse are popular for spotting migrating gray whales. Around 20 species of

whales and porpoises have been seen around Point Reyes. At nearby Chimney Rock, a breeding colony of northern elephant seals can be observed. California sea lions and harbor seals also frequent the park. Less obvious, but no less interesting, are shoreline invertebrates such as geoduck and gaper clams, hermit crabs, mole crabs, basket whelk snails, and the jellyfish known as by-the-wind sailor. The best way to learn about these odd creatures is to take a ranger-led beach walk.

✳ Padre Island ✳
NATIONAL SEASHORE
Gulf of Mexico

This Texas Gulf Coast park near Corpus Christi preserves the longest tract of undeveloped barrier island in the world. Padre Island's 70 miles of sandy beach, the great majority of which remains pristine, offer you the chance to find solitude and enjoy the crashing surf, the salty sea breeze, and the raucous sounds of birds. But it's a unique group of reptiles—sea turtles—that makes Padre Island such a special place for natural history lovers. All five species of sea turtles found in the Gulf of Mexico are officially classified as either threatened or endangered, and all five have occurred at Padre Island. The Kemp's ridley, the world's most endangered sea turtle, has been the focus of recovery efforts in Texas, and breeding in the national seashore has increased to more than 120 nests annually. In June, park visitors can attend releases of hatchling sea turtles at an incubation facility on the Gulf of Mexico. The western (non-Gulf) side of Padre Island is also fascinating. Laguna Madre is a rare hypersaline lagoon,

Assateague Island's marshes and estuaries teem with wading birds, such as egrets and herons.

with a salt content much higher than normal ocean water. Its complex ecosystem provides vital nursery areas for shrimp and other marine invertebrates and fish.

✳ Assateague Island ✳
NATIONAL SEASHORE
Marsh Trail

This 37-mile-long Atlantic Ocean barrier island at the Maryland–Virginia state line offers many of the pleasures people associate with seashores, from swimming to fishing to beachcombing. Yet there's plenty here for those who'd like to explore nature, especially marshes and estuaries teeming with life. The half-mile Life of the Marsh Trail wanders through cordgrass, saltgrass, and glasswort, some of the components that make salt marshes the most productive of all wetlands. To explore Chincoteague Bay further, you can hike or take canoes to backcountry campsites. Intriguing animals such as horseshoe crabs, ghost crabs, and blue crabs frequent Assateague shores, while bottlenose dolphins swim offshore. Even the famed Assateague ponies have a marine connection and have been shaped by the seaside environment. These small, shaggy horses are descended from stock brought to the island in the 1600s by local planters. Their small size is thought to be a result of their poor diet (mostly cordgrass and beach grass), and their chubby look comes from the amount of water they must drink to offset the salt they take in.

chapter six

learning experiences

guided boat tours

Seeing our national parks from the water

Put away the hiking boots and give tired feet a rest at these national parks, where scenic beauty can be enjoyed from a boat, barge, canoe, or kayak. Some of these tours are the sit-back-and-relax type, while a few require paddling. All feature guides who will help visitors see and appreciate the surrounding landscape and wildlife.

 Everglades
NATIONAL PARK
Ten Thousands Islands
and Whitewater Bay

This South Florida national park is a very big and very wild place, with relatively few ways for the average person to access areas away from roads and visitor centers. Canoeing and kayaking open up new opportunities, but can be daunting for inexperienced paddlers. For alternatives, head to the Gulf Coast Visitor Center at Everglades City, in the western part of the park, and sign up for a ranger-guided boat or canoe trip. Boat tours of the Ten Thousands Islands area are offered daily; narrated by a naturalist, the tours last 1.5 hours and you'll likely see wading birds, alligators, and other wildlife on the relaxed cruise. Or, bring a canoe or kayak—or rent one—and join a park ranger on a paddling trip for a more intimate look at the Ten Thousand Islands. On selected dates the park even offers evening canoe trips. Call the Gulf Coast Visitor Center *(239-695-3311)* for schedules. In the Flamingo area, in the

southern part of the park, boat tours explore the Whitewater Bay backcountry north of Florida Bay. Contact the Flamingo Visitor Center *(239-695-3311)* for information.

Acadia
NATIONAL PARK
Frenchman Bay, Baker Island,
and Little Cranberry Island

The rocky coast of Maine ranks with America's most beautiful landscapes, and Mount Desert Island certainly has its share of the rugged scenery: crashing waves, tall lighthouses, conifer-draped mountains, and hardwood forests that blaze red and gold in autumn. Viewing the shore from the water is an exciting experience, and from mid-May into fall Acadia National Park offers a variety of ranger-guided boat trips that focus on diverse topics. The Baker Island Cruise *(207-288-2386)* takes you to a small island, with a hike to explore nature and history. The Dive-In Theater Cruise *(800-979-3370)* travels through Frenchman Bay looking for seals, porpoises, and birds, while a diver brings undersea creatures on board so passengers can get an up close look. On the Frenchman Bay Cruise *(207-288-4585),* you set sail on a 151-foot-long, four-masted schooner, the *Margaret Todd,* with narration covering local wildlife and history. The Islesford Historical Cruise *(207-276-5352)* travels to Little Cranberry Island for a visit to the Islesford Historical Museum, and also explores glacier-carved Somes Sound, the only fjord on the Atlantic coast of the United States. Check with the national park for schedules and departure locations.

✴ Apostle Islands ✴
NATIONAL LAKESHORE
Heart of the Archipelago

Northern Wisconsin's Apostle Islands National Lakeshore encompasses 12 miles of Lake Superior shoreline on the mainland, but the attraction for most is the park's 21 islands, many of them officially designated wilderness. Historic lighthouses are located on six of the islands; some offer guided tours in summer, led by park rangers or volunteers. The most popular way to experience an overview of the Apostle Islands is the 55-mile

The Apostle Islands' deeply eroded, colorful shorelines are best appreciated while cruising the waters of Lake Superior.

Island Princess Grand Tour boat cruise that travels through the heart of the archipelago, offered daily by an authorized park concessionaire from late May to mid-October *(800-323-7619, www.apostleisland.com)*. Featuring narration on local history from knowledgeable guides, the trip lasts 3.25 hours and passes lighthouses on close-in Raspberry and northern-most Devils Islands, as well as coastal caves and rock formations. Two other tours offered are the Islander Lighthouse Cruise, a two-hour afternoon excursion, and the Evening Lighthouse Cruise, a three-hour-plus sunset tour that visits sea caves and the beacons at Devils Island and Raspberry Island.

> *During the canal's heyday, canal boats often got caught in "traffic-jams" up to five-miles long, sometimes waiting several days to unload their goods in Georgetown.*

☆ Chesapeake & Ohio Canal ☆
NATIONAL HISTORICAL PARK
Georgetown and Great Falls
Mule-Pulled Barges

In what was for the time a massive construction project, investors in 1828 began building a commercial canal from the District of Columbia along the Potomac River into Maryland. Twenty-two years and more than 180 miles of construction later, the Chesapeake & Ohio Canal began carrying barges of coal, lumber, and produce from the interior of the United States to the East Coast. Flood damage and competition from railroads put it out of business within a few decades. Now partly restored as part of the national historical park, the C & O Canal takes you back to those 19th-century days, as park rangers in period dress narrate tours aboard replica 1870s-era canalboats pulled by sure-footed mules. The boat travels at a leisurely pace while rangers describe what life was like for the families who lived and worked on the canal. Along the way, passengers get to experience going through one of the canal's locks. The boat rides are offered Wednesday through Sunday in spring, summer, and fall, at visitor centers in Georgetown (a Washington, D.C., neighborhood) and Great Falls (in Potomac, Maryland); call for dates and times. Tours last about an hour, and except for group reservations, are offered on a first-come, first-served basis.

☆ Voyageurs ☆
NATIONAL PARK
Evening Starwatch Tour and
Guided Canoe Tours

During its summer season this northern Minnesota national park offers several guided boat and canoe tours at all three of its visitor centers: Rainy Lake, Kabetogama, and Ash River. One, the North Canoe Voyage, lets participants paddle a 26-foot replica of the type of craft used by the original voyageurs, legendary fur traders of the late 18th and early 19th centuries who paddled canoes between northwestern Canada and Montreal. Various ranger-guided excursions aboard the motorized *Voyageur* and *Otter* tour boats journey to an abandoned gold mine, stop in at the historic 1913 Kettle Falls Hotel, look for bald eagles and other wildlife, visit a scenic rock garden, and cruise the lakes at sunset; there's even a late-night Starwatch Tour offered bimonthly in July and August. The guided canoe tours are free, all other tours charge a fee; reservations are highly recommended. Check the park website for a complete list of scheduled tours.

☆ Glacier ☆
NATIONAL PARK
Many Glacier, Two Medicine Lake, Rising Sun, and Lake McDonald

Although best known for its spectacular glacier-carved mountains and famed Going-to-the-Sun Road, Glacier National Park in Montana also encompasses some fabulously scenic lakes. Glacier Park Boat Company *(406-257-2426, www.glacierparkboats .com),* an authorized concessionaire, offers narrated boat cruises in four locations: Many Glacier (cruising on both Swiftcurrent Lake and Lake Josephine), Two Medicine Lake, Rising Sun (St. Mary Lake), and Lake McDonald. Tours run 45 minutes to 1.5 hours in length. Knowledgeable guides provide commentary on the park, expounding on the cultural and natural history of the area and pointing out geological features and wildlife. In addition, at all lakes except McDonald, you have the option of disembarking for a guided hike, exploring on foot for a half day, and returning on a later cruise back to the departure point. At St. Mary Lake, the hike goes to St. Mary Falls; at Many Glacier the hike reaches Grinnell Lake; and the Two Medicine hike visits Twin Falls.

☆ Lake Chelan ☆
NATIONAL RECREATION AREA
Journey to Stehekin

Most activities at this remote and beautiful area in north-central Washington center on the small community of Stehekin, which can be reached only by boat, seaplane, or trail. Historic sites, waterfalls, and varied outdoor activities attract visitors, and trails lead into the wilderness of the adjacent South Unit of North Cascades National Park. The National Park Service–operated Golden West Visitor Center in Stehekin, open daily from mid-March through mid-October, offers advice, backcountry camping permits, and ranger-led programs. Getting to Stehekin by boat is definitely a big part of the adventure, as the concessionaire-operated *Lady of the Lake II (509-682-4584, www.ladyofthelake.com)* ferries passengers across spectacular Lake Chelan from its south end to Stehekin in the north, making scheduled stops along the way at Moore Point, Lucerne, Prince Creek, and Fields Point. Set in a valley gouged out by glaciers, the 55-mile-long lake is the third deepest in North America, behind only Crater Lake and Lake Tahoe. The scenic trip passes areas such as the Narrows, where the lake is constricted to a quarter mile wide, and Domke and Bridal Veil Falls. While the boat serves more as a ferry service, the captain does offer light narration along the way; the one-way trip takes 4 hours. A speedier option is the *Lady Express,* run by the same company; it does the trip in 2.5 hours.

☆ Pictured Rocks ☆
NATIONAL LAKESHORE
Lake Superior Shoreline

The handsomely colored Pictured Rocks of Michigan's Upper Peninsula formed as sandstone in an ancient shallow sea. Along 15 miles of the Lake Superior shore these rocks create scenes of great beauty, in places rising from the water as cliffs 180 feet high. Bands of color reveal minerals in the sandstone: red and orange for copper, green and blue for iron, black for manganese, and white for calcium carbonate. Although the Pictured Rocks can be viewed from some land lookout sites, the best way to see them is from the water. From mid-May to mid-October, a park concessionaire *(800-650-2379, www.picturedrocks.com)* operates a tour boat that departs the town of Munising and cruises along the Lake Superior shoreline for about three hours. Noteworthy sites along the way include Miners Castle (one "turret" of the castle fell in 2006, but it remains a striking rock formation), Rainbow Cave, Indian Head, and Spray Falls.

☆ Channel Islands ☆
NATIONAL PARK
Santa Cruz Island's Painted Cave
by Kayak

The five main islands of this national park off the southern California coast, sometimes called the "Galápagos of North America" for their biological diversity, feature abundant wildlife and striking scenery. Channel Islands is one of the least visited national parks, with most people seeing it via commercial boat tours. (A few arrive on private boats or by seaplane.) Park-authorized concessionaires *(805-642-1393, www.islandpackers.com; 805-965-1985, www.condorcruises.com)* operate boats leaving from harbors in Ventura, Oxnard, and Santa Barbara, with tours offering looks at seals, sea lions, dolphins, whales, sea otters, and the largest breeding colonies of seabirds in southern California. Sea kayaking allows even closer exploration of island shores, including Santa Cruz Island's Painted Cave, one of the largest and deepest sea caves in the world. Several concessionaires (see the park website) offer

guided sea kayak trips, giving inexperienced paddlers a greater degree of confidence and safety in dealing with weather and sea conditions that can change quickly.

☆ Curecanti ☆
NATIONAL RECREATION AREA
Upper Black Canyon of the Gunnison River
and Curecanti Needle

Located along the Gunnison River just upstream from Black Canyon of the Gunnison National Park, Curecanti encompasses three reservoirs and part of the famed Black Canyon, a place of awe-inspiring cliffs rising high above the river. From Memorial Day weekend through Labor Day weekend, the park offers ranger-guided boat tours of the Upper Black Canyon, cruising past tall rock walls, waterfalls, and the famous Curecanti Needle, a 700-foot-high granite spire with a distinctive pointed shape. The tour begins at the Pine Creek boat dock off U.S. 50; the 1.5-mile round-trip hike to the dock includes a stairway with 232 steps.

☆ Cruise Crater Lake ☆

One of the most unusual national park boat trips is the daily two-hour, ranger-guided cruise around Oregon's Crater Lake *(July–mid-Sept.)*, the deepest lake in the United States. Occupying the caldera (collapsed magma chamber) of Mount Mazama, a volcano that exploded 7,700 years ago, Crater Lake is known for water of such deep, rich blue that it seems almost unnatural. Some tours allow you to disembark and explore Wizard Island, a cinder cone that grew from an eruption after the caldera formed. Wizard Island hikers, then, are climbing a volcano inside another volcano.

bus & shuttle drives

Enjoying the views while someone else does the driving

At some national parks—the more popular ones—buses and shuttles serve multiple purposes: They transport many more visitors much more efficiently, they generally take passengers to the most popular places, and they reduce the impact on the environment so these national parks will still be here for our grandchildren.

✶ Acadia ✶
NATIONAL PARK
Island Explorer Routes

In coastal Maine's Acadia, park officials try to alleviate chronic vehicular congestion with propane-powered Island Explorer buses *(207-667-5796, www.exploreacadia.com),* which have carried millions of passengers into and around the park since their debut in 1999. From late June and into October, buses travel along eight routes, covering a lot of ground, but the Island Explorer is a transportation system, not a tour bus. Shuttle drivers may share the history of the area, but their real function is to get you to where you want to go, and generally that means recreational areas as well as iconic sites such as Sand Beach and Thunder Hole at the ocean's edge and to the Jordan Pond House in the interior of the park. The free bus service stops at campgrounds, carriage road entrances, and trailheads found along the routes. In addition to regular stops, drivers will pick up pedestrians who flag them down along the road. So take a bus . . . and get lost.

✶ Yosemite ✶
NATIONAL PARK
Yosemite Valley Shuttle System

The Yosemite Valley Shuttle System in California's Yosemite National Park casts such a wide net across the valley floor, it needs to operate several routes just to cover a smidgen of the park's wealth of breathtaking ground. Yosemite Village is the Grand Central Terminal of the operation, with bus drivers arriving to pick up passengers as early as 7 a.m., and the year-round valley shuttle picking up and dropping off at a variety of service and lodging locations. The reach of the fleet increases between mid-June and early September aboard the El Capitan shuttle that makes five stops at hiking trails, riverfront beaches, and a picnic area near the mountain. Farther south, from spring to fall there's easy access to the Mariposa Grove of Giant Sequoias on free buses that come with an added feature: Passengers can still get in even when the parking lot is full. Even Wawona visitors get a bonus with a daily summertime service that runs all the way from here to Yosemite Valley.

✴ Rocky Mountain ✴
NATIONAL PARK
Bear Lake Route and Others

In Colorado's Rocky Mountain National Park, a line of gleaming white low-sulfur diesel buses provide you with an enormous convenience. Once inside the park, the shuttle buses, running from roughly Memorial Day to the beginning of October, operate along three routes on the eastern side of the park. The Bear Lake Route takes passengers along the picturesque Bear Lake corridor, past its iconic views of the surrounding mountains and into deeper reaches of the park, with drop-offs at hiking trailheads and the shores of Bear Lake. The Moraine Park Route leads to campgrounds, trailheads, and the Moraine Park Museum. The Hiker Shuttle is specifically designed to get you from the town of Estes Park to popular sites between the town and Glacier Basin as early as 6:30 a.m.

✴ Zion ✴
NATIONAL PARK
Springdale and Zion Canyon Shuttles

Travelers who arrived at Zion in the late 1990s would have been among the two million-plus visitors who entered the park in their own vehicles.

A shuttle bus conveys park visitors through the heart of Utah's Zion Canyon, made more tranquil by the lack of cars.

Things changed, and today two shuttle bus routes snake through the park—one roams among a half dozen stops throughout Springdale and the second travels along the Zion Canyon Scenic Drive, stopping at eight locations, including the historic Zion Lodge, the picnic areas at the Grotto, the hanging gardens at Weeping Rock, and then traveling as far north as the Temple of Sinawava, gateway to the fascinating and surreal Narrows. As the bus enters the winding road, like a CinemaScope film, the scenery grows larger and more fantastic as the bus delves deeper into the canyon where, gradually, the cliffs start to tower overhead. The canyon shuttle sets off from the Zion Canyon Visitor Center and provides free transportation April through October.

> [I]n the early 20th century, the official stance of the Department of the Interior was that no automobiles would be allowed in the national parks ... [T]he opening of Yellowstone to automobiles in 1915 signaled the beginning of a new era.

☆ Denali ☆
NATIONAL PARK & PRESERVE
Denali Park Road Bus

Alaska's Denali covers a lot of ground—about 6 million acres—so it's natural that the park has two transportation systems: shuttle buses and camper buses. The park has only a single paved road, and after a relatively brief 15 miles, the Denali Park Road turns to an avenue of rock and gravel open only to mass transit. A variety of services transports visitors from the park entrance to sites along an incredible 92-mile stretch that dead ends in the ancient gold-mining community of Kantishna. While the driver negotiates the rough road over mountains and beside cliffs, past boreal forests and subarctic tundra, passengers get to marvel at the remote and wild landscape. It's great to observe the wilderness and perhaps enhance the visit with a casual day hike, but for a more demanding experience roll into the park aboard a camper bus that accommodates passengers, backpacks, and bicycles. For a fee, leave the driving to bus lines that provide narrated tours and highlight specific areas of the park including its tundra wilderness, the remnants of Kantishna, and the park's own natural history. Be sure to bring groceries and be prepared to spend some time. Even on shuttle buses, round-trips can last up to 13 hours.

☆ Grand Canyon ☆
NATIONAL PARK
South Rim Shuttles

Not only is the Grand Canyon in Arizona deep and wide, it is also very, very long. Even the most popular overlooks on the South Rim are spread far and wide. During the peak season of summer, four shuttle routes help expand the reach of visitors. Even bicyclists can load their bikes onto racks and hitch a ride. Departing about every 15 to 30 minutes from the Canyon View Information Plaza, the buses roll to dozens of stops along the South Rim. Buses on the Village Route pick up and drop off passengers at stops including the hotels, bookstore, general store; the Kaibab Trail Route leads to vistas such as Pipe Creek and Yaki Point to the east; and the Hermits Rest Route takes passengers to several spectacular overlooks along the bus-only accessible road on the far western end of the South Rim. Making things even easier, a wonderfully convenient line heads out of the park and down to Tusayan, the small community just outside the park's southern border, where many park visitors leave their cars.

☆ Mount Rainier ☆
NATIONAL PARK
Longmire and Paradise
Weekend Shuttles

For travelers arriving from Kansas or Iowa or Florida or some other flatland state, there are several reasons to opt for the weekend shuttle that rolls the dozen miles between the park's Longmire Historic District and Paradise. One is the cost (free), two is the fact they won't have to face the dense traffic that collects around Paradise each weekend, and, three, buses also help protect the park's environment by reducing greenhouse gases. But perhaps the best reason is that these visitors are probably unaccustomed to dealing with the twisting roads that climb into the hills. The shuttle driver takes care of all of that and then throws in stops at Cougar Rock Campground, Narada Falls, and the Comet Falls Trailhead—which, by the way, are three more reasons to step aboard. Need a fourth? On weekends buses roll as far west as the town of Ashford, 20-some miles from Paradise.

☆ Point Reyes ☆
NATIONAL SEASHORE
Whale-Watching Shuttles and More

There aren't many transit systems that include a stop to watch whales. That's one reason why thousands of people leave the cities and head to California's Point Reyes—especially from late December into mid-April, when hundreds of migrating gray whales swim up from their summer grounds off the Baja Peninsula to return back to the Bering Sea. During this time, to prevent congestion on weekends and holidays, Sir Francis Drake Boulevard is closed to private vehicles, and a fleet of buses provide transportation from Drakes Beach to the headlands and Point Reyes Lighthouse and Chimney Rock, where

☆ The Reds of Glacier ☆

Captured in vintage photographs and on thousands of mid-century home movies are images of low-profile "touring sedans" that once ferried passengers throughout our parks. At one time, hundreds of these vehicles rolled down scenic roads and to vista points at Yellowstone, Yosemite, and Bryce Canyon, but as a new car culture took over after World War II, these classics were slowly nudged aside.

But not at Glacier.

Credit the topographical demands of the Going-to-the-Sun Road, where sheer drops and tight turns demanded that drivers keep both eyes on the road. Even in the late 1990s, when park officials examined ways to alleviate pollution, reduce development, and protect the park's environment, the cherished "Reds" (so named for the vehicles' color scheme of a slick red body and sharp black accents) were considered such a fundamental part of Glacier's heritage that a drive was on to find ways to keep them in service.

They finally found an answer—and a partner: the Ford Motor Company. With Ford engineers and designers at the wheel, among the changes the Reds were given in their makeover was a switch to liquid propane, which burns 93 percent cleaner than gasoline; a stronger and more modern chassis, which supported a new body comprised of lighter materials; and the addition of ergonomic seats, a modern instrument panel, and various energy-saving and environmentally friendly extras. What remained of the old bus? Perhaps the most important thing: Its appearance. Committed to preserving a design that is both classic and contemporary, both Glacier and Ford managed to retain the vehicle's low profile, its multiple doors, the convenient rollback canvas top, and, of course, the iconic color scheme. The Reds roll on.

elephant seals roost and whales splash past. This service makes it easier for guests to switch their focus to the magical sight of whales swimming, spouting, and breaching in the cold, gray waters offshore (be sure to bring the binoculars). Bus tickets are sold at the Kenneth C. Patrick Visitor Center at Drakes Beach.

☆ Gettysburg ☆
NATIONAL MILITARY PARK
Battlefield Bus Tours

Arguably the most recognized and important battle of the Civil War, the Battle of Gettysburg was fought not only in the town, but all around it. While rangers

Newly modernized, Glacier's historic Red Buses from the 1930s still navigate the Going-to-the-Sun Road.

at the visitor center fill you in on the highlights of major battles and the story of the cemetery and its dedication, the Park Service itself doesn't run interpretive battlefield bus tours to such major sites as Little Round Top and The Wheatfield. The most practical option may be the popular double-decker bus tours *(717-334-6296, www.gettysburgbattlefield tours.com)* or even aboard a fleet of restored 1930s Yellowstone buses *(717-334-8000, www.historic tourcompany.com)*; these commercial operations are operated by park-approved vendors and led by knowledgeable guides. Each is convenient, each is very informative, and each has the ability to cover the countryside, provide the lay of the land, and reveal historical facts that can help determine where to return later in a private vehicle.

☆ Colonial ☆
NATIONAL HISTORICAL PARK
Williamsburg, Jamestown,
and Yorktown Links

The three neighboring Virginia cities of Colonial National Historical Park—Colonial Williamsburg, Jamestown, and Yorktown—are conveniently linked through the efforts of Colonial Williamsburg *(757-229-1000, www.colonialwilliamsburg.org)*, which operates the Historic Triangle Shuttle to and from the other two sites from spring and into fall. Streamlining the process, additional shuttles await passengers in Jamestown to take them to historic sites within the city, including Historic Jamestowne, the Jamestown Settlement, and the Glasshouse. Where the shuttle buses stop at the Yorktown Battlefield Visitor Center, the county picks up the slack by providing the Yorktown Trolley *(757-890-3500)*, which takes passengers to stops within the historic village and to the Yorktown Victory Center. No shuttle service operates between Yorktown and Jamestown.

books about u.s. parks

Great destinations for bookworms

Since as early as the 1870s, when Yellowstone was the focus of federal protection—and several popular books—authors have found plenty of inspiration in America's national parks. Thousands of books about the parks have been published, ranging from historical fiction and murder mysteries to classics of conservation, nature, and outdoor adventure.

Bob Flame: Rocky Mountain Ranger
DORR G. YEAGER
Fiction: Set in Rocky Mountain National Park

Originally published in 1935, this classic young adult novel set in Rocky Mountain National Park was recently re-released in paperback and still makes edge-of-your-seat reading after all these years. Chief naturalist at Rocky Mountain in the early 1930s, Dorr G. Yeager mixes fact and fiction to spin a realistic tale of high adventure along the Continental Divide. His courageous protagonist is allegedly a composite of men who actually worked in Rocky Mountain at the time. As the story unfolds, Bob Flame and the other park rangers battle poachers, rescue tourists lost in the backcountry, and set out on dangerous ski patrols above tree line. Yeager was especially hard on poachers, a huge problem during the national park's early days. "He'll have six months to think things over," Flame declares after arresting an illegal hunter, "and when he comes out I'll bet he'll have reached the conclusion that those three does were pretty expensive meat." The book's popularity encouraged more people to visit Rocky Mountain and other national parks, and ingrained in the public's mind the image of the intrepid, idealistic, and fearless ranger dedicated to preserving America's natural treasures.

The Killer Angels
MICHAEL SHAARA
Fiction: Set Around Gettysburg

Winner of the 1975 Pulitzer Prize for fiction, *The Killer Angels* is a classic of historical fiction and battlefield literature. Although technically fiction, the story is largely based on real events that unfolded in and around Gettysburg, Pennsylvania, between June 30 and July 3, 1863, during a battle that for all intents and purposes decided the outcome of the Civil War and the survival of the Union. Michael Shaara spins his tale from the perspective of several main characters, grand strategists like Confederate leader Robert E. Lee and Union commander George Meade to courageous frontline heroes like

Maj. Gen. George Pickett (commanding a Division of Virginians) and Col. Joshua Chamberlain (commanding the 20th Maine Infantry). Told in chronological order and packed with maps that show how the combat played out over four days, the book makes an excellent companion for anyone visiting Gettysburg National Military Park. Shaara's inspiration for the book was a 1966 family visit to the national park unit, a trip that also inspired his son Jeffrey Shaara to write about the Civil War in two historical novels of his own (Gods and Generals and The Last Full Measure).

Oh, Ranger! True Stories From Our National Parks
EDITED BY MARK J. SAFERSTEIN
Nonfiction: Stories from a Wide Variety of U.S. National Parks

Inspired by the 1928 memoir of Horace M. Albright, the first superintendent of Yellowstone National Park, *Oh, Ranger!* provides a fascinating insider's look at everyday life in the National Park Service. The book's short stories were penned by current and former park rangers; some of the accounts are lighthearted and funny, others poignant and heartrending, and every single one of them true. The tales range from a dolphin rescue at Canaveral National Seashore to human search and rescue in the Grand Canyon, from surviving a hurricane at Cape Hatteras National Seashore to how the national parks of Washington, D.C., were impacted by the events of September 11, 2001. While Yellowstone, Yosemite, and other celebrated national parks provide much of the literary fodder, many lesser known

> *Harpers Ferry Center publishes official [NPS] handbooks that provide more comprehensive information about a park and expanded discussion of concepts and issues ... [M]any of these handbooks are available online.*

parks are also covered in the book, places like Saguaro National Park in Arizona, El Malpais National Monument in New Mexico, Wind Cave National Park in South Dakota, and Timucuan Ecological and Historical Preserve in Florida. All profits from sales of the book are donated to national park education programs as well as the National Park Service employee and alumni association.

Lost in My Own Backyard: A Walk in Yellowstone National Park
TIM CAHILL
Nonfiction: Backcountry Adventures in Yellowstone National Park

Globetrotting adventure writer Tim Cahill takes on a subject close to home—Yellowstone—in this humorous and informative tale of hiking the world's first national park. Cahill earned his reputation writing about far-off places like the Andes and East Africa before turning his attention to an area less than 100 miles from his Montana home. During his summer-long Yellowstone walkabout, Cahill moves between glaciers to geysers, muses on the strange microbiology of the park's thermal wonders, watches midnight moonbeams over waterfalls, and has more than his share of animal encounters while contemplating the concept and value of preserving wilderness. The book also doubles as a convenient guide to those looking to hike the Yellowstone country themselves. The first half describes a variety of Cahill's favorite day hikes; the second half details longer and much more ambitious backcountry routes. The author also provides a bibliography of his favorite books on Yellowstone.

The Man Who Walked Through Time
COLIN FLETCHER
Nonfiction: Account of a Backpacking Journey
Through Grand Canyon National Park

Considered by many as the founding father of the modern backpacking movement, Colin Fletcher was already an avid walker when he decided in 1963 to trek the Grand Canyon from one end to the other via routes deep inside the canyon. Heat, height, and poisonous snakes were just three of the dangers he faced during the two-month trek. His account of the journey is a remarkable study in man's ability to survive in a hostile environment, as well as a fascinating look at Arizona landmark's geology, wildlife, and ancient human history. It's also an interesting insight into backpacking in an era before freeze-dried foods, portable hydration systems, GPS, or cell phones. The book is a reminder that even in the most crowded of parks during the most popular of seasons, there are still remote trails and secluded campsites for those who dare to step off the beaten track.

Our National Parks
JOHN MUIR
Nonfiction: A Naturalist's Take

Scottish-American naturalist John Muir may be most closely associated with Yosemite, but he actually spent time tramping many of America's early national parks. This 1901 book, comprising articles first published in the *Atlantic Monthly*, offers Muir's insights and observations on Sequoia, Mount Rainier, and other natural wonders that would soon receive federal protection. Muir points out that America's wild areas should be viewed as "fountains of life" where people can renew their health and spirit rather than just places for harvesting timber, digging for minerals, or siphoning water for irrigation. "I have done the best I could to show forth the beauty, grandeur, and all-embracing usefulness of our wild mountain forest reservations and parks," Muir writes, "with a view to inciting the people to come and enjoy them, and get them into their hearts, that so at length their preservation and right use might be made sure."

The National Parks: America's Best Idea
DAYTON DUNCAN AND KEN BURNS
Nonfiction: Companion Book
to PBS Documentary

The literary companion to the hit television series of the same name, *The National Parks: America's Best Idea* explores the origin, growth, and sociopolitical background of the U.S. National Park System like few books that have come before. Historical black-and-white photographs blend with dramatic color images and a surprisingly lively text that takes readers all the way from early parks like Yellowstone and Yosemite and the legacy of Theodore Roosevelt, through the Depression-era expansion under FDR, the new western parks created in the 1960s alongside Lyndon Johnson's Great Society program, and Jimmy Carter's highly contentious campaign to protect Alaska's wilderness treasures. Delving deep into the national soul, Duncan and Burns try to determine what it is about Americans that made them dream up something so unprecedented in human history, and conversely how the national parks have impacted American culture. As Burns writes in the introduction: "For the first time in human history, land—great sections of our natural landscape—was set aside, not for kings or noblemen or the very rich, but for everyone, for all time."

Ranger Confidential: Living, Working and Dying in the National Parks
ANDREA LANKFORD
Nonfiction: Accounts From Rangers in Yellowstone, Yosemite, Denali, and Elsewhere

The fourth book from ranger-turned-writer Andrea "Andy" Lankford, *Ranger Confidential* dispenses with wilderness romance and cuts straight to the heart of how difficult it can be to manage America's national parks. Compiled from eight years of interviews, research, and Lankford's own encounters, the book delves into the everyday trials, tribulations, and triumphs of today's park rangers. Garnered from Yellowstone, Yosemite, Great Smoky Mountains, Denali, and other parks, many of the stories reflect the seemingly incompatible task of protecting nature from human impact while at the same time expediting tourism. As a former law enforcement ranger in parks like Cape Hatteras, Zion, and Grand Canyon, Lankford is well acquainted with the skill set that modern rangers are required to master: police officer and history teacher, traffic warden and animal behavior expert, search-and-rescue whiz and public relations specialist, often all on the same shift. Lankford's other books include *Biking the Grand Canyon Area* and *Haunted Hikes: Spine-tingling Tales and Trails From North America's National Parks*.

An eloquent writer, naturalist John Muir successfully advocated for the preservation of wilderness.

The Swamp: The Everglades, Florida and the Politics of Paradise
MICHAEL GRUNWALD
Nonfiction: History of the Everglades

Did the Florida Everglades (rather than hanging chads) swamp Vice President Al Gore's run for the White House in 2000? That's just one of the many interesting ideas and opinions floating in Michael Grunwald's excellent history of the Everglades and environs. An award-winning reporter for the *Washington Post,* Grunwald chronicles the sad modern history of one of the world's most important wetlands: the last stand of the indigenous Seminole Indians; the millions of birds slaughtered in the name of fashion; the invasion of the sugar barons and the property kings; the "re-plumbing" of the vast grassland by the U.S. Army Corps of Engineers in order to divert water for commercial and residential use; and finally the 1990s fight over whether a new super airport for Miami should be developed on the edge of the Everglades—a controversy that cost Gore vital votes in a state that ultimately decided the 2000 presidential campaign. But not all is doom and gloom. Grunwald also examines the personalities on both sides of the political spectrum that have helped save the Everglades from even greater misfortune, including President Bill Clinton's landmark ecosystem restoration plan, signed into law in December 2000 and the most expensive environmental scheme in U.S. history.

Western National Parks' Lodges Cookbook
KATHLEEN BRYANT
Nonfiction: Cookbook Featuring Recipes
From 15 Lodges in Ten Western Parks

Veteran *Arizona Highways* writer Kathleen Bryant morphs from red rock to red chili in this mouth-watering account of gourmet grub in western national parks. Stunning photography of both the scrumptious food and the historic lodges makes *Western National Parks' Lodges Cookbook* a must-have for the home library of any park aficionado. But the book excels on several other levels as well: a history of the lodges, a tribute to the men who designed and built them, and a practical cookbook for those who might want to re-create national park flavors in their own kitchens. Bryant's tome is packed with more than 70 signature recipes gleaned from chefs at 15 lodges in ten different parks. The dishes range from rare reptilian treats like rattle-snake empanadas at the Furnace Creek Inn in Death Valley National Park (try making those at home) to Pacific-Southwest fusion foods like the wild Alaska salmon tostadas with organic greens and tequila vinaigrette served at the El Tover Dining Room in Grand Canyon National Park. Some dishes are simple, others complex; all are sublime.

☆ Nevada Barr ☆

In the tradition of Agatha Christie and Dashiell Hammett, author Nevada Barr has created a contagious series of mystery books set around a dynamic central character. The star of her dozen plus whodunits is Anna Pigeon, an adventurous National Park Service law enforcement ranger who always gets her man.

Each book takes place in a different park, starting with *Track of the Cat*, a 1993 novel set in Guadalupe Mountains National Park in Texas that won both the Agatha and Anthony Awards for best first mystery. Since then, Anna Pigeon has tracked down bad guys in Big Bend, Dry Tortugas, Glacier, Isle Royale, Mesa Verde, Lassen Volcanic, Yosemite, Carlsbad Caverns, and Rocky Mountain National Parks, as well as Natchez Trace Parkway, Statue of Liberty National Monument, and Cumberland Island National Seashore.

Barr's life is nearly as fascinating as her fictional ranger. Born and raised in the Sierra Nevada mountains, she studied drama and acting in college and worked nearly two decades in stage, film, and radio before turning her eye to writing. Her introduction to national parks was a series of seasonal ranger jobs that took her to Guadalupe Mountains, Isle Royale, Mesa Verde, and other places where her novels would be set.

live exhibits

Interpreting the role of domesticated animals in U.S. history

The Park Service watches over myriad aspects of our country's history, from the Lincoln Memorial in the District of Columbia to Native American cliff dwellings in Colorado, from the textile mills of Lowell, Massachusetts, to Civil War–era forts. But not all the historic aspects of our parks are inanimate. In some cases, parks portray America's past by hosting "exhibits" that live and breathe—not to mention whinny, moo, squeal, and bleat.

Several parks incorporate domestic animals into their interpretation of earlier times. These aren't the bears, deer, or elk of nature-oriented parks, but cattle, pigs, and other farm dwellers, which give visitors a more complete and accurate view of historical times.

At Theodore Roosevelt National Park in North Dakota, visitors can enjoy a small herd of longhorn steers, recalling the 19th-century days of western cattle drives, specifically the Long X Trail, a route that passed through what is now the park and was once used by ranchers to move cattle from the southern United States to lush pastures in the upper Great Plains.

Some of the longhorns at Theodore Roosevelt National Park came

from Grant-Kohrs Ranch National Historic Site in Montana, a working ranch where you can observe activities connected with raising cattle. Grant-Kohrs is also home to the horses cowboys need for herding cattle, and even chickens typical of a frontier homestead.

In southern Virginia, Booker T. Washington National Monument preserves the site of the tobacco

plantation where Washington was born to an enslaved mother in 1856, before going on to become the first president of Tuskegee Institute (now Tuskegee University) in Alabama. To present a true picture of the boyhood of the famed "Great Educator," the park keeps sheep, pigs, horses, and chickens typical of an antebellum tobacco farm in the Virginia Piedmont.

CARL SANDBURG HOME N.H.S.

Quite possibly the most fascinating domestic animals within the National Park Service can be seen at Carl Sandburg Home National Historic Site in Flat Rock, North Carolina. The beloved poet died in 1967, and his house has been a park since 1974, displaying thousands of books and other personal items. Surprisingly to many, Sandburg's wife, Lilian, was renowned in her own right as a breeder of champion goats.

"In the community, people knew more about Mrs. Sandburg than they knew about Carl Sandburg," says park interpreter Greg Litten. "In fact, when the Sandburgs moved down here in 1945, it was specifically to be in a good location where Mrs. Sandburg could continue raising the goats she had started breeding at their farm in Michigan."

CONNEMARA FARMS

Today, you can tour the red dairy barn on the 267-acre Connemara Farms property and learn about Mrs. Sandburg's influential career in the livestock industry.

"Mrs. Sandburg had about 250 goats from three different breeds, all chosen for good milk production," Litten says. "She was a smart woman and a good manager who knew about genetics, and she raised some real champion producers. She won all sorts of national awards. One of her goats, Jennifer II, produced around 3 gallons of milk a day for almost a year, which was a world record for a good 20 years."

Milk from Mrs. Sandburg's goats was widely distributed in western North Carolina, and her breeding methods helped improve the genetic makeup and milk production of dairy goats nationwide. She shared her knowledge with other goat breeders, and shipped goats to developing nations worldwide to help farmers improve their herds. Director of the American Dairy Goat Association for more than ten years, Mrs. Sandburg remained a strong advocate of the health benefits of goats' milk until she gave up management of her farm in 1965.

"The park's herd is much smaller than what Mrs. Sandburg was working with, because she had workers to help out," Litten says. "We maintain a herd of about 15 or 16 goats of the same breeds that she was managing: Nubian, Saanen, and Toggenburg. There's a few kids born each year, so a few other goats are sold off."

The park is managed as a living, interactive interpretive exhibit, demonstrating goat breeding and Mrs. Sandburg's life. "When you come here you see a vegetable garden like the one that Mrs. Sandburg planted, which would have helped them live sustainably," says Litten. "The goats are all part of her herd's direct bloodline."

INTERACTIVE EXHIBIT

Twice a day, you can watch park rangers and volunteers milk the herd of dairy goats. Some of the milk is used in cheesemaking demonstrations. "When it comes to the actual cheese production, that's a kind of a specialized job," Litten says. "Just a few of the rangers do that."

In a program called FRESH (Flat Rock Exceptional Sandburg Helpers), local young people come to the park to help with the goat operation. "Some of these students take goats to the local fair to show them," Litten says. "And some of the FRESH kids have grown up and become rangers."

A certain number of park visitors are city people who rarely, if ever, set foot on a working farm. "We maintain the goat operation for a lot of reasons," Litten says, "and one of them is to let people make that connection: Where does our food come from?"

field excursions

Hands-on learning in the national parks

Learning is a lifelong process, but when there's a chance to learn while actually *living*, well, that may be the ultimate educational experience. Partnering with some national parks are field institutes that offer courses often led by historians, scientists, authors, and other experts who can turn an ordinary vacation into educational adventures.

⁕ Glen Canyon ⁕
NATIONAL RECREATION AREA
Grand Circle Field School

In many ways this section of Arizona appears to be just a stark and spare landscape, yet hidden in plain view is an entirely new world to discover, one that the Grand Circle Field School reveals through an inter-generational curriculum that includes hikes, fossil research, and even cowboy sing-alongs. Whether learning at base camp or on a wilderness experience aboard a combination houseboat/photography expedition, students will find themselves navigating red-rock canyons with the park's mountains, canyons, deserts, ruins, petroglyphs, and abandoned homesteads framing lessons in archaeology, geology, biology, history and botany. Some courses are Lodge and Learn getaways that focus on the lives of wolves, buffalo, and prairie dogs, as well as birds of prey. The school also offers guided hikes into the Vermilion Cliffs, filled with remote gulches, grottoes, and canyons. School: *505-797-8540, www.grandcirclefieldschool.org.*

⁕ Grand Canyon ⁕
NATIONAL PARK
Grand Canyon Field Institute

Arizona's vast Grand Canyon has the dimensions to conceal countless marvels and mysteries—many of which can be solved in more than a hundred courses that snake down canyon trails, trek into the deepest recesses, and flow down the Colorado River. Many courses are simple—yoga courses, a casual walk along the rim, and even writing retreats—but many are designed to lead students into a more natural (and demanding) environment. Courses range from brutal to beautiful, so beware of physical limitations before embarking on a course. Art instructors know where to find the most perfect plants and flowers and how to sketch, paint, and photograph them. There's loveliness in and around the canyon and, in a number of à la carte classes, found in the sky as well. Far from the city lights, astronomy classes will reveal the sort of heavens our ancestors enjoyed. Now we can enjoy it, too. School: *866-471-4435, www.grandcanyon.org/fieldinstitute.*

⭐ Great Smoky Mountains ⭐
NATIONAL PARK
Great Smoky Mountains Institute

Lessons at the Great Smoky Mountains Institute are designed to touch upon one or more of three "strands": sense of place, diversity, and stewardship. Considering this Tennessee–North Carolina park's heritage, it's a smart combination. Clear-cutting led to a host of environmental tragedies, and the story of the ecosystem's rescue became a logical foundation for the institute's lessons. Relocated when this area became a park, the families of Cades Cove left behind a unique mountain culture whose story is shared in courses on cultural diversity. Logging inspires day hikes that celebrate the largest old-growth forest east of the Mississippi, just as streams and rivers and wetlands are used to explain the hydrology, structure, and habitats of the southern Appalachian Mountains. The park's myriad habitats make it a photographer's paradise. Courses focused on light, composition, and equipment take place in fields of wildflowers and at vantage points perfect for sunrise and sunset scenes. Lastly, the autumn Appalachian Celebration offers a festive exploration of the region's culture in music, storytelling, food, and dance. School: *865-448-6709, www.gsmit.org.*

Geologic eye candy, the Vermilion Cliffs serve as a natural classroom for students of the Grand Circle Field School.

✵ Arches and Canyonlands ✵
NATIONAL PARKS
Canyonlands Field Institute

Canyonlands Field Institute uses the combined acreage of Arches and Canyonlands—more than 400,000 acres—and several thousand more outside their boundaries as its campus. Lessons and courses are taught at national monuments, national forests, on Indian reservations. Seminars can be personalized, so a one-day hike could become a multiday hike that tacks on river running and camping. Attend a lecture, enroll in a literary symposium, learn how to conduct oral histories, embark on a river study course with a group, or get away from everyone by

---

☆ More Field Institute Opportunities ☆

Olympic National Park—Olympic Park Institute (360-928-3720, www.olympicparkinstitute.org): K-12, customized programs, family programs, and teacher training; four hours to ten days.

Sequoia and Kings Canyon National Parks—Sequoia Field Institute (559-565-4251, www.sequoia history.org): Creative arts and adventure (kayaking, nature walks, backpacking trips, and winter activities) programs; one day to one week.

World War II Valor in the Pacific National Monument—Arizona Memorial Museum Association (808-282-5086, www.pacifichistoricparks.org): A six-day course promotes understanding of the attack and the ensuing war.

Yosemite National Park—Yosemite Conservancy (209-379-2321, www.yosemiteconservancy.org): Day hikes, backpacking, cultural and natural history, writing, photography, birding, and art classes.

---

reserving a fleet of rafts for a private excursion. A natural history course may be as simple as a nature hike or one that requires the use of a cooking yurt followed by an overnight in a teepee. Exploring this land on water can cover myriad topics: While polishing skills at white-water rafting and kayaking, students also absorb information on geology, water plants, wildlife, and human and cultural history. School: *435-259-7750, www.canyonlandsfieldinst.org.*

✵ Zion ✵
NATIONAL PARK
Zion Canyon Field Institute

The soft swirl of mountains and the odd colorations found in Zion's rocks and canyons are only part of this southern Utah park's personality. It has far more to offer. The institute offers field experiences for dedicated adventurers and participatory options for families. Some last a few hours, others take three days, and overall the range is as wide as Zion itself with studies of insects, lizards, and snakes; and of botany through native plant seed propagation, low desert wildflowers, and explorations to the hanging gardens of Zion. Geology is a natural, with lessons that explain the mysteries and evolution of the land from canyon floor to canyon rim. Art courses in poetry, painting, journaling, and photography, meanwhile, draw inspiration from the land, flowers, and sky. School: *435-772-3264, www.zionpark.org.*

✵ Denali ✵
NATIONAL PARK & PRESERVE
Alaska Natural History Institutes

The hands-on programs presented by naturalists, biologists, botanists, authors, and artists at Denali that touch on adventure, creative arts, and field seminars have become very popular. A frontier expanse of forest, mountains, tundra, slopes and bogs and rain forest, this landscape is home to prolific wildlife and sometimes rarely seen wildflowers and rivers filled with trout. Field excursions may involve wildlife tracking and studying the habitat of sheep, caribou, moose, wolves, and grizzly bears. Rafting expeditions disappear into the wilderness in search of some of Denali's 165-some species of birds. Attending classes here won't be a night at the Ritz. Some courses involve hiking, kayaking, and no-frills rustic camping, which may be offset by sessions in which you literally draw inspiration from your surroundings in drawing, painting, and photography classes. As broad as the course selection is, however, everything boils down to a simple lesson: preservation and conservation. School: *866-257-2757 or 907-274-8440, www.alaskainstitutes.org.*

✳ Joshua Tree ✳
NATIONAL PARK
Desert Institute

Courses at Joshua Tree in southern California are designed to appeal to a cross-generational student body, so lessons may be as practical as learning to read a compass and map, as novel as mastering the art of stellar navigation, as thrilling as tracking an animal, or as demanding as scaling the park's tallest peak. Some guided hikes explore and explain how this harsh land shaped the existence of the ancient people who lived here, while another brings students up to date on the very active, but seldom recalled, gold-mining operations launched here in the 1890s and relaunched by necessity during the Depression. In a unique twist on standard botany lessons, after searching for edible desert plants a final exam includes ways to prepare and eat them at a fire pit cookout. Another course looks at how snakes have managed to adapt to an ecosystem of extreme temperatures and a scarcity of water. Many

courses focus on the creative arts, including the re-creation of Native American pottery and baskets. The barren landscape magnifies the profile of anything that survives here, so painters and photographers have the inspiration—and instruction—to capture the park's unique beauty. School: *760-367-5535, www.desertinstitute.homestead.com.*

✳ North Cascades ✳
NATIONAL PARK
North Cascades Institute

Classes in the fields of art, literature, and science at North Cascades Institute have been developed to get attendees past the implied barriers of the

Joshua Tree's desert biodiversity features prominently in many of the Desert Institute's field classes.

Washington park and deeper into its forests, higher into its mountains, and farther down its rivers so the resonance of nature helps change thinking and lead to preservation and conservation. Programs are geared for all ages and personalities; courses can range from dainty to dangerous, as passive as silk painting and wildflower photography to more active programs that involve multiday backcountry treks to explore the upper Skagit River, hone map- and compass-reading skills, and teach how to track bears and cougars. A variety of lessons help students embrace the outdoors through combination canoe trek/yoga courses, improve their journaling and poetry skills, and interpret the land through watercolors. School: 360-854-2599, www.ncascades.org.

In the 1930s, Yellowstone National Park set out to revive the wild buffalo herd. To meet this important goal, the park set up a buffalo ranch on the northern edge of the Lamar Valley.

☆ Point Reyes ☆
NATIONAL SEASHORE
Point Reyes Field Seminars

The institute features courses nearly as varied as the seashore's dramatic coastline landscape, with field courses whose duration (as little as four hours) and price (around $50) make them readily accessible and equally popular among long-distance travelers as well as day-trippers heading in from nearby San Francisco. Glimpses of the natural world are captured in classes that interpret the environment through paints, pastels, and pencils, while scientists and naturalists help focus observational skills on insects, examine the medical and nutritional value of plants and mushrooms, lead kayaking expeditions on Tomales Bay and other waterways, and conduct evening hikes that skirt past mudflats to a vantage point to see the setting sun. Given the coastline's unique biodiversity, popular day- and weekend-long courses study songbirds, pelagic seabirds, shorebirds, raptors, and ducks and other migratory fowl, while photography courses focus on these birds as well as landscapes, flowers, waves, and sunsets. School: 415-663-1200, www.ptreyes.org.

☆ Yellowstone ☆
NATIONAL PARK
Yellowstone Association Institute

Northwestern Wyoming's fascinating human and natural history provides the content for the Yellowstone Association Institute's curriculum. Budding naturalists can learn about the park's wolves, raptors, and bison as well as geological marvels including hot springs, mud pots, and geysers, while curious historians can learn about the days when tourists arrived via horse and buggy and U.S. Army soldiers were on patrol against poachers, vandals, and robbers. Yellowstone's abundance of natural beauty inspires art courses with plein air painting sessions, sketch classes, and instruction in photographing the park's thermal features and brilliant autumn leaves. Some courses reach back in time to turn city slickers into mountain men (or women) capable of identifying footprints and scat to track animals, studying the habitat and behavior of birds, and learning how beavers change our environment by building their own. And if one's vision of Yellowstone includes mountains, forests, and a gently flowing stream, sign up for fly-fishing lessons. School: 406-848-2400, www.yellowstoneassociation.org.

ranger programs

Get smart at the parks

No matter which national park toured, you will always leave knowing more than when you arrived. Rangers are passionate about their parks and want everybody to understand what humans and nature have conspired to create. As such, they offer park visitors one-of-a-kind programs that greatly enhance the learning experience.

☆ Mount Rushmore ☆
NATIONAL MEMORIAL
Evening Lighting Ceremony

At nearly any time of day, the spectacle of Mount Rushmore is already awe-inspiring. Then comes nightfall and the spectacular 30-minute Evening Lighting ceremony. Held from around mid-May into September, the presentation is one of the most popular ranger-led programs at any national park. At the spacious amphitheater, patriotic music plays as dusk starts to shade the four heroic faces on the mountain. The evening's program begins when a ranger strides to the center of the stage to explain the story behind the sculpture, take questions from the audience, and then introduce "Freedom: America's Lasting Legacy," a short film that stirs up potent levels of patriotism that reach a crescendo when, to the musical accompaniment of "America the Beautiful" and sing-along favorite "The Star-Spangled Banner," the faces are slowly illuminated. To wrap it all up, active and retired military personnel are invited to the stage to assist during the flag retreat.

☆ Gettysburg ☆
NATIONAL MILITARY PARK
Living History Programs

Credit the incredible stories woven into the Battle of Gettysburg that keep this national park in Pennsylvania atop the must-see list. Supplementing the ranks of uniformed rangers each summer are living historians who appear in period dress while adapting the persona of someone related to the battle. In addition to an impressive daily total of 18 ranger programs, guests may join a rotating cast of characters who share firsthand stories of their experiences here. There may be the expectant mother who saddled up to show Union soldiers local roads, the *New York Times* reporter who covered the battle only to find his dying son in the field, a sketch artist on assignment, a reporter from the London *Times*, or troops coming to Gettysburg to remember their fellow soldiers. You can always learn something from a ranger, but a completely new level of learning is reached when you suspend your disbelief and listen to the stories of people who were actually there.

✵ Carlsbad Caverns ✵
NATIONAL PARK
Evening Bat Show

At New Mexico's Carlsbad Cavern, a few hundred thousand bats peel themselves off the ceiling to take off for dinner each evening. From Memorial Day weekend to mid-October, just before sunset, a ranger stands near the natural amphitheater created by the cave entrance and shares information about bats and the importance of protecting them. With a little luck, the 30-minute talk will end just as the first bats appear from deep within the cave, a small trickle slowly turning into an aerial stampede as thousands swarm into the sky. You are cautioned to remain quiet, as voices and the high-frequency pitch of flash cameras can distract the bats. As summer passes the size of the maternal colony grows, the baby bats having grown enough to take flight and hunt for themselves.

✵ Bryce Canyon ✵
NATIONAL PARK
Full Moon Hike

Utah's Bryce Canyon is a geological wonder. One of the park's most popular ranger programs is the bimonthly Full Moon Hike offered between May and October. This hike shines a new light on the hoodoos—the towering spires that are the icons of Bryce. With visitors lining up as early as 6 a.m. for the 60 tickets awarded for each of the night's walks, the two-hour experience offers the best of all worlds. Bryce is seen in an unusual natural state, with the full moon illuminating the canyon and the casual evening walk infused with lessons in geology, wildlife,

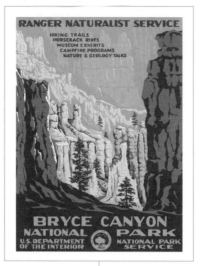

and astronomy. More than likely, this evening walk will inspire a pre-dawn rise to catch a spectacular sunrise above Bryce, Inspiration, or Sunset Points. Depending on demand, rangers may lead walks into the canyon although guests are welcome to go on their own.

✵ Minute Man ✵
NATIONAL HISTORICAL PARK
"Who Were the Minute Men" Living History Presentation

Guests begin to understand the passion behind the Battles of Lexington and Concord—the first skirmishes of the Revolutionary War—by watching the excellent multimedia show in the visitor center in Concord, Massachusetts, and then traveling to the Hartwell Tavern inside the park's 18th-century living history site, where a ranger decked out as a colonial-era soldier presents "Who Were the Minute Men?" to explain the roots and role of the Minute Men and militias—and concludes the presentation with a bang by demonstrating how to fire a musket. The park is long and narrow, and some sites may require the use of a car to reach them, but rangers are stationed at most sites to answer questions about the history of the place. To help visitors become fully immersed in the stories of the Revolution, a 3.5-hour walking tour covers several miles of the Battle Road Trail, illustrating the amazing story of how a ragtag group of citizen soldiers drove the British back to Boston. In addition to costumed rangers, nearly every weekend costumed interpreters come to the park to present mock trials or town meetings while reenactors portraying Minute Men congregate around Hartwell Tavern, sometimes setting up camp and celebrating like it's 1776.

☆ Lava Beds ☆
NATIONAL MONUMENT
Guided Lava Tube Tours

When the heat of the California summer becomes too severe, it's a welcome relief to find a place to get out of the sun—like inside a 55°F lava tube that snakes beneath the landscape of this national park. During the summer, once a day on weekdays and twice daily on weekends, rangers are ready to get down to business, which means getting their groups down below ground. Unlike limestone caves which evolve over hundreds of thousands of years, lava tubes are created relatively quickly and from a powerful geological force. The nearly 20 tunnels created here offer three levels of difficulty, so there will always be a balance of opportunities. On a ranger-led exploration guests don gloves and helmets and carry flashlights and descend into the catacombs for about an hour. In easier caves you are able to follow a lighted and paved trail, and in more difficult tubes you get a quick introduction to the serious challenges of caving. At any time of the year, this is also an activity that can be done without a ranger leading the way. Dressed for the experience, anyone can purchase cave maps at the visitor center and explore the chilly tubes solo. And if a summertime exploration piques an interest in caving, consider returning in the winter for the reservation-only, extremely limited admission Crystal Ice Cave guided tour.

☆ Fossil Butte ☆
NATIONAL MONUMENT
Aquarium in Stone, Hands-on Presentation

While Wyoming's Fossil Butte is not the largest national park in America, it quite likely has the oldest exhibitions. Preserved across and below this sagebrush-filled landscape are an inestimable number of fossils from the Eocene epoch, in cosmic terms

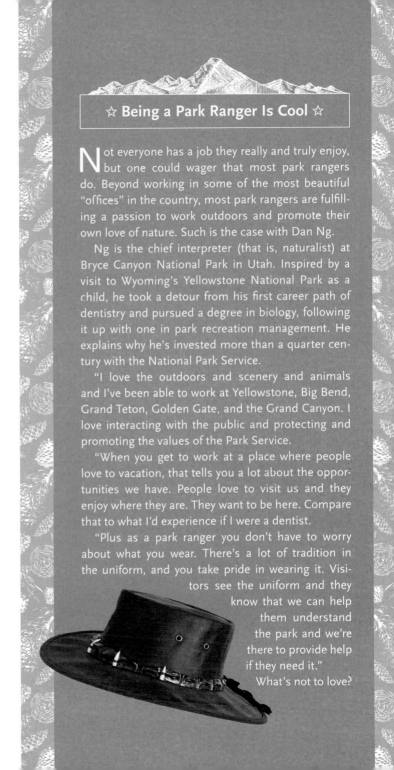

☆ Being a Park Ranger Is Cool ☆

Not everyone has a job they really and truly enjoy, but one could wager that most park rangers do. Beyond working in some of the most beautiful "offices" in the country, most park rangers are fulfilling a passion to work outdoors and promote their own love of nature. Such is the case with Dan Ng.

Ng is the chief interpreter (that is, naturalist) at Bryce Canyon National Park in Utah. Inspired by a visit to Wyoming's Yellowstone National Park as a child, he took a detour from his first career path of dentistry and pursued a degree in biology, following it up with one in park recreation management. He explains why he's invested more than a quarter century with the National Park Service.

"I love the outdoors and scenery and animals and I've been able to work at Yellowstone, Big Bend, Grand Teton, Golden Gate, and the Grand Canyon. I love interacting with the public and protecting and promoting the values of the Park Service.

"When you get to work at a place where people love to vacation, that tells you a lot about the opportunities we have. People love to visit us and they enjoy where they are. They want to be here. Compare that to what I'd experience if I were a dentist.

"Plus as a park ranger you don't have to worry about what you wear. There's a lot of tradition in the uniform, and you take pride in wearing it. Visitors see the uniform and they know that we can help them understand the park and we're there to provide help if they need it."

What's not to love?

A ranger enthralls visitors with stories of Carlsbad Caverns before leading them through the cave's Natural Entrance.

a relatively recent 50 million years ago. Each summer, on Fridays and Saturdays a ranger leads guests to the hands-on program Aquarium in Stone, the title revealing that the arid butte known as Fossil Lake is what remains of an ancient lake bed, the floor sprinkled with the impressions of creatures that lived—and died—here. After traveling through an aspen grove, guests reach an area where researchers are combing the rock to find the fossilized remains of dragonflies, fish, snakes, turtles, and other prehistoric creatures and foliage. You may be able to assist the scientists and, if you're lucky, locate a fossil that will be removed and researched and then displayed

with hundreds of other highly detailed fossils at the visitor center. The fact that guests get to see how these samples are discovered, uncovered, and preserved creates a fascinating program.

☆ Mammoth Cave ☆
NATIONAL PARK
Wild Cave Tours

Claustrophobes should beware the special tours at Kentucky's Mammoth Cave that travel beyond the regular guest experience and deep into a challenging and chilly (mid-50s) subterranean world. In addition to a two-hour tour for kids ages 8–12 and a crawling trek for families with kids 10 and older, the wildest option is the Wild Cave Tour. How wild? Dressed out in caving gear (helmet, gloves, knee-pads, light) guests follow the ranger/caver deep into sections of the cave that lack lights and amenities. But thoughts of finding a restroom (reached at an underground lunchroom about two hours into the experience) may be put on hold as novice spelunkers deal with more immediate concerns, such as moving from a relatively large section of cave that reduces to the size of a kneehole in a desk before reducing again to narrow passages as small as just 9 inches high. Before signing up for the 5-mile jaunt, be certain that you can handle the pressure of living like a mole—because once inside, it's hard to get out.

Each year more than 120,000 volunteers donate over 4 million hours of service in the national parks. They come from every state . . . to help preserve and protect America's natural and cultural heritage.

☀ Wright Brothers ☀
NATIONAL MEMORIAL
Family Nights and Kitebuilding Programs

It's hard to believe that the inspiration for the modern aviation age came from the minds of a couple kids. After their father presented young Wilbur and Orville Wright with a toy called a Penaud helicopter, the seed was planted that would eventually help the two conquer the mysteries of flight. It's with this same sense of discovery and creativity that rangers here facilitate a number of programs that inspire kids—and adults—to think creatively and understand the importance of perseverance. During summertime at this North Carolina park, Family Nights rangers explain the principles of flight and then, using old toys, demonstrate with balloons, paper airplanes, puddle jumpers (a propeller on a stick that dates back to the 14th

century), and ornithopters (flying birds) how flight can be achieved. Next, kids are invited to make their own paper airplanes based on patterns the rangers provide or, even better, following in the footsteps of the Wright brothers by creating airplane designs themselves. The rangers also host kitebuilding classes, providing the materials and instruction to help kids get their aircraft soaring in the winds of Kitty Hawk. The regularly scheduled presentation in the flight room is educational and inspiring as rangers detail the long and arduous process the Wrights faced in the development of their flyer. According to a ranger, it's a lesson parents want their kids to learn, underscoring that instant fame is fleeting and hard work, imagination, and persistence will triumph.

☀ Canyon de Chelly ☀
NATIONAL MONUMENT
Natural and Navajo History Hikes

Canyon de Chelly isn't just in the northeast section of Arizona. The entire canyon is contained within the Navajo Nation, and to explain its history are rangers and local guides, many of whom are Native Americans, authorized and certified to share the story of the canyon. These are more than just nature walks. Depending on how much time is available, hikes range from simple three-hour treks to demanding weeklong expeditions that explore more remote reaches of the canyon. For guests who'd prefer not to go on foot, guides also lead horseback and Jeep tours that can expand the roaming range as well as awareness of the region's past, from natural and geological history to facts about Navajo and ancient Pueblo people.

outfitted adventures

Experts in the fine art of outdoor encounters

For those who'd rather leave the planning to the experts, outfitters provide ready-made national park tours. With an emphasis on outdoor adventure, most trips feature hiking, biking, boating, or all three. They range from budget camping trips, where everyone pitches in, to luxury journeys with stays at park lodges and meals in fine restaurants.

✷ Backroads ✷
NATIONWIDE
Biking, Hiking, and Rafting Immersion

Californian Bill Hale started Backroads in 1979 as a way to create "epic experiences" for people. While all of Backroads' excursions are active, Hale says an even bigger part of the Backroads experience is cultural immersion. The outdoor adventure company offers more than 200 trips each year, including multisport adventures in a number of U.S. national parks. One of the newest trips is a Crater Lake family multisport in the Cascades Range of southern Oregon. The itinerary includes a pedal around Crater Rim Drive with jaw-dropping views of the deep caldera; white-water rafting on the Deschutes River near Bend; and a hike along a portion of the Pacific Crest Trail. Among the overnight stops on the five-day tour are Crater Lake Lodge and a dude ranch. Other Backroads itineraries feature Bryce Canyon, Zion, and the Grand Canyon, as well as Yellowstone and the Grand Tetons. Outfitter: *www.backroads.com.*

✷ Austin Lehman Adventures ✷
NATIONWIDE
Luxury Hiking and Rafting

Dan Austin and Paul Lehman created one of the world's first boutique adventure travel outfits in 1985. They pioneered a new type of travel that combined adrenaline and luxury, small groups led by experienced guides with a mandate to experience places like a local would. Twenty-five years later, that's still their trademark. ALA's multisport jaunt through Glacier National Park is typical of what one can expect on one of their trips, a mosaic of hiking backcountry trails over granite and ice, rafting the unfettered Flathead River, making like Lance Armstrong on the Going-to-the-Sun Road, and retiring at night in the comfort of one of the park's legendary lodges. Austin Lehman offers journeys in more than a dozen parks in total, trips like Bull Moose to Bucking Broncos in Yellowstone and Grand Teton, and a Greatland Multisport Adventure in Alaska that combines hiking, biking, kayaking, and small-ship cruising. Outfitter: *www.austinlehman.com.*

☀ Country Walkers ☀
NATIONWIDE
Slow and Steady Walking Tours

Walking is the best way to absorb the geography and culture of a place. And that's what Country Walkers is all about: immersion via slow and steady footsteps. This is ambling for those who don't do it as part of everyday life, either as part of a group or self-guided using Country Walkers' maps, notes, and inside tips. The guided trips cover a dozen different parks from Alaska to Acadia. The Olympic Peninsula adventure is par for the course, a leisurely weeklong wander through most of the park's highlights, including the tide pools and seamounts of Kalaloch and the temperate rain forest of the Hoh River region. Nights are passed in the comfort of the park lodges. The hiking is rated easy to moderate, with everyone putting in 4 to 9 miles per day. Outfitter: *www.countrywalkers.com.*

☀ Natural Habitat ☀
NATIONWIDE
Animal Encounters

As its name suggests, Natural Habitat specializes in close encounters of the animal kind all around the globe. In the United States, the Colorado-based

Glacier hikes are the highlight of many outfitters' trips to the vast wilderness parks in Alaska.

adventure travel company throws out some pretty wicked wildlife trips. One unique trip revolves around photographing the winter wonders and wildlife of Yellowstone and Grand Teton. In addition to the bison and elk that congregate around the geyser fields in winter, the trip also includes a trek into secluded reaches of the Lamar Valley in search of wolves. Accommodation on the eight-day adventure includes the Mammoth Hot Springs Hotel and Old Faithful Snow Lodge; much of the transportation is via snow coaches. "We have often used the word 'luxury' in our materials," says Nat Hab spokesman Matt Kareus. "But we actually mean the luxury of the experience—of getting into places where no one else goes, having experiences that are truly unique and life enriching." Outfitter: *www.nathab.com*.

> *Throughout time, people have sought out Glacier's rugged peaks, clear waters, and glacial-carved valleys; its landscape giving both desired resources and inspiration to those persistent enough to venture through it.*

✷ O.A.R.S. ✷
NATIONWIDE
Aquatic Adventures

America's premier white-water outfitter organizes aquatic adventures in a number of national parks from its base in the San Francisco Bay Area. The granddaddy of them all is a three-week run down the Colorado River between Lee's Ferry and Lake Mead. Done in reinforced wooden dories or rubber rafts, the trip takes 18 to 19 days and is without doubt the ultimate Grand Canyon river trip. Highlights include the fern grottoes of Elves Chasm, swimming in the incredible turquoise pools of Havasu Canyon, exploring the ancient Pueblo granaries of Nankoweap peninsula, and conquering rapids that would put any theme-park roller coaster to shame.

Rafters camp along sandbanks at night and take their meals over open fires beneath the soaring redrock walls. There's plenty of time for casual swims, side hikes, and wildlife-watching. O.A.R.S. also organizes a combined Yosemite hiking and Tuolumne River rafting trip, as well as multiday float trips in five other parks including Dinosaur National Monument. Outfitter: *www.oars.com*.

✷ Adventure Center ✷
NATIONWIDE
Budget Camping Adventures

Oakland's Adventure Center cut its teeth in the 1980s on budget tours for young people and backpackers. While they are still dedicated to adventure at affordable prices, the company now attracts clientele of all ages and interests. From Cape Cod to Mount Rainier, the Adventure Center offers more than two dozen itineraries that touch in whole or part on U.S. national parks. Most nights are spent tent camping. Participants share cooking duties with the guides. And a hot shower every day is not a given. Some of the national park trips revolve around hiking while others are multisport. The 12-day Western Discovery includes seven different park units between San Francisco and Las Vegas. Among the trip's many adventures are biking Yosemite Valley, camping in Nevada's Great Basin, a full day of hiking in Zion, boating on Lake Powell, and ranger-guided walks around the Grand Canyon. One of the more hardcore trips is a 15-day Alaska walking adventure in Denali, Kenai Fjords, and Wrangell–St. Elias. Outfitter: *www.adventurecenter.com*.

☀ Road Scholar ☀
Educational Outings
in Spectacular Settings

A nonprofit organization dedicated to lifelong learning opportunities for older adults, Road Scholar offers fascinating low-cost travel opportunities with an educational angle. Formerly known as Elderhostel, the group rebranded its programs "Road Scholar" in 2009 to emphasize the combination of journey and learning that characterizes every trip. National parks are among their more popular programs. Road Scholar visits more parks than any other travel outfitter in the entire country—46 in total—including off-the-beaten-path destinations like Assateague Island National Seashore in Maryland and Virginia, New River Gorge National River in West Virginia, Canyon de Chelly National Monument in northern Arizona, and Capitol Reef National Park in central Utah. Trips often combine more than one park, like a southwestern Colorado adventure that includes Great Sand Dunes, Mesa Verde, Black Canyon of the Gunnison, and Colorado National Monument. Outfitter: *www.roadscholar.org*.

A so-called hiker's paradise, Glacier National Park is one of the premier destinations for backpacking trips.

☀ St. Elias Alpine Guides ☀
ALASKA
Alaskan Wilderness Challenges

Nobody does Alaska like McCarthy-based St. Elias Alpine Guides. Deep-wilderness backpacking, rafting wild and scenic rivers, climbing the continent's highest peaks, extreme mountain climbing, backcountry ski touring, and even kite skiing on remote ice fields—these guys do it all. While most of their adventures take place in and around Wrangell–St. Elias National Park and Preserve, they also venture into Denali and the Chugach Mountains. Many of the company's most extreme adventures (like scaling 18,000-foot Mount St. Elias) are designed for experienced hikers, climbers, or backpackers craving world-class wilderness challenge. But the company also offers easy one-day glacier hikes and river rafting out of McCarthy, as well as relatively easy four-day trips to places like Skolai Pass and Iceberg Lake that sample a small portion of the Wrangell wilderness. Participants fly in by bush plane (landing in a grassy meadow or rocky glacial field), pitch their tents at some jaw-dropping location, and spend the days doing day hikes on glaciers, lakeshores, and wildlife trails and the nights curled up inside the tent, sipping hot chocolate and swapping tales of the day. Outfitter: *www.steliasguides.com*.

⁜ REI Adventures ⁜
NATIONWIDE
Guided Multisport Adventures

The adventure travel arm of the outdoor equipment store organizes guided trips—hiking, biking, paddling, and more—in and around many national parks. Its portfolio includes a multisport and bear camp adventure in Alaska's Kenai Fjords, a Glacier Bay cruise and kayak combo, a family adventure trip to Washington's San Juan Islands, four days of camping and kayaking on Yellowstone Lake, and an amphibious (hike and kayak) exploration of Lake Powell in Glen Canyon National Recreation Area. Led by highly experienced guides, most of these trips are rated moderate and in many cases no previous experience is required. Camping is normally at remote campsites, in tents or alfresco (camper's choice), the meals prepared by both guides and guests. Outfitter: *www.rei.com/adventures*.

☆ Rail Journeys to National Parks ☆

Once upon a time luxury trains provided transport to the gateways of many national parks. Nowadays only a few of the vintage lines remain, as well as a few new ones.

- **Alaska Railroad** *(www.alaskarailroad.com):* This rail line runs between Anchorage and Fairbanks, traveling up the eastern edge of Denali National Park and Preserve. It stops at a station only 100 yards from the park's visitor center. Another branch runs from Anchorage to Seward, gateway to Kenai Fjords National Park
- **Amtrak** *(www.amtrakvacations.com):* This company offers a dozen trips with national park elements, including the Glacier Park Discovery Tour between Chicago and Seattle and the Peak to Pacific ride between Denver and San Francisco that includes a side trip to Yellowstone.
- **Grand Canyon Railway** *(www.thetrain.com):* Perhaps the most notable, this historic railway runs from Williams, Arizona, to the South Rim of the Grand Canyon. Since the last spike was driven in 1901, the line has carried numerous dignitaries to the canyon including Teddy Roosevelt, John Muir, and Clark Gable.

⁜ National Geographic Expeditions ⁜
NATIONWIDE
Photography Workshops

From Yellowstone National Park to Gettysburg National Military Park, National Geographic trips touch on many different parks. But given the organization's reputation for incredible images, the weekend photography workshops are among the most appealing trips. The chromatic adventures actually stretch over four days in four very photogenic cities: New York, Tucson, San Francisco, and Washington, D.C. At first glance it may seem like these destinations have little in common with Yosemite. But when you think about the fact that the Statue of Liberty, the Golden Gate Bridge, the Lincoln Memorial, and Arizona's most amazing saguaro cactus forests are either managed by the Park Service or located inside national parks, the connection becomes crystal clear. The workshops—lead by professional instructors and well-known NG photographers like Catherine Karnow, Bob Sacha, David Alan Harvey, and Nevada Weir—are designed for amateurs keen on taking their digital photographic skills to the next level. Outfitter: *www.nationalgeographicexpeditions.com*.

ten best parks
literary pilgrimages

Insight into the lives of great writers

In the first decades after the Revolutionary War, the United States lived in the cultural shadow of Europe. As the 19th century progressed, home-grown writers, artists, and composers made their marks in the arts world. The following national parks showcase the lives of some of our nation's finest writers.

✳ New Bedford Whaling ✳
NATIONAL HISTORICAL PARK
Herman Melville

Thousands of American students have written essays on *Moby-Dick* and the symbolism of Ahab's pursuit of the white whale. The novel ranks among the great achievements of modern literature and contains some of the most beautiful writing ever put on paper. Herman Melville based much of his 1851 story on his own experiences on a whaling ship. He embarked from New Bedford, Massachusetts (which he described as "perhaps the dearest place to live in, in all New England"), in 1841 and returned to Boston in 1844. At New Bedford Whaling National Historical Park, you learn how fortunes were made from whale oil and relive the voyages of whalers. The park's Seamen's Bethel has been a house of worship for mariners since 1832. Melville attended services here and later wrote about the chapel's marble memorials to sailors lost at sea. The pulpit in the shape of a ship's bow was added in 1961, based on Melville's description of a pulpit in *Moby-Dick*.

✳ Edgar Allan Poe ✳
NATIONAL HISTORIC SITE
Edgar Allan Poe

Debate about Edgar Allan Poe's literary qualities—not to mention his personal character—began during his lifetime, intensified at his early death (at age 40), and continues today. There can be no doubt, though, that few writers have been as influential as the Boston native known as the master of the macabre. His chilling horror tales are still avidly read, and stories such as "The Murders in the Rue Morgue" cause many to credit him with having invented the detective story. Poe's chronically underfinanced life forced him to move often. The house that is now Edgar Allan Poe National Historic Site was his Philadelphia home for about a year beginning in 1843. You are greeted by a sculpture of a raven, a reminder of Poe's renowned poem "The Raven" (in which the bird utters the ominous word "Nevermore"). Exhibits include recordings of Poe's works narrated by actors such as Vincent Price, Basil Rathbone, and Christopher Walken.

Theodore Roosevelt's Sagamore Hill home on Long Island holds a wealth of the President's personal possessions.

★ Sagamore Hill ★
NATIONAL HISTORIC SITE
Theodore Roosevelt

Famously described by historian Henry Adams as embodying "pure act" for the decisive force of his personality, Theodore Roosevelt did more in his lifetime than a dozen ordinary people. The 26th U.S. President, he was also a soldier, rancher, conservationist, adventurer, voracious reader, and respected author. He published a historical study, *The Naval War of 1812*, while still in his early 20s; it was just one of some 18 books he would write on subjects including history, biography, nature, and government, as well as his autobiography. Sagamore Hill, on New York's Long Island near the town of Oyster Bay, was his home from 1884 until his death in 1919, and as such, the rambling, 23-room Victorian house is full of original Roosevelt family furnishings and personal items, including his Rough Rider hat from the Spanish-American War, his gold-plated shaving kit, hunting trophies, and a ring containing a strand of Abraham Lincoln's hair. The Sagamore Hill Nature Trail winds through a forest of oaks and tulip trees along the same path Roosevelt and his family took on many swimming and camping excursions.

☀ Arches ☀
NATIONAL PARK
Edward Abbey

Almost everyone will find something to be upset about in Edward Abbey's life and works, and that would no doubt please the renowned conservationist and writer, who died in 1989. In his most famous book, the 1975 novel *The Monkey Wrench Gang,* he sympathetically portrays a group dedicated to (non-violent) sabotage against environmentally destructive projects in the Southwest. The book made Abbey a villain to dambuilders and developers and something of a saint to environmentalists, yet Abbey criticized liberals, advocated gun ownership, and was proudly politically incorrect. Without a doubt, though, he widened the public discussion of the value of wilderness and individualism. Abbey was hugely influenced by the stark landscapes of the West. In the 1950s he worked as a ranger at Utah's Arches National Monument (now a national park), an experience that shaped his first literary success, the 1968 memoir *Desert Solitaire: A Season in the Wilderness.* To see the rock formations of Arches at sunrise is to understand how this terrain could create such passion in Abbey and fire his beliefs that human presence can only diminish the wilderness.

☀ North Cascades ☀
NATIONAL PARK
Jack Kerouac, Gary Snyder, and Philip Whalen

The striking landscape of Washington's North Cascades—glacier-sculpted mountains dotted with alpine lakes, waterfalls, rocky streams, and the largest collection of glaciers in the lower 48 states—has the power to inspire anyone, but it holds a special place in the American literary movement known as the Beat Generation. Three Beat writers—novelist and poet Jack Kerouac, poet and environmental

☆ Literary Role of National Parks ☆

A number of other authors have written works associated with our national parks, in both fiction and nonfiction:

- Colin Fletcher: His *Man Who Walked Through Time* chronicles the author's 1963 adventure hiking the length of the Grand Canyon.
- Peter Matthiessen: His *Shadow Country,* which won the National Book Award in 2008, revised and combined three novels set in Florida's Ten Thousand Islands area, now comprising part of Everglades National Park.
- John Muir: Though best known as a naturalist and conservationist, he wrote many influential books and essays, including *The Yosemite* and *Travels in Alaska.* He is remembered at Muir Woods National Monument and John Muir National Historic Site, both in California.
- Nevada Barr: She has written a series of mysteries featuring fictional national park ranger Anna Pigeon, including *Track of the Cat* (set in Guadalupe Mountains National Park) and *High Country* (Yosemite National Park).
- Tennessee Williams. His Pulitzer Prize–winning 1947 play, *A Streetcar Named Desire,* was shaped by the cultural melting pot of New Orleans, a unique city whose heritage is the focus of one unit of Jean Lafitte National Historical Park and Preserve.

activist Gary Snyder, and poet Philip Whalen—all worked for a time as fire lookouts on mountain peaks here in the 1950s. Kerouac, perhaps most famous of the three for books such as *On the Road,* was stationed atop 6,102-foot Desolation Peak, now in Ross Lake National Recreation Area, part of the North Cascades park complex. His experience was reflected in his novel *Desolation Angels*. Snyder worked on 8,127-foot Crater Mountain, in Pasayten Wilderness just east of the national park, and on 6,106-foot Sourdough Mountain in the park's North Unit, where Whalen also worked. All three peaks can be climbed by physically fit hikers; none require technical mountaineering skills.

★ Carl Sandburg Home ★
NATIONAL HISTORIC SITE
Carl Sandburg

Known as the "poet of the people," Carl Sandburg was born the son of an immigrant railroad worker and dropped out of school after the eighth grade to work and travel the country—experiences that shaped his political beliefs and poetry. He won Pulitzer Prizes for both poetry and a biography of Abraham Lincoln. In 1945, Sandburg and his wife, Lilian, bought a house and property in Flat Rock, North Carolina, primarily so she could have a place to raise her prize-winning dairy goats. The house was always full of music and friends—not to mention more than 15,000 books. Sandburg died here in 1967 at the age of 89. You can see thousands of family items, from teapots to clothing to guitars on which Sandburg performed folk songs. The Park Service maintains a small herd of goats, and rangers demonstrate milking and cheesemaking seasonally.

The park includes more than 5 miles of trails through the woods and fields, where Sandburg felt it was important "to go away by himself and experience loneliness" at times.

★ Longfellow ★
NATIONAL HISTORIC SITE
Henry Wadsworth Longfellow

For a time in the mid-19th century, Henry Wadsworth Longfellow was arguably the most famous living writer, not just in the United States but worldwide. Poems such as "The Song of Hiawatha," "Paul Revere's Ride," "The Courtship of Miles Standish," and "Evangeline" earned him enough money that he resigned his teaching position at Harvard University and devoted himself to writing and translation. Longfellow spent the rest of his life in the house on Brattle Street in Cambridge, Massachusetts, a gift from his father-in-law in 1843. Guests who stopped by included Nathaniel Hawthorne, Ralph Waldo Emerson, Charles Dickens, and Oscar Wilde. The house had gained fame even before the poet's residence, though: In 1775, during the Revolutionary War, George Washington used it as the headquarters of his Continental Army for nine months. Today, the national historic site seasonally offers small-group tours of the house, allowing you to see Longfellow's library, study, bedrooms, family portraits, and paintings by artists such as Gilbert Stuart and Albert Bierstadt. The formal gardens are open year-round.

★ Eugene O'Neill ★
NATIONAL HISTORIC SITE
Eugene O'Neill

A life punctuated with sorrows provided background material for the plays of Eugene O'Neill, winner of four Pulitzer Prizes and a Nobel Prize for literature. Born in a hotel on New York City's Broadway, O'Neill suffered from alcoholism and depression, married three times, and had difficult relationships with his children. When O'Neill and his third wife, Carlotta, bought a 158-acre ranch near

Danville, California, in 1937, he hoped he could live and work there permanently. He and Carlotta lived in the house, called Tao, for seven years, during which he wrote the plays *The Iceman Cometh, Long Day's Journey Into Night,* and *A Moon for the Misbegotten.* Illness and the circumstances of World War II forced the O'Neills to leave in 1944. O'Neill never completed another play and died in Boston in 1953. Private vehicles are not allowed at the historic site; you must take a shuttle bus from Danville. After a guided tour of the home, there's time for a walking tour of the grounds as well.

> The Italian composer Giacomo Puccini's (1858–1924) opera, Madame Butterfly, includes a passage from the "Star Spangled Banner"; Puccini used the opening notes of the anthem as a motif for the character of Lt. B. F. Pinkerton, U.S.N.

☆ Adams ☆
NATIONAL HISTORICAL PARK
Henry Adams

Members of the political Adams family are the stars of this site in Quincy, Massachusetts, most notably John Adams, second U.S. President, and his son John Quincy Adams, sixth President. The park preserves their birthplaces, as well as the Old House, built in 1731, which was home to John Adams and John Quincy Adams; the latter's son, Civil War minister to Great Britain Charles Francis Adams; and Charles Francis's sons, scholars and historians Henry Adams and Brooks Adams. The latter two individuals provide the literary connection to the site. Though Brooks was an author, the real literary lion of this site is Henry, whose autobiography—in truth, more of a collection of philosophical essays— *The Education of Henry Adams,* won the Pulitzer Prize in 1919 and endures as one of the most studied and discussed books of the 20th century. The Adamses rank among the most influential families

in American history. The historic structures that nurtured them can be visited only on guided tours, which also allow you to see the 1870s Stone Library, built according to the will of John Quincy Adams and now housing more than 14,000 volumes. The grounds include an orchard and a formal garden.

☆ Fort McHenry ☆
NATIONAL MONUMENT & HISTORIC SHRINE
Francis Scott Key

On September 13, 1814, American lawyer and amateur poet Francis Scott Key was under British detention on a ship in the Baltimore harbor, conducting negotiations related to the ongoing War of 1812. That night, American military post Fort McHenry came under heavy bombardment from British ships, and as night fell Key was unsure of the battle's outcome. "By the dawn's early light," though, he saw "the star-spangled banner" still flying over the fort—a sign that the British attack had failed. Key was inspired to write a poem he called "Defence of Fort McHenry." Set to the melody of a British drinking song, it became a popular patriotic tune, and in 1931 was officially designated the national anthem of the United States, with the name "The Star-Spangled Banner." Today, Fort McHenry is a national monument and historic shrine, the only National Park Service site with that designation. You can take a self-guided tour to see military memorabilia, an electric battle map, barracks, commander's quarters, guardhouse, and powder magazine. Flag changes are held twice daily, weather permitting.

chapter seven

discovering history

ten best parks
age of discovery
Where Europeans staked their claims to American soil

The discoveries of Christopher Columbus sparked a land rush in the Americas, with the Spanish, French, English, and Russian powers, among others, scrambling to establish colonies and monopolize the riches of the New World. Proof of their cultural marks can be found in parks commemorating the nation's colonial era.

☆ San Juan ☆
NATIONAL HISTORIC SITE
Spanish Colonists, 1508

The second oldest European settlement in the New World after Santo Domingo, San Juan, Puerto Rico, was settled by Spanish colonists in 1508—only 16 years after Columbus "discovered" America. By 1521, they had relocated from the Spanish Main to a small offshore island that offered better living conditions and defensive possibilities. Soon after, the Spanish began construction of the first in a series of sandstone fortifications that compose the heart of today's park as well as the oldest European structures in the entire National Park System. Castillo San Cristóbal is the largest of these, a sprawling citadel that took more than 150 years to complete (1634–1790). But the hulking El Morro (primarily built 1639–1689) is the most famous, a triangular bastion overlooking the harbor mouth that fell only once in battle during its 400-year history. El Morro also bears the distinction of firing the first American shot of World War I—a 1915 salvo against a German warship. Daily ranger talks and walks (in English and Spanish) relate the history of the forts and the Spanish in Puerto Rico. Or you can explore the meandering ramparts on their own, trekking the top of the walls or the waterfront Paseo del Morro trail.

☆ De Soto ☆
NATIONAL MEMORIAL
Hernando de Soto, 1539

While Juan Rodríguez Cabrillo was sailing the California coast and Francisco Vásquez de Coronado was trekking the Southwest, another intrepid Spaniard, Hernando de Soto, was on a meandering four-year journey through the American Southeast. Far more than the other two expeditions, De Soto's venture would forever change the lives of the native people with whom he came into contact. De Soto landed somewhere near present-day Tampa Bay, Florida, with a legion of 600 men and more than 200 horses in 1539. They set off northward on an odyssey that would take him across the Great Smoky Mountains

The foundations of El Morro, a triangular Spanish colonial bastion in San Juan, Puerto Rico, date back to 1539.

and all the way to the banks of the Mississippi River, where De Soto died from a fever. The marathon expedition and its aftermath are explored in a short film and displays at the Bradenton, Florida, memorial visitor center. A living history exhibit called Camp Uzita operates during the winter season *(Dec.–April)*, with rangers and volunteers dressed as 16th-century Spaniards and Native Americans. Ranger-led kayak tours of the park's mangrove swamp and shallow coastal waters are offered May to November. The first landing is reenacted during a one-day festival each April.

☆ Cabrillo ☆
NATIONAL MONUMENT
Juan Rodríguez Cabrillo, 1542

Perched at the entrance to San Diego Bay, this small but popular national monument commemorates the first European to navigate the U.S. West Coast, as well as California's maritime heritage and unique coastal ecosystems. Juan Rodríguez Cabrillo had already earned fame as the captain of Hernán Cortés's crossbowmen during the Spanish conquest of Mexico, and then as a gold miner and shipbuilder in Guatemala, before agreeing to lead the first Spanish voyage along the California coast in 1542. Cabrillo and his three ships sailed north along the California coast, going as far as today's Russian River, north of San Francisco; he would die on the return trip from complications of an injury suffered in a skirmish with indigenous warriors. His expedition laid the groundwork for the Spanish settlement of California and a string of Franciscan missions that would eventually stretch between San Diego and Sonoma. His historic first landing is reenacted on the bayshore below the visitor center during the Cabrillo Festival each October. The park also includes the iconic Old Point Loma Lighthouse (1855)—replete with 19th-century furnishings—and a number of historic coastal defense batteries. Terraces provide astonishing bird's-eye views of San Diego Bay and the vast Pacific. Trails lead through pristine coastal chaparral vegetation and along sandstone cliff tops above tide pools.

OCTOBER 2 1672

Spanish colonial officials broke ground for the Castillo de San Marcos, a coquina fort in St. Augustine, Florida, that would be largely completed by 1695. Later a U.S. Army post, it is now Castillo de San Marcos NM.

☆ Coronado ☆
NATIONAL MEMORIAL
Francisco Vásquez de Coronado, 1540

Francisco Vásquez de Coronado led the only European land army ever to invade U.S. territory. In 1540, the conquistador marched 339 Spanish soldiers and more than a thousand native allies from Mexico City into what is now Arizona. Coronado and his entourage trekked to Kansas and back on a futile two-year search for the Seven Cities of Cibola and their legendary riches. They found instead a flourishing Pueblo Indian culture and natural treasures like the Grand Canyon. Located on the Arizona–Mexico border, this park reflects on the significance of the 16th-century expedition and its lasting historical and cultural impact on the Southwest. The visitor center displays Spanish colonial armor and other artifacts, as well as a short film about the expedition. Hike the monument's 8 miles of mountain and valley trails, through high desert, grassland and woodlands, to see a landscape little changed since the 16th century.

☆ Fort Raleigh ☆
NATIONAL HISTORIC SITE
First English Settlement in the New World, 1587

Sponsored by Sir Walter Raleigh in 1585, the nation's first English settlement was the ill-fated Roanoke Colony, established on the coast of today's North Carolina. The venture failed after less than a year and Raleigh dispatched a second voyage in 1587, a group of 116 men, women, and children who populated what came to be called the "Lost Colony" because they were never seen nor heard from again. No definite proof has ever been found as to why or how the colony disappeared. The modern park includes a visitor center and museum, an archaeological dig that yielded a number of significant 16th-century artifacts, Elizabethan Gardens landscaped in the style of the time, and a reconstruction of the earthen fort. The park's most renowned feature is the Waterside Theater, where the Roanoke Island Historical Association presents Paul Green's outdoor symphonic drama *The Lost Colony* on summer nights *(late May–late Aug., www.thelostcolony.org)*.

✳ St. Croix Island ✳
INTERNATIONAL HISTORIC SITE
First French Colony in North America, 1605

With a charter from France's Henry IV in hand, French explorer Pierre Dugua de Monts led a 1604 expedition to the Bay of Fundy and established a small colony on St. Croix Island in the middle of the river of the same name that now separates Maine and New Brunswick. Among the 74 settlers were cartographer Samuel de Champlain and Mathieu de Costa, a skilled translator and the first known black man to set foot in Canada. Nearly half the group perished in the winter, and come spring, the French moved their first North American colony to Port Royal, Nova Scotia. An interpretive trail (on the Maine coast opposite the island) spins the tale of these intrepid souls, and during the summer rangers give history talks. Visits to St. Croix Island itself are discouraged because of its fragile ecosystem.

✳ Salinas Pueblo Missions ✳
NATIONAL MONUMENT
Franciscan Missions, 1622

In an attempt to spread Christianity in the New World, Spanish Franciscan friars arrived in the upper Rio Grande region in the late 15th century and by the 1620s had made their way to the remote Salinas region on the eastern side of the Manzano Mountains, named after the area's salt lakes (salinas) and salt trade. Abó (1622) was the first of a small string of missions the Franciscans created among the local Tiwa and Tompiro peoples. But owing to persistent famine, drought, and Apache raids, as well as extreme distance from other Spanish colonial hubs, the friars were gone within 75 years. The ruins of their wondrous red-rock churches can be seen in the park's three historical segments—Quarai, Abó, and Gran Quivira—linked by the Salt Missions Trail (N. Mex. 55); the small but interesting visitor center is located in the town of Mountain Air, New Mexico.

✳ Colonial ✳
NATIONAL HISTORICAL PARK
British Colonial Establishment, 1607

This park bookends the British colonial era in the New World, from the establishment of Jamestown (1607) to the landmark Battle of Yorktown (1781) that ended British rule in the 13 Colonies. Perched on either side of the Virginia Peninsula, the park's two anchor segments are connected by the 24-mile Colonial Parkway, which meanders through heavily wooded countryside and Colonial Williamsburg. The settlement at Jamestown eventually grew into the first capital of a Virginia Colony that would play a pivotal role in the American Revolution 169 years later. One of the National Park System's more popular units, this park offers a wide range of activities from living history tours of Jamestown to interpretive talks on the Yorktown battlefield.

✳ Roger Williams ✳
NATIONAL MEMORIAL
Puritan Colonization, 1631

Fleeing religious intolerance in England, Puritan minister Roger Williams arrived in Massachusetts in 1631. Speaking out against the narrow-minded ways of his fellow colonists, Williams was convicted of sedition and heresy, and in 1635 fled the colony in order to avoid arrest. He established a settlement among the Narragansett Indians west of the Seekonk River, christening the new colony Providence and dedicating it to both religious freedom and separation of church and state—two principles on which the United States was later founded. Located in downtown Providence, Rhode Island, the park celebrates the theologian and guiding light of American idealism. The visitor center includes displays and a short film on Williams's life; the grounds include outdoor exhibits set around what was once the town's common (public open area).

☆ Sitka ☆
NATIONAL HISTORICAL PARK
Russian Foothold, 1741

Although the Russians were late starters in the European bid for North America, their presence in Alaska endured from 1741 to 1867, when the territory was sold to the United States. This national historical park commemorates the site of the most significant skirmish between Russian forces and Alaska's indigenous people—the 1804 Battle of Sitka—as well as the settlement the Russian fur traders built there afterward. The region's Russian and Native American heritage is explored at the park visitor center and the adjacent Southeast Alaska Indian Cultural Center. Trails lead to totem poles and the historic battleground on a peninsula between Sitka Sound and the Indian River. Separate from the main park, the Russian Bishop's House sits in the middle of modern Sitka town. Built in 1843, the imposing log structure is one of the oldest remaining Russian colonial structures in North America. In addition to living quarters restored with period furnishings, the house also boasts the richly decorated Russian Orthodox Chapel of the Annunciation. The nearby St. Michael's Cathedral is a faithful reproduction of the 1848 original that burned down in the 1960s.

☆ Historic Places of Worship ☆

Faith was one of the leading reasons why Europeans colonized America, and our parks now safeguard some of the nation's oldest places of worship.

Concepción, San José, San Juan Capistrano, and Espada, San Antonio, Texas: Franciscan friars built these four Spanish colonial churches in the early 18th century with the goal of converting the indigenous populations to Christianity. Strung together in the San Antonio Missions National Historical Park, the missions blend Moorish, Gothic, and baroque features. All are active Roman Catholic congregations.

Gloria Dei (Old Swedes' Church), Philadelphia, Pennsylvania: A national historic site preserves this single oldest church in the park system, opened in 1700 on the site of an even older Lutheran chapel by descendants of the New Sweden colony (1638–1655). Services are held in the small brick structure Sunday mornings; however, the congregation is now Episcopal.

Old North Church, Boston, Massachusetts: This 1723 church is now part of the Boston National Historical Park. Sexton Robert Newman flashed two lanterns from its steeple on the night of April 18, 1775, to warn local patriots that the British were coming. An active Episcopal congregation, services are held on Sunday. The Georgian-style church is also home to the oldest church bells (1744) in North America.

Touro Synagogue, Newport, Rhode Island: Now a national historic site, this 1762 synagogue is the nation's oldest place of Jewish worship and the only synagogue surviving from the colonial era. The congregation was created in 1658 by Sephardim fleeing the Spanish Inquisition. The Orthodox Congregation Jeshuat Israel renders Shabbat services on Friday evening and Saturday morning; separate seating for men and women, and proper attire required.

rock art & petroglyphs

An artistic glimpse into the soul of ancient Americans

Rock art reflects the artistic skills of the ancient peoples who once populated many of our parks. There are two basic forms: chipped or carved petroglyphs and painted pictographs. The art is often hard to date and even more difficult to interpret, especially the more abstract motifs, and the true meaning of many images remains a mystery.

✳ Petroglyph ✳
NATIONAL MONUMENT
Rinconada Canyon

With more than 24,000 images, this desert park on the western outskirts of Albuquerque, New Mexico, safeguards one of the largest and most significant rock art anthologies in North America. Created by both indigenous Pueblo people and Spanish settlers between 400 and 700 years ago, the petroglyphs reflect stark cultural differences between the two groups. The Pueblo Indians used rock art to preserve and pass along information about their culture, history, and spiritual beliefs. Their favorite subjects were human and animal figures, and geometric designs. Some of the ancient motifs—like the flute-playing Kokopelli—are still popular in local culture. The Spaniards, who came later, were more likely to render Christian crosses or livestock brands in the dark basalt faces. The park is divided into three units along a 17-mile stretch of the volcanic West Mesa Escarpment. Rinconada Canyon, close to the visitor center, boasts more than 1,200 petroglyphs of both Native American and Hispanic origin. The Boca Negra section offers three trails and several hundred images. Farther north, the Piedras Marcadas section yields more than 5,000 petroglyphs near the remains of an ancient Pueblo town that is still largely unexcavated. Guided walks and Native American craft events are park staples.

✳ Canyonlands ✳
NATIONAL PARK
Horseshoe Canyon

Some of North America's oldest and most impressive rock art is found in one of the park system's most secluded segments—Horseshoe Canyon in central Utah. Rendered in ocher and white, the ethereal pictographs of the Great Gallery are masterpieces of the Barrier Canyon Style, 20 humanoid images spread along 200 feet of rust-colored rock. Devoid of arms and legs, the life-size tapered figures are thought to date from the Late Archaic period (2000 B.C.–A.D. 500), when Paleo-Indians occupied

Etched during the Late Archaic period, the humanoid figures of Canyonlands' Great Gallery never fail to impress.

the canyon. Their artistic merit is reflected in the fact they were reproduced (on a canvas mural) for a 1941 exhibit at the Museum of Modern Art in New York. A separate unit from the rest of Canyonlands, Horseshoe Canyon is accessed via an unpaved road between the town of Green River and Utah 24 (near Capital Reef National Park). Drive time is roughly 90 minutes from Green River (47 miles). From the west rim parking area, a footpath and equestrian trail leads down to the Great Gallery. The 6.5-mile round-trip hike averages six hours; a permit is needed for horse or mule transit. You can join ranger-guided walks to the Great Gallery on autumn weekends.

> *The dark coating found on many rock surfaces is called desert varnish. This natural patina is formed from iron and manganese oxides fixed with clay particles by microorganisms to the rock.*

☆ Chaco Culture ☆
NATIONAL HISTORICAL PARK
Una Vida and Sun Dagger
at Fagada Butte

It's hard to imagine today given its windswept loneliness and isolation, but Chaco Canyon in New Mexico was once the bustling cultural, economic, religious, and political hub of the Four Corners region. The golden age lasted for roughly 400 years, from around A.D. 850 to the 13th century, when the ancient Pueblo people inexplicably abandoned the area. Part of their legacy is a rich collection of rock art. Una Vida ("one life") is the most important of these, an eclectic petroglyph gallery created on a sandstone panel behind the great house of the same name. Human figures, handprints, geometric designs, dogs, birds and other animals are among the many motifs. The ruins and rock art are reached via a half-mile trail from the park's visitor center. Even more remarkable is the Sun Dagger petroglyph atop Fajada Butte on the other side of the visitor center. Three upright stone slabs cast rays of sunlight and shadow onto spiral patterns on the face of an ancient astronomical calendar etched on a rock face. In such a way, the ancient Pueblo people marked lunar and solar cycles. Near the sprawling Pueblo Bonito ruins, the quarter-mile Petroglyph Trail leads to images of humans and animals.

☆ Dinosaur ☆
NATIONAL MONUMENT
Prehistoric Human Figures
at Cub Creek and Swelder Shelter

As well as being a rich depository of dinosaur bones, this national monument that straddles the border between Colorado and Utah also boasts one of the nation's most dazzling petroglyph treasures. A thousand years ago the Fremont people hunted, cultivated, and expressed their artistic skill in this part of the American West. Although their style and substance varied throughout the region, the Fremont rock art found at Dinosaur tends to feature human-like figures with trapezoidal bodies, abstract or geometric designs, and animal figures such as birds, snakes, lizards, and bighorn sheep. Five of the "art galleries" at this park are relatively easy to reach, especially Cub Creek (with its lizard motifs and strange horned human figures) and Swelter Shelter near the western visitor center. A sixth art gallery, at McKee Springs on the park's northern fringe, is more isolated, and often unreachable during inclement weather, but well worth the effort to view some of the nation's most outstanding prehistoric human figures.

✵ Capitol Reef ✵
NATIONAL PARK
Capitol Gorge's Fremont Gallery

Between A.D. 600 and 1300, a prehistoric society called the Fremont Culture populated much of the Basin and Range region between the Rocky Mountains and the Sierra Nevada, including the long north–south ridge called Capitol Reef. Between hunting, gathering, and primitive cultivation they somehow found time to express their inner artist in both petroglyphs and pictographs. The park's most important rock art gallery is deep in Capitol Gorge near the visitor center and Fruita ghost town. A short hike from the parking turnout brings you to a rock wall decorated with human-like shapes and geometric designs. Some of the anthropomorphic forms are quite elaborate, clad in clothing, jewelry, and headdresses. Some even sport distinct facial expressions. As with so much of the ancient rock art found in North America, modern researchers have yet to ascertain exactly what the images mean or why the Fremont people felt compelled to render them in such profusion. Late 19th-century settlers passing through the gorge etched their names and dates on the nearby Pioneer Register. Another rich area for rock art is the Bureau of Land Management-administered Grand Staircase–Escalante National Monument, which abuts the southern end of Capitol Reef.

✵ El Morro ✵
NATIONAL MONUMENT
Inscription Trail

They may not have had the artistic flair of today's taggers, but those people who rendered the thousands of inscriptions on El Morro collectively created the nation's most important graffiti gallery. Drawn by the fresh water of an oasis-like pool at the base of the 250-foot headland, generations of Spanish explorers,

☆ A Starring Role in Films ☆

More than 400 movies have been shot on location in America's national parks, with the landscapes playing a starring role in the films.

Some of the scenes in which these landscapes starred are the stuff of Hollywood legend, like the edge-of-your-seat finale from Alfred Hitchcock's thriller *North by Northwest,* in which Cary Grant battles enemy agents on the face of Mount Rushmore. The alien rendezvous at the end of *Close Encounters of the Third Kind* famously transpires at the base of Devils Tower. And Charleton Heston's spacecraft crash-landed into Lake Powell at the start of *Planet of the Apes.*

With their rugged outdoor scenery, national parks are especially suited for Westerns. *How the West Was Won* used Bent's Old Fort and the Badlands. The Badlands also starred in the 1990 Oscar winner *Dances With Wolves.* Although much of *Butch Cassidy and the Sundance Kid* was set in what is now Canyonlands, key scenes were filmed at Zion. Clint Eastwood, meanwhile, scowled and squinted his way across the desolate dunes of White Sands in *Hang 'Em High.*

Just because a national park is old, large, or famous doesn't make it a Hollywood darling. Despite their size and acclaim, Yellowstone and the Grand Canyon have appeared in very few films. On the other hand, the Illinois & Michigan Canal National Heritage Corridor has provided backdrops for at least 20 movies, Glacier more than 35 films, and Death Valley more than 45.

and American soldiers and settlers, paused here to drink and presumably reflect on what they were doing in the middle of the Southwest desert. They carved their names, dates, and messages in the soft sandstone, a 300-year record of who passed this way and to some extent what they were thinking at the time. They may have been inspired by the petroglyphs that already existed at El Morro, the artwork of the ancient Pueblo people who once lived in mudbrick dwellings atop the headland. Exhibits at the visitor center at this national monument in western New Mexico trace 700 years of human history at El Morro. The half-mile Inscription Trail leads to the main gallery, more than 2,000 individual "tags." Another trail leads to the crest of the bluff and the ruins of Atsinna ("place of writing on rock") pueblo, where the area's earliest artists lived.

✳ Petrified Forest ✳
NATIONAL PARK
Puerco Pueblo: Newspaper Rock

It may look like an arid, uninhabitable wilderness today, but once upon a time the Painted Desert of northern Arizona supported human communities. Among the relics they left behind are the rock art at several sites in the narrow central portion of the park. Puerco Pueblo reached its zenith around A.D. 1300, when as many as 200 people may have lived there, including artists who carved human, geometric, and astronomical images into nearby rocks. One of the more celebrated images marks the summer solstice each June. Ranger walks at Puerco Pueblo include both ruins and petroglyphs. The aptly named Newspaper Rock was indeed a way for ancient people to communicate the most important ideas and events of their time. More than 650 petroglyphs are carved into boulders at the base of a cliff. Modern visitors can peruse "all the news

Native Americans once lived in the landscape of Petrified Forest; traces remain of their communities.

that's fit to etch" through free spotting scopes at the Newspaper Rock viewpoint. More remote rock art can be viewed on special ranger-guided walks into the park's normally off-limits wilderness areas.

✳ Hawaii Volcanoes ✳
NATIONAL PARK
Puu Loa Petroglyphs
on Chain of Craters Road

Born and literally raised by volcanic forces, Hawaii lends itself perfectly to rock art. Native Hawaiians even have their own name for petroglyphs—*kii pohaku*. The archipelago's largest gallery is found on the Big Island, a collection of more than 23,000 images called the Puu Loa Petroglyphs. Found near the ocean end of Chain of Craters Road, the motifs range from simple holes or dots punched in the lava rock, to geometric designs, human forms, sailing canoes, feathered capes, and cryptic images. Most are thought to date from before the first European landfall on the islands. Because local women once buried the umbilical cords of their newborns nearby, some anthropologists think the dots and circles at Puu Loa may be an ancient "birth registry" or family record. Other images are thought to represent important journeys, historical events, and expressions of human age or good health. Many of the petroglyphs are visible from a boardwalk at the end of a short trail that starts in the turnoff at milepost 16.5 of Chain of Craters Road.

☀ Lava Beds ☀
NATIONAL MONUMENT
Big Painted Cave and Symbol Bridge

Long after the magma had cooled, humans ventured into the inland mountains of northern California and transformed rough lava surfaces into works of art. Interestingly, most of the petroglyphs were rendered on lakeside cliffs or boulders, while the most popular canvas for pictographs were the large lava tubes. Researchers believe the local Modoc people and their predecessors created the Lava Beds pictographs between A.D. 500 and 1600. The park's petroglyphs are believed to be even older, although no one has been able to determine exactly how old. The best places to view pictographs are Big Painted Cave and Symbol Bridge along the 0.8-mile Symbol Bridge Trail in the heart of the park. The independent Petroglyph Section east of Tule Lake has the best rock carvings, especially the towering cliff face at Petroglyph Point. In addition to dots, zigzag lines, and human figures, Lava Beds rock art is known for its astronomical motifs, leading researchers to speculate that the area's ancient artists had a fascination with the night sky.

☀ Virgin Islands ☀
NATIONAL PARK
Reef Bay and Petroglyph Trail

One of the enduring mysteries of the Caribbean is who created the geometric shapes and strange humanoid faces now found in the mountains of Virgin Islands National Park. The images were most likely carved by Taino Indians who lived on the island of St. John before the arrival of the first Europeans. Archaeological digs at Cinnamon Bay have yielded evidence that Taino Indians once inhabited the island's northern shore. However, given the petroglyphs' similarity to rock art rendered by the Ashanti people of West Africa, an alternative theory attributes the artwork to African slaves who worked the island's sugar plantations. Hidden deep in the interior, the artworks grace a dark-gray rock face above a jungle pool, reached by following the Reef Bay Trail southward from Centerline Road. A short spur trail (0.3-mile Petroglyph Trail) runs off to the rock art. The realm of dragonflies, frogs, tiny fish, and wild orchids, the pond also offers insight into Virgin Islands nature. Rangers lead a guided hike to the area two or three times per week. The 5.5-hour journey includes boat transportation from the beach at the end of the trail back to the visitor center at Cruz Bay.

native american culture

Evocative traces of once flourishing civilizations

The European colonization of the United States brought millions of people in search of land. As forests were cut and prairies fenced and plowed, Native American nations were forced into smaller and smaller homelands, decimated by wars and diseases. Much of their civilization has disappeared, but these sites preserve evidence of their past.

✶ Mesa Verde ✶
NATIONAL PARK
Pueblo Cliff Dwellings

Unquestionably one of the world's most important archaeological sites (as well as among the most visually impressive), Mesa Verde in 1906 became the first primarily archaeological site designated a national park, and in 1976 was declared a cultural World Heritage site. More than 4,000 individual archaeological sites exist within this southwestern Colorado park, the most famous of them a series of large, beautiful cliff dwellings set into canyon walls. Though this plateau was populated by people known as the ancient Pueblo people from about A.D. 550 to 1300, it was only during the last century of occupation that they built and resided in the elaborate cliff dwellings. The structures here were abandoned in the late 13th century for unknown reasons. Plan your trip to Mesa Verde during the period from late spring through fall, when all facilities are open, including the most impressive cliff dwellings: Spruce Tree House, Cliff Palace (the largest cliff dwelling in North America), Balcony House, and Long House. Some can be seen only on ranger-led tours, while smaller ruins such as Cedar Tree Tower can be explored on your own. A visit to the Chapin Mesa Archaeological Museum is a must first stop. Watch an orientation film, see dioramas representing daily life in an ancient Pueblo village, and learn details about Mesa Verde from exhibits and artifacts.

✶ Little Bighorn Battlefield ✶
NATIONAL MONUMENT
Battle of Little Bighorn

Still studied and argued about after more than 130 years, the Battle of the Little Bighorn remains one of the most mythic military clashes in American history. On June 25–26, 1876, in what is now southeastern Montana, forces of the Seventh Cavalry of the U.S. Army met several thousand Lakota Sioux and Cheyenne, led by warriors such as Crazy Horse, Gall, and White Bull. The Lakota and Sioux gained one of the most decisive victories of the prolonged Plains Indian Wars of the late 19th century, in what

Cliff Palace at Mesa Verde National Park is one of the most stunning examples of ancient Pueblo architecture.

became known as "Custer's Last Stand." Controversial Lt. Col. George Armstrong Custer was one of 263 Army soldiers and attached personnel killed in the battle; the Lakota Sioux and Cheyenne suffered an unknown number of casualties. Formerly known as Custer Battlefield National Monument, the park for decades had no memorials to Native Americans who fought and died, nor was their viewpoint significantly acknowledged in historical presentations. That oversight has changed today, and park staff offer a more balanced view of the events surrounding Little Bighorn.

> *Items missing from the pre-Spanish Indian culture [from around Montezuma Castle National Monument] include metals, livestock, wheeled vehicles, and writing.*

☆ Chaco Culture ☆
NATIONAL HISTORICAL PARK
Pueblo Bonito and
Other Chacoan Great Houses

Archaeologists recognize this Native American site in northwestern New Mexico as having been the major regional center for the people known as the ancient Pueblo culture. Chaco's political and economic influence in the period A.D. 850 to 1250 extended to communities many days' journey away. Visitors know the park as one of the largest and most striking collections of Native American structures in the Southwest. One highlight is Pueblo Bonito, a Chacoan "great house": a very large multistory public building with associated kivas (formal ceremonial rooms). Pueblo Bonito once rose four stories high and contained more than 600 rooms and 40 kivas; it remains a sacred place to several American Indian tribes. Five other major archaeological sites are located around the 9-mile Canyon Loop Drive, including Casa Rinconada, which contains the largest kiva in the park. Many of the structures at Chaco Canyon seem to have been aligned to observe astronomical events, a tradition continued in today's park with the Chaco Night Sky Program presenting astronomy programs from April to October.

☆ Hopewell Culture ☆
NATIONAL HISTORICAL PARK
Mound City Group
and Large Earthworks

This fascinating park in south-central Ohio showcases the Native American culture that dominated the forested regions of eastern North America from 200 B.C. to A.D. 500. The Hopewell culture encompassed political and spiritual beliefs of various tribes, and was characterized by the construction of tall burial mounds and large earthworks in geometric patterns. For example, a parallelogram-shaped earthwork encloses 111 acres, and a 13-acre rectangular enclosure contains at least 23 mounds. The Mound City Group, Seip Earthworks, and Hopewell Mound Group complexes feature self-guided walking trails. The park's museum displays some of the thousands of artifacts found in the earthworks, including knives, pipes, animal effigies, masks, arrowheads, copper ornaments, pottery, and tools.

✴ Poverty Point ✴
NATIONAL MONUMENT
Earthen Mounds

This site in the bayou country of northeastern Louisiana once ranked among the largest population centers in the world. At the height of its power, about 1500 B.C., the community here was a sprawling complex of tall earthen mounds and concentric semicircular ridges, a focal point of trade and, probably, religious activities. Archaeologists believe that the earthworks were built by a hunter-gatherer society, contradicting earlier theories that an agricultural lifestyle was required to support such extensive construction effort. A 2.6-mile hiking trail winds through the ridges and past a massive earthen mound measuring 700 by 640 feet at its base and rising 70 feet high. Some have speculated that the mound's shape is that of a flying bird, or possibly something resembling a tree of life.

✴ Canyon de Chelly ✴
NATIONAL MONUMENT
Cliff-Ledge Dwellings

The attractions of this park in northeastern Arizona are threefold: ruins of ancient dwellings perched on cliff ledges, spectacular walls of red sandstone rising hundreds of feet above valley floors, and a community of Navajo families whose heritage dates back 2,000 years. Canyon de Chelly is administered cooperatively by the Park Service and the Navajo Nation, with access more limited than in most parks. Two roads wind along canyon rims, offering superb vistas, and one publicly accessible trail leads down to the canyon floor. Otherwise, you must be accompanied by a ranger or Navajo guide. The 18-mile South Rim Drive and the 17-mile North Rim Drive pass sites such as Mummy Cave Ruin, one of the park's largest structures, and the amazing spectacle of Spider Rock, an eroded pinnacle rising 800 feet above the canyon floor. At several places you can see the pastures, fields, and traditional hogan houses of modern Navajo farm families on the canyon floor.

✴ Bandelier ✴
NATIONAL MONUMENT
Ancient Pueblo Structures near
Rio Grand

Like Chaco Canyon, another New Mexico park, Bandelier preserves structures built by the people of the ancient Pueblo culture. This site near the Rio Grande displays different construction techniques, though, utilizing volcanic ash geologically "welded" into a soft rock called tuff. The people who lived here from about A.D. 1150 to 1550 used blocks of tuff to build structures on the canyon floor and excavated shallow caves into the adjacent cliff face to shelter other structures. You must be adventurous and physically fit to see all of Bandelier: Reaching some sites requires climbing wooden ladders and narrow stone stairways.

✴ Knife River Indian Villages ✴
NATIONAL HISTORIC SITE
Northern Plains Indians Earth Lodge

The nomadic lifestyle of many Plains Indians means that few physical traces of their communities remain. This park, in central North Dakota at the confluence of the Knife and Missouri Rivers, interprets the history of the Hidatsa and Mandan people, Northern Plains Indians who built earthen lodges. The Lewis and Clark expedition passed through this area in October 1804, encountering a thriving community of around 4,500 people, who welcomed them and let them build a fort where they could spend the winter. While here, Lewis and Clark hired Toussaint Charbonneau, a French-Canadian fur trapper living with the Hidatsa, as an interpreter; his wife, Sacagawea, accompanied him. Later, the villages suffered greatly from smallpox, a European disease against which they had no immunity. The Mandan population was reduced by 90 percent and the Hidatsa by half. In 1845, they left their Knife River villages and moved upriver along the Missouri. The park preserves a reconstructed earth lodge and walking trails wind through village sites where depressions of other lodges can be seen.

☆ Walnut Canyon ☆
NATIONAL MONUMENT
Sinagua Culture Architecture

Set in a beautiful canyon near Flagstaff, Arizona, this park protects elaborate structures of rock, mud, and wood built on alcoves set back into near-vertical sandstone walls. The people who lived here from A.D. 1100 to 1250 are known by archaeologists as the Sinagua culture. The name comes from the early Spanish explorers' description of the nearby San Francisco Mountains. (*Sin agua* means "without water," which isn't exactly true.) Ruins of Sinagua pueblos can be seen also at other Arizona sites such as Montezuma Castle and Tuzigoot National Monuments. Building their homes into cliff walls may have had several advantages for the Sinagua, including safety from attack, protection from weather, and moderation of temperature extremes. Physically

☆ Petroglyph National Monument ☆

Near Albuquerque, New Mexico, can be found a spectacular collection of petroglyphs: rock art produced by carving or pecking away at the dark "desert varnish" (a mineral patina) on boulders or cliff faces. Around 24,000 petroglyphs have been located in this striking volcanic landscape. Most of the rock art—handprints, snakes, birds, deer, and mysterious abstract figures—is thought to have been created between 1300 and the late 1600s, the earlier examples by American Indians and those after 1540 by both Indians and the Spaniards who by then occupied the area.

fit, you can descend into the canyon via the steep 0.9-mile Island Trail to see 25 rooms of the cliff dwellings, with more visible across the canyon.

☆ Gila Cliff Dwellings ☆
NATIONAL MONUMENT
Mogollon Culture Stone-and-Wood Structures

One of this park's attractions is its setting in the rugged Gila National Forest, adjacent to a 558,000-acre wilderness area. Traveling to the site through the mountains of southwestern New Mexico creates the proper mood for a trip back in time. There's mystery, too: No one knows why people of the Mogollon culture built stone-and-wood structures in cliffs here around A.D. 1270, only to abandon the site after just a few decades. Seeing the dwellings, set in shallow caves in the cliffs, requires taking a trail that climbs 175 feet from the valley floor. Guided tours of the cliff dwellings are offered daily. Don't miss the short Trail to the Past, which leads to pictographs (rock paintings) and to a single isolated Mogollon dwelling in a small canyon.

ten best parks
revolutionary war

Cities, towns, and battlefields that determined America's fate

Most of us think of Boston and Philadelphia as the cradles of the American Revolution, and Yorktown as the place where it finally ended after eight long years of warfare. But as several national parks demonstrate, this conflict waged up and down the Atlantic seaboard and far inland, a group effort by all 13 Colonies to expel the Redcoats.

✴ Boston ✴
NATIONAL HISTORICAL PARK
Old South Meeting House and More

Many of the ideas and actions that sparked the American Revolution came about in Boston and nearby Charlestown, and it's that theme that ties together the 16 historic sites that compose this park. The landmarks and two visitor centers are spread along the 2.5-mile Freedom Trail between Boston Common and Bunker Hill. The Boston Massacre Site marks one of the earliest episodes, the 1770 slaughter of five unarmed civilians by British troops. Old South Meeting House is where thousands of colonists gathered in 1773 to protest "taxation without representation" and launch the Boston Tea Party. Paul Revere kept his eye on the Old North Church to see if British forces were advancing by land or sea in April 1775. Two months later, the war's first large-scale battle was waged at Bunker Hill. The park's Charlestown Navy Yard portion pays homage to Boston's rich maritime heritage, from the Revolution through World War II.

✴ Valley Forge ✴
NATIONAL HISTORICAL PARK
1777–78 Winter Encampment
of the Continental Army

The events of the winter of 1777–78 at Valley Forge testify to the sacrifice and sheer grit it took to fight the Revolutionary War. At the close of the war's third year, George Washington chose a remote location west of Philadelphia as a winter encampment for the Continental Army. Most of his 12,000 troops were already ill equipped and underfed, and the cold, wet weather further demoralized the Patriots. Roughly a sixth of the army perished from disease that winter. You can explore Valley Forge via ranger-led tours, cell phone tours, and 90-minute trolley tours, as well as on 18 miles of hiking and biking trails. Living history presentations are offered on weekends (*April–Sept.*), but the highlight is a reenactment of the March Out of the Continental Army on June 19. Set along the banks of the Schuylkill River near Norristown, Pennsylvania, the park is especially evocative when viewed beneath a blanket of fresh snow.

The Union Jack marks the British position on Yorktown Battlefield, site of the last major battle of the Revolutionary War.

☆ Colonial ☆
NATIONAL HISTORICAL PARK
Battle of Yorktown

Yorktown was the last major land battle of the Revolutionary War. In the summer of 1781, British commander Charles Cornwallis had encamped along the York River in order to resupply and plan an attack against rebel forces in Virginia. After a French fleet routed the Royal Navy in the Chesapeake Bay, Cornwallis found himself suddenly trapped between the river and a large French-American army under the command of George Washington. A three-week siege convinced Cornwallis and his 8,300 troops that the situation was hopeless and the British surrendered on October 19. It was another year before the Treaty of Paris officially ended the war, but Yorktown was the final British hurrah. The battleground serves as the eastern anchor of the eclectic park. Many of the original redoubts and batteries remain, explored along a 7-mile Battlefield Tour Road and 9-mile Encampment Tour Road. The visitor center offers a short orientation film on the siege and audio tours of both routes, as well as information on historic house tours and interpretive programs.

☆ Independence ☆
NATIONAL HISTORICAL PARK
Site of the Official
Declaration of Independence

In Philadelphia the 13 Colonies made their rebellion official—a Declaration of Independence from Britain adopted by the Continental Congress on July 4, 1776. This downtown park preserves dozens of structures and thousands of relics related to America's struggle for liberty and her early years of the independence. Most sites are within easy walking distance of one another. Independence Hall—where the Continental Congress met—takes pride of place, with surviving copies of the Declaration of Independence, Articles of Confederation, and Constitution on display. The 2,080-pound bell that once pealed from the hall's trademark steeple is now across the street at the Liberty Bell Center. Other key buildings include Congress Hall (where the U.S. Senate and House of Representatives convened 1790–1800) and the Old City Hall (where the Supreme Court adjudicated during that same decade). The park offers a number of guided tours (including a Ring Up History self-guided, cell phone tour).

☆ Minute Man ☆
NATIONAL HISTORICAL PARK
Lexington Common

Nobody knows for sure who fired the "shot heard 'round the world" on Lexington Common, but that first bullet sparked a chain of bloody events on April 19, 1775, that made war between Britain and the 13 Colonies inevitable. Minute Man preserves several key battlegrounds, as well as the heritage of the Patriot militia that defeated elite British troops. The Redcoats had been dispatched to the area to seize rebel arms and supplies. After a skirmish in Lexington, they marched to Concord to complete their mission, only to be met by colonial "minute men"—militiamen trained to fight on a moment's notice—at North Bridge. Routed, the British began a long and costly retreat to Boston. The 5-mile Battle Road Trail follows their route between Concord and Lexington, winding past historic houses, skirmish points, and the spot where Paul Revere was captured.

☆ Guilford Courthouse ☆
NATIONAL MILITARY PARK
British Victory at
Guilford Courthouse

Few other battles in U.S. military history proved so fortuitous to the losing side as the 1781 clash at Guilford Courthouse. The battle in the North Carolina Piedmont country was the culmination of a 16-month British campaign to retake the southern colonies (Georgia and the Carolinas). Nathanael Greene amassed 4,400 colonial troops at Guilford on March 15 in an effort to stymie that plan. On the other side were Gen. Charles Cornwallis and 1,900 highly trained Redcoats and Hessian allies. Ninety minutes later—after an intense British bayonet charge—the fighting was over and the Americans in tactical retreat. But the British suffered 28 percent casualties. Severely weakened, Cornwallis adjourned to Yorktown to lick his wounds, a strategic blunder that would lead to the end of the war just seven months later. Films, exhibits, and original artifacts at the visitor center bring the bloody

Our national parks honor various foreigners who helped the Americans win the Revolution.

Marquis de Lafayette (1757–1834): The young Frenchman was instrumental in bringing the French into the war as America's ally. He is honored at several parks including Valley Forge and Yorktown.

Baron de Kalb (1721–1780): A major general in the Continental Army, Bavarian-born de Kalb came to the Colonies with Lafayette and distinguished himself as a field commander in the Southern theater. He was killed in the 1780 Battle of Camden in South Carolina.

Baron von Steuben (1730–1794): A German aristocrat-soldier, he wintered with Washington at Valley Forge and fought at Yorktown. He introduced discipline to the Continental Army and penned the nation's first military training manual.

Louis Lebègue Duportail (1743–1802): A French military engineer, Duportail helped organize the Valley Forge camp and coordinate the siege at Yorktown.

Thaddeus Kościuszko (1746–1817): This Polish freedom fighter helped fortify Philadelphia, orchestrated the defenses at Saratoga, and helped Nathanael Greene decide on Guilford Courthouse as the place to take on the Redcoats.

Casimir Pulaski (1747–1779): Pulaski is known as the "father of the American Cavalry." Mortally wounded at the 1779 Battle of Savannah, his memory lives on in the name of a citadel at the mouth of the Savannah River—now Fort Pulaski National Monument.

clash to life; the battlefield itself is best explored with the aid of a narrated road tour CD. A rousing battle reenactment is staged on one weekend each March.

☆ Ninety Six ☆
NATIONAL HISTORIC SITE
Star Fort and Stockade Fort

Set in the backwoods of South Carolina, the town of Ninety Six was the site of two different Revolutionary War clashes. A thriving crossroads long before the Revolution, Ninety Six was named in the (mistaken) belief that it was 96 miles from an important Cherokee village. By the advent of the Revolution, it was populated by residents both for and against independence, who took up arms against one another in November 1775. The latter prevailed, transforming Ninety Six into a Loyalist stronghold for much of the war. In the summer of 1781, Nathaniel Green and his Continental troops managed to capture the town but not the earthworks Star Fort, even after a 28-day siege. The original eight-pointed fort is still there, in surprisingly good shape, as are many of the siege trenches and a reconstruction of the 1781 Stockade Fort. Costumed volunteers portray Revolutionary-era soldiers and citizens in living history events during the summer months, an evening candlelight tour in October, and a French and Indian War weekend in April.

☆ Saratoga ☆
NATIONAL HISTORICAL PARK
Battles of Saratoga

The 1777 Battles of Saratoga turned the military tide in favor of the rebels, boosted colonial confidence, and brought France into the war as an economic and military ally. The two battles unfolded 18 days apart, as Gen. Horatio Gates and his men moved to block the advance of Gen. John Burgoyne's British army down the Hudson Valley. The Redcoats won the first skirmish with the ragtag Colonial troops on September 19. But they incurred significant casualties and were ill prepared for a second battle on October 7 that ended in a decisive Colonial win and a humiliating surrender by Burgoyne. A one-way road takes you to various sites on the heights above New York's Hudson River where the fighting took place. Two separate (but nearby) park segments safeguard the restored house of American general Philip Schuyler and the 155-foot-high Saratoga Monument.

> **MAY 16 1914**
> *A bronze statue of Commodore John Barry ... first American naval officer to capture an enemy vessel in the Revolutionary War, was dedicated in Franklin Park, part of National Capital Parks in Washington, DC.*

☆ Morristown ☆
NATIONAL HISTORICAL PARK
Billet of Washington's Continental Army

Dubbed the military capital of the American Revolution, Morristown played a pivotal role in rebellion against British rule. Located about halfway between New York and Philadelphia, the small central New Jersey town was a natural choice for George Washington to billet the Continental Army during the months when fighting was next to impossible. Their first sojourn in Morristown was January to May 1777 after crossing the Delaware River and defeating British forces at Trenton. But it was the second stay, during the harsh winter of 1779–1780, which earned the town lasting repute. During that winter, Washington's troops suffered severe discomfort, disease, and starvation. Hundreds mutinied, but the vast majority stayed with their commander-in-chief. The park comprises four segments, including

Washington's Headquarters (in the Ford Mansion) and Fort Nonsense in modern Morristown, as well as the Jockey Hollow and New Jersey Brigade encampment areas in the nearby countryside. A park for all seasons, Morristown's 27 miles of trails are ideal for hiking and biking in fair weather, or cross-country skiing and snowshoeing in winter.

☆ George Rogers Clark ☆
NATIONAL HISTORICAL PARK
Fort Sackville at Vincennes

While the big set piece battles were waging in the East, a small group of Virginians and their allies were waging war with the British along the western frontier. The seven-month Illinois Campaign ended in February 1779, when American commander George Rogers Clark and his men forced the Redcoats to relinquish Fort Sackville at Vincennes, in what is now southern Indiana. After an 18-day march through horrific winter weather, much of it in freezing floodwater, the combined force of Americans, Frenchmen, and Indians took the British by surprise: They laid siege to the wooden stronghold and within two days had convinced the inhabitants that surrender was the only option. Their fortitude and courage unfolds on seven murals inside the George Rogers Clark Memorial, painted by Ezra Winter in the early 1930s. Clark's victory had long-lasting implications: It secured the Ohio River Valley and lower Great Lakes Region for the fledgling United States. In the words of Clark himself: "Great things have been affected by a few men well conducted."

saratoga national historical park

Author Joe Yogerst's Interview with Park Ranger Eric Schnitzer

The Hudson River Valley near Saratoga Springs, New York, defines bucolic, a mosaic of farms, fields, and slowly meandering water framed by heavily wooden bluffs. Gazing across this serene scene today, it's hard to imagine that one of the pivotal events of American history—and by extension, Western civilization—took place amid these pastoral landscapes more than two centuries ago.

In the autumn of 1777, Gen. John Burgoyne led a British force down from Canada with the goal of driving a stake through the heart of the American Revolution, splitting the Colonies and their insurgent forces by taking control of the Hudson Valley. The rebels were fully aware of British intentions—and how vital it was to thwart the invasion; they sent a ragtag army under the leadership of Horatio Gates to face the well-trained and far better armed Redcoats.

Two battles played out, an initial confrontation on September 19 and a follow-up on October 7. They were far from being the largest or bloodiest clashes of the war for American independence, and neither was especially remarkable

in terms of military tactics. The significance of these twin battles derives from what probably would have happened if the Colonial forces had not prevailed.

"Saratoga was a turning point in the war," park ranger and historian Eric Schnitzer tells me as we walk the Bemis Heights overlooking the Hudson at Saratoga National Historical Park. "The battles came at a time when it really looked like the rebels would lose the war and the Colonies would not gain their

independence." As author Richard Ketchum points out in his excellent book on the battle: "At Saratoga, the British campaign that was meant to crush the American rebellion ended instead in a surrender that changed the history of the world."

In addition to capturing an entire British army and terminating their plan to cut the Colonies in half, the Patriot victory quelled Loyalist sentiment in a state that could have easily gone either Patriot or British at that point in time; persuaded the French they should finally enter the conflict as an American economic and military ally; and most importantly gave the American public and military a much needed boost in morale. "Talk about a reversal of fortune," says Schnitzer. "Saratoga really did convince people that we could beat the British."

VISITING SARATOGA N.H.P.

Most visitors pick up a map at the visitor center and drive the 10-mile, one-way loop road through the largest of the four segments that compose the park. Visitors can also tap into a cell phone tour or download an MP3 audio tour from the park's website. People are also encouraged to explore the park on foot or bike. Those who crave in-depth information can hire an Official Saratoga Battlefield Guide for a customized tour that can take anywhere from 2.5 to 4 hours.

Special events are another Saratoga staple: Music on the Menu lunchtime programs that feature live tunes from the Revolutionary War, a living history Anniversary Encampment in September, and a combined reading of the Declaration of Independence and naturalization ceremony for new Americans on the Fourth of July.

And some people, says Schnitzer, just come for the greenery. "One of the things we really prize here at Saratoga," says the ranger, "is the natural beauty. The field and forest configuration is very similar to what it was like at the time of the battles."

FALL OF 1777

Sitting on the porch of the Neilson House, an 18th-century cabin that still stands in the middle of the battlefield, I try to imagine the scene in the fall of 1777, the Patriots poised on the heights and the Redcoats approaching along the river below. Burgoyne got wind of the American ambush and sent the bulk of his forces on a sweep around the enemy flank.

Realizing what was about to happen, Gen. Benedict Arnold convinced an apprehensive Gates to pounce on the British in the woods. The daring move caught the British by surprise and cemented Arnold's reputation as a brilliant combat general. Although the Americans staged a tactical retreat, they had successfully blocked the British advance.

Dug in around the Great Ravine, Burgoyne and his men waited

nearly three weeks for reinforcements from New York City. Short on supplies and with winter closing in, the British general decided on a last-gasp attack. Arnold was the star again, leading a furious charge that overwhelmed the Redcoats. During the attack, Arnold was severely wounded with an injury that would end his field career and contribute to his infamous betrayal of the American cause.

THE UNNAMED HERO

Near the end of my day at Saratoga, I swing past the Breymann Redoubt to visit the Boot Monument—a soldier's leg rendered in marble near the spot where the controversial American general fell in battle. Benedict Arnold's name does not appear on the effigy, but the inscription dedicates the monument to "the most brilliant soldier of the Continental Army." Nowhere else in the nation is a bona fide traitor immortalized. But that's how crucial Arnold was to American success at Saratoga, and how important these battles were to the birth of the nation.

"Everything came into play the way it did because of Benedict Arnold's decisions," says Schnitzer. "The battles would not have played out like they did and we may not have had the great turning point in the Revolutionary War."

capital attractions

Green spaces and memorial places in Washington, D.C.

A pre-planned city, Washington, D.C., has more than lived up to the vision of George Washington, architect Pierre-Charles L'Enfant, and others who took an active part in its creation. The Park Service manages many of the national capital's parks, monuments, and memorials—some of them national symbols and global icons.

✷ National Mall ✷
DISTRICT OF COLUMBIA
Capitol Building to Lincoln Memorial

A stroke of urban planning genius, the National Mall runs nearly 2 miles between the Capitol building and the Lincoln Memorial. The broad, grassy passage is often described as America's front yard. Inspired by the gardens of Versailles, French-born architect and engineer Pierre-Charles L'Enfant included the grand avenue in his 1791 blueprint for the new American capital. From political demonstrations and rock concerts to presidential Inaugurations and outdoor art exhibits, the Mall has hosted tens of thousands of events, including some of the most memorable in American history. Dozens of landmarks are set within its bounds, from presidential shrines like the Ulysses S. Grant Memorial and Washington Monument to poignant military tributes like the World War II Memorial, Korean War Veterans Memorial, and Vietnam Veterans Memorial. The Mall also borders great storehouses of culture and knowledge like the Smithsonian Institution museums and the National Gallery of Art. With the Tidal Basin and East Potomac Park included within its official boundaries, the park also offers vibrant nature.

✷ President's Park ✷
THE WHITE HOUSE
The White House and Its Parks

Perched on the northern edge of the Mall, this unit of the park system includes the chief executive's mansion and all of the green space and monuments surrounding this famous residence. White House tours need to be booked well in advance through your local member of Congress. The visitor center presents a 30-minute film on the history of the White House, as well as exhibits on the First Families and other presidential topics. Best place for photos is the pedestrian-only stretch of Pennsylvania Avenue and adjoining Lafayette Park on the north side, an open space where there is almost always someone or some group practicing their First Amendment right to free speech. The Ellipse park on the south side is where the National Christmas Tree glimmers each year.

✳ Chesapeake & Ohio Canal ✳
NATIONAL HISTORICAL PARK
Historic Waterway

This 184.5-mile waterway facilitated transportation along the Potomac River between the District of Columbia and Cumberland, Maryland. Gouged out between 1828 and 1850, the canal opened the upper Potomac basin to waterborne commerce with the rest of the East Coast. The first 10 miles of the C&O hug the eastern bank of the Potomac. The visitor center offers displays, maps, and information, as well as rides on reproduction canal boats pulled by mules through Georgetown's bygone warehouse district (*June–Oct.*). Rangers also lead interpretive walks on a variety of local topics. The towpath between Georgetown and the Maryland border is especially good for hiking and biking.

✳ Thomas Jefferson Memorial ✳
NATIONAL MEMORIAL
Tidal Basin and Monument

There isn't a more sublime building in all of Washington than this memorial to the third U.S. President, its Ionic columns and dome reflected in the Tidal Basin

Exquisitely sited and designed, the Thomas Jefferson Memorial commemorates America's third President.

or silhouetted by sunset over the Potomac. Thomas Jefferson was the architect of so many American ideals, in particular those enshrined by the Declaration of Independence. Designed by John Russell Pope and inspired by the Pantheon in Rome, the white marble memorial was dedicated in 1943. The interior is graced by a 19-foot bronze statue of Jefferson, the wall engraved with passages from his writings on liberty, equality, and freedom of religion. Rangers lead walking and bike tours, but in many respects this is a memorial best explored alone, reflecting on the inspiration and influence of the man.

The iconic Washington Monument stands at the center of the National Mall in Washington, D.C.

✴ Lincoln Memorial ✴
NATIONAL MEMORIAL
Lincoln Statue and Speeches

A surge of emotion overcomes visitors the first time they ascend the stairs at this memorial and see Daniel Chester French's immortal statue of Abraham Lincoln gazing down at them. The Lincoln Memorial is a masterful blend of architecture and ideas. Henry Bacon's timeless design, completed in 1922, features 36 Doric columns representing the 36 states of the union at the time of Lincoln's assassination. The interior walls bear passages from the 16th President's Gettysburg Address and 1865 Inaugural speech, and allegorical murals by Jules Guerin that reflect Lincoln's lofty ideals and momentous accomplishments. The serene structure rests on an emotive site at the western end of the Mall, its facade glimmering in the Reflecting Pool. The memorial has long been a place of pilgrimage for those seeking freedom, justice, and truth, most notably Dr. Martin Luther King, Jr., who delivered his "I Have A Dream" speech here in 1963.

✴ Washington Monument ✴
NATIONAL MEMORIAL
Tribute to Father of Our Nation

The Washington Monument soars above the District of Columbia as a tribute to the first President. In 1836, architect Robert Mills won a competition to design a lasting memorial to the former commander-in-chief. But lack of funding and disagreement over the architectural merit of Mills's design—an Egyptian-style obelisk surrounded by a Greek-style colonnade with a rooftop statue of Washington driving a chariot—forced the government to scale back his grand vision. Political squabbling and the Civil War also took their toll; it took nearly 50 years for the monument to be finally completed, in 1884. The bottom third of the 555-foot tower is finished with a slightly different colored white marble than the upper two-thirds, one consequence of the delay-plagued construction. An elevator whisks you to the observation deck and its consummate views of the nation's capital.

☆ Rock Creek ☆
PARK
1,700 Acres of
Urban Greenspace

From urban playground to commuter corridor—Rock Creek is many things to many people. Despite its modern vibe, this park is actually one of the oldest federally operated parks, set aside in 1890 as a "pleasure ground" for the American people. More than twice the size of New York's Central Park, Rock Creek encompasses more than 1,700 acres and stretches roughly 10 miles from north to south, fat at the top and increasingly skinny at the bottom as the creek meanders toward the Potomac. The park offers many diversions: more than 25 miles of hiking trails and 13 miles of equestrian paths; a boating center where kayaks, canoes, and rowing shells are available for rent; an 18-hole golf course and 25 tennis courts. The park's Carter Barron Amphitheatre comes alive in summer with a wide variety of music, drama, and dance. The nature center offers all sorts of exhibits on park flora and fauna, as well as the only planetarium operated by the National Park Service.

☆ Theodore Roosevelt Island ☆
NATIONAL MEMORIAL
88-Acre Island
In the Potomac River

One of the guiding lights of conservation, Theodore Roosevelt was responsible for the creation of myriad national parks and monuments, the U.S. Forest Service, and 50 wildlife refuges. The 88-acre Theodore Roosevelt Island in the middle of the Potomac River

☆ Presidential Park Honorees ☆

- **George Washington:** A national monument marks the Virginia spot where the first President was born.
- **John Adams and John Quincy Adams:** A Boston-area park preserves the childhood home of the second and sixth Presidents.
- **Martin Van Buren:** A national historic site protects the eighth President's Hudson Valley estate.
- **Abraham Lincoln:** Three park units document the migration of the Lincoln family across the Midwest.
- **Ulysses S. Grant:** The general turned President is remembered at Grant's Tomb in New York City and the family farm near St. Louis.
- **James A. Garfield:** The Ohio home of the 20th President, not far from Cleveland, is now a park unit.
- **Theodore Roosevelt:** The nature-loving 26th President is recalled in several park units.
- **William Howard Taft**: The 27th President spent his childhood at a house in Cincinnati.
- **Herbert Hoover:** An Iowa site explores the rural childhood and Quaker upbringing of the 31st President.
- **Franklin Roosevelt:** The 32nd President and his wife, Eleanor, are buried on the grounds of the Hudson Valley home where Roosevelt grew up.
- **Harry Truman:** The Missouri home and farm where the "People's President" lived for more than 50 years is now a park.
- **Dwight Eisenhower:** The 34th President spent the last decades of his life at a farm near Gettysburg.
- **John Kennedy:** The Brookline, Massachusetts, house where Kennedy was born is now a historic site.
- **Lyndon Johnson:** A park in the Texas Hill Country preserves the home and ranch of the 36th President.
- **Jimmy Carter:** The 39th President's hometown Plains High School, local train depot, and boyhood farm make up this site in southwest Georgia.

commemorates the 26th President's legacy. Hiking trails and boardwalks wind through lush forest and marshland, where deer, beaver, and fox roam. The memorial plaza features a bronze statue of the ex-Rough Rider and granite slabs inscribed with some of his memorable quotes about nature and conservation. Native Americans used the island as a seasonal fishing village and later patriot-politician George Mason transformed the isle into a private estate. Other than a brief period during the Civil War when Union troops were stationed there, the island has been uninhabited since the 1830s, when the Mason family vacated.

Du Pont Circle in Washington, DC, part of National Capital Parks, contains a fountain by Daniel Chester French honoring the [Civil War] naval hero [Commodore Samuel Francis Du Pont].

☆ George Washington ☆
MEMORIAL PARKWAY
Road to Mount Vernon

This meandering roadway connects more than 20 scenic, nature, recreation, and historic areas on both sides of the Potomac in the Washington, D.C., metropolitan area. The parkway was conceived in the 1930s as a tribute to the nation's revolutionary hero and first President, a leafy route through areas that Washington often traversed by horse or carriage. It has since evolved into so much more, an eclectic urban green space where you can participate in a dozen activities on any given day, from bird-watching, biking, and boating to outdoor concerts and ranger-guided history walks. Among the park's varied segments are the U.S. Marine Corps Iwo Jima Memorial, Clara Barton National Historic Site, Theodore Roosevelt Island, LBJ Memorial Grove-on-the-Potomac, Dyke Marsh Wildlife Preserve, and 800-acre Great Falls Park. The parkway also provides access to adjacent landmarks like Arlington National Cemetery and the C&O Canal. There is no visitor center, but regular interpretive programs are available at seven segments, including Claude Moore Colonial Farm (living history), Glen Echo Park (carousel tours), and Dyke Marsh (bird walks).

☆ National Capital Parks-East ☆
DISTRICT OF COLUMBIA
Oxen Hill Farm and
12 Other Urban Parks

A tribute to historical preservation and environmental rebirth, this collection of 13 parks gives visitors a compelling reason to explore a part of the nation's capital that until recently was far off the tourist trail. The park's 8,000 acres encompass museums and nature areas, historic golf courses and farmland, hiking trails and even campgrounds all within a dozen miles of Capitol Hill. NCP-E is rich in African-American history, including the Cedar Hill home of famed abolitionist Frederick Douglass, the Mary McLeod Bethune Council House, and the home of author Carter G. Woodson. Among its outstanding nature areas are Kenilworth Park and Aquatic Gardens, the only original marshland left inside the District, famous for both its water lilies and wildlife that includes beaver, otter, fox, and more than a hundred bird species. Animals of a different ilk are the focus at Oxon Hill Farm, where activities include milking cows, feeding chickens, and scenic wagon rides. Among the NCP-E's recreational offerings is hiking the 8 miles of wooded trails at Greenbelt Park in suburban Maryland.

ten best parks
civil war

Learning about the conflict that divided our country

The four bloody years of the Civil War, 1861–65, tested the unity of a nation not yet a century old. More than 600,000 died in battle or of disease, and issues such as slavery, states' rights, lingering discrimination, and Reconstruction shaped the American psyche for decades. The following Civil War sites are essential places to visit.

☆ Gettysburg ☆
NATIONAL MILITARY PARK
Battle of Gettysburg

Most historians consider the series of clashes that took place in southern Pennsylvania on July 1–3, 1863, to have been the pivotal events of the Civil War. Coming from heartening victories in Virginia, Confederate Gen. Robert E. Lee hoped that fresh triumphs in Union territory might demoralize northern politicians and pressure them to grant independence to the South to avoid further bloodshed of a continuing war. Instead, Lee was forced to retreat after three days of fighting that resulted in 51,000 total casualties for both sides, making Gettysburg the bloodiest battle of the war. Never again would the Confederacy reach so far into the North or come so close to winning the war. With an expansive visitor center opened in 2008, Gettysburg National Military Park provides you with an excellent and evocative look at this defining moment in American history. A film entitled "A New Birth of Freedom" and the historic Gettysburg Cyclorama (a 360-degree painting depicting Pickett's Charge, the climactic event of the battle) are both must-sees. Near the visitor center is the Soldiers' National Cemetery, where President Abraham Lincoln delivered the famed Gettysburg Address on November 19, 1863. You can take a self-guided tour of the battlefield (using a recorded audio narration), or hire a licensed guide who will give accounts of the battle while driving. Park guides have encyclopedic knowledge and are well worth the additional fee.

☆ Antietam ☆
NATIONAL BATTLEFIELD
Battle of Antietam

Civil War buffs revere Antietam for its preservation of the look of the battlefield, allowing you to accurately visualize events of September 17, 1862. On that date, the Army of the Potomac, led by Maj. Gen. George B. McClellan, held off a push into western Maryland by Confederate forces led by Gen. Robert E. Lee, who had to retreat after a battle that had momentous consequences: President Abraham Lincoln had been waiting for a Union victory before declaring freedom for enslaved people in the South. Five days after Antietam, he issued the preliminary Emancipation Proclamation. From that point forward, the Civil War's aim was both to preserve the Union and end slavery. Among park attractions are a self-guided, 8.5-mile auto tour through the battlefield and the Pry House Field Hospital Museum (limited hours), located in the house that served as McClellan's headquarters. The museum features a re-creation of a wartime operating theater. Lincoln visited the Pry House two weeks after the battle.

★ Vicksburg ★
NATIONAL MILITARY PARK
Siege of Vicksburg

Though often overshadowed by the Battle of Gettysburg, which ended a day earlier, the long siege of Vicksburg, Mississippi, ranks among the Civil War's most important events. The 47-day siege ended with Confederate surrender on July 4, 1863. President Abraham Lincoln famously called Vicksburg the "key" to the Confederate South and stated that "the war can never be brought to a close until that key is in our pocket." At Vicksburg—one of the war's most accurately laid out

Many of the major military parks stage an annual reenactment of their key battle, bringing history to life.

battlefield memorial sites—you can stand where soldiers stood and imagine the Union siege of the city, when opposing forces were so close they could call out to each other during lulls in the fighting. A museum displays the Union iron-clad gunboat U.S.S. *Cairo,* sunk in the nearby Yazoo River in 1862; it was the first warship ever sunk by an electronically detonated torpedo. Park activities include living history programs, artillery and rifle firings, and interpretive talks.

JUNE 28 1865

Two-and-a-half months after Gen. Robert E. Lee's surrender at Appomattox, the Confederate ship Shenandoah committed the last offensive action of the Civil War . . .

✴ Shiloh ✴
NATIONAL MILITARY PARK
Battle for Corinth

In early 1862, Union forces moved across western Tennessee with the intention of capturing Confederate railroad lines at Corinth, Mississippi. Pausing at a small log church named Shiloh Meeting House near Pittsburg Landing, the Union Army commanded by Maj. Gen. Ulysses S. Grant was surprised on April 6 by a Southern attack. Though first gaining the upper hand, Confederates were forced to retreat the following day to Corinth. Some 100,000 men did battle those two days, with close to a quarter of them killed, wounded, or missing in action. With a larger Union force approaching, they abandoned the rail crossroads. On October 3–4, Confederates tried and failed to recapture Corinth in a fierce battle. Shiloh National Military Park encompasses much of the April 1862 battlefield at Pittsburg Landing as well as an interpretive center 22 miles away at Corinth. The Shiloh site offers a 9.5-mile auto tour route with 14 stops at important locations such as Bloody Pond, the Hornet's Nest, and the spot where Confederate Gen. Albert Sidney Johnston was killed. The military park features more than 150 commemorative monuments, 600 troop position markers, and 229 authentic Civil War–era cannon; there's also a national cemetery at the Shiloh site. Both the Corinth and Shiloh sites feature living history programs, including the annual reenactment of the Battle of Shiloh.

✴ Chickamauga & Chattanooga ✴
NATIONAL MILITARY PARK
Battle of Lookout Mountain: Base for Sherman's March

Noted for its mountaintop vistas and its well-preserved battlefields (it was established just 30 years after the Civil War), this park straddling the Georgia–Tennessee border is a favorite of military strategists, who have long studied how geography affected battle tactics. Major engagements took place at the two main sites here in September and November 1863, as Union and Confederate forces contended for control of Chattanooga's rail lines, roads, and strategic position on the Tennessee River. The Union victory in the Battle of Lookout Mountain on November 24, 1863, allowed Maj. Gen. William T. Sherman to use Chattanooga as a base for his decisive 1864 march to Atlanta. The Chickamauga Battlefield Visitor Center displays the historic Fuller Gun Collection of more than 300 weapons, while the Lookout Mountain Battlefield Visitor Center houses the massive "Battle Above the Clouds" painting depicting Union movement at the November clash.

✷ Fredericksburg & Spotsylvania ✷
County Battlefields Memorial
NATIONAL MILITARY PARK
Battles of Chancellorsville and
Wilderness and Spotsylvania Court House

Four battles in Northern Virginia in the years 1862–64 earned this area a terrible distinction as "the bloodiest landscape in North America." More than 15,000 were killed and 85,000 wounded in the engagements: the December 1862 Battle of Fredericksburg, one of the biggest Union defeats of the Civil War; the May 1863 Battle of Chancellorsville, often called Confederate Gen. Robert E. Lee's greatest victory (though the South suffered

Confederate Gen. Robert E. Lee surrendered his troops at Appomattox Court House on April 9, 1865.

a major setback in the death of legendary Lt. Gen. Thomas J. "Stonewall" Jackson); and the May 1864 Battles of Wilderness and Spotsylvania, part of Union Lt. Gen. Ulysses S. Grant's drive toward the Confederate capital of Richmond. Only the first two sites have visitor centers, so exploration of the park should begin at one of them. Despite the suburban sprawl that has grown up around these locations, their historical importance makes them must-see sites on any Civil War traveler's itinerary.

✷ Manassas ✷
NATIONAL BATTLEFIELD PARK
First and Second Battles of Bull Run

"Manassas: End of Innocence" is the name of a film shown at the visitor center in this Northern Virginia park, and with good reason: Both Union and Confederate forces entered the first major land battle of the Civil War on July 21, 1861, imagining a quick and easy victory. Northern troops thought they would quickly vanquish the ragtag Southerners, while the "Rebs" believed that one skirmish would cause the North to grant them independence. The Union was soundly defeated and forced to flee to Washington, D.C.; the Confederates learned that the North had no intention of ending the fight quickly. Both sides realized that the war would be long, difficult, and bloody. A larger battle at the same location in late August 1862 also ended in a victory for the South, and marked the high-water mark of Southern military success. A hiking trail near the visitor center focuses on the first battle, while sites of the second battle can be seen on a driving tour of the area. A popular feature is an equestrian statue of Gen. Thomas "Stonewall" Jackson. He got his nickname at the First Battle of Bull Run, when another Confederate general supposedly pointed out "Jackson standing like a stone wall" in the face of Union attack.

⋇ Fort Donelson ⋇
NATIONAL BATTLEFIELD
Battle of Fort Donelson

This park in north-central Tennessee was the site of a vital Union victory in February 1862. It opened the way for the Union to capture Nashville, and as the first significant Union triumph of the war it gave an important boost to Northerners' spirits. (It also brought to public attention the victorious officer, Brig. Gen. Ulysses S. Grant.) Much of this park along the Cumberland River looks very much as it did during the battle. A 6-mile driving tour leads to the remains of the earthen-walled fort, the batteries from which Confederate cannon fired on Union gunboats, the place where Union soldiers camped on the night before the fort's surrender, and the road along which the Confederate forces almost escaped.

⋇ Appomattox Court House ⋇
NATIONAL HISTORICAL PARK
Lee's Surrender

In early April 1865, Confederate Gen. Robert E. Lee found his forces exhausted, surrounded, and outnumbered, and reluctantly concluded that surrender was his only option. He sent a message to Union Lt. Gen. Ulysses S. Grant, and the two men met in the parlor of a private home in the town of Appomattox Court House, in south-central Virginia. Their meeting essentially ended the long, bloody Civil War. The park's centerpiece is a reconstruction of the home of Wilmer and Virginia McLean, where the generals met and set in motion the reunion of a long-divided nation. The parlor is furnished with both original and reproduction items. Original structures within the park include houses, cabins, offices, stores, and the 1819 Clover Hill Tavern. The visitor center is located in a reconstruction of the county courthouse, and exhibits include the pencil

☆ First Shots of the Civil War ☆

For a look at the Civil War's beginning, tour **Fort Sumter National Monument** in Charleston, South Carolina. The state seceded from the Union in December 1860, and on April 12, 1861, Confederates began artillery bombardment of Union-held Fort Sumter, on an island at the entrance of Charleston Harbor. The post surrendered the next afternoon, and Fort Sumter remained under Confederate control until February 1865, when Southern forces abandoned Charleston. By then, Union bombardment had left Sumter in ruins. Today, ferries take visitors to the island, but much of the story of the buildup to the war is told at the park visitor education center near the Charleston waterfront.

used by Lee to make corrections to the terms of surrender. The 4-mile History Trail, a hiking path, leads to several sites associated with the meeting.

⋇ Pea Ridge ⋇
NATIONAL MILITARY PARK
Battle of Pea Ridge and Elkhorn Tavern

One of the best preserved of all Civil War sites, this park in northwestern Arkansas was the location on March 7–8, 1862, of the "battle that saved Missouri for the Union." The 4,300-acre park encompasses the entire area of the battle, in which Confederate troops heading north with the intention of capturing St. Louis were forced to retreat—an outcome so significant that many historians believe Pea Ridge was the most important Civil War battle west of the Mississippi. More than two dozen interpretive displays are set along a 7-mile driving tour, including a reconstruction of the Elkhorn Tavern that served as a hospital and headquarters for the Confederates.

forts

America's archetypical frontier architecture

Simple wooden stockades or defensive earthworks were the first permanent structures built by colonists and settlers—to protect against wild animals, indigenous attacks, and raids by rival European powers. Forts were also vital to the American westward push, erected as fortified trading posts and U.S. Army outposts.

✳ Bent's Old Fort ✳
NATIONAL HISTORIC SITE
Bent's Fort

For most of the 1830s and '40s, Bent's Fort was the only permanent settlement along the Santa Fe Trail between Missouri and the Mexican towns of the Rio Grande Valley. Built by Charles and William Bent and Ceran St. Vrain on the north bank of the Arkansas River in territory now part of Colorado, the adobe stronghold was a meeting place for fur trappers, Cheyenne and Arapahoe traders, westward-bound explorers, and U.S. Cavalry detachments probing the outer edges of American territory. The fort was a staging post for John C. Frémont's western explorations, and Kit Carson worked as a hunter for the Bent brothers during his trapper years. The fort was destroyed in 1849, cause unknown. It was reconstructed in 1976 with the help of original paintings, sketches, and diaries, and now serves as the fulcrum for the park. Living history interpreters lead guided tours during the summer months, culminating in the annual Fur Trade Encampment in early October.

✳ Castillo de San Marcos ✳
NATIONAL MONUMENT
San Marcos

In contrast to other U.S. bastions, San Marcos is a typical Iberian design, a hulking masonry star fort similar to those found throughout the Spanish colonies, but rare on mainland North America. Construction began in 1672 and continued for more than 20 years as the Spanish sought to protect St. Augustine—their Florida capital—from pirates and rival European powers. Lacking quality stone, in a stroke of genius the engineers used coquina—conglomerate shell similar to limestone—as the primary building material. When the British laid siege in 1702, the coquina walls easily absorbed the shock of the cannonballs and Spain won the day. Over the next 200 years, the citadel had several masters, including the British (1763–1784) and the Confederacy (1861–62). Its most controversial era was the 1870s, when it housed Native American prisoners of war, most notably Cheyenne warrior, artist, and theologian David Pendleton Oakerhater.

☆ Dry Tortugas ☆
NATIONAL PARK
Fort Jefferson

Fort Jefferson is the focal point of secluded Dry Tortugas, in the Gulf of Mexico about 70 miles from Key West. Set on one of seven keys that make up the park, the fort was planned as a post for defending Florida and the Gulf Coast. Construction started in 1846 but was never fully completed; more than 16 million bricks went into the hexagonal ramparts that surround the 11-acre citadel. Jefferson remained in Union hands during the Civil War and never fired a shot in anger. During most of its active service, the fort served as a military prison or quarantine station. You reach the fort via boat or seaplane from Key West. Activities are limited to the visitor center and a self-guided tour; beyond the fort, the park offers a wide array of outdoor adventures, including scuba and snorkel, camping, fishing, and bird-watching.

☆ Fort Laramie ☆
NATIONAL HISTORIC SITE
Fort Laramie

Fort Laramie played a pivotal role in Manifest Destiny as a trading post, military stronghold, and way station for thousands of people heading west on

Fort Jefferson, one of the largest 19th-century coastal forts built for defensive purposes, never actually saw battle.

☆ Forts on National Trails ☆

Given their function as military bastions and trading posts, many of the fortifications on our list are found along the Park Service's National Trails System (*www.nps.gov/nts/index.htm*).

- Bent's Old Fort is a secluded waypoint on the northern branch of the **Santa Fe National Historic Trail** between Missouri and New Mexico.
- Fort Smith is near the western end of the **Trail of Tears National Historic Trail,** which follows the two routes that thousands of Native Americans from five southeast tribes walked from their homelands to the Indian Territory, today's Oklahoma.
- Fort Vancouver lies on the **Lewis and Clark National Historic Trail**—the path that the explorers took from the Mississippi River to the Pacific coast—and is near the western end of the **Oregon National Historic Trail** that so many 19th-century settlers trod.
- Fort Stanwix in upstate New York lies astride the **North Country National Scenic Trail,** a meandering route that runs all the way between the Hudson River and North Dakota.
- Fort McHenry offers a historic port-of-call on the watery **Captain John Smith Chesapeake National Historic Trail** through the tidelands of Virginia, Maryland, and Delaware.
- Fort Point overlooks the Golden Gate near the western end of the **California National Historic Trail** and the northernmost point of the **Juan Bautista de Anza National Historic Trail,** which traces the route of the 18th-century explorer through Arizona and California.
- Fort Laramie overlooks four national historic trails—**Oregon** and **California**, **Mormon Pioneer**, and **Pony Express**—that follow the same route through much of Nebraska and Wyoming.

the California, Oregon, and Mormon Trails. Fur trader William Sublette founded the fort in 1834 on a strategic site near the confluence of the Laramie and North Platte Rivers, in today's southeast Wyoming. By the late 1840s, the federal government had purchased the fort and set about transforming Laramie into a forward base for confronting and pacifying the Plains Indians. In 1890, with the Indian threat over, Fort Laramie, now looking more like a small town than a military post, was abandoned. Eleven of the original structures have been restored and decorated with period furnishings and artifacts. The visitor center is housed in the old commissary storehouse. Overlooking the grassy parade ground are the comfy Captain's Quarters, the New Guardhouse (with a collection of artillery pieces), and the two-story "Old Bedlam"—named after the famous English asylum because of the rambunctious behavior of the bachelor officers who bunked there.

☆ Fort McHenry ☆
NATIONAL MONUMENT & HISTORIC SHRINE
Fort McHenry

Constructed in 1798 to defend Baltimore from seaward attack, the star-shaped Fort McHenry was no different than dozens of other forts along the Atlantic seaboard—until September 13, 1814, when British Royal Navy warships appeared at the harbor entrance. They pounded McHenry for 25 hours before deciding the fort would not fall. Watching from a nearby truce ship was Washington lawyer Francis Scott Key, who shortly after penned a poem called "The Defence of Fort McHenry" as an ode to the brave American defenders. Set to the tune of a popular British drinking song, Scott's ditty rose in popularity through the 19th century but didn't become the official U.S. national anthem until 1931. Park activities range from flag ceremonies and interpretive programs to morning bird walks in the nearby wetlands and the summer Twilight Tattoo Ceremony and Concert series.

⭐ Fort Point ⭐
NATIONAL HISTORIC SITE
Fort Point

Fort Point sits perched in spectacular fashion on a rocky shore directly beneath San Francisco's Golden Gate Bridge. Completed in 1861, the thick brick bastion was designed to protect California's leading port and goldfields from foreign attack and Confederate naval raids. With 7-foot thick walls and three levels of arched masonry casemates, the fort was the only one of its kind on the West Coast, large and strong enough to withstand a six-month siege. Fort Point was abandoned after the 1906 earthquake and nearly transformed into a federal prison until Alcatraz got the nod instead. The redbrick structure is now considered a masterpiece of mid-19th-century military architecture. The fort is opened to the public five days a week *(Thurs.–Mon.)*. Special interpretive events include a Civil War reenactment in August and candlelight tours once a month during the winter.

⭐ Fort Smith ⭐
NATIONAL HISTORIC SITE
Fort Smith

This southwest Arkansas park preserves the remains of two forts. The first, Fort Smith (1817–1824), was built by the U.S. Army at the highest navigable point on the Arkansas River but was soon abandoned; the

UNITED STATES DEPARTMENT OF THE INTERIOR
NATIONAL PARK SERVICE

FORT MARION
NATIONAL MONUMENT
ST. AUGUSTINE, FLORIDA

stone foundations are visible on a bluff at Belle Point. A second, larger fort was started in 1838 as a U.S. Army post on the edge of the recently created Indian Territory. It later served as a training ground for the Mexican War and was occupied by both sides during the Civil War. By the early 1870s, Fort Smith was transformed into a U.S. federal court and jail, one that prisoners dubbed "Hell on the Border." During his 14 years on the bench (1875–1889), infamous Judge Isaac C. Parker sentenced 160 men to death.

The visitor center occupies the former barracks-courthouse-jail building; a reconstruction of the gallows stands behind. A riverside path leads to the Trail of Tears Overlook, which commemorates the forced removal of Cherokees and four other southeast tribes to the Indian Territory in the 1830s.

⭐ Fort Stanwix ⭐
NATIONAL MONUMENT
Fort Stanwix

Strategically located about halfway between New York City and Canada, Fort Stanwix played pivotal roles in both the French and Indian War and the American Revolution. Named after British Gen. John Stanwix, who oversaw its construction in 1758, the wooden fort was also guardian of the Oneida Carry, a vital portage link on the trade route between the Hudson Valley and the eastern Great Lakes region. After the French and Indian War, the fort stood abandoned until 1776, when colonial troops garrisoned it in order to block a major British invasion route from Canada and aid the Patriots' Oneida Indian allies. Redcoats besieged Stanwix in the summer of 1777, but the nearby Battle of Oriskany gave the defenders the diversion they needed to counterattack and lift the siege. The fort later featured in relations between settlers and the upstate Indian nations but then fell into disrepair. It was painstakingly rebuilt in the 1970s on its original site in the middle of what is now modern Rome, New York. In addition to three short trails—one of them along a portion of the Oneida Carry—the national monument offers guided tours, historic weapons demonstrations and living history programs, especially during the summer months.

> *June 28 1865: [T]he 1st Kansas Colored Volunteer Infantry . . . participated in the Battle of Island Mound, Missouri, becoming the first African American soldiers from a northern state to engage Confederate soldiers.*

✷ Fort Sumter ✷
NATIONAL MONUMENT
Fort Sumter

This squat citadel at the mouth of Charleston harbor is the stuff of American myth and legend. Construction on the coastal defense post started after the War of 1812 and was still unfinished when, in the first shots (and bloodshed) of the Civil War, Confederate guns opened fire on the fort on April 12, 1861—a 34-hour Rebel barrage that ended in surrender of the Union troops inside. One of those inside was artillery officer Abner Doubleday, one of the early advocates of baseball, and there are those who say that home plate derives its shape from Fort Sumter's pentagonal outline. The only way to reach the island is by private boat or concessionaire ferry from the Park Service's Visitor Education Center in the Charleston waterfront or Patriot's Point on the opposite side of the bay. The Visitor Education Center renders an excellent introduction to the political, social, and economic factors that sparked the Civil War. Once on the island, you can join a ranger-led tour of the fort that includes the parade ground, the excellent fort museum, and the rooftop of Battery Isaac Huger with its historic flags display. The park's third unit—Fort Moultrie, a brick fort that dates to 1809 and which was reconstructed around 1898 due to heavy damage received in the Civil War—is located on Sullivan's Island on the other side of the harbor entrance.

✷ Fort Vancouver ✷
NATIONAL HISTORIC SITE
Fort Vancouver

Fort Vancouver was born as a commercial operation, the bustling headquarters and supply depot of Britain's Hudson Bay Company (HBC) in western North America. Founded in 1824 as a fur-trading post in the lower Columbia River Valley, the fort grew into the hub of a vast trade network and the most populous "town" on the Pacific coast between Alaska and Mexico, home to around 600 people from more than 35 ethnic and tribal groups. HBC continued business at the fort long after the Oregon Country became part of the United States in 1846. The U.S. Army moved in when the British left in 1860 and stayed until 1948, when the fort became part of the park system. The park has two units: the Fort Vancouver site in Vancouver, Washington, and the McLoughlin House site, which preserves two pioneer-era homes in Oregon City, Oregon. Much of the fort has been rebuilt. Ranger, audio, and self-guided tours are just three ways to experience the park. The fort stages a number of special events each year, including the 1860s Cannon Salute on Memorial Day and the Brigade Encampment in June.

ten best parks
monuments & memorials

Tributes to American heroes and ideals

Ranging from global icons to faraway battlefields and evoking both natural disasters and human tragedies, national parks in the form of monuments and memorials stir the soul in their remembrance of American heroes or the ideals on which this nation was founded. These dedicated places always generate reflection.

☆ Statue of Liberty ☆
NATIONAL MONUMENT
New York Harbor

World-renowned icon of freedom and democracy, beacon to immigrants all around the globe, Lady Liberty is one of our planet's most recognizable landmarks. A gift from the people of France to the United States, the Statue of Liberty Enlightening the World was created in Paris by sculptor Frédéric-Auguste Bartholdi and engineer Gustave Eiffel, stuffed into 214 crates, and shipped across the Atlantic in a French warship. It's now hard to imagine given her famous green patina, but Lady Liberty was a dark copper brown when reassembled on Bedloe's Island in 1886. She is literally draped in metaphors: The seven points of her crown represent the seven seas and seven continents; the tablet in her left hand is inscribed with the date of American independence; her torch lights the path to freedom. Visitors can ogle the New York skyline and harbor through the lofty "jewel" windows of her crown. The national monument also includes the federal immigration station on Ellis Island, where more than 12 million people entered the United States between 1892 and 1954.

☆ World War II Valor in the Pacific ☆
NATIONAL MONUMENT
Hawaii, California, and Alaska

This sprawling park encompasses nine wartime sites in three Pacific Rim states—Hawaii, California, and Alaska. The U.S.S. *Arizona* Memorial in Pearl Harbor is by far the most visited, a striking modern structure hovering above the rusty remains of the sunken battleship where 1,177 U.S. sailors lost their lives on December 7, 1941. The nearby U.S.S. *Utah* and U.S.S. *Oklahoma* Memorials are also part of the park, as are a string of mooring quays on Pearl Harbor's "Battleship Row" and six chief petty officer's bungalows on Ford Island. The Alaska portion includes historical sites on three Aleutian islands—the remains of a Japanese military base on Kiska, the frozen battlefield on Attu, and a B-24 bomber crash site on Atka. The park's

Mount Rushmore has become an American icon, attracting hundreds of thousands of visitors each year.

most controversial element is the Tule Lake Segregation Center National Historic Landmark in northern California, where more than 18,000 Japanese Americans were locked away until after the war.

⭐ Flight 93 ⭐
NATIONAL MEMORIAL
Pennsylvania

This stirring memorial recalls the sacrifice of those aboard United Flight 93 on September 11, 2001. One of four airplanes hijacked that day by Middle Eastern terrorists, Flight 93 was on its way from Newark to San Francisco when four men commandeered the cockpit and diverted the Boeing 757 toward Washington, D.C. Authorities believe they planned to crash the plane into the White House or U.S. Capitol. Learning of the other hijackings by cell phone, passengers fought to regain control of the flight. During this struggle, the aircraft crashed into a field in Somerset County, Pennsylvania, killing everyone. The first phase of a permanent monument, replacing the temporary one in place since shortly after 9/11, is slated for completion in 2011. The design centers around a "Sacred Ground" memorial at the impact site that features a wall inscribed with the names of the 40 heroes aboard the flight.

✷ Mount Rushmore ✷
NATIONAL MEMORIAL
South Dakota

"American history shall march across that sky-line," quipped Gutzon Borglum when he first saw the Black Hills in the early 1920s. The Danish-American sculptor spent the next 17 years turning that vision into a larger-than-life reality, the faces of four Presidents—Washington, Jefferson, Lincoln, and Roosevelt—carved in granite on a South Dakota mountainside. Borglum successfully crafted a lasting monument to the American spirit and the country's ideals of freedom and liberty. His artwork has become a symbol of the United States around the globe. The Avenue of the Flags (representing the U.S. states and territories) leads from the parking area to the excellent Lincoln Borglum Museum, named after the artist's son, who supervised completion of the memorial after his father died in 1941. The Presidential Trail takes you to wooden viewing platforms directly beneath the famous faces, as well as the studio where Borglum rendered plaster scale models of the presidential faces.

✷ Johnstown Flood ✷
NATIONAL MEMORIAL
Pennsylvania

The only unit of the park system that revolves around a natural disaster, this memorial in southwestern Pennsylvania recalls an 1889 deluge that took the lives of more than 2,200 people and revolutionized the way that Americans respond to major calamities. On the afternoon of May 31, rain-filled Lake Conemaugh burst South Fork Dam, sending an estimated 20 million gallons of water downstream in a wave that reached 40 feet in height. About an hour later, the deluge smashed into Johnstown, a

☆ Footnotes in History ☆

While many of the parks enshrine icons of American history, there are also those dedicated to the memory of obscure events, some of them bizarre enough to bring to mind that old saying: Truth is stranger than fiction.

San Juan Island National Historical Park in Washington State pays tribute to the Pig War, an 1859 conflict between the United States and Britain for control of the islands in Puget Sound. Hostilities broke out when an American settler shot a British-owned pig that was eating his potatoes, and nearly escalated into full-blown warfare before cooler heads prevailed. In the end, the only casualty was the spud-loving porker.

One of the enduring mysteries at **Grand Canyon National Park** is what happened to Glen and Bessie Hyde. The newlyweds vanished in 1928 during a romantic adventure honeymoon rafting the Colorado River in the bottom of the canyon. They were never seen again, dead or alive. Their unsolved disappearance has generated several legends as to what might have befallen them as well as Elvis-like sightings.

After years of plundering ships in the Caribbean and along the Atlantic Coast, the notorious pirate Blackbeard (Edward Teach) finally met his match in what is now **Cape Hatteras National Seashore.** In November 1718, a pair of Royal Navy ships ambushed Blackbeard's *Adventure* in Ocracoke Inlet. According to legend, it took 25 stab wounds and five bullets to finally dispatch the infamous brigand, his headless body then tossed overboard at a spot now called Teach's Hole.

burgeoning steel town and railroad hub, washing much of the town away. Clara Barton and her newly formed American Red Cross spearheaded the relief effort. A visitor center shows a riveting film about the disaster. Paths lead through the old lake bed and remains of the dam. In summer, rangers lead van tours of flood-related sights. Every May 31, the victims are remembered in a ceremony during which 2,209 lit candles are displayed on the grounds.

☆ Little Bighorn Battlefield ☆
NATIONAL MONUMENT
Montana

Waged June 25–26, 1876, the Battle of the Little Bighorn was an epic clash of cultures, the culmination of several hundred years of westward expansion and Native American retreat. There were heroic personalities on both sides: Sitting Bull, Crazy Horse, and Lt. Col. George Armstrong Custer. Nobody knows for certain why Custer ordered the ill-fated attack rather than wait for reinforcements. Perhaps he underestimated the number of Lakota, Cheyenne, and Arapahoe encamped in the valley of Montana's Little Bighorn River or perhaps it was merely hubris on the part of a military leader. Regardless, Custer and more than 260 of his men perished. The elongated battlefield is best explored via the 5-mile self-guided auto tour. Places were members of the Seventh Cavalry fell are marked by simple white headstones erected in 1890. They are most abundant atop Last Stand Hill, where Custer's command

was surrounded and obliterated. Red granite pillars mark the known spots where Cheyenne and Lakota warriors fell in battle.

☆ Jefferson ☆
NATIONAL EXPANSION MEMORIAL
Missouri

Named after the President who purchased the Louisiana Territory from Napoleon and dispatched Lewis and Clark to explore America's new frontier, this striking memorial graces the west bank of the Mississippi River in St. Louis. Erected in the 1960s, the 630-foot-tall Gateway Arch is a soaring monument to the energy, curiosity, and ambition that stoked America's westward expansion in the 19th century. Designed by famed Finnish-American architect Eero Saarinen, the stainless steel arch is a giant upside-down version of a catenary curve—the ideal shape of a hanging chain. You can ride a tram to the top for a view across St. Louis and the Mississippi Valley. At the bottom of the arch, the Museum of Westward Expansion pays tribute to the settlers, soldiers, cowboys, prospectors, and Native Americans who helped shaped America's frontier mosaic. The Old Courthouse forms another section of the park, dedicated in 1828 and the scene of numerous landmark trials, including the first two sessions of the 1847 Dred Scott case that had such a profound impact on slavery.

☆ Chamizal ☆
NATIONAL MEMORIAL
Texas and Mexico

Wedged between the bustling urban centers of El Paso, Texas, and Ciudad Juarez, Mexico, Chamizal is a green oasis in the middle of what is otherwise unrelenting desert and urban sprawl. The memorial commemorates a landmark 1963 treaty between the

United States and Mexico that solved a long-running border dispute caused by the natural meander of the Rio Grande over the previous century. American authorities had to relocate more than 5,000 people on the U.S. side and cede 437 acres of South El Paso to Mexico. In turn, Mexico had to relinquish claims to Cordova Island in the middle of the river. Both governments shared the cost of cementing the river and building new ports of entry on either side. Chamizal also celebrates the shared heritage of the border region in murals, museum displays, and three art galleries with revolving exhibits. The park features a wide variety of activities, including ranger-guided history and culture programs, the Armchair Explorer video travel series, children's arts-and-crafts and book-reading events, as well as live music and dance with a Southwest flavor.

✶ Perry's Victory & International ✶ Peace Memorial
NATIONAL MEMORIAL
Ohio

"We have met the enemy and they are ours," wrote Master Commandant Oliver Hazard Perry after his celebrated naval victory during the War of 1812. The enemy in this case was a British fleet trying to slip into U.S. waters from Canada. And the place was the southern shore of Lake Erie, an archipelago off the Ohio coast that now serves as the setting for a park that commemorates both war and peace. The memorial column rises 352 feet above South Bass Island and overlooks the spot where the furious maritime battle raged on September 10, 1813.

The Americans prevailed, capturing all of the enemy warships and ending the threat of British invasion via the Great Lakes. You can hop an elevator to an open-air observation deck near the top of the monument. In the summer, rangers give interpretive talks on the battle, the War of 1812, and other topics. Living history demonstrations unfold on summer weekends, with rangers and volunteers clad in period military uniforms and civilian garb.

✶ War in the Pacific ✶
NATIONAL HISTORICAL PARK
Guam

One of the last stepping-stones across the Pacific to the Japanese mainland, the island of Guam was the scene of fierce fighting between Allied troops and the Japanese Imperial Army in the summer of 1944. The park is unique in that it honors not just the Americans who fought and died on Guam, but also Allied troops from eight other nations, the Japanese troops who fell here, and the native Chamorro (Guam natives) who were killed or wounded during the conflict. The T. Stell Newman Visitor Center has movies, exhibits, and artifacts relating to the War on the Pacific, as well as maps and information on visiting the hundred historic buildings, bunkers, caves, and memorials that make up the park. The Agat Beach and Asan Beach Units, where Allied forces came ashore in 1944, are easy to reach via Maritime Drive (Route 1). Some of the more secluded units— like Mount Alifan, site of the Japanese command post—are much more difficult to reach owing to steep topography and thick vegetation.

african-american struggle

Stepping-stone on the road to equal rights

The legacy of slavery cast a deep shadow over American history, first denying nearly all rights to people of African descent and later severely discriminating against them in education, business, social interaction, and other areas. At these sites, travelers can learn of the African-American struggle for equal rights and meet heroes of that quest.

☆ Martin Luther King, Jr. ☆
NATIONAL HISTORIC SITE
The King Center

Born in Atlanta, Georgia, in 1929, Martin Luther King, Jr., became one of the most important figures of the 20th century. His passionate advocacy of equal rights for African Americans, while emphasizing the importance of nonviolent protest, helped shape the civil rights movement of the turbulent 1960s. Felled by an assassin's bullet in 1968, he nonetheless set in motion changes that reformed American society in profound ways. This historic site in Atlanta's Sweet Auburn neighborhood interprets several locations connected with King. The visitor center includes exhibits and audiovisual presentations on King and the civil rights movement. The 1922 Ebenezer Baptist Church is where King's grandfather and father preached, where he was baptized and ordained as a minister, where he joined his father as co-pastor in 1960, and where his funeral was held. The King Center includes exhibits on King's life and work as well as his gravesite, an eternal flame, and a reflecting pool that serves as a place for contemplation. The house where King was born and where he lived until age 12 is furnished with items from the 1930s and '40s. It can be visited only on a ranger-led tour, limited to 15 participants. The tours are popular; arrive early to secure a spot.

☆ Frederick Douglass ☆
NATIONAL HISTORIC SITE
Cedar Hill House

As national and international momentum grew to end slavery in the mid-19th century, Frederick Douglass wrote and spoke eloquently for abolition, using his own life experience as inspiration. Born into slavery in 1818, Douglass learned to read despite his lack of formal schooling and escaped to the free North. His 1845 autobiography brought him fame; he became a newspaper publisher and served in various government positions, including U.S. minister to Haiti. Cedar Hill, his estate in southeastern Washington, D.C., is now Frederick Douglass

National Historic Site, where you can see exhibits on Douglass's life, watch a 17-minute film entitled "Frederick Douglass: Fighter for Freedom," and tour the house (with many original furnishings and personal items) and 9-acre grounds.

☆ Brown v. Board of Education ☆
NATIONAL HISTORIC SITE
Monroe Elementary School

In a 1954 case popularly known as *Brown* v. *Board of Education*, the U.S. Supreme Court ruled that schools segregated by race violated the constitutional principle of "equal protection." It was the beginning of the end of segregated schools in America, and one of the most important landmarks in the struggle for African-American rights. Brown v. Board of Education National Historic Site is located in Topeka, Kansas, where in 1951 an African-American girl named Linda Brown was refused enrollment in an all-white school near her home. The setting is the former Monroe Elementary School, once a school for African-American students (and attended by Linda Brown). Exhibits include a film entitled "Race and the American Creed," and galleries on

The 1965 Selma-to-Montgomery March played a pivotal role in the granting of voting rights to African Americans.

☆ Tuskegee Institute ☆

A small university in east-central Alabama boasts an honored legacy in African-American history. Tuskegee Institute (now Tuskegee University) in 1881 hired as its first president a young teacher named Booker T. Washington, who became one of the most respected educators in the country's history. Among the staff he hired was George Washington Carver, a renowned botanist who worked to improve the lives of poor farmers. In World War II, Tuskegee trained African-American military pilots who gained fame as the "Tuskegee Airmen." Some campus buildings were designed by Robert R. Taylor, the first African-American graduate of the Massachusetts Institute of Technology. In recognition of these and other accomplishments, the school has been designated both a national historic landmark and a national historic site.

the themes of Education and Justice and the legacy of the historic legal case. Interactive displays and video help tell the story of the fight for civil rights in America.

☆ Little Rock Central High School ☆
NATIONAL HISTORIC SITE
Central High School

Though *Brown* v. *Board of Education* outlawed school segregation in 1954, the ruling was effectively ignored in some parts of the country. In 1957, nine black students were barred from attending all-white Central High School in Little Rock, Arkansas, precipitating a tense confrontation between federal and local forces after President Eisenhower ordered federal military troops to escort the students. The "Crisis at Little Rock" was a milestone in the civil rights movement and is commemorated today at this national park unit, which encompasses the only still functioning high school within a national historic site. A visitor center adjacent to the school presents exhibits on the desegregation crisis, as well as audio-visual programs on the events in Little Rock during the fall of 1957. Tours of Central High School itself are available only with advance reservation to groups of ten or more.

☆ Selma to Montgomery ☆
NATIONAL HISTORIC TRAIL
Edmund Pettus Bridge to
Alabama State Capitol

On March 7, 1965, a predominantly African-American group in Selma, Alabama, began what they hoped would be a peaceful walk to protest racial discrimination. Marchers were soon brutally attacked by police, however. Scenes from "Bloody Sunday" were shown on television and in newspapers around the world causing outrage. Two weeks later, marchers successfully completed a five-day walk to the Alabama State Capitol in Montgomery, 54 miles to the east. By the time they reached their goal, the 3,000 people who had begun had grown to 25,000, a gathering addressed by famed civil rights leader Dr. Martin Luther King, Jr. The Selma-to-Montgomery March helped ensure the passage of the federal Voting Rights Act of 1965, which helped African Americans gain political representation. Travelers on this historic trail can visit sites including the Martin Luther King, Jr., Walking Tour and the Edmund Pettus Bridge (where the police attack occurred) in Selma; the Lowndes County Interpretive Center, located midway between Selma and Montgomery; and the Dexter Avenue King Memorial Baptist Church, the Rosa Parks Museum, and the Civil Rights Monument in Montgomery.

☆ Tuskegee Airmen ☆
NATIONAL HISTORIC SITE
Tuskegee Hangar

Racial discrimination was still a fact of life in the U.S. military as World War II began. African Americans were generally relegated to noncombat roles, and none was allowed to be a pilot in the Army Air Corps (the precursor to today's Air Force). This historic site in eastern Alabama honors the hundreds of men who participated in an experimental training program and overcame discrimination to become pilots, bombardiers, navigators, instructors, and maintenance staff. During combat the "Tuskegee Airmen" distinguished themselves for skill and bravery, helping break down barriers to integration in the military. Visitors to the site can see interpretive films and (on weekends) tour a museum in a restored hangar, which contains historic aircraft, model airplanes, audiovisual presentations of personal recollections from airmen, and exhibits on the unit's accomplishments in and out of combat.

☆ Booker T. Washington ☆
NATIONAL MONUMENT
Booker T. Washington Birthplace

Born into slavery in 1856, Booker T. Washington once wrote, "I had the feeling that to get into a schoolhouse . . . would be about the same as getting into paradise." A dedicated believer in the power of education, he worked tirelessly to gain more opportunities for African Americans. At the age of 25, Washington was named the first president of Tuskegee Institute (now Tuskegee University) in Alabama. Booker T. Washington National Monument is located at the site of the tobacco plantation where Washington was born, 25 miles southeast of Roanoke, Virginia. The visitor center contains exhibits on his life and legacy. The short Plantation Trail passes reconstructions of buildings like those that would have been on the farm, including a replica of the kitchen cabin where Washington lived as a boy. The park includes a garden and a farm area where sheep, pigs, horses, and chickens are raised.

☆ Harpers Ferry ☆
NATIONAL HISTORICAL PARK
Last Stand: Fire Engine House

A federal armory at the confluence of the Potomac and Shenandoah Rivers was the target of a raid in 1859 by abolitionist John Brown and his band

At Tuskegee University, a statue of Booker T. Washington illustrates him lifting the "veil of ignorance."

of followers, who hoped to seize weapons, arm enslaved African Americans, and start a battle to end slavery in the United States. Though Brown was captured, tried for conspiracy, and hanged, his actions had far-reaching influence and inspired further abolitionist sentiment and anti-slavery activities. During the Civil War, Confederate and Union troops fought repeatedly over the weapons and manufacturing equipment at Harpers Ferry. In 1867, missionaries established Storer College, one of the country's first integrated schools. Aimed primarily at educating formerly enslaved persons, Storer included famed writer and orator (and former slave) Frederick Douglass as a trustee. Harpers Ferry eventually became a place of pilgrimage for African Americans and played an important role in the early civil rights movement. Today's park, in what is now the panhandle of West Virginia, includes a visitor center, the John Brown Museum, a blacksmith shop, a dry-goods store, and the fire engine house where Brown made his last stand.

> **MARCH 11 1941**
>
> *Henry Ford participated in ceremonies dedicating the George Washington Carver Museum at Tuskegee Institute, Alabama . . . [T]he museum is part of Tuskegee Institute National Historic Site.*

☆ George Washington Carver ☆
NATIONAL MONUMENT
George Washington Carver Birth Site

Born during the Civil War on a small farm in southwestern Missouri, George Washington Carver overcame his early enslavement to become an internationally renowned botanist. He was especially known for his promotion of the peanut and the sweet potato as he tried to help poor southern farmers find alternatives to cotton as a crop. In his work at the Tuskegee Institute in Alabama, and by the impact of his personality, Carver inspired African Americans struggling to attain equal rights. The national monument preserves his birth site, a farm owned in the 19th century by Moses and Susan Carver. Daily guided tours are offered, as are programs on subjects ranging from nature study to pioneer farm life to art (Carver was an avid and accomplished painter). The Science Discovery Center honors Carver's strong belief in the ability of science to improve people's lives.

☆ Boston African American ☆
NATIONAL HISTORIC SITE
Black Heritage Trail:
Abiel Smith School

Within this historic site stands the largest area of pre–Civil War black-owned structures in the United States, with houses, businesses, schools, and churches that were part of a thriving African-American community on the north side of Boston's Beacon Hill. Park rangers lead visitors around sites on the Black Heritage Trail, a 1.6-mile walking tour that lasts around 1.5 hours. A National Park Service visitor center is located in the 1835 Abiel Smith School, used by African-American students during the era of segregated education. Other sites on the trail include the Robert Gould Shaw and Massachusetts 54th Regiment Memorial, honoring African Americans who fought in the Civil War; Charles Street Meeting House, an early center of the fight for equal rights; the John J. Smith House, an important hub for abolitionist activities; and the Phillips School, once segregated but later one of the first schools to accept African-American students.

ten best parks
science & industry
Celebrating technological advances that shaped the world

Among the eclectic sites administered by the Park Service are many that recognize the hard work, invention, and economic achievements that moved America into the industrial age and beyond. These parks allow a look behind the scenes at the nuts and bolts of how things work, from simple blacksmithing to the space age.

☆ Thomas Edison ☆
NATIONAL HISTORICAL PARK
The Phonograph, Electric Lights, and Motion Pictures

How could first place *not* go to the man who literally changed the world with his inventions, yet modestly claimed that "genius is 1 percent inspiration and 99 percent perspiration"? Born in 1847, Thomas Edison invented or improved a long list of things, but he's most famous for three: the phonograph, electric lighting, and the motion picture. Called the "Wizard of Menlo Park" (in New Jersey, where he did his early work), Edison later moved to new, much larger laboratories at West Orange, New Jersey, now preserved as a national historical park. Edison proudly called his West Orange headquarters "the best equipped and largest laboratory extant . . . facilities superior to any other for rapid and cheap development of an invention." His labs are said to be the model for future research facilities such as Bell Laboratories. You can tour the laboratories where Edison worked until his death in 1931, see interpretive videos, and admire examples of his inventions. Tours are also available of Glenmont, Edison's 29-room Queen Anne–style mansion, and the estate grounds and outbuildings. The main lab tour is self-guided, but ranger-led programs are offered throughout the day, delving deeper into various aspects of the Wizard's productive life.

☆ Wright Brothers ☆
NATIONAL MEMORIAL
1903 Flyer

Humans have dreamed of flying since our brains got big enough to feel jealousy toward birds. True flight had to wait, however, until two bicycle-builders from Dayton, Ohio, turned their obsession into reality on the barrier island sand dunes of North Carolina. On December 17, 1903, at a place called Kill Devil Hills, Wilbur and Orville Wright succeeded in the first sustained powered flights in a heavier-than-air machine, and a new age of transportation had begun. The memorial to their achievement includes functional replicas of their 1903 Flyer (the original is in the Smithsonian National Air and Space Museum in Washington, D.C.), and a 1902 glider that the brothers used to test steering mechanisms before they tried motorized flight. The park features reconstructions, based on photographs, of their hangar and living quarters. You can walk along the exact flight paths taken by the Wright brothers plane on that day in 1903; the brothers took turns flying the plane, making four attempts to sustain flight, and Wilbur was at the controls for the final and longest attempt—852 feet, lasting 59 seconds. Private pilots can land their own small planes at the park on the 3,000-foot First Flight Airstrip.

✯ Golden Spike ✯
NATIONAL HISTORIC SITE
Transcontinental Railroad Line

Today, when it is possible to jet from Boston to Los Angeles in a few hours and make computer measurements smaller than an angstrom, it might be hard to imagine the excitement that swept across America on May 10, 1869, when a telegraph operator in northern Utah sent the simple word "DONE" along the wires. It meant that two teams working toward each other from east and west had met at Promontory Summit, completing the first transcontinental railroad line and making possible a trip by train from the Atlantic to the Pacific: no more wagon trains, no more weeks-long voyages around Cape Horn. Nothing before had so unified the United States, both practically and psychologically. At Golden Spike National Historic Site you can see exhibits on the transcontinental railroad

As early as the 1830s' men were asking for a transcontinental Railroad but no one could believe that rails could cross the "Great Desert." Those who believed in a railroad from the east to the west were considered by most as "crazy."

and the effort required to bring it to reality, and drive part of the original rail route via an auto-tour route that passes construction sites, hill cuts, and the Chinese Arch, a natural limestone arch named in honor of the thousands of Chinese workers who labored on the rails. Modern reproductions of the two steam locomotives that met at Promontory Summit hold demonstration runs between May 1 and Labor Day.

✯ Lowell ✯
NATIONAL HISTORICAL PARK
Waterpower Textile Mills

It was in the northeastern Massachusetts town of Lowell that an important period of American industrialization began in the early 19th century. A group of businessmen established a planned city using waterpower to run textile mills, visualizing it as a more humane place than the gloomy factory towns of England. Employing mostly immigrants and "mill girls" (young unmarried women from around New England), the mills fueled a population growth in Lowell from about 2,500 in 1826 to more than 33,000 in 1850, when the city was one of the world's leading textile producers. Various economic factors caused almost all the mills to close by the 1930s, but some have been restored or renovated for purposes ranging from museums to art galleries. It's fascinating to see raw cotton turned into cloth on 19th-century looms, or to take a tour of the canals that used water from the Merrimack River to run vast amounts of machinery. There's even a video called "Lowell Blues" on Beat Generation writer Jack Kerouac, a Lowell native. Not only is Lowell National Historical Park an educational and entertaining experience, it's a fine example of a beleaguered community finding ways to reinvigorate itself.

✳ Saugus Iron Works ✳
NATIONAL HISTORIC SITE
Iron and Steel Industry

In the 17th century, settlers of the Massachusetts Bay Colony needed a variety of manufactured goods to help them build and set up houses and clear and farm the land. When the goods they'd brought from Europe wore out, they needed replacements; beginning in 1646, they could obtain them from Saugus Iron Works, the first complete ironmaking factory in colonial America, churning out hoes, nails, saws, axes, hinges, skillets, pots, and much more. Today's national historic site features a blast furnace, forge, rolling mill, warehouse, and working water wheels, all reconstructed based upon extensive archaeological excavations. A museum displays many of the artifacts found on the site. Though Saugus operated only 22 years, it gave a vital boost to the United States iron and steel industry.

In North Carolina in 1903, the Wright brothers made the first successful flights with a heavier-than-air machine.

A 19th-century merchant ship replica sits moored at Salem, Massachusetts, once a vital trading center.

☆ Salem Maritime ☆
NATIONAL HISTORIC SITE
Maritime Trading Center

Relive the days when sailing ships set out on voyages around the globe at this park on the Massachusetts coast. Privateers (essentially government-sanctioned pirates) operated from Salem during the Revolutionary War, and in the decades after American independence, the port saw vast quantities of goods arriving from Europe and the Far East, making this one of the new nation's most important trade centers (and the home of one of America's first millionaires). The

historic site features a modern replica of the tall ship *Friendship*, which was launched in 1797 and captured by the British in the War of 1812. Also part of the park are wharves dating back to 1762 and the 1819 Custom House, where author (and Salem native) Nathaniel Hawthorne worked from 1846 to 1848.

☆ Keweenaw ☆
NATIONAL HISTORICAL PARK
Copper Mining

Thanks to geology, the Keweenaw Peninsula of northern Michigan was the site of the world's richest known deposit of 97 percent pure copper. "Copper fever" struck the area in the 1840s, and by the end of the decade this region of Michigan's Upper Peninsula was producing 85 percent of the nation's supply of the mineral. Mining continued until the 1960s, and today's park allows you to recall those boom years. Here you can tour underground mine shafts, see the Quincy Mine, where the world's largest steam-driven hoist reached 9,260 feet down into the earth, and admire the results of some of the wealth created, such as an 1899 opera house and a 1908 mansion built by a mine owner. The Finnish American Heritage Center, on the campus of Finlandia University in Hancock, recognizes the heritage of the great number of Finns who came to work the mines in the 19th century.

☆ Springfield Armory ☆
NATIONAL HISTORIC SITE
Military Weapons

Some of America's most famous weapons used by the military, including the Springfield rifle of the Civil War, the bolt-action Springfield Model 1903 of World War I, and the powerful Springfield M-1 Garand rifle of World War II, were developed and manufactured at this site in central

Massachusetts. Founded in 1777 and given official status by George Washington in 1794, the Springfield Armory continued to produce most of the country's military weapons until 1968. The armory's influence went far beyond guns: Manufacturing methods developed here, such as the use of interchangeable parts, were eventually utilized in the mass production of many industrial items. The museum at Springfield Armory National Historic Site houses a vast collection of muskets, rifles, pistols, machine guns, swords, and bayonets, as well as exhibits highlighting innovative production techniques.

✳ Steamtown ✳
NATIONAL HISTORIC SITE
Steam Train

Nearly everyone is fascinated by the sights, the sounds, the smells, and the raw power of steam locomotives. Vital to the United States' growth and economic development, but doomed by the greater efficiency of the diesel-electric locomotive, steam had largely disappeared from railroading by the 1950s. Nonetheless, a significant number of steam-train enthusiasts keep that colorful era alive in many places around the country, especially at Steamtown National Historic Site in Scranton, Pennsylvania. Located within the railroad yard of the Delaware, Lackawanna, and Western Railroad, the park displays a collection of passenger and freight cars and steam locomotives, including an impressive *Big Boy* built in 1941 for the Union Pacific and a 1903 freight engine (the park's oldest locomotive) built for the Chicago Union Transfer Railway Company. The visitor center shows an 18-minute film, "Steel and Steam." Steamtown offers train rides seasonally, but call ahead for times; the schedule varies depending on staff and equipment availability.

✳ Minuteman Missile ✳
NATIONAL HISTORIC SITE
Nuclear Defense

The Cold War, the stalemate between the United States and the Soviet Union that inspired the phrase "mutually assured destruction," was one of the defining historical themes of the 20th century. Several states were home to Minuteman nuclear missiles, each stored underground in a concrete "silo," with a crew ready in case an Emergency War Order arrived with a command to launch. At this western South Dakota national historic site, you can tour the above ground Launch Control Facility Delta-01 and the underground Launch Control Center, where crew members could remotely launch missiles from ten silos. A few miles away is Launch Facility Delta-09 (a missile silo), with an inoperative Minuteman inside. Tours begin at a visitor contact station at exit 131 on I-90. Make reservations in advance, because the cramped space in these sites means space on tours is very limited.

☆ Transatlantic Communication ☆

What is now **Cape Cod National Seashore** in Massachusetts was the site of one of the 20th century's most significant events, when on January 18, 1903, Guglielmo Marconi presided over the first public two-way wireless communication between North America and Europe. Messages from President Theodore Roosevelt and King Edward VII were exchanged in Morse code, opening a new era in long-distance communication. Unfortunately, little remains of Marconi's historic wireless station: Facilities were torn down or abandoned to decay, and coastal erosion has even eaten away most of the land on which the station stood.

presidential footprints

Finding inspiration within and beyond the Beltway

Since 1789, when George Washington took the first presidential oath of office, our Chief Executives have left the nation with stories of achievement, compassion, conservation, tragedy, and incredible vision. Their imprints have been left on homes, monuments, battlefields, and even hardscrabble western landscapes.

✴ Gettysburg ✴
NATIONAL MILITARY PARK
Site of Lincoln's Gettysburg Address

No one knew when Abraham Lincoln followed the lengthy two-hour speech of famed orator Edward Everett that he would make perhaps the most well-known and impactful speech in American history. Lincoln had been invited to Gettysburg by local attorney David Wills to appear at the dedication of a portion of part of one battlefield as a national cemetery. At the dedication the "few appropriate remarks" he delivered became known as the Gettysburg Address, ten sentences that summed up the nation's past, present, and, what Lincoln hoped, its future. Within two minutes, the "United States *are* . . ." became "the United States *is* . . ." and there was no doubt that with a Union victory, Lincoln would unite the nation. When the President sat down after his comments, few in the crowd realized that he had even made a speech at all—it was only after he provided copies to friends and the press that his words became a part of the American story.

This is still hallowed ground, and the vivid stories of the battles and Lincoln's healing words are an essential stop for anyone interested in stories of war . . . and peace.

✴ Mount Rushmore ✴
NATIONAL MEMORIAL
Sculpture of Four Presidents

This fabled sculpture has been celebrated (and parodied) in hundreds of media from postcards to dinner plates, yet visitors who round the corner on U.S. 16A near Keystone forever remember their first sight of the enormous four faces. Native Americans, however, have every right to take issue with the placement of the work, a spiritual site they knew as the Six Grandfathers when sculptor Gutzon Borglum was recruited in 1924 to honor four legendary Presidents. There soon followed 14 years of blasting, drilling, and chiseling. Dedicated in 1941, the mountain reveals the faces of George Washington, Thomas Jefferson, Abraham Lincoln, and Theodore Roosevelt, selected respectively for their contributions

Site of a horrific battle, Gettysburg is where Lincoln delivered a now famous speech on the principles of human equality.

to the birth, growth, development, and preservation of our nation. Quite inspiring in the daytime, the experience may be even more stirring at dusk. About an hour before sunset each evening between May and September, people entering the amphitheater will hear patriotic music filling the valley. Following a short film on the history of the project, after dark the four faces are gradually illuminated with the ceremony closing as everyone sings "The Star-Spangled Banner."

✴ President's Park ✴
THE WHITE HOUSE
Presidential Residence

Perhaps America's most iconic government building (the U.S. Capitol runs a close second), until Theodore Roosevelt stamped its name on stationery in 1901, the White House had been called the President's Palace, Presidential Mansion, President's House, and, more often, the Executive Mansion. The history that's happened here is astounding. Beyond wars and social programs and Presidents steering America from fledgling nation to global superpower, think of John and Abigail Adams (the *first* First Family to live here), hanging their laundry to dry in the East Room or the raucous celebration of Andrew Jackson's 1829 Inauguration when supporters came in and trashed the place. Then there's Theodore Roosevelt losing sight in his left eye when sparring with a boxer; Warren G. Harding's alleged trysts with Nan Britton in a White House antechamber; and John F. Kennedy's humorous observation about living at the White House and serving as the nation's Chief Executive: "The pay is good and I can walk to work."

✴ Denali ✴
NATIONAL PARK & PRESERVE
Mountain Named for
President McKinley

What does an Alaska national park and preserve have to do with a politician from Ohio? A 20,320-foot-tall mountain that crowns the Alaska Range. Known by the indigenous Athabaskan as Denali, meaning "the great one," the mountain has more bulk and a steeper incline than Mount Everest. But as with many American places first named by indigenous peoples, Manifest Destiny led to imperialistic name changes. That's what happened here in 1896 when William Dickey, a gold prospector and fan of presidential nominee William McKinley, saw Denali and unilaterally decided to name the peak Mount McKinley after the presidential candidate who advanced a monetary gold standard (his opponent favored silver). While the name seemed to be as stable as the mountain—especially after the unfortunate assassination of McKinley in 1901—time passed, and today locals, Alaska natives, mountaineers, visitors, and Alaska's Board of Geographic Names more frequently are inclined to refer to Mount McKinley by its original name. Another bad break for the 25th President? The former Mount McKinley National Park was absorbed when Denali National Park and Preserve was created in 1980.

✴ Lyndon B. Johnson ✴
NATIONAL HISTORICAL PARK
Ranch of the 36th President

In a state that prides itself on being large, it seems the Lone Star State was right on track when it produced Lyndon Baines Johnson, a President who seemed larger than Texas. As his political and personal fortunes increased, LBJ purchased a ranch of nearly 1,600 acres in the heart of Texas Hill Country, roughly 15 miles east of Fredericksburg. He donated it to the National Park Service in December 1972, a month before his death, but the ranch remained the home of his widow, Lady Bird, until her death in 2007. In one of the most unusual presidential home tours, you pick up a map and narrative CD at the LBJ State Park across the Pedernales River and then follow directions around the ranch, passing the one-room schoolhouse Johnson attended, well-stocked wildlife enclosures, the grave of the former President, and guided tours inside the main home. Don't miss the state park, either, where there's an exhibit on the botany of Hill Country. Fitting, since Lady Bird was a dedicated conservationist who advanced nationwide beautification projects, including planting roadside wildflowers—notably the ubiquitous bluebonnets that bloom in Texas fields each spring.

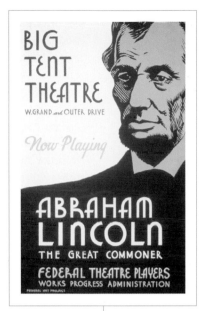

✮ Harry S Truman ✮
NATIONAL HISTORIC SITE
Truman's Missouri Home

Despite guiding the nation through perhaps the most transitive eight years in its history (atomic age, United Nations, Marshall Plan, GI Bill, integration of the military, etc.), President Harry Truman returned to his Independence, Missouri, home in 1953 with an approval rating of only 22 percent. In ensuing decades as the nation dealt with a string of political and presidential scandals, Truman's reputation was burnished with nostalgia and recognition of the honesty and work ethic of the "uncommon common man." Today, new generations of admirers arrive in Independence to visit his presidential library and homestead. With its gingerbread trim, peaked gables, and wrap-around porch, the 14-room Victorian home could have been used in Grant Wood's iconic "American Gothic." The home also reveals something else about Truman who was, for decades, paying off the debt of his failed haberdashery. He didn't actually own the house until after the death of its owner, his mother-in-law, Madge Gates Wallace, in 1952.

✮ Ford's Theatre ✮
NATIONAL HISTORIC SITE
Assassination Site of
President Abraham Lincoln

On April 14, 1865, Good Friday, the Civil War was largely over. Robert E. Lee had surrendered to Grant at Appomattox and President Abraham Lincoln was given something he had prayed for—a chance to govern states that were, once again, *united*. Looking forward to a well-deserved evening out, he and wife Mary headed a few blocks from the White House in Washington, D.C., to Ford's Theatre to see the comedy *My American Cousin*. Shortly after 10 p.m., famed actor and Confederate sympathizer John Wilkes Booth snuck into the President's private booth and fatally wounded Lincoln with a single shot. When the President died at 7:22 the following morning, Ford's Theatre was written into history. Although nearly a century and a half has passed, the tragedy of the evening still seems fresh. Due

Gateway Arch, symbol of westward migration

to a multiyear restoration completed in 2009, the theater's interior still evokes the age of Lincoln, and the basement museum displays fascinating exhibits, including a handbill from the play, Booth's diary, and the small pistol Booth wielded.

☆ Theodore Roosevelt ☆
NATIONAL PARK
26th President's Ranch

On February 12, 1884, 25-year-old Theodore Roosevelt welcomed the birth of his first child, Alice. Two days later, as he was grieving over the death of his mother that morning, he also learned he had lost his 22-year-old wife (also named Alice) from

an undiagnosed kidney disease concealed by the pregnancy. Overwhelmed, Roosevelt left his infant daughter with his sister and escaped into the Black Hills of North Dakota to find peace and a physical outlet for his anguish. Already an avid outdoorsman, his two years in the Wild West would later affirm his reputation as "The Cowboy President" and confirm, in his own words, that "It was here that the romance of my life began." In the 1880s, these were the Badlands and, by and large, they still are. The same wildlife Roosevelt knew (and often hunted)—bison, elk, deer, antelope, and wild horses—still roam the grasslands, and nearly 200 species of birds, many catalogued, sketched, and studied by the professorial cowboy, still flitter across the 70,000-plus acres of "grim fairyland." It took a tragedy to compel Roosevelt to retreat to the Dakotas, but it took time here and inner strength to return to his daughter, remarry, and, at 42, become America's youngest President.

☆ Jefferson ☆
NATIONAL EXPANSION MEMORIAL
Gateway to the
Lands of the Louisiana Purchase

New Yorkers boast about trading $24 worth of beads for Manhattan, but the rest of the nation could argue that an even better swap was trading $15 million for more than 800,000 square miles of land that *doubled the size of the nation*. President Thomas Jefferson was the prime mover in the Louisiana Purchase of 1803, and the subsequent exploration of the new land and what lay beyond it revealed the extent of the extraordinary purchase he had made. To commemorate the purchase and mark a site near where explorers Lewis and Clark passed on their epic trek, the Jefferson National Expansion Memorial—better known as the Gateway

Arch—was completed in 1965. As the centerpiece for the Mississippi riverfront complex, the stainless steel arch is a dynamic testament to the vision of Jefferson. In a spacious subterranean area below the arch, museums, theaters, and exhibits celebrate the efforts of pioneers and explorers—and add a special tribute to the construction crews who built the arch. To complete the experience, you can ride a string of cars inside the arch that take people to an observation area below the arch's 630-foot peak. Through the windows looking east are America's origins, and to the west the fulfillment of Jefferson's vision.

✴ George Washington Birthplace ✴
NATIONAL MONUMENT
Popes Creek Plantation

The Father of Our Country was born in 1732 to Augustine and Mary Washington in a home 80 miles downstream of Mount Vernon, the first President's adult home. His father's Popes Creek Plantation—on the southern shore of the Potomac River, near land settled by the Washington family in 1657—is long gone, but what has been preserved has been done to a level that could be recognizable to George Washington today. The house the Father of our Country was born in burned down in 1779; its appearance is unknown. A "memorial house," based on designs of 18th-century well-to-do Virginia homes, was built here in the 1930s to honor the 200th anniversary of Washington's birth and is filled with period pieces. The park stages several demonstrations by costumed interpreters at the Living Colonial Farm, including taking care of its heritage livestock, tobacco curing, and wool spinning. A 1-mile walking path leads to the gravesites of Washington's father, grandfather, and great-grandfather.

☆ Presidents and Our National Parks ☆

America's Chief Executives have had a tremendous impact on the history and expansion of the country's National Park System. In 1864, Abraham Lincoln set aside Yosemite Valley "for public use, resort and recreation . . . inalienable for all time." President Grant sanctioned the protection of Yellowstone. But until Woodrow Wilson authorized the formation of the National Park Service (NPS) in 1916 and brought these parks under its wings, they and other future national parks were operated by a variety of organizations.

With the arrival of the NPS, most Presidents continued to encourage the development and expansion of the service. Franklin Roosevelt placed all historic war sites under its jurisdiction; Harry S Truman dedicated Everglades National Park in 1947; and in the early 1950s Dwight Eisenhower launched Mission 66, a ten-year plan to expand park services for guests in time for the Golden Anniversary of the NPS. In the mid-1960s, LBJ enacted a series of congressional measures, passing the Wilderness Act of 1964, the Land and Water Conservation Fund Act of 1965, the National Historic Preservation Act of 1966, and, in 1968, both the Wild and Scenic Rivers Act and the National Trails System Act.

In the decades since, a succession of other measures to obtain and protect valuable lands and historic sites was made easier with the establishment of the National Environmental Policy Act (1969), Endangered Species Act (1973), Archaeological Resources Protection Act (1979), and the monumental Alaska National Interest Lands Conservation Act of 1980 that added more than 47 million acres to the park system. The NPS will continue to grow . . . as long as federal funding continues to keep pace.

chapter eight

sleeping & eating

ten best parks
historic lodges
Where the accommodation is part of the park experience

M any national parks feature inns or lodges that immerse visitors in history: the days when railroads were opening new areas to travel, when architects using native materials created designs now called "parkitecture." Some lodges lack many modern amenities, but as in all real estate, the attraction is location, location, location.

☆ Yellowstone ☆
NATIONAL PARK
Old Faithful Inn (1904):
Largest Log Hotel in the World

The entire area around Yellowstone's iconic Old Faithful geyser in northwestern Wyoming is a national historic district, with a major highlight being the 1904 Old Faithful Inn, itself a national historic landmark. One of the few remaining log hotels in the United States, and the largest log hotel in the world, the inn was designed by Robert C. Reamer with asymmetry meant to reflect the disorder of the natural world; its steeply pitched roof mimics mountain peaks. Seven hundred feet long and seven stories tall, Old Faithful Inn boasts a lobby with a 65-foot-high ceiling and a huge fireplace built of volcanic rhyolite stone. No matter how many photos of the lobby visitors may have seen, they are always awestruck seeing it in person for the first time. The inn's rustic design had a major influence on subsequent architecture in other parks. Enlarged in 1915 and 1927 (under Reamer's supervision), the inn now

has 327 rooms. It goes without saying that, for a legendary inn such as Old Faithful, it's mandatory to make reservations as far in advance as possible. *Lodge: 307-344-7901, www.yellowstonenationalpark lodges.com.*

☆ Grand Canyon ☆
NATIONAL PARK
El Tovar Hotel (1905):
South Rim

Just after the turn of the 20th century, the Atchison, Topeka, & Santa Fe Railway built a spur line north from Williams, Arizona, to the Grand Canyon to haul copper from a proposed mine. As it turned out, there wasn't enough copper to be profitable. So the railroad hired architect Charles Whittlesey to build a hotel on the South Rim to draw tourists (i.e., train passengers). Opened in 1905, El Tovar Hotel has elements of a Swiss hunting lodge—a popular design theme of the time. Since then, the hotel, a national historic landmark, has hosted Theodore Roosevelt (twice), William Howard Taft, Albert

Einstein, Western author Zane Grey, Bill Clinton, and thousands of other guests who have marveled at the canyonside views. Though the lobby and other public areas look much as they did in 1905, the rest of the hotel was extensively refurbished in 2005; all 78 rooms have a range of modern amenities. No matter how appealing El Tovar's interior is, however, nothing can compete with the grand spectacle just 20 feet from its front door. Free park shuttle buses take guests to shops, visitor centers, and scenic overlooks along the South Rim. Lodge: *888-297-2757, www.grandcanyonlodges.com*.

☆ Yosemite ☆
NATIONAL PARK
Ahwahnee Hotel (1927):
Yosemite Valley Views

The Ahwahnee Hotel's major attraction is one that dates from even before its opening in 1927: The hotel was specifically sited to provide views of California's Yosemite Valley, one of the most spectacular landscapes on Earth. With Half Dome, Yosemite Falls, Glacier Point, and other iconic natural landmarks out its windows, the Ahwahnee offers guests a chance to get out and explore the valley before

Seemingly hewn from its surroundings, Yosemite's spectacular Ahwahnee Hotel has been welcoming guests since 1927.

day-trippers arrive. The hotel's impressive rock-and-wood facade holds a secret: The "redwood" is actually concrete, shaped and stained to look like wood. Designers wanted to lessen the possibility of fire, a constant danger in all-wood buildings before the days of sprinkler systems. More than 5,000 tons of stone and 1,000 tons of steel were brought to the park during construction. The Ahwahnee's design blends elements of art deco, Native American, Middle Eastern, and arts and crafts styles. The Great Lounge features a massive stone fireplace and ten floor-to-ceiling windows with stained-glass panels, and the unique Mural Room boasts wood paneling and a large mural of Yosemite flora and fauna. Lodge: 801-559-4884, www.yosemitepark.com.

Presidents Hoover and Roosevelt made the Two Medicine Chalets their headquarters in Glacier . . . During his famous Fireside Chat made from the chalets, FDR told his radio audience about the park.

☆ Voyageurs ☆
NATIONAL PARK
Kettle Falls Hotel (1913):
Boundary Waters

The expansive lakes of northern Minnesota were attracting tourists in the late 19th century, with steamboats providing access to remote areas. In 1913, a hotel was opened at Kettle Falls, a passage between Namakan and Rainy Lakes where Ojibwe Indians and voyageurs (French–Canadian fur trappers) once portaged their birchbark canoes. All sorts of semi-scandalous legends grew up about the early days of this inn, located on the border between the United States and Canada, especially concerning bootlegging in the Prohibition era. One family owned and operated Kettle Falls Hotel for 70 years, welcoming guests that included Charles Lindbergh and John D.

Rockefeller, among others, and serving hearty meals to travelers. In 1976, the hotel was placed on the National Register of Historic Places. Now located within Voyageurs National Park, the hotel was extensively renovated in 1987. Kettle Falls can be reached only by boat or floatplane, with water shuttles available from Ash River. With its red roof, striped awnings, and long veranda with rocking chairs, the hotel looks as homey and inviting as it truly is. Lodge: 218-240-1724, www.kettlefallshotel.com.

☆ Crater Lake ☆
NATIONAL PARK
Crater Lake Lodge (1915):
Rimside Views of Crater Lake

The fact that this Oregon lodge is only partly historic is a little disappointing to architecture buffs, but there's plenty of good news to offset that fact. Completed in 1915, Crater Lake Lodge has had a checkered history, and at one point was in danger of demolition. Structural problems led to it being extensively rebuilt before its reopening in 1995. The picturesque Great Hall is largely original, however; and the lodge's overall rustic style is reflective of the 1920s, in keeping with other national park inns of the era. Guests can learn about the lodge's past in the Exhibit Room, just off the lobby. The recent renovation means that rooms are more up-to-date than those at many park historic inns, and there's one more priceless attribute: The lodge sits right on the rim of Crater Lake, one of North America's most scenic natural wonders. Lodge: 888-774-2728, www.craterlakelodges.com.

☆ Volcano House ☆

Volcano House, in Hawaii Volcanoes National Park, has long ranked with the most distinctive lodges in the National Park System. Perched on the rim of Kilauea Crater, the hotel has been in operation in one form or another since the mid-19th century and famously offers a splendid vista into the sometimes-active crater. The present 1941 establishment replaced an 1877 building whose guests included Mark Twain and Franklin D. Roosevelt. Unfortunately, Volcano House was closed in 2010 by park officials, who were concerned about conditions and maintenance. Its reopening has tentatively been set for 2012, but as of this writing the hotel's future is uncertain.

☆ Glacier ☆
NATIONAL PARK
Many Glacier Hotel (1915):
Railroad-built Chalet

The imposing, five-story Many Glacier Hotel sits in a spectacular location in the northern part of this Montana national park, surrounded by rugged glacier-shaped peaks such as the great promontory of Grinnell Point. Swiftcurrent Lake is just steps away. Opened in 1915 by the Great Northern Railway, the hotel was designed to attract tourists who would arrive by rail; today it's reached by a road that runs alongside Swiftcurrent Creek and Lake Sherburne. Hikers will find lots of nearby opportunities on trails that range from flattish and easy to long-distance treks up into the park's backcountry; guided boat tours leave from the hotel's dock. A national historic landmark, Many Glacier Hotel was designed with a Swiss-chalet theme. Major renovations are planned for the hotel after the 2010 season. Lodge: *406-892-2525, www.glacierparkinc.com.*

☆ Great Smoky Mountains ☆
NATIONAL PARK
LeConte Lodge (Begun 1926):
Hike-in Experience

LeConte Lodge isn't for everybody, but guests who appreciate its solitude, simplicity, and beautiful surroundings return year after year. No roads lead to this Tennessee establishment, the only lodging in Great Smoky Mountains National Park; getting to the lodge requires a hike of at least 5 miles. (The lodge brings in supplies three times a week on llamas.) There's no electricity or telephone, and bath time means using buckets and wash basins (bring your own washcloth and towel). Kerosene lanterns provide light, and propane heaters take some of the chill out of the elevation of 6,360 feet. Hearty meals are served family style, and guests retire to one of the extremely basic cabins or lodge units. At LeConte Lodge, rustic really means rustic. Still interested? Once here, guests enjoy birdsong, fabulous Great Smokies sunrises and sunsets, relaxing rocking chairs, and the feeling that they've left the modern world far, far away. Lodge: *865-429-5704, www.leconte-lodge.com.*

☆ Oregon Caves ☆
NATIONAL MONUMENT
Chateau at the Oregon Caves (1934)

A national historic landmark, this rustic hotel opened in 1934 and still retains an amazing degree of that era's ambience, with original furnishings, local wood construction, and even a 1930s-style coffee shop. The restaurant emphasizes local meat, produce, wines, and microbrews. Built on a hillside, the Chateau at first glance appears to be somewhat compact, but a rear view shows that it's actually six stories tall. The building seems to nestle among the surrounding Douglas-firs and other conifers, and that environment is reflected in the interior, largely constructed of native wood. Large, rough-hewn logs support ceiling beams in the lobby, and the stair balusters and rails are natural tree branches. Lodge: *877-245-9022, www.oregoncaveschateau.com.*

✶ Shenandoah ✶
NATIONAL PARK
Big Meadows Lodge (1939)

Set near the halfway point of 105-mile-long Skyline Drive in Virginia's Shenandoah National Park, Big Meadows took its name from the large, grassy ridgetop area where it was built in 1939. Local stone and wood (much of it from chestnut trees, now virtually extinct) were used in construction, and the result is a lodge that well matches its Appalachian Mountains environment. The original lodge has 29 rooms, but a variety of other rooms and cabins have been added since the facility opened; newer rooms tend to be larger and have more amenities. The park's Harry F. Byrd, Sr. Visitor Center is located in the Big Meadows area, and a wide array of hiking and horseback trails are nearby, including easy access to the Appalachian Trail. It's not far to Lewis Falls, one of dozens of waterfalls in the park. Lodge: *888-896-3833, www.visitshenandoah.com.*

✶ Death Valley ✶
NATIONAL PARK
Inn at Furnace Creek (1927)

Well before a national park was established at the hottest, driest, and lowest spot in the United States, a borax-mining company built a beautiful lodge on a hill at the mouth of Furnace Creek Wash. Local mines had closed, and the company was looking for a way to make money from the narrow-gauge railroad it had built to ship ore. Opened in 1927, the inn was built in the Spanish mission style, with stucco walls, towers, arches, and a red tile roof. Thanks to the skills of its architects and landscape designers, the Inn at Furnace Creek blends nicely with the desert surroundings, its colors matching the Funeral Mountains that serve as its backdrop. Over time, the inn has developed into a true luxury oasis, with palm trees, beautiful gardens, and a spring-fed swimming pool. There could hardly be a more comfortable respite from one of the most hostile environments on Earth. As a bonus, guests can play a round at the world's lowest-elevation golf course, an 18-hole layout more than 200 feet below sea level. Lodge: *760-786-2345, www.furnacecreekresort.com.*

As dawn breaks, mist rises off Swiftcurrent Lake in Glacier National Park's Many Glacier region.

backcountry lodges/cabins

Wilderness with a roof overhead

Many national parks offer accommodations that can only be reached by foot or boat, or by remote, little-traveled roads. Such is the case with each of the following lodgings, where guests get a roof over their heads and varying levels of comfort and services, but always a sense of connection with the beauty of the park surrounding them.

⭐ Denali ⭐
NATIONAL PARK & PRESERVE
Camp Denali

Camp Denali rests on a ridge amid open expanses of tundra 90 miles deep into the park. When it was built by hand as a labor of love in the early 1950s, the camp of hand-hewn spruce-log cabins stood on the edge of the park. When the park tripled in size in 1980, Camp Denali remained as a 67-acre inholding. The camp retains a sense of rusticity befitting its roots and setting even as it has developed luxe touches and an upscale eco-lodge vibe. Guests are treated to handmade quilts on the beds and fresh produce from the camp's own organic greenhouse, served in a new timber-frame dining hall. But they still need to walk outside to use a private outhouse and stroll a few minutes to use the communal showers. The only access is by way of Camp Denali's own shuttle bus, and it's a full day's journey via the gravel park road that includes pauses for a buffet lunch and wildlife viewing. A stay (three-, four-, or seven-day stints) at the camp is filled with hikes,

drives, and canoeing with staff naturalists as well as occasional evening programs with guest naturalists and artists. Those programs are held in the camp's log lodge, which is also the central reading room, stocked with Alaska books, and gathering place. And then there's the view—the breathtaking presence of Mount McKinley and 11 major peaks of the Alaska Range. Lodge: *www.campdenali.com*.

⭐ Yosemite ⭐
NATIONAL PARK
Yosemite High Sierra Camps

Five nights of backpacking in the High Sierra would ordinarily dictate carrying a 50-pound pack, but hikers who book Yosemite's High Sierra Camps get a backcountry experience that entails toting nothing more than a daypack filled with some clothing layers and toiletries. Everything else is waiting at each of the five camps, strategically located around a 53-mile loop. Each camp has tent cabins, cots with blankets, and a chuck wagon that doles out ample breakfasts, dinners, and to-go trail lunches.

Most hikers start from the Tuolumne Meadows Lodge (8,500 feet) to acclimate to the altitude, and proceed counterclockwise. Book early; the camps often fill a year in advance. Lodge: *www.yosemitepark.com.*

★ **Ross Lake** ★
NATIONAL RECREATION AREA
Ross Lake Resort

This Washington State resort has all the trappings of a rustic old fishing lodge, but plenty of nonfishing types have discovered the serenity of Ross Lake Resort's roadless setting on the south end of 20-mile-long Ross Lake. The 15 self-catering floating cabins are modest but well furnished. Bedding, a full kitchen, and a barbecue are provided, but guests must bring their own food. Access is by ferry from Diablo Lake—the resort truck meets the ferry and shuttles guests in on a 2-mile private road. Guests can rent the resort's boats or kayaks, hike, or honor the heritage of the place by fishing for wild rainbow trout or bull trout. A popular day trip is to rent a boat, motor 14 miles up the lake to the Desolation Peak Trailhead, and make the 4-mile,

The aurora borealis dances across the night sky above Camp Denali in Denali National Park and Preserve.

4,000-foot pilgrimage to the peak, where Beat Generation writer Jack Kerouac spent a summer as a fire lookout. Lodge: *www.rosslakeresort.com*.

⭐ Grand Canyon ⭐
NATIONAL PARK
Phantom Ranch

Phantom Ranch dates from an era (1922 to be exact) when national parks, or more specifically, railroads near the parks, needed fine accommodations to attract passengers to their rail lines. The Santa Fe Railroad and Fred Harvey Company enlisted architect Mary Colter to design an oasis destination on the site of an old prospectors' camp for well-heeled, mule-mounted tourists—a place where they could relax, splash in Bright Angel Creek, and enjoy fine dining. The mule trip to the bottom of the canyon became *the* signature trip in Arizona's Grand Canyon National Park, and remained so for decades. Today, more hikers and river runners than mule riders make the trek to the complex of stone cabins and dormitories that lies in the shade of cottonwood trees. Hikers need to be in good shape to make the round-trip 10.5-mile journey to the canyon bottom. Mule trippers get first dibs on the cabins; most other visitors stay in the dorms, and everyone dines in the dining room. Reservations open on the first of every month for vacancies 13 months in the future; reserve early as they go very fast. Lodge: *www.grandcanyonlodges.com/phantom-ranch*.

⭐ Glacier ⭐
NATIONAL PARK
Sperry and Granite Park Chalets

Two backcountry chalets in Montana's Glacier National Park offer guests a dash of creature comfort minus grid-associated niceties. Guests will not get hot showers or electricity, but they will be served three squares a day at Sperry and have access to the facilities to cook their own meals at Granite Park. Most important, guests get the silence of the backcountry—both chalets are set amid Glacier's signature jagged peaks and wildflower meadows, and both are reachable only by foot—or hoof *(www.swanmountainoutfitters.com/glacier)*, in the case of Sperry. The 17-room, 1913 Sperry Chalet rewards a 6.7-mile approach via Sperry Trail. Granite Park is a simple 12-room shelter right on the Continental Divide, 7.6 miles from Logan Pass on the Highline Trail. Both chalets make great base camps for day hikes. From Sperry, for example, it's a spectacular 3.5-mile hike to Sperry Glacier. Lodge: *www.sperrychalet.com, www.graniteparkchalet.com*.

⭐ Haleakala ⭐
NATIONAL PARK
Wilderness Cabins

Here's a very different version of a romantic Hawaiian getaway: snuggling into one of Haleakala's three remote hike-in cabins, built by the Civilian Conservation Corps in the 1930s. Each is high on the mountain where the night air is brisk and clear. Amenities amount to cooking facilities (propane stove) and utensils, plus firewood to fuel a wood stove. Guests bring their own sleeping bag and use a nearby pit toilet. The main attractions of the cabins are location, location, and location. Holua Cabin, 3.7 miles down the Halemauu Trail, is set in native shrubland, where petrels sing at night. Kapaloa

Cabin, 5.6 miles via Keoneheehee Trail, is in the middle of a cinder desert; it's a place to stargaze and tell ghost stories over a howling wind. It's the most private of the three; the others have campgrounds nearby. Paliku Cabin, 9.2 miles via Keoneheehee Trail, is in cloud forest and can be very wet. All three are very popular, especially on full-moon nights. Lodge: *www.fhnp.org/wcr.*

> *U.S. Army cavalrymen stationed in [Yellowstone] constructed a network of simple log structures 10 to 15 miles apart—a day's travel on horseback or skis. Today [there are] 38 such patrol cabins, some of which date back to 1910.*

☆ Great Smoky Mountains ☆
NATIONAL PARK
LeConte Lodge

The shortest route to LeConte Lodge is a 5.2-mile hike that ascends 3,800 feet, so once guests arrive, they've earned the right to sit in a rocking chair and soak up the Great Smoky view near the top of Tennessee's 6,593-foot Mount LeConte. The lodge's weathered cabins, with their pine bunks and grouted log walls, virtually define the term "rustic." There's no electricity, and bathing involves a bucket and sponge. But guests get comfort-food dinners and breakfasts served family style in the wood-and-stone dining room, and they can order a sack lunch for the trail. The big attractions are sunrise and sunset, which are best viewed from Myrtle Point, a short hike up from the lodge. But a rocking-chair view is perfectly acceptable. Lodge: *www.leconte-lodge.com.*

☆ Wrangell–St. Elias ☆
NATIONAL PARK & PRESERVE
Kennicott Glacier Lodge

Alaska's Kennicott Glacier Lodge is everything a lodge in the middle of the country's largest national park should be: remote (eight-hour drive or two-hour flight from Anchorage to nearby McCarthy), quiet (no cars on lodge property), and gloriously situated, with views of the Chugach and Wrangell Mountains, and the Kennicott-Root Glacier confluence is so close guests can hear the trickling of glacial meltwater. To get there, guests drive to the end of Alaska 10, walk across the Kennicott River on a footbridge, and meet the lodge shuttle for the 5-mile drive in. Built in 1987 to reflect the copper-mining heritage of surrounding Kennicott, now a ghost town preserved by the park, the 25-room lodge feels like a prospector's retreat replete with family-style meals. The lodge is a home base for hikes on Root Glacier, float trips on the Kennicott River, or strolls through the old mining town, which boomed between the early 1900s and 1938. The lodge offers three meals a day, shared bathrooms, an exquisite porch overlooking the glaciers, and a sense of congeniality befitting such a remote yet comfortable hostelry. Lodge: *www.kennicottlodge.com.*

☆ Virgin Islands ☆
NATIONAL PARK
Maho Bay Camps and Concordia Eco-Tents

When Maho Bay opened its 114 tent cottages arrayed on a steep hillside abutting the national park on the north end of St. John in 1976, no one had heard the term "eco-resort," but the lodge was a prototype for many a back-to-nature hostelry to follow. The wood-frame, canvas-sided, and screened cottages and are linked to each other and communal bathhouses by wooden walkways amid lush tropical foliage—the feel is akin to sleeping in a tree house. It's a short

Whether you're bird-watching from the back porch of a remote lodge or scanning the horizon from a high point on the trail, whatever is worth seeing in the parks is worth seeing well—which is why good binoculars might be the best travel investment you can make.

If possible, resist buying bargain basement. Cheap (under $100) binos will magnify, but their optics are poor. They cause eyestrain that you might not be aware of; rather, you just lose interest in looking through them. When you shop, spend some time outdoors comparing models, and hold a fixed gaze for at least 30 seconds for each. You'll note differences.

If you're looking at 7x42s, the 7 means magnification; an object will appear seven times closer than with the naked eye. Figures of 7, 8, and 10 are common. Magnification of 10 may sound good, but it's hard to handhold. The image will be shaky. The 42 is the diameter of the objective lens in millimeters. A larger number means more light-gathering ability—in other words, better low-light performance. That's important, because the best wildlife viewing is early in the morning or at dusk. With compact binoculars, say, 8x20, you get shirt-pocket convenience, but just average low-light performance.

Lots of other factors figure in to a binocular's cost as well, such as fully multicoated lenses that sharpen the view and sturdy construction that holds barrel alignment. Almost always, higher priced binos merit their costly price tags, something you'll forget on seeing that elusive critter.

walk down to three beaches, or a short hike to Leister Bay for a snorkeling adventure out to Water Lemon Cay. At Concordia, on the southeast end of the island, the ambience is more arid, but the views of cliffs and ocean are just as dramatic. The 25 ecotents each have a private bath and shower. Guests can drive or take a taxi to either place, but there's no need for a car afterward. Both camps serve meals and provide kitchen facilities for cooking, and the trails and beaches of the national park are right outside the tent flap. Lodge: *www.maho.org.*

☆ Chesapeake & Ohio Canal ☆
NATIONAL HISTORICAL PARK
Historic Lockhouses

Staying in one of the three houses in Maryland once occupied by Chesapeake & Ohio Canal lockkeepers is similar to sleeping inside a historic landmark, which is exactly the case. The lockhouses, which stand right beside the canal towpath, are each decked out in period furnishings and stocked with literature about the canal's history, so it's easy for guests to immerse themselves in a historic journey during their stay. Lockhouse 22, at Pennyfield, might provide the most authentic experience of its mid-1830s heritage—a quiet, secluded location with no electricity or plumbing. Guests park nearby and tote in everything they need. Lockhouse 49, at Four Locks, is also quiet (although it's near a popular Potomac River boat ramp), but it has electricity and is furnished in 1920s style—the era when the canal ceased operation. Lockhouse 6, in the Bethesda neighborhood of Brookmont, is more urban (indoor plumbing and electricity) and is furnished in a 1950s fashion. The C&O Canal Trust is planning to rehab more of the old canal quarters as part of its effort to preserve and interpret the historic canal. Lodge: *www.canalquarters.org.*

ten best parks
cabins

Your home in the wilderness—four trusty walls

Cabins can be a compromise between the ease and convenience of a hotel, and the "roughing it" quality of camping. The parks have some cabins that offer comfortable modern furnishings, and others with only very primitive accommodations. All have in common a prime location in stunning environs and the potential to be cozy hideaways.

☆ Yellowstone ☆
NATIONAL PARK
Shoshone Lodge and
Guest Ranch

Wyoming's Yellowstone National Park has become an emblem of the American West, and that's not surprising given its claim to spectacles like free-ranging herds of bison, spouting geysers, and rugged mountain peaks. Into the bargain, though, Yellowstone has become host to hordes of visitors, especially in the summer months. The rustic log cabins at Shoshone Lodge and Guest Ranch, just 4 miles outside the East Entrance to Yellowstone, offer a restful antidote to days spent navigating crowds at Old Faithful and Yellowstone Lake. At the foot of the Absaroka Mountains, backed by the rushing waters of Grinnell Creek, Shoshone is a lovely, secluded retreat with cabins that have a range of amenities, from kitchenettes fully stocked with cookware and utensils, to more basic setups with just a microwave and refrigerator. All the cabins have electricity, running water, and even luxuries like TVs and wireless Internet. They're

spotlessly clean, and each unit has a front porch furnished with wooden rockers or gliders. The lodge also has a restaurant and gift shop. For guests who desire more activity after a day of exploring Yellowstone, the ranch offers horseback rides through the mountains, or guests can strike out on their own and hike up to some beautiful overlooks of the surrounding area. Lodge: *www.shoshonelodge.com.*

☆ Catoctin ☆
MOUNTAIN PARK
Camp Misty Mount

Catoctin Mountain Park in Maryland is set in beautiful mountain scenery, but it has the advantage of an interesting history, too—it was formed to create jobs during the Great Depression. Within the park, the Park Service–operated Camp Misty Mount—a camp of wood-and-stone cabins that date from 1936—is a great place to go and spend a week in the summer or fall. The cabins' original architectural detail and craftsmanship are largely intact and the accommodations are basic, but clean. The cabins have cots, mattresses, and electric lights inside (but no electrical outlets), and picnic tables and grill rings outside. Guests need to bring their own bedding, cookware, and food storage devices. There are dining facilities and bathrooms located centrally in the camp, and the small camp store sells charcoal, ice, and other basic provisions. Guests desiring extra privacy should ask for one of the cabins located off the main loop. The changing leaves in Catoctin are beautiful and the crisp autumn evenings refreshing, so plan a visit for the fall. Cabins: *www.nps.gov/cato/ planyourvisit/mistymount.htm.*

> *Rapidan Camp [in Shenandoah] was the first complex specifically designed as a presidential retreat [by President Hoover]. It eventually consisted of 13 buildings connected by a network of paths and stone or wood bridges…*

✷ Kenai Fjords ✷
NATIONAL PARK
Three Public-use
Wilderness Cabins

Kenai Fjords National Park, at the tip of Kenai Peninsula in Alaska, is still truly outback territory. The Ice Age lives on here—Harding Icefield, parent of nearly 40 glaciers, lies at the heart of the park, much of which is still untrammeled wilderness. For guests wishing to immerse themselves in this unspoiled setting, Kenai has two cabins on the Kenai Fjords coast for public use during the summer months, and one available for use during the winter months. The summer-use cabins are accessible only by floatplane, water taxi, private vessel, or charter boat; the cabins need to be reserved well in advance of a planned visit. Holgate Cabin—on the Holgate Arm of the Aialik Bay—offers great views of Holgate Glacier from its front porch, and guests may see bears ambling over the cobble beach nearby in search of berries. Aialik Bay Cabin looks out over the Aialik Glacier, and at low tide you can walk out over the bay for more than a mile and poke around in the tide pools. Willow Cabin, the winter-use cabin, is propane heated and accessible only by snowmobile, cross-country skis, snowshoes, or dogsled, but a stay there will intimately acquaint you with the stillness and pristine beauty of an Alaska winter. Cabins: *www .nps.gov/kefj/planyourvisit/lodging.htm.*

✷ Shenandoah ✷
NATIONAL PARK
Big Meadows Lodge, Skyland Resort,
and Lewis Mountain Cabins

Shenandoah National Park, which stretches along the ridgeline of the Blue Ridge Mountains, offers nice options for cabin lodging. All are situated along the park's famous Skyline Drive, which runs for 105 miles, the length of the Virginia park. Both Big Meadows Lodge and Skyland Resort, at mileposts 51 and 41.7 respectively, offer comfortable cabins with electricity and private bathrooms, and meals are available at the nearby lodges. Skyland Resort also has three family cabins with living areas, separate bedrooms, and kitchenettes. Lewis Mountain Cabins, at milepost 57.5, offers both single and double-room cabins. A stay here is a truly restful experience—the setting is peaceful, and early rising guests may catch sight of white-tailed deer and other wildlife before they seek the refuge of the deep woods during the day. All the cabins have heat, electricity, private bathrooms, and bedding provided. There are outdoor grilling rings for cooking, but guests need to bring utensils and food storage devices. A nearby camp store sells provisions. Lodge: *www.visitshenandoah.com.*

☀ Cape Lookout ☀
NATIONAL SEASHORE
Great Island Cabins
and Long Point Cabins

North Carolina's secluded Cape Lookout National Seashore is still largely undeveloped and perfect for travelers seeking a primitive beach camping experience. The park offers basic rental cabins on two of the park's three barrier islands. The Great Island Cabins on the South Core Bank are individual units that each sleep between 4 and 12 people and have hot water, basic furnishings, and a kitchen and private bath. At North Core Banks, the Long Point Cabins are duplex cabins that sleep six people to a side. Each of these six-person units has all the amenities of the Greater Island Cabins, and several also have air-conditioning. The duplex cabins share porches and decks, with nice views across the beach to the ocean. In keeping with the primitive character of Cape Lookout, the cabins on both islands are pretty spartan, so guests need to bring their own bedding and cookware. Cabins: *www .nps.gov/calo/planyourvisit/lodging.htm.*

☀ Yukon–Charley Rivers ☀
NATIONAL PRESERVE
Seven Public-use Cabins

Traversed by the mighty Yukon River and encompassing the entire course of the smaller Charley River and other minor waterways, the park has seven cabins available for public use, all of which are easily accessed from the Yukon River. These cabins are primitive, offering basic accommodations, but their real charm lies in their historical resonance. Nation Bluff Cabin, for instance, was built in 1934 by a trapper; Slaven's Public Use Cabin is just 100 yards from Slaven's Roadhouse, a restored 1930s roadhouse; and Coal Creek Camp was a 1930s gold-mining camp in which one cabin has been renovated for public use.

In addition to their handy proximity to the Yukon River—the main means of accessing the different regions of the park—these cabins provide an interesting window into the land's history and past use. Lastly, the no-fee cabins are occupied on a first-come, first-served basis. Cabins: *www.nps.gov/yuch/planyour visit/publicusecabins.htm*

☀ Isle Royale ☀
NATIONAL PARK
Rock Harbor Lodge

Isle Royale National Park, a remote island in Lake Superior about 15 miles from the coast of Ontario, can be reached only by boat or seaplane, and visitors

Shenandoah's Skyland Resort, at the highest point on Skyline Drive, offers stunning views of the park.

who make the effort to get there usually stay a few days. The only lodging facility on the island is Rock Harbor Lodge at Rock Harbor, which has 20 cottages with kitchenettes and private baths. Utensils, dishware, and bedding are provided, and all units have studio-type living areas and electric heat. Cottage guests also get one half-day use of a canoe, which can be used to get to sights like Lookout Louise, one of the most beautiful overlooks on the island, and Raspberry Island, home to a living bog. Guests also have easy access to hiking trails that lead to attractions like Scoville Point, surrounded on three sides by Lake Superior, and 938-foot Mount Franklin. Lodge: *www.isleroyaleresort.com*.

★ Grand Teton ★
NATIONAL PARK
Spur Ranch Cabins

Grand Teton National Park in northwestern Wyoming boasts dramatic scenery, with the jagged profile of the Teton Range towering over placid glacial lakes and valleys. For a comfortable stay in the park, rent a cabin at Spur Ranch Rental Cabins. The setting is stunning—the ranch is situated on the banks of the Snake River, and there are breathtaking views of the snowcapped Tetons. There are one- and two-bedroom units available, and the cabins are clean, cozy, and evoke rustic western living with their handcrafted lodgepole-pine furnishings. Each cabin has a kitchen

In wintertime, Yosemite National Park has much to offer visitors who love the cold and snow.

equipped with everything guests will need to prepare their meals, and a porch on which they can relax afterward; there are also grills outside the cabins. The Spur Ranch complex has a grocery store, deli, and even a wine shop for last-minute provisions. Spur Ranch is within easy reach of all the hiking, touring, fishing, and exploring that Grand Teton has to offer. Cabins: *www.dornans.com.*

☆ Olympic ☆
NATIONAL PARK
Kalaloch Lodge: Bluff and Log Cabins

All but 5 percent of Olympic National Park is officially designated wilderness, and not a single road actually passes through its heart. Guests wishing to explore the park's interior will need to do a lot of legwork—literally. For a restful haven after a day of hiking and climbing, rent a cabin at Kalaloch Lodge sitting high on a bluff in the 73-mile strip of the park's protected Pacific coastline. The cabins are just steps away from beautiful sandy beaches. The Bluff Cabins overlook the Pacific; the Log Cabins sit a row back from the Bluff Cabins, but are only a few steps farther from the beach. The Bluff and Log Cabins both have units with varying levels of amenities, from fully outfitted kitchenettes and fireplaces to more basic furnishings. From Kalaloch, it's only about 30 miles to the famous 7,980-foot Mount Olympus and the subalpine forests and alpine meadows of the park's interior. Lodge: *www.olympicnationalparks.com.*

☆ Yosemite ☆
NATIONAL PARK
The Redwoods: Privately Owned Homes

Lodging in California's Yosemite National Park is neither cheap nor easily booked. The Redwoods, located 4 miles inside the south entrance to the park, offers 130 vacation homes, ranging from one-bedroom

☆ Phonograph Nelson ☆

The Nation Bluff cabin in the Yukon–Charley Rivers National Preserve was built by an interesting character. The reclusive trapper Christopher "Phonograph" Nelson constructed it in 1934, and while local lore attributes his nickname to a couple different causes, the most popular is that when he actually had human company, he unleashed on them a torrent of thoughts that invited no response and made him sound like the playing of a phonograph record. Legend also has it that poor old Phonograph Nelson was something of a lonely heart. He wanted a wife to share in his wilderness existence, the story goes, so he sent away for a mail-order bride, but when he went to fetch her, she was so rotund that his dogs weren't up for the task of pulling her home in his sled. She found another suitor and Nelson never did marry, but he trapped and skinned pretty much every large animal found in the Yukon Territory.

rustic log cabins to six-bedroom spacious modern homes. All the homes are outfitted with kitchens and fireplaces, and are fully stocked with linens, bedding, and cookware. There are two markets and a post office within walking distance of The Redwoods, and the complex is beautifully situated between the Chilnualna Creek and the South Fork of the Merced River. It's about a 30-minute scenic drive to Yosemite Valley in the heart of the park. One catch—each of the homes at The Redwoods is privately owned, so the decor and level of comfort will vary from home to home, and generally speaking, guests get what they pay for. But the location is superb, and these cabins and homes are a convenient, scenic base from which to base rambles in the famous park. Lodging: *www.redwoodsinyosemite.com.*

just-outside-the-park lodging

Intriguing parkside lodges in which to bunk down

Nearly as much as their nature, America's national parks have long been celebrated for their grand (and often quirky) lodgings. Some of the oldest and best establishments are located right outside the park gates, in adjoining towns or wilderness and rural areas that perpetuate the vibe of that particular park.

☆ Acadia ☆
NATIONAL PARK
Bar Harbor Grand Hotel

An incredibly faithful reproduction of David Rodick's Guest House, the Bar Harbor Grand gazes down on Main Street in the largest town on Mount Desert Island, gateway to Acadia National Park. The original hotel started out as a small guesthouse in 1866 and was for a time, after the completion of the second expansion in 1881, at the height of Bar Harbor's popularity as a Victorian seaside resort for wealthy travelers, the largest hotel in Maine with more than 400 rooms. By 1906 the era was over and the Rodick demolished. Yet here it is again, looking just like the old black-and-white photos, four stories and twin towers with a long veranda across the front, a reproduction of the hotel as it appeared in 1875. The reproduction period decor and flora prints in the Grand's 70 rooms also bring to mind the long ago. The hotel is a short hike, bike, or drive from the rambling national park, and within walking distance of in-town attractions like Acadia Guides Mountain Climbing School and the Improv Acadia comedy club. The harbor is close at hand, for ranger-led boat excursions to more secluded parts of Acadia. Hotel: *888-766-2529 or 207-288-5226, www.barharborgrand.com.*

☆ Glacier ☆
NATIONAL PARK
Prince of Wales Hotel

Set against a backdrop of jagged snowcapped peaks, the Princes of Wales is one of several classic wilderness lodges developed by the Great Northern Railroad during the early part of the 20th century. Located in Waterton Lakes National Park in southern Alberta, the hotel is just over the U.S.–Canada border from Montana's Glacier National Park. Although named after the future King Edward VIII of England—who later abdicated and became the Duke of Windsor—the 1920s building is more Swiss Alpine than British Empire. The seven stories rise to a massive, green A-frame roof capped with a 30-foot bell tower. But don't expect fondue in the

Buffalo Bill's Pahaska Tepee, just outside Yellowstone National Park, is filled with memorabilia from the showman's life.

Royal Stewart Dining Room: the menu mixes trendy Italian dishes and Canadian classics like rainbow trout, Alberta surf and turf, and grilled Atlantic salmon. And don't miss afternoon tea in the lobby, Earl Grey and scones with a fabulous view over Middle Waterton Lake. The 86 rooms, decked out with dark wooden furniture and earthy fabrics, feature lake or mountain views. Hotel: *403-859-2231, www.glacierparkinc.com/prince_of_wales.php.*

☆ Yellowstone ☆
NATIONAL PARK
Pahaska Tepee:
A Legacy of Buffalo Bill Cody

Pahaska means "longhair" in the Lakota Sioux language, a reference to the stylish locks of the man who founded this wilderness lodge in 1904 on the eastern edge of Yellowstone National Park—Buffalo Bill Cody. Although ostensibly a hunting camp for Cody and his friends, Pahaska was also part of the consummate showman's ongoing efforts to promote tourism in the Yellowstone country by way of Cody, Wyoming, and the Shoshone River Valley. "He picked the best spot in the valley," says current owner Bob Coe. The heart of the complex, located just outside the park's East Entrance, is a two-story log mansion where Buffalo Bill housed, fed, and entertained his guests. Tours of the rustic manse are given daily during the summer season; the interior is filled with old black-and-white photographs, antique furnishings, and an odd assemblage of other relics sure to whet the curiosity of anyone. Modern-day guests stay in comfortable log and A-frame cabins scattered through the pine forest behind the old lodge. In today's on-demand world, Pahaska

Tepee is refreshingly unplugged: no television, Internet, cell phone service, or other distractions. But there is plenty of wildlife. Elk, deer, and bison frequently wander the grounds, while moose and bear are often spotted along the nearby Shoshone River. Trail rides, trout fishing, and white-water rafting number among the lodge activities offered to guests. Hotel: *800-628-7791 or 307-527-7701, www.pahaska.com.*

☆ Yosemite ☆
NATIONAL PARK
Evergreen Lodge

One mile from the Hetch Hetchy Entrance to Yosemite National Park, Evergreen Lodge straddles a ridge between two branches of the Tuolumne River. The Main Lodge (built in 1921), recreation buildings, and cabin clusters are scattered across 22 acres of old-growth forest in a part of the Yosemite region little explored by outsiders. Silence, solitude, and comfort are what Evergreen is all about, a place to get away from it all and back to nature without totally roughing it. Cabins feature private bathrooms and balconies, gourmet coffeemakers, satellite radio, DVD players, and daily maid service; for those who need to stay connected, the rec halls have Wi-Fi. And just in case guests forget this is California, a new massage cabana lays on deep tissue, hot stone, reflexology, and other treatments. Daytime activities run the full gamut, from excursions inside the national park to biking, hiking, fly-fishing, geo-caching, and white-water rafting. Dinners at the lodge always feature a great selection of California wines. The action continues through the evening with s'mores around the outdoor fireplace, movies, or kid's crafts in Tuolumne Hall, or live music and shooting pool at the Tavern. Hotel: *209-379-2606, www.evergreenlodge.com.*

⚝ Mount Rushmore ⚝
NATIONAL MEMORIAL
Hotel Alex Johnson

The "Residence of Presidents" in downtown Rapid City, South Dakota, has hosted six American heads of state over the last 90 years. The nine-story Alex Johnson still looks much as it did on opening day in 1929, the redbrick facade topped by a faux-Tudor crown and the hotel's trademark neon sign. Native American motifs dominate the lobby with its huge stone fireplace, massive chandeliers, and intricately painted wood-beam ceiling. In recent years the historical ambience has been complemented by a thorough updating of the 143 guest rooms to 21st-century standards including flat-screen TVs, modern bathrooms, iPod docks, Wi-Fi, and comfy king beds. The Presidential Suite is a masterpiece of handcrafted woodwork and one-of-a-kind light fixtures. Other recent additions include a corner coffee shop on the ground floor and Wicked Spa with its array of massages, facials, and other treatments. Rapid City is closest to Mount Rushmore National Memorial, but four other park system units are less than an hour's drive from the hotel: Wind Cave, Jewel Cave, Badlands, and Minuteman Missile. Hotel: *800-888-2539 or 605-342-1210, www.alexjohnson.com.*

⚝ Shenandoah ⚝
NATIONAL PARK
Inn at Little Washington

A small luxury lodge on the eastern flank of Shenandoah National Park, the Inn at Little Washington is both a marvelous place to base a stay in the region and an incredible way to stimulate your taste buds. The town of "Little" Washington (pop. 183) takes its name from the man who originally surveyed the area in 1749, none other than young George

---

☆ Classic National Park Souvenirs ☆

National parks have certainly sparked more than their fair share of key chains and snow globes, but they have also inspired mementoes that now rank as endearing period pieces and even high art.

Many classic park souvenirs display a touch of class—like a lady's compact featuring a photo of **Glacier** or a bronze serving tray embossed with an image of **Crater Lake,** both from the 1930s; and sterling silver sugar shovel and nut scoop embossed with **Yellowstone** scenes from the 1920s. Others reflected something of the park, for example, the **Great Smoky Mountains** miniature iron skillet ashtray.

Some mementoes are clever, such as the 1920s vintage Fred Harvey **Grand Canyon** miniature mail pouch with 12 black-and-white photographs inside. While others—like colorful wooden **Isle Royale** fishing lures from the 1950s—were intended to be useful.

Others just make you scratch your head. In the 1940s, **Yosemite** gift shops stocked wooden phone book covers with taffeta ribbons and a bear carved on top. Some early souvenirs literally gave away part of the park: **Petrified Forest** sold small chunks of petrified wood with tiny metal dinosaurs glued to the top.

Southwestern parks seemed to spark a number of drink-related items. In the 1950s, a collectible frosted tumbler full of iced tea was exactly what you wanted to have in your hand in **Death Valley** or **Joshua Tree.** Among vintage **Grand Canyon** keepsakes are copper shot glasses and elaborate beer steins.

How much are these souvenirs worth now? It depends on age, condition, rarity, and sheer novelty. A **Glacier** mountain goat wood carving by artist John L. Clarke now fetches in excess of $1,200. First edition books by the 19th-century national park explorers and surveyors can go for as much as $2,000.

Washington. The inn didn't come along until 1978, when chef/owner Patrick O'Connell and his partner converted an old wooden gas station and garage into a quaint colonial boutique hotel with sweeping views of the Virginia country-side. The 18 guest rooms, each unique, were created by London stage designer Joyce Evans and are furnished with pieces made on both sides of the Atlantic. Many boast private balconies or gardens. O'Connell has also developed the property into a bastion of fine dining that draws gourmands from as far away as Washington, D.C. His farm-to-table kitchen—based on fresh local ingredients—has garnered numerous accolades including James Beard and Wine Spectator Awards. Hotel: 540-675-3800, *www.theinnatlittlewashington.com.*

> *Many of the hotels [in Estes Park] are electric lighted; many have rooms with private baths; and several also have private cottages and tents accommodating from one to six persons. [1919]*

☀ Everglades ☀
NATIONAL PARK
Ivey House

With no overnight lodging available inside Everglades National Park, the next best thing are accommodations on the edge of the park, like the Ivey House in Everglades City. Family-owned and -operated, this tropical bed-and-breakfast was founded by naturalist guide David Harraden more than 30 years ago as one of Florida's first eco-lodges. Guest rooms are spread across three buildings: the historic Lodge, a remodeled 1928 boardinghouse; the old Cottage; and the modern, 18-room Inn with its swimming pool inside a screened-in courtyard. Guests gather in the great room at night to swap wildlife tales and other adventures. The Ivey offers a range of Everglades adventures, including sunrise and mangrove kayak trips, as well as overnight, guided adventures into the national park. The gray-bearded Harraden leads many of the trips himself. For guests wishing to explore on their own, the lodge also rents kayaks, canoes, and camping equipment, and organizes van and powerboat shuttle transport to popular put-in spots. Hotel: 877-567-0679 or 239-695-3299, *www.iveyhouse.com.*

☀ Hawaii Volcanoes ☀
NATIONAL PARK
Kilauea Lodge

As an interesting point of history, the boutique hotel Kilauea Lodge started life in 1938 as a rustic YMCA outpost called Camp Hale O Aloha. For decades it hosted Hawaiian school kids on outings to Hawaii Volcanoes National Park. Despite its conversion into a modern hotel, the lodge retains much of the old Civilian Conservation Corps ambience, especially in the main building with its Fireplace of Friendship constructed of stones and coins from 32 countries. Just a mile outside the park, the lodge is perfectly situated for close encounters of the volcanic kind. For guests who crave an urban escape, Hilo is only 30 minutes up the road. The 12 rooms are all different; some of them have fireplaces and private balconies. Two offsite homes—a 1929 summerhouse and golf course cottage—are also available. Sunday brunch in the lodge restaurant is a local tradition, as are the dinners prepared by chef/owner Albert Jeyte; the menu includes treats like duck à l'orange, leg of antelope filet, rock lobster, and Cajun-style ahi tuna. Hotel: 808-967-7366, *www.kilaualodge.com.*

✱ Olympic ✱
NATIONAL PARK
Lake Quinault Lodge

Opened in 1926, rustic Lake Quinault Lodge perches on the secluded southwest side of Olympic National Park overlooking the lake of the same name. The three-story main building, with its shingled sides and steeply pitched roof, looks like something out of a Brothers Grimm fairy tale. Guests gather at night for dinner in the Roosevelt Dining Room and chats around the great fireplace in the lounge. Accommodations include fireplace rooms, spacious lakeside rooms, and pet-friendly boathouse rooms in an annex even older than the main lodge. A broad lawn runs down to a lakeshore perfect for boating, fishing, or swimming. Hiking and biking are also popular with guests. Outdoor swimming pool, sauna, and massage service round out the amenities. The Quinault Rain Forest section of the park is on the lake's north shore, easily reached by road or boat; Olympic's Queets Valley and Kalaloch Coast segments are nearby as well. Hotel: 800-562-6672 or 360-288-2900, *www.olympicnationalparks.com/ accommodations/lake-quinault-lodge.aspx.*

✱ Rocky Mountain ✱
NATIONAL PARK
Stanley Hotel: Colorado's Celebrated Hotel

Inventor and entrepreneur F. O. Stanley (famous for the Stanley Steamer automobile) arrived in Estes Park in 1903 hoping that Colorado's pure mountain air would cure his tuberculosis. Within months he was on the road to recovery, and he would summer in Estes Park the rest of his life. Stanley built a guesthouse for his well-heeled Eastern friends, a huge wooden, whitewashed structure that would soon morph into Colorado's most celebrated hotel. Theodore Roosevelt, "Unsinkable" Molly Brown, Enrico Caruso, and John Philip Sousa are among those who stayed during its heyday. A young writer by the name of Stephen King came in 1974 seeking inspiration; the book that came from that stay, *The Shining*, became a horror classic. Nowadays the Stanley is the epitome of an elegant, old wilderness escape, the rooms modernized, but not at the expense of bygone character and charm. Nearly every window offers stunning Rocky Mountain views and a park entrance gate is just 15 minutes up the road. The hotel's restored concert hall offers a slate of live music throughout the summer. Hotel: 800-976-1377 or 970-577-4000, *www.stanleyhotel.com.*

Just outside Rocky Mountain National Park, in Estes Park, the Stanley is Colorado's most celebrated hotel.

park rooms to beg for

Suite dreams in all shapes and sizes

What are the ten most coveted hotel rooms in America's national parks? They range from historic cabins and carriage barns to Caribbean hideaways and poolside bungalows where Hollywood stars once frolicked. Each of these amazing rooms is equally as impressive as its natural surroundings.

✴ Grand Canyon ✴
NATIONAL PARK
Bright Angel Lodge:
Buckey O'Neill Suite

Not the kind of place you want to sleepwalk, the Buckey O'Neill Suite is just steps from the Grand Canyon's edge, a wonderfully rustic cabin that's the oldest continuously standing structure on the South Rim. Arizona politician turned prospector William "Buckey" O'Neill built the cabin in the 1890s while searching for copper in the region. He later volunteered for Theodore Roosevelt's Rough Riders and died at the Battle of San Juan Hill. Part of Bright Angel Lodge, the cabin betrays its pioneer origins with solid log walls, wood-shingle roof, and old-fashioned green door and window frames. The bygone vibe continues inside with log paneling and a stone fireplace. Yet Buckey is not without its modern contrivances, including a mini fridge and telephone service. The suite is very popular with Grand Canyon regulars and should be booked at least six months in advance. Lodge: *www.grandcanyonlodges.com*.

✴ Golden Gate ✴
NATIONAL RECREATION AREA
Cavallo Point Lodge:
Frank House

San Francisco swank meets vintage Army architecture at Cavallo Point Lodge, set along the Marin County waterfront of Golden Gate National Recreation Area. Once upon a time this was Fort Baker, a post–Civil War outpost. The 24 whitewashed structures around the parade ground were built as housing for the officers and their families. More than a century later, Frank House is the resort's most lavish unit, a two-story clapboard manse with more than 1,100 square feet of living space, including two bedrooms, a living room, and a full kitchen. There aren't many places even in hotel-rich San Francisco where guests can wake up with the Golden Gate Bridge hovering above their toes, or where they can lounge in a glass-enclosed sun porch with Alcatraz looming in the distance. Stylish walnut furnishings, leather armchairs, period details, and a funky modern fireplace complete the picture. Lodge: *www.cavallopoint.com*.

☆ Death Valley ☆
NATIONAL PARK
Furnace Creek Resort:
Pool Bungalow

"All the advantages of hell without the inconveniences," is how an early 20th-century newspaper report described Death Valley. The same could be said today for the fabulous Pool Bungalow at the Furnace Creek Resort. Definitely designed for a romantic tryst, the stand-alone bungalow was made for no more than two, with doors that open onto private stairs that lead to the resort's deliciously sinful pool area. Opened in 1927, the resort (and its lush Garden of Eden setting) has long drawn the Hollywood crowd to the desert, a guest list that includes Bette Davis, Jimmy Stewart, and Claudette Colbert. Clark Gable and Carole Lombard honeymooned here. The spring-fed pool is the main attraction, but there's plenty of other ways to keep busy, including a yoga class in the adjacent garden, tennis beneath the lights, wicked treatments in the massage rooms directly beneath the bungalow, and exotic room service meals like rattlesnake empanadas and prickly pear cactus–date buns. Lodge: *www.furnacecreekresort.com.*

A stylish oasis, the pool at Death Valley's Furnace Creek Resort offers refreshing relief from the desert heat.

Many Presidents have made a point of visiting the oldest and grandest national parks. Barack Obama is the latest, with a 2009 summer vacation in Yellowstone that saw the President reprise part of a national park–hopping tour he did as a kid.

Yellowstone has always been a favorite destination. Chester Arthur was the first to visit, in 1883, exploring the park on a horse. Jimmy Carter fished in Yellowstone Lake. Bill Clinton lunched at the Old Faithful Inn and visited geysers with the First Lady. Gerald Ford even spent a youthful summer (1936) there as a ranger.

Not surprisingly, nature-loving Theodore Roosevelt paid several memorable visits to national parks. During his 1903 trip to Yosemite, TR was led into the wilderness by none other than John Muir. Sixty years later, John F. Kennedy came to the Yosemite Valley and stayed at the Ahwahnee Hotel.

Given its proximity to the nation's capital, Shenandoah has been a favorite of several Presidents, including Herbert Hoover who spent many a day wondering the woods around Camp Rapidan. FDR dedicated the park in 1936 and returned later during his long Presidency. With six parks to his credit, FDR also owns the record for most presidential visits.

George W. Bush jumped right into trailbuilding in Rocky Mountain National Park. Harry Truman happily cavorted through the snows of Mount Rainier. Ronald Reagan went underground at Mammoth Cave. William Howard Taft argued with a military aide over whether he could ride a horse into the Grand Canyon. And in a show of bipartisanship, Richard Nixon and his predecessor Lyndon Johnson visited Redwood National Park together in 1969 to dedicate the Lady Bird Johnson Grove of big trees. The list goes on.

☆ Cuyahoga Valley ☆
NATIONAL PARK
Inn at Brandywine Falls:
The Granary

One of the few bed-and-breakfasts found inside a national park, the Inn at Brandywine Falls recalls the days when Ohio's Cuyahoga River was an integral part of America's industrial revolution. James Wallace, owner of the local mill, constructed the clapboard complex in 1848, and it passed down to modern times seemingly untouched from those halcyon days. Set in the old carriage barn behind the main house, The Granary is the inn's largest and most lavish accommodation, albeit elegance with a rustic touch. The two-story suite is framed in wood-plank floors and hand-hewn ceiling beams, heated with a wood-burning Franklin stove and decorated with family heirlooms and antiques. A king-size bed is tucked up on the sleeping loft. Downstairs on the main floor is a parlor (with a double bed for extra guests) and a small kitchenette with fridge and microwave. The Granary's bathroom boasts a jumbo Jacuzzi tub. The staff can bring breakfast in bed, or guests can eat with everyone else in the big house dining room, a hearty Ohio farm breakfast that varies slightly from day to day. Lodge: *www.innatbrandywinefalls.com*.

☆ Virgin Islands ☆
NATIONAL PARK
Maho Bay Camp:
Harmony Studios

These chic shacks cling to a jungle slope high above Maho Bay on the north shore of St. John, offering comfort amid unparalleled Caribbean scenery. A dozen spacious suites decorated in bright Caribbean colors, all are equipped with kitchenettes (with fridge and microwave) and private decks with full or partial views of the blue-green sea. Each studio easily sleeps two to six people and has its own private bathroom. As part of Maho Bay, guests can partake of all the dining and recreation options—including tours of the national park—available in the original tented camp at the bottom of the hill, including access to the white-sand strand. Like the rest of the eco-camp, the studios employ sustainable design, including solar power, rainwater collection, and roof scoops that channel breezes through the studios. Many of the materials that went into constructing the units were recycled from old lumber, plastic, rubber, and glass. Lodge: *www.maho.org*.

> *A young James A. Garfield, 20th President of the United States, worked briefly as a mule boy on the Ohio & Erie Canal, an important cultural resource within Cuyahoga Valley National Park.*

✵ Cumberland Island ✵
NATIONAL SEASHORE
Greyfield Inn: Library Suite

Guests needn't bring their own reading material for a stay at the Greyfield Inn, especially if they make plans to sleep in the Library Suite, named after the adjacent sitting room and its copious collection of bygone novels, historical accounts, and biographies. The Carnegies of steel fame once owned much of Georgia's Cumberland Island and built fabulous mansions as both vacation homes and year-round residences. Greyfield (erected in 1900 for Margaret Carnegie Ricketson) is still owned and operated by Carnegie descendants, and is still lovingly decorated as it was a century ago with antiques and family mementoes, making it ideal for a romantic getaway. The sumptuous Library Suite is the only guest room in the main house with an en suite bath, a factor that makes it especially hard to reserve without booking months in advance. A four-poster king bed adds to its allure, as do the views out the back window over Cumberland Sound and the marsh along Old House Creek. Located on the house's main floor, the suite is also steps away from the cozy little bar and the spacious living room where guests gather at night to swap stories about their day on the Georgia barrier island. Each stay includes breakfast, picnic lunch, and a gourmet dinner. Lodge: *www.greyfieldinn.com*.

✵ Yosemite ✵
NATIONAL PARK
Ahwahnee Hotel:
Mary Curry Tresidder Suite

Yosemite National Park in California has spawned plenty of famous men (John Muir, Stephen Mather, Ansel Adams), but author, naturalist, and hotelier Mary Curry Tresidder was undoubtedly the "first lady" of the valley. The suite occupies a private apartment built in the Ahwahnee Hotel in 1928 for the Tresidder family. Mary lived here the better part of 40 years, running the hotel with a very personal touch and penning books like *Trees of Yosemite*. It was converted into a guest room after Mary's death in 1970. Also called the "Queen's Room" because Queen Elizabeth II and Prince Philip stayed there in 1983, the suite sprawls across the lodge's secluded sixth floor and features fabulous views of Yosemite Valley and its celebrated granite walls. Among the suite's features are craftsmen cabinets and a four-poster canopy bed. A black-and-white portrait of Mary (in a rocking chair) hangs above the suite's sitting area. Her ghost is said to haunt the entire floor, fussing over the guests in much the same manner as Mary did in real life, making sure everything is copacetic. Lodge: *www.yosemitepark.com*.

✶ Bryce Canyon ✶
NATIONAL PARK
Lodge at Bryce Canyon:
Historic Deluxe Cabins

Built in the late 1920s, the deluxe cabins at Utah's Bryce Canyon still look much as they did 80 years ago, tucked into the pines about 100 yards from the canyon rim. Gilbert Stanley Underwood's design is classic national park: log slab siding anchored by stone corner piers, rough rubble masonry chimneys, and steep gable roofs with cedar shingles. The interiors retain their original wooden siding and stone fireplaces (although gas has replaced wood). Latter-day improvements include queen-size beds and full bathrooms. Each cabin boasts a private porch with views of the surrounding forest and a wonderful whiff of pine throughout the day. Their location close to the canyon's Rim Trail makes the cabins ideal for those who cherish sunrise and sunset views or photography. Lodge: *www.brycecanyonforever.com.*

✶ Yellowstone ✶
NATIONAL PARK
Lake Yellowstone Hotel:
Presidential Suite

Living up to its lofty moniker, the Presidential Suite at the Lake Yellowstone Hotel hosted both Warren Harding (1923) and Calvin Coolidge (1927) while on official visits to the Wyoming national park. Their wives no doubt found the spacious second-floor room an oasis of luxury in the middle of the wilderness. The suite wraps around the hotel's southwestern corner, overlooking timberland on one side and the broad sweep of Yellowstone Lake on the other. It was created along with the rest of the hotel in 1891 and refurbished by master park architect Robert Reamer a decade later. The double front door opens onto a large living room flanked by two nice-size bedrooms, each furnished with antiques and reproductions. Brass beds complement the bygone vibe. The artwork reflects Yellowstone wildlife themes, in particular the etched glass panel of grizzly bears fishing for salmon. Although the two bathrooms and kitchenette are thoroughly modern, the rest of the suite is resolutely unplugged to retain its rustic ambience—even Presidents must do without television and DVD players. Lodge: *www.yellowstonenationalparklodges.com.*

✶ Grand Teton ✶
NATIONAL PARK
Jenny Lake Lodge:
Water Lily Suite

All of the rooms at Jenny Lake Lodge are named after local wildflowers, but only one is outfitted for Grand Teton romance—the Water Lily Suite. The lodge was born as a dude ranch in the early 1920s and only recently transformed into a swank wilderness hotel that features a main building and 37 log cabins. Yet modern amenities (like a Jacuzzi whirlpool tub) do not detract from the rustic ambience of a suite that features handmade quilts, peeled-wood furniture, and a wood-burning stove for those cool Wyoming nights. Water Lily is Jenny Lake Lodge's largest and most secluded cabin. Out back is a porch equipped with rocking chairs with a view through thick forest to a nearby meadow. A hearty breakfast and five-course dinner, included in the room rate, are taken in the lodge dining room. Like the Water Lily Suite, they are sumptuous affairs, with entrees such as pan-seared duck breast in a pomegranate glaze with toasted almond couscous. Lodge: *www .gtlc.com/lodging/jenny-lake-lodge-overview.aspx.*

ten best parks
culinary delights
National park feasts for the palate rather than the eyes

Adding flavor—literally—to any vacation is indulging in the local cuisine, be it a spicy Southwestern meal, a pie made of northern Rockies berries, or fish from the Great Lakes. Many of the private restaurants inside the national parks emphasize local flavors, with an emphasis on fresh ingredients grown or raised in the region.

✷ Acadia ✷
NATIONAL PARK
Jordan Pond House: Popovers for Tea

Partake in a tradition that stretches back more than 130 years by munching popovers with strawberry jam, butter, and tea on the back lawn of Jordan Pond House in Maine's Acadia National Park. Both the house and nearby lake are named after the pioneering Jordan family, who established a farm here in the 1840s. Thirty years later the property transformed into a pleasant country café to serve the growing number of tourists flocking to Mount Desert Island. Popovers have been a specialty since the very start. And they seem to taste even better when admiring Pemetic Mountain and the Bubbles across the lake. The popovers are also served à la mode with homemade ice cream. And if that still doesn't satisfy your sweet tooth, consider a dollop of blueberry or chocolate sauce. Jordan Pond's cappuccino coffee and chai tea also complement the popovers. Restaurant: *www.thejordanpondhouse.com.*

✷ Glacier ✷
NATIONAL PARK
Eddie's Café: Huckleberry Pie

One of the great debates in Montana (and throughout the northern Rockies) is who makes the best huckleberry pie. Eddie's Café in Apgar village certainly makes a bid for the pie title and just about everything else one can make with huckleberries. Their menu includes buttermilk pancakes with huckleberry syrup, huckleberry yogurt, salads with huckleberry vinaigrette, grilled chicken with huckleberry barbecue sauce, huckleberry milk shakes, huckleberry lemonade and ice tea, huckleberry-flavored coffee, deep-dish huckleberry cobbler, and huckleberry-peach pie à la mode. Visitors could easily huckleberry their way across the whole region. The Mountain Lounge at St. Mary's Lodge makes a pretty mean huckleberry martini. The Whistle Stop Restaurant in East Glacier and Park Café in St. Mary are both known for their huckleberry pies. There's even a huckleberry cannery in Hungry

Horse, Montana (near the park's West Gate), with a factory shop that sells pies, fudge, licorice, taffy, and jams flavored with Montana's favorite berry. Restaurant: *www.eddiescafegifts.com*.

✷ Wrangell–St. Elias ✷
NATIONAL PARK & PRESERVE
McCarthy Lodge:
Copper River Salmon

It doesn't get any fresher than this: Alaska salmon straight from the Copper River and served with nouvelle cuisine flourish in the dining room at the McCarthy Lodge. This far out in the middle of nowhere, most folks are happy with basic grub. But the lodge bucks that trend with culinary maestro Joshua Slaughter, who combines superfresh local ingredients with sophisticated cooking techniques and presentation. The lodge's signature dish is Copper River red salmon, caught by angler Ralph Lohse in local streams and served medium rare with a tarragon-mustard sauce and locally grown greens. The restaurant's eclectic wine list (another pleasant surprise in the wilderness) includes Chardonnays and Pinots and perfectly complements the fish. Decorated with old black-and-white photographs and pioneer mementoes, the rustic lodge has been around

The United States' vast differences in regional cuisines are showcased in numerous national park eateries.

since 1916, when the entire building was moved to McCarthy from the coastal town of Katalla, where it was part of a fish cannery. Slaughter is also known for his 12- to 20-course tasting menus, often composed on the fly with whatever takes his fancy that day. The menus are dynamic and change frequently but might include cucumber cantaloupe intermezzo or pork loin in an onion sauce with balsamic mustard. Restaurant: *www.mccarthylodge.com*.

Many Alaskans live off the land ... Subsistence fishing and hunting provide a large share ... The state's rural residents harvest about 22,000 tons of wild foods each year—an average of 375 pounds per person.

for an additional cost, everything is paired to amazing wines. Hungry park visitors who pop into Murray Circle for lunch can dig into a five-course mini-degustation that includes a leafy salad, chips and dip, chilled sweet pea gazpacho soup, a choice of three entrées, and chocolate torte with coconut tapioca for dessert. Restaurant: *www.murraycircle.com*.

☆ Golden Gate ☆
NATIONAL RECREATION AREA
Murray Circle Restaurant: Degustation Menus

Even in a region known for its fine dining, the national park restaurants in the San Francisco Bay Area stand out, in particular the Murray Circle Restaurant on the Marin side of the Golden Gate. Located in Fort Baker, part of the Golden Gate National Recreation Area, the restaurant is part of the upscale Cavallo Point Lodge, the Michelin one-star eatery revolves around Bay Area regional cuisine, pioneered by the legendary Chez Panisse restaurant 30 years ago and perfected by Murray Circle executive chef Joseph Humphrey. The genre blends fresh local, organic, and sustainable ingredients with French, Spanish, and Mediterranean cooking techniques to create dishes unique to northern California. Humphrey's 14-course Grand Tasting Menu features many of his trademark dishes: quail with cherries and soy beans; wood-grilled venison with avocado, daikon, and hazelnuts; and chicken and foie gras with hand-cut spaghetti carbonara;

☆ Blue Ridge ☆
PARKWAY
Mabry Mill Restaurant: Grits

Nothing is more evocative of good old-fashioned Southern cooking than grits, the cornmeal porridge that goes with any meal. Founded in 1910 along the Blue Ridge, Mabry Mill produces its own stone-ground cornmeal for the restaurant's hush puppies, spoon bread, griddlecakes, muffins, and illustrious grits. Guests can eat them piping hot with melted butter or stone cold (sliced and fried in pork drippings). The dining experience is enhanced on summer and autumn weekends, when live bluegrass often invades the grounds. Guests can also take a self-guided tour of the old historic buildings, including a blacksmith shop, whiskey still, and the much photographed water mill, its gray-plank profile reflected in the adjacent pond. Traditional Appalachian crafts are another Mabry staple, including ranger-led demonstrations on how to grind maize into cornmeal. The gift shop sells cornmeal that can be used to make grits, bread, or cakes back home. Mabry Mill is located at milepost 176 along the Blue Ridge Parkway, not far from Rocky Knob Visitor Center. Restaurant: *276-952-2947*.

☆ Isle Royale ☆
NATIONAL PARK
Rock Harbor Dining Room:
Lake Superior Trout

As any lakeside eatery should, the Rock Harbor Dining Room boasts several mouthwatering seafood dishes, including wonderfully fresh Lake Superior trout. The 8-ounce filet is oven baked with lemon and herbs and served with the veggie of the day and wild rice pilaf. Much of the trout comes from the nearby Edisen Fishery, started in 1895 by local fishermen and still in operation. The fishery's log buildings are on the National Register of Historic Places. Located on Isle Royale's northeast shore, the dining room is part of Rock Harbor Lodge, the only overnight accommodation in the Michigan park. Restaurant: *www.rockharborlodge.com*.

☆ Yellowstone ☆
NATIONAL PARK
Obsidian Dining Room:
Bison Short Ribs

In a rare happenstance for a national park, in Wyoming's Yellowstone you can eat what you see wandering around inside the park. The buffalo served at half a dozen park restaurants doesn't derive from local herds, however, but rather ranch-raised bison from neighboring states. At the Old Faithful Snow Lodge, the Obsidian Dining Room's finger-licking short ribs are braised in local Moose Drool beer and served with buttermilk mashed potatoes; they come in 3- and 6-ounce portions. The kitchen also serves an awesome bison tenderloin cooked with fried shallots and rosemary in a Cabernet sauce. Restaurant: *www.yellowstonenationalparklodges.com*.

☆ Death Valley ☆
NATIONAL PARK
Furnace Creek Inn:
Jalapeño Molten Cheesecake

Celebrate a trip deep into eastern California's Death Valley with a dish that's equal parts mouthwatering and mouth scorching. Cheese and jalapeños are a natural combination, found in many Mexican and Southwest stalwarts. But whether jalapeño molten cheesecake is an appetizer or dessert, well, that's up to individual diners. Chef Michelle Hanson at the Furnace Creek Inn makes the delicacy with two hard cheeses (jack and mozzarella), plus cream cheese, sour cream, tortilla chips, and eggs blended and baked together. The cheesecake's kick comes not just from the peppers, but also the onion, garlic, and dash of Tabasco. The coup de grâce is a dollop of prickly pear jelly and a strip of "frizzled" cactus. The inn's dining room serves several other offbeat desert dishes, too, including a crispy cactus appetizer served with yellow tomato salsa, house guacamole, and the aforementioned prickly pear jelly. Restaurant: *www.furnacecreekresort.com*.

☆ Crater Lake ☆
NATIONAL PARK
Crater Lake Lodge:
Citrus Duck

The dining room at Crater Lake's namesake lodge culls many of its ingredients from the surrounding hinterland: fresh produce from the Willamette Valley, cheese and wine from the Rogue River Valley, halibut and other seafood from the Pacific, and duck from Oregon's manifold lakes, rivers, and ponds.

The lodge's citrus duck is a classic of Pacific Northwest regional cuisine, oven baked and basted with a citrus-chili glaze and served with fresh sautéed greens and long-grain wild-rice pilaf. Keeping to the aquatic theme, start a meal with Oregon mussel meunière, wild salmon satay in a dijonnaise sauce, or Northwest clam chowder with smoked bacon. A national historic landmark built in 1915 and renovated in the late 1990s, Crater Lake Lodge and its dining room summon a rustic wilderness experience of solid rock walls, wood-beam ceilings, and large windows with views of the stunningly blue Crater Lake. Restaurant: *www.craterlakelodges.com*.

☆ Mesa Verde ☆
NATIONAL PARK
Metate Room:
Masa Chicken Asadero

Nobody does Southwest cuisine like the Metate Room. Perched at around 8,000 feet on the edge of Mesa Verde in Colorado, this upscale eatery at the Fair View Lodge serves endless views and savory dishes in equal measures. The masa chicken asadero is to die for, a chicken breast stuffed with green chilis and asadero cheese and breaded in cornmeal dough (masa), served with green chili mashed potatoes and a smoked jalapeño cream sauce. Chef Brian Puett's other modern interpretations of heritage food include medallions of pork tenderloin dusted with cinnamon and chili powders; prickly pear shrimp cocktail; and an out-of-this-world Nanescatha pizza made with black-bean hummus, roasted peppers, cilantro, and cotija cheese on traditional Navajo flat bread. The modern decor carries Southwest touches with its Native American carpets and pottery. Metate's panorama overlooks the desert canyons to the east of Mesa Verde, a view that nearly trumps the food. Restaurant: *www.visitmesaverde.com*.

☆ National Park–inspired Libations ☆

As they are apt to do anywhere on the planet, bartenders in national park bars create cocktails with local names and flavor.

Bright Angel Bar on the South Rim of the **Grand Canyon** boasts some of the most imaginative beverages, including Cactus Lemonade (vodka and lemonade with a splash of prickly pear cactus syrup), Grand Gold (Hornitos Reposado tequila, sweet and sour, lime and a splash of Grand Marnier), and Kaibab Coffee (made with Bailey's and walnut liqueur).

In **Yellowstone,** the **Bear Pit Bar** at the Old Faithful Inn offers several local libations. The Mud Pot blends Bacardi rum, Kahlúa, and a touch of cream into a concoction that really does resemble the park's celebrated paint pots. The Cutthroat Cooler is a summer's day combo of sparkling wine, peach schnapps, and grenadine. An off-the-card drink is the Rocky Mountain (Expletive Deleted), which brings together Jack Daniels, Amaretto, and Rose's lime juice.

With its views of Half Dome and Glacier Point, the **Ahwahnee Bar** is a great place to sit and sip in **Yosemite Valley.** The signature drink is El Capitini—The First Ascent, made with Absolut vodka, Cointreau, and pomegranate juice and served with a keepsake carabineer. The bar staff created the martini to commemorate the first ascent of El Capitan in 1958.

The **Taproom** at Skyland Resort in **Shenandoah National Park** has cooked up a number of specialty drinks with Appalachian themes. Prohibition Punch is an eclectic blend of orange-flavored liqueur, orange and lemon juices, moonshine, rum, and Grenadine. A Copper Kettle Cooler mixes moonshine with French and Italian vermouth and a splash of lemon. The Stony Man Camp Cooler combines rose wine with cranberry juice and Sprite for a sweet tangy fizz.

campgrounds

Experiencing your environs close-up

One of the best ways to see a national park is to camp in the heart of it. Some campgrounds stand out from the rest, distinguished by their beautiful and secluded settings, excellent facilities, and proximity to great things to do. The following sites meet those criteria, providing campers with some exceptional spots to pitch a tent.

✴ Theodore Roosevelt ✴
NATIONAL PARK
Cottonwood Campground

Best known for its rugged, badlands terrain and its rich variety of wildlife, Theodore Roosevelt National Park in North Dakota is a great place to camp if you want little company, access to water, and a striking setting. The best option here is Cottonwood Campground in the park's South Unit, located near the banks of the Little Missouri River. The sites are quite private, the surroundings beautiful, and there are modern bathrooms centrally located. Camping here puts you close to some of the park's biggest attractions, including the Scenic Loop Drive, but it also offers the chance to experience the park's wildlife firsthand. Bison roam freely through the park—there are between 200 and 400 of them in the South Unit alone—and you sometimes spot them in the campground, or wake in the morning to find fresh bison tracks outside your site where one wandered through during the night. Though seeing these huge, magnificent beasts can be a thrilling experience, do give them a wide berth—a provoked bison is not the kind of anecdote you want to take away from your camping experience.

✴ Sequoia ✴
NATIONAL PARK
Cold Springs Campground

California's Sequoia National Park is well known for its sequoia trees, so giant and ancient that legend has it a logger in 1888 needed five days and a team of five men to cut down a tree. But the park also has dramatic canyons, rock formations, rivers, and giddy elevations with stunning overlooks. At an elevation of 7,500 feet, the small Cold Springs Campground, in the Mineral King area, assures access to spectacular views and is also near the famed sequoia groves. Shaded by aspens and evergreens, the campsites are tent only—the winding, rocky road to the campground isn't navigable by trailers and RVs. Each campsite has a picnic table and fire pit with a grill; there are pit toilets and drinking water in the campground.

✳ Sleeping Bear Dunes ✳
NATIONAL LAKESHORE
D. H. Day Campground

The setting of Sleeping Bear Dunes, along 31 miles of beautiful Lake Michigan's southern shoreline, makes it a wonderful place for a camping trip. The D. H. Day Campground offers a happy medium between roughing it in the backcountry and camping with the ease of modern conveniences: It's rustic camping with vault toilets and spigots in a peaceful lakeshore setting. The 88 campsites at D. H. Day Campground are nicely shaded and screened from one another by trees and brush, and from almost all areas of the campground, campers have very easy access to the gorgeous, unspoiled white-sand beaches of Lake Michigan or any of the 21-inland lakes. On a clear day, campers can get up early and take the short walk to the beach to see the sun rise over the lake. In the evening, campers can participate in a ranger-led program on the local culture, the lake's ecology, or the history of the logging and shipping in the area. Each campsite has a fire ring that people can gather around to stay cozy in the cool Michigan evenings. Campsites are available only on a first-come, first-served basis, so try to arrive early in the day to snag a good spot.

Early risers at one of Assateague Island's oceanside campsites set their lines and settle back to greet the sun.

✳ Acadia ✳
NATIONAL PARK
Blackwoods and Seawall Campgrounds

Acadia National Park's beautiful, classic campgrounds are popular for good reason. The park's two primary campgrounds—Blackwoods and Seawall—have lovely wooded campsites that are within a ten-minute walk of the Maine Atlantic coast. Blackwoods Campground is located on the east side of the island, closer to some of Acadia's major features like the network of historic, broken-stone carriage roads and the Park Loop Road. Seawall, on the west side of Mount Desert Island, is less crowded and provides a more private camping experience, though it's also farther from the park's big attractions. Both campgrounds reserve the majority of their sites for tents, though there are some sites that accommodate RVs and pop-ups; each campground has cold running water, picnic tables, fire rings, and showers and a camp store within a half mile.

✳ Assateague Island ✳
NATIONAL SEASHORE
Oceanside and Bayside Campsites

Assateague Island National Seashore in Maryland is a stunning place to camp; a good campsite provides sweeping views of the bay or of the Atlantic fringed by long beaches. The white noise at night is the rush of surf. The bird-watching is spectacular, and lucky campers will glimpse the wild ponies that roam the island, too. There are several types of waterfront camping available: oceanside or bayside drive-ins for RVs and trailers, or oceanside or bayside walk-ins for tents. All the campsites have a picnic table and upright grill, and there are chemical toilets, cold-water showers, and drinking water located in each camping area. The tranquility and loveliness of the setting attracts people time and time again,

Campers on Assateague Island thrill to the sight of the island's famed wild horses.

but beware the mosquitoes, especially in summer. Come armed with repellent, and since camping on the beach doesn't afford a lot of shade, bring a shade tent or umbrella to deflect the sun during the day.

✳ Natural Bridges ✳
NATIONAL MONUMENT
Near Bridge View Drive Overlooks

In the arid canyon country of southeastern Utah, Natural Bridges National Monument preserves three striking natural bridges, formed when the relentless action of water eroded thin sandstone walls into arch-like features. The only place to lodge in the park—and actually, within 25 miles of it—is the campground located beyond the visitor center. Its size, only 13 campsites, combined with its remote location guarantees a relatively uncrowded stay, and the sites are spacious and nicely screened from each other. The campground is primitive; the closest drinking water is at the visitor center, less than a mile away. Each campsite has a fire grill, picnic table, and tent pad. Rangers offer evening campfire programs at the campground during the summer. The greatest things about this campground, however, are its remarkable setting and its proximity to Bridge View Drive, along which are overlooks of the Sipapu, Kachina, and Owachomo Bridges.

☆ Rocky Mountain ☆
NATIONAL PARK
Moraine Campground

The high-mountain landscape of Rocky Mountain National Park in Colorado makes for some magnificent camping, and Moraine Campground, in a ponderosa pine forest at an elevation of 8,100 feet, is a great place to set up a tent. The campground can accommodate just about any kind of camping, from trailers, RVs, and tents, to tent-only walk-ins. There are stunning views of the snowcapped Rockies from many of the sites, so come early, if possible, to claim a site; the campsites can be reserved for stays Memorial Day weekend through September, while the rest of the year is first come first served only. Each campsite has a picnic table and fire grate; restrooms, water spigots, and vault toilets are located centrally, but there are no showers in the park. Moraine also has a beautifully maintained amphitheater for evening campfire programs in the summer, and hiking trails to Cub, Fern, Bear, and Odessa Lakes originate at or near the campground.

☆ Point Reyes ☆
NATIONAL SEASHORE
Coast Camp, Sky Camp, and Tomales Bay

For backcountry camping with coastal scenery, Point Reyes National Seashore in California can't be beat. Backcountry camping is the only kind permitted in Point Reyes, and the hike-in campgrounds are set in different surroundings, so you will have no trouble finding a setting that speaks to you. If proximity to the shore is a necessity, Coast Camp has sites

☆ Firewood Pests ☆

In many national park campgrounds, notices ask that campers not bring their own firewood in to burn at their campsite; some parks have even implemented bans on firewood that isn't purchased or gathered within the campground. This may seem like a finicky Park Service requirement, but there's actually an important reason behind it. Invasive exotic pests like the emerald ash borer, elm bark beetle, and chestnut blight fungus have decimated entire populations of native ash, elm, and chestnut trees in some states. In an effort to contain these epidemics, scientists are trying to quarantine the areas in which pests have infected and killed trees so that they do not spread to healthy tree populations elsewhere in the country. Campers may never know it, but the firewood they bring into the campground to burn at an evening campfire could contain the larvae of one of these pests, and just like that, the pests are introduced to the area and the quarantine is all for naught. So do right by our beautiful native trees—some of which are now severely threatened—by using only the wood the park provides on the premises.

tucked into a grassy coastal valley with the beach and tide pools only 200 yards away, while Wildcat Camp sits in an open meadow on a bluff overlooking the ocean. For stillness and deep seclusion, Glen Camp is quite isolated and deep in a wooded valley, screened from ocean breezes. Sky Camp, on the western side of Mount Wittenberg and at a higher elevation (1,017 feet), has beautiful vistas of Point Reyes, Drakes Bay, and the Pacific. Boat-in campers should head to Tomales Bay, on the west side of the national seashore beaches, made up of small sandy coves backed by steep cliffs. All of the camps are tranquil and free from crowds and cars. But this also means they're popular, so book ahead if a visit to this park includes a weekend.

> On August 25, 1916, the National Park Service Organic Act established the National Park Service and set it forward on this mission: "... to conserve the scenery and the natural and historic objects and the wild life therein ..."

☆ Lassen Volcanic ☆
NATIONAL PARK
Manzanita Lake Campground

Lassen Volcanic National Park in the Cascade Range in northern California is so named because of the 30 volcanic domes within its boundaries, but there are quite a few other natural features to be discovered here. These include lovely Manzanita Lake, which formed when a volcanic dome collapsed and the resulting avalanche dammed up a creek. This site is the setting for Manzanita Lake Campground, a beautiful place from which to base an exploration of the park. To start, there's trail access from the campground to the lake, which affords striking views of Lassen Peak opposite. Manzanita Lake is also a very popular spot for fishing (catch-and-release only), swimming, and boating; the Loomis Museum (which has information, exhibits, and videos about

the area) and an amphitheater for evening programs are less than a mile away from the campground. Each campsite has a picnic table and campfire ring, and the campground has flush toilets and drinking water. For other amenities, the Camper Store close by has a laundromat, hot showers, and some groceries.

☆ Denali ☆
NATIONAL PARK & PRESERVE
Savage River Campground

Home to grizzlies and gray wolves, expansive wilderness, and the tallest mountain in North America, Denali has something else going for it too—sheer size. Larger in area than the state of New Hampshire, the Alaska park has a lot to offer. Set up camp at Savage River Campground at mile 13 on Park Road, the only road that goes into Denali. Away from the activity of the park entrance, Savage River is the smallest of the three campgrounds in Denali accessible by vehicle. The individual sites are screened by brush. An old gravel road leads through the campground toward its namesake river where, beyond the dense tree cover, there are beautiful, open views of the surroundings. On clear days, Mount McKinley towers in view from the campground. Each campsite has a picnic table and fire grate; flush and pit toilets and spigots for potable water are scattered throughout the campground, and an amphitheater hosts evening ranger programs on everything from grizzlies to glaciers. Campers can launch recreational activities—hiking, picnicking, and touring—via free shuttle buses at the nearby Savage and Mountain Vista rest areas.

rv campgrounds
Establishing base camp . . . all across America

National parks strike a pretty good balance when it comes to RV camping. Full hookups are rare, but most camping areas more than compensate with some of the nation's most spectacular scenery. Enjoy the comfort of a rolling home as well as ranger programs, walks on the beach, brilliant night skies, and unparalleled beauty.

✳ Canyonlands ✳
NATIONAL PARK
Willow Flat and Squaw Flats Campgrounds

Before setting out for Canyonlands, note that only two paved roads lead into this sprawling southeastern Utah park—a sign that RV camping here will be different. The Willow Flat Campground in Islands in the Sky features 12 sites (only one of which is pull-through) so count on there being a high demand for these slots in peak season. At Squaw Flats, a total of 26 sites make camping in the Needles more popular—that and the fact that there are bathrooms, water, and picnic tables here. But whether the site is seriously primitive or just very primitive, the reason campers come here for an overnight (or more) is for easy access to the park's numerous overlooks where walking a few dozen yards will reveal a canyon that's 2,000 feet deep and a landscape that stretches out for a hundred miles. Later that evening comes front row seating before one of the darkest night skies in the country, a fact that literally expands the universe. Park rangers host night-sky programs in the summer, revealing to participants with the aid of far-seeing telescopes—or perhaps even the naked eye—new stars and constellations and, in a way, a whole new world.

✳ Grand Teton ✳
NATIONAL PARK
Flagg Ranch and Colter Village

Of Grand Teton's six campgrounds only two—Flagg Ranch, 5 miles north of the park off John D. Rockefeller Memorial Parkway *(800-443-2311, www.flaggranch.com)*, and Colter Village *(800-628-9988, www.gtlc.com)*—offer RV campsites with hookups, and one is designated tent only. So why bring an RV here instead of opting for a hotel? Because here campers can go to sleep under a blanket of stars that are not dimmed by city lights and then awake to see the first rays of light kissing the Teton Range. In the morning, the east-facing range receives a constantly changing flood of light that first affects the color of the sky and then fills in the crevices and cracks, peaks and pinnacles. Another RV advantage is having easier access to the trails and activities of the park long before outsiders arrive, such as paddling upon Jackson Lake when the surface is still and glassy and having the luxury to experience this place in an unparalleled sense of peace and solitude. In addition to the morning light show, which makes for dramatic photographs, travelers may find themselves sharing their campsite with a passing deer or moose or, to be fair, bear, but the free-roaming menagerie is a vivid reminder that one is living on the land, experiencing it in full—and not in a hard-wired hotel cube.

An RV rolls through Canyonlands, a geologic wonderland of red-rock canyons, mesas, and buttes.

☆ Assateague Island ☆
NATIONAL SEASHORE
Oceanside and
Bayside and Oceanside Campgrounds

Although Baltimore, Philadelphia, Norfolk, Richmond, and Washington, D.C., arc around this thin strip of a park in Maryland, it's not necessarily an easy place for urban dwellers to reach. After drivers run the gauntlet and clear the dense commercial traffic heading to Ocean City, a town sprawled across two states (Maryland and Virginia), a lonely country road sweeps into the protected seashore on Assateague Island, where the names of Assateague's two campgrounds—Bayside and Oceanside—enticingly say it all. Park the RV at Bayside and to the west is the Sinepuxent Bay, a small portion of larger Chincoteague Bay. Nearby along the waterfront are areas for clamming and crabbing and launching a canoe, while on the east side of the entry road is Oceanside Campground where, just beyond the dunes, Atlantic Ocean waves crash onto the shore. Campers frequenting this area can enjoy lazy days stretched out on the sands, walking along forest and dunes trails, warming themselves around a fire ring or, even better, enjoying the night sky by the light of a beachfront blaze. At the southern end of the island, there's a lighthouse, walking trails, and the Chincoteague Wildlife Refuge—but no camping.

☆ Lassen Volcanic ☆
NATIONAL PARK
Butte Lake Campground

This remote California park—it's out in the wilderness far from Carson City and Sacramento—is swaddled in ponderosa pine, lodgepole pine, and Douglas-and white fir. When setting up camp, there won't be any hookups anywhere and only a lone laundromat graces the eight campgrounds here—six of which are open to RVs where the camper may be parked a mile high or up around 10,000 feet in thin air. The rustic campgrounds offer some pull-through spaces, many back-in, and many campsites subject to change

without notice when ice and snow and falling trees necessitate a makeover. Each location sits in close proximity to hiking trails as well as natural features, such as a river or lake, or in the case of Butte Lake Campground, nearby lava beds and Cinder Cone. Campers will most appreciate the nighttime swirl of stars overhead, and the peace and serenity that comes with camp-imposed "quiet hours" that last a luxuriously long time, from 10 p.m. until 10 a.m.

✷ Great Smoky Mountains ✷
NATIONAL PARK
Elkmont, Smokemont,
Cades Cove, and More

Sandwiched between the village of Cherokee on the east and the hyperactive tourist draws of Gatlinburg and Pigeon Forge on the west, this national park straddling Tennessee and North Carolina offers travelers the chance to escape and do something different: Relax. This park allows campers to slip into nature and slip out of range of cell phone signals and fudge shops. The nature of the Smokies is found at approximately 1,000 sites spread across ten campgrounds—all but Big Creek (RVs not allowed) are suitable for RV camping and offer better site separation and thicker vegetation than at open-air camps; none have electrical or water hookups, however, and each has a maximum RV length limit. Get a jump on the day with almost instant access to

the activities—fishing and paddling and swimming in streams, exploring quiet hiking trails, and reaching the Cades Cove Loop which, due to the presence of historic structures left behind by mountain families, will be packed with cars by mid-morning. Savvy RVers will be on the road early, perhaps unloading the bicycles and taking advantage of special two-wheels-only access to Cades Cove on Wednesday mornings. In the high season, many of the campgrounds host evening ranger programs. Sites at Elkmont, Smokemont, Cades Cove, and Cosby Campgrounds can all be reserved for stays mid-May through October; all other campgrounds are filled on a first-come, first-served basis.

✷ Glacier ✷
NATIONAL PARK
Lake McDonald, St. Mary Lake,
Avalance, and Many Glacier Campgrounds

There are more than a dozen campgrounds and more than 1,000 sites sprinkled across northwestern Montana's Glacier National Park, a spectacular northern Rockies wilderness. Although 5 of the 13 campgrounds are off-limits to RVs, an RVer will have trouble choosing a site from the remaining options available, among them the many beautiful lakeside campgrounds along Lake McDonald and St. Mary Lake; the beautiful forest-set Avalanche Campground beside the Going-to-the-Sun Road; and Many Glacier Campground, near Swiftcurrent Lake. Beware: RV excursions may be affected by size restrictions on the Going-to-the-Sun Road (21 feet long, 8 feet wide, 10 feet high), however, since snappy turns can limit navigation. Passing that test, overnight guests soon learn that campgrounds are usually given the best placement in the parks and that being here after the day crowds are gone is a magical experience—one heightened by the sight of spectacular star formations, and the night followed by sunrises creeping over the Continental Divide, illuminating peaks on the Livingston and Lewis Ranges of the Rocky Mountains. Better than coffee, this is the best part of waking up.

☆ Mount Rainier ☆
NATIONAL PARK
Ohanapecosh, Cougar Rock,
and White River Campgrounds

In one of the most picturesque areas of the country, this Washington State national park is easily one of the most popular areas for RV camping. That's the good news. The downside is that since the park was created in a time when mobile campers were small, many large RVs won't be able to navigate the tight turns on some of the park roads. At the park's three campgrounds open to RVs, limits on RVs range from 27 to 35 feet, with trailers limited between 18 and 27 feet. Should the rig fit, prepare for a pleasing RV experience. In the southeast corner of the park, the Ohanapecosh Campground is bisected by the crystal-clear Ohanapecosh River, a snowfield-fed swift ribbon of water that exemplifies the beauty of the Pacific Northwest. At Cougar Rock Campground in the southwest corner of the park, the real attraction is easy access to great recreational activities including photography, hiking, climbing, fishing,

mountain biking, and nightly ranger programs during the summer. White River Campground is near the popular Sunrise area. Although weather narrows the window of access to RV camping in Mount Rainier, the range of services and activities—let alone views of the iconic snowcapped mountain surrounded by forests of western hemlock, Douglas-fir, and western redcedar—makes Mount Rainier well worth the drive.

☆ Grand Canyon ☆
NATIONAL PARK
Mather, Desert View,
and North Rim Campgrounds

Anyone who's ever visited Arizona's Grand Canyon has seen tourists leave their cars, walk to the rim, and depart ten minutes later, certain that they had fully experienced the Grand Canyon. Not even close. As RVers know, it takes days to even begin to appreciate this natural phenomenon, which is why they prefer to roll into the park's campgrounds, put out the lawn chairs, and sit a spell. On the South Rim, the most popular site is Mather Campground, which is within a short shuttle bus ride from the rim and close to services that include a library, amphitheater, market, and laundry. Attached to the campground, Trailer Village (operated by Xanterra) offers specialty sites for RVs—one of the rare national park locations where full hookups are offered. A more remote option, Desert View is about 25 miles east, and while smaller RVs are welcome, the calendar isn't as accommodating—it's only open between May and October. So, too, is the North Rim's namesake campground, which sits among ponderosa pines. None of the park-operated campgrounds offer full hookups, but they do have dump stations. Make reservations well in advance, because even though the canyon's immense, the campgrounds are not.

✯ Acadia ✯
NATIONAL PARK
Blackwoods and Seawall Campgrounds

Acadia National Park shares Maine's Mount Desert Island with pockets of privately owned land and the village of Bar Harbor. It's an interesting situation, and one that benefits RV campers who can roll into the campgrounds of Blackwoods or Seawall knowing that they're well within the park, close to the coast, sheltered by red spruce and white pine and fir trees, and within walking distance of rocky and sandy beaches. RVs up to 35 feet have the advantage of pull-through camping at sites that add an extra layer of privacy to an already secluded area courtesy of lush vegetation. And thanks to the park's layout, when a camper can't handle another dinner of grilled hot dogs and s'mores, it is only a few miles to the village of Bar Harbor, from where, following a meal at a local restaurant, it's only a short drive back to the best room in town: the RV.

✯ Rocky Mountain ✯
NATIONAL PARK
Aspenglen, Timber Creek, Glacier Basin,
and Moraine Park Campgrounds

The pleasure of finding a site within Colorado's Rocky Mountain National Park will largely depend on how much someone wants to see alpine meadows and how pleased they'd be to go to sleep to the call of coyotes and awake to the bugling of elk and if they'd love to be surrounded by some of the highest mountains in America, where dozens on either side of the Continental Divide peak out at more than 12,000 feet. Each of the park's four drive-in campgrounds open to RVs sit above 8,000 feet—Aspenglen at 8,200 feet, Timber Creek at 8,900 feet, Glacier Basin at 8,500 feet, and Moraine Park at 8,160 feet—each connect with hiking trails, and two,

---

☆ Camping Sense ☆

The hiker's adage "take only pictures, leave only footprints," is one that applies to campers as well. But camouflaging the impact of multiple overnights can be a little bit trickier. For campers, the ideal of "leave no trace" is a collection of simple rules that will convince the next camper that you were never even here. That may be tough on your ego, but better for the planet. Rule one: Don't book a site that's not appropriate for the size of your RV—call in advance to make sure there's clearance for your unit. Two: Try to keep your RV atop the gravel pad, leave plastics and aluminum in recycling bins, and dump gray water in the appropriate drains. Three: Do not dig pits, chop down trees, or blaze new trails—for that matter, don't build huge blazes; keep campfires confined on the concrete grill pads. Last, remember where you are: You are a guest in the wilderness. Out of respect to your neighbors—both human and not—be quiet during "quiet hours" and do not feed curious animals looking for a handout. It's not only illegal, it habituates them to humans, an unwanted situation.

Moraine and Glacier Basin, are along the shuttle bus route, which makes sneaking out to Estes Park free and convenient. A mountain pine beetle infestation has wiped out much of the timber around Timber Creek and Glacier Basin, so campers have to bring their own shade (a canopy works wonders). There are no electric, water, or sewer hookups at any of the campgrounds; all but Aspenglen have a dump station. Check with the park for size restrictions and when, or if, generators can be run. Rangers stage educational presentations almost nightly at each of the campground's amphitheaters.

chapter nine

other wonders

places to say "i do" or "i will"

Finding the perfect setting *in* the perfect setting

Many romantic stories have been written in our national parks, where quiet sanctuaries amid the widespread grandeur and lovely settings designed by nature serve as the perfect backdrop for a marriage proposal or wedding. Ceremonies are usually low-key and discreet (permits and restrictions apply), but romance is ever present.

✳ Glen Canyon ✳
NATIONAL RECREATION AREA
Crenellated Shoreline of Lake Powell

The waters of Lake Powell stretch into million-year-old sandstone canyons and seep up cliff walls, creating nearly 2,000 miles of shoreline that feather throughout the serpentine 186-mile-long lake set on the Utah–Arizona border. The lake's multiple fingers in this 1.25-million-acre national recreation area create natural sanctuaries where couples can escape and find themselves alone among the region's spectacular cliffs, buttes, smooth sands, color-changing canyons, and deep blue waters. In these dramatic settings visitors can be at one with nature . . . and together with their intended.

✳ Cape Cod ✳
NATIONAL SEASHORE
Atlantic Shoreline at Sunrise

Sweet sea breezes, curling waves that have been kissing the sand for millennia, and 44,600 acres of pristine shoreline create a setting that rivals the spiritual peace of the grandest cathedrals. Among the ecosystems of this Massachusetts peninsular preserve are grasslands, heathlands, woodlands, and forests, as well as hidden lakes and ponds. And if the park's endless Atlantic coast beaches—some 40 miles' worth—are the church, the soft sand dunes are nature's pews. Arrive before dawn and as day breaks, a well-timed proposal can lead to a new chapter that begins in the glow of sunrise. Thanks to nature and the local resident turned President who signed the papers to preserve it (a young man named John F. Kennedy), this national seashore and its untamed wilderness will always be here to offer suitors—and their grandchildren—a magical place to create family memories.

✳ Grand Teton ✳
NATIONAL PARK
Inspiration Point

With a ticket in hand and an engagement ring at the ready, arrive at the landing at the Jenny Lake Visitor Center and board an open boat to Mount St.

The warm and picturesque Virgin Islands make for the perfect beach wedding destination.

John and a trail that leads to Inspiration Point. The walk is easy and quite picturesque as it passes Hidden Falls and its river rapids before arriving at Inspiration Point (elev. 7,200 feet), an overlook dominated by a view of Jenny Lake with Mount St. John and Grand Teton to the rear. The dramatic vista will be unforgettable, especially because this is where he or she said yes. Return to seal the deal at Grand Teton, where weddings are often held at one of the Signal Mountain summit turnouts, adding unique vistas to wedding photographs. Couples at this Wyoming park can bring the wedding indoors in the Menors Ferry Historic District, where the Chapel of the Transfiguration boasts a broad window that frames the tallest of the Teton peaks.

> ### 1832
> *The third floor attic [in the Great Falls Tavern, C & O Canal] served as "the honeymoon suite" and privacy could be secured for those with 50 cents and a marriage certificate.*

☆ Virgin Islands ☆
NATIONAL PARK
Trunks Bay Beach

High on the list of exotic wedding locations, the tropical Trunks Bay Beach on the U.S. Virgin Island of St. John offers the option for a shoes-free ceremony. That's actually a good idea considering that rolling waves tend to soak the feet of bride and groom. Consistently placed among the world's ten best beaches by people who have the enviable task of ranking beaches, Trunk Bay Beach is sandwiched between crystal-clear, blue-green Caribbean waters and a tropical potpourri of coconut palms and seaside grapes. When the traditionally casual ceremony begins, guests may sit in folding chairs (or on the sand) and the bride and groom may opt for a floral arrangement of colorful orchids (or settle for seaweed). By nature, Trunk Bay weddings are laid-back and natural, and the ceremony could just as easily conclude with a surfing contest as with a kiss. With nature and human nature setting the pace, often the only guideline couples follow is timing their first kiss as man and wife to a Technicolor Caribbean sunset.

☆ Hot Springs ☆
NATIONAL PARK
Historic Bath Houses

There aren't many towns in America where one side of the street is the city itself and the other a national park that shares the city's name. In fact, Hot Springs in Arkansas may be the *only* one. For centuries, Quapaw Indians tapped into naturally healing, heated, and therapeutic mineral waters that were later utilized by 20th-century entrepreneurs as the centerpiece of a gilded age resort—and those are reasons enough to visit Hot Springs. Add a lovely grand hotel, the Oaklawn Park racetrack, a gorgeous circa-1880s promenade, and a commanding view of the Ouchita Mountains from a circuitous drive to the top of 1,060-foot Hot Springs Mountain, and there's every reason to visit. The National Park Service has preserved several historic bathhouses: Buckstaff and Quapaw are in operation and Fordyce is restored as a museum. After taking the plunge in a mineral-rich bath, after being kneaded into muscle-melting bliss, while sipping iced lemonade and relaxing in plush robes, the mood may be right to take advantage of the town's heritage and hot springs and ask . . . "Will you?"

★ Yosemite ★
NATIONAL PARK
Bridalveil Fall

About a century ago, wealthy travelers would invest nearly a week to travel from San Francisco to Yosemite. Then, it'd take *another* week to reach the park's lodges via horseback. Their determination proves that Yosemite is a special setting for a proposal or, perhaps, a wedding. In the park's 1,200 square miles are forests, fields, mountains, valleys, rivers, and streams—and, of course, waterfalls. Bridalveil Fall which, by name alone, deserves to be a member of the wedding party. A favorite for photos and a marvelous backdrop for bride and groom, the fall plunges 620 feet down a sheer cliff, exploding in great froths of water at its base and sending spray far and wide. Ceremonies at its base may only be performed between 8 a.m. and noon between June and September, so shoot for this limited window of opportunity—Bridalveil can provide a most iconic and memorable wedding memory.

★ Olympic ★
NATIONAL PARK
Ruby Beach

While some people wed wearing rose-colored glasses, couples that wed on the south side of Olympic National Park do so on rose-colored sands. Actually, the hue is hard to see, but the name of Ruby Beach does have a magical ring to it thanks to colored gemstone fragments sprinkled in the sand. The coastal setting is surrounded by a jumble of driftwood trees; boulders and coastal monoliths being slapped by churning waves; and the fringe of Olympic's tangled rain forest wilderness of redcedar, hemlock, spruce, and a soft pad of mosses and bright ferns. For couples accustomed to the area and its weather (which leans toward brisk and

The charmingly rustic Yosemite Chapel sits amid unparalleled scenery in Yosemite National Park.

misty most days), this Washington State location may be the Pacific Northwest counterpart to the Virgin Island's Trunk Bay.

★ Golden Gate ★
NATIONAL RECREATION AREA
Marin Headlands

Scattered around the San Francisco Bay Area, the Golden Gate National Recreation Area touches three counties and features an assortment of sites, including beaches, forests, trails, decommissioned military bases, and a lighthouse, so the odds of finding a romantic place to propose are very high—and the odds approach 100 percent in the Marin Headlands.

Here overlooks, a lighthouse, and vista points reveal a montage of the Pacific Ocean, the Golden Gate Strait, the Golden Gate Bridge, and, in the distance, San Francisco and its iconic skyline. One of the most picturesque settings in America, the headlands can help anyone begin their own classic love story.

☆ Great Smoky Mountains ☆
NATIONAL PARK
Cades Cove Historic Churches

Prior to the establishment of Great Smoky Mountains National Park in 1934, Cades Cove was the center of the Smoky Mountains community. Even at the dawn of the modern age, residents here still lived a somewhat pioneer lifestyle, but one enjoyed in a spacious and pastoral valley surrounded by low and lovely mountains. The residents were compelled to leave, but they left behind three historic churches—Methodist, Missionary Baptist, and Primitive Baptist. Each is a wonderfully unadorned no-frills house of worship that comes without heat or electricity—each charmingly rustic. Make reservations well in advance (only two weddings are allowed each day at any location), and advise guests to allot extra time. The Cades Cove Loop is a one-way road that becomes quite congested during the park's peak season, so it may take a while for your guests to arrive—and for newlyweds to depart.

☆ Vanderbilt Mansion ☆
NATIONAL HISTORIC SITE
Formal Gardens

The Hudson River Valley has long been associated with romance, even in the mid-19th century inspiring landscape artists influenced by romanticism. Representative of the gilded-age country place, the Vanderbilt Mansion National Historic Site offers the perfect romantic setting for a wedding. Slightly removed from the baronial 54-room, beaux arts mansion, the Italian-style Formal Gardens are open to small wedding parties of up to 30 guests. Even without access to the house itself, the 3-acre Formal Gardens—terraced and landscaped gardens filled with approximately 6,000 colorful annuals, perennials, and hundreds of rose bushes, and completed with statuary, fountains, and an inky black reflecting pool—add a touch of romance to a ceremony worthy of a Vanderbilt.

☆ Yosemite (Marryin') Sam ☆

For couples who dream of marrying in a chapel in a valley, one national park rises to the top of their list of where to wed: Yosemite.

That's because Yosemite offers a chance to be married in a chapel in THE valley.

Moved to its present site beside Southside Drive in 1901, the circa-1879 Yosemite Chapel offers couples the rare privilege of exchanging vows in a house of worship in a national park. The simple wooden chapel is an excellent example of early chapel architecture in the Sierra Nevada, one that is as plain as its surroundings are majestic. It looks familiar and comforting. The interior consists solely of several rows of wooden  pews, hanging lights, a simple altar, and a single cross. But the sanctuary can be enhanced with candles, flowers, ribbons, and accoutrements limited only by the wedding budget. Without frills or adornment, the sincerity of the chapel—the first structure in Yosemite National Park placed on the National Register of Historic Places (1973)—shines through.

arts & gardens

Where America's boundless creativity blooms

The national parks may be best known as galleries of natural beauty, but they also preserve and reflect America's human artistry. The inventory of creatively focused parks runs the gamut from manicured formal gardens and musical icons to the homes of celebrated American artists and historic theaters that still stage events.

☆ Frederick Law Olmsted ☆
NATIONAL HISTORIC SITE
Fairsted House

As the father of landscape architecture and the nation's paramount parkmaker, Frederick Law Olmsted (1822–1903) spent the latter half of the 19th century designing and redefining the very essence of urban green space. He is most renowned as the creator of New York's Central Park. But he also designed the nation's first state park (Niagara Falls), created the master plans of both Stanford and the University of California at Berkeley, landscaped the Chicago World's Fair of 1893, helped preserve Yosemite Valley, and designed thousands of green spaces—parks, gardens, cemeteries, residential neighborhoods, college campuses, arboretums, landscaped roadways—in 24 different states. Olmsted's beloved Fairsted house in Brookline, Massachusetts, forms the nucleus of this historic site. Olmsted founded the world's first professional landscape design firm here in 1883. In addition to living quarters and studio space, the house also contains archives with more than a million original blueprints, photographs, and design-related documents. The site reopens in 2011 after a three-year renovation.

☆ International Peace Garden ☆
NORTH DAKOTA–MANITOBA, CANADA
Border Carin and Floral Clock

This unusual park along the U.S.–Canada frontier—about a third of the garden grows in North Dakota, the remainder in Manitoba—serves as a lasting tribute to friendship between North American neighbors that share a common language, colonial origin, and so many other bonds. The National Park Service helped create the garden in the early 1930s and maintains a close relationship with the international nonprofit that manages the park today. The garden's eclectic landscapes include woodlands, flower beds, and man-made lakes. Among highlights are the famous border cairn (made with stones gathered on either side of the border), a large floral clock that changes colors with the seasons, floral versions

Music—specifically jazz—is the focus of the unique New Orleans Jazz National Historical Park.

of the Maple Leaf flag and the Stars and Stripes, and a bell tower that chimes every 15 minutes to the sound of London's Westminster. The North American Game Warden Museum and 9/11 Memorial comprising ten steel girders from the fallen Twin Towers are the most recent additions. Campsites and cabins are available inside the park. The actual border crossing is open around the clock. You don't need to go through customs to access the garden, but you do need to clear U.S. or Canadian customs upon exiting.

> [T]he 100th U.S. Congress resolved that "Jazz is hereby designated as a rare and valuable national American treasure to which we should devote our attention, support, and resources to make sure it is preserved, understood and promulgated."

✴ Marsh-Billings-Rockefeller ✴
NATIONAL HISTORICAL PARK
Mansion, Formal Garden, and Carriage Barn

This park in central Vermont is a beacon of early American conservation, environmentalism, and sustainable living. The property originally belonged to mid-19th-century diplomat and linguist George Perkins Marsh, author of *Man and Nature,* a landmark work on ecology and mankind's negative impact on the planet. Philanthropist and railroad magnet Frederick H. Billings purchased the estate and much of the surrounding land in 1869 and set about rehabilitating its distressed forests and farms along the lines suggested by Marsh. Conservationists Laurance Spelman Rockefeller and his wife Mary French (Billings' granddaughter) became stewards of the property in the 1950s and later donated it to the National Park Service. Today's park pays tribute to these landmark environmentalists, as well as the reforestation and progressive farming methods pioneered here. The hub of the park is the old Marsh estate on the north bank of the Ottauquechee River in Woodstock. Rangers lead guided tours of the Marsh-Billings-Rockefeller Mansion (1805) and formal garden, while the history of conservation is explored at the visitor center in the Carriage Barn (1895). You can also hike deep into the woods, climb Mount Tom, or explore the Billings Farm and Museum.

✴ New Orleans Jazz ✴
NATIONAL HISTORICAL PARK
Louis Armstrong Park and Jazz Walk of Fame

Like the music it seeks to honor and preserve, this park unit in the French Quarter of old New Orleans is energetic, eclectic and often free-form. The park pays tribute to a unique American invention and revolves around the people and places that shaped the city's jazz heritage. The temporary visitor center on Peters Street will soon give way to a new facility in Louis Armstrong Park as the place where one can join interpretive talks and walks, watch video documentaries, and relish live jazz. The park stages concerts every Wednesday (12–1 p.m.) and Saturday (2–3:30 p.m.) throughout the year, as well as special programs. All events are free. The park has created two self-guided audio tours available via cell phone or MP3 download. The Jazz Walk of Fame leads people between 16 lampposts marked with musical biography placards in Algiers Point on the south bank of the Mississippi River, a short ferry ride from the French Quarter. The Jazz History Tour covers 11 sites in and around the French Quarter pivotal to the birth and development of local jazz.

☆ Saint-Gaudens ☆
NATIONAL HISTORIC SITE
Aspen House

As one of the driving forces behind the 19th-century American Renaissance in art and architecture, Augustus Saint-Gaudens (1848–1907) created much of what we now consider classic American iconography. From double eagle coins and commemorative medals to presidential busts and dramatic equestrian statues, the Irish-born artist immortalized the American spirit and history in bronze, copper, marble, and gold. His long-time summerhouse, gardens, and studios—and more than a hundred of his works—are the focus of this park near Cornish, New Hampshire, in the gorgeous Connecticut River Valley. The grounds and gardens are open year-round; Aspet House (the sculptor's home) and the studios are only open Memorial Day through October. Ranger-guided programs offered in season include an hour-long art walk and 20-minute house tour. Classical music concerts are staged in the Little Studio on many summer Sundays, carrying on a tradition established by Saint-Gaudens himself. The park also hosts the Park Service's oldest artist-in-residence program. Figurative sculptors chosen for the program spend the summer and fall working at Ravine Studio and interacting with the curious.

☆ Ford's Theatre ☆
NATIONAL HISTORIC SITE
Site of Lincoln's Assassination

Ford's Theatre in the District of Columbia is seared into America's collective soul as the place where a great man fell to an assassin's bullet. *Our American Cousin* was playing on April 14, 1865, when celebrated actor John Wilkes Booth, an ardent Confederate sympathizer, slipped into the presidential box and shot Abraham Lincoln. The mortally wounded

☆ Get Art Schooled in the Parks ☆

- **Saint-Gaudens National Historic Site,** New Hampshire: Saint-Gaudens offers beginning sculpture workshops for grown-ups, teens, and children, as well as more advanced training in skills like casting, moldmaking, and patination. All classes are conducted by the artist-in-residence.
- **Weir Farm National Historic Site,** Connecticut: Visitors are encouraged to try their hand at plein air painting and sketching as part of a Take Part in Art program that includes the free distribution of watercolors, pastels, graphite, and colored pencils, as well as special events like A Brush With Nature, during which professional artists share their passion and techniques.
- **Yosemite National Park,** California: The Yosemite Art and Education Center offers free art classes spring through fall, including watercolor, sketching, pastels, and pen and ink instruction. All ages are welcome and classes are held outdoors (weather permitting). Art supplies can be purchased at the center. Yosemite Outdoor Adventures organizes advanced multiday classes in outdoor painting, nature photography, and Native American basketmaking.
- **Wolf Trap National Park for the Performing Arts,** Virginia: Wolf Trap tenders a full slate of educational art programs for children, including interactive workshops with visiting performers. Adult instruction is available in a wide range of disciplines, from guitar and African drumming to opera and musical theater.

President was carried across Tenth Street to the Petersen boardinghouse, where he was pronounced dead early the following morning. The federal government expropriated the theater shortly after, declaring that Ford's would never be used again for public amusement. In the early 1930s both the theater and Petersen House were turned over to the National Park Service. Despite that earlier decree, Ford's was restored into an active theater in the 1960s and now presents a wide array of stage productions. The basement Ford's Theatre Museum displays numerous Lincoln Presidency and assassination artifacts, such as Booth's derringer pistol, as well as the bloodstained pillow from Lincoln's deathbed. For information and tickets on current productions log onto *www.fords.org*.

☆ Wolf Trap ☆
NATIONAL PARK FOR THE PERFORMING ARTS
Open-air Performing Arts Center

Wolf Trap has long held a special place in the hearts of Washington, D.C.–area theater and music aficionados. According to local legend, wolves really did run wild, once upon a time, in these Northern Virginia woods. Catherine Filene Shouse, an ardent supporter of the arts, donated Wolf Trap to the National Park Service in 1966 along with the funds to develop the property into a cultural node. The hundred-plus shows that take the stage each year range from opera, symphony, and Shakespeare, to classic rock, Broadway musicals, and stand-up comedy. In summer, the park's main stage, the 7,000-capacity Filene Center, offers both covered seats and outdoor seating on a sprawling lawn perfect for picnicking during a performance. Children's events are held in the nearby Theatre-in-the-Woods. The Wolf Trap Foundation, which operates the facility in partnership with the National Park

Service, also organizes wintertime performances at an indoor theater called The Barns at Wolf Trap. Rangers conduct backstage tours of the Filene Center October through March. For information on current shows log onto *www.wolftrap.org*.

☆ Thomas Cole ☆
NATIONAL HISTORIC SITE
House and Old Studio

When Englishman Thomas Cole (1801–1848) arrived in the United States at the age of 17, he had trained as an engraver's assistant and calico designer's apprentice. Within a decade, he was the country's leading landscape painter, a founding member of

After decades spent shuttered, Ford's Theatre, site of Lincoln's assassination, again stages productions.

the National Academy of Design, and had launched a new art movement called the Hudson River school that came to define the nation's obsession with the great American wilderness. The name derives from Cole's love affair with upstate New York, in particular the Catskills. From 1827 he was a regular at Cedar Grove farm and later married the owner's niece. You can take guided tours of the federal-style Main House (1815) and the Old Studio (1839) where he painted, as well as watch a film on Cole at the visitor center, hike along the Hudson River School Art Trail, or indulge in Cedar Grove's famous Sunday Salons with noted artists, writers, and scholars.

✳ Vanderbilt Mansion ✳
NATIONAL HISTORIC SITE
Architecture and Grounds

Although named after one of the nation's most renowned families, this park in New York's Hudson Valley is actually dedicated to an era in American history: the gilded age, the period between the Civil War and the turn of the 20th century when the United States grew into an industrial powerhouse. A spin-off of that success was super-wealthy families like the Vanderbilts and fabulous country homes like the Vanderbilt Mansion. Constructed in 1896–99 as a country home for Frederick William Vanderbilt, the sprawling estate includes the ornate, 54-room mansion, copious woodland, and three terraced Italian-style gardens that were Frederick's pride and joy. An avid gardener and flora aficionado, the tycoon often labored in the gardens himself and was a frequent winner of plant and flower awards at horticulture shows. The

gardens withered after Vanderbilt's 1938 death but were revived starting in the 1980s by a group of local gardeners called the F. W. Vanderbilt Garden Association. Working in conjunction with the Park Service, the club organizes guided garden tours, plant sales, alfresco wine tastings, and other events. A free summer lawn concert series called Music in the Parks is also hosted at the mansion.

✳ Weir Farm ✳
NATIONAL HISTORIC SITE
Retreat for Artists

American impressionist landscape artist Julian Alden Weir (1852–1919) purchased this Connecticut property on a whim in 1882. Collector Erwin Davis offered to trade the 153-acre farm for $10 and a single painting from the artist's private collection. Craving a country escape, Weir accepted the deal and moved in a year later with his wife. Over the next 36 years, the farm served as a creative retreat for many of Weir's artist friends, among them John Singer Sargent, Childe Hassam, and John Twachtman. After Weir's death in 1919, sculptor Mahonri Mackintosh Young (1877–1957) and painter Sperry Andrews (1917–2005) also lived and worked at the farm, with Andrews staying until his death, long after the Park Service had acquired the property. Ranger-led walks explore the farm's artistic, agrarian, and geological legacies. The visitor center hosts rotating art and history exhibitions. You can meander through the farm buildings on their own or hike bucolic trails to the Weir Pond and the nearby Weir Preserve. (The house and studio are closed for ongoing renovation until 2012.)

hike-to views

A little sweat for a lot of unforgettable scenery

There are hundreds upon hundreds of miles of trails in America's national parks, and hiking them could keep a person busy for years. But in the interest of time, and to give a person a sweeping scope of a park, here are a few hikes that lead to incredible views of the most majestic and distinctive landscapes our parks have to offer.

☆ Sleeping Bear Dunes ☆
NATIONAL LAKESHORE
Sleeping Bear Point Trail

On the banks of Lake Michigan on Michigan's Lower Peninsula, Sleeping Bear Dunes National Lakeshore is perfectly situated for challenging hikes to rewarding views. For beautiful overlooks on Lake Michigan and the surrounding landscape, take the Sleeping Bear Point Trail—it's a 2.8-mile loop over sandy terrain to sweeping views of the lake, surrounding dunes, and South and North Manitou Islands. As far as elevation goes, it isn't a terribly strenuous hike, but scrambling up dunes as sand falls away under foot will make that 2.8 miles feel like much more; however, the vistas from the top of the dunes are well worth the effort. To shorten the hike, simply backtrack to the trailhead after reaching some of the most impressive viewpoints, which come fairly early in the loop. And if the views of Lake Michigan prove captivating, there's a spur off the loop that leads down to the shoreline itself.

☆ Crater Lake ☆
NATIONAL PARK
Mount Scott and Garfield Peak Trails

Crater Lake, one of Oregon's crown jewels, was formed when a volcano exploded with such force that its summit collapsed, leaving a caldera 6 miles wide that filled with water. There are more than 100 miles of trails within the park, but a couple short trails will take hikers to views that display the full splendor of Crater Lake. For panoramic views of the east side of the park, the lake, and even Mount Shasta, take the 2.5-mile trail (one way) up Mount Scott to an elevation of 8,929 feet, the highest point in the park. The trailhead for this roughly three-hour round-trip hike is about 14 miles east of Park Headquarters along Rim Drive. For an easier, shorter hike, try the Garfield Peak Trail, which originates east of Crater Lake Lodge along the caldera rim and ascends 1,000 feet to stunning views of Crater Lake, and a wonderful vantage point on Phantom Ship, an eerie-looking island rock formation that comprises 400,000-year-old lava flows. The hike is 1.7 miles one way and will take between two and three hours to accomplish round-trip.

★ Badlands ★

NATIONAL PARK
Notch Trail and White River Valley

The crumpled, distinctive landforms of Badlands National Park create one of the most desolately beautiful landscapes in the American West. Most people view the South Dakota park through the windows of their car, but a badlands experience will be much richer on foot, taking advantage of one of the stunning hikes through the bluffs. The trails are generally pretty short, but that doesn't mean a person won't sweat—the ascents are steep. The 1.5-mile Notch Trail meanders through a canyon and then ascends so sharply that the Park Service has installed a log ladder to help hikers clamber up. The trail passes numerous jagged gullies, canyons, and spires that water carved out of sandstone to create the contorted badlands formations. Eventually the trail comes out onto a ledge—the "Notch"—which rewards hikers with sweeping views of the White River Valley basin below, an expanse

Trails in Sleeping Bear Dunes offer timeless views of sandy dunes and sweeping panoramas of Lake Michigan.

periodically interrupted by weird upthrust rock formations. It's badlands scenery at its most awesome, and everybody who sees it will be glad they ventured out of the car. This hike should probably be reserved for the sure of foot—much of the trail is over loose, unstable terrain that threatens to fall away under foot.

> The U.S. Lighthouse Board cared for the statue as the first electric lighthouse or "navigational aid" 1886–1902, followed by the War Department 1902–1933 and since 1933 she has been cared for by employees of the National Park Service.

✳ Golden Gate ✳
NATIONAL RECREATION AREA
Lands End

Lands End in the Golden Gate National Recreation Area has the San Francisco Bay Area's most turbulent and rocky coast, with headlands sculpted by driving wind and waves. Treacherous rocky outcroppings, lying in choppy Pacific waters off the coast with only their tips jutting above the surf, have been the cause of many shipwrecks, remnants of which can still be seen from the cliffs above the shore. To see it up close, take the Lands End segment of the Pacific Coastal Trail, beginning at the Merrie Way Trailhead off Point Lobos Avenue, and walk north along the edge of the city. Go at low tide for a chance to see the wrecks of the *Ohioan,* a freighter lost in 1937; and two tankers, the *Lyman Stewart* (sank 1922) and the *Frank Buck* (sank 1937); off to the northeast stands Mile Rock, one of the deadly outcroppings responsible for ships' demises, and Mile Rock Lighthouse. About half a mile along the trail, a set of stairs leads down to Mile Rock Beach— it's worth the climb down (and later back up) for a close-up look at the strength and ferocity of the Pacific waters along this section of the coast. A short trail leads to Mile Rock Lookout, also worth a quick side trip. Head back up to the Pacific Coastal Trail and continue north to Eagles Point Overlook, where a wooden viewing platform and staircase on the cliff offer thrilling panoramic views of the entrance to San Francisco Bay. For a slice of history, duck into the Victorian-age Sutro Baths ruins near the end of the trail.

✳ Statue of Liberty ✳
NATIONAL MONUMENT
Staircase Views of New York Harbor

The rigorous, almost vertical—and some might say claustrophobic—climb to the crown of the Statue of Liberty National Monument rewards the hearty with unparalleled views from the top. The narrow, 354-step spiral staircase that ascends to the crown from the statue's pedestal was closed after the September 11, 2001, attacks, but was reopened to the public in the summer of 2009. Only 240 people are allowed up to the crown each day (purchase the crown ticket at the same time as the ferry ticket), and those privileged few enjoy stunning panoramic views of the Manhattan skyline and New York Harbor. Almost as intriguing is the close-up view afforded of the interior iron framework that supports the massive copper shell of the statue. A gift from France in the late 19th century, the statue was designed by sculptor Frédéric-Auguste Bartholdi and the iron framework was engineered by Gustave Eiffel. So put on light clothing (temperatures in the crown well exceed those on the ground), mentally prepare, and start climbing— burning quads will be forgotten upon catching sight of the views.

⁎ Zion ⁎
NATIONAL PARK
Angels Landing: Look Down into Canyon

Famed for its jagged rock outcroppings, yawning gorges, and narrow canyons flanked by striated cliffs, Utah's Zion National Park offers classic hiking. From the trailhead at the Grotto picnic area, hike the 5-mile trail to Angels Landing. The trail was cut into solid rock in 1926 and has a series of 21 short switchbacks on the 1,500-foot climb. The scene from the top is spectacular and gives dizzying views into the depths of Zion Canyon, as well as an impressive perspective on the other canyons, cliffs and gullies that score the landscape passed en route. This hike is not for those with a fear of heights—the route to the top is very steep, and at points, the ground next to the trail falls away to steep drop-offs. Chains anchored along part of the route serve as handholds to help hikers climb.

⁎ Carlsbad Caverns ⁎
NATIONAL PARK
Natural Entrance to the Cave

A descent of nearly 750 feet into the depths of Carlsbad Caverns takes you into one of the world's most famous caves. The Natural Entrance route leads 1.25 miles down a steep corridor past spectacles like the Boneyard, a mass of limestone so dissolved and perforated that it's said to resemble Swiss cheese more than bones; and Iceberg Rock, a single 200,000-pound boulder that fell from the cave ceiling thousands of years ago. This steep hike is strenuous, so only those in good health should undertake it. From the lunchroom area into which the Natural Entrance corridor opens, a path leads into the stunning 14-acre Big Room, one of the largest cave rooms in the world. It contains spectacular, sometimes bizarre natural features with names to match, such as the Bottomless Pit, Painted Grotto, and Giant Dome.

⁎ Glacier ⁎
NATIONAL PARK
Hidden Lake Nature Trail

In Montana's Glacier National Park, the Hidden Lake Nature Trail in the Logan Pass area offers a relaxing 3-mile round-trip excursion to the kind of scenery for which the park is renowned. The boardwalk trail begins at the Logan Pass Visitor Center; the slightly raised walkway helps protect the alpine meadow beneath. Keep an eye out for mountain goats, bighorn sheep, or pika on nearby Clements Mountain and Mount Reynolds along the way. At trail's end is

An American icon symbolizing freedom and democracy, Lady Liberty stands tall in New York Harbor.

a captivating overlook of Hidden Lake 750 feet below, glistening in its glacier-carved basin, with Bearhat Mountain rising behind it. On a clear day, Sperry Glacier might be visible, a mere remnant of the massive ice sheets that sculpted Glacier's topography. The trail is very popular, so go early to the avoid crowds.

☆ Rocky Mountain ☆
NATIONAL PARK
Twin Sisters Peak

For a classic summit hike, look no further than the Twin Sisters Peak Trail in Colorado's Rocky Mountain National Park, famous for its mountain scenery. The Twin Sisters Peaks are two adjacent summits near the park's eastern boundary. Starting at the Lily Lake Visitor Center, this 3.5-mile trail (one way) ascends to a high saddle between the peaks, climbing 2,388 feet using a series of well-cut switchbacks. The trail ends at an elevation of about 11,400 feet, getting steeper and more rugged the higher it goes. Take breaks on the way up to enjoy views of Longs Peak, Mount Meeker, and Estes Cones. From the saddle, short, rough scrambling trails lead to either summit—the west peak is easier to reach. From here, the 360-degree views of the Continental Divide, Great Plains, and Estes Park area are phenomenal.

☆ Lewis and Clark ☆
NATIONAL HISTORIC TRAIL
Lolo Trail

One of most challenging mountainous sections Lewis and Clark encountered during their epic expedition across the West was the Lolo Trail, their path across the Bitterroot Mountains for about 120 miles through Montana and Idaho. Today, the Lolo Motorway—Forest Service Road 500, a primitive dirt road built in the 1930s—follows much of the original Lolo Trail and provides access to points that the explorers

☆ Lewis and Clark on the Lolo Pass ☆

Hikers today thrill to the view from the Indian Post Office on the Lolo Trail in the Bitterroot Mountains. But the members of the Corps of Discovery at that same spot back in 1805 were not nearly so euphoric. The Lewis and Clark expedition reached the Bitterroot Valley in mid-September as the weather was worsening, but Lewis and Clark knew they had no choice but to start over the mountains. They began their ascent on September 11, and for ten punishing days battled frostbite, malnutrition, and exhaustion as they struggled through the pass before finally breaking out of the mountains onto Weippe Prairie on September 20. They passed the spot marked by the Indian Post Office on September 16 in knee-deep snow and frigid temps, and Clark wrote in his journal that day, "I have been wet and as cold in every part as I ever was in my life, indeed I was at one time fearfull my feet would freeze in the thin Mockirsons which I wore . . . men all wet cold and hungary." Their courage during this ordeal is something to bear in mind when standing in the same spot today and taking in the glorious view of the Bitterroots.

wrote about in their journals. Enter the Motorway in Idaho off U.S. 12 via Forest Service Road 107, and then drive east about 5 miles past Devil's Chair and Howard's Camp to the marker for the Indian Post Office. Stop and make the short hike to the mysterious cairn of rocks—their origin and purpose uncertain—at the site that Lewis and Clark passed in 1805. At 7,033 feet, this is the highest point on the Lolo Trail; take a few minutes to admire the stunning views of the Bitterroot Range, an achingly beautiful landscape little changed from when Lewis and Clark passed through.

urban escapes

Green spaces near city places

Most people, even dedicated urbanites, need a break now and then from concrete jungle, round-the-clock noise, and exhaust fumes. Some American cities are lucky enough to have units of the National Park System right on their doorsteps, offering recreation and natural beauty within easy reach of millions.

✳ Gateway ✳
NATIONAL RECREATION AREA
New York Harbor, New York,
and New Jersey

With three units located around New York Harbor in both New York and New Jersey, Gateway is just a subway or bus ride away for residents of America's largest metropolis. Some come to swim or sun on beaches, others to bike or jog miles of trails, to fish or kayak, to visit historic sites, or to go on a wildflower walk. And these activities are just the beginning of the year-round offerings at Gateway, a getaway perfect for everything from chilling out to learning a new skill at one of dozens of ranger-led programs. Camping areas allow city folk to sample life in the wild, while buildings at Fort Tilden in Queens have been converted into an arts center. Fort Tilden is just one of six decommissioned forts or military air fields open to the public within Gateway; the Sandy Hook Proving Ground was the first U.S. Army weapons testing grounds, established in 1874. Brooklyn's Jamaica Bay Wildlife Refuge,

the only wildlife refuge in the park system, ranks among the most popular bird-watching sites in the region, with marsh, fields, woods, and ponds. Other sites within the park offer golf and even places for flying model airplanes. If you can't find something to do at Gateway, you're just not looking closely enough.

✳ Golden Gate ✳
NATIONAL RECREATION AREA
San Francisco Bay Area

Want to hike through one of the world's most beautiful forests? Want to visit the legendary prison where Al Capone and "Machine Gun" Kelly were locked up? Want to go hang gliding, enjoy a quiet picnic, admire an art collection, or visit a Cold War–era missile site? All of this and a lot more is possible at Golden Gate, a collection of some three dozen separate units stretching for 70 miles on or near the Pacific Coast, both north and south of San Francisco. A short list of attractions here would include Marin Headlands, a natural area at the north end of the Golden Gate Bridge; Alcatraz Island, former home of an infamous federal prison; Crissy Field, a restored tidal marsh and renowned windsurfing center; Ocean Beach, the longest beach in the Bay Area and a mecca for serious surfers; Point Bonita Lighthouse, a still active beacon; the reconstructed Cliff House and the Sutro Baths, the latter now in ruins; and Muir Woods National Monument, a grove of magnificent coast redwood trees. Bay Area residents treasure these and other park sites, all contributing to making one of the nation's most attractive cities even more appealing.

☆ Urban National Parks ☆

National park? Isn't that a huge tract of wilderness far removed from civilization, with perhaps high mountains and vast forests? That was a common perception until the 1960s and '70s, when the first nature- and recreation-oriented "urban" national park units were established (as distinguished from, for example, historic sites such as Statue of Liberty National Monument). Fire Island National Seashore (near New York City), Indiana Dunes National Lakeshore (near Chicago), Gateway National Recreation Area (in and around New York City), and Golden Gate National Recreation Area (in and around San Francisco) were among the first sites dedicated to the idea that urban residents, too, deserve national parks. These and similar National Park System sites across the country now provide a taste of the natural world to countless people who might otherwise experience it only on television or the Internet.

☆ Rock Creek ☆
PARK
Washington, D.C.

Stretching for 10 miles along the waterway for which it's named, this green space in northwestern Washington, D.C., is beloved by residents of the nation's capital. Jogging, biking, skating, golf, soccer, horseback riding, and tennis are among the more popular activities, while picnicking and bird-watching offer more contemplative pursuits. The park closes some streets to auto traffic on weekends and holidays, creating peaceful paths even more removed from the busy world of government and business just beyond its boundaries. With a nature center, a planetarium, historical exhibits, and a concert venue, Rock Creek more than fulfills its 1890 mandate to be "a public park or pleasure ground for the benefit and enjoyment of the people of the United States."

☆ Santa Monica Mountains ☆
NATIONAL RECREATION AREA
Los Angeles into
Ventura County

The world's largest urban national park, Santa Monica Mountains National Recreation Area spans almost 40 miles from Los Angeles westward into Ventura County, its many separate units covering nearly 240 square miles. Within the designated area are state and local parks, ranging from historic sites to wild areas offering solitude in a region of freeways, shopping malls, and near-endless suburbs. The 65-mile-long Backbone Trail System traverses the rugged Santa Monica Mountains, its entire length open to hikers, while some segments are available for mountain biking and horseback riding. Located in the land of Hollywood and Beverly Hills, the park has inevitable movie and television connections: Many movies and TV shows were filmed

A rainbow arcs across the Santa Monica Mountains, playground to millions of urban residents in the Los Angeles area.

at Paramount Ranch in Agoura Hills, now home to fine hiking trails; Peter Strauss Ranch, along Mulholland Highway, was donated to the park by actor Strauss, who wanted to preserve its natural beauty; Will Rogers State Historic Park, just off Sunset Boulevard, preserves the estate of the famed humorist and actor who died in 1935. One of the park's most fascinating historical attractions is Rancho Sierra Vista/Satwiwa in Newbury Park, where the Satwiwa Native American Indian Culture Center interprets the heritage of the Chumash and Tongva-Gabrielino people who once lived here. In

the northern part of the national recreation area, Cheeseboro Canyon boasts extensive hiking trails and woodlands of the imposing valley oak, a tree species found only in California.

✳ Cuyahoga Valley ✳
NATIONAL PARK
Cleveland and Akron, Ohio

Connecting the Ohio cities of Cleveland and Akron, Cuyahoga Valley boasts a combination of attractions that can justifiably be called unique in the National Park System. Consider that visitors can ride a restored railroad train, attend a summer concert by the famed Cleveland Orchestra, go cross-country skiing, drive a scenic byway, jog or bike alongside the historic Ohio & Erie Canal, attend a theater performance, play golf, go horseback riding, or admire some of the most beautiful waterfalls in the eastern United States—all within the boundaries of Cuyahoga Valley National Park. Running for 22 miles through the heart of the park, the Cuyahoga River once served as a poster child for pollution (it actually caught fire several times when massive oil slicks ignited). Though still no model of purity, the river has recovered enough that fish, birds, and other wildlife now abound along its tree-shaded length. Several villages within the park provide amenities such as dining, shopping, and bike rental. In the southwestern part of the park, Hale Farm and Village *(Mem. Day–Oct.)* is a living history attraction that re-creates 19th-century farm life in the Cuyahoga Valley.

> *Boston Light Station, part of Boston Harbor Islands [NRA], is visited every year by the Flying Santa . . . started by William Wincapaw in 1929. The Flying Santa delivers food, toys, and other necessities to lighthouses across New England.*

✷ Boston Harbor Islands ✷
NATIONAL RECREATION AREA
Boston Harbor

In a world where open space is hard to find near cities, the National Park Service finds innovative ways to bring nature and recreational activities to urban residents. One good example is Boston Harbor Islands National Recreation Area, a collection of 34 islands and peninsulas close to the historic Massachusetts capital, administered through a partnership among federal, state, and local government agencies and private businesses. "Minutes away, worlds apart" is the park's slogan, and a visitor sea kayaking around Grape Island or hiking a trail at Worlds End, a 244-acre peninsula overlooking Hingham Harbor, would agree that the congestion of downtown Boston seems far removed. For great views of the Boston skyline, head to Spectacle Island, which has the highest point in the park, 157 feet above sea level, as well as 5 miles of hiking trails. History is represented at places such as Little Brewster Island, home to the country's oldest light station, and 19th-century Army post Fort Warren on Georges Island.

✷ Indiana Dunes ✷
NATIONAL LAKESHORE
Gary, Michigan City, and Chicago

A very high percentage of the nearly 2 million annual visitors to Indiana Dunes come simply to sunbathe or swim along 15 miles of sandy Lake Michigan shore. In itself, that resource makes the park a treasured getaway for residents of Chicago and nearby cities such as Gary and Michigan City, Indiana. Beyond the beach, though, trails wind through natural habitats of surprising biodiversity, with rare plants and butterflies living among the dunes, savannas, marshes, prairies, and woodlands. Miller Woods, Cowles Bog, Heron Rookery, and Ly-co-ki-we are among the best trails for nature lovers, while the Mount Baldy Trail ascends a 126-foot dune for a panoramic view of Lake Michigan. Mount Baldy is a "moving" dune, pushed about 4 feet a year by prevailing winds. For a glimpse into the area's past, visit restored Chellberg Farm, where three generations of a family of Swedish farmers lived.

✴ Chattahoochee River ✴
NATIONAL RECREATION AREA
Atlanta

Residents of Atlanta benefit today from planning decisions made in the 1970s, when public officials began working to protect 48 miles of the Chattahoochee River on the edge of the city. As Atlanta has grown, the various units of the national recreation area endure as green spaces for picnicking, hiking, mountain biking, horseback riding, and nature enjoyment. The river itself is extremely popular for canoeing, kayaking, tubing, and rafting, as well as fishing for trout, bass, and catfish. (Because river water comes from the dam on Lake Sidney Lanier, it's mostly too cold for comfortable swimming even in summer.) Of the many separate units within the park, the Cochran Shoals area may be the most popular, with a 3-mile trail and a wetlands boardwalk. Concessionaires rent kayaks, canoes, and inner tubes at several locations along the Chattahoochee.

✴ Mississippi River ✴
NATIONAL RIVER & RECREATION AREA
Minneapolis and St. Paul

With various units spanning 72 miles of the Mississippi River in the vicinity of the Twin Cities of Minneapolis and St. Paul, this park is actually a consortium of state, regional, county, and municipal areas, ranging from city parks to museums and from wildlife refuges to historic sites. The Park Service owns only 35 of the recreation area's 54,000 acres, but coordinates activities and assists travelers from its visitor center in downtown St. Paul. Other visitor centers are located in various units including Minnehaha Park in Minneapolis, home of 53-foot-tall Minnehaha Falls, mentioned in Longfellow's poem "Song of Hiawatha." Citizens of the Twin Cities happily avail themselves of the area's opportunities for hiking, cross-country skiing (Fort Snelling State Park is a favorite), and canoeing. The 12.7-mile stretch of the Mississippi between the Crow River boat ramp and the Coon Rapids Dam offers excellent scenery and wildlife far different from the commercial waterway downstream.

✴ Biscayne ✴
NATIONAL PARK
Miami

Ninety-five percent of the 172,000 acres of this Florida Atlantic coast park is water—but that only makes it more of an attraction for residents of Miami, where boating is a way of life for many people. Within sight of downtown skyscrapers, Biscayne National Park offers diving, snorkeling, canoeing, and kayaking, as well as islands to visit for those with their own power boats. Exploring Biscayne Bay, one can see part of the world's third largest coral reef, as well as more than 500 species of fish, sea turtles, manatees, dolphins, and occasionally American crocodiles. Some of the larger keys (coral islets) in the national park offer camping and hiking (winter is best for avoiding mosquitoes). Tropical hardwood forests host rare and endangered birds and butterflies. One oddly historic hiking path is the infamous "Spite Highway," a road bulldozed in the 1960s by developers trying to ruin the environment and prevent the creation of a national park here. The 7-mile route on Elliott Key has slowly recovered from the intentional destruction, with native vegetation masking the scar.

island escapes

Crossing the water to get away from it all

Solitude, romance, adventure, excitement—all these words and more come to mind when travelers think of island getaways. The National Park System encompasses hundreds of islands, some large and some tiny, and many beckon visitors to enjoy their charms for a few hours or an entire vacation.

☆ Isle Royale ☆
NATIONAL PARK
Lake Superior Island, Michigan

Wild and remote, yet not forbiddingly so in either category, Isle Royale offers a true North Woods experience to those who venture across Lake Superior's frigid waters to reach it. The largest island in the world's largest freshwater lake, Isle Royale provides commercial lodging, developed campgrounds, and unspoiled wilderness during its season of mid-April through October. (The park closes completely in winter.) Most people access the island via one of four ferries that leave from Minnesota or Michigan, though a few take a half-hour seaplane flight. Travelers can hike through mixed coniferous and hardwood forest, kayak along rocky shores, or camp beside gorgeous lakes, falling asleep to the howling of wolves and waking to the "laughter" of loons. Various boat services and ranger-guided trips give you the chance to explore Isle Royale in countless ways, from roughing it to (comparatively) leisurely tours. A day trip to Isle Royale is possible, but such a visit leaves only a few

hours to enjoy the park; plan for a sojourn of at least a few days. Good preparation is key to an enjoyable trip, as is a realistic knowledge of physical limitations and not trying to do too much, either on land or paddling.

☆ Cumberland Island ☆
NATIONAL SEASHORE
Atlantic Barrier Island, Georgia

Beautiful beaches and a wilderness area of wetlands and woodlands make this 18-mile-long Georgia barrier island a great choice for a relaxing getaway or an adventure trip. There's plenty for history buffs, too, beginning with American Indian shell mounds and continuing through European settlement, African-American slavery and post-emancipation communities, and a period when the island was a favored retreat of the wealthy Carnegie family (some of their mansions still stand on the island). Regular ferry service provides access to Cumberland Island from St. Marys, Georgia; private boats can also anchor near the island, and some hardy paddlers reach it by kayak. There's still private property on Cumberland,

and an inn providing accommodations, but extensive wilderness and sandy Atlantic beaches make this island special for those who bike its roads or hike its trails.

⭐ Channel Islands ⭐
NATIONAL PARK
Southern California Islands

Despite its location off the coast of heavily populated southern California, Channel Islands National Park receives relatively light visitation. Those people who do make the boat (or seaplane) trip across the Santa Barbara Channel can explore five major island groups that are home to globally significant biodiversity. These islands, in fact, are sometimes called the "Galápagos of North America." From ultrarare birds to blue whales, the world's largest animal, Channel Islands is a wildlife film come to life. All the islands are reachable for day-trippers (the closest, Anacapa, is a 90-minute boat trip from the mainland), and even a brief visit will bring sightings of seals, sea lions, sea otters, whales (more than two dozen species have been seen in the waters off the islands), and the largest colonies of seabirds in southern California.

A storm rages off the coast of Cumberland Island, a unique barrier island chock-full of natural and cultural heritage.

Developed campsites are found on all five islands, and backcountry camping is allowed on Santa Cruz and Santa Rosa. For a real adventure, sea kayakers can explore striking sea cliffs and Painted Cave, one of the world's largest and deepest sea caves. Found on Santa Cruz, the cave is nearly a quarter mile long.

There are many endangered species that rely on barrier islands such as Cumberland. They include wood storks, piping plovers, least terns, gopher tortoises, manatees and sea turtles.

⭐ Acadia ⭐
NATIONAL PARK
Isle au Haut, Atlantic Coast, Maine

Most of this beautiful national park is located on an island—Mount Desert Island, off the coast of central Maine—but make the extra effort to visit the park's Isle au Haut, a much smaller island (about 5,500 acres) 20 miles southwest of Mount Desert. Isle au Haut is reached by a mail boat from the little town of Stonington, a circumstance that limits the number of visitors. Much of the island can be seen on a day trip, exploring trails that wind through woodland and meadows and along rocky shores. More solitude is available by reserving a campsite at Duck Harbor. Sleeping on Isle au Haut makes it possible to enjoy sunrises and sunsets on the island, a lovely place that seems more remote than its location would indicate.

⭐ Cape Lookout ⭐
NATIONAL SEASHORE
Atlantic Barrier Islands, North Carolina

The Outer Banks of North Carolina are deservedly popular: a series of Atlantic Ocean barrier islands with expansive beaches, great fishing, historic beacons, and excellent wildlife-watching opportunities. Cape Lookout National Seashore, comprising three main islands—North Core Banks, South Core Banks, and Shackleford Banks—can be reached only by commercial ferries from four communities on the North Carolina mainland and has only minimal facilities. (Vehicles can be transported on some ferries.) As a result, the islands of Cape Lookout draw fewer visitors and offer more solitude than other Outer Banks islands. Other reasons to visit include seeing the 163-foot-high lighthouse, touring historic Portsmouth Village, admiring the wild horses, collecting seashells, camping in a primitive site far from other people, or simply enjoying the sun, sand, and salt breeze of a deserted beach.

⭐ Apostle Islands ⭐
NATIONAL LAKESHORE
Lake Superior Islands, Wisconsin

After getting information at the visitor center in the small town of Bayfield, in northern Wisconsin, catch a boat ride out to explore some of the 21 islands of this Lake Superior park. Eighteen of the islands allow camping, and six boast historic lighthouses. Eighty percent of Apostle Islands National Lakeshore is designated wilderness, which means unspoiled island environment. Sea kayaking is a popular way to travel around the islands (rentals are available from park concessionaires), but Lake Superior's notoriously changeable weather and rough water means paddling experience is strongly recommended. If interested in a true escape, consider this: Almost half the camping on the 21 islands takes place on just one of them, Stockton Island. Wilderness camping is available, and the park has established a camping zone system to assure solitude.

✳ Gulf Islands ✳
Gulf Coast Islands, Florida and Mississippi

This Gulf Coast park includes 12 separate units in both Florida and Mississippi, on the mainland and on islands. But true island lovers will be most interested in the four Mississippi islands where primitive camping is allowed: East Ship, Horn, Petit Bois, and part of Cat. With stunning white-sand beaches—originating as eroded quartz in the Appalachian Mountains and washed down to the Gulf of Mexico by rivers—these undeveloped islands offer beauty, nature, and solitude for visitors who have their own boats or who take charter boats for the 12-mile trip from the mainland. (Watch for bottlenose dolphins during the crossing.) Swimming, fishing, hiking, bird-watching, and beachcombing are all popular activities. Campers must bring their own food and water to the islands (plus extra supplies in case weather delays a return to the mainland), as well as the usual insect repellent, mosquito netting, sunblock, and first-aid gear. It's strictly a policy of "pack it in, pack it out" on these remote islands, but the wild and lonely place makes the planning and preparation worthwhile.

Boating is a way of life in the coastal waters surrounding Acadia National Park.

✯ Sleeping Bear Dunes ✯
NATIONAL LAKESHORE
North and South Manitou Islands,
Lake Michigan, Michigan

Most people visit this Michigan park, on Lake Michigan's eastern shore, to swim, play on the tall dunes, or visit historic sites on the mainland. Some, however, have discovered the park's two wild islands, North and South Manitou. The former, about 8 by 4 miles, is managed as wilderness open for backpacking, except for a 20-acre area around a small village. South Manitou, about 3 by 3 miles, is more developed, with camping allowed only in three official park campgrounds. Along with several historic buildings, South Manitou has a 104-foot-tall lighthouse, dating from 1871, that offers a panoramic view of Lake Michigan. Commercial ferries leave from the town of Leland to reach North and South Manitou Islands.

✯ Biscayne ✯
NATIONAL PARK
Elliott, Boca Chica, and Adams Keys, Florida

The watery wonderland of Biscayne National Park—95 percent of this Miami-area park is composed of Biscayne Bay and the Atlantic—has more to offer than just scuba diving, snorkeling, and boating. You can take a commercial tour boat to see Elliott Key, once home to a thriving maritime community and now a park site with camping, swimming, and a 7-mile hiking trail. Boca Chica Key, also reachable by tour boat, offers camping and a 65-foot-high ornamental lighthouse built by a businessman who once owned the island. When open, the lighthouse observation deck provides a great panorama of the bay and the city skylines beyond. Those with their own boats can tour Adams Key, once the site of an exclusive fishing club where several U.S. Presidents visited. The best way to explore Biscayne's islands is

☆ Wizard Island ☆

One of the most striking and fascinating islands in the National Park System is 320-acre Wizard Island, which rises 765 feet above the brilliant blue water of Oregon's Crater Lake. The lake itself was formed when water collected in a caldera, or collapsed volcanic summit. Wizard Island (named for a fancied resemblance to a sorcerer's hat) is a classic cinder cone, built of material ejected from the caldera floor after the main volcanic explosion. Seasonal boat tours take visitors to Wizard Island, where a 0.9-mile trail ascends to a small crater at the top.

via kayak or canoe, which can traverse shallow channels and lagoons to see wildlife such as sharks, rays, wading birds, and possibly a manatee or sea turtle.

✯ Theodore Roosevelt Island ✯
NATIONAL MEMORIAL
Potomac River Island, District of Columbia

What is an 88-acre island in a metropolitan area doing on a list of wilderness islands? In its own way, this District of Columbia park in the Potomac River is a treasured green getaway, a peaceful respite from city life for residents of the national capital. Acquired in 1932 to honor our greatest conservationist President, Theodore Roosevelt Island comprises 2.5 miles of hiking trails through woods that seem removed from civilization, as well as a statue of Roosevelt and stone monuments inscribed with some of his quotations. Had this park been accessible during his Presidency, there's no doubt that T.R. would have skipped out on Cabinet meetings now and then to enjoy nature here, just as he enjoyed roaming nearby Rock Creek Park to watch birds and partake in the "strenuous life" he always advocated.

ten best parks
underappreciated parks
Overlooked gems awaiting your discovery

Yellowstone and the Grand Canyon deserve the appreciation they receive, but the National Park System includes nearly 400 units, scores of lesser known sites that well reward a visit—and that are far less crowded than big-name parks. From vast wilderness to varied history, from swamp to desert, these places should be more famous.

⋆ Great Basin ⋆
NATIONAL PARK
Alpine Lakes, Gnarled Bristlecone Pines, a Glacier, and Lehman Caves

Feel the urge to climb a 13,000-foot mountain? Want to tour a beautiful cave? Eager to backpack to alpine lakes and through high desert where few others venture? Want to marvel at some of the oldest living things on Earth? All that and more awaits at this park in eastern Nevada, where glacier-sculpted, 13,063-foot Wheeler Peak rises like an outpost of the Rocky Mountains in the Great Basin. A beautifully scenic drive climbs to more than 10,000 feet on Wheeler's flank, providing fabulous views with minimal effort. At the road's end, an easy hike leads to groves of picturesquely contorted bristlecone pines, some more than 3,000 years old. Wheeler is also home to the southernmost glacier in the Northern Hemisphere (small, but geologically unique). After exploring the mountains, take a ranger-guided tour of Lehman Caves, where paths snake through marble and limestone passages featuring strange

helictites, delicate argonite crystals, and rare formations called cave shields. Travelers to Great Basin National Park can find these attractions in a place that sees only about 90,000 visitors a year.

⋆ Buffalo ⋆
NATIONAL RIVER
America's First National River: The Ozarks, Northwestern Arkansas

This beautiful northwestern Arkansas stream was designated America's first official national river in 1972, after years of controversy pitting those who wanted to protect its crystal-clear water, lush forests, and spectacular bluffs against those who wanted the river dammed to form a sprawling reservoir. People who canoe or raft the 135-mile Ozark river today— the spring white water on the upper parts or the gentle flat water of its lower reaches—give thanks that the conservationists won. Three official wilderness areas along its length add to the "wild" quality of the river. At places like Steel Creek, sheer sandstone cliffs rise 400 feet from the water's edge, and

The setting sun paints the wide-open skies above the Kelso Dunes at Mojave National Preserve with vivid colors.

all along the river are gravel bars for primitive camping, swimming holes for cooling off on a summer day, and rewarding hiking trails. There's even a ghost town on the lower river: Rush, where zinc was once mined. All in all, Buffalo National River preserves some of the finest scenery in the central United States, as well as one of the country's best float streams.

> At about 600 feet in height, Kelso Dunes in Mojave National Preserve are the third tallest in North America. When quantities of the sands move, they sometimes create a booming sound.

⭐ Big Cypress ⭐
NATIONAL PRESERVE
Wetlands and Swamps

There aren't very many big cypress trees in this southern Florida park; rather, it's named for the expansive size of the forests in Big Cypress Swamp, covering hundreds of thousands of acres. The park offers many of the attractions of Everglades National Park, just to the south, with only a small fraction of the visitation. Driving either of Big Cypress's two scenic roads will bring into view alligators and abundant birdlife, including such striking species as wood stork, anhinga, white ibis, purple gallinule, and snowy egret. The Turner River, Upper Wagonwheel, and Birdon Road Loop Drive passes for miles alongside canals built for drainage long ago, now creating a virtual roadside zoo of wildlife.

⭐ Colorado ⭐
NATIONAL MONUMENT
Southwest Red-rock Country

The red-rock country of the Southwest is justifiably famous for its spectacular canyons, buttes, spires, and other sandstone formations. Colorado National Monument offers a splendid array of eroded cliffs and pinnacles in an accessible and easily toured location, without the crowds and long-distance drives associated with more famous sites in the region. Much of the park can be seen on the 23-mile Rim Rock Drive, which can be reached just a few minutes off I-70 near Grand Junction, Colorado. Trails here range from the short, easy Window Rock Trail to more strenuous hikes such as the route into Monument Canyon, which passes major rock sculptures including Independence Monument (a 450-foot-high sandstone monolith), Kissing Couple, and the Coke Ovens.

⭐ Wrangell–St. Elias ⭐
NATIONAL PARK & PRESERVE
Glaciers and Boreal Forests

Although Alaska's Denali National Park and Preserve draws more visitors, the state's Wrangell–St. Elias deserves recognition as well. It is the largest national park in the United States and site of 9 of the 16 highest mountains in the country. Many outfitters and concessionaires offer adventure tours into the park, from river rafting to sea kayaking to scenic flights to guided glacier hikes. There's another option, too: Travelers can (with care and depending on weather) explore the park on two mostly unpaved roads, which provide access to trailheads, campsites, and historic sites. The McCarthy Road runs 61 miles through boreal forest to the tiny community of McCarthy, following an old railroad right-of-way and crossing rivers on high trestles. Nearby are the remains of a once-thriving copper mine, now a national historic landmark. The 42-mile Nabesna Road passes through spectacular mountain landscape and offers the chance to see Dall sheep, among other wildlife. Lucky visitors might come across caribou, moose, grizzly (brown) and black bears, mountain goats, gray wolves, coyotes, red foxes, wolverines, and porcupines. Both these drives are challenging and require planning and preparation, but offer thrilling experiences as a reward.

☆ Wind Cave ☆
NATIONAL PARK
Cave and Grasslands

The film shown in the visitor center at this South Dakota park is entitled "Wind Cave: One Park, Two Worlds"—an apt slogan. Not only does the park feature Wind Cave, with passages full of unusual and beautiful formations, the 44-square-mile landscape above ground is home to a diverse array of wildlife. In 1903, this site became the first park in the world created to protect a cave, noted primarily for its outstanding display of boxwork, an unusual formation of thin calcite fins resembling honeycombs. Eventually Wind Cave came to be recognized as the world's fourth largest cave. Various ranger-guided tours are offered, including one suitable for people

☆ Least Visited National Parks ☆

If "underappreciated" equaled "least visited," several remote parks in Alaska, most of them accessible only by airplane or boat, would be atop the list. In 2009, Aniakchak National Monument and Preserve had only 14 recorded visitors. Even a well-known site such as Katmai National Park and Preserve had only 43,035, or less than half the visits Great Smoky Mountains National Park gets in one day in July. The most visited National Park Service unit? The Blue Ridge Parkway, with more than 16 million annual visits.

with physical limitations. Before or after a cave tour, driving or hiking in the park can bring sightings of bison, elk, pronghorn, mule deer, coyotes, and prairie dogs. The park's approximately 450 bison move around as they graze; it's easier to see the appealing little prairie dogs, whose colonies are easily visible near roads.

☆ Mojave ☆
NATIONAL PRESERVE
Desert Landscape

This expansive southern California park doesn't show up often on travelers' radar screens, and that's a shame—at least in one way. For those who love Mojave National Preserve, its very remoteness, unpeopled landscapes, and opportunities for solitude are among its best features. Adventurous travelers can explore tall sand dunes, volcanic cinder cones, the world's largest forest of Joshua trees, and the remnants of a history of mining, ranching, and military activity. The preserve encompasses three of the four major North American deserts—Mojave, Great Basin, and Sonoran—and spans an elevation range from 7,929 feet atop Clark Mountain to 880 feet in the desert. All this adds up to a great biological diversity including, after wet winters, colorful displays of desert wildflowers.

☆ Jean Lafitte ☆
NATIONAL HISTORICAL PARK & PRESERVE
Southern Louisiana History:
Cajun Cooking, Music, and History

Sometimes people ask why this multifaceted park is named for Jean Lafitte, a notorious 19th-century pirate and smuggler who traded in slaves and lived mostly outside the law. The answer . . . well, it's complicated, just like the cultural landscape of southern Louisiana. Even today, this melting pot reflects the influence of pre-Columbus America, France, Spain, England, Africa, the Canary Islands, Germany, the Caribbean, the Confederate States, and many other places. You can learn a lot about local history at any or all of the six separate sites in this park, which spread across southern Louisiana from the swamps of the Mississippi River Delta to the prairies farther west. One can take a history walk in the French Quarter of New Orleans, see abundant wildlife in a nature preserve, attend a live radio broadcast of Cajun music in an old-time theater, visit the site of the famed 1815 Battle of New Orleans, watch a Cajun-cooking demonstration, and enjoy many other activities—too many to be summarized here. In few places in American do unique traditions endure as they do along the bayous and marshes of southern Louisiana.

PLEASE

Keep The Park Clean

✴ Chaco Culture ✴
NATIONAL HISTORICAL PARK
Ceremonial, Trade, and Administrative Center of the Ancient Pueblo People

Other Native American sites in the Southwest are more famous—including Mesa Verde in Colorado and Canyon de Chelly in Arizona—but none was more important in its day than the communities that developed in Chaco Canyon, in what is now northwestern New Mexico. Only this park's remoteness and distance from major highways have kept it from greater renown as a historical destination. From around A.D. 850 to 1250, Chaco Canyon was a major ceremonial, trade, and administrative center for the culture called the ancient Pueblo, with elaborate and spectacular public architecture that matched its highly developed social organization. For reasons unknown, the center's inhabitants abandoned the site in the mid-13th century. In recognition of its importance, Chaco Culture National Historical Park and associated locations (including Aztec Ruins National Monument, 60 miles north) have been designated a World Heritage site. The park's 9-mile Canyon Loop Drive accesses six major archaeological sites, including "great houses": very large multistory public buildings with adjacent kivas, or ceremonial rooms. Truly awe-inspiring in both its appearance and historical significance, Chaco Culture is well worth the journey to see it.

✴ Sunset Crater Volcano ✴
NATIONAL MONUMENT
Six Million Years of Volcanic Activity

Too few of the millions of people who visit Arizona's Grand Canyon each year detour to this fascinating park just northeast of Flagstaff. Set in a landscape full of dozens of symmetrical cones and other evidence of six million years of volcanic activity, Sunset Crater is a classic example of a cinder cone, named for the reddish oxidized material at its top. Many volcanic features can be seen along trails, including lava "squeeze-ups," spatter cones, and lava bubbles. No climbing is allowed on Sunset Crater Volcano, so symmetrical that it looks like every child's drawing of a volcano. To see what the terrain is like, though, you can climb to the top of nearby Lenox Crater.

park contacts

National Park Service
1849 C St., NW
Washington, DC 20240-0001
email: asknps@nps.gov
www.nps.gov

A

Abraham Lincoln Birthplace
National Historic Site
2995 Lincoln Farm Road
Hodgenville, KY 42748-9707
270-358-3137
www.nps.gov/abli/

Acadia
National Park
PO Box 177
Bar Harbor, ME 04609-0177
207-288-3338
www.nps.gov/acad/

Adams
National Historical Park
135 Adams Street
Quincy, MA 02169-1749
617-773-1177
www.nps.gov/adam/

African Burial Ground
National Monument
290 Broadway, First Floor
New York, NY 10007-1823
212-637-2019
www.nps.gov/afbg

Agate Fossil Beds
National Monument
301 River Road
PO Box 27
Harrison, NE 69346-2734
308-668-2211
www.nps.gov/agfo/

Alagnak Wild River
Katmai National Park & Preserve
PO Box 7
King Salmon, AK 99613-0007
907-246-3305
www.nps.gov/alag/

Alibates Flint Quarries
National Monument
c/o Lake Meredith National
Recreation Area
PO Box 1460
Fritch, TX 79036-1460
806-857-3151
www.nps.gov/alfl/

Allegheny Portage Railroad
National Historic Site
110 Federal Park Road
Gallitzen, PA 16641-2000
814-886-6100
www.nps.gov/alpo/

American Samoa
National Park of American Samoa
Pago Pago
American Samoa 96799-0001
684-633-7082
www.nps.gov/npsa/

Amistad
National Recreation Area
HCR-3, Box 5-J
Del Rio, TX 78840-9350
830-775-7491
www.nps.gov/amis/

Andersonville
National Historic Site
496 Cemetery Road
Andersonville, GA 31711-9707
229-924-0343
www.nps.gov/ande/

Andrew Johnson
National Historic Site
12 Monument Avenue
Greeneville, TN 37744-1088
423-639-3711
www.nps.gov/anjo/

Aniakchak
National Monument & Preserve
PO Box 7
King Salmon, AK 99613-0007
907-246-3305
www.nps.gov/ania/

Antietam
National Battlefield
PO Box 158
Sharpsburg, MD 21782-0158
301-432-5124
www.nps.gov/anti/

Apostle Islands
National Lakeshore
415 Washington Avenue
Bayfield, WI 54814-4809
715-779-3397
www.nps.gov/apis/

Appalachian
National Scenic Trail
Appalachian Trail Conservancy
PO Box 807
Harpers Ferry, WV 25425-0807
304-535-6331
www.nps.gov/appa/

Appomattox Court House
National Historical Park
PO Box 218
Appomattox, VA 24522-0218
434-352-8987
www.nps.gov/apco/

Arches
National Park
PO Box 907
Moab, UT 84532-0907
435-719-2100
www.nps.gov/arch/

Arkansas Post
National Memorial
1741 Old Post Road
Gillett, AR 72055-9707
870-548-2207
www.nps.gov/arpo/

Arlington House,
The Robert E. Lee Memorial
c/o George Washington
Memorial Parkway
Turkey Run Park
McLean, VA 22101-0001
703-235-1530
www.nps.gov/arho/

Assateague Island
National Seashore
7206 National Seashore Lane
Berlin, MD 21811-2540
410-641-1441
www.nps.gov/asis/

Aztec Ruins
National Monument
84 County Road 2900
Aztec, NM 87410-9715
505-334-6174
www.nps.gov/azru/

B
Badlands
National Park
PO Box 6
Interior, SD 57750-0006
605-433-5361
www.nps.gov/badl/

Bandelier
National Monument
HCR 1, Box 1, Suite 15
Los Alamos, NM 87544-9701
505-672-3861
www.nps.gov/band/

Bent's Old Fort
National Historic Site
35110 Highway 194 East
La Junta, CO 81050-9523
719-383-5010
www.nps.gov/beol/

Bering Land Bridge
National Preserve
PO Box 220
Nome, AK 99762-0220
907-443-2522
www.nps.gov/bela/

Big Bend
National Park
PO Box 129
Big Bend National Park, TX
   79834-0129
432-477-2251
www.nps.gov/bibe/

Big Cypress
National Preserve
HCR 61, Box 110
Ochopee, FL 34141
239-695-2000
www.nps.gov/bicy/

Big Hole
National Battlefield
PO Box 273
Wisdom, MT 59761-0723
406-689-3155
www.nps.gov/biho/

Big South Fork
National River & Recreation Area
4564 Leatherwood Road
Oneida, TN 37841-9544
423-569-9778
www.nps.gov/biso/

Big Thicket
National Preserve
3785 Milam Street
Beaumont, TX 77701-4724
409-839-2689
www.nps.gov/bith/

Bighorn Canyon
National Recreation Area
PO Box 7458
Fort Smith, MT 59035-7458
406-666-2412
www.nps.gov/bica/

Biscayne
National Park
9700 SW 328 Street
Homestead, FL 33033-5634
305-230-7275
www.nps.gov/bisc/

Black Canyon of the Gunnison
National Park
102 Elk Creek
Gunnison, CO 81230-9304
970-641-2337
www.nps.gov/blca/

Blue Ridge
Parkway
199 Hemphill Knob Road
Asheville, NC 28803-8686
828-271-4779
www.nps.gov/blri/

Bluestone
National Scenic River
c/o New River Gorge National River
PO Box 246
Glen Jean, WV 25846-0246
304-465-0508
www.nps.gov/blue/

Booker T. Washington
National Monument
12130 B.T. Washington Hwy.
Hardy, VA 24101-9688
540-721-2094
www.nps.gov/bowa/

Boston African American
National Historic Site
46 Joy Street
Boston, MA 02114-4025
617-742-5415
www.nps.gov/boaf/

Boston Harbor Islands
National Recreation Area
408 Atlantic Avenue, Ste. 228
Boston, MA 02110-3349
617-223-8666
www.nps.gov/boha/

Boston National Historical Park
Charlestown Navy Yard
Visitor Center
Boston, MA 02129-4543
617-242-5601
www.nps.gov/bost/

Brices Cross Roads
National Battlefield Site
c/o Natchez Trace Parkway
2680 Natchez Trace Parkway
Tupelo, MS 38804-9718
662-680-4025
www.nps.gov/brcr/

Brown v. Board of Education
National Historic Site
1515 SE Monroe Street
Topeka, KS 66612-1143
785-354-4273
www.nps.gov/brvb/

Bryce Canyon National Park
PO Box 170001
Bryce Canyon, UT 84717-0001
435-834-5322
www.nps.gov/brca/

Buck Island Reef
National Monument
Danish Customs House
Kings Wharf
2100 Church Street, #100
Christiansted, VI 00820-4611
340-773-1460
www.nps.gov/buis/

Buffalo National River
402 North Walnut
Suite 136
Harrison, AR 72601-1173
870-365-2700
www.nps.gov/buff/

C

Cabrillo
National Monument
1800 Cabrillo Memorial Drive
San Diego, CA 92106-3601
619-557-5450
www.nps.gov/cabr/

Canaveral National Seashore
308 Julia Street
Titusville, FL 32796-3521
321-267-1110
www.nps.gov/cana/

Cane River Creole
National Historical Park
400 Rapides Drive
Natchitoches, LA 71457-3100
318-352-0383
www.nps.gov/cari/

Canyon de Chelly
National Monument
PO Box 588
Chinle, AZ 86503-0588
928-674-5500
www.nps.gov/cach/

Canyonlands
National Park
2282 S. West Resource Blvd.
Moab, UT 84532-3406
435-719-2100
www.nps.gov/cany/

Cape Cod
National Seashore
99 Marconi Site Road
Wellfleet, MA 02667-0250
508-771-2144
www.nps.gov/caco/

Cape Hatteras
National Seashore
1401 National Park Drive
Manteo, NC 27954-2708
252-473-2111
www.nps.gov/caha/

Cape Krusenstern
National Monument
PO Box 1029
Kotzebue, AK 99752-0029
907-442-3890
www.nps.gov/cakr/

Cape Lookout
National Seashore
131 Charles Street
Harkers Island, NC 28531-9702
252-728-2250
www.nps.gov/calo/

Capital Parks
National Capital Region
1100 Ohio Drive, SW
Washington, DC 20242-0001
202-485-9880
www.nps.gov/ncro/

Capitol Reef
National Park
HC 70, Box 15
Torrey, UT 84775-9602
435-425-3791
www.nps.gov/care/

Capulin Volcano
National Monument
PO Box 40
Capulin, NM 88414-0040
505-278-2201
www.nps.gov/cavo/

Carl Sandburg Home
National Historic Site
1928 Little River Road
Flat Rock, NC 28731-9766
828-693-4178
www.nps.gov/carl/

Carlsbad Caverns
National Park
3225 National Parks Highway
Carlsbad, NM 88220-5354
505-785-2232
www.nps.gov/cave/

Carter G. Woodson Home
National Historic Site
c/o Mary McLeod Bethune Council
   House NHS
1318 Vermont Avenue, NW
Washington, DC 20005-3607
202-673-2402
www.nps.gov/cawo/

Casa Grande Ruins
National Monument
1100 Ruins Drive
Coolidge, AZ 85228-3200
520-723-3172
www.nps.gov/cagr/

Castillo de San Marcos
National Monument
1 Castillo Drive South
St. Augustine, FL 32084-3699
904-829-6506
www.nps.gov/casa/

Castle Clinton
National Monument
c/o Federal Hall National Memorial
26 Wall Street
New York, NY 10005-1907
212-344-7220
www.nps.gov/cacl/

Catoctin
Mountain Park
6602 Foxville Road
Thurmont, MD 21788-0158
301-663-9388
www.nps.gov/cato/

Cedar Breaks
National Monument
2390 W. Highway 56 #11
Cedar City, UT 84720-4151
435-586-9451
www.nps.gov/cebr/

Cedar Creek & Belle Grove
National Historical Park
77181/2 Main Street
PO Box 700
Middletown, VA 22645-9500
540-868-9176
www.nps.gov/cebe/

Chaco Culture
National Historical Park
PO Box 220
Nageezi, NM 87037-0220
505-786-7014
www.nps.gov/chcu/

Chamizal
National Memorial
800 S. San Marcial Street
El Paso, TX 79905-4123
915-532-7273
www.nps.gov/cham/

Channel Islands
National Park
1901 Spinnaker Drive
Ventura, CA 93001-4354
805-658-5730
www.nps.gov/chis/

Charles Pinckney
National Historic Site
c/o Fort Sumter National Monument
1214 Middle Street
Sullivans Island, SC 29482-9748
843-881-5516
www.nps.gov/chpi/

Chattahoochee River
National Recreation Area
1978 Island Ford Parkway
Atlanta, GA 30350-3400
770-399-8070
www.nps.gov/chat/

Chesapeake & Ohio Canal
National Historical Park
1850 Dual Highway, Ste. 100
Hagerstown, MD 21740-6622
301-714-2201
www.nps.gov/choh/

Chickamauga & Chattanooga
National Military Park
PO Box 2128
Fort Oglethorpe, GA 30742-0128
706-866-9241
www.nps.gov/chch/

Chickasaw
National Recreation Area
1008 West Second Street
Sulphur, OK 73086-0201
580-622-3161
www.nps.gov/chic/

Chimney Rock
National Historic Site
PO Box F
Bayard, NE 69334-0680
308-586-2581
www.nps.gov/chro/

Chiricahua
National Monument
12856 E. Rhyolite Creek Rd.
Willcox, AZ 85643-9737
520-824-3560
www.nps.gov/chir/

Christiansted
National Historic Site
Danish Customs House
Kings Wharf
2100 Church Street, #100
Christiansted, VI 00820-4611
340-773-1460
www.nps.gov/chri/

City of Rocks
National Reserve
PO Box 169
Almo, ID 83312-0169
208-824-5519
www.nps.gov/ciro/

Clara Barton
National Historic Site
5801 Oxford Road
Glen Echo, MD 20812-1201
301-320-1410
www.nps.gov/clba/

USA 25
North Dakota 1889

Colonial
National Historical Park
PO Box 210
Yorktown, VA 23690-0210
757-898-3400
www.nps.gov/colo/

Colorado
National Monument
Fruita, CO 81521-0001
970-858-3617
www.nps.gov/colm/

Congaree
National Park
100 National Park Road
Hopkins, SC 29061-9118
803-776-4396
www.nps.gov/cong/

Constitution Gardens
c/o National Mall & Memorial Parks
900 Ohio Drive, SW
Washington, DC 20242-0004
202-426-6841
www.nps.gov/coga/

Coronado
National Memorial
4101 East Montezuma
  Canyon Road
Hereford, AZ 85615-9376
520-366-5515
www.nps.gov/coro/

Cowpens
National Battlefield
PO Box 308
Chesnee, SC 29323-0308
864-461-2828
www.nps.gov/cowp/

Crater Lake
National Park
PO Box 7
Crater Lake, OR 97604-0007
541-594-2211
www.nps.gov/crla/

Craters of the Moon
National Monument & Preserve
PO Box 29
Arco, ID 83213-0029
208-527-3257
www.nps.gov/crmo/

Cumberland Gap
National Historical Park
PO Box 1848
Middlesboro, KY 40965-3848
606-248-2817
www.nps.gov/cuga/

Cumberland Island
National Seashore
PO Box 806
St. Marys, GA 31558-0806
912-882-4335
www.nps.gov/cuis/

Curecanti
National Recreation Area
102 Elk Creek
Gunnison, CO 81230-9304
970-641-2337
www.nps.gov/cure/

Cuyahoga Valley
National Park
15610 Vaughn Road
Brecksville, OH 44141-3018
216-524-1497
www.nps.gov/cuva/

D

Dayton Aviation Heritage
National Historical Park
PO Box 9280
Wright Brothers Station
Dayton, OH 45409-9280
937-225-7705
www.nps.gov/daav/

De Soto
National Memorial
PO Box 15390
Bradenton, FL 34280-5390
941-792-0458
www.nps.gov/deso/

Death Valley
National Park
PO Box 579
Death Valley, CA 92328-0579
760-786-3200
www.nps.gov/deva/

Delaware Water Gap
National Recreation Area
Bushkill, PA 18324-9410
570-588-2451
www.nps.gov/dewa/

Denali
National Park & Preserve
PO Box 9
McKinley Park, AK 99755-0009
907-683-2294
www.nps.gov/dena/

Devils Postpile
National Monument
PO Box 3999
Mammoth Lakes, CA 93546-3999
760-934-2289
www.nps.gov/depo/

Devils Tower
National Monument
PO Box 10
Devils Tower, WY 82714-0010
307-467-5283
www.nps.gov/deto/

Dinosaur
National Monument
4545 E. Highway 40
Dinosaur, CO 81610-9724
970-374-3000
www.nps.gov/dino/

Dry Tortugas
National Park
c/o Everglades National Park
40001 State Road 9336
Homestead, FL 33034-6733
305-242-7700
www.nps.gov/drto/

E

Ebey's Landing
National Historical Reserve
PO Box 774
Coupeville, WA 98239-0774
360-678-6084
www.nps.gov/ebla/

Edgar Allan Poe
National Historic Site
532 North Seventh Street
Philadelphia, PA 19123-3502
215-597-7130
www.nps.gov/edal/

Effigy Mounds
National Monument
151 Highway 76
Harpers Ferry, IA 52146-7519
563-873-3491
www.nps.gov/efmo/

Eisenhower
National Historic Site
1195 Baltimore Pike, Suite 100
Gettysburg, PA 17325-7034
717-338-9114
www.nps.gov/eise/

El Malpais
National Monument
123 East Roosevelt Avenue
Grants, NM 87020-2017
505-285-4641
www.nps.gov/elma/

El Morro
National Monument
Route 2, Box 43
Ramah, NM 87321-9603
505-783-4226
www.nps.gov/elmo/

Eleanor Roosevelt
National Historic Site
4097 Albany Post Road
Hyde Park, NY 12538-1997
845-229-9115
www.nps.gov/elro/

Eugene O'Neill
National Historic Site
PO Box 280
Danville, CA 94526-0280
925-838-0249
www.nps.gov/euon/

Everglades
National Park
40001 State Road 9336
Homestead, FL 33034-6733
305-242-7700
www.nps.gov/ever/

F

Federal Hall
National Memorial
26 Wall Street
New York, NY 10005-1907
212-825-6888
www.nps.gov/feha/

Fire Island National Seashore
120 Laurel Street
Patchogue, NY 11772-3596
516-289-4810
www.nps.gov/fiis/

First Ladies
National Historic Site
331 S. Market Avenue
Canton, OH 44702-2107
330-452-0876
www.nps.gov/fila/

Flight 93
National Memorial
109 West Main Street, Ste. 104
Somerset, PA 15501-2066
814-443-4557
www.nps.gov/flni/index.htm

Florissant Fossil Beds
National Monument
PO Box 185
Florissant, CO 80816-0185
719-748-3253
www.nps.gov/flfo/

Ford's Theatre
National Historic Site
c/o National Mall & Memorial Parks
900 Ohio Drive, SW
Washington, DC 20242-0004
202-426-6924
www.nps.gov/foth/

Fort Bowie
National Historic Site
3327 S. Old Fort Bowie Road
Bowie, AZ 85605-0158
520-847-2500
www.nps.gov/fobo/

Fort Caroline
National Memorial
12713 Fort Caroline Road
Jacksonville, FL 32225-1240
904-641-7155
www.nps.gov/timu/

Fort Davis
National Historic Site
PO Box 1379
101 Lt. Henry Flipper Drive
Fort Davis, TX 79734-1456
432-426-3225
www.nps.gov/foda/

Fort Donelson
National Battlefield
PO Box 434
Dover, TN 37058-0434
931-232-5706
www.nps.gov/fodo/

Fort Frederica
National Monument
Route 9, Box 286-C
St. Simons Island, GA
  31522-9710
912-638-3639
www.nps.gov/fofr/

Fort Laramie
National Historic Site
965 Gray Rocks Road
Fort Laramie, WY 82212-0086
307-837-2221
www.nps.gov/fola/

Fort Larned
National Historic Site
1767 KS Highway 156
Larned, KS 67550-9321
620-285-6911
www.nps.gov/fols/

Fort Matanzas
National Monument
c/o Castillo de San Marcos
National Monument
1 Castillo Drive South
St. Augustine, FL 32084-3699
904-471-0116
www.nps.gov/foma/

Fort McHenry
National Monument &
Historic Shrine
End of East Fort Avenue
Baltimore, MD 21230-5393
410-962-4290
www.nps.gov/fomc/

Fort Necessity
National Battlefield
One Washington Parkway
Farmington, PA 15437-9514
724-329-5512
www.nps.gov/fone/

Fort Point
National Historic Site
Fort Mason, Building 201
San Francisco, CA 94123-1304
415-556-1693
www.nps.gov/fopo/

Fort Pulaski
National Monument
PO Box 30757
Savannah, GA 31410-0757
912-786-5787
www.nps.gov/fopu/

Fort Raleigh
National Historic Site
c/o Cape Hatteras National Seashore
1401 National Park Drive
Manteo, NC 27954-2708
252-473-5772
www.nps.gov/fora/

Fort Scott
National Historic Site
PO Box 918
Old Fort Boulevard
Fort Scott, KS 66701-0918
620-223-0310
www.nps.gov/fosc/

Fort Smith
National Historic Site
PO Box 1406
Fort Smith, AR 72902-1406
479-783-3961
www.nps.gov/fosm/

Fort Stanwix
National Monument
112 E. Park Street
Rome, NY 13440-5816
315-338-7730
www.nps.gov/fost/

Fort Sumter
National Monument
1214 Middle Street
Sullivans Island, SC 29482-9748
843-883-3123
www.nps.gov/fosu/

Fort Union
National Monument
PO Box 127
Watrous, NM 87753-0127
505-425-8025
www.nps.gov/foun/

Fort Union Trading Post
National Historic Site
15550 Highway 1804
Williston, ND 58801-8680
701-572-9083
www.nps.gov/fous/

Fort Vancouver
National Historic Site
612 E. Reserve Street
Vancouver, WA 98661-3811
360-816-6230
www.nps.gov/fova/

Fort Washington Park
National Capital Parks, East
1900 Anacostia Drive, SE
Washington, DC 20020-6722
301-763-4600
www.nps.gov/fowa/

Fossil Butte
National Monument
PO Box 592
Kemmerer, WY 83101-0592
307-877-4455
www.nps.gov/fobu/

Franklin Delano Roosevelt
Memorial
c/o National Mall &
    Memorial Parks
900 Ohio Drive, SW
Washington, DC 20242-0004
202-426-6841
www.nps.gov/fdrm/

Frederick Douglass
National Historic Site
1411 W Street, SE
Washington, DC 20020-4813
202-426-5961
www.nps.gov/frdo/

Frederick Law Olmsted
National Historic Site
99 Warren Street
Brookline, MA 02445-5930
617-566-1689
www.nps.gov/frla/

Fredericksburg & Spotsylvania
County Battlefields Memorial
National Military Park
120 Chatham Lane
Fredericksburg, VA 22405-2508
540-373-6122 or 540-786-2880
www.nps.gov/frsp/

Friendship Hill
National Historic Site
c/o Fort Necessity National Battlefield
One Washington Parkway
Farmington, PA 15437-9514
724-329-5512
www.nps.gov/frhi/

G
Gates of the Arctic
National Park & Preserve
201 First Avenue, Doyon Building
Fairbanks, AK 99701-4848
907-457-5752
www.nps.gov/gaar/

Gateway
National Recreation Area
Public Affairs Office
210 New York Avenue
Staten Island, NY 10305-5019
718-354-4606
www.nps.gov/gate/

Gauley River
National Recreation Area
c/o New River Gorge National River
PO Box 246
Glen Jean, WV 25846-0246
304-465-0508
www.nps.gov/gari/

General Grant
National Memorial
122nd Street & Riverside Drive
New York, NY 10027-3703
212-666-1640
www.nps.gov/gegr/

George Rogers Clark
National Historical Park
401 S. Second Street
Vincennes, IN 47591-1001
812-882-1776
www.nps.gov/gero/

George Washington Carver
National Monument
5646 Carver Road
Diamond, MO 64840-8314
417-325-4151
www.nps.gov/gwca/

George Washington
Memorial Parkway
Turkey Run Park
McLean, VA 22101-0001
703-289-2500
www.nps.gov/gwmp/

George Washington Birthplace
National Monument
1732 Popes Creek Road
Washington's Birthplace, VA
  22443-9688
804-224-1732
www.nps.gov/gewa/

Gettysburg
National Military Park
1195 Baltimore Pike, Suite 100
Gettysburg, PA 17325-1080
717-334-1124
www.nps.gov/gett/

Gila Cliff Dwellings
National Monument
HC 68, Box 100
Silver City, NM 88061-9352
575-536-9461
www.nps.gov/gicl/

Glacier
National Park
PO Box 128
West Glacier, MT 59936-0128
406-888-7800
www.nps.gov/glac/

Glacier Bay
National Park & Preserve
PO Box 140
Gustavus, AK 99826-0140
907-697-2232
www.nps.gov/glba/

Glen Canyon
National Recreation Area
PO Box 1507
Page, AZ 86040-1507
928-608-6200
www.nps.gov/glca/

Golden Gate
National Recreation Area
Fort Mason, Building 201
San Francisco, CA 94123-1304
415-561-4700
www.nps.gov/goga/

Golden Spike
National Historic Site
PO Box 897
Brigham City, UT 84302-0897
435-471-2209
www.nps.gov/gosp/

Governors Island
National Monument
Battery Maritime Building, Slip 7
10 South Street
New York, NY 10004-1900
212-825-3045
www.nps.gov/gois/

Grand Canyon
National Park
PO Box 129
Grand Canyon, AZ 86023-0129
928-638-7888
www.nps.gov/grca/

Grand Portage
National Monument
PO Box 426
170 Mile Creek Road
Portage, MN 55605-0426
218-475-0123
www.nps.gov/grpo/

Grand Teton
National Park
P.O. Drawer 170
Moose, WY 83012-0170
307-739-3300
www.nps.gov/grte/

Grant-Kohrs Ranch
National Historic Site
266 Warren Lane
Deer Lodge, MT 59722-0790
406-846-2070
www.nps.gov/grko/

Great Basin
National Park
100 Great Basin National Park
Baker, NV 89311-9700
775-234-7331
www.nps.gov/grba/

Great Egg Harbor
National Scenic & Recreational River
c/o National Park Service,
Northeast Region
200 Chestnut Street
Philadelphia, PA 19106-2818
215-597-1581
www.nps.gov/greg/

Great Sand Dunes
National Park & Preserve
11500 Highway 150
Mosca, CO 81146-9798
719-378-6300
www.nps.gov/grsa/

Great Smoky Mountains
National Park
107 Park Headquarters Road
Gatlinburg, TN 37738-4102
865-436-1200
www.nps.gov/grsm/

Greenbelt Park
6565 Greenbelt Road
Greenbelt, MD 20770-3207
301-344-3948
www.nps.gov/gree/

Guadalupe Mountains
National Park
HC 60, Box 400
Salt Flat, TX 79847-9400
915-828-3251
www.nps.gov/gumo/

Guilford Courthouse
National Military Park
2331 New Garden Road
Greensboro, NC 27410-2355
336-288-1776
www.nps.gov/guco/

Gulf Islands
National Seashore
1801 Gulf Breeze Parkway
Gulf Breeze, FL 32561-5000
850-934-2600
www.nps.gov/guis/

Gulf Islands
National Seashore
3500 Park Road
Ocean Springs, MS 39564-9709
228-875-9057
www.nps.gov/guis/

H
Hagerman Fossil Beds
National Monument
221 North State Street
PO Box 570
Hagerman, ID 83332-0570
208-837-4793
www.nps.gov/hafo/

Haleakalā
National Park
PO Box 369
Makawao, Maui, HI 96768-0369
808-572-4400
www.nps.gov/hale/

Hamilton Grange
National Memorial
414 West 141st Street
New York, NY 10031
212-666-1640
www.nps.gov/hagr/

Hampton
National Historic Site
535 Hampton Lane
Towson, MD 21286-1397
410-823-1309
www.nps.gov/hamp/

Harpers Ferry
National Historical Park
PO Box 65
Harpers Ferry, WV 25425-0065
304-535-6029
www.nps.gov/hafe/

Harry S Truman
National Historic Site
223 North Main Street
Independence, MO 64050-2804
816-254-9929
www.nps.gov/hstr/

Hawaii Volcanoes
National Park
PO Box 52
Hawaii National Park, HI 96718-0052
808-985-6000
www.nps.gov/havo/

Herbert Hoover
National Historic Site
110 Parkside Drive
West Branch, IA 52358-0607
319-643-2541
www.nps.gov/heho/

Hohokam Pima
National Monument
c/o Casa Grande Ruins
National Monument
1100 Ruins Drive
Coolidge, AZ 85228-3200
520-723-3172
www.nps.gov/pima/

Home of Franklin D. Roosevelt
National Historic Site
4097 Albany Post Road
Hyde Park, NY 12538-1997
845-229-9115
www.nps.gov/hofr/

Homestead
National Monument of America
8523 West State Highway 4
Beatrice, NE 68310-6743
402-223-3514
www.nps.gov/home/

Hopewell Culture
National Historical Park
16062 State Route 104
Chillicothe, OH 45601-8694
740-774-1126
www.nps.gov/hocu/

Hopewell Furnace
National Historic Site
2 Mark Bird Lane
Elverson, PA 19520-9505
610-582-8773
www.nps.gov/hofu/

Horseshoe Bend
National Military Park
11288 Horseshoe Bend Road
Daviston, AL 36256-6524
256-234-7111
www.nps.gov/hobe/

Hot Springs
National Park
101 Reserve Street
Hot Springs, AR 71901-4195
501-623-2824
www.nps.gov/hosp/

Hovenweep
National Monument
McElmo Route
Cortez, CO 81321-8901
970-562-4282
www.nps.gov/hove/

Hubbell Trading Post
National Historic Site
PO Box 150
Ganado, AZ 86505-0150
928-755-3475
www.nps.gov/hutr/

I
Independence
National Historical Park
143 S. Third Street
Philadelphia, PA 19106-2778
215-597-8787
www.nps.gov/inde/

Indiana Dunes
National Lakeshore
1100 N. Mineral Springs Rd.
Porter, IN 46304-1299
219-395-8585
www.nps.gov/indu/

Isle Royale National Park
800 East Lakeshore Drive
Houghton, MI 49931-1895
906-482-0984
www.nps.gov/isro/

J
James A. Garfield
National Historic Site
8095 Mentor Avenue
Mentor, OH 44060-5753
440-255-8722
www.nps.gov/jaga/

Jean Lafitte
National Historical Park & Preserve
419 Decatur Street
New Orleans, LA 70130-1035
504-589-3882
www.nps.gov/jela/

Jefferson National
Expansion Memorial
11 North 4th Street
St. Louis, MO 63102-1882
314-655-1600
www.nps.gov/jeff/

Jewel Cave
National Monument
R.R. 1, Box 60AA
Custer, SD 57730-9608
605-673-8300
www.nps.gov/jeca/

Jimmy Carter National
Historic Site
300 N. Bond Street
Plains, GA 31780-0392
229-824-4104
www.nps.gov/jica/

John D. Rockefeller, Jr.
Memorial Parkway
c/o Grand Teton National
Park, P.O. Drawer 170
Moose, WY 83012-0170
307-739-3300
www.nps.gov/grte/

John Day Fossil Beds
National Monument
32651 Highway 19
Kimberly, OR 97848-9701
541-987-2333
www.nps.gov/joda/

John Fitzgerald Kennedy
National Historic Site
83 Beals Street
Brookline, MA 02446-6010
617-566-7937
www.nps.gov/jofi/

John Muir
National Historic Site
4202 Alhambra Avenue
Martinez, CA 94553-3883
925-228-8860
www.nps.gov/jomu/

Johnstown Flood
National Memorial
733 Lake Road
South Fork, PA 15956-3602
814-495-4643
www.nps.gov/jofl/

Joshua Tree
National Park
74485 National Park Drive
Twentynine Palms, CA 92277-3533
760-367-5500
www.nps.gov/jotr/

K

Kalaupapa
National Historical Park
PO Box 2222
Kalaupapa, HI 96742-2222
808-567-6802
www.nps.gov/kala/

Kaloko-Honokohau
National Historical Park
73-4786 Kanalani Street, #14
Kailua Kona, HI 96740-2608
808-329-6881
www.nps.gov/kaho/

Katmai
National Park & Preserve
PO Box 7
King Salmon, AK 99613-0007
907-246-3305
www.nps.gov/katm/

Kenai Fjords
National Park
PO Box 1727
Seward, AK 99664-1727
907-224-7500
www.nps.gov/kefj/

Kennesaw Mountain
National Battlefield Park
905 Kennesaw Mountain Drive
Kennesaw, GA 30152-4855
770-427-4686
www.nps.gov/kemo/

Keweenaw
National Historical Park
25970 Red Jacket Road
Calumet, MI 49913-0471
906-337-3168
www.nps.gov/

Kings Canyon
National Park
47050 Generals Highway
Three Rivers, CA 93271-9651
559-565-3341
www.nps.gov/seki/

Kings Mountain
National Military Park
2625 Park Road
Blacksburg, SC 29702-7325
864-936-7921
www.nps.gov/kimo/

Klondike Gold Rush
National Historical Park
319 Second Avenue S.
Seattle, WA 98104-2618
206-553-7220
www.nps.gov/klse/

Klondike Gold Rush
National Historical Park
PO Box 517
Skagway, AK 99840-0517
907-983-2921
www.nps.gov/klgo/

Knife River Indian Villages
National Historic Site
PO Box 9
Stanton, ND 58571-0009
701-745-3300
www.nps.gov/knri/

Kobuk Valley
National Park
PO Box 1029
Kotzebue, AK 99752-1029
907-442-3890
www.nps.gov/kova/

Korean War Veterans Memorial
c/o National Mall & Memorial Parks
900 Ohio Drive, SW
Washington, DC 20242-0004
202-426-6841
www.nps.gov/kwvm/

L
Lake Chelan
National Recreation Area
810 State Route 20
Sedro-Woolley, WA 98284-1263
360-856-5700
www.nps.gov/noca/

Lake Clark
National Park & Preserve
Clark National Preserve
4230 University Drive
Suite 311
Anchorage, AK 99508-4626
907-271-3751
www.nps.gov/lacl/

Lake Mead
National Recreation Area
601 Nevada Highway
Boulder City, NV 89005-2426
702-293-8920
www.nps.gov/lake/

Lake Meredith
National Recreation Area
PO Box 1460
Fritch, TX 79036-1460
806-857-3151
www.nps.gov/lamr/

Lake Roosevelt
National Recreation Area
1008 Crest Drive
Coulee Dam, WA 99116-0037
509-633-9441
www.nps.gov/laro/

Lassen Volcanic
National Park
PO Box 100
Mineral, CA 96063-0100
530-595-4444
www.nps.gov/lavo/

Lava Beds
National Monument
1 Indian Wells Headquarters
Tulelake, CA 96134-8216
530-667-2282
www.nps.gov/labe/

Lewis and Clark
National Historical Park
92343 Fort Clatsop Road
Astoria, OR 97103-9803
503-861-2471
www.nps.gov/lewi/

Lincoln Boyhood
National Memorial
3027 E. South Street
Lincoln City, IN 47552-1816
812-937-4541
www.nps.gov/libo/

Lincoln Home
National Historic Site
413 S. Eighth Street
Springfield, IL 62701-1905
217-492-4241
www.nps.gov/liho/

Lincoln Memorial
c/o National Mall & Memorial Parks
900 Ohio Drive, SW
Washington, DC 20242-0004
202-426-6841
www.nps.gov/linc/

Little Bighorn Battlefield
National Monument
PO Box 39
Crow Agency, MT 59022-0039
406-638-2621
www.nps.gov/libi/

Little River Canyon
National Preserve
2141 Gault Avenue North
Fort Payne, AL 35967-3673
256-845-9605
www.nps.gov/liri/

Little Rock Central High School
National Historic Site
2120 Daisy Bates Drive
Little Rock, AR 72202-5212
501-374-1957
www.nps.gov/chsc/

Longfellow
National Historic Site
105 Brattle Street
Cambridge, MA 02138-3407
617-876-4491
www.nps.gov/long/

Lowell National
Historical Park
67 Kirk Street
Lowell, MA 01852-1029
978-970-5000
www.nps.gov/lowe/

Lyndon B. Johnson
National Historical Park
PO Box 329
Johnson City, TX 78636-0329
830-868-7128
www.nps.gov/lyjo/

Lyndon Baines Johnson
Memorial Grove on the Potomac
c/o George Washington
Memorial Parkway
Turkey Run Park
McLean, VA 22101-0001
703-289-2500
www.nps.gov/lyba/

M
Maggie L. Walker
National Historic Site
c/o Richmond National
Battlefield Park
3215 East Broad Street
Richmond, VA 23223-7517
804-771-2017
www.nps.gov/mawa/

Mammoth Cave
National Park
PO Box 7
Mammoth Cave, KY 42259-0007
270-758-2328
www.nps.gov/maca/

Manassas
National Battlefield Park
12521 Lee Highway
Manassas, VA 20109-2005
703-754-1861
www.nps.gov/mana/

Manzanar
National Historic Site
PO Box 426
Independence, CA 93526-0426
760-878-2932
www.nps.gov/manz/

Marsh-Billings-Rockefeller
National Historical Park
54 Elm Street
Woodstock, VT 05091-1023
802-457-3368
www.nps.gov/mabi/

Martin Luther King, Jr.,
National Historic Site
450 Auburn Avenue, NE
Atlanta, GA 30312-0526
404-331-5190
www.nps.gov/malu/

Martin Van Buren
National Historic Site
1013 Old Post Road
Kinderhook, NY 12106-3605
518-758-9689
www.nps.gov/mava/

Mary McLeod Bethune Council
House National Historic Site
1318 Vermont Avenue, NW
Washington, DC 20005-3607
202-673-2402
www.nps.gov/mamc/

Mesa Verde National Park
PO Box 8
Mesa Verde National
Park, CO 81330-0008
970-529-4465
www.nps.gov/meve/

Middle Delaware
National Scenic River
c/o Delaware Water Gap National
Recreation Area
Bushkill, PA 18324-9410
570-588-2435
www.nps.gov/dewa/

Minidoka National
Historic Site
221 North State Street
PO Box 570
Hagerman, ID 83332-0570
208-837-4793
www.nps.gov/miin/

Minute Man
National Historical Park
174 Liberty Street
Concord, MA 01742-1705
978-369-6993
www.nps.gov/mima/

Minuteman Missile
National Historic Site
21280 SD Highway 240
Philip, SD 57567-7102
605-433-5552
www.nps.gov/mimi/

Mississippi
National River & Recreation Area
111 E. Kellogg Boulevard
Suite 105
St. Paul, MN 55101-1256
651-290-4160
www.nps.gov/miss/

Missouri
National Recreational River
508 East Second Street
Yankton, SD 57078-4422
402-336-3970
www.nps.gov/mnrr/

Mojave
National Preserve
2701 Barstow Road
Barstow, CA 92311-6609
760-252-6100
www.nps.gov/moja/

Monocacy
National Battlefield
4801 Urbana Pike
Frederick, MD 21704-7307
301-662-3515
www.nps.gov/mono/

Montezuma Castle
National Monument
PO Box 219
Camp Verde, AZ 86322-0219
928-567-5276
www.nps.gov/moca/

Moores Creek
National Battlefield
40 Patriots Hall Drive
Currie, NC 28435-0069
910-283-5591
www.nps.gov/mocr/

Morristown
National Historical Park
30 Washington Place
Morristown, NJ 07960-4242
973-539-2016
www.nps.gov/morr/

Mount Rainier
National Park
Tahoma Woods, Star Route
Ashford, WA 98304-9751
360-569-2211
www.nps.gov/mora/

Mount Rushmore
National Memorial
Highway 244
Bldg. 31, Suite 1
Keystone, SD 57751-4404
605-574-2523
www.nps.gov/moru/

Muir Woods
National Monument
Mill Valley, CA 94941-2696
415-388-2596
www.nps.gov/muwo/

N
Natchez
National Historical Park
PO Box 1208
Natchez, MS 39121-1208
601-446-5790
www.nps.gov/natc/

Natchez Trace
National Scenic Trail
c/o Natchez Trace Parkway
2680 Natchez Trace Parkway
Tupelo, MS 38804-9718
662-680-4025
www.nps.gov/natt/

Natchez Trace Parkway
2680 Natchez Trace Parkway
Tupelo, MS 38804-9718
662-680-4025
www.nps.gov/natr/

National Capital Parks-East
1900 Anacostia Dr., SE
Washington, DC 20020
202-690-5185
www.nps.gov/nace/

National Mall
c/o National Mall & Memorial Parks
900 Ohio Drive, SW
Washington, DC 20242-0004
202-485-9880
www.nps.gov/nama/

Natural Bridges
National Monument
HC 60, PO Box 1
Lake Powell, UT 84533-0101
435-692-1234
www.nps.gov/nabr/

Navajo
National Monument
HC 71, Box 3
Tonalea, AZ 86044-9704
928-672-2700
www.nps.gov/nava/

New Bedford Whaling
National Historical Park
33 William Street
New Bedford, MA 02740-6222
508-996-4095
www.nps.gov/nebe/

New Orleans Jazz
National Historical Park
419 Decatur Street
New Orleans, LA 70130-1035
504-589-4806
www.nps.gov/jazz/

New River Gorge
National River
PO Box 246
Glen Jean, WV 25846-0246
304-465-0508
www.nps.gov/neri/

Nez Perce
National Historical Park
36063 HWY 95
Spalding, ID 83540-9715
208-843-7001
www.nps.gov/nepe/

Nicodemus
National Historic Site
304 Washington Avenue
Nicodemus, KS 67625-9719
785-839-4233
www.nps.gov/nico/

Ninety Six
National Historic Site
PO Box 496
Ninety Six, SC 29666-0496
864-543-4068
www.nps.gov/nisi/

Niobrara
National Scenic River
146 S. Hall Street
PO Box 319
Valentine, NE 69201-2104
402-376-1901
www.nps.gov/niob/

Noatak
National Preserve
PO Box 1029
Kotzebue, AK 99752-0129
907-442-3890
www.nps.gov/noat/

North Cascades
National Park
810 State Route 20
Sedro-Woolley, WA 98284-1263
360-856-5700
www.nps.gov/noca/

O

Obed Wild & Scenic River
PO Box 429
Wartburg, TN 37887-0429
423-346-6294
www.nps.gov/obed/

Ocmulgee
National Monument
1207 Emery Highway
Macon, GA 31217-4399
478-752-8257
www.nps.gov/ocmu/

Olympic
National Park
600 East Park Avenue
Port Angeles, WA 98362-6757
360-565-3000
www.nps.gov/olym/

Oregon Caves
National Monument
19000 Caves Highway
Cave Junction, OR 97523-9716
541-592-2100
www.nps.gov/orca/

Organ Pipe Cactus
National Monument
10 Organ Pipe Drive
Ajo, AZ 85321-9626
520-387-6849
www.nps.gov/orpi/

Ozark
National Scenic Riverways
404 Watercress Drive
Van Buren, MO 63965-0490
573-323-4236
www.nps.gov/ozar/

P
Padre Island
National Seashore
PO Box 181300
Corpus Christi, TX
  78480-1300
361-949-8173
www.nps.gov/pais/

Palo Alto Battlefield
National Historical Park
1623 Central Blvd. #213
Brownsville, TX 78520-8326
956-541-2785
www.nps.gov/paal/

Pea Ridge
National Military Park
PO Box 700
Pea Ridge, AR 72751-0700
501-451-8122
www.nps.gov/peri/

Pecos National
Historical Park
PO Box 418
Pecos, NM 87552-0418
505-757-7200
www.nps.gov/peco/

Pennsylvania Avenue
National Historic Site
c/o National Mall & Memorial Parks
900 Ohio Drive, SW
Washington, DC 20242-0004
202-426-6841
www.nps.gov/paav/

Perry's Victory & International
Peace Memorial
PO Box 549
93 Delaware Avenue
Put-in-Bay, OH 43456-0549
419-285-2184
www.nps.gov/pevi/

Petersburg
National Battlefield
1539 Hickory Hill Road
Petersburg, VA 23803-4721
804-732-3531
www.nps.gov/pete/

Petrified Forest
National Park
PO Box 2217
Petrified Forest, AZ 86028-2217
928-524-6228
www.nps.gov/pefo/

Petroglyph
National Monument
6001 Unser Blvd., NW
Albuquerque, NM 87120-2033
505-899-0205
www.nps.gov/petr/

Pictured Rocks
National Lakeshore
PO Box 40
Munising, MI 49862-0040
906-387-3700
www.nps.gov/piro/

Pinnacles
National Monument
5000 Highway 146
Paicines, CA 95043-9770
831-389-4485
www.nps.gov/pinn/

Pipe Spring
National Monument
HC 65, Box 5
Fredonia, AZ 86022-9600
928-643-7105
www.nps.gov/pisp/

Pipestone
National Monument
36 Reservation Avenue
Pipestone, MN 56164-1269
507-825-5464
www.nps.gov/pipe/

Piscataway Park
National Capital Parks, East
1900 Anacostia Drive, SE
Washington, DC 20020-6722
301-763-4600
www.nps.gov/pisc/

Point Reyes
National Seashore
Point Reyes, CA 94956-9799
415-464-5100
www.nps.gov/pore/

Port Chicago Naval Magazine
National Memorial
c/o Eugene O'Neill National
  Historic Site
PO Box 280
Danville, CA 94526-0280
www.nps.gov/poch/

Potomac Heritage
National Scenic Trail
National Park Service
PO Box B
Harpers Ferry, WV 25425-0030
304-535-4014
www.nps.gov/pohe/

Poverty Point
National Monument
c/o Poverty Point State
Commemorative Area
PO Box 248
Epps, LA 71237-0248
318-926-5492
www.nps.gov/popo/

Prince William
Forest Park
18100 Park Headquarters Rd.
Triangle, VA 22172-1644
703-221-7181
www.nps.gov/prwi/

Puuhonua o Honaunau
National Historical Park
PO Box 129
Honaunau, HI 96726-0129
808-328-2326
www.nps.gov/puho/

Puukohola Heiau
National Historic Site
PO Box 44340
Kawaihae, HI 96743-4340
808-882-7218
www.nps.gov/puhe/

R

Rainbow Bridge
National Monument
c/o Glen Canyon National
Recreation Area
PO Box 1507
Page, AZ 86040-1507
928-608-6200
www.nps.gov/rabr/

Redwood
National Park
1111 Second Street
Crescent City, CA 95531-4198
707-464-6101
www.nps.gov/redw/

Richmond
National Battlefield Park
3215 East Broad Street
Richmond, VA 23223-7517
804-226-1981
www.nps.gov/rich/

Rio Grande
Wild & Scenic River
c/o Big Bend National Park
PO Box 129
Big Bend National Park, TX
  79834-0129
432-477-2251
www.nps.gov/rigr/

Crested Honeycreeper

Rock Creek Park
3545 Williamsburg La., NW
Washington, DC 20008-1207
www.nps.gov/rocr/

Rocky Mountain
National Park
1000 Highway 36
Estes Park, CO 80517-8397
970-586-1206
www.nps.gov/romo/

Roger Williams
National Memorial
282 North Main Street
Providence, RI 02903-1240
401-521-7266
www.nps.gov/rowi/

Rosie the Riveter/World War II Home
Front National Historical Park
1401 Marina Way South
Suite C
Richmond, CA 94804
510-232-5050
www.nps.gov/rori/

Ross Lake
National Recreation Area
810 State Route 20
Sedro-Woolley, WA 98284-1263
360-856-5700
www.nps.gov/noca/

Russell Cave
National Monument
3729 County Road 98
Bridgeport, AL 35740-9770
205-495-2672
www.nps.gov/ruca/

S

Sagamore Hill
National Historic Site
20 Sagamore Hill Road
Oyster Bay, NY 11771-1899
516-922-4788
www.nps.gov/sahi/

Saguaro
National Park
3693 South Old Spanish Trail
Tucson, AZ 85730-5601
520-733-5100
www.nps.gov/sagu/

St. Croix Island
International Historic Site
PO Box 247
Calais, ME 04619-0247
207-454-3871
www.nps.gov/sacr/

St. Croix
National Scenic Riverway
401 N. Hamilton Street
St. Croix Falls, WI 54024-0708
715-483-2274
www.nps.gov/sacn/

St. Paul's Church
National Historic Site
897 South Columbus Avenue
Mount Vernon, NY 10550-5018
914-667-4116
www.nps.gov/sapa/

St.-Gaudens
National Historic Site
139 Saint-Gaudens Road
Cornish, NH 03745-9704
603-675-2175
www.nps.gov/saga/

Salem Maritime
National Historic Site
Custom House
174 Derby Street
Salem, MA 01970-5186
978-740-1660
www.nps.gov/sama/

Salinas Pueblo Missions
National Monument
PO Box 517
Mountainair, NM 87036-0496
505-847-2585
www.nps.gov/sapu/

Salt River Bay National Historical
Park & Ecological Preserve
Danish Customs House
Kings Wharf
2100 Church Street, #100
Christiansted, VI 00820-4611
340-773-1460
www.nps.gov/sari/

San Antonio Missions
National Historical Park
2202 Roosevelt Avenue
San Antonio, TX 78210-4919
210-534-8833
www.nps.gov/saan/

San Francisco Maritime
National Historical Park
Bldg. E, Fort Mason Center
San Francisco, CA 94123
415-447-5000
www.nps.gov/safr/

San Juan Island
National Historical Park
PO Box 429
Friday Harbor, WA 98250-0429
360-378-2240
www.nps.gov/sajh/

San Juan
National Historic Site
Fort San Cristobal
501 Calle Norzagaray
San Juan, PR 00901-1213
787-729-6777
www.nps.gov/saju/

Sand Creek Massacre
National Historic Site
PO Box 249
Eads, CO 81036-0249
719-438-5916
www.nps.gov/sand/

Santa Monica Mountains
National Recreation Area
401 West Hillcrest Drive
Thousand Oaks, CA 91360-4223
805-370-2301
www.nps.gov/samo/

Saratoga
National Historical Park
648 Route 32
Stillwater, NY 12170-1604
518-664-9821
www.nps.gov/sara/

Saugus Iron Works
National Historic Site
244 Central Street
Saugus, MA 01906-2107
781-233-0050
www.nps.gov/sair/

Scotts Bluff
National Monument
190276 Old Oregon Trail
PO Box 27
Gering, NE 69341-9700
308-436-4340
www.nps.gov/scbl/

Selma to Montgomery
National Historic Trail
7002 US Highway 80
Hayneville, AL 36040-4612
334-877-1984
www.nps.gov/semo/

Sequoia
National Park
47050 Generals Highway
Three Rivers, CA 93271-9651
559-565-3341
www.nps.gov/seki/

Shenandoah
National Park
3655 US Highway 211 East
Luray, VA 22835-9051
540-999-3500
www.nps.gov/shen/

Shiloh
National Military Park
1055 Pittsburg Landing Road
Shiloh, TN 38376-9704
731-689-5275
www.nps.gov/shil/

Sitka
National Historical Park
106 Metlakatla Street
Sitka, AK 99835-7665
907-747-6281
www.nps.gov/sitk/

Sleeping Bear Dunes
National Lakeshore
9922 Front Street
Empire, MI 49630-9797
231-326-5134
www.nps.gov/slbe/

Springfield Armory
National Historic Site
1 Armory Square
Springfield, MA 01105-1299
413-734-8551
www.nps.gov/spar/

Statue of Liberty
National Monument
Liberty Island
New York, NY 10004-1467
212-363-3200
www.nps.gov/stli/

Steamtown
National Historic Site
150 South Washington Avenue
Scranton, PA 18503-2018
570-340-5200
www.nps.gov/stea/

Stones River
National Battlefield
3501 Old Nashville Highway
Murfreesboro, TN 37129-3095
615-893-9501
www.nps.gov/stri/

Sunset Crater Volcano
National Monument
6400 N. Highway 89
Flagstaff, AZ 86004-2759
928-526-0502
www.nps.gov/sucr/

T

Tallgrass Prairie National Preserve
PO Box 585
226 Broadway
Cottonwood Falls, KS 66845-9728
620-273-6034
www.nps.gov/tapr/

Thaddeus Kosciuszko
National Memorial
c/o Independence National
Historical Park
143 S. Third Street
Philadelphia, PA 19106-2818
215-597-7130
www.nps.gov/thko/

Theodore Roosevelt Birthplace
National Historic Site
28 E. 20th Street
New York, NY 10003-1399
212-260-1616
www.nps.gov/thrb/

Theodore Roosevelt Island
National Memorial
c/o George Washington Memorial
Parkway
Turkey Run Park
McLean, VA 22101-0001
703-289-2500
www.nps.gov/this/

Theodore Roosevelt
National Park
PO Box 7
Medora, ND 58645-0007
701-623-4466
www.nps.gov/thro/

Theodore Roosevelt Inaugural
National Historic Site
641 Delaware Avenue
Buffalo, NY 14202-1079
716-884-0095
www.nps.gov/thri/

Thomas Cole
National Historical Site
PO Box 426, 218 Spring St
Catskill, NY 12414
518 943-0652
www.nps.gov/thco/

Thomas Edison
National Historical Park
Main Street & Lakeside Avenue
West Orange, NJ 07052-5515
973-736-0550
www.nps.gov/edis/

Thomas Jefferson
Memorial
c/o National Mall & Memorial Parks
900 Ohio Drive, SW
Washington, DC 20242-0004
202-485-9880
www.nps.gov/thje/

Thomas Stone
National Historic Site
6655 Rosehill Road
Port Tobacco, MD 20677-3400
301-934-6027
www.nps.gov/thst/

Timpanogos Cave
National Monument
R.R. 3, Box 200
American Fork, UT 84003-9803
801-756-5239
www.nps.gov/tica/

Timucuan
Ecological & Historic Preserve
13165 Mt. Pleasant Road
Jacksonville, FL 32225-1227
904-641-7155
www.nps.gov/timu/

Tonto
National Monument
HC 02, Box 4602
Roosevelt, AZ 85545-8148
928-467-2241
www.nps.gov/tont/

Touro Synagogue
National Historic Site
85 Touro Street
Newport, RI 02840
401-847-4794
www.nps.gov/tosy/

Tumacacori
National Historical Park
PO Box 67
Tumacacori, AZ 85640-0067
520-398-2341
www.nps.gov/tuma/

Tupelo
National Battlefield
c/o Natchez Trace Parkway
2680 Natchez Trace Parkway
Tupelo, MS 38804-9718
662-680-4025
www.nps.gov/tupe/

Tuskegee Airmen
National Historic Site
c/o Tuskegee Institute
National Historic Site
P.O. Drawer 10
Tuskegee Institute, AL 36087-0010
334-724-0922
www.nps.gov/tuai/

Tuskegee Institute
National Historic Site
PO Drawer 10
Tuskegee Institute, AL 36087-0010
334-727-3200
www.nps.gov/tuin/

Tuzigoot
National Monument
PO Box 219
Camp Verde, AZ 86322-0219
928-567-5276
www.nps.gov/tuzi/

U

Ulysses S. Grant
National Historic Site
7400 Grant Road
St. Louis, MO 63123-1801
314-842-1867
www.nps.gov/ulsg/

Upper Delaware
Scenic & Recreational River
274 River Road
Beach Lake, PA 18405-9737
570-729-8251
www.nps.gov/upde/

V

Valley Forge
National Historical Park
1400 N. Outer Line Drive
King of Prussia, PA 19406-1009
610-783-1000
www.nps.gov/vafo/

Vanderbilt Mansion
National Historic Site
4097 Albany Post Road
Hyde Park, NY 12538-1997
845-229-9115
www.nps.gov/vama/

Vicksburg
National Military Park
3201 Clay Street
Vicksburg, MS 39183-3469
601-636-0583
www.nps.gov/vick/

Vietnam Veterans Memorial
c/o National Mall & Memorial Parks
900 Ohio Drive, SW
Washington, DC 20242-0004
202-485-9880
www.nps.gov/vive/

Virgin Islands Coral Reef
National Monument
PO Box 710
Cruz Bay, St. John, VI 00831-0710
340-776-6201
www.nps.gov/vicr/

Virgin Islands
National Park
PO Box 710
Cruz Bay, St. John, VI 00831-0710
340-776-6201
www.nps.gov/viis/

Voyageurs
National Park
3131 Highway 53
International Falls, MN
  56649-8904
218-283-6600
www.nps.gov/voya/

W

Walnut Canyon
National Monument
6400 N. Highway 89
Flagstaff, AZ 86004-2759
928-526-3367
www.nps.gov/waca/

War in the Pacific
National Historical Park
460 N. Marine Drive
Piti, GU 96915
671-472-7240
www.nps.gov/wapa/

Washington Monument
c/o National Mall & Memorial Parks
900 Ohio Drive, SW
Washington, DC 20242-0004
202-485-9880
www.nps.gov/wamo/

Washita Battlefield
National Historic Site
RR1, Box 55A
Cheyenne, OK 73628-9725
580-497-2742
www.nps.gov/waba/

Weir Farm
National Historic Site
735 Nod Hill Road
Wilton, CT 06897-1309
203-834-1896
www.nps.gov/wefa/

Whiskeytown
National Recreation Area
PO Box 188
Whiskeytown, CA 96095-0188
530-242-3400
www.nps.gov/whis/

White House
c/o National Capital Region
1100 Ohio Drive, SW
Washington, DC 20242-0001
202-619-6344
www.nps.gov/whho/

White Sands
National Monument
PO Box 1086
Holloman AFB, NM 88330-1086
505-679-2599
www.nps.gov/whsa/

Whitman Mission
National Historic Site
328 Whitman Mission Road
Walla Walla, WA 99362-7299
509-522-6360
www.nps.gov/whmi/

William Howard Taft
National Historic Site
2038 Auburn Avenue
Cincinnati, OH 45219-3025
513-684-3262
www.nps.gov/wiho/

Wilson's Creek
National Battlefield
6424 W. Farm Road 182
Republic, MO 65738-9514
417-732-2662
www.nps.gov/wicr/

Wind Cave
National Park
R.R. 1, Box 190, Hwy. 385
Hot Springs, SD 57747-9430
605-745-4600
www.nps.gov/wica/

Wolf Trap National Park
for the Performing Arts
1551 Trap Road
Vienna, VA 22182-1643
703-255-1800
www.nps.gov/wotr/

Women's Rights
National Historical Park
136 Fall Street
Seneca Falls, NY 13148-1517
315-568-2991
www.nps.gov/wori/

World War II Memorial
c/o National Mall & Memorial Parks
900 Ohio Drive, SW
Washington, DC 20242-0004
202-426-6841
www.nps.gov/nwwm/

World War II Valor in the Pacific
National Monument
Pearl Harbor
1 Arizona Memorial Place
Honolulu, HI 96818-3145
808-422-2771
www.nps.gov/valr/

Wrangell–St. Elias
National Park & Preserve
PO Box 439
Copper Center, AK 99573-0439
907-822-5234
www.nps.gov/wrst/

Wright Brothers
National Memorial
c/o Cape Hatteras National Seashore
1401 National Park Drive
Manteo, NC 27954-2708
252-441-7430
www.nps.gov/wrbr/

Wupatki
National Monument
6400 N. Highway 89
Flagstaff, AZ 86004-2759
928-679-2365
www.nps.gov/wupa/

Y

Yellowstone
National Park
PO Box 168
Yellowstone National Park,
  WY 82190-0168
307-344-7381
www.nps.gov/yell/

Yosemite
National Park
PO Box 577
Yosemite National Park, CA
  95389-0577
209-372-0200
www.nps.gov/yose/

Yucca House
National Monument
c/o Mesa Verde National Park
PO Box 8
Mesa Verde National
Park, CO 81330-0008
970-529-4465
www.nps.gov/yuho/

Yukon–Charley Rivers
National Preserve
201 First Avenue
Doyon Building
Fairbanks, AK 99701-4848
907-457-5752
www.nps.gov/yuch/

Z

Zion
National Park
Springdale, UT 84767-1099
435-772-3256
www.nps.gov/zion/

authors' 10 best national parks

Robert E. Howells

Yosemite National Park
Mojave National Preserve
Joshua Tree National Park
Olympic National Park
Death Valley National Park
Channel Islands National Park
Grand Teton National Park
Everglades National Park
Santa Monica Mountains National Recreation Area
Redwood National Park

Olivia Garnett

Harpers Ferry National Historical Park
Crater Lake National Park
Sleeping Bear Dunes National Lakeshore
Devils Tower National Monument
Natchez Trace National Scenic Trail
Badlands National Park
Whitman Mission National Historic Site
Theodore Roosevelt National Park
Lewis and Clark National Historic Trail
Montezuma Castle National Monument

Gary Mckechnie

Zion National Park
Death Valley National Park
Grand Canyon National Park
Wright Brothers National Memorial
Mesa Verde National Park
Statue of Liberty National Monument
Franklin Delano Roosevelt National Historic Site
Minute Man National Historical Park
Valley Forge National Historical Park
Nez Perce National Historical Park

Jeremy Schmidt

Yellowstone National Park (Old Faithful at minus 40 degrees)
Glacier National Park (Highline Trail north of Logan Pass)

Grand Canyon National Park (Tonto Plateau trail in spring)
Everglades National Park (Chickee camping—Chickees are floating platforms in backcountry)
Voyageurs National Park (Loons calling at dawn)
Yosemite National Park (Brink of Nevada Falls)
Grand Teton National Park (Lake Solitude)
Olympic National Park (Hoh River Trail)
Canyonlands National Park (Needles District trails)
Navajo National Monument (Betatakin ruins on guided walk)

Mel White

Rocky Mountain National Park (hike from Bear Lake to Fern Lake trailhead)
Big Bend National Park (Rio Grande, Chihuahuan Desert, and Chisos Mountains)
Acadia National Park (biking the carriage roads)
Point Reyes National Seashore (underrated wildlife-watching site)
Blue Ridge Parkway (amazing fall foliage)
Buffalo National River (great canoeing under awesome sandstone bluffs)
Saguaro National Park (hiking among giant cactus)
Theodore Roosevelt National Park (bison roaming the High Plains)
Dry Tortugas National Park (spring birding extravaganza)
National Mall and Memorial Parks (a history lesson in stone)

Joe Yogerst

Channel Islands National Park
Cumberland Island National Seashore
Golden Gate National Recreation Area
Hawaii Volcanoes National Park
Little Bighorn Battlefield National Monument
National Mall & Memorial Park
Olympic National Park
Wrangell–St Elias National Park & Preserve
Yellowstone National Park
Yosemite National Park

index

Boldface indicates illustrations.

Illustrations Credits

Cover: (UP LE), Marc Adamus/Aurora Photos; (UP CTR), Jonathan Larson/iStockphoto.com; (UP RT), Galyna Andrushko/Shutterstock; (CTR RT), zschnepf/Shutterstock; (CTR LE), Whit Richardson/Aurora Photos; (LO LE), Nicholas Roemmelt/iStockphoto.com; (LO CTR), RiverNorthPhotography/iStockphoto.com; (LO RT), Pierre Chouinard/Stockphoto.com. Back cover: (UP LE), urosr/Shutterstock; (UP CTR), Corey Rich/Aurora Photos; (UP RT), Oleksandr Buzko/iStockphoto.com; (CTR LE), Alaska Stock Images/NationalGeographicStock.com; (CTR RT), Matt Propert; (LO LE), zschnepf/Shutterstock; (LO CTR), Jeffrey M. Frank/Shutterstock; (LO RT), Tim Starr, National Geographic My Shot.

1, Library of Congress; 2-3, Jim Richardson; 5, Devochka i zaicheg/Shutterstock; 6, David S. Boyer; 8, Triff/Shutterstock; 10, ejwhite/Shutterstock; 11, Eliza Snow/iStockphoto.com; 13, Jonathan Larson/iStockphoto.com; 15, David Davis/Shutterstock; 16, spherical image/Shutterstock; 17, Sasha Buzko/Shutterstock; 20, Melissa Farlow/NationalGeographicStock.com; 21, BogdanBoev/Shutterstock; 23, uros ravbar/iStockphoto.com; 24, StudioSmart/Shutterstock; 25, Frances A. Miller/Shutterstock; 27, William Cheung/iStockphoto.com; 28, Chris Leachman/Shutterstock; 30, Library of Congress; 32, Lowell Georgia; 35, Dwight Smith/Shutterstock; 37, Nicholas Roemmelt/iStockphoto.com; 38, Natalia Bratslasky/Shutterstock; 40, Ray Rope/iStockphoto.com; 42, Stephen Alvarez/NationalGeographicStock.com; 45, Library of Congress; 47, Chris Johns; 48, Eric Isselee/Shutterstock; 51, Natalia Bratslavsky/Shutterstock; 53, W. Robert Moore; 55, Christian Muscat/Shutterstock; 57, Lijuan Guo/Shutterstock; 59, Natalia Bratslavsky/Shutterstock; 60, Ashok Rodrigues/iStockphoto.com; 63, swinner/Shutterstock; 64, Tomo Jesenicnik/Shutterstock; 67, Courtesy National Park Service; 68, alpxn/iStockphoto.com; 71, Annie Griffiths Belt; 73, Library of Congress; 74, Kathleen Revis; 75, Thomas Barrat/Shutterstock; 77, Doug Lemke/Shutterstock; 79, sandsun/iStockphoto.com; 80, Lilyana Vynogradova/Shutterstock; 82, Olivier Renck/Aurora/Getty Images; 85, Luminis/Shutterstock; 87, David S. Boyer and Arlan R. Wiker; 88, Ray Roper/iStockphoto.com; 90, Maria Stenzel; 92, Michael Westhoff/iStockphoto.com; 93, Library of Congress; 94, Nathan Shahan/Shutterstock; 95, David Rock/Shutterstock; 97, Kelly Pollak/iStockphoto.com; 99, marekuliasz/Shutterstock; 100, Bruce Dale; 103, Corey Rich/Aurora Photos; 104, Irina Rogova/Shutterstock; 106, Library of Congress; 108, iceprotector/Shutterstock; 111, Dean Conger; 113, Jose Azel/Aurora Photos; 116, Geir-Olva Lyngfjell/iStockphoto.com; 118, Mark Fisher/Aurora Open/Getty Images; 119, Library of Congress; 120, forbis/Shutterstock; 122, SeDmi/Shutterstock; 123, Ecoasis/Shutterstock; 125, Harrison Shull/Shullphoto.com/Aurora Photos; 127, scusio-9/Shutterstock; 128, David Morgan/iStockphoto.com; 130, Kipp Schoen/iStockphoto.com; 133, Sam Abell; 135, Eduardo Luzzatti Buye/iStockphoto.com; 137, CROM/Shutterstock; 138, Oksana Perkins//Shutterstock; 141, Giorgio Fochesato/iStockphoto.com; 142, Arkady/Shutterstock; 143, Skip Brown/NationalGeographicStock.com; 146, George H. H. Huey; 149, Danita Delimont/Alamy; 150, Khomulo

Anna/Shutterstock; 152, Perig/Shutterstock; 153, Harrison Shull/Aurora Photos; 155, Dean Conger; 157, Tina Darby/Shutterstock; 158, Rudi Tapper/iStockphoto.com; 159, Adrov Andriy/Shutterstock; 160, Pgiam/iStockphoto.com; 162, Tom Baker/Shutterstock; 164, Dan Barnes/iStockphoto.com; 166, Igor Grochev/Shutterstock; 167, Eric Isselee/Shutterstock; 169, Paul Chesley; 171, Alexander Kosev/Stockphoto.com; 172, Raymond Gehman/NationalGeographicStock.com; 174, Tom Bean/Getty Images; 176, Library of Congress; 177, Veniamin Kraskov/Shutterstock; 179, Charles Schug/Shutterstock; 182, Bates Littlehales; 184, Julie Quarry/Alamy; 185, OlegD/Shutterstock; 187, Library of Congress; 189, Alaska Stock Images/NationalGeographicStock.com; 190, Pelana/Shutterstock; 191, James Kay/Stock Connection/Aurora Photos; 192, Brian Maebius/rangerdoug.com; 195, Jodi Cobb, National Geographic Photographer; 197, Library of Congress; 198, Supri Suharjoto/Shutterstock; 200, Oleksandr Buzko/iStockphoto.com; 202, Danny E Hooks/Shutterstock; 205, James L. Stanfield; 206, David Mathies/Shutterstock; 207, nito/Shutterstock; 209, ElementalImaging/iStockphoto.com; 210, Le Do/Shutterstock; 212, Stacey Putman/Stockphoto.com; 214, Ray Roper/Stockphoto.com; 215, Eric Foltz/Stockphoto.com; 217, Bonita R. Chesier/Shutterstock; 219, amygdala_imagery/iStockphoto.com; 220, ramplett/iStockphoto.com; 221, Alekcey/Shutterstock; 223, Jim Richardson; 224, Steve and Donna O'Meara/NationalGeographicStock.com; 225, photoHare/Shutterstock; 228, Pierre Chouinard/Shutterstock; 231, Eric Foltz/iStockphoto.com; 233, Pgiam/iStockphoto.com; 235, Ivonne Wierink/Shutterstock; 236, George F. Mobley; 237, Library of Congress; 239, Mooneydriver/iStockphoto.com; 241, Anthony Ricci/Shutterstock; 242, Ray Roper/iStockphoto.com; 244, Wire_man/Shutterstock; 245, Michael Cook/iStockphoto.com; 246, Lawrence Long/iStockphoto.com; 248, Oleg_Mit/Shutterstock; 250, dpshp/iStockphoto.com; 251, Library of Congress; 252, Ray Roper/iStockphoto.com; 253, Frank Leung/iStockphoto.com; 255, Michael Nichols, NGP; 257, David Parson/iStockphoto.com; 258, Rich Reid/NationalGeographicStock.com; 259, Dee Golden/Shutterstock; 260, Rich Harris/iStockphoto.com; 261, Rich Harris/iStockphoto.com; 263, George F. Mobley; 264, Library of Congress; 265, Maxim Kulko/Shutterstock; 266, James P. Blair; 267, Eric Isselee/Shutterstock; 269, Christopher Russell/iStockphoto.com; 271, mlwinphoto/iStockphoto.com; 273, James L. Amos; 274, Le Do/Shutterstock; 276, Raymond Gehman; 278, Brian Maebius/rangerdoug.com; 281, Wesley Pohl/iStockphoto.com; 284, Rhonda Suka/iStockphoto.com; 287, Library of Congress; 288, Library of Congress; 290, Elena Butinova/Shutterstock; 291, Eric Isselee/Shutterstock; 293, urosr/Shutterstock; 295, Eric Foltz/iStockphoto.com; 298, Brian Maebius/rangerdoug.com; 299, stevedangers/Stockphoto.com; 300, Michael Nichols, NGP; 303, Alaska Stock Images/NationalGeographicStock.com; 305, Doug Marshall/Aurora Photos; 308, William Albert Allard; 310, Madlen/Shutterstock; 312, Valerii Kaliuzhnyi/iStockphoto.com; 314, Michael Lok/iStockphoto.com; 316, Yaroslave Radlovskiy/iStockphoto.com; 319, Dave Rock/Shutterstock; 321, Ray Roper/Stockphoto.com; 322, Phil Schermeister; 323, Irafel/Shutterstock; 325, Jeffrey M. Frank/Shutterstock; 326, RoxyFer/Shutterstock; 327, Library of Congress; 330, Bates

Littlehales; 331, Adam Korzekwa/iStockphoto.com; 332, IgorGolovniov/Shutterstock; 334, Valerii Kaliuzhnyi/Shutterstock; 335, Elnur/Shutterstock; 337, Jeremy Edwards/iStockphoto.com; 338, Matt Propert; 342, DenGuy/iStockphoto.com; 344, Library of Congress; 347, Varina and Jay Patel/Shutterstock; 349, Library of Congress; 352, RiverNorthPhotography/iStockphoto.com; 353, Eric Isselee/Shutterstock; 354, photographer/Shutterstock; 357, Library of Congress; 359, Library of Congress; 363, Pgiam/iStockphoto.com; 364, Juanmonino/iStockphoto.com; 367, Dwight Nadig/iStockphoto.com; 368, Connes/Shutterstock; 369, Library of Congress; 370, Steve Geer/iStockphoto.com; 372 (LE), Brad Wieland/iStockphoto.com; 372 (CTR), Brad Wieland/iStockphoto.com; 372 (RT), Brad Wieland/iStockphoto.com; 374, Galen Rowell/Corbis; 377, Ric Ergenbright/Corbis; 379, Ralph Clevenger/Corbis; 380, photo25th/Shutterstock; 382, StudioSmart/Shutterstock; 385, Richard Nowitz/NationalGeographicStock.com; 386, StudioCampo/iStockphoto.com; 389, Lee Foster/Alamy; 390, akiyoko/Shutterstock; 393, RiverNorthPhotography/iStockphoto.com; 395, Roberto Soncin Gerometta/Alamy; 398, James Steidl/Shutterstock; 400, John Shepherd/iStockphoto.com; 402, Library of Congress; 405, Aimin Tang/iStockphoto.com; 406, James L. Stanfield; 410, Condor 36/Shutterstock; 412, R. Gino Santa Maria/Shutterstock; 414 (LO), elsar/Shutterstock; 414 (UP), Koksharov Dmitry/Shutterstock; 416, Randy Lincks/Alamy; 418, Simon Phipps/iStockphoto.com; 419, Brendan Howard/Shutterstock; 421, Smithsonian Institution Collections, National Museum of American History, Behring Center; 423, Roxana Bashyrova/Shutterstock; 424, James L. Stanfield; 425, Library of Congress; 427, Melissa Farlow/NationalGeographicStock.com; 429, iladm/Shutterstock; 432, EtiAmmos/Shutterstock; 433, Thomas Barrat/Shutterstock; 435, Slavoljub Pantelic/Shutterstock; 437, Raymond Gehman/NationalGeographicStock.com; 439, Paul Lemke/iStockphoto.com; 442, Eri Foltz/iStockphoto.com; 445, Library of Congress; 446, Matt Propert; 447, Paul Fries/iStockphoto.com; 448, Jeff Banke/Shutterstock; 449 (LO), Ray Roper/iStockphoto.com; 449 (UP), Ray Roper/iStockphoto.com; 450, tomograf/iStockphoto.com; 451, Sylvana Rega/Shutterstock; 452, blinow61/Shutterstock; 453 (UP LE), Ray Roper/iStockphoto.com; 453 (LO RT), Lawrence Long/iStockphoto.com; 454 (UP LE), tomograf/iStockphoto.com; 454 (LO RT), Sylvana Rega/Shutterstock; 455, EtiAmmos/Shutterstock; 456, Sylvana Rega/Shutterstock; 457, Ray Roper/iStockphoto.com; 458, EtiAmmos/Shutterstock; 459 (UP RT), Sylvana Rega/Shutterstock; 459 (LO LE), Jeff Banke/Shutterstock; 460, Sylvana Rega/Shutterstock; 461, blinow61/Shutterstock; 462, tomograf/iStockphoto.com; 463 (LO LE), Ken Brown/iStockphoto.com; 463 (UP RT), Sylvana Rega/Shutterstock; 464, tomograf/iStockphoto.com; 465, Ray Roper/iStockphoto.com; 466, tomograf/iStockphoto.com; 467 (UP LE), Brendan Howard/Shutterstock; 467 (LO), Sylvana Rega/Shutterstock; 469, IgorGolovniov/Shutterstock; 470, Ken Brown/iStockphoto.com.

National Geographic
The 10 Best of Everything:
National Parks

Robert E. Howells, Olivia Garnett, Gary Mckechnie,
Jeremy Schmidt, Mel White, Joe Yogerst, *Authors*

Published by the National Geographic Society
John M. Fahey, Jr., *President and Chief Executive Officer*
Gilbert M. Grosvenor, *Chairman of the Board*
Tim T. Kelly, *President, Global Media Group*
John Q. Griffin, *Executive Vice President;*
President, Publishing
Nina D. Hoffman, *Executive Vice President;*
President, Book Publishing Group

Prepared by the Book Division
Barbara Brownell Grogan, *Vice President and*
Editor in Chief
Marianne R. Koszorus, *Director of Design*
Barbara Noe, *Senior Editor*
Carl Mehler, *Director of Maps*
R. Gary Colbert, *Production Director*
Jennifer A. Thornton, *Managing Editor*
Meredith C. Wilcox, *Administrative Director, Illustrations*

Staff for This Book
Caroline Hickey, *Project Manager*
Robert E. Howells, *Contributing Editor*
Jane Sunderland, *Text Editor*
Sanaa Akkach, *Art Director*
Jane Menyawi, Matt Propert, *Illustrations Editors*
Linda Makarov, *Designer*
Judith Klein, *Production Editor*
Britany Brown, Lynsey Jacob, Sally Young, *Researchers*
Marshall Kiker, *Illustrations Specialist*
Elizabeth L. Newhouse, Lise Sajewski, Mary Stephanos,
Contributors
Melissa Phillips, Lindsey Smith, *Design Interns*

Manufacturing and Quality Management
Christopher A. Liedel, *Chief Financial Officer*
Phillip L. Schlosser, *Senior Vice President*
Chris Brown, *Technical Director*
Nicole Elliott, *Manager*
Rachel Faulise, *Manager*
Robert L. Barr, *Manager*

Acknowledgment:
Fact notes from the National Park Service website, www.nps.gov.

The National Geographic Society is one of the world's largest nonprofit scientific and educational organizations. Founded in 1888 to "increase and diffuse geographic knowledge," the Society works to inspire people to care about the planet. National Geographic reflects the world through its magazines, television programs, films, music and radio, books, DVDs, maps, exhibitions, live events, school publishing programs, interactive media and merchandise. *National Geographic* magazine, the Society's official journal, published in English and 32 local-language editions, is read by more than 35 million people each month. The National Geographic Channel reaches 320 million households in 34 languages in 166 countries. National Geographic Digital Media receives more than 13 million visitors a month. National Geographic has funded more than 9,200 scientific research, conservation and exploration projects and supports an education program promoting geography literacy. For more information, visit nationalgeographic.com.

For more information, please call 1-800-NGS LINE
(647-5463) or write to the following address:

National Geographic Society
1145 17th Street N.W.
Washington, D.C. 20036-4688 U.S.A.

For information about special discounts for bulk purchases,
please contact National Geographic Books Special Sales:
ngspecsales@ngs.org

For rights or permissions inquiries, please contact National Geographic Books
Subsidiary Rights: ngbookrights@ngs.org

Library of Congress Cataloging-in-Publication Data
The 10 best of everything national parks : 800 top picks from parks coast to coast.
     p. cm.
Includes index.
ISBN 978-1-4262-0734-1
1. National parks and reserves--United States. I. National Geographic
Society (U.S.) II. Title: Ten best of everything national parks.
E160.A142 2011
917.3--dc22

                                          2010039588

Printed in China

10/RRDS/1

ALSO AVAILABLE IN THIS SERIES

TWO MUST-HAVE COMPANION GUIDES FOR GLOBE-TROTTING CONNOISSEURS

FOR IN-DEPTH INFORMATION ON YOUR FAVORITE PARKS

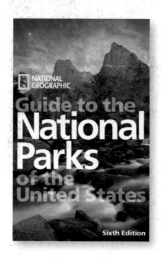

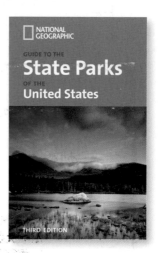

Available wherever books are sold. Visit www.nationalgeographic.com/books